Canada and the United States: The Civil War Years

৯৩ BY THE SAME AUTHOR

These New Zealanders
British Imperialism: Gold, God, Glory
Historiography of the British Empire-Commonwealth
Recent Trends and New Literature in
Canadian History
The Cold War: From Yalta to Cuba
Malaysia (with John Bastin)
Canadian-West Indian Union: A Forty-Year Minuet
The Age of Imperialism
The Historian as Detective
Pastmasters (with Marcus Cunliffe)
The Blacks in Canada

Robin W. Winks

CANADA and the UNITED STATES

The Civil War Years

HARVEST HOUSE, MONTREAL

CANADA AND THE U.S.A.
THE CIVIL WAR YEARS

This is a revised paperback
edition of the hardcover book
published by The Johns Hopkins
Press, Baltimore 18, Md. in
1960. Except for the new matter
and the errata, the present
edition is complete and synonymous
with the original in every detail.

Copyright © Canada by Harvest House Ltd.
First paperback edition — January 1971
ISBN 88772-117-6
Library of Congress Catalog Card No. 77-150658.

Deposited according to law in the
Bibliothèque Nationale du Québec
1st quarter, 1971
For information address Harvest House Ltd.
1364 Greene Avenue, Montreal 215, Quebec, Canada
Printed and bound in Canada.

To my wife, Avril, who will not read it

℘ PREFACE

> Question on British Foreign Office examination:
> "What are the most important things in the world?"
> Successful answer: "Love, and Anglo-American relations."

THERE IS NO COUNTRY IN THE WORLD, INCLUDING GREAT BRITAIN, TO which Canada is tied so closely by blood and by geography as she is to the United States. On a front of nearly 5,000 miles, two of the world's great democracies face each other. For a distance as great as that between London and Cape Town or between New York and Buenos Aires, Canada and the United States share a frontier line noted for its lack of fortifications. This line is especially significant for the Dominion of Canada, for she is the only major country in the world with but a single neighbor. Canada has been subjected to the cultural, political, economic, and social influences of that neighbor to a far greater extent than are nations bounded by two or more ethnically diverse peoples. Canadians have long been aware of the overwhelming importance to them of this relationship.

The people of the United States, at least in thoughtful segments of society, also have become increasingly aware of the importance of the Dominion. [1] There are good reasons for these manifestations of

---

[1] For an examination of the growth of university interest in Canadian affairs, see Reginald G. Trotter, "Canadian History in the Universities of the United States," *Canadian Historical Review*, VIII (Sept., 1927), 190–217; Edith E. Ware, ed., *The Study of International Relations in the United States: Survey for 1934* (New York, 1934), pp. 280–299, and Ware, ed., *Survey for 1937* (New York, 1938), pp. 224–241; and Robin W. Winks, "Thirty Years After: Canadian History in the Universities of the United States," *CHR*, XL (March, 1959), 38–50, which contains a bibliography of additional articles.

interest. Canada guards the roof of the New World, America's air-age
back door to and from the Soviet Union, as the Distant Early Warning, Mid-America, and Pinetree lines demonstrated. Continental
rather than national defense became a reality with the establishment
of NORAD, the North American air defense system. Trade between
the United States and Canada is the world's greatest in volume, and
each is the other's most important customer. Under normal conditions,
traffic on the Detroit River alone is heavier than the combined traffic
through the Suez and Panama canals.

Geographically each nation reaches into the heart of the other.
Over half of the population of Canada lives south of the forty-ninth
parallel, and Ontario sweeps into the United States nearly as far south
as New York City. Maine, on the other hand, juts up sharply
between the old Canadas and the Maritime Provinces, so that even
today the chief route of travel between Nova Scotia and Canada's
capital, Ottawa, is through the United States. For the most part, the
people of Canada's regions have closer contact with a like region in
the United States than they have with each other. Nova Scotians often
resemble their Maine neighbors more than they resemble their fellow
citizens from British Columbia. Across the high plains of the West,
the Dakotas merge imperceptibly into the Prairie Provinces. Manitobans
go not to Toronto, halfway across the continent, but to Minneapolis
to shop. British Columbia has at least as close economic ties with
Seattle as with Ottawa or Montreal. Then, too, disputes with Canada
over the St. Lawrence Seaway, diversion of water from the Columbia
River, the perennial fisheries question, trade relations, wheat subsidies,
and problems of oil markets and foreign investments have forced
thinking Americans to consider Canadian-American relations with
less equanimity. Canada's recent foreign policy has demonstrated to
many Americans that the Dominion is a sovereign nation of importance
in international circles.

American scholarly interest in Canada has kept pace with this more
general awareness, accelerating since the Dominion's independent entry
into World War II. Significantly, the single most important contribution to the study of Canadian-American relations has been a
cooperative series of twenty-five volumes for the Carnegie Endowment
for International Peace under the editorship of James T. Shotwell.
Written by some of the ablest Canadian and American scholars, this
project was completed in 1945 with John Bartlet Brebner's superb

analysis of the creation of the *North Atlantic Triangle*.[2] But few of these volumes deal intensively with any short period of time or any limited subject, and while free of any explicit thesis, they tend to reflect the sponsor's natural hope for international peace. The series was written during the years when Anglo-American solidarity was discovered to be a necessity for the survival of the democratic ideal.

This necessity is no less urgent today than it was three decades ago. And if the Anglo-American connection is to be understood, we must know more of the history of the Commonwealth. New sources and improved methods for research are available to the scholar today, and the study of America's relations with all of the members of the Commonwealth, individually and collectively, at the level of the monograph, has been well begun, as a glance at the various lists of doctoral dissertations in progress throughout the United States and the Commonwealth reveals. The easy cliché, bright and sparkling from much wear, is giving way to the collective facts and the cautious interpretations upon which the scholar may build his broader works of synthesis, from which in turn new clichés may arise.

It was natural that the concept of a "century of peace" on the North American continent would have particular appeal in a world that could not find peace in its time. Under the impact of the growing liberal interpretation of history it became a textbook cliché that for nearly a hundred and fifty years the United States and Canada have been a joint example to the world of good neighborhood. The tradition of a "century of peace" could not stand the test of historical scholarship, however, for in 1950 Colonel Charles P. Stacey, then historian for the Canadian army, demonstrated in a pioneering article that the tradition, like so many, was based on a myth.[3] From 1815 until 1871 the British North American provinces felt themselves open to attack from an America that many provincials considered to be emotional, untrustworthy, and grasping. The United States seemed

---

[2] (New Haven and Toronto). For a brief description of the intended scope of the series, see Ware, ed., *Survey for 1934*, pp. 299–304. It is worth noting that five of the six standard surveys of Canadian-American relations have been written by Canadian, not American, scholars.

[3] "The Myth of the Unguarded Frontier, 1815–1871," *American Historical Review*, LVI (Oct., 1950), 1–18, and *The Undefended Border: The Myth and the Reality* (Ottawa, 1955).

certain that the British colonies would gravitate toward Washington, for the monarchical way of life, root of an older code threatened by the rising winds of democracy and republicanism, was said to be doomed. In the meantime, the provinces could be ignored or, when useful for America's domestic needs, Britain could be pricked through them, her "Achilles heel in North America." Peace between nations takes on greater urgency when it is understood that it has been tested by ordeals greater than mere debate and that harmonious relations, if even now established, are a thing of very recent vintage.

The period of the American Civil War, 1861-1865, was one of unusual tension along the border. From the Civil War emerged two nations, for not only was the Union preserved, but the Confederation of Canada was hastened as the war revealed its awesome lesson of the destructive fruits of separatism. Canada's political institutions owe much to the Civil War ; the war is a part of its history. And the conflict's central figure, Abraham Lincoln, has become a continental figure, one embraced by Canadians as eagerly as by Americans. One of the two earliest Lincoln Fellowships outside the United States was in Hamilton, Ontario, and Toronto has its own Civil War Round Table. Canada was represented at the Springfield observance of the Sesquicentennial of Lincoln's birth, and when the National Library of Canada and the Library of Congress jointly observed library week in 1959, the American gift to Canada was a microfilm of the Robert Todd Lincoln Collection of the Papers of Abraham Lincoln. [4] Several etchings of the Civil War President enhance the University of Alberta's art gallery, a city in western Canada honors Nancy Hanks Lincoln with a street name, and at least three prominent and highly successful Canadian politicians—Sir Wilfrid Laurier, Liberal Prime Minister, 1896-1911 ; John G. Diefenbaker, Conservative Prime Minister, 1957–1963 ; and Leslie Frost, Premier of Ontario, 1949–1961—have claimed on the hustings to be "fervent admirers of Lincoln." Not only does America's sixteenth President belong to the ages ; he belongs to the nations. [5]

[4] Hye Bossin, *In the Spirit of Abraham Lincoln* (Hamilton, 1954), p. 6; H. F. Rissler, "The Sesquicentennial of Lincoln's Birth," Ill. State Hist. Soc., *Journal*, LII (Summer, 1959), 295; Dept. of External Affairs, *Canadian Weekly Bulletin* (May 27, 1959), p. 5; *The Lincoln Sesquicentennial Intelligencer*, I (June, 1959), 3; L.C., *Information Bulletin* (April 13, 1959), pp. 201-205.
[5] On Laurier, see p. 363; on Diefenbaker, see "Prairie Lawyer," *Time* (Aug. 5, 1957), p. 25; Milton Mackaye, "Canada's Amazing Prime Minister," *Saturday Eve-*

The writer hopes that he has made some contribution to the history of Canada, to the history of diplomacy, and to imperial history, as well as to the continuing story of the Civil War. He feels that by discounting British North American affairs during the war, while subjecting other aspects of Anglo-American relations to close scrutiny, American scholars have tended to neglect a vital factor in British foreign policy. Of course, Britain's colonies in North America also had considerable influence on her colonial policy by their very existence. This is a study of Canadian-American relations, and to a lesser extent of Canadian nation-building, however, and the author does not intend it to be an investigation of British colonial administrative history, although he trusts that some new light may be thrown on the imperial situation. The writer also hopes that within the scope of his study he has been able to make some contribution that goes beyond G. M. Young's classic description of diplomatic history as "what one clerk said to another clerk," that where it is revisionist it will not seem presumptuous, and that where it is strictly factual it will at least warrant the reviewer's conveniently damning label, "useful."

ACKNOWLEDGMENTS

Originally submitted as a doctoral dissertation to the Department of History at The Johns Hopkins University, and subsequently revised and shortened, this book has benefited from the criticism and encouragement of several scholars. Charles S. Campbell, Jr., formerly of The Johns Hopkins and now at The Claremont Graduate School, directed this study in its initial stages and provided perceptive criticism of subsequent drafts. C. Vann Woodward, then also of The Johns Hopkins, read the entire manuscript in an early draft and rooted out a plethora of defects. Samuel Flagg Bemis of Yale University read the first third of an intermediate draft and gave willingly of his deeply informed criticism, while John Morton Blum, also of Yale, spent many hours of a typically busy and productive summer offering stylistic advice that improved the manuscript measurably. Thomas C. Mendenhall, formerly of Yale and now President of Smith College, criticized Chapter Twelve so that it might be a taut ship. Mason

ning Post (Aug. 30, 1958), p. 15; and London (Ont.) *Free Press*, March 14, 1960; on Frost, see McKenzie Porter, "Leslie Frost's Masquerade as the Common Man," *MacLean's* (May 23, 1959), pp. 14, 69.

Wade, when at the University of Rochester, suggested several pertinent French-Canadian sources, while Adolphe Robert, as President of the Association Canado-Américaine in Manchester, New Hampshire, commented on an early draft of the first portion of Chapter Ten.

Colonel Charles P. Stacey, then Director of the Historical Section of the Canadian Army and now on the faculty of the University of Toronto, read the entire manuscript and detected numerous errors of fact. Colonel Stacey was one of the first to encourage the writer in this project, as were the late Fred Landon of the University of Western Ontario and the late John Bartlet Brebner of Columbia University, and it is based upon the foundation that these three scholars so ably laid. W. L. Morton, then of the University of Manitoba, and Gerald Craig of the University of Toronto, brought their knowledge of the period to bear upon all or nearly all of the manuscript, while J. M. S. Careless and Elisabeth Wallace, also of Toronto, helped the writer in his efforts to understand George Brown and Goldwin Smith respectively. That the volume undoubtedly retains many flaws in style and errors in fact, all of which are the sole responsibility of the writer, is due entirely to his slowness as a pupil rather than to these, his teachers.

Ideally scholarly research and writing is a cooperative endeavor, and the writer has been fortunate in receiving the added and sometimes unsolicited aid and counsel of many who not only subscribe to but practice this ideal. Literally hundreds of people supplied anecdotes concerning Canadian enlistments in the Northern armies or public opinion during the Civil War, volunteered diaries, answered queries, and verified information. Ultimately most of the anecdotes and much of the information fell to the writer's bluc pencil—and it well may be suggested that even more should have done so—but whether such material was used or not, the writer is nonetheless indebted to those who offered it, and he hopes that the many who helped him will not feel that he is ungrateful when forced to refer to them by that most unsatisfactory of abbreviations, "too numerous to mention."

The writer is particularly grateful to Martin B. Duberman of Princeton, who permitted him to read portions of his manuscript biography of Charles Francis Adams ; to Lyman H. Butterfield of the Adams Manuscript Trust, who gave the author permission to quote from Adams' microfilm diary ; and to the late Joe Patterson Smith of Illinois College, who furnished valuable transcripts relating to Baring Brothers and Company. Several others who provided specific materials are acknowledged in the footnotes relating to their contributions.

Others helped in various ways and cannot be omitted, even for the sake of brevity. These include Lewis B. Mayhew of Michigan State University, David Spring and the late Sidney Painter of The Johns Hopkins, Glyndon G. Van Deusen of the University of Rochester, Clifton K. Yearley, then of the University of Florida, W. A. Ross of St. Albans, Vermont, Gabriel Nadeau of Rutland and Lienne Tétrault of Southbridge, Massachusetts, Ella Lonn of Baltimore, Eleanor Poland of Kansas City, Missouri, Peter Waite of Dalhousie University, Lewis G. Thomas of the University of Alberta, the Right Reverend Thomas B. Fulton, Chancellor of the Archdiocese of Toronto, Mrs. A. Woodburn Langmuir—daughter of George T. Denison—and Hye Bossin of Toronto, F. L. Britton of Hamilton, Constance Kerr Sissons of Whitby, Ontario, Edgar A. Collard of the Montreal *Gazette,* Mme Wilfrid Rouleau, also of Montreal, and Philip Van Doren Stern of New York City.

To the staff of what must be the most accessible of archives, tho Public Archives of Canada—where one may work through the night with but a single guard on the floor below—and especially to William Ormsby, Wilfred Smith, Rolland Labonté, and the former Dominion Archivist, W. Kaye Lamb, go particular thanks. Others at institutions visited by the writer who went far beyond the duties of their calling to provide materials were Mrs. Julia B. Carroll and Mrs. Patricia Dowling of the Foreign Affairs Section at the National Archives in Washington ; Margaret Butterfield of the Rush Rhees Library at the University of Rochester ; G. W. Spragge, as Archivist of Ontario ; D. H. Bocking and Allan R. Turner of the Saskatchewan Archives Board ; J. Russell Harper, then of The New Brunswick Museum ; D. C. Harvey, then Archivist of Nova Scotia ; Jean C. Gill, then Librarian of the Legislative and Public Library of Prince Edward Island ; Willard Ireland, Archivist of British Columbia ; Bruce Peel, Librarian of the University of Alberta ; Violet Taylor of the Toronto Public Library ; Laura A. Ekstrom of the State Historical Society of Colorado ; Francis C. Haber, then Librarian at the Maryland Historical Society ; Russell Reid of the State Historical Society of North Dakota ; Richard G. Wood of the Vermont Historical Society ; and Malcolm D. MacGregor of the Marine Historical Association at Mystic, Connecticut.

Without exception the librarians at the following institutions at
which the author worked also gave generously of their time : the
Parliamentary Library of Canada ; the legislative libraries of Alberta,
British Columbia, New Brunswick, Nova Scotia, and Ontario ; Univer-
sity of British Columbia, University of Saskatchewan, University of
Western Ontario, University of Toronto, Carleton University, Queen's
University, l'Université Laval, Dalhousie University, University of
New Brunswick, Acadia University ; the public libraries of Vancouver,
Edmonton, Ottawa, Hamilton, Montreal, Halifax, and Saint John ;
the Newfoundland Museum ; the Cambridge Military Library and the
Maritime Museum, both in Halifax ; and in the United States, the
Library of Congress, the New London Historical Society, the American
Antiquarian Society, the State Historical Society of Wisconsin, the
University of Colorado, the University of Illinois, the University of
Kentucky, the University of Vermont, Cornell University, the Houghton
and Widener Memorial libraries of Harvard University, the Yale
University Library, Connecticut College, Radcliffe College, the Enoch
Pratt Free Library and the library of the Peabody Institute in
Baltimore ; the public libraries of Seattle, Rochester (New York),
New York City, Detroit, and Boston ; the Boston Athenaeum, and
l'Union Saint-Jean-Baptiste d'Amérique, Woonsocket, Rhode Island.

Many institutions that the writer was unable to visit made him
feel as though he had done so, so prompt and thorough was their
cooperation. The Alabama Department of Archives and History
furnished a valuable photostat, the Trevor Arnett Library at Atlanta
University provided transcripts, Duke University Library supplied a
microfilm of the pertinent papers of Clement C. Clay, The Filson
Club in Louisville and the University of North Carolina Library made
diaries available, the Ohio Historical Society sent microfilms of the
papers of Joshua Giddings and Syracuse University supplied photostats
of others. The Clements Library of the University of Michigan sent
extracts from newspapers, the Brant Historical Society Museum
produced a photostat of a scarce article, the State Archivist of
Washington sent Verifax materials, the Illinois State Historical Society
loaned a rare pamphlet, and the Western Reserve Historical Society
provided a copy of a crucial manuscript. Other institutions that
provided books and other materials include the Historical Society of
Pennsylvania, the Historical Society of Montana, the Mississippi
Department of Archives and History, the Confederate Memorial Literary

Society of Richmond, the Buffalo Historical Society, the New York State Library, the Maine Historical Society, the Henry E. Huntington Library, the University of Chicago, the University of Oklahoma, the University of Maine, Stanford University, l'Université de Sherbrooke, the Glenbow Foundation in Calgary, the Provincial Library of Manitoba, the Jordan (Ontario) Historical Museum of the Twenty, the Lennox and Addington Historical Society, and of course the Public Record Office of Great Britain.

The writer would like to thank The Johns Hopkins University for financial aid for research and the Department of History of Yale University for making extensive typing services available. Six years' association with the departments of the two universities has shown him the nature of true scholarship even where he has been unable to achieve it himself. Mrs Ruthanne Baldwin of Baltimore and Mrs. Adelaide Amore of New Haven cheerfully suffered the writer's scrawl to type various drafts. The editors of *The American Neptune, The Canadian Historical Review*, and *North Dakota History* gave permission to use material that first appeared in their journals.

The writer's greatest debt remains to his parents, teachers both, who encouraged him in an early interest in history, and to his wife, who neither typed nor proofread the manuscript, but who supplied that which is most important of all, companionship.

A NOTE ON TERMINOLOGY

To use the term "Canadian-American relations" for the Civil War period technically is perhaps somewhat inaccurate. In 1861–1865 "Canada" was but one of several British Colonies, called provinces, to the north of the United States. "Canada," correctly used, applied only to the present-day provinces of Ontario and Quebec, which also were called "the united Canadas," "the united provinces," or more simply, "the Canadas." At this time "Canada West" and "Canada East" referred to Ontario and Quebec respectively, and to what had been called "Upper Canada" and "Lower Canada," respectively, earlier in the nineteenth century. All of these terms were used in correspondence in the 1860's. The present study is intended to include all of the present-day Dominion. This, in 1861–1865, consisted of the united Canadas ; of the Maritime Provinces of Prince Edward Island, New Brunswick, and Nova Scotia ; of

Newfoundland ; of the Hudson's Bay Company's territory ; and of the Crown Colony of British Columbia and the colony of Vancouver Island, which were separate units at the time. This entire area colloquially was referred to as "Canada" even during these years, and since reputable historians have used this inaccuracy for some time, the present writer feels no obligation to correct them. It could be argued that "the United States" also is employed inaccurately throughout, for the present study deals with Confederate as well as Federal relations with the provinces. However, the verdict of the Civil War— also a term that is controversial—seems sufficient justification for this terminology.

Robin W. Winks
New Haven, Connecticut
March, 1960

ᖇᖇ PREFACE TO THE SECOND EDITION

FIRST BOOKS ARE LIKE FIRST CHILDREN, IN THAT ONE ALWAYS LIKES to see them do well. I am naturally pleased, therefore, to see this volume, now over ten years old, reissued in such a way as both to bring it before a larger public and to make possible the correction of errors which appeared in the first edition. I am grateful to Professors Gerald Craig and Charles P. Stacey, of the University of Toronto, and Peter Waite of Dalhousie University, as well as the late Kenneth MacKirdy of Waterloo University, who pointed out to me most of the errors on the following errata page (p. XXIV).

In a decade, one's perspective on a subject changes. Were I able to revise more fully, I would now place less emphasis on the "inextricably bound . . . system of defense and . . . pattern of economic interchange" mentioned on page 380. The Introduction, in its references to Negroes in Canada, would require some alterations, although these are now available to interested readers in two recent explorations I have attempted, *The Blacks in Canada* (New Haven, 1971) and "Josiah Henson and Uncle Tom," an introduction to the 1969 reprint edition of the 1881 version of *An Autobiography of the Rev. Josiah Henson* . . . (Reading, Mass.) I have also been able to follow up certain minor leads relating to Maine (see page 107) in FO 5, 846 ; in the papers of Sir William Francis Drummond Jervois, which I found in 1966, and which I am now using for a biography ; and on the *Labuan* (see page 126) in FO 97, 42 and 43. Michael Brennan, of Egham, Surrey, has written (May 4, 1962) to me to say that he has found John C. Braine's Islington (London) birth certificate, which removes the mild doubts I expressed on page 245. I have not been able to gain access to the papers of Lord Lyons, now at Arundel Castle, which are being sorted. Nonetheless, despite the massive wave of Civil War books which appeared during the Civil War Centennial of the 1960's, very little has been written to prompt any revisions in the text.

It may be said, however, that my wife has fulfilled my prediction.

London
November, 1970

xvii

ABBREVIATIONS USED

AHR and A.H.A.—*American Historical Review* and Association.
BMW to/from GCC—British Minister to Washington to/from Governor-in-Chief of Canada, L.C. photostats. Original document in related series at P.A.C. also was examined when available.
BRH—*Le Bulletin des Recherches Historiques.*
B—Papers of the Admiralty, P.A.C.
C—Military Correspondence, P.A.C.
CD—Consular Dispatches, United States, N.A. Followed by post name.
CFA—Reports from Minister to Great Britain, Charles Francis Adams, to Department of State, N.A.
CFA Diary—Charles Francis Adams' Diary.
CHR and C.H.A.—*Canadian Historical Review* and Association.
CO—British Colonial Office Records, P.R.O., on photostats at P.A.C. and L.C.
CSA—Confederate States Archives, L.C.
DL—Interdepartmental Domestic Letters, Department of State, N.A.
E—Papers of the Executive Council of Canada, P.A.C.
FO—British Foreign Office Records, P.R.O., on photostats at L.C.
G—Papers of the Governor General of British North America, P.A.C. Sub-divided into series numbers.
GBI—Instructions to Minister to Great Britain, N.A.
ITC—Instructions to United States Consuls, N.A.
L.C.—Library of Congress, Washington, D.C.
MC—Miscellaneous Correspondence, Department of State, N.A.
MVHR—*Mississippi Valley Historical Review.*
N.A.—National Archives, Washington, D.C.
NBL—Notes to the British Legation, N.A.
NFBL—Notes from the British Legation, N.A.
O.P.A.—Ontario Provincial Archives, Toronto.
OR—*The War of the Rebellion: A Compilation of the Official Records of the Union and Confederate Armies* (Washington, 1880–1901).
ORN—Rush, Richard, *et. al., Official Records of the Union and Confederate Navies in the War of the Rebellion* (Washington, 1894–1927).

P.A.C.—Public Archives of Canada, Ottawa.
P.A.N.S.—Public Archives of Nova Scotia, Halifax.
PP—Great Britain, *Parliamentary Papers.*
P.R.O.—Public Record Office, London.
T.P.L.—Toronto Public Library.
W.R.—War Records, N.A.

Collections of private papers are cited in full on the first occasion, with their place of deposit indicated. Subsequent abbreviations are based on surnames. Abbreviations not listed above, and documentation, are modeled on William R. Parker, comp., *The MLA Style Sheet* (Rev. ed., Washington, 1951).

ဢ CONTENTS

CONTENTS

Canada and the United States: The Civil War Years

৯ ERRATA

On page 25, for Golden Smith read Goldwin Smith, as it appears correctly elsewhere ;

On page 26, for Labrador read Quebec ;

On page 59, note 17, for *Traditions* read *Tradition* ;

On page 70, for continued her voyage read made her way ;

On page 78 and note 31 on page 79, for Frederick Rogers read Frederic Rogers ;

On page 85, note 47, for *Soie* read *Sorel* ;

On page 103, for formalized read formal ;

On page 105, note 1, for [George T. Denison] read [H. B. Wilson] ;

On page 118, note 37, insert George Bennett as editor of *The Concept of Empire* ;

On page 121, note 45, for 1919 read 1909 ;

On page 144, for pulsillanimous read pusillanimous ; for Gloucester, Canada, read Gloucester County ;

On page 156, for James McLaughlin read John McLaughlin ;

On page 160, for Alexander S. Johnston read Alexander S. Johnson ;

On page 161, for Sir John Rose read John (shortly Sir John) Rose ;

On page 163, for Barcley Sound read Barkley Sound ;

On page 164, for San Juan de Fuca read Juan de Fuca ;

On page 166, note 24, for *Period* read *Era* ;

On page 248, for St. Mary Bay read St.Mary's Bay ;

On page 249, for St. Margaret Bay read St.Margaret's Bay ;

On page 259, for aids read aides ;

On page 267, for Windsor University read King's College, Windsor ;

On page 282, for reconsideration read government ;

On page 306, for *Telegram* read *Telegraph*, and again on page 311, note 26, and page 367, note 11.

On page 313, note 29, for O.P.A. read P.A.C. ;

On page 350, for Conservative read Liberal ;

On page 388, for Story), and W.C. Milner read Story and W.C. Milner) ;

Corresponding corrections should also appear in the Index.

one ϼϽ INTRODUCTION

"The United States is the affirmation of the
revolutionary process; Canada the negation."
BRUCE HUTCHISON

HAD THE PEOPLE OF BRITISH NORTH AMERICA BEEN ABLE TO HEAR, DURING
the nineteenth century, the frequent declarations by certain Mid-
western politicians in the early part of the following century that the
United States always had followed a policy of isolation, they probably
would have been amused. Although the North American republic
generally had been successful in avoiding entanglements and alliances,
permanent or temporary, in Europe, it definitely had not pursued such
a policy in the New World.

The Monroe Doctrine, supposed bulwark against such entanglements, was not isolationist. With respect to the New World it was
given an increasingly internationalist interpretation from the time of
James K. Polk's presidency. The Doctrine in its original form did not
include the British provinces within its orbit, but in the years before
the Civil War many American expansionists avowed that the provinces
violated the spirit of Monroe's supposed intent. The United States
never had professed to follow a policy of isolation on the North
American continent, and she frequently had been embroiled in major
and minor disputes with her neighbors. After 1854 she had close connections through a reciprocal trade treaty with most of Britain's North
American provinces and hence with Britain herself.

British North America also made it impossible for the mother
country to follow a policy of isolation toward North America in time
of emergency. Any policy with respect to Europe had to be shaped
with the realization that strategically "Britain's back door" stood wide

open to attack in North America. She could not concentrate her entire force in Europe for fear of an American war, and she could not garrison the provinces heavily for fear of a European war. This lesson had been made clear during the Napoleonic era when the first of the world wars engulfed the United States as well. During the war the United States unsuccessfully had attempted to seize the coveted colonies. Again, in 1837, when rebellion swept across the Canadas like summer lightning, the United States, while passing a strict neutrality act, had provided the rebels with shelter and indirect aid. Throughout the nineteenth century the British provinces were a collective hostage through which the United States could win concessions from Great Britain. Even after confederation in 1867 Canada continued to thwart American efforts to relax into a position of continental isolation. Whether colony or dominion, loose string of provinces or member of a Commonwealth, Canada has not escaped participation in every major European war. Partially because the United States could not allow Canada to fall to a European invader, the United States has found isolation from Europe's wars impossible.

In 1861 British North America consisted of five provinces stretching from Lake Superior to the Atlantic Ocean, of two colonies on the far Pacific coast, and of a vast unsettled area in between. The united provinces of Upper and Lower Canada, combined as a single province administratively, but still divided culturally and geographically into Canada West and Canada East, dominated the British-owned half of the continent. Along the Atlantic coast were New Brunswick, Nova Scotia, and Prince Edward Island, the first two of considerable importance because of their strategic locations and their dominance over the fisheries, the last a tiny island cut off from the rest of the world. In all of these provinces a governor general, resident in Quebec, Canada East, represented the presence of the Crown. The governor-generalship of British North America generally was considered one of the most important administrative positions that Her Majesty's Colonial Office could bestow. The three Maritime Provinces also had their own lieutenant governors or administrators. Each of the provinces had considerable local autonomy with elected assemblies and appointed executive councils. Among the Atlantic Provinces, but not included under the governor general's immediate jurisdiction, was Newfoundland, an isolated island that enjoyed less autonomy than her mainland neighbors. On the Pacific coast were the colonies of Vancouver Island

and British Columbia, technically separate but under a single governor. In between lay the vast territory of the Hudson's Bay Company, controlled from London, administered from Fort Garry on the Red River by a resident governor, and also outside the governor general's jurisdiction.

All of these areas, save the two island Atlantic Provinces, had close contacts with the United States. When anti-imperialism was at its height in England, it was British North America, so dangerously close to the United States, that was considered for independence first.[1] The Little Englanders argued that loyalty suffered a sea-change, that the trans-Atlantic colonies, in particular, of the European powers grew to independence almost as a law of nature. And British North America was likely to breed war with the United States because of her very existence.

The peace that Canada and the United States observed during the nineteenth century was often an uneasy one. Only since 1871 has the so-called undefended frontier truly been undefended. From 1783 to 1871 Great Britain and the provinces felt that an American invasion was possible, and the United States, in turn, resented the presence of a foreign flag on North American soil. Both nations kept the frontier in a state of partial defense throughout these years, and when there was no shooting war, there was what one Canadian newspaper preferred to call "a war in anticipation."[2]

From the very beginning, events conspired against friendly relations. Briefly Nova Scotia had considered joining the other American colonies in rebellion and had sent delegates to the Second Continental Congress. Loyalists driven from the rebellious colonies virtually had created Upper Canada, and it was Upper Canada, as Canada West or Ontario, that later populated the Prairie Provinces. These loyalists, sincere in their conviction that rebellion against the Crown had been unwise, were forced to begin a new life, and they nursed a hatred for the Republic.

---

[1] For example, see R. L. Schuyler, "The Climax of Anti-Imperialism in England," *Political Science Quarterly*, xxxvi (Dec., 1921), 537–560.

[2] Montreal *Witness*, Dec. 30, 1861. Carl Sandburg has called the period 1860–1861 a "Cold War." This phrase carries unfortunate twentieth-century connotations, which do not apply here. See Sandburg, *Lincoln Collector: The Story of Oliver R. Barrett's Great Private Collection* (New York, 1949), p. 248, and William Clark, *Less than Kin: A Study of Anglo-American Relations* (London, 1957), p. 1. Clark refers to the period 1817–1871 as one of "competitive coexistence."

The War of 1812 had served to inject this same hatred into a new generation. The emerging tradition of the "century of peace" was tempered in the fire of severe trial long after 1815.

Great Britain made some effort to maintain a semblance of a balance of power in North America from 1817 to 1850. This balance came to depend more and more on salt-water superiority and less and less on equality along the Great Lakes. By 1850 Britain was recognizing that the only means of keeping the provinces from entering the political orbit of the United States was to take the calculated risk of having them partially enter its economic orbit. In 1854 a reciprocity treaty, the first Britain ever negotiated on behalf of a colony and the first ever signed by the United States, was forced upon the Republic when Britain rigorously enforced the Convention of 1818 against American fishermen. While the Maritime Provinces were dissatisfied with the treaty, it brought prosperity to the united Canadas and helped to end efforts on the part of some of the merchants of Montreal to have Canada East annexed to the United States. If the reciprocity treaty frustrated annexation, and if it was intended as part of a *détente* in Anglo-American relations,[3] it also created additional friction. In the years of industrial growth before the Civil War, protectionist sentiment in Canada grew rapidly, and in 1859 the Canadas changed from a specific to an ad valorem basis for levying duties and placed a higher tariff on manufactured goods. This, one group in the United States contended, violated the spirit of the reciprocal agreement

During these same years the American frontier had been pushed rapidly westward. Between 1850 and 1860 population of the area that became Minnesota increased 2,730 per cent. As new railroads hungrily licked northwestward for more land, Americans moved closer to the territory of the Hudson's Bay Company, a land that Canadians considered part of their own manifest destiny. Since 1858, it was rumored, American agents had been engaged in renewed annexationist activities on the Pacific coast. When thousands of gold-seekers swept north from California to the gold fields of British Columbia in 1859, it appeared to some that the omnivorous Americans soon would cut Canada West off from expansion to the western sea. In 1860 William H. Seward, a powerful Republican expansionist, declared in a platform speech at

---

[3] On this view see Max Beloff, "Great Britain and the American Civil War," *History*, n.s., xxxvii (Feb., 1952), 43; R. W. Van Alstyne, "British Diplomacy and the Clayton-Bulwer Treaty, 1850–1860," *Journal of Modern History*, xi (June, 1939), 149–183.

St. Paul that he hoped to see the time when that city would be the center of an America that embraced the entire continent. Although much of the annexation sentiment of American orators was political pap, it seemed apparent that the West could not be held by the British company much longer, for even the residents of the Red River settlement were beginning to complain of their lack of representative government.

Something of a *rapprochement* between Great Britain and the United States took place in 1860. Despite some discord over the reciprocity treaty, the two nations seemed to be on far friendlier terms than at any time since the Treaty of Ghent. The only outstanding issue between them was a jurisdictional dispute over the San Juan Islands in Puget Sound. The dispute, arising out of an imprecise boundary definition in the Treaty of 1846, which had settled the major Oregon territorial question, was not serious because neither nation wished to have it so. In June, 1859, one Captain George Pickett, acting under the orders of Brigadier General William S. Harney, Commander of the Oregon Department, had occupied the principal island of the group. Governor James Douglas of Vancouver Island and British Columbia had protested Pickett's action, and Secretary of War John B. Floyd had sent General Winfield Scott to the islands to arrange a *modus vivendi*. The American troops were moved to one end of the island, and a joint occupation, beginning on March 13, 1860, was peaceably arranged, despite General Harney's continued declarations that the islands were part of Washington territory.[4]

It also was in 1860 that Queen Victoria's eldest son, the Prince of Wales, visited the United States. This was the first time since the Revolution that a member of the royal family had visited the Republic, and there were some trepidations in the mind of the Duke of Newcastle, who accompanied the Prince, concerning the behavior of recent Irish immigrants to America during the visit. Newcastle, an imperialist of the old school, was impressed by what he saw in British North America. The colonies seemed to be a bulwark of the Empire, and

---

[4] See Hugh L. Keenleyside and Gerald S. Brown, *Canada and the United States: Some Aspects of their Historical Relations* (Rev. ed., New York, 1952), pp. 190–196, for a lucid summary of the San Juan episode. On the Far West see R. L. Reid, "John Nugent: The Impertinent Envoy," *British Columbia Historical Quarterly*, VIII (Jan., 1944), 71, and J. W. Pratt, "The Ideology of American Expansion," in Avery O. Craven, ed., *Essays in Honor of William E. Dodd by His Former Students at the University of Chicago* (Chicago, 1935), pp. 335–353. Other works on expansionism are cited in Chapter Nine.

despite anti-imperialistic rumblings in England, he determined that
they should be retained. The Prince dedicated the new Victoria Railway Bridge spanning the St. Lawrence River at Montreal, was fêted at
Halifax (where the American consul's daughter asked for a dance
with "Mr. Wales"), was present at the laying of the cornerstone for
the new Canadian Parliament buildings at Ottawa, and watched
Blondin, the famous balancing artist, walk across Niagara Falls on a
tightrope.

The Prince, traveling as Baron Renfrew in the United States, found
an unexpectedly warm welcome. A flotilla of illuminated steamers
and three hundred torch-bearing firemen greeted him when he arrived
at Detroit. At Chicago an excited mayor honored him, at Springfield
happy crowds cheered him, in western Illinois numerous grouse, which
he promptly shot, entertained him, and in Washington a worried
President, James Buchanan, assured him of American friendship. Newcastle, agreeably surprised that there was no unpleasant incident to mar
the visit, wrote to the Prime Minister, Viscount Palmerston, in glow-
ing terms:

> There could be but two causes for such a demonstration: personal
> love of the Queen, which amongst this people is a passion, and
> rapidly growing affection for England, which I am thoroughly con-
> vinced this visit will speedily ripen into a firm and (if properly
> watched and fostered) an enduring attachment . . . . I think I am
> not too sanguine in saying now that we shall leave the United States
> on the 20th a faster friend to our country than they have been since
> their separation.[5]

The Prince of Wales was entertained in Boston on October 18,
1860. On that day he marched by Breed's Hill to shake hands with one
Ralph Farnham, the last survivor of the Battle of Bunker Hill, and with

[5] John Martineau, *The Life of Henry Pelham, Fifth Duke of Newcastle, 1811–1864*
(London, 1908), pp. 299–300. Of the many sources of information on the tour
the most informative were P.A.C., G 1, 153: Newcastle to Head, April 23, 1861;
G. D. Englehart, *Journal of the Progress of H.R.H. the Prince of Wales through
British North America, and his Visit to the United States, 10th July to 15 Nov.,
1860* (London, 1860); T. B. Gough, *Boyish Reminiscences of His Majesty the
King's Visit to Canada in 1860* (London, 1910), pp. 162–178; James Macauley,
ed., *Speeches and Addresses of H.R.H. The Prince of Wales: 1863–1888* (London,
1889), pp. 7–9; Victor Tremblay, "Le Prince de Galles nous visite," *Saguenayensia*,
1 (June, 1959), 51–56; and David C. Mearns, *Lincoln and the Image of America*
(Hamilton, Ont., 1953), p. 2.

Farnham's seventy-year-old daughter. Shortly thereafter the Prince and his suite steamed from Portsmouth for England in H.M.S. *Hero*. Massed bands played the anthems of both nations, and as he sailed away he could have seen, had he chosen to look back, the British and American flags intertwined on the hills overlooking the harbor. On November 2 *The Times* of London pronounced itself convinced that there would be eternal peace between the nations.

A year later the same newspaper thought that war was inevitable, for the apparent *rapprochement* of 1860 was short-lived. With the outbreak of civil war in the United States, the great gulf of ignorance between the countries, as illuminated by *The Times'* confession to "habitual indifference to American affairs," [6] took its effect. The British North American provinces, on the other hand, were thought to be in a position to interpret the war and its issues to the mother country, to dispel some of the ignorance that existed concerning the United States. For it was not only the constitutional issues involved in sectionalism and secession of which the English were uninformed. Many Englishmen knew less about the United States than they knew of central Africa, and novels with supposed American settings that told of monkeys and tropical foliage in Illinois, of ice caps in Maine and elephants in South Carolina, found readers in the British Isles.

British North Americans had cause to know more about the United States and, in particular, about her "peculiar institution" of slavery. There had been slavery in the provinces themselves, but the practice had been limited in the eighteenth century, and after 1833, when Great Britain abolished slavery in all of her colonies, the provincials became increasingly hopeful for the ending of slavery in the United States as well. After 1850 the people of the provinces had given close attention to events in the Republic, for in that year the Fugitive Slave Act was passed. The act spurred thousands of Negroes across the border into the provinces and particularly into Canada West.

The census figures for 1851 and 1861 show something of the influx of escaped slaves. In the former year eight thousand Negroes lived in Canada West and only eighteen in Canada East. By the outbreak of the Civil War there were over eleven thousand in Canada West, a still negligible one hundred and ninety in Canada East. The Negro population of New Brunswick increased nearly fifty per cent during the ten years, from eleven hundred to sixteen hundred. The Negro was more prevalent in Nova Scotia than elsewhere, for one person in fifty was

*Feb. 17, 1858.

a Negro, the population increasing from five thousand to six thousand during the decade. There were, therefore, approximately nineteen thousand Negroes in the provinces in 1861, according to the census report, plus an estimated four thousand Negroes on the Pacific coast.[7]

These census figures are unreliable, however, and other sources have placed the Negro population of the provinces as high as seventy-five thousand by 1861. Sixty thousand is the commonly accepted estimate for all of British North America, at least twenty thousand of whom crossed the border in the final decade. In 1861 the American Missionary Association estimated that forty thousand Negroes lived in Canada West alone, a figure that recent scholars have revised to thirty thousand.[8]

After 1850 the people of the Canadas, in particular, were supporters of abolitionism. There was some effort to segregate schools, especially in Canada West, where over half of the Negro population was living in three counties, and the last segregated school did not close until 1891, but most Canadians favored freedom for the Negro and a certain degree of equality of opportunity. This feeling can be overemphasized, however, unless one realizes that many of the abolitionists did not share today's concept of social and economic equality. The Negro was to be free, but he was not to forget his station in life. Toronto, Hamilton, London, Halifax, and Saint John all had their Black Halls, Negro quarters, "African" churches, and Darky Lanes. The Negroes, often from choice and sometimes from pressure, continued to live a segregated life in the provinces. But they were free, a few were prosperous, and except during the coldest winters they seemed content.[9]

[7] Canada, Board of Registration and Statistics, *Census of the Canadas, for 1851–52* (Quebec, 1853), I, 36–37, 107, 317; *Census of the Canadas, 1860–61* (Quebec, 1863), I, 43, 79; and Anti-Slavery Society of Canada, *First Annual Report . . .* (Toronto, 1852), p. 17. The Pacific coast estimate appears in Matthew Macfie, *Vancouver Island and British Columbia* (London, 1865), p. 388.

[8] Fred Landon, "The Negro Migration to Canada after the Passing of the Fugitive Slave Act," *Journal of Negro History*, v (Jan., 1920), 22; Ida Greaves, *The Negro in Canada* (Orillia, Ont., 1931), pp. 33–34. On the estimate of the American Missionary Association see Landon's two articles, "The Negro Refugees in Canada West, 1848–1864," *American Missionary*, n.s., XVI (Nov., 1924), 296–297; and "The Work of the American Missionary Association among the Negro Refugees in Canada West, 1848–1864," Ontario Hist. Soc., *Papers and Records*, XXI (1924), pp. 198–205; and the 1861 *Report* of the Association. The present writer has in progress a general history of the Negro in Canada.

[9] On segregation see the Toronto *Globe*, Oct. 15, 1861; O.P.A., Education Office: Dennis Hill to Egerton Ryerson, Mar. 22, 1852; "Two Brothers," *The United*

It was at Chatham, in Canada West, that John Brown met with several Negroes and three whites in May of 1858 to plan a blow against the South, and Southerners never forgave Canadians for this.[10] It was to Canada that three of the Secret Six who supported Brown fled following the raid at Harper's Ferry, and while there one of them, Samuel Gridley Howe, wrote to abolitionist Theodore Parker:

> I look with the more interest upon Canada, because it seems to me she is to be the great and reliable ally of the Northern States, in the coming struggle with slavery. When the lines are fairly drawn what an immense moral aid it will be to the North to have such a population as that of Canada (especially Canada West) at her back! [11]

George Brown, editor of the powerful Toronto *Globe*, knew of the Chatham meeting in advance and supported the abolitionists. Slavery, he wrote, polluted the entire continent: "The leprosy of the atrocious system affects all around it. . . . We are in the habit of calling the people of the United States 'the American,' but we too are Americans; on us, as well as on them, lies the duty of preserving the honour of the continent." [12] Brown also drew a parallel between the veto power of

---

States and Canada as Seen by Two Brothers in 1858–1861 (London, 1862), p. 107; "T.D.L.," *A Peep at the Western World* (London, 1863), p. 15; W. H. and J. H. Pease, "Opposition to the Founding of the Elgin Settlement," *CHR*, xxxviii (Sept., 1957), 202–218; and T. L. Spraggins, "Negro Colonization on the Eve of the Civil War," *The Negro Educational Review*, ix (April, 1958), 65–77.

[10] J. C. Hamilton, "John Brown in Canada," *Canadian Magazine*, iv (Dec., 1894), 134; J. L. Hubard, "Mr. Hamilton's Sketch of Brown," *ibid.* (March, 1895), 487–489; Fred Landon, "Canadian Negroes and the John Brown Raid," *Jour. of Negro Hist.*, vi (April, 1921), 174–182.

[11] L. E. Richards, ed., *Letters and Journals of Samuel Gridley Howe* (Boston, 1906–1909), ii, 447: March 25, 1860. A search of the John Brown Papers at the L.C. and Massachusetts Historical Society, and of the Franklin B. Sanborn Papers at the University of Atlanta was not revealing. Literature on Brown is extensive and rapidly growing, and most of it contains passing reference to the Chatham meeting or to Howe, Sanborn, and George L. Stearns, Brown's supporters who fled to Canada, or to Frederick Douglass, the Negro leader, who also temporarily took refuge in Canada. The definitive historiographical study is J. C. Malin, *John Brown and the Legend of Fifty-Six* (Philadelphia, 1942), while a valuable bibliographical essay appears in C. Vann Woodward, "John Brown's Private War," in Daniel Aaron, ed., *America in Crisis* (New York, 1952), pp. 109–130.

[12] March 24, 1852, quoted in Fred Landon, "The Anti-Slavery Society of Canada," *Jour. of Negro Hist.*, iv (Jan., 1919), 39.

the South and that of French Canada, and he hoped that he soon would see "the overthrow of two equally baleful dominations—the Slavocracy of the South and the French Priestocracy of the North." Sir Edmund Head, Governor General of British North America from 1854 to 1861, had taken an interest in the racial problem in the United States, and he too had foreseen the possibility of a civil war over slavery, as had the editors of such newspapers as the Toronto *Leader* and the Napanee *Bee*.[13]

Most of the communities along the border served, at one time or another, as terminals for the underground railroad. Fugitive slaves crossed the border from Detroit, Cleveland, and Buffalo, from upper New York and Vermont. They crossed the Great Lakes in open boats to land at the tiny ports in Canada West or trekked north into the Maritime Provinces. Economically they created no tension, for they turned to heavy labor in the cities or, in Canada West, farmed and worked on the railroads, although there was some slight resentment expressed by French Canadians over their presence. But psychologically they had a great impact on the people of British North America.[14]

So too did Harriet Beecher Stowe's *Uncle Tom's Cabin*, which was published in Toronto and Montreal in 1852. The Toronto *Globe* printed selections from the book, including the famous fifth chapter, and the book itself sold in the thousands and reportedly made confirmed abolitionists of many Canadians. The story was even more exciting when it was realized that the prototype of Uncle Tom, the Reverend Josiah Henson, who had escaped to the Canadas in 1830, was living at the colony of Dawn, near Dresden, in Canada West.[15] Even

[13] *Globe*, Sept. 5, 1860; *Leader*, Dec. 22, 1859; *Bee*, Nov. 16, 1850, the last quoted in W. S. Herrington, ed., "The Newspapers of the County," Lennox and Addington Hist. Soc., *Papers and Records*, x (1919), 7–8.

[14] G 1, 153: Newcastle to Head, Jan. 8, 1861. Many of the articles of Fred Landon, in particular "The Underground Railroad Along the Detroit River," *Michigan History*, xxxix (March, 1955), 63–68; "A Daring Canadian Abolitionist," *ibid.*, v (Oct., 1921), 364–373; "Captain Charles Stuart, Abolitionist," *Western Ontario History Nuggets*, no. 24 (London, 1956); and "Abolitionist Interest in Upper Canada," *Ontario History*, xliv (Oct., 1952), 165–172, deal with the underground railroad. See also John Nettleton, "Reminiscences, 1857–1870," Huron Institute, *Papers and Records*, ii (1914), 15.

[15] Toronto *Globe*, March 2, 1938; J. L. Beattie, *Black Moses: The Real Uncle Tom* (Toronto, 1957); Aileen Ward, "In Memory of 'Uncle Tom,'" *Dalhousie Review*, xx (Oct., 1940), 335–338; Fred Landon, "When Uncle Tom's Cabin Came to Canada," *Ontario Hist.*, xliv (1952), 1–5; Jean Tallach, "The Story of Josiah Henson," Kent Hist. Soc., *Papers and Records*, vii (1951), 43–52.

today *Uncle Tom's Cabin* is the "American classic" that Canadian school children know best. It probably served to make many men vow, as did the young Wilfrid Laurier, who was one day to be Prime Minister, that slavery must be destroyed.[16]

Now, on March 1, 1861, as Abraham Lincoln prepared to take office as President of a troubled United States, the Most Reverend John J. Lynch, Bishop of Toronto, received Pope Pius IX's endorsement to change the name of a tiny church above Niagara Falls to "Our Lady of Peace" so that it might become a pilgrim's shrine to North American harmony. Early in 1861 the Federal government of the United States had reason to believe that the people of British North America would view a civil war with, at worst, a highly benevolent neutrality, and at best, active aid to the free-soil states. There was cause, they felt, to assume that the provinces would form an alliance of the spirit with the North.[17]

[16] Arthur A. Hauck, *Some Educational Factors Affecting the Relations between Canada and the United States* (Easton, Pa., 1932), p. 22. For the even greater impact of Mrs. Stowe's book as a play, see Harry Birdoff, *The World's Greatest Hit: Uncle Tom's Cabin* (New York, 1947), pp. 144–185. On Laurier see John I. Cooper, *Montreal, the Story of Three Hundred Years* ([Montreal], 1942), pp. 80–81.

[17] Archives, Archdiocese of Toronto: Papal Brief, Pius IX, March 1, 1861 and Archbishop Lynch, Pastoral Letters, April 25, 1876; F. H. Severance, "Niagara's Consecration to Peace," Buffalo Hist. Soc., *Publications*, XVIII (1914), 98–99. See also *History of the Archdiocese of Toronto* (Toronto, 1892); *History of St. Patrick's Church, Niagara Falls, Ontario* (Niagara Falls, Ont., 1945); and Roger Duhamel, "La Politique étrangère du Canada," *Ecrits du Canada Français*, II (1955), 105.

two ⪻ SHIFTING TIDES OF OPINION

> "There is some misunderstanding between the Northern and Southern states . . . ."
> ALEXANDER MC NEILLEDGE

DURING THE WINTER OF THE SECESSION CRISIS BRITISH NORTH AMERICAN public opinion was, for the most part, in sympathy with the Federal government of the United States. The British colonials tended to be abolitionists. They were inclined to consider the disruption of the American democracy due to moral issues, and at first they regarded arguments to the contrary as sophistries. This sympathy with the Northern states was evident only so long as the main issue in the secession crisis appeared to be slavery. In January the editor of the Toronto *Globe* probably spoke for many when he declared that he had "waded through many speeches delivered by men in and out of Congress" since Lincoln's election and had "totally failed to find any one good and sufficient reason for destroying the union." He added, in explanation of his paper's columns bursting with American news, that Canadians were deeply interested in the fate of the American Union, for they knew that any fundamental change in the Republic would alter the future of the entire continent.[1] British North Americans were in general agreement that a war fought to free the slave, while a terrible price to pay, would remove a blot from the American character.[2]

By the time of the firing on Fort Sumter many British North Ameri-

[1] Jan. 7, 1861. The quotation at the head of the page appears in P.A.C., McNeilledge Diary, M-113, R2: 889, 15.

[2] For one example, see P.A.C., Thomas D'Arcy McGee Papers: McGee to James Sadlier, Feb. 15, 1861.

cans were beginning to reconsider their sympathy for the North. During the spring it became increasingly evident to them that the Republican administration did not intend to fight a war for abolition, and with the common bond of abolitionism removed, the people of the provinces reviewed their position with respect to the North more analytically. The people of the British provinces knew little of the President-elect's character or abilities, they distrusted his administrative officers, and they generally were unable to understand the constitutional issues involved in secession or the justice of a war over union.

The Southern states resented the sentiments of the *Globe* and its abolitionist brethren. After John Brown's raid at Harper's Ferry, Governor Henry A. Wise of Virginia had hinted at international subversion of the American (i.e. Southern) way of life by a "sectional organization" originating in the Canadas, and he had predicted that the war on abolitionists would be carried into the Negro-welcoming provinces.[3] He probably agreed that there was no country in the world "so much hated by slaveholders as Canada."[4] *De Bow's Review* summed up abolitionists as "the vile, sensuous, animal, brutal, infidel, superstitious Democracy of Canada and the Yankees."[5] It seemed that by its own profession British North America rather clearly was aligned in sentiment with the North, and that it had little or no sympathy for the slave states. When it became apparent that the provinces were, in fact, not pro-Northern, there was an anti-Canadian reaction in the North.

During the secession winter the colonials found sufficient cause to continue to disparage the South. In February New Brunswickers were indignant over the tarring and feathering of a fellow provincial in Savannah because he entertained Negroes on his vessel and declared that Negroes were as good as white men. Shortly thereafter Governor Wise of Virginia reportedly renewed his attack on the Canadas, calling upon outgoing President James Buchanan to demand from Britain a promise that Negroes would be returned forcibly from their sanctuary within the provinces to a life of slavery in the South.

The British press groped to understand the crisis and its meaning

[3] Va., Senate, *Journal*, 1859, pp. 9–25; Toronto *Globe*, Dec. 28, 1859.
[4] S. R. Ward, *Autobiography of a Fugitive Negro* (London, 1855), p. 158. See also R. J. Zorn, "Criminal Extradition Menaces the Canadian Haven for Fugitive Slaves, 1841–1861," *CHR*, XXXVIII (Dec., 1957), 284–294.
[5] Quoted in Fred Landon, "Canadian Opinion of Southern Secession, 1860–61," *CHR*, I (Sept., 1920), 258.

for the Crown in North America. Opinion was divided over whether or not the United States government should use force to compel the Southern states to remain in the fold, but at first, in the British North American provinces at least, there was general agreement that the dissolution of the Union was unfortunate and that the Southern leaders were responsible for it. On January 7 *The Times* of London, to which most Canadian papers rather slavishly looked for guidance, found the secession of South Carolina to be the bitter fruit of the South's own aggressive policy, and it declared that slavery was the sole cause of the crisis.

Throughout the crisis and the war itself the Toronto *Globe*, Canada's leading newspaper, was the chief Canadian advocate of what was thought to be the Northern position. It warred upon all apologists for slavery. Some of its reform fever undoubtedly was due to a circulation race with the Toronto *Leader* or was intended to embarrass the conservative government then in power, but much of it was sincere. The *Globe* was the most widely read newspaper in the British North American provinces, claiming a circulation in 1862 of thirty thousand.[6] As the voice of the Clear Grit or Reform party in the united Canadas, it was the chief spokesman for the "representation by population" demands of Canada West. In this sense it often was considered to be too American in its political philosophy. Nationalistic, far more interested in Canada's future than in England's past, and youthfully exuberant, it launched crusades against a strangely wonderful assortment of evils. To the mind of George Brown, its politically ambitious editor, slavery was the most virulent of these evils. Both in his birthplace, Scotland, and in New York City, where he had lived, Brown had imbibed abolitionism. He carried it with him to Toronto and attempted to make it part of his Victorian reform creed there. He expressed his sincerity by aiding fugitive Negroes and by giving financial aid to Negro families resident in Canada West. On slavery as the cause of the war Brown wrote: "We are in a position to speak with confidence to the anti-slavery men of Great Britain . . . to tell them that slavery is the one great cause of the American rebellion, and that the success of the North is the death-knell of slavery."[7]

[6] J. M. S. Careless, "George Brown and the Toronto *Globe*," unpub. Ph. D. diss. (2 vols., Harvard, 1949), p. 117. Careless, *Brown of the Globe: The Voice of Upper Canada, 1818–1859* (Toronto, 1959), as its title indicates, does not reach the war period.

[7] Quoted in John Lewis, *George Brown* (Toronto, 1912), p. 116.

Possibly more than any other newspaper in the provinces, the *Globe* could claim, at least on domestic issues, to formulate rather than merely to guide, to guide rather than merely to express, the opinion of the people, and with it as his lever Brown was attempting to force himself into the ranks of the mighty. In addition to the obvious virtues of its editorials, its full coverage of news, and its reprinted English articles, the *Globe* was a powerful force because it frequently "scooped" its rivals. In 1867 Brown would print a substantially correct draft of the Confederation Bill, then before the British Parliament in London, four days before an official copy reached Ottawa. During the Quebec Conference in 1864 Brown would have the earlier speeches into print and on the streets while the official banquet was still in progress. In 1861 he made telegraphic arrangements for war reports that put the *Globe* far in advance of the rest of the colonial press.[8]

Despite the *Globe*'s intensive efforts, British North American interest in the Civil War did not remain focused on slavery. Conservative opinion took its cue from *The Times*. By March "The Thunderer" reconsidered its judgment that slavery was the chief issue and avowed that the tariff controversy was equally important. A week later *The Times* removed the qualification, concluding that slavery was not an issue at all and that the basic causes of the approaching war were purely economic.[9] In this case at least two conservative Canadian papers did not wait for *The Times*' guidance. The powerful Montreal *Gazette* announced on January 10 that the origin of disunion lay in economic conflicts. The first major Canadian newspaper to give explicit support to the Southern cause, the *Gazette* initiated a column of "Southern News" and thereafter regularly reported on the movements of the new President of the Confederacy, Jefferson Davis. The *Gazette*'s editors, John Lowe and Brown Chamberlin, were close friends of Liberal-Conservatives John A. Macdonald and George-Etienne Cartier, then the leaders of the Canadian government, and they did not hesitate to use the constitutional crisis in the United States in order to discredit George Brown and the Reform party.[10]

The following week the Toronto *Leader,* semi-official spokesman

---

[8] *Globe*, May 1, 1861.

[9] March 12, 19, 1861. See M. A. Jones, "Sectionalism and the Civil War," in H. C. Allen and C. P. Hill, eds., *British Essays in American History* (New York, 1957), p. 179.

[10] Wilfred Campbell, "Four Early Canadian Journalists," *Can. Mag.*, XLIII (Oct., 1914), 557.

for the Liberal-Conservative party of Canada West, cautiously approached the same position. The *Leader* became the chief defender of the Southern cause in British North America, and during the war years it rose to challenge the *Globe* for circulation leadership. Many of its editorials were pointed replies to Brown, written by Charles Lindsey, a competent conservative-by-conviction, who, with the aid of George Sheppard, a disgruntled former employee of Brown, gave the paper what dignity it had. Its owners, James Beaty, an Irish leather merchant of little education but shrewd business instincts, realized that in contention lay sales.[11]

During the spring the British North American press shifted from a consideration of abolition to problems that had a more immediate bearing upon the provinces themselves. Journalists began to assess the practical effect on the provinces of a full-scale war across the border. As it became apparent that Lincoln was not going to wage a holy war against slavery, British North Americans began to consider less idealistic aspects of the problem. By late spring many British North Americans probably would have agreed with Thomas Carlyle that the Civil War was merely the burning out of a dirty chimney. The people of the provinces remembered, as Carlyle apparently did not, however, that the sparks from a neighbor's chimney can be dangerous.[12]

Amateur geopoliticians searched for the significance that the war must hold for the provinces. Would a Northern victory increase or

[11] *Leader*, Jan. 19, 1861. There were several newspapers in Canada West that built their circulation on war news. Most provincial newspapers devoted at least a page of each issue to American news, and some had several pages devoted to battle reports, troop movements, and political speeches. They frequently complained of the inaccuracy of the news received, of how it contradicted itself, and of how much that they had to print was only rumor. This is quite true: A check of the news content shows many inaccuracies, and the telegrams printed in each issue frequently were in error, obviously being the distillation of rumor. Nevertheless, the significant fact is not whether the news was correct or not, but that there was an overwhelming demand for it. By 1863 a number of new enterprises had been established chiefly on the strength of the public demand for American news and communities of only a thousand people were supporting up to four newspapers, which contained the same news filtered through different editorial policies. For an analysis of the British North American press reaction to the Civil War, see Chapter Eleven.

[12] On the shift in opinion see Toronto *Globe*, July 23, 1861; Ottawa *Citizen*, Feb. 19, June 14, 1861; Yarmouth *Herald*, April 8, 1861; [Newburgh] *North American*, Aug. 19, 1862; L. B. Shippee, *Canadian-American Relations, 1849–1874* (New Haven, 1939), p. 113; Thomas Hodgins, *British and American Diplomacy affecting Canada, 1782–1899* (Toronto, 1900), p. 55.

decrease the possibility of annexation? A rumor that the United States had thought to prevent civil war by foreign war, with the Canadas as the target, stirred old fears. A Southern triumph would create a balance of power in North America, some said, or even would give the Canadas an opportunity to hold the balance, while a Northern victory would unleash American expansionism once again.[13] On the other hand, a Northern defeat also might be followed by an invasion, for the North might seek British territory in compensation for its losses. The war, the *Leader* intoned, was for power, union, and empire. William H. Russell, traveling reporter for *The Times*, noted how prevalent was the idea that the Federals would keep their armies in good humor at the end of the war by trying to annex the Canadas, and in Montreal he found this feeling fostered by knots of Southern families resigned to "a sort of American Siberia." George Brown countered the *Realpolitik* that purported to favor the South with the argument that a Northern victory would be far safer for the Canadas since an independent South would mean sporadic warfare on the continent for decades to come, and such local fighting would threaten peace anywhere in North America.[14]

British North Americans also debated the effect upon the idea of popular government of successful secession from the American Union. George Sheppard of the Toronto *Leader* filled columns of other pro-Southern papers, especially the Ottawa *Citizen*, with his defenses of the Confederacy. "I see nothing that shd [*sic*] occasion regret in the fact of separation," he wrote to a friend, for "the principles of popular government do not suffer . . . . Nay, the South, in asserting state sovereignty, gives an impetus to democratic principles . . . ." The Union would never be repaired, he predicted, and the Confederacy would be "*the* Confederacy of the continent." [15] Others felt that separation would cause popular government to suffer: from London Joseph

[13] "A Monarchy, or a Republic! Which?," *British American Magazine*, II (Dec., 1863), 114; Brougham Villiers [F. J. Shaw] and W. H. Chesson, *Anglo-American Relations, 1861–1865* (New York, 1920), p. 15.

[14] *Leader*, March 14, 1861, Jan. 16, 1862; Russell, *Canada, Its Defences, Conditions and Resources* (Boston, 1865), pp. 74–76.

[15] Sheppard to Charles Clarke, Jan. 24 and Feb. 4, 1861, quoted in J. J. Talman, ed., "A Canadian View of Parties and Issues on the Eve of the Civil War," *Journal of Southern History*, V (May, 1939), 251. This article contains a list of the dispatches that Sheppard wrote. See also Talman, "George Sheppard, Journalist, 1819–1912," Royal Soc. of Canada, *Transactions*, XLIV, ser. 3 (June, 1950), 119–134; and Rochester *Democrat and American*, Oct. 11, 1861.

Parkes, English reform politician and Benthamite, wrote to Edward Ellice, British-Canadian financier and merchant, that it was evident that a federal system of government was "the worst of all popular schemes of rule . . . . It is clear," he wrote, ". . . that the 'American Constitution' is non-adhesive and is wanting in expansive power. I am moaning—sincerely thinking that this young but great Republic will discredit the Cause of Liberalism and democratic government . . . ." But he, too, felt that Southern secession would assure the British provinces continued independence from the United States. "It is in truth," he said, "a wholly unexpected National Suicide." [16]

The question of how best to help the Negro was another matter the newsmen discussed. Northerners seemed to have no real interest in the Negro, they said. A severe race riot in Detroit was followed by an attack by American workmen on an inoffensive Negro settlement at Oil Springs, in Canada West, in which one Negro was injured, and British troops later were to be sent to Windsor to quell a race riot fomented by visiting Detroiters.[17] Some observers argued that a Southern victory would mean the end of slavery, for the South, as an independent nation, would be faced with an aggressive Northern neighbor that would utilize the pressure of world opinion to force the South to free her slaves. If the North won, Lincoln would be forced to allow slavery to continue in order to conciliate the subdued states.[18] On the other hand, George Brown said, this argument ignored the fact that an independent South would be a nation whose entire way of life was a vindication of slavery. He argued that, even if it were true that most of the Northerners were fighting for union, emancipation would be a by-product of victory.[19] Some of the Canadian abolitionists found a way out of their quandary by deciding that the slave would be better off after the Union was dissolved because he then could find freedom by crossing the Mason-Dixon line and would not have to travel all of the way to the British North American provinces.

The more British North Americans considered the plight of the

[16] P.A.C., Edward Ellice Papers, A-1: Jan. 3, 15, Feb. 22, 1861.

[17] Montreal *Gazette*, Nov. 20, 1861; Orlo Miller, *A Century of Western Ontario: The Story of London, 'The Free Press,' and Western Ontario, 1849–1949* (Toronto, 1949), p. 140.

[18] For example, see Brampton *Times*, quoted in Toronto *Globe*, Oct. 15, 1861; Ellice Papers, A-7: Ellice to Ellice, Jr., Nov. 17, 1861; Viscount Crichton, *A Tour in British North America and the United States, 1863* (Dublin, 1864), p. 37.

[19] Toronto *Globe*, Oct. 15, 1861.

Negro and the effect of the war on the provinces, on liberalism, or on law and order, the more they began to reformulate their original opinion of the crisis. In general, conservatives tended to find more reasons for giving up any ideological affinity that they may temporarily have formed with Northern abolitionists than did followers of the liberal persuasion. But many of the liberals also were hard put to support the North in the war. In effect, both political groups split into opposing factions over the implications of Southern secession. The conservatives seemed more inclined to accept the Southern view that human bondage was necessary in the hotter climates in order to assure a labor supply. The same lack of a declaration by Lincoln of a crusade to stamp out slavery that had disorganized the liberal body of opinion made it possible for most of the conservatives to close ranks and attack the North for insincerity. But there also were conservatives who found the idea of a rebellion against established authority, and the use of extralegal force as opposed to parliamentary persuasion to bring about change, too contrary to Burkean ethics to accept.

The liberals may have been more inclined than the conservatives to accept the Northern war aims, but they were far from unanimous in this. If there were liberals who felt that the United States had represented the world's finest experiment in democracy or who opposed the South because of slavery, there also were liberals who championed the South for her nationalism. This group felt that the war was one for Southern independence and that the Confederacy was a testimony to the vitality of the right to revolution and to the Lockean conception of government. There was some crossing of political lines in the provinces on the basis of differing philosophical viewpoints toward the use of revolution as a means of producing change.

The firing upon Fort Sumter in the early morning of April 12 and Lincoln's "setting on foot," as he phrased it, of a blockade of the Southern coasts on April 19 told the world that the ways of peace were not to prevail and that the democratic experiment now was to be tested severely. The provincial press ceased to debate theoretical points and turned its attention to the actuality of war. For the most part, British North Americans still responded with guarded declarations in favor of the North. The *Globe* continued to lead the way, predicted a Northern victory, and asked that Canadians practice a benevolent neutrality toward the North, since "the North has as noble a cause to fight for as any for which blood has ever been shed . . . ." The

Three Rivers *Enquirer* probably spoke for most of the British Canadians of the provinces when it "most earnestly and energetically protested against the slightest recognition, either direct or indirect being taken of the government of Jefferson Davis . . . ." The French-Canadian press, comparatively silent during the secession months, also asked for strict neutrality, and generally found the firing upon "Fort Sumpter" a tragedy.[20]

In the Maritimes, distant from the sources of the news, the press at first was hesitant to accept the fact that war had begun, for "so much contradictory intelligence was afloat with regard to the States, seceded, and seceding, and to secede—that the whole agitation at times appeared to be nothing more serious than a tempest of words." Once accepted, the news fell "flat on the ear, its force having been broken by previous rumors and much speaking." Nevertheless, the Maritimes' leading Liberal-Conservative newspaper was not inclined to feel that the matter was very serious.[21]

Those who had felt that the Southern states would be permitted to rejoin the Union with their slave system intact were implying that the Federal government was more concerned with preserving the Union than with any serious attempt to end slavery. In the face of Lincoln's own pronouncement in his first inaugural address to this effect, it was difficult for many British North Americans to continue to support the Northern states once the war actually began. While the Toronto *Globe* remained faithful to the Northern cause, the colonial press, in general, was unprepared to give moral support to Lincoln and his advisors once it became apparent that blood was about to be shed to preserve the Union. The old fears of Northern imperialism were refocused on the person of William H. Seward in particular, and the new Secretary of State's actions in his first weeks in office, combined with a prolonged and scurrilous attack upon the provinces by the widely distributed New York *Herald*, effectively terminated an uneasy affinity. In England Thomas Carlyle again epitomized the growing attitude with an epigram: "Why, the difference between the North and the South in relation to the nagur is just this—the South says to the

[20] *Globe*, Jan. 16, April 12, 16, May 27, Sept. 2, 1861; *Enquirer*, May 4, 1861. Quebec *Le Canadien*, April 17, 1861, is typical of several French-language newspapers examined. See also Duhamel, "La Politique étrangère," pp. 106–107.

[21] Fredericton *Head Quarters*, April 17 and May 1, 1861: ". . . the whole affair is merely a temporary, but not dangerous disarrangement of the brain of the American people . . . ."

nagur, 'God bless you! and be a slave,' and the North says, 'God damn you! and be free.' " [22] So it seemed.[23]

[22] Quoted in Yvonne ffrench, ed., *Transatlantic Exchanges: Cross-Currents of Anglo-American Opinion in the Nineteenth Century* (London, 1951), p. 200.

[23] Gertrude E. Gunn, "New Brunswick Opinion on the American Civil War," unpubl. M.A. thesis (Univ. New Brunswick, 1956), arrives at the same conclusion for the one province as the present writer does for British North America as a whole. Basing her study on many New Brunswick newspapers, Miss Gunn found that secession was deplored, but that during 1861 Lincoln's refusal to wage war on slavery, combined with the Northern defeat at Bull Run, a renewed consideration of the economic effect of the war on the province, the fear of annexation, and the abusive New York press, caused the colonists to turn from the North (pp. 184–185).

three 𝓫 THE NORTHERN POLICY-MAKERS

"I need not tell you . . . that Nations drift into wars . . . ."
JOHN BRIGHT *to* CHARLES SUMNER

IN THE MONTHS OF SECESSION, AS SOUTH CAROLINA, MISSISSIPPI, FLORIDA, Alabama, Georgia, Louisiana, and Texas declared themselves free of the Union, the British colonists looked to the man who had been elected President of the United States in November, 1860. Abraham Lincoln virtually was unknown to the people of British North America. The Toronto *Globe,* which prided itself on its coverage of American news, had found little cause to mention him until February, 1860,[1] and two months after his nomination by the Republicans the paper considered him "a fourth-rate lawyer." [2] His nomination over William H. Seward, the prominent Senator from New York, was puzzling. The Canadian press interpreted his election as a sign that a civil war would not be forced upon the distracted Republic, for Lincoln seemed as weak as his predecessor, Buchanan, and was not thought to be a man who would "rock the boat."

The British North Americans therefore turned with particular and favorable interest to Lincoln's inaugural address. By now the *Globe* evinced a "great confidence in the man. We believe," it said, "that he has a purpose and is determined to carry it out." The *New Brunswick Courier* of Saint John found the address "clear, explicit, straightforward, fearless and to the point." The conservative Toronto *Leader* damned with faint praise: "If we cannot admire Mr. Lincoln's tawdry and corrupt school boy style, it is impossible not to give him credit

---

[1] Fred Landon, "Canadian Opinion of Abraham Lincoln," *Dalhousie Rev.,* II (Oct., 1922), 329. But see *Globe,* Nov. 5, 1858.
[2] July 20, 1860. Also see *The Globe* for May 12, July 12, Aug. 18, 1860.

for the good sense he displays in recognizing the gravity of the crisis, and in abstaining from all threats of coercion . . . ." [3] Most of the press found the inaugural address calm, logical, and restrained.

A tall, gangling, awkward Westerner who hardly could be expected to cope with the machinations of skilled party chieftains, if they chose to seek a foreign quarrel, Abraham Lincoln was, some felt, a man without "one statesmanlike opinion," a man not even rising to "the dignity of the commonplace." [4] While Lincoln had professed a desire to see England, and while his taste in literature ran to English poetry, his knowledge of things English was slight, although he apparently tried to correct this, for he drew David Hume's huge history from the Congressional Library.[5] He twice had visited Canada West,[6] but his knowledge of things British North American was almost nonexistent. However his understanding of human beings was unmatched. He was to grow in office so rapidly that he soon was promoting a highly successful foreign policy. Soon he and Seward would be consulting together whenever it seemed necessary, not waiting for the Tuesday and Friday Cabinet meetings. On walks and drives, after Seward's nine o'clock breakfast, on Sundays while the President was being barbered, they would plan each step as the need arose.[7] Doing so, they were to grow in statesmanship together.

If British North Americans were relieved by Lincoln's inaugural address, they were exercised over his choice of administrative officers. In January the British minister to Washington, Lord Lyons, had warned his Foreign Secretary, Lord John Russell, that it was almost certain that Seward would be Lincoln's Secretary of State. Seward was well known for his expressed desire to extend the blessings of American democracy to the Canadas. Wrote Lyons of Seward: "His view of the relations between the United States and Great Britain has always been that they are a good material to make political capital of. He thinks at all events

---

[3] *Globe*, March 5, 1861; *Courier*, March 9, 1861; *Leader*, March 5, 1861.

[4] Saint John *Morning Freeman*, July 9, 1861. See also Halifax *Church Record*, April 18, 1862.

[5] Jay Monaghan, *Diplomat in Carpet Slippers* (Indianapolis, 1945), p. 277.

[6] In 1848 (T. I. Starr, "The Detroit River and Abraham Lincoln," Detroit Hist. Soc., *Bulletin*, III [Feb., 1947], 4-6) and with Mrs. Lincoln in 1857 (Paul M. Angle, *Lincoln, 1854-1861, Being the Day-by-Day Activities of Abraham Lincoln from January 1, 1854 to March 4, 1861* [Springfield, Ill., 1933], p. 187; Ruth P. Randall, *Mary Lincoln, Biography of a Marriage* [Boston, 1953], pp. 169-170).

[7] J. M. Scovel, "Recollections of Lincoln and Seward," *Overland Monthly*, XXXVIII (Oct., 1901), 265.

that they may be safely played with without any risk of bringing on a war." Seward, Lyons reported, had declared that England would never go to war with the United States. Lyons, who thought otherwise, feared that Seward might try to divert civil war and further his own popularity by invoking a foreign quarrel, although Lyons did not think that Seward would push his anti-British tendencies to the point of actual war. Seward, Lyons added, had offered a facetious explanation for his attitude—that by taking up the cry against Britain he was acting from friendship, "to prevent the other Party's appropriating it and doing more harm with it than he had done." [8]

William Henry Seward, twenty-sixth Secretary of State of the United States, had had no previous diplomatic experience and was not deeply schooled in international law. At fifty-nine he was at the height of his power politically, assuming the role of premier, he felt, under a figurehead President who would have to lean upon him for advice on matters domestic as well as foreign. Like "a huge bird chiseled in stone," [9] Seward sat in his smoke-filled office and searched for a way to avert a civil war. Nearly every morning, quite early, he could be seen walking through Lafayette Square, dressed in his conservative black suit, smoking and thinking. In the evenings, seated deep in a chair in order to conceal his short stature, sipping wine or brandy, he would assure his friends that all would be well, shock the tender-skinned with his oaths, and search for an answer to how he, the true leader of the nation, could end the crisis.

At the outset Seward had much of the diplomat's artifice, and he once had said that he would answer only questions to which he did not know the answers. However, he was to grow in his office so rapidly that he became, in the opinion of one eminent historian, "one of the greatest figures that ever conducted American foreign policy." [10] An opportunistic politician who was distrusted by the British when he accepted his portfolio, Seward was to develop under his own responsibilities and through his close association with Lincoln into a states-

[8] Thomas L. W. Newton, *Lord Lyons, A Record of British Diplomacy* (London, 1913), I, 30: Jan. 7, 1861.

[9] Agnes Macdonell, "America Then and Now: Recollections of Lincoln," *Magazine of History, with Notes and Queries*, XVII (1919), 51.

[10] Dexter Perkins, "William Henry Seward," *University of Rochester Library Bulletin*, VII (Autumn, 1951), 1. For an opposite Canadian view see Hector Charlesworth, *The Canadian Scene, Sketches: Political and Historical* (Toronto, 1927), pp. 196–197.

man whom the British minister came to consider a vital instrument for continued international peace. Yet, he lacked the greatness of Lincoln, for some flaw in his character produced a conceit that contrasted sharply with his President's singular humility. As Golden Smith, a visiting English historian, found, Seward had "too much cleverness."

Although he was as subtle as Lincoln, Seward lacked the depth of character that must temper subtlety. The New Yorker was too driven by competitive spirit, too eager for total victory, too anxious to impress those about him with the brilliance of his diplomacy, to be entirely consistent, to follow a principled policy unhesitatingly, or to forsake the public opportunities afforded by his position for the quieter channels of good diplomacy. In his diplomacy he often was too legalistic, too willing to hide behind a technicality that followed the letter but not the spirit of the law, but in this he could be wildly inconsistent. He showed a limited range of view in his dealings with British North America in particular, and he seemed unable to place himself in his opponent's position, to visualize his own policy as viewed from without.

Seward's supreme self-confidence was shown in, and his actions were colored by, his conviction that he would determine the policy of the Lincoln administration.[11] Before Lincoln's inauguration he received many letters from followers who proclaimed their faith in his leadership, and many, like one Thomas Fitnam, who later received a consular post in British North America, reported that the people looked to Seward alone for settlement of the nation's troubles. Fitnam helped italicize his way into office: "*. . . no public man . . . has ever been placed in a better position than you are now, either for the weal or woe of the human race. It is for you to say what will be done.*" If Seward would only seize the opportunity he could be "the *Pater Patria* of the second great epoch in our national history," Fitnam concluded.[12] It is of little wonder, with his self-esteem fed by many such letters, that Seward thought of himself as premier. His concept of his office

[11] E. D. Adams, *Great Britain and the American Civil War* (New York, 1925; reissued as 2 vols. bound in one, with identical pagination, New York, 1957), I, 115; W. E. Baringer, *A House Dividing: Lincoln as President-Elect* (Springfield, Ill., 1945), pp. 87–89, 135–136, 326–327; George F. Milton, *The Rise of Presidential Power, 1789–1943* (Boston, 1944), pp. 124–127. *The Times* also thought that the United States would follow Seward, not Lincoln.

[12] Univ. Rochester Lib., William H. Seward Papers: Fitnam to Seward, Feb. 19, 1861.

as a premiership was partially true, however, for not since the tenure of John Quincy Adams was the office so important or did it intrude so fully into the lives of average Americans.

Since the reciprocity treaty was signed in 1854, Seward, as Senator from New York, had informed himself of Canadian affairs, and in 1857 he had traveled, with his son Frederick, throughout the British North American provinces. They went as far north as Mingan, in Labrador, which few British North Americans had seen. In 1859 Seward had broadened his horizons further by an extended tour of Europe. The presence among Seward's large pamphlet collection of considerable material on British North America would indicate that he informed himself by study as well as by travel. Since 1850 he had been an outspoken annexationist of the "ripe fruit" persuasion—that the British colonies soon would fall into Uncle Sam's basket without being picked. It was feared in the provinces that he might try to hasten the ripening. By the spring of 1861 he seemed ready to put his prediction of expansion into effect. To many Canadians it seemed probable that Lincoln was not the man to control Seward.[13]

Next to Lincoln and Seward the most important figure in shaping foreign policy was the senior Senator from Massachusetts, abolitionist Charles Sumner, who was Chairman of the Senate Foreign Relations Committee. Sumner was a man of unimpeachable morals, but he was, at times, perhaps too ready to substitute his own moral law for the law of nations. He had hoped to be Secretary of State and, failing that, minister to Great Britain. Seward, whom Sumner regarded as unqualified for the portfolio, passed over the Senator to select Charles Francis Adams of Massachusetts for the Court of St. James's. Sumner knew that Adams was Seward's personal choice and that Lincoln had not been entirely pleased with the selection of Adams.[14] Sumner also realized

[13] Frederick W. Seward, *Reminiscences of a War-Time Statesman and Diplomat, 1830–1915* (New York, 1916), pp. 115–128; Frederick Bancroft, *The Life of William H. Seward* (New York, 1900), I, 73. See also H. W. Temple, "William H. Seward," in Samuel Flagg Bemis, ed., *The American Secretaries of State and Their Diplomacy* (New York, 1928; reissued in double volumes with identical pagination, New York, 1958), VII, 3–115.

[14] Seward Papers: Robert Hadfield to Seward, Jan. 14, 1861; Charlestown (Mass.) *Advertiser,* May 29, 1861, Detroit *Free Press,* May 25, 1861, Chicago *Times,* June 29, 1861, quoted in H. C. Perkins, *Northern Editorials on Secession* (New York, 1942), II, 959–983. Hadfield went to England where he prepared "interminable notes" on reciprocity and annexation for Charles Francis Adams (CFA Diary: Oct. 30, Nov. 2, 5, 1861).

that Seward was more interested in domestic than foreign affairs. The huge volumes of Wheaton in the State Department library went unread save by Chief Clerk William Hunter, and Phillimore's ponderous work on international law sat on the shelves with its pages uncut.[15] Sumner, who could quote Wheaton, Phillimore, or Vattel with ease, truly was interested in foreign affairs and especially so in English matters. He also maintained an interest in British North America and later gave many pamphlets on Canadian politics to Harvard University. While somewhat mollified by his elevation to the Chair of the Committee, Sumner hardly worked harmoniously with Seward during 1861, as some biographers imply. The breach apparently began during the secession winter when Seward was working in the interest of reconciliation rather than abolition, and the appointment of Adams, rather than Sumner, brought the breach into the open.

Sumner was considered to be Britain's friend. British North Americans and Englishmen looked to him for an antidote to Seward's expected anti-British advice to the President. The Duke of Argyll, who wrote to Sumner frequently, rejoiced that Sumner's position gave him a chance to control Seward's "reckless spirits." Sumner's correspondence with British statesmen often gave him an opportunity to criticize Seward, and he was not loath to undermine the Secretary in this manner. Sumner also wrote to Governor John A. Andrew of Massachusetts that Seward had put foreign relations "in a bad way through the grossest mismanagement." He felt that England would not be troublesome provided she was not stirred up by a "sinister influence," and Seward, he felt, was such an influence. Actually, Sumner probably contributed to the strain on Anglo-American relations by keeping alive the idea that Seward wanted war long past the time when the Secretary had realized the uselessness and danger of such a policy.[16]

The British would have been shocked to learn that Charles Sumner himself was thinking in terms of annexation of the Canadas. During the secession crisis Sumner seemed willing to "let the erring sisters go," and he was giving at least some thought to the arguments of

[15] Charles F. Adams [Jr.], "Declaration of Paris Negotiations, 1861," Mass. Hist. Soc., *Proceedings*, XLVI (1912), 43; Adam Gurowski, *Diary, from November 18, 1862 to October 18, 1863* (New York, 1864), III, 183.

[16] Harvard Univ., Charles Sumner Papers, CXXXV: June 4, 1861, and Sumner to Francis Lieber, Dec. 16, 24, 1861; Mass. Hist. Soc., John A. Andrew Papers: May 24, 1861; E. L. Pierce, *Memoir and Letters of Charles Sumner* (Boston, 1893), IV, 37: Sumner to Rudolph Schleiden, June 2, 1861; New York *Herald*, Dec. 31, 1861.

such newspapers as the New York *Herald* that the British provinces might be seized as compensation. In this way the North could jettison the states that were economically, culturally, and geographically opposed to the "Northern way of life" and could obtain an equally large territory that, except for French Canada, would be economically and geographically compatible. Late in 1860 Sumner privately had spoken of compensating for any loss by annexation of the Canadas, and Ohio's Senator Benjamin Wade, in a speech on the floor of the Senate on December 17, had discussed the idea, predicting a brief war, an expanding South, and a disgruntled New England turning northward. On January 29 Edward Everett had recorded in his diary the summary of a long conversation with Sumner, who made no secret of his thoughts. A leading diplomatic historian of the period has implied that Sumner's bitterness over not receiving the post to Great Britain arose partly from his desire to negotiate a cession of the provinces. In public, however, he did no more than talk vaguely of annexation while sending up trial balloons to see whether an intensely abolitionist stand would be supported by his colleagues and the country.[17]

In February the New York *Herald* had professed to see a new policy emerging: The North was going to give up all of the slave states except Delaware and Maryland and was going to expand through the Canadas to the Pacific. The *Herald* reported that Salmon P. Chase, Secretary of the Treasury - designate, had originated the scheme and that Sumner, Horace Greeley of the New York *Tribune,* and Joshua Giddings, soon to be Consul General to British North America, supported it. The New York *Times* felt that nothing was more certain than a union of the North with Canada, and the Boston *Daily Atlas and Bee* also was urging such a policy on the administration. The

---

[17] E. D. Adams, I, 55; Laura A. White, "Charles Sumner and the Crisis of 1860–61," in Craven, ed., *Essays in Honor of William E. Dodd,* pp. 156–158. That Sumner's ideas were known is shown by a letter from one Gardner Brewer, a Boston merchant, who wrote to support the idea of compensation (Sumner Papers: Jan. 30, 1861). Sumner's *Works,* which he edited himself, contain no reference to his annexationism at this time. The letters among his papers for the first months of 1861 are so few in contrast to those of other months as to lead one to suspect that Sumner destroyed some of his correspondence. W. C. Ford found evidence that he may have destroyed some of his letters to and from Governor Andrew for the period February to April, and Andrew's own letterbook for the same period also is missing. See Ford, "Sumner's Letters to Governor Andrew, 1861," Mass. Hist. Soc., *Proc.,* LX (April, 1927), 223.

Herald declared that the United States would become a third- or fourth-rate power if the Canadas were not annexed. Asserting that Canadians desired complete independence and claiming that they could have it only by identifying their fortunes with the North, the New York paper concluded that there was "no necessity for hostilities [with Canada], and no probability of any taking place." According to the *Herald,*

> The contracted views of the people of Lower Canada will be enlarged and expanded by an infusion of the Anglo-Saxon element and the energy of the people of the free States, who, being cut off from a Southern field of enterprise, must, by the law of their nature, expand northward and westward. Such is the degree of manifest destiny, and such the programme of William H. Seward, Premier of the President elect.[18]

"Compensation" had support from other sources as well. Governor Andrew of Massachusetts supported the idea, hoping for a confederation of New England and the Maritime Provinces, and Cassuis M. Clay, soon to be minister to Russia, went to Washington to urge upon Lincoln the Doctrine of Compensation. It is possible that the British statesman William Gladstone gave ear to the compensation plan, for in 1904 the historian Goldwin Smith asserted that Gladstone had written to him suggesting that if the North would let the South go, the provinces might be permitted to join the Union. The London *Economist* opined that if the provinces wanted to join the North to compensate her, such a move would be a practical way of cutting British military expenditures.[19]

Lincoln's foreign appointments, like those of his predecessors, were made to placate his Cabinet members and to fulfill political obligations, not to send the most able men to the posts best suited for them. In a notebook, opposite the names of all legations and consulates, he had

[18] *Tribune,* Feb. 4–6, 1861; *Times,* Feb. 9, 1861; *Bee,* Feb. 20, 1861, quoted in White, p. 157; *Herald,* Feb. 9, 1861.
[19] Andrew Papers: Clay to Andrew, Feb. 2, 1861; A. G. Browne, *Sketch of the Official Life of John A. Andrew* (Boston, 1868), p. 66; F. L. Bullard, "What Goldwin Smith Did for Uncle Sam during the Civil War," *Lincoln Herald,* LII (Dec., 1950), 23; *Economist,* Feb. 23, 1861. The London *Press* facetiously declared that the provinces should annex the Northern states to save the better class of American citizens from the dangers of the mob (March 23, 1861, quoted in *Littell's Living Age,* 3rd ser., XIII [May, 1861], 438).

noted the name of a deserving friend or of an important follower of
a member of his checkered Cabinet. To important posts in England
and the British provinces went dilettante diplomats, party loyalists
who felt such spoils were but "earthly acknowledgment" of their
service to the party.[20] In the British provinces these men were the
closest contact that thousands of colonials had with the sovereignty
of the United States. The wonder is not that many of the appointees
did poorly but, rather, that some performed their duties with so much
intelligence and initiative. Five men, in particular, should be singled
out in this regard. Charles Francis Adams performed with distinction
as minister to the Court of St. James's. Thomas Dudley, Chairman of
the Republican State Executive Committee of New Jersey, went to
Liverpool and served ably. James Q. Howard of Ohio, who was one
of Lincoln's campaign biographers, acted wisely throughout the war
at Saint John, New Brunswick. Melville M. Jackson of Wisconsin was
made consul at Halifax, and he became one of the North's most capable and energetic representatives. Finally, David Thurston of Massachusetts, who was consul at Toronto, served as the administration's
capable "troubleshooter" in the Canadas.

The only direct administrative contact that the United States had
with British North America was through the Consulate General at
Montreal, a position acknowledged by the State Department to be "the
most important and interesting to the United States of all" consular
offices.[21] Lincoln sent Joshua Giddings, a leading Ohio abolitionist,
to this key post. Giddings was inexperienced in diplomacy, untutored
in international trade, and unwell, and he soon was suspect to the
Canadians. He never seemed to put the function of his office first in
his mind. He was interested in the position chiefly because it could
enable him to "make a little money" to leave to his children at his death.
Salmon P. Chase had failed to obtain a judgeship for him, and in March
Giddings went to Washington to ask for a consul's post. Despite the
opposition of Vice-President Hannibal Hamlin, Giddings, with the
support of Chase, Lincoln's Secretary of the Navy Gideon Welles,
Secretary of War Simon Cameron, and Postmaster General Montgomery Blair, received the appointment to Montreal. Fellow abolitionist Gerrit Smith wrote that Giddings would find the anti-slavery at-

---

[20] Monaghan, pp. 16, 68; Henry J. Carman and Reinhard H. Luthin, *Lincoln and the Patronage* (New York, 1943), p. 99; F. B. Weisenberger, "Lincoln and His Ohio Friends," *Ohio Historical Quarterly*, LXVIII (July, 1959), 223–256.

[21] N.A., ITC, XXXII, 539: Seward to Giddings, Nov. 7, 1862.

mosphere of the Canadas a "delight to breath." [22] The new Consul General was to receive some rude shocks.

Giddings was not suited for any task calling for tact, for exceptional energy, or for diplomatic skill. He was so pressed for money as to consider pocketing the government's rent allotment when it appeared that offices could be had without charge, and he was such an intense abolitionist as to turn violently against the Canadians when he found that they were not willing to violate their neutrality to help the North. Although other consuls in British North America were severely overworked, Giddings alone, despite holding the chief office, took time to carry on a vast correspondence with friends in America, to write a polemical history of the United States, and to report, when queried by the State Department, that there was very little to do in the office. Yet he later declared that he had so much to do that a secretary was essential, for which his salary, one of the largest in the service, did not seem adequate, and eventually David Thurston had to complete part of Giddings' task. His attitude of self-importance was shown when he wrote to his son that his two-room office would be open on the Queen's Birthday in May: ". . . I expect Her Majesty and I will be the two greatest men [*sic*] in town on that day." [23]

On the whole, British North Americans could find little that was cheering in Lincoln's selection of Cabinet officers or consular officials. Even the Commander of the Northern army, General Winfield Scott, was an object of distrust, for he was known to harbor annexationist views. One of his favorite stories, ominously enough, was of his participation in the battle of Chippawa, fought on Canadian soil in 1814.[24] But Seward remained the chief figure of British concern.

As Lyons had feared, Seward was thinking of ending the domestic crisis quickly by stirring up the old national antipathies. Seward was

[22] Ohio St. Archeological and Hist. Soc., Joshua R. Giddings Papers: Giddings to son Grotius, Jan. 29, and Chase to Giddings, Jan. 31, 1861, also Giddings to J. Giddings, Jr., March 7, and Smith to Giddings, April 9, 1861; Syracuse University, Gerrit Smith Miller Collection: Giddings to Smith, June 24, Nov. 13, 1861; Boston Public Library, William Lloyd Garrison Papers: Giddings to Garrison, June 12, 1862; Roy P. Basler, ed., *The Collected Works of Abraham Lincoln* (New Brunswick, 1953–55), IV, 284: c. March 15, 1861.

[23] Giddings Papers: Giddings to J. Giddings, Jr., May 21, 1861; G. W. Julian, *Life of Joshua R. Giddings* (Chicago, 1892), p. 391.

[24] Charles W. Elliott, *Winfield Scott, the Soldier and the Man* (New York, 1937), p. 599; Frederick W. Seward, p. 169: May, 1861.

reminded that he might use the dormant San Juan controversy to wring concessions from Great Britain,[25] but he wanted something more drastic than concessions. In this he was not alone, for unknown to Seward others were thinking of a foreign quarrel as a means of re-kindling the nation's supposed common patriotism. Among these were Senator Sumner and the obscure army captain on the Pacific coast, George E. Pickett.

[25] Seward Papers: T. R. Stoddard to Seward, Feb. 19, 1861.

four 〜 WILLIAM H. SEWARD AS
WOULD-BE PREMIER

"The post of a Minister, and even of a Premier, has no temptations for me."

WILLIAM H. SEWARD, *1849*

WHEN WILLIAM H. SEWARD BECAME SECRETARY OF STATE, HE LOOKED upon himself as Lincoln's premier. Seward could remember a day in Boston in 1848 when he was the main speaker of the evening and Lincoln was but an unknown Congressman from Illinois sitting on the same platform. Now he labored to make his policy of conciliation and delay with respect to the South Lincoln's as well. In this he succeeded for a short time, but, on March 29, 1861, Lincoln told his Cabinet that the Federal forts in the South must be retained in order to preserve the Union and that Fort Sumter was to be reinforced. The Secretary failed to realize that with this decision the President had taken the reins of government.[1]

Seward responded on April 1 with his now famous memorandum, "Some Thoughts for the President's Consideration." In it he declared that the administration was without a policy either foreign or domestic. He suggested that Lincoln should "seek explanations from Great Britain and Russia, and send agents into Canada, Mexico and Central America to rouse a vigorous continental spirit of independence on this continent against European intervention." What there was to explain Seward did not say, but his additional recommendation that Congress should be convened to declare war on France or Spain if their explanations were not satisfactory made his purpose clear—

[1] E. D. Adams, *Great Britain and the American Civil War*, I, 118.

to divert public feeling from a domestic war by arousing the presumed common nationalism of all sections of the nation. He would not evade the responsibilities of carrying out this policy if the President devolved it upon the Cabinet, Seward wrote.

Lincoln replied the same day that his would be the guiding hand in whatever was done and that he hoped for peaceful relations with all nations. This was a second clear statement by Lincoln that he, not Seward, would exercise the powers of the presidential office, but the Secretary, while yielding on the immediate issue, continued to work at cross-purposes to his President at least until the fall of Fort Sumter on April 13. Following that event, but before the secession of Virginia, Seward made one final effort to conciliate at least the upper South by sending Rudolph Schleiden, minister from the Republic of Bremen, to confer with Alexander H. Stephens, Vice-President of the Confederacy, at Richmond. With Schleiden's return to Washington on April 27 from his unsuccessful mission, Seward realized that his hopes of conciliating the South were illusory and turned again to the "foreign war panacea," which he had indirectly suggested in his memorandum on the first of the month.

The diplomatic corps in Washington probably knew that Seward was thinking in terms of a foreign war. In January Seward had declared to Schleiden that domestic peace could be maintained, if "the Lord would only give the United States an excuse for a war with England, France, or Spain." [2] Now, frustrated in his attempts to promote a domestic policy of conciliation and appeasement, Seward wrote his famous "Dispatch No. 10" of May 21 to Adams to read to Russell. In draft form this dispatch was so belligerent as to be an open insult to Great Britain. For the third time, however, Lincoln stayed Seward's hand by modifying the dispatch and by instructing Adams to use it merely as a personal guide to general policy, communicating only the parts of it that seemed necessary. Since Adams saw that a foreign war was neither an honorable nor a practical means of solving the domestic problem, he could be counted on to maintain a pacific policy. Slowly Seward came to realize that he could not dominate Lincoln and that while his advice would be heeded on specific matters, he must bow to the President's general policies and direction.

Lord Lyons had been aware of Seward's attitude and already had

[2] R. H. Lutz, "Rudolf Schleiden and the Visit to Richmond, April 25, 1861," *A.H.A., Annual Report* (1915), p. 210, and quoted in E. D. Adams, I, 124.

warned Russell of the possibility of war. Even after someone, probably Sumner,[3] "leaked" the information to Lyons that Seward's proposed policy had been rejected by the administration, the minister continued to fear that the Secretary might regain his supposed influence. On May 20 Lyons wrote to Russell that the Americans viewed British North America as the weak point in British policy and that many, including Seward, mistakenly thought that there was a strong pro-American feeling in the provinces and were advocating the annexation of the Canadas to compensate for the impending loss of the South.[4] Since Lyons feared that Lincoln was too unschooled in foreign affairs to oppose Seward, he felt that Britain should make some demonstration of her readiness to defend her colonies. Lyons therefore wrote to Sir Edmund Head, the Governor General of the British North American provinces, to suggest that defensive measures be set afoot.

Lyons apparently was afraid that Seward might try to promote the San Juan question into a major issue. In January he had written Russell that he was anxious to settle the dispute. There was some cause for Lyons' fear. On March 16 Lincoln asked the Senate for advice on whether to submit the controversy to arbitration. In the West Captain George Pickett, who later returned to the South to win fame at Gettysburg, was working, possibly with the knowledge of General Harney and Governor Stevens of the Washington Territory, to promote a war with Britain.[5] Pickett, reasoning as naively as Seward, felt that a foreign war would avert a domestic one, and he sought to draw British troops on San Juan Island into a compromising position. He failed to realize that a minor dispute over a few unimportant islands, while possibly capable of being promoted into a *casus belli*, hardly would reconcile the two antagonistic sections on the far-away East coast. Senator Sumner saw this clearly, and as his first official act as Chairman of the Senate Foreign Relations Committee he delivered a report, on March 19, that recommended submitting the dis-

[3] Charles F. Adams, Jr., *Autobiography* (Boston, 1916), p. 103; *The Diary of Gideon Welles, Secretary of the Navy under Lincoln and Johnson* (Boston, 1911), I, 368.

[4] Newton, *Lord Lyons*, I, 41.

[5] *Ibid.*, p. 30: Jan. 7, 1861; L. C. Pickett, *Pickett and His Men* (Atlanta, 1899), pp. 123–124; Alfred Tunem, "The Dispute over the San Juan Islands Water Boundary," *Washington Historical Quarterly*, XXIII (Oct., 1932), 294–297. L. J. Edson, *The Fourth Corner: Highlights from the Early North West* (Bellingham, 1951), p. 105, discounts L. C. Pickett's account.

pute to arbitration.[6] Congress postponed consideration of Sumner's report until December. Even then Lyons continued to fear an incident on San Juan Island in which the United States might find an excuse for a sudden declaration of war against Great Britain. Lyons' continuing suspicions about Seward, long after the Secretary had given up his schemes for a foreign war, colored Anglo-American relations for at least the rest of the year and led Lyons to misinterpret some of Seward's subsequent actions.

During the winter of 1860–1861 the Colonial and Foreign Offices had taken cognizance of the delicate situation in the United States and had expressed to Lyons their concern over the future of the reciprocity treaty and the question of maintaining British neutrality. Lyons had warned the Foreign Office that there was considerable feeling against the treaty in the North, and Colonial Secretary Newcastle had suggested to Governor General Head that it might be well to conciliate feeling in the United States during the crisis. It was not in the British interest to have the reciprocity issue become entangled in a civil war.[7] To forestall any event that might compromise British neutrality, Newcastle had indicated, in a dispatch to Head on January 16, the general course to be pursued in dealing with persons or shipping belonging to any of the Southern states. Newcastle advised Head to treat any question that arose "without reference to any political considerations with a simple view of facilitating as far as possible the operation of peaceful commerce" and to remain aloof from "any demonstration likely to give umbrage to either party in the United States or to wear the appearance of partisanship on either side." When any vessel belonging to "either party" entered any harbor within the British North American provinces, Head was to allow the vessel the facilities usually accorded to the United States, even though she might hoist "some unusual or unknown flag or claim some new national character." Head was not to recognize any vessel in any other capacity than that of the United States, however.[8]

---

[6] The report is printed in *The Works of Charles Sumner* (Boston, 1875–80), v, 484–491.

[7] FO 5, 962: Lyons to Russell, Nov. 4, 1864; Beckles Willson, *Friendly Relations: A Narrative of Britain's Ministers and Ambassadors to America, 1791–1930* (London, 1934), pp. 212–213. Actually, from October, 1860, to January, 1861, Head was absent, and Sir Fenwick Williams was administering the office. See Henry J. Morgan, *Sketches of Celebrated Canadians* (Montreal, 1865), p. 740.

[8] G 1, 153: Newcastle to Head, Jan. 1, 16, 1861, 1–3, and enclosed, Lyons to Russell, Nov. 5, 1860, 7–26; E 4, 14: 130.

When hostilities began in South Carolina, two of the British provinces expressed their concern for the welfare of the United States in terms that Her Majesty's government considered less than neutral. On April 13 the Prime Minister of Nova Scotia, Joseph Howe, informed the House of Assembly of the events in Charleston harbor. Led by Howe, former Provincial Secretary Charles Tupper, and Attorney General Henry Harrington, the Assembly adopted a resolution offered by former Prime Minister J. W. Johnston, which expressed sympathy and regret for the United States "without expressing any opinion upon the points in controversy." The following month the assembly of Prince Edward Island moved a resolution of sympathy, which it sent to Lieutenant Governor George Dundas, asking that it be communicated to Seward.[9]

This resolution never reached the Secretary of State. Dundas sent it to Lyons for approval, and the minister replied that it would be unwise for the legislative bodies of the British provinces to communicate directly with the United States, and that if he were asked to communicate all such resolutions made, he might have to communicate some "not consonant with the policy of Her Majesty's Government, or not calculated to be agreeable to the Government of the United States." He felt that informing the United States Government of official sentiment in the provinces by resolution was an unwise procedure: "The American people are rather touchy on such points, and it is by no means easy, even with the best intentions to speak of their affairs in a manner entirely acceptable to them." Edward Ellice put much the same thought less diplomatically to his friend, Joseph Parkes: "What a strange race of madmen—only fit for a lunatic asylum—our old calm, calculating and sagacious friends in the north country have become!"[10]

Possibly hoping to get the Governor General to make a show of support for the North, which might help to bolster the waning pro-Northern sentiments of the British North American people, or which might make the border states more hesitant about secession, Seward sent a special agent to Quebec to discuss the war with Head. At a cabinet meeting on April 12 Seward fulfilled one of the suggestions contained in his memorandum of April 1 by proposing to send some-

[9] N.S., House of Assembly, *Debates and Proceedings, 1861:* April 13; P.E.I., Legislative Council, *Debates and Proceedings, 1861:* 467.
[10] G 8D, 30: Lyons to Russell, May 18, 321–326, enc. in Newcastle to Dundas, June 15, 1861, 311–313; Ellice Papers, A-7, 5: Aug. 11, 1861.

one to the Canadas "to keep political feelings right." He recommended George Ashmun,[11] who was to be paid $10 a day for his work, given a commission for three months, and extended an advance of $500 on account.[12] Seward informed Ashmun that he had reason to believe that the authorities and people of the provinces entertained "erroneous views in regard to the states [*sic*] of affairs" in the United States, and that Ashmun had been selected to "impart . . . correct information on the subject . . . of the motives and prospects of citizens in some of the Southern States who are avowedly disloyal to the Union" and to report to the State Department whatever he learned.[13]

George Ashmun was a former Congressman from Springfield, Massachusetts, who had served with Lincoln in the House of Representatives. A Yale graduate and a writer for the Springfield *Republican*, he had been an old-line Whig and anti-slavery man. When Lincoln had offered his famous "spot resolutions" of 1846 to the House, Ashmun had supported them.[14] Later he was to serve as one of the four civilian pallbearers at Lincoln's funeral. Now living in Washington, Ashmun was in contact with most of the Republican party members. He had led the delegation that notified Lincoln of his nomination, and after the election Ashmun's name had been mentioned for a Cabinet post until he told Lincoln that he would accept no office.[15] In March of 1861 Ashmun had visited Head in Quebec while representing the English interests of the Grand Trunk Railway in some negotiations there. He also was well known to Seward and had written him during

[11] Ashmun's name frequently appears as "Ashman," for this is the spelling that Head, Lyons, and Russell used in their dispatches. The confusion over spellings has led some writers to confuse George Ashmun of Massachusetts with a George Ashman of Illinois who was among Lincoln's personal guard at one time.

[12] The pay is cited in Howard K. Beale, ed., *The Diary of Edward Bates, 1859-1866*, A.H.A., *Annual Report* for 1930, IV (Washington, 1933), 182. The commission and advance are mentioned in N.A., Foreign Affairs, "Special Agents," XXI: "George Ashnum [*sic*], April 13, 1861, Canada," no. 188, and cited in George F. Milton, *Abraham Lincoln and the Fifth Column* (New York, 1942), p. 49, without source.

[13] F. L. Bullard, "Abraham Lincoln and George Ashmun," *The New England Quarterly*, XIX (June, 1946), 198-200.

[14] George S. Merriam, *The Life and Times of Samuel Bowles* (New York, 1895), I, 35; Richard Hooker, *The Story of An Independent Newspaper* (New York, 1924), p. 49. Ashmun, born in Massachusetts in 1804, the son of a Senator, was trained in the law. He died in 1870 in Springfield (Yale Univ., *Obituary Records of Graduates of Yale College . . . 1870-80* [New Haven, 1880], p. 17).

[15] F. F. Browne, *The Every Day Life of Abraham Lincoln* (Chicago, 1913), p. 243; Baringer, *House Dividing*, p. 119.

the secession crisis to thank him for his speeches of "Crowning Excellence" and "Substantial Elements." [16] Ashmun seemed a logical choice for an executive mission to the provinces.

Almost immediately the news of Ashmun's commission was given to the press, either directly from a Cabinet member or from a Cabinet member to Sumner and from Sumner to a reporter. Within four days of the appointment the New York *Herald* revealed that Ashmun was on a secret mission to Canada.[17] Seward at once wrote Ashmun an abrupt letter annulling the appointment, declaring that the trip, "having, through means unknown to this Department, been announced in the public journals," would no longer serve a useful purpose.[18] Seward's action would indicate that Ashmun was to be a propagandist, for only in this capacity would public knowledge of his appointment have undermined the mission. Ashmun was told to consider his mission terminated when he had received the communication and to return his instructions to the department.

As soon as Lord Lyons somewhat belatedly read of the mission in the Boston *Post*, he informed Seward that official communication with the Canadian authorities should be made through his office and not by special agent. Seward refused to give Lyons any information concerning Ashmun but assured the minister that "no agents were employed for any objects affecting the relations between Canada and the United States." [19] This statement was true in fact as of four days before their talk, and it is at least possible that Seward officially had annulled Ashmun's appointment precisely so that he could report to Lyons, who would make inquiries, that there was no official mission to the Canadas. Seward could leave it to Ashmun to complete his trip in an unofficial capacity. There was a strong possibility that his dispatch would not reach Ashmun, who had left Washington two days before, until he reached Quebec anyway, and the significant omission of any request that the $500 advanced to Ashmun be returned may have implied that Ashmun could keep the money and use it when necessary. Since communication between Washington and the North had been broken on April 17 by the burning of a railway bridge near Baltimore, Seward

[16] P.A.C., Baring Papers: Ashmun to Samuel G. Ward, March 5, 1861; Seward Papers: Jan. 14, 1861.

[17] April 17, 1861. It was another three days before any other paper that was examined by the writer printed the story (Boston *Post*, April 20, 1861).

[18] "Special Agents," xxi: April 18, 1861.

[19] Lyons to Russell, April 22, 1861, and quoted in Alexander Somerville, *Canada, A Battle Ground* (Hamilton, 1862), p. 10.

must have known that his message would be delayed and that Ashmun might not receive it at all.

Head probably would have welcomed Ashmun and could have talked with him freely had publicity not been given to the mission. The Governor General liked Ashmun for his scintillating conversation and for his knowledge of world affairs. Head wrote to Samuel Ward, the American agent for the Baring Brothers, who had introduced Ashmun into official circles in the Canadas, about the *Herald* article. He said that the impression in Quebec was that Ashmun was coming "to feel the way . . . with reference to the disposition of the people . . . towards the Northern States" and that if Lyons shared this impression it would be very difficult to communicate with Ashmun in any confidential manner. "I shall tell him candidly the awkwardness which has been produced by these reports," Head promised. "Personally I shall be very glad to see him." He added that in his official capacity he had not known whether Ashmun was on any other than a railroad mission to the provinces, and implied that, had it not been for the article, he would have liked to have received Ashmun unofficially to learn what he could of the situation in Washington. Head already had written to a friend in the Colonial Office that he did not think it would "be a pleasant thing to have 100,000 or 200,000 men kicking their heels with arms in their hands on our frontier and all the habits acquired in a Southern Civil War." Other than Ashmun, almost his only contact in the United States at the time was with George Ticknor in Boston, and the famed scholar of Spanish literature hardly could furnish him with the information that Ashmun might supply.[20] As he implied, Head might have been prepared to report, if the necessity had arisen, that Ashmun again was in the Canadas on railroad business only. The exposure of the mission by the *Herald* made it impossible for Head to do so.

Seward's message apparently reached Ashmun while he was in Quebec. Although upset by the peremptory tone of his recall, Ashmun acted as Seward may have hoped that he would and in the capacity of private citizen remained in Quebec until he had learned everything he could. On May 3 he visited with Head in the presence of two Liberal-Conservative members of the Governor General's Executive Coun-

[20] G 20, 83: April 20, enc. in Ward to Head, May 1, 1861; P.R.O., George Cornewall Lewis Papers: Head to Lewis, April 24, 1861, quoted in D. G. G. Kerr, *Sir Edmund Head: A Scholarly Governor* (Toronto, 1954), p. 217; Toronto *Leader*, Oct. 28, 1861.

cil, George-Etienne Cartier and Philip Vankoughnet. Ashmun explained that Seward had sent him to present "the true position" of the United States during its domestic crisis, and Head informed him that is was improper for a governor general to have any official contact with a foreign power. Ashmun impressed the Governor General with his frankness, and when he emphatically declared that "he would talk to no one and return at once" to Washington if Head desired that he do so, Head told him to remain and to talk with whom he pleased, the provinces having "nothing to conceal, nor any desire to impede his intercourse with anybody."[21]

It thereby was with Head's permission that Ashmun met with Alexander Tilloch Galt, the Canadian Minister of Finance. This was a natural liaison, for both men had a mutual interest in the Grand Trunk Railway. Galt told Ashmun that there had been a general renewal of anti-Americanism in the Canadas and that a strong shift in public opinion against the North was in progress. Ashmun reported to Seward that he, too, could sense this shift.[22]

When Head informed Newcastle of Ashmun's presence, the Colonial Secretary approved the Governor General's conduct and instructed him to "continue quietly to discourage all Missions whether from the United States or from the Southern Confederacy." Lord John Russell sent a dispatch to Lyons telling him that he should "not conceal from Mr [.] Seward the unfavorable impression" that the sending of a secret agent to the provinces had made on Her Majesty's government. Russell also spoke of his displeasure to Adams.[23]

Later, Lyons wrote to Head that Seward had taken "credit to himself for having recalled Mr. Ashman [*sic*] in finding that his mission was ill looked upon."[24] Lyons stated that the mission was withdrawn because of his strong protest while Ashmun had indicated to Head that there was no official mission at all. Lyons was incorrect, for Seward had terminated the mission as soon as it was made public and before the minister had protested, but probably partially in anticipation of

[21] Seward Papers: Ashmun to Seward, May 13, 1861 (misdated April); BMW from GCC, vii: Head to Lyons, May 3, 1861.

[22] Oscar D. Skelton, *Life and Times of Sir Alexander Tilloch Galt* (Toronto, 1920), p. 314, quotes Galt's letter to his wife from Washington, Dec. 5, 1861, in which he says, "I got here on Saturday night, and was fortunate enough to meet Mr. Ashman [*sic*], whom you may recollect at Quebec."

[23] G 2, 7: June 1, 1861; G 1, 165: 446; G 1, 153: May 16, enc. in Newcastle to Head, June 1, 1861, 446–448.

[24] Newton, i, 50: Aug. 2, 1861.

the protest. In either case, the question of cause and effect involved must have reacted in Head's thoughts against Ashmun.

Ashmun's mission proved to be a diplomatic blunder. It annoyed Lyons and Russell and led them further in their distrust of Seward. By placing Head in an embarrassing position in the eyes of his conservative Council, it forced him to decline to discuss the war with a friend who might have had several unofficial talks with him in the future, had his position not been published. The most serious result of the mission was that Russell was able to excuse to Adams the dispatching of extra British troops to British North America, arguing that Ashmun's mission proved the need for re-inforcments there to assure Her Majesty's neutrality.[25]

Seward's diplomacy with respect to the provinces hardly had produced his first mistake when he rushed into two more errors, adding to the growing British distrust of the North. On April 20 a group of merchants from Chicago, who feared an invasion by anti-Unionists from Kentucky, voted to send an agent to the Canadas to purchase arms and ammunition. The British consul at Chicago, J. E. Wilkins, ultimately notified Head that the Chicagoans trusted that the agent would be well received because of the "known desire on the part of the people of Canada to cultivate friendly commercial relations with the Western States" and to promote use of the St. Lawrence route by Western producers. Wilkins added that the merchants understood that no assistance could be expected from the Canadian authorities in their official capacities, and that the agent already was on his way.[26] By implying that the people of the Canadas would sell arms to an American agent solely because they needed the reciprocity treaty and American trade, the Chicago merchants insulted sincere Canadian opinion and made it difficult for a Canadian to praise the North without appearing to sell his soul for trading privileges.

The following day Governor E. D. Morgan of New York sent Amaziah C. Jones, Justice of the Supreme Court of that state, to Head to purchase or borrow from the Canadian Government 50,000 Minié rifles. During the same week Head received a similar request from the Governor of Ohio. He replied at once to both requests, although they were communicated to him outside the proper channels, explaining that he could not sell any military supplies because of a statutory

[25] CFA: Adams to Seward, June 28, 1861.
[26] FO 5, 763: Lyons to Russell, n.d., no. 177; G 1, "Correspondence Relating to the Fenian Invasions and the Rebellion of the Southern States," 1: April 21, 1861, 1.

provision against allowing arms belonging to the local militia to be taken from the united Canadas. This provision had been inserted in the Militia Act at his request to prevent Canadian troops from selling their arms in the United States. Head informed both governors that Lord Lyons was the proper medium of communication between the United States and the Canadas and softened his refusal by adding that he could "sympathize deeply with the feelings of all patriotic Americans in the present crisis . . . ." [27]

In the meantime the agent from Chicago had reached London, Canada West. Acting on the agent's behalf, the local militia commander at London, one Lieutenant H. C. R. Beecher, telegraphed directly to Captain S. Retallack, the Governor General's Military Secretary and principal *aide-de-camp:*

> Southern Border of Illinois threatened with invasion. She has plenty of men. No arms. Governor and Committee Chicago Citizens have sent to procure them. They know there are plenty here . . . . No Time to reach Quebec. Danger imminent. Please lay matter before his Excellency. Pray they may have one thousand or more . . . . They would wish new and they would thankfully take any . . . .

Retallack did not present Beecher's request to Head, and he replied that he refused to correspond by telegraph on the subject. "Nothing belonging to the govt [.]," he warned, was "to be touched or moved at the peril of those who attempt it." [28]

Requests submitted to the government could not be honored, of course, for it was contrary to British neutrality to sell arms to either belligerent in a civil war. However, private merchants could sell arms and did so later. That Head was correct in his action there is no doubt, but that Retallack was unnecessarily harsh also seems evident. Retallack handled the request in such a routine manner that it remained virtually unnoticed by the Governor General. When Governor Andrew of Massachusetts also requested arms, Head apparently was not informed.[29]

Seward unwisely lent his support to the efforts to obtain Canadian arms. He wrote to Lyons on May 3 that he had learned that the

[27] *Ibid.*: Morgan to Head, April 22, p. 1, and Head to Wilkins and Head to Morgan, both April 25, 1861, p. 2, and also in FO 5, 763: 2; G 1, 463: Head to Newcastle, April 25, 1861.
[28] FO 5, 763: April 22, and n.d., 1861.
[29] BMW from GCC, VII: Head to Lyons, May 8, 1861.

provinces would not sell to "a *State* as such" and that he inferred that the Government of Canada would sell to the several states through the Federal government. As the arms that the State of Ohio wanted to purchase were intended for her troops mustering into the Army of the United States, Seward, with the President's approval, requested a sale direct to Ohio. He also asked for the same treatment of the application from New York. Lyons replied by sending copies of the answers that Head had sent to Wilkins and Morgan. Head reported the requests to Newcastle and received a general approval of his actions together with instructions that he should neither sell nor lend arms to either faction in the United States.[30]

With the Canadian supply of arms blocked, the states turned to the Maritime Provinces. Governor Israel Washburn, Jr., of Maine sent one George Dyer to learn from H. T. Manners-Sutton, the Lieutenant Governor of New Brunswick, what he could of Maritime attitude. Dyer told Manners-Sutton that he felt certain that there would be general agreement with the Governor that the "suppression of Rebellion [was] an object in which British North America and indeed all civilized communities were interested . . . ."[31] The Governor interpreted this as an effort to obtain information on the probability of British recognition of the Confederacy as well as a hint that the United States would regard as inapplicable to the present contest the rules that she had enforced against Great Britain during the Crimean War with respect to recruiting. He undoubtedly read Dyer's intent correctly, and he linked it with an attempt in the previous week, by the officer in charge of raising the Maine militia, to purchase arms from the New Brunswick militia. Manners-Sutton had forbidden such a transaction. Newcastle approved his action and forbade the sale of arms from the Maritime Provinces as well.[32]

These failures to obtain British arms demonstrated clearly and quickly a point to which Northerners, aware of the general praise that they once had received in the Canadian press, had been blind: "strict neutrality" was to be the British policy in North America as elsewhere.

[30] NBL, 8: May 3, 1861, 419–420; G 1, 299: Lyons to Head and Lyons to Seward, both May 3, 1861, 60, 66; G 1, 153: Newcastle to Head, May 25, 26, 1861, 418–419, 434–435; G 2, 165: 434; NFBL, 41: Lyons to Seward, original, May 3, and enc., Head to Morgan, extract, April 25, 1861.

[31] P.A.C., CO, New Brunswick, 188: Manners-Sutton to Newcastle, May 13, 1861, 134.

[32] *Ibid.*: June 20, 1861.

In the midst of the emotional weeks following the actual outbreak of the war, this seemed to many like hypocrisy on the part of the British. In a war viewed as a moral crusade, the crusaders generally think there is no such thing as neutrality, and especially in this civil war, a war fought for "the benefit of civilization itself," Northerners thought the British, who themselves opposed slavery, inconsistent. In May and June, following the Ashmun and arms incidents, the Northern press professed to have found an "unexpected enemy" at America's back door. When news of the Queen's neutrality proclamation of May 13 arrived, it only gave an official seal to what already had been apparent in the British provinces.

A third venture by Seward, also in late April and early May, compounded the respective impressions that the Canadians were hostile and Seward an expansionist. On April 27 Governor Andrew of Massachusetts personally warned Head that the Canadian iron steamer *Peerless,* then on Lake Ontario, had been purchased by "the rebels." Andrew trusted that the Governor General would "take all possible steps to stop this piratical cruizer [*sic*] at the canals or elsewhere." [33] Head was alarmed that the North might try to seize the *Peerless* or other ships on the slightest suspicion, or that they might even damage the canals to prevent the escape of such vessels to the sea, and he wrote confidentially to Sir Fenwick Williams, Commander of Her Majesty's forces in North America, suggesting that guards be placed along the canals with all haste. Head also apprised Lyons of the request from Andrew, adding that he had not told the Governor that the proper medium of communication was through the legation in Washington only because he "feared such an intimation would seem a mockery" at a time when communications between the Northern states and Washington were interrupted or entirely cut off.[34]

[33] G 1, 463: Head to Newcastle, April 29, 1861.
[34] P.A.C., Governor General's Letterbook: April 29, June 13, 1861; New Brunswick Museum, Saint John, Sir William Fenwick Williams Papers: Head to Williams, April 29, 1861. Head was referring to the fact that no official communications were received from Lyons in Washington from the afternoon of April 17 until the afternoon of April 26, for the railway bridges between Washington and Baltimore had been damaged. Because of this it was the British Consul General at New York, Edward M. Archibald, whose dispatch was the first received in the Foreign Office informing Russell of the outbreak of war. Archibald wrote that the South had provoked the war and that the North would crush her completely. Archibald's comments contrast with the more formal and neutral dispatches from Head and Lyons. All three men privately were pro-Northern, but only the Consul

Lyons and Seward discussed the *Peerless* on May 1. The vessel was believed to carry a British flag and to have regular British papers, but it was thought to be destined for Southern use. Seward suggested that the Governor General, "with or without instructions from Lyons," should have it detained. Lyons warned Seward that if the ship's papers were in order Head had no legal power to hold it, and the Secretary replied that he would not "require" such directions. Seward went on to add, however, that the American government could not tolerate the fitting out of "piratical vessels" on Canadian waters and that he would order the seizure of the *Peerless* on receipt of reliable information that she had been sold or was about to be sold to the insurgents, regardless of the flag or papers she might bear. Lyons protested "unequivocally and without reservation" at the time and later in writing. Seward replied that regardless of the protest he already had issued the orders. He added that he sent his order "with no feelings of hostility against the Government of Great Britain" and implied that he had the President's approval for the projected seizure.[35] Within the hour after he had received Seward's note, Lyons wired Head to explain the situation. He believed that Seward was trying to bluff Britain, and he still feared that the Secretary hoped for a foreign quarrel. Head replied that he rejoiced to find that a "clear and emphatic" protest against Seward's order had been made, but he gave no indication of what he would do if the *Peerless* were seized.[36]

Seward's note to Lyons contains several features of interest. One cannot avoid comparing it with the Secretary's belligerent draft of Dispatch No. 10, which was as close to a threat of war as he made to Great Britain. Lincoln had revised that note, but he probably had not seen the seizure order, since it was written and delivered within a few hours of Lyons' meeting with Seward. In conjunction with the dispatch

---

General felt in a position to reveal his sentiments. See Edith J. Archibald, *Life and Letters of Sir Edward Mortimer Archibald* (Toronto, 1924), pp. 118-128. Archibald has been called the "Walter Hines Page of the Civil War" (P.A.C., Charles Hibbert Tupper Papers, 4, M-109: no. 3274).

[35] G 1, 299: Lyons to Head, May 2, 1861; NBL, 8: May 1, 1861, 417-419.

[36] BMW to GCC, 9: May 1, 2, 1861; BMW from GCC, 7: May 7, 1861; Bancroft, *Seward*, II, 225. Bancroft apparently confused the dates involved in the *Peerless* and Ashmun affairs, for he sees the two as related, Ashmun being sent to the Canadas to persuade Head to act in seizing the vessel. This could not have been the case, for Ashmun was appointed on April 13, while the first intimation of a desire to prevent the sailing of the *Peerless* was not until April 27, well after Ashmun's commission had been withdrawn.

to Adams of May 21, this note to Lyons supports the argument that Seward still was determined to test the British attitude and perhaps find cause for war with her. Certainly the note could have created a heated situation, for Seward was well aware of Britain's extreme sensitivity to violations of her flag, especially at sea. Had the *Peerless* been captured by American forces, Great Britain undoubtedly would have made demands, as she did during the *Trent* affair the following November, which could have been used by Seward as a *casus belli*. The note also shows Seward's early tendency to send orders directly to naval officers, by-passing the Secretary of the Navy, a further indication that at this time he viewed himself as a premier. It is possible, of course, to consider the note in another light: that Seward had borrowed a leaf from Sumner's book and was sending out a feeler to learn how rigorously the British government would enforce her neutrality on the North American continent itself. The note was sent, it should be remembered, before Queen Victoria had proclaimed British neutrality.

The fate of the *Peerless* remains unknown. Seward later wrote Adams that Head apparently had detained her, for she did not sail and was not used by the Confederates.[37] A careful search of the records of the Governor General and of Lord Lyons reveals no indication that the ship was detained. It is probable that Head investigated the *Peerless*, found no evidence of its being sold to the Confederacy, and permitted it to continue with its regular business. Certainly no one acted upon Seward's order.

Seward had accomplished nothing by his tactics. He again had created an unfavorable impression on both Head and Lyons [38] and had given Lord John Russell an additional cause for sending troops to the provinces, a cause that the Foreign Secretary was quick to impress upon Adams.[39] By her own actions British North America again had given evidence of her official neutrality, and when Queen Victoria's proclamation of May 13 arrived from London, it only gave imperial status to Head's previous decisions to maintain strict neutrality in accordance with his interpretation of his January instructions from

[37] U.S., Dept. of State, *Foreign Relations of the United States: Diplomatic Papers, 1861* (Washington, 1861), pp. 111–112: Seward to Adams, July 1.

[38] Bancroft, II, 225, correctly surmises that Seward's action was poorly received, but feels that it possibly was his action that prevented the *Peerless* from going to the Confederates. The present writer could find no documentary evidence to support this view.

[39] *Foreign Relations, 1861*: Adams to Seward, June 14.

Newcastle. Seward did not accept either of Head's decisions gracefully, and when news of the Queen's proclamation was received
Seward raged "like a caged tiger" and "swore he would send [it] to
hell." [40] He instructed Adams to tell Russell how "shocked, offended
and disgusted" the American people were, adding philosophically,
"You and I and Lord Lyons . . . and Lord Palmerston, will . . .
be forgotten before the respect and affection cherished in this country
towards England will have recovered the tone they had when the
Prince of Wales returned nine months ago from our shores to his
own." [41] Despite overstatement Seward probably was close to the
truth, for these nine months had brought profound changes in public
opinion while strengthening British distrust of the Secretary of State.

Lyons indicated how well Seward had nurtured his fears when he
gave some credence to a report that the Secretary of State was plotting
to seize the Canadas. The rumor had an air of truth about it, for it was
reported to the British Consul General at New York, Edward M.
Archibald, on June 1, the same day that the anti-British New York
Herald attacked Lyons for alleged secessionist proclivities, and part
of the rumored plot was that the *Herald* was being subsidized by the
United States government to promote annexation of the provinces.
The informant, one George Manning, claimed to be a British subject
and, as Archibald noted, had "rather a chequered" history. Manning
claimed that he had been in the Neapolitan Service as a Colonel of
Engineers, that he had accompanied General Winfield Scott from
Vera Cruz to Mexico, and that he was the father-in-law of the late
Count George Esterhazy, quondam minister from Austria to Prussia.

Manning reported having overheard Seward's son plan to buy several newspapers in the Canadas to agitate for union with the United
States. The senior Seward, he heard, was to finance the project from
the "United States Secret Service fund," a headquarters was to be
established at Buffalo, and Hamilton Merritt, a Canadian merchant who
was well known for promoting trade with the United States, was to be
the "Territorial Governor" when Canada West was absorbed by the
Republic. Manning declared that Moses Perley, the British Fishery
Commissioner, was to co-operate with the former American Consul
General in the provinces, Israel Andrews, in carrying out a similar
project in New Brunswick. Haste was imperative, for the plotters

[40] Sumner Papers: July 26, 1869.
[41] GBI, XVII: June 21, 1861, 438–439.

feared that Great Britain might send additional troops to the Canadas. Manning added that he had read two letters written by the Secretary of State that corroborated the conversation.

The Consul General rushed the report to Lyons, who sent it on to Russell marked "Secret" with the comment that while some parts of the statement showed "great improbability," there was "only too much reason to believe that Mr. Seward would see with pleasure disturbances in Canada." Lyons declared that Perley would have no part in such a plot and thought it unlikely that Andrews would either. A copy of the statement also was sent to Head in Quebec. It is significant that Archibald and Lyons chose to consider Manning's story seriously. Apparently both men felt that Seward was quite capable of formulating such a scheme.[42]

Governor General Head may have felt Seward capable of plotting to seize the Canadas, but he quickly supplied information that laid Lyons' mind at ease. In 1856, he recalled, Manning had visited him in Toronto while using the name "Alexander St. George" and had told him a story of much the same kind. At that time as well Seward had been the "Arch-conspirator," and both Perley and Merritt had been named. John A. Macdonald, then the Attorney General for Canada West, had been in the room with Head and had heard the entire account. Neglecting to mention that in 1856 he had believed Manning,[43] Head added, "It is utterly incredible that the same man should have two opportunities of detecting by fortunate accident Mr. Seward's plots against Canada . . . ."[44]

Plotting seemed to be part of the summer air. Archibald wrote Lyons

[42] FO 5, 765: Archibald to Lyons, June 1, enc. in Lyons to Russell, June 3, 1861. The conversation on which Manning eavesdropped was said to have occurred in New York City on the evening of Friday, May 13. The writer has checked the Department of State's dispatches, as well as penciled notations made on inter-departmental memoranda, for this date, and some appear to have notations in Frederick Seward's hand. A check of railroad schedules for 1861, while by no means conclusive, since many unlisted trains ran during the war months and few ran on time, would seem to indicate that there was no train that Seward could have used for going to and from New York City in the time allowed. There are, in addition, many flaws in Manning's statement, which raise doubts about his veracity. His reference to Seward's son is quite indefinite, since Seward had three sons. Seward also had a nephew who was prone to put in appearances at New Jersey and New York resorts claiming to be one of Seward's sons.

[43] D. G. G. Kerr, pp. 132-133.

[44] FO 5, 766: Head to Lyons, June 9, extracted in Lyons to Russell, June 13, 1861.

about preparations by a group called the 69th Irish Reserve for invading Canada West from Buffalo.[45] Word filtered from the camps that the Yankees had a new marching song, sung to the tune of "Yankee Doodle": [46]

> Secession first he would put down
> Wholly and forever,
> And afterwards from Britain's crown
> He Canada would sever.

On Independence Day an officer of the "Order of the North Star" asked Sumner for support in agitating for Canadian independence and for eventual union of the provinces with the United States. The writer, who said he was a Canadian, hoped Sumner would help establish a "Brotherhood of Liberty," which would embrace all of the continent. And rumor took many forms, as when the Duke of Newcastle told his confidant, Edward Watkin, President of the Grand Trunk Railway Company, that he had heard that Maine now wanted to be annexed to British territory.[47]

By the end of the summer of 1861 many British North Americans no longer were pro-Northern. With slavery discounted as a moral bond between the North and the provinces, with Seward showing apparent hostility and highhandedness in his diplomacy, and with the natural spread of rumor as time elapsed, public opinion in British North America was shifting into new channels. The tactless handling of Ashmun's mission, Head's refusal to sell British arms to the Northern states, and Seward's belligerent attitude during the *Peerless* affair had muddied the waters of the short-lived Anglo-American *rapprochement* in North America. The colonists were confused, for they did not understand the North's war aims, and they felt they understood all too clearly Seward's machinations. Unwilling to espouse the cause of the South merely because they did not understand the cause of the North, the British abolitionists now had a tendency to invoke Carlyle's plague on both houses. During the summer it was not uncommon to find editorial pages filled with condemnation of the South followed with damnation of the North. The Napanee *Standard* seems typical of

---

[45] FO 5, 765: June 4, extracted in Lyons to Russell, June 10, 1861.

[46] Quoted in Keenleyside and Brown, *Canada*, p. 113.

[47] Sumner Papers, LII: Augustus Watson to Sumner; Edward Watkin, *Canada and the United States: Recollections, 1851 to 1886* (London, 1887), p. 65: July 17, 1861. This rumor came up again in 1864–1865.

this viewpoint. Pointing out that the South had started the war, the *Standard* encouraged readers to see the Southern aristocrat as a man of "incredible grossness, lolling on couches while being fanned by slaves, taking incredible sexual liberties with Negro women," who were released from "that which is worse than death" only by death itself. The paper insisted that slavery was the sole cause of the war. But, the *Standard* added, instead of striking a blow against the slave system, the North had chosen to fight for "a figment," "a shadow"—union, and the North would lose the war so long as the Northern troops had only this "bosh" for inspiration. What was needed was a great Cause to fight for, such as a crusade to make the world safe for all races.[48]

During the late summer and early fall three new factors further changed public opinion. An especially heated election was fought in the united Canadas in which the alleged efforts of the opposition party to "Americanize" the provinces were a major campaign issue. The first contingent of British re-inforcements for the depleted North American garrisons arrived to the accompaniment of much pageantry. In October Seward issued a general defense circular, which was interpreted in the provinces as a threat. It is these events that now must be considered.

[48] W. S. Herrington, ed., "Extracts from the Napanee Standard, 1862-3," Lennox and Addington Hist. Soc., *Papers and Records*, XII (1926), 11–16. Several citations in support of the various generalizations made in this chapter concerning newspaper opinion are brought together, and opinion is analyzed, in Chapter Eleven.

five ॐ POISONING THE WELL

> "The truth is that you can't live without enemies, and
> the best enemies are the ones nearest home."
>
> V. S. PRITCHETT

A FORTNIGHT AFTER NEWS OF THE FIRING UPON FORT SUMTER REACHED
London the imperial government decided to reinforce the North
American garrisons. There were only 4,300 regular imperial troops in
British North America in 1861, and the provinces themselves could
furnish but another 10,000 ill-trained volunteers. In Canada West few
volunteer companies had been meeting regularly. Wellington County
probably was typical, taking from April to August to form four small
detachments. Ordnance was insufficient, and ten thousand rifles and
four million cartridges sent to the Canadas in 1856 had been withdrawn. Lord Lyons was suggesting that the best way to prevent a
sudden attack from the United States was "manifest readiness to
prevent one," and Head agreed. In embarking on a preparedness program, the British government indicated that it took the possibility of
a Northern invasion seriously. In July substantial reinforcements
sailed for the New World with considerable haste.[1]

The troops were not sent "quietly," in the manner that Newcastle
later was to suggest, but, rather, to the accompaniment of considerable
fanfare. The largest ship in the world, *The Great Eastern*, was com-

---

[1] Great Britain, *Hansard's Parliamentary Debates, 1861*: CLXIII, col. 2194, May 17;
G 1, 154: Newcastle to Head, July 16, 1861, 91–92; P.A.C., Nova Scotia, Dispatches,
CV: Newcastle to Mulgrave, Aug. 20, 1861, 242; Newton, *Lord Lyons*, 1, 39–40:
May 22, 1861; Charles P. Stacey, *Canada and the British Army, 1846–1871* (London,
1936), p. 118; Charles Clarke, *Sixty Years in Upper Canada, with Autobiographical
Recollections* (Toronto, 1908), p. 116.

missioned to carry the troops to North America, and after being converted by Birkenhead artisans into a troop ship, she took on board
2,144 officers and men of the Royal Artillery. They were equipped
with the new Armstrong gun and were accompanied by 473 women
and children. With 3,000 people on board, counting the crew, the huge
ship carried twice the passengers of any previous ocean-going vessel.

This was an unprecedented number of reinforcements to send abroad
at one time. Had they been sent to North America in smaller groups,
they might have attracted little attention, but the Northern press
hardly could ignore the largest ship in the world. The ship's new
captain, thirty-year-old James Kennedy, had a flair for showmanship
that nearly matched the vessel. He seized the opportunity to goad the
ship across the Atlantic, reducing speed neither for fog, nor for ice-
bergs, nor for the Cunard liner *Arabia*, which he nearly hit, to set a
record crossing time of eight days and six hours. In Quebec the
performance continued, the city's ferries working two days to carry
Kennedy's passengers to shore, while enterprising lakesmen from as
far away as Toronto organized excursions to see the leviathan. When
the vessel slipped back down the St. Lawrence late in August with a
cargo of dry deals, many predicted that she would return with ten
thousand more reinforcements.[2]

In England a few voices spoke out to suggest that reinforcing
British North America in such a manner was likely to anger the United
States, while others objected to the great expense involved in this display of British power. Although *The Great Eastern* was not employed
again, Prime Minister Palmerston declared that preparedness meant
peace, and he explained that the troops were sent at the request of the
British Commander in North America, Sir Fenwick Williams, who
feared filibustering expeditions by discharged American soldiers when
the civil conflict was over. As the St. Lawrence River normally froze
over by late in November, it would be impossible to reinforce the
garrisons again until spring, Palmerston said, so that it seemed wise
to begin the process during the summer.[3]

---

[2] New York *Herald*, Aug. 23, 1861; Montreal *Gazette*, July 20–Aug. 28, 1861;
Toronto *Globe*, July 29–Aug. 26, 1861; New York *Times*, July 27–Aug. 20, 1861.
James Dugan, *The Great Iron Ship* (New York, 1953), pp. 96–101, describes the
voyage. He mistakenly attributes the sending of reinforcements to a Fenian threat.
George Gale, *Quebec 'Twixt Old and New* (Quebec, 1915), p. 191, describes the
reception in Quebec.

[3] *Hansard's, 1861*: CLXIII, cols. 1516–21, June 24, and cols. 937–938, June 11;
Anthony Ashley, *The Life of Henry John Temple, Viscount Palmerston: 1845–*

Only a few people professed to see no relationship between the new troops and the American war. In May local elections in Newfoundland had been accompanied by serious internal disturbances, which had led to a request for reinforcements. But the new troops had been sent to the provinces as well as to Newfoundland. *The Times'* correspondent, William H. Russell, explained to that august journal's former American correspondent, J. C. Bancroft Davis, that Britain feared that the three hundred thousand troops then in Federal uniform might not be controllable if the campaign were short, as it was expected to be.[4] When Adams asked Russell why additional troops were being sent, the Foreign Secretary replied that reinforcement of the garrisons was "only a proper measure of precaution, in the . . . disordered condition of things," and cited the *Peerless* affair and the Northern efforts to purchase arms. Others chose to regard the troops as imperial police who were to control the borders in case of a large influx of runaway slaves or to prevent violations of British neutrality from within the provinces. Seward appeared to agree, for he professed to welcome the presence of fresh British troops on the continent to prevent the Confederacy from converting the commerce or neutrality of the provinces to the South's advantage. On the other hand, the Toronto *Globe* was convinced that the soldiers were not needed for any purpose and that their sole benefit would be to make "more dollars chink on the counters of our shop-keepers."[5] Whatever the reason for the presence of the reinforcements, they served to inform the British North Americans that the mother country considered the provinces to be in some danger. They also broadcast this intelligence to the people of the North.

Despite the reinforcements, Canada West in particular showed concern, for her lake ports were not in a state of defense. Governor General Head was well aware of the exposed position of the Canadas. For five years he had been noting how easily the Yankees could march to Quebec. On June 23 he conferred with Dennis Donohoe, the British consul in Buffalo, about American naval forces on the Great Lakes.

1865 (London, 1876), II, 226: Palmerston to Newcastle, Sept. 1, 1861; Stacey, *Army*, p. 119.

[4] C 369: C. Trollope to Retallack, May 17, 1861, 152–162; L. M. Sears, ed., "The London *Times'* American Correspondent in 1861: Unpublished Letters of William H. Russell in the First Year of the Civil War," *Historical Outlook*, XVI (Oct., 1925), 253: June 29, 1861. See also Ottawa *Citizen*, July 23, Nov. 8, 1861.

[5] CFA, 77: Adams to Seward, June 14, 1861; *Foreign Relations, 1861*, pp. 105–106; GBI: July 1, 1861, p. 445; *Globe*, Aug. 15, 1861.

While escorting the Queen's second son, Prince Alfred, through Canada West, Head also seized the opportunity to make personal sketches of the American defenses on the lakes, and in July he provided a special guard for the Beauharnois and Cornwall canals.[6]

Former outposts on the Isle au Noire in the St. Lawrence River and at Penetanguishene on Georgian Bay were serving as juvenile reformatories, old Fort Malden was being used as a branch of the provincial lunatic asylum, and the Welland Canal, on the Niagara frontier, was indefensible. American commercial shipping on the Great Lakes gave the United States a great advantage over Britain, for Canadian shipping, even if converted to a war footing, could not hope to equal American. In addition, the Admiralty's lake charts were badly out of date. Finally, Great Britain had not maintained gunboats on the lakes up to the maximum allowed by the Rush-Bagot agreement. The Canadian government had a number of small vessels used for pilotage, attending to buoys, and relieving lighthouses, which could carry small guns, of course, but they were no match for the potential of the U.S.S. *Michigan*, which was serving as a recruiting vessel at Buffalo, on Lake Erie.[7]

Head was disturbed by the presence of the *Michigan*, for the ship far exceeded the tonnage provision of the Rush-Bagot agreement. Lyons drew Seward's attention to the fact,[8] and Seward conferred with the Secretary of the Navy, Gideon Welles. Welles reported, somewhat erroneously, that the *Michigan*, of 582 tons, had been built in 1844 and carried a single gun of eight inches in diameter, that it was used exclusively for recruiting purposes and for artillery practice for the new seamen, and that it was a *casus foederis*.[9] Welles' tonnage re-

[6] G 12, 18B: Head to Newcastle, June 25, 1861; G 1, 154: Newcastle to Head, July 18, 1861, 107–109; W. B. Kerr, "Dennis Donohoe: First British Consul in Buffalo, 1857–1864," Univ. of Buffalo, *Studies*, xiv (Jan., 1937), 48.

[7] P.A.C., B 29, vi: R. Collinson to Monck, Sept. 30, 1861; F. C. Bald, "Fort Malden —Offspring of Detroit," Detroit Hist. Soc., *Bulletin*, iv (Oct., 1947), 8.

[8] NFBL, 42: Aug. 31, 1861, 17.

[9] In spite of the displacement limitation of the Rush-Bagot agreement, the 685-ton *Michigan* had been launched at Erie in 1843. She began cruising in 1844 with only one of the six guns for which her plans had provided, since the agreement limited armaments to a single eighteen-pounder. In 1905 her name was changed to *Wolverine*, in 1943 she was stricken from the navy list, and she was scrapped in 1949. See M. H. Gluntz, "Naval Construction on the Great Lakes," U.S. Naval Institute, *Proceedings*, lxxxiii (Feb., 1957), 133–145, which is reprinted in *Inland Seas*, xiii (Winter, 1957), 256–268; and H. R. Spencer, "A Great Lady Passes," *ibid.*, v (Spring, 1949), 55–56.

port was incorrect, and even on the basis of his own statement the ship apparently was well over the provision that each nation would maintain not more than four vessels of not over one hundred tons' burden. Surprisingly conciliatory, Seward told Lyons that if the British government desired it, he would be happy to reconsider the case. Actually, the United States had wanted to take the *Michigan* out to the Atlantic where it could be used against the Confederacy, but the ship was too large to pass through the Welland Canal.[10]

Lyons, Head, and a vocal portion of the Canadian press refused to be comforted. When the first reinforcements were sent to the colonies, imperial and provincial governments alike expected that the civil war would end within the year. Lyons consistently reported that the period of maximum danger to British North America would come in the month following the end of the war, when the North might unleash its growing army upon the Canadas. If the war ended shortly, perhaps with the first major battle, an invasion was possible during the summer. Should the war last until winter, the period of danger would be the spring of 1862, Lyons reasoned. In June he talked with a number of congressmen, and he felt they showed "a state of mind so utterly unreasonable as to border upon frenzy." He was convinced that Seward shared their delusion that the North could carry on a war simultaneously with Great Britain and the South, provided that French aid, which Lyons felt the congressmen expected, was received.

Therefore, on June 6 Lyons strengthened his warnings by sending Lord John Russell a coded telegram that warned that "a sudden declaration of war by the United States against Great Britain appears to me to be by no means impossible, especially as long as Canada seems open to invasion."[11] A democracy, Lyons said, could not be trusted to act rationally in moments of severe strain, and the danger of invasion was imminent if Britain gave any appearance of yielding. Lyons felt that the only safe means of preventing war were "manifest readiness . . . inflexibility in conduct, [and] firmness and conciliation in language." He added that in such a war it was not in the British interest to give a lasting check to the prosperity of the Americans or even "unnecessarily to wound their pride." They should be brought to terms

[10] G 10, 2: Head to Newcastle, June 15, 1861, 100; NBL, 9: Sept. 12, 1861, 2–3.
[11] FO 5, 765: received June 25, quoted in cipher telegram sent same day. The original cipher dispatches of the Governor General, as well as the coding book, are in the P.A.C.

at once by the prompt and vigorous use of a greatly superior naval force, for "the spirit, the energy, and the resources of this people, would insure their providing powerful means of defending themselves and annoying an enemy, if time were allowed them." [12]

Because the imperial administration already had shown itself willing to let the provinces have their independence, there was some debate in Great Britain as to whether Englishmen should or would fight to save the distant colonies. In the event of armed aggression it generally was agreed that Great Britain had a moral obligation to defend any of the provinces. Newcastle told Head that in 1860, when he was in Albany with the Prince of Wales, Seward had said that should he become President he would make it his policy to abuse England and to find an excuse for war with her if necessary. Newcastle thought it wise, therefore, to continue to increase the forces in the Canadas and to "assume quietly an attitude of preparation." At the same time, he was not so pessimistic as Lyons, for he felt that Seward was indulging in bravado for political consumption, and he advised Head to make sufficient allowance for Seward's "hyper-American use of the policy of bully and bluster." [13]

The American press denounced Britain's "quiet" rearmament program as evidence of hostility to the Republic. Tension along the border increased as rumors spread. The New York *Times* pointed out that the troops had been brought to police the frontier and to prevent possible Confederate abuse of neutral territory, but the New York *Herald* suggested an armistice between the North and South for two or three years to permit their combined armies to conquer British and Russian North America, Cuba, Jamaica, and Central America.[14] In turn, the Canadian press often was quick to accept rumor as fact, as when it generally stated that Fort Porter, at Buffalo, was being garrisoned by the Federal government for a possible invasion of Canada West.

The period of strain also produced the first of several flurries of public speeches and polemical literature. A number of Canadians wrote jeremiads on an "inevitable war." The chief of the pamphleteers was Colonel George Taylor Denison from Toronto, whose pamphlet

[12] FO 5, 765: June 8, 1861.
[13] Halifax *Morning Chronicle*, July 18, 1861; James Ferguson, *Notes of a Tour in North America in 1861* (London, 1861), p. 32; Martineau, *Newcastle*, pp. 301–303.
[14] *Times*, July 27, 1861; *Herald, passim*, June and July, 1861.

Canada—Is She Prepared for War?, published under the *nom de plume* of "A Native Canadian," was cited by the *Globe* as an example of war-mongering, although Denison closely followed Lord Lyons' reasoning in his concept of the war danger. It would be impossible for an exposed neutral to avoid some border warfare, he reasoned, and with the coming of peace a great body of unemployed soldiers, schooled in the ways of war, would be seeking new worlds to conquer. But polemics probably were the least of the factors contributing to the growing tension.[15]

During the month of the arrival of British reinforcements the most important of the British North American provinces, the united Canadas, held an election. Fear of the "Americanization" of Canada nearly always had played some role in Canadian elections, and the role was particularly prominent in July of 1861. The possibility of a Northern invasion could be used by the Liberal-Conservative party, then in power, to promote the usual crisis argument that one should not change horses in the middle of a stream. In addition, the conservatives could argue that the Clear Grits and other Reform or liberal groups were foisting American ideas upon the voters. These ideas, the conservatives did not hesitate to say, had been proved to be undesirable, since the internecine war to the south indicated that the American form of representative government was self-destructive.

Factors other than a Tory desire to stay in office caused manifestations of anti-Americanism in the election of 1861.[16] One was the rise of expansionist sentiment among the political leaders of both parties in Canada West. The Canadas often had proposed unifying all the British North American provinces into a single nation, for the Canadas would be predominant in such a nation, even as Ontario and Quebec are today. Several of the political leaders of Canada West especially were interested in unification, for the success of any transcontinental nation north of the United States would depend to a great extent upon incorporating the Hudson's Bay Company's territory between Canada West and British Columbia. The merchants of Canada West hoped to

[15] *Globe*, March 30, 1861; Denison, *Soldiering in Canada* (Toronto, 1901), p. 49; Denison, *The National Defences: or, Observations on the Best Defensive Force in Canada* (Toronto, 1861).

[16] There is no scholarly study of the election of 1861 in the Canadas. Such a study is a definite need if one is to understand either the confederation movement in the provinces or Canadian-American relations during the Civil War.

dominate this vast Western area, and if the prairie settlements could be made an economic appendage to Toronto, that city could supplant Montreal as the financial capital of the provinces and become the chief metropolis of the new nation.

This sense of the manifest destiny of Canada West was strong among the Reform or liberal elements of the province. George Brown used the Toronto *Globe* to preach his form of expansionism, and his close friend and fellow journalist William McDougall consistently pointed out that the war to the south was giving Canadians an opportunity to extend their influence over the Western areas and to replace St. Paul as the economic capital of the region. Thus the party that generally was disposed to take a favorable view of the North in the Civil War also was the party that had cause to promote the argument that America's disadvantage was the province's advantage. In effect, both parties in Canada West served to increase anti-Americanism, the Liberal-Conservative party from principle and the Reform group from expediency. Whichever way the voter cast his ballot, he was reminded that the United States had been and again would be a menace to British and Canadian interests.

John A. Macdonald, Tory leader in Canada West, did not join those who feared an invasion from the United States. However, he was willing to assert that his opponents were pro-American if it would help to keep his party in office.[17] When a supporter of William McDougall, who was then Member of Parliament for North Oxford, hinted that reformers might have to look across the border for support, Macdonald charged the liberals with "looking to Washington." At Whitby, McDougall was burned in effigy by a mob of six hundred of Macdonald's supporters. In each hand of the effigy was a sign that read "Look to Washington," over its heart one that proclaimed "Annexation," and at its hatband a placard labeling the figure "Traitor Mc-Doughall" [*sic*]. Shortly before the election the Tories printed a Voter's Guide, which warned of the menace of "Clear Grit treason." A clearly subversive and highly powerful organization was working to plant the republican institutions of the United States among the Canadians, the guide said, and the "Revolutionary Designs of the Red

---

[17] Donald G. Creighton, *John A. Macdonald: The Young Politician* (New York, 1953), pp. 308–314. For some of Creighton's afterthoughts on Macdonald, see his essay in Claude T. Bissell, ed., *Our Living Traditions: Seven Canadians* (Toronto, 1957), pp. 48–62.

Republicans" would have to be stopped by a demonstration of loyalty to the true principles of monarchy.[18]

Railroad magnates in the Canadas also added to the fears of annexation. The united Canadas had a well-integrated railroad system in 1861, which linked Sarnia, Canada West, with Portland, Maine via Toronto and Montreal. The Grand Trunk Railway had been constructed as a wide-gauge road so that Canadian trade would have to pass through Montreal and would siphon into Portland during the winter. Rail traffic could not pass to competing cities in the United States, or from Montreal to the port of Boston, without breaking bulk, for the Northern states, except for Maine, used a narrower-gauge track. This railroad line had been constructed with capital from Montreal, Portland, and London, and in part it represented an effort to challenge Boston's position as the Northeast's chief all-year seaport.[19]

In competition with the Grand Trunk Railway was the Great Western Railroad in Canada West, which connected Niagara Falls and Toronto with Windsor, opposite Detroit. This line had been financed by some of the Americans who had backed the New York Central, which in 1861 ran from Albany to Buffalo. The financiers wanted a direct connection across the lower peninsula of Canada West from Buffalo to Detroit, for such a route would be considerably shorter than that around the southern shore of Lake Erie. However, although the line was built, the powerful Grand Trunk interest had been able to persuade the Liberal-Conservative party, then in office, to require the route to be of the same width as the Grand Trunk line. This integrated the Canadian system but forced a change of bulk at the Suspension Bridge at Niagara Falls if cargo were to flow from the New York Central across Canada West to Detroit.[20]

The Montreal railroad interest defended the forced integration of the two principal Canadian railroad systems by arguing that the broad gauge was a defense measure since it presumably would make invasion

---

[18] P.A.C., John A. Macdonald Papers, 337: Thomas Moody to McDonald [sic], July 7, 1861; *ibid.*, 297: "The Voters' Guide: A Campaign Sheet," dated June 20, 1861.

[19] For a succinct account of the building of the railroad line, see Alfred D. Chandler, Jr., *Henry Varnum Poor: Business Editor, Analyst, and Reformer* (Cambridge, Mass., 1956), pp. 12–19, 230.

[20] George R. Taylor and Irene D. Neu, *The American Railroad Network, 1861–1890* (Cambridge, Mass., 1956), pp. 15–22; George P. deT. Glazebrook, *A History of Transportation in Canada* (Toronto, 1938), pp. 172–187.

from New York more difficult.[21] Railroad authorities like Thomas C. Keefer of Hamilton supported this argument,[22] but there is no evidence that military tacticians considered the gauge difference of any great value. Since no less than seventeen Northern railroad lines, any one of which could carry an invading army, ran to the British North American border, the fact that trains could not pass immediately across the border was of only secondary significance, for a rail could be shifted inward to make the track serviceable.[23]

During the election of 1861 the railroad interests within the Liberal-Conservative party further compounded anti-Northern sentiment in the provinces by repeating their argument concerning the need for defense. The Montreal railroad leaders had good reason to want to increase apprehension over a Northern invasion, for they were trying to persuade the Colonial Office to subsidize a new intercolonial railway extension from Rivière du Loup, Canada East, to the Maritime Provinces. The Montrealers were now in competition with the chief railway figure of Maine, John A. Poor, who had revived an old plan to tap the Maritimes by constructing a line from Portland to Saint John, New Brunswick. This line, the Western Extension plan or European and North American Railway, would prevent Montreal from dominating the Maritime Provinces as she then dominated the Canadas.[24]

Railroad competition between the Western Extension and intercolonial plans was intense during the Civil War, and the advocates of the latter did not hesitate to brand Poor an imperialist who was the advance agent of American annexationism. They took their case not only to the Colonial Office but to the British North American people as well. From mid-1861 until at least March, 1865, the Liberal-Conservative party and the Montreal railroaders helped to promulgate the

[21] Montreal *Witness*, Dec. 26, 1861; Sarnia *Observer*, Dec. 27, 1861; Quebec *Le Canadien*, Aug. 29, 1862; A. W. Currie, "Sir Edward Watkin: A Canadian View," *Journal of Transport History*, III (May, 1957), 31–40.

[22] *On the Military and the Commercial Importance of Completing the Line of Railway from Halifax to Quebec* (London, 1862); "Travel and Transportation," *Eighty Years' Progress in British North America* (Toronto, 1863), pp. 245–246.

[23] On the number of lines see Halifax *Morning Chronicle*, July 30, 1863, and William J. Wilgus, *The Railway Interrelations of the United States and Canada* (New Haven, 1937), p. 41. A. W. Currie, in his *The Grand Trunk Railway of Canada* (Toronto, 1957), p. 490, considers the suggestion that the broad gauge would prevent invasion fanciful.

[24] See Edward C. Kirkland, *Men, Cities and Transportation: A Study in New England History, 1820–1900* (Cambridge, Mass., 1948), I, 215–222.

"bogey of annexationism" in order to further their own interests. A voluminous literature on the railroad controversy joined the hundreds of pamphlets on patriotism, defense, and the election, to further "poison the well" of Canadian-American relations.[25]

The Liberal-Conservatives won the election, but in doing so they helped bring resentment against the North to a new pitch—and this in the crucial month of July, the month of the first battle of Bull Run. Pressured into advancing into Virginia before he felt ready, Union General Irvin McDowell attacked the Confederate troops under General P. G. T. Beauregard on July 21. A Northern triumph had seemed certain at first, and the disorganized retreat that the Northern troops made a few hours later appeared all the more disgraceful by contrast. The North had snatched defeat from the jaws of victory. The Confederate officers did not follow up their advantage, but for two days Washington lay open to attack from without and to abuse by drunken and discouraged Northern soldiers from within. Viewed strategically the battle meant little, but viewed psychologically it meant much.

President Lincoln had told Congress at the opening of its special session on July 4 that the United States had the "general sympathy" of the world.[26] The disgrace of defeat destroyed much of this sympathy. Those Britishers who had contended from the outset that "Yankees" could not fight now seemed to have proof. In the Canadas the Tory press loudly proclaimed that the test of battle had shown the Southern cause to be just. For the first time those who had wanted to cheer the South on but who had remained silent for fear of the Northern army found their voices. Others who might support the North while the controversy was only a debate now found, to their horror, that blood actually had been shed, and these, both now and even more loudly later as the dreary war continued to stain the

[25] Poor, *Organization of the European and North American Railway Company* (New York, 1866); E. R. Burpee, *Report of the Survey of the Extension of the European and North American Railway to the American Boundary* (Fredericton, 1865); Alice R. Stewart, "The State of Maine and Canadian Confederation," *CHR*, xxxiii (June, 1952), 148–164; F. N. Walker, ed., *Daylight through the Mountains* (Montreal, 1957), p. 350. A large number of railway pamphlets may be consulted in the Keefer Railway Collection of the Hamilton, Ontario, Public Library.

[26] The address appears in John G. Nicolay and John Hay, eds., *The Complete Works of Abraham Lincoln* (New York, 1905), vi, 297–325, and in James D. Richardson, *A Compilation of the Messages and Papers of the Presidents, 1789–1897* (Washington, 1896–99), v, 20–31.

countryside, decried the spilling of blood for a lost and thereby to them unjust cause. For they came increasingly to believe that the cause of union was irretrievably lost.

When news of the debacle reached the Canadas, some of the Liberal-Conservatives celebrated with champagne. Two of John A. Macdonald's followers marched into the Canadian Legislative Assembly while it was in session to raise three cheers for the Confederate states.[27] A comment that probably was typical of conservative opinion of the North after Bull Run was recorded in the diary of one intelligent observer: the "impertinent threats of the Northerners to invade Canada after they have 'whipped the Secessionists' (which they never can do) has caused all Canadians to scorn and laugh at them." [28]

A few weeks later, as the first pain of the defeat at Bull Run began to subside in the North, the New York press and the major British North American newspapers reprinted a dispatch written for *The Times* by that newspaper's American correspondent, William H. Russell, which described the disorganized flight of Northern troops and congressmen back across the Potomac River after the battle. Personally Russell was pro-Northern, although the conservative *Times* was not, and Russell's exciting account, read today, is amusingly cool and correct. Russell did not attempt to describe the battle, which he did not see. His original dispatch dealt only with the disorderly retreat. But if the account seemed comical to the British reader, it seemed needlessly insulting to the soldiers who had endured the dust, heat, and sweat of Manassas Junction and to the people of the North who now feared a Confederate invasion. Without explicitly doing so, Russell seemed to have smeared the North with the stains of incompetence, cowardice, and buffoonery. In the late summer, when he traveled to the Canadas in search of cooler nights and friendlier faces, some of his hosts expressed their surprise that he had left the Northern states alive.[29]

[27] Fred Landon, ed., "Extracts from the Diary of Mrs. John Harris, 1857–77, of London, Ontario," London *Free Press*, July 14–Nov. 17, 1928, art. 4; Toronto *Globe*, July 29, 1861; William T. R. Preston, *My Generation of Politics and Politicians* (Toronto, 1927), p. 25.

[28] Francis Paget Hett, ed., *The Memoirs of Susan Sibbald, 1783–1872* (London, 1926), p. 318: Aug. 23, 1861.

[29] Rupert Furneaux, *The First War Correspondent: William Howard Russell of The Times* (London, 1944), p. 153. *The Times* soon replaced the pro-Northern Russell with the lesser known but strongly pro-Southern Charles McKay, author of travel books on the South and on the British provinces.

British North Americans never quite recovered from Bull Run. They continued to talk, even as late as 1864, as though one British soldier could defeat ten Northerners, although the Union army of 1864 had little resemblance to the inexperienced band of 1861. The Canadian press began to throw sharp jibes at the Northerners who drilled so assiduously and accomplished so little. The British North American attitude toward defense became strangely polarized: either that Canada West, in particular, was completely indefensible or, conversely, that a handful of troops could defend it. In either case the result was a lack of local interest in defensive measures.

The British War Office had planned to send three more regiments of reinforcements to the Canadas at the end of the summer. However, as the addition of 2,500 more men to the Canadian garrison would raise it above its pre-Crimean War level, other voices in Britain began to question the need to continue the economically burdensome operation. On September 2 *The Times* declared that if the troops were being sent merely as a demonstration to awe the United States, it was a foolish gesture, for they would provide less than two men per mile of frontier line. It was equally foolish if it were a gesture to show that Great Britain would protect the provinces, for the Canadians alone were capable of raising fifty thousand men of their own if only required to do so, enough to defeat Yankees who lacked any knowledge of scientific warfare and who ran in battle. British troops, *The Times* argued, were needed in Europe and in New Zealand, where another war with the Maori threatened, and not in North America.

In September Newcastle concluded that the provinces were safe until the next spring, and he suggested keeping the three regiments in readiness in England rather than submitting them to the rigors of the long Canadian winter. Sending reinforcements earlier on *The Great Eastern* had been a wise move, he said, both because of the patriotic spirit they would infuse into the colonies and because of the effect upon Lincoln and Seward of a demonstration of force, but more troops might make the colonists too dependent on the mother country for their defense. The plan to send further reinforcements to the provinces was suspended with the expectation that in case of a sudden need *The Great Eastern* could rush troops up the St. Lawrence until quite late in the year.[30]

Before Newcastle's decision reached Quebec, Governor General

[30] Martineau, pp. 302–303: Newcastle to Head, Sept. 3, 1861; *The Times*, Sept. 9, 1861.

Head anticipated the question of Canadian dependence on British troops. He reported that the Canadians were not disposed to defend themselves. If a war with the North began, he wrote, it probably would be from an imperial cause and not from a Canadian grievance. Since the colony would have no voice in choosing a war policy, and since there were "no causes of difference with the Government of the United States arising out of the affairs or interests of Canada," the colony would be involved in war "only as a part and an exposed part of the Empire." The Canadian people were loyal to the Crown, Head insisted, but simply because the frontier happened to be "a line of weakness through which an enemy might wound England" was not a sufficient reason for charging the province with the burden of defense "in a war caused by interests in no degree of a local . . . character . . . ." [31]

Nor was the Foreign Office quite so sanguine as the Colonial and War Offices. Palmerston continued to urge Earl Russell to send troops to North America, and in mid-September Russell hurried precautionary instructions to Lyons on how he should conduct himself in case the United States chose to break off relations with Great Britain. However, even this eventuality would not be too serious, Russell apparently thought, for Lyons was to retire briefly to Canada East in the expectation that any misunderstanding would not last for long. [32]

In the meantime Seward quietly had been placing special agents along the British North American border, dipping into the Secret Service fund in order to pay them. Seward felt they could augment the reports from the dozen or so consuls whom he was appointing to the provinces. Already a substantial group of Confederates was present in British North America, consisting largely of stranded tourists or young men bent on making their fortunes by running the blockade, and Seward had written to recommended police officers asking if they would accept positions as agents to watch Confederate movements north of the border. [33] The regular consuls filed copies of newspaper editorials critical of the Lincoln administration, commented on public opinion, and began to report on the presence of known Confederates. Some of the consuls probably were appointed as agents or, as the Canadians were wont to say, as spies, for they often had little

[31] G 9, 38: Sept. 9, 1861, 191–197.
[32] Newton, I, 52: Sept. 13, 1861.
[33] MC: H. Walworth to Seward, Oct. 8, and T. H. Canfield to Seward, Oct. 16, 1861, are typical of several replies.

commercial business to transact and, in two cases at least, were located in areas where legitimate trade practically was nil. In the long run it was the consuls rather than the special agents who proved to be the most valuable "listening posts" in the provinces.[34]

Seward was not quiet in all of his acts with respect to British North America, however, and he soon gave added support to the Canadian feeling that he was pursuing an aggressive policy. On October 10, after he had learned from Adams that Britain did not intend to send another detachment of reinforcements to North America until spring, he issued a preliminary circular letter to the governors of all of the Northern seaboard and lake states recommending that they take measures to place the ports and harbors under their jurisdiction in a state of defense. Seward still was viewing the war unrealistically, for the following day he wrote Sumner that the rebellion was "already arrested" and charged that what success it did attain was due largely to "the timidity . . . of British Statesmen and the British Press . . . ."[35] On October 14 Seward issued a second circular letter to the same effect as the first.[36]

Seward's biographer, Frederic Bancroft, has interpreted the circular letter as the Secretary's means of letting Europe know that the North could increase her own measures for defense along the British North American border and that, as he had said earlier, he was not disturbed by the presence of the British reinforcements.[37] Had Seward intended the circular as a gesture of this nature, however, he surely would have issued it at the time when the reinforcements arrived in Quebec amidst such fanfare. Lyons thought that the circular was a "trial balloon" to test public feeling once again on the subject of a quarrel with

[34] See, for example, a typically excellent dispatch from M. M. Jackson to Seward in CD, Halifax, IX: Sept. 5, 1861, reporting the presence of no less than eleven British warships in Halifax harbor, including the flagship *Nile*. See also CI, 28: Seward to Giddings, July 3, 1861, 551–552.

[35] Sumner Papers, LIII: Oct. 11, 1861.

[36] James Morton Callahan, in *American Foreign Policy in Canadian Relations* (New York, 1937), p. 272, feels that Seward probably issued the circular because the British were sending troops to the Canadas. This could not have been the case, for Seward issued no circular of this nature when troops were sent and both his preliminary and final defense circulars came after he had learned from Adams that the reinforcement operation had been halted. See CFA, 77: Sept. 19, recd. Oct. 8, 1861; FO 5, 772: Lyons to Russell, Oct. 18, 1861; New York *Herald* and New York *Times*, both Oct. 17, 1861.

[37] *Seward*, II, 212.

England,[38] and it is possible that he was correct, especially in the light of Seward's letter to Sumner, which partially blamed Britain for the internecine war. Seward knew that further reinforcements were not on the way, so he could test the wind safely with his circular letter. On the other hand, the reason that Seward gave to Lyons for issuing the circular—that Confederate agents were thought to be in the provinces to promote British intervention in the war—was a plausible one at the time and, viewed with hindsight, a wise one. The circular gave publicity to the possibility of Confederate attempts to embroil the United States and Great Britain in war. Seward showed himself awake to what was to become a reality nearly three years later when the Confederate government actually embarked upon such a plan.

Now it is known that there were no official Confederate agents in British North America so early in the war, for Confederate foreign policy showed a lack of imagination throughout the conflict. Intent upon prying diplomatic recognition from Great Britain or France, the South did not turn to an attempt to embroil the North in war with Britain as early as Seward and others expected. The South failed to realize that intervention might be won elsewhere than in London. Had Southerners turned to the policy of embroilment earlier, working from the British provinces at the outset, the policy might have been successful, for if there had been a raid by Confederates from the Canadas in 1861 while Seward was casting about for a possible *casus belli* with Britain, as there was in 1864, he might have seized upon it and fallen into a Southern trap. It often is stated that Seward's "foreign war panacea" was shelved by Lincoln. Of lesser, but nonetheless considerable, importance is the fact that there simply was not even a mildly legitimate excuse for war with Britain early in 1861, and Seward probably would not have deliberately engineered one without a proper façade.

The defense circular, whatever Seward's intentions, produced a hostile reaction in the provinces. It seemed to furnish more evidence of America's "childish irritability" over the fact that the nations of the world had not combined together, with England in the lead, "to go mad with despair at the mere prospect of the Republicans shooting one another." [39] Most of the provincial press viewed the circular letter as a threat, and a ludicrous one in view of Bull Run, or as retaliation for

[38] FO 5, 472: to Russell, Oct. 18, 1861.
[39] *The Times*, Oct. 8, 1861. See also Toronto *Globe*, June 3, 1861.

the public manner in which Britain had poured troops into the provinces.[40]

The Toronto *Globe* tried to allay the suspicions that the circular aroused, and on October 19 used its issuance for an occasion to analyze the shifting balance of power on the continent. George Brown was one Canadian who was not hypnotized by Bull Run, for he was aware of the growing strength of the American armies. Brown predicted an "exhaustive war" that would last many years, ending with a Northern victory, after which the North would be too depleted to attack Great Britain. Even a second-rate state like Canada, he said, could swing the balance in favor of the South near the long war's end, if this seemed desirable. Brown felt that Lincoln and Seward realized this, that the circular was a wise precaution taken to prevent aid being given to the South by "English aristocrats," and that it was aimed not at the provinces but at Britain. Canada, in fact, was in an enviable position as a possible kingmaker on the North American continent, Brown concluded, and might grasp the crown for herself.

Throughout 1861 the British North American provinces were filled with an uneasy people—uneasy not because they feared an immediate invasion, which few did, but rather because they found themselves taking an increasingly anti-Northern view of the war. Most of them probably would have liked to favor the Northern cause, for it once had seemed the cause of righteousness. Most British North Americans knew that although the North might be fighting for union, the Negro still would benefit from a Northern victory.[41] But the growing friction along the border, the imperial government's evident concern over possible attack, Seward's apparent hostility, and an exacerbating election had driven the colonial away from even an alignment of sympathy with the Yankee. The British North American was trying to rationalize his growing antagonism. What he needed was a dramatic event, an act that would crystallize opinion, some Northern gesture against either the provinces or the mother country that would confirm the rightness of the rationalizations. This event was not long in coming. President Lincoln, who early in the year had declared that there was "nothing gone wrong," was to find that everything domestic and foreign could go wrong at once.

[40] Several newspapers quoted in Cleveland *Leader* and Toronto *Globe*, both Oct. 19, 1861.

[41] For example, see G 14, 26: T. G. Anderson to James M. Mason, Nov. 14, 1861; Toronto *Globe*, June–Sept., 1861, *passim*, which quotes editorials from other newspapers.

six 🐎 "ONE WAR AT A TIME":

THE *TRENT* AFFAIR

> "Most Americans are born drunk . . . . Americans do
> not need to drink to inspire them to do anything."
>
> G. K. CHESTERTON

YOUNG GEORGE JOHNSON HAD FOUND THAT STEWART'S RESTAURANT WAS the best place in Halifax for his lunchtime snack. He always could look forward to a lively discussion on the American war with the other young men who were beginning their careers in the nearby banks, warehouses, and produce markets. The war had caught the imagination of Johnson as it had that of most Haligonians, and he was especially eloquent in defending the chivalrous and strong-willed Southerners from the fanatical Northerners who were trying to foist an unwanted government upon the South. He never had been to the South, or even to "the Boston States" for that matter, but he had read the local newspapers and had thought about the issues involved in the Civil War as clearly as he could. Johnson stood almost alone in defense of the South, although those who were wont to charge the South with treason were wavering. Today Johnson was determined to win them over.

The men were stamping the snow from their feet when the door burst open to admit a breathless boy. Johnson was in the midst of an argument concerning Northern press abuse of Great Britain. The boy was gone in a moment, but he had stayed long enough to shout his message: "The Yankees have just held up an English ship. They've kidnapped the rebels!" That he was not strictly accurate did not matter. Very little that the Haligonians heard was strictly accurate.

It was enough for Johnson's final triumph. "It's war certain," he said, turning to his friends. "Damn me if I ever speak for a Yank again," one of the "Federals" replied. It was November 19, and the "rebels" held a unanimous decision in the battle of Stewart's Restaurant. Haligonians were "swung round like a gate." [1]

It was an exciting week in the Canadas as well. In Montreal General Tom Thumb was at the Mechanics' Hall, playing the roles of Charles IV, Montezuma, and Cortez "simultaneously," and LaRue's Panopticon of eighty thousand moving models of men and animals enacting the Sepoy Rebellion was attracting half the population. The other half was enjoying the annual Montreal Steeple Chase at the race course, having a glass of soda water from a splendid new silver soda fountain that had opened opposite the French Cathedral, or watching Mr. A. J. Davis, the "Man Born without Arms, Thighs, or Knee Joints," exhibit himself to the accompaniment of a brass band. In Canada West one Marcus Gunn was holding a regular Sunday evening séance to contact some "Spirit members in the spirit Spheres," but the conditions did not seem favorable. [2] He received, instead, very different news, news that came "like a thunder-clap in a summer sky" [3] to British North Americans—news of what since has become famous as "the *Trent* affair," a series of events that served to crystallize wavering opinion in the provinces.

The Confederate government had dispatched two distinguished former senators of the United States to Europe. James Murray Mason of Virginia, best known as the father of the Fugitive Slave Act, had been chosen to match wits with Adams in London while John Slidell of Louisiana, a man whose abilities were held in particularly high regard in the North, was on his way to Paris. On November 7 they had sailed from Havana on a British merchantman and mail packet, the *Trent*. On the following day Captain Charles Wilkes of the *San Jacinto* stopped the *Trent*, placed the two commissioners under arrest and removed them, technically by force, from the ship. Wilkes returned with his prisoners to the mainland, arriving on November 17, while the *Trent* continued her voyage to England. [4]

---

[1] See Johnson, "The Trent Affair," Nova Scotia Hist. Soc., *Collections*, xvi (1912), 41–59; G. Gunn, "New Brunswick Opinion," p. 185; Skelton, *Galt*, p. 313.

[2] P.A.C., Marcus Gunn Diary, II, 310: Nov. 17, 1861. A transcript is in the Lawson Memorial Library, University of Western Ontario.

[3] Watkin, *Recollections*, p. 86. Thereafter the British North American press reported Captain Charles Wilkes' every move to the end of the war. For a typical example, see Halifax *Acadian Recorder*, Oct. 11, 1862.

[4] The details of the seizure are too well known to be repeated here. The standard

The *Trent* affair came at a moment when the newspapers of North America had had little of significance to report for some time. There had been no battle of importance since July and no noteworthy diplomatic development, except for Seward's defense circular. Northern newspapers, eager for the smallest success to report to the people, "welcomed and exaggerated" the news, and their victory-starved readers gave to Wilkes' brash act every sign of approval, fêting and acclaiming him wherever he went.[5]

In the British North American provinces news of the incident "set the whole country ablaze." [6] Canadian editors had been reduced to repeating tested truths about righteousness, preparedness, and neutrality.[7] The seizure fell on hungry presses like manna in the midst of drought. Even to highly insular, almost unconcerned, Prince Edward Island it brought a "profound sensation." [8]

Official reaction to the news of the seizure of the envoys was prompt and vigorous. The new Governor General of British North America,

---

accounts include: Charles F. Adams, "The Trent Affair," Mass. Hist. Soc., *Procs.,* XLV (Nov., 1911), 35–148; R. H. Dana, "The Trent Affair: An Aftermath," *ibid.* (March, 1912), 508–530; Fred Landon, "The Trent Affair of 1861," *CHR,* III (March, 1922), 48–55; Arnold Whitridge, "The Trent Affair, 1861: An Anglo-American Crisis that Almost Led to War," *History Today,* IV (June, 1954), 394–402; T. L. Harris, *The Trent Affair* (Indianapolis, 1896); and Evan John [E. J. Simpson], *Atlantic Impact, 1861* (London, 1952). The most recent articles are V. H. Cohen, "Charles Sumner and the *Trent* Affair," *Jour. of So. Hist.,* XXII (May, 1956), 205–219, and David Large, "Friends and the American Civil War: The Trent Affair," Friends' Hist. Soc., *Journal,* XLVIII (Autumn, 1957), 163–167. Daniel Henderson, *The Hidden Coasts* (New York, 1953), is the only full-scale biography of Wilkes; W. W. Jeffries, "The Civil War Career of Charles Wilkes," *Jour. of So. Hist.,* XI (Aug., 1945), 324–348; J. D. Hill, "Charles Wilkes: Turbulent Scholar of the Old School," U.S. Naval Institute, *Procs.,* LVII (July, 1931), 866–887; L. M. Sears, *John Slidell* (Durham, 1925); Beckles Willson, *John Slidell and the Confederates in Paris* (New York, 1932); and Stephen McQ. Huntley, *Les Rapports de la France et la confédération pendant la Guerre de Sécession* (Toulouse, 1932), provide additional information on Wilkes and the seizure.

[5] Bancroft, *Seward,* II, 228; Cohen, pp. 205–206. See also Toronto *Globe,* Dec. 4, 1861; Albany *Evening Journal,* Dec. 2, 1861.

[6] Fredericton *Head Quarters,* Nov. 20, 1861; Ottawa *Citizen,* Nov. 19, 26, 1861; Saint John *New Brunswick Courier,* Nov. 23, 1861; Clarke, *Sixty Years,* p. 119; J. Travis Mills, *Great Britain and the United States: A Critical Review of their Historical Relations* (London, 1920), p. 44.

[7] Barrie *Northern Advance,* Nov. 13, 1861; Toronto *Globe,* Nov. 11, 1861, quotes several such editorials from Canadian newspapers.

[8] Duncan Campbell, *History of Prince Edward Island* (Charlottetown, 1875), p. 147.

Lord Monck, who had taken office less than a week before the news arrived, decided to strengthen provincial defenses on his own authority without waiting for word from London, which he knew could not arrive until December. Charles Stanley, fourth Viscount Monck, was an Irishman from Tipperary who had legal training. At forty-two, Monck was entering an office for which he had no particular qualifications other than those that were least tangible but most important— energy, tact, and an immense capacity for patience. He had served in the House of Commons for seven years and had been a Lord of the Treasury in Lord Palmerston's government from 1855 to 1858. Since then he had been a landed gentleman out of office, a situation that Palmerston corrected when he returned to the prime-ministership. Monck's position carried a function of greater importance than in any other colonial dependency, for the Governor General was tied closely to foreign as well as to colonial policy. Monck was to remain in his position until 1868 and thus became the first Governor General of the Dominion of Canada. During this time he was to conclude that his "most anxious and responsible duties" were those involved in helping conduct foreign relations with the United States.[9]

Monck wanted the provincial militia, which had been drilling spasmodically, prepared for action.[10] He instructed the British Military Commander in North America, Sir Fenwick Williams, not to use the telegraph for the communication of any important or secret information and directed Williams to make his preparations "*as quiet as possible*, not on account of the Americans but lest an alarm and panic should be excited amongst our people . . . ." Although there were not enough arms in the Canadas to supply the sedentary militia, Monck did not want Williams to forward any from Halifax, for he felt that this alone might create the panic that he feared.[11]

The Governor General had to contend with a number of defensive problems. He considered his main task to be the expediting of defensive measures in Canada West. The Canadian government had asked for

[9] There is no biography of Viscount (later first English Baron) Monck, and he left no memoirs, although his sister-in-law Frances Monck, did. See T. B. B[rowning]'s sketch in Leslie Stephen and Sidney Lee, eds., *Dictionary of National Biography, Supplement* (London, 1922), XXII, 1055-56.

[10] For a list of regimental histories too numerous to cite here, many of which contain incidental information on the defense movement in the provinces, see C. E. Dornbusch, *The Canadian Army, 1855-1955: Regimental Histories and A Guide to the Regiments* (Cornwallville, New York, 1957).

[11] Williams Papers: Monck to Williams, Nov. 28, 1861.

a military report on proposed British strategy in case of war, and on November 29 the report, prepared by a captain in the Royal Engineers, chilled the administration with its conclusions that extensive concentrations of troops would be needed along the Beauharnois, Cornwall, and Welland canals, where much fighting would take place, and that immediately upon the outbreak of war colonial and imperial troops would have to seize Fort Montgomery at Rouse's Point and Fort Niagara below Buffalo, both in New York state, if Montreal and Toronto were to be held against an invader. Construction on a new battery to defend Toronto began on December 2. Anticipating the arrival of more troops, Monck had his military secretary make inquiries concerning navigation on the lower St. Lawrence and learned that, although ice was forming below Quebec, the river would be open at least to Bic, at the head of the military wagon road, for several days. When four United States revenue boats dropped anchor at Kingston following a gale, the local commander sent an officer aboard them ostensibly to ask whether they had suffered any damage but actually to examine them for the presence of heavy guns. When the gale-lashed revenue cutters slipped down the St. Lawrence River for Boston, Monck rejoiced that the American force on the lakes was thus reduced and concluded from their departure that the American government did not intend war, at least until spring.[12]

During the same weeks Lieutenant Governor Arthur Gordon of New Brunswick and Charles Hastings Doyle, Commander of the British troops in Nova Scotia, conferred on Maritime defenses. They found that Saint John and Woodstock, in New Brunswick, were virtually defenseless, and the provincial legislature, which did not anticipate a war, was unwilling to provide funds for defensive purposes. Doyle felt that a portion of the province west of the Saint John River would have to be given up to an invader but that the interior of the province, and thus the land approaches to Nova Scotia, could be defended successfully. The Maritime Provinces also could be protected by issuing letters of marque and by mounting guns at key points along the Nova Scotian coast. According to Joseph Howe, leader of the liberals in Nova Scotia, who offered every able-bodied man in the

[12] *Ibid.*: Nov. 26, 29, 1861; C 1671: Doyle to Lewis, Oct. 1861, p. 1; C 696: H. Bouchier to R. Rollo, Nov. 24, 25, 1861, pp. 145-150; Toronto *Leader*, Dec. 3, 1861; transcripts from James W. Brown Diary: Oct. 23, Dec. 4, 1861. The writer wishes to thank the owner of the diary, Miss Dorothy E. Coaté, of Rosseau, Ontario, and Fred Neal of Fredericton for making transcripts available.

province for military service, the major weakness in Maritime defense was that the frontier could not be armed quickly due to the lack of railroad connections. However, Howe had an ulterior motive, for he wrote from London whence he had gone on a mission to obtain Colonial Office support for the Inter-colonial Railway project.[13]

Acting independently of London and Quebec, Earl Mulgrave, the Lieutenant Governor of Nova Scotia, also put the machinery of defense into motion. He sent young George Johnson to Portland to assess sentiment there. Johnson went on to Boston, Springfield, and New York City on his own initiative, and he reported to Mulgrave that in these centers there seemed to be no general clamor for war.[14]

In the first week of December, still acting without word from London, Monck obtained his Executive Council's sanction for issuing arms to local troops and for forming companies of artillery and engineers. Sir Fenwick Williams set out on a tour of inspection of the most strategic border points, while Lyons and Monck continued to emphasize the need for "vigilance and quiet" until they had heard from the Colonial and Foreign offices.[15] Monck submitted estimates to the Executive Council for an extensive plan of fortifications at Toronto with the warning that he would not take the responsibility for leaving such measures undone. He wanted no additional powers, however, for he feared that the people of the provinces might panic if they learned that he had been given emergency powers, and he felt that the regular Militia Act gave him sufficient authority. By the provisions of the act the Governor General could accept the services of any body of men who volunteered, and he received a number of such applications by the end of November. In any case Monck did not have sufficient arms with which to equip those who already had volunteered.

The Militia Act empowered the Governor General to call out the men in case of "war, invasion or insurrection, or imminent danger" from them. He did not wish to order the Militia to prepare for a war that had not begun and that he hoped would be averted. As long as men were being organized and trained and plans for defense were being made Monck felt there was little more of an unostentatious nature that he could do. Several thousand militia could drill and be prepared for an invasion without an official proclamation of emer-

---

[13] G 8B, 62: Gordon to Newcastle, Nov. 25, 1861, 11–14, with encs.; P.A.C., Joseph Howe Papers, VIII: Howe to Mulgrave, Nov. 30, 1861, 150–161.
[14] Saint John *Morning Freeman*, Dec. 28, 1861; Johnson, p. 50.
[15] Williams Papers: Monck to Williams, Dec. 5, 11, 1861; the latter quotes Lyons.

gency, just as volunteers could be used to build defenses for Kingston and Toronto. This plan had the obvious virtue of not calling Northern attention to the defensive measures taken in the provinces and of avoiding the implied threat to or fear of the United States that the calling up of militia might be taken to indicate.[16]

Lacking news from London concerning the crisis, Monck turned to the North. The best way to learn of Washington's attitude was to send someone directly to the capital, and he did this early in December. The Canadian Finance Minister, Alexander Galt, had planned to confer with Seward, Chase, and Lincoln about a growing rumor that the reciprocity treaty was to be abrogated. What could be more logical than to have Galt make his journey now? [17] In Washington Galt saw Ashmun once again and talked with Seward. The Secretary gave Galt no encouragement, and the Canadian may have winced when he noted the large, unframed photograph of the Duke of Newcastle, the Prince of Wales, and former President Buchanan that still sat on Seward's mantelpiece, a mute reminder of better times. Galt also found little to cheer him in the President's Annual Message, and he failed to see Chase at all.[18]

In his annual report to the President, Secretary of War Simon Cameron had recommended giving immediate attention to fortifications on the Great Lakes. "Aggressions are seldom made upon a nation ever ready to defend its honor and repel insults," he wrote, and advised the Federal government to "show the world that while engaged in quelling disturbances at home" the North could protect itself from attack from abroad. Lincoln incorporated part of Cameron's advice into his Annual Message.

When the President submitted his first Annual Message to Congress on December 3, he did not mention the *Trent* affair, to Galt's discomfort. Lincoln did defend the October circular, however, and he recommended harbor improvements and the establishment of arms depots on the frontier. Somewhat vaguely he said that America's relations with other nations, while "less gratifying" than formerly, were "more satisfactory than a nation so unhappily distracted . . . might reasonably have apprehended." When speaking of domestic

---

[16] P.A.C., MS. Group 10, 17A, 5: Monck to Williams, Nov. 30, 1861, 19–23; G 2, 8: Monck to Newcastle, Dec. 19, 1861, 337.

[17] Transcripts of Galt's letters, as cited from Skelton's biography, appear in the P.A.C., Alexander T. Galt Papers, 1.

[18] Skelton, *Galt*, p. 314: Galt to his wife, Dec. 5, 1861.

affairs the President argued at length that there was no suitable natural line between the North and South upon which to base a national boundary.[19] He appeared to be invoking the "rule against unnatural boundaries" that had become part of the creed of Manifest Destiny,[20] and since much of British North America blended imperceptibly with the United States, it was alarming to the colonials to have this concept publicly used by the President. A portion of the provincial press also gave a hostile interpretation to Lincoln's suggestion that "adequate and ample" measures be taken to maintain public defense "on every side," and the Toronto *Leader* viewed this as proof that Lincoln intended war.[21] A few of the British North American newspapers found the Message brief, sensible, and moderate,[22] but others thought it "tame and insipid," ponderous and tedious, and even illiterate.[23]

Two days later the House of Representatives determined to refer that part of the Message that dealt with lake defenses to a select committee instead of to the standing Committee on Military Affairs, as was customary. Some of the representatives from border states hoped to dip into the pork-barrel for construction of local fortifications. While expressing no outwardly hostile sentiment toward Britain, the House also adopted a resolution instructing the Committee on Roads and Canals to inquire into the feasibility of enlarging the Illinois and Michigan Canal in order to make possible steam navigation between the Mississippi River and the Great Lakes. Finally, the Committee on Military Affairs was directed to inquire into the expediency of fortifying the mouth of the Columbia River and the islands of Puget Sound. However, by the time the various committees had prepared their reports the immediate crisis had passed.[24]

Galt succeeded in interviewing Lincoln on December 4, and he used the occasion to discuss Seward's defense circular with the President.

---

[19] U.S., *Congressional Globe*, 37th Cong., 2nd Sess., Appendix, pp. 1–17; *Foreign Relations, 1862*, pp. 3–13.

[20] See Albert K. Weinberg, *Manifest Destiny* (Baltimore, 1935), pp. 212–215, and J. A. Hawgood, "Manifest Destiny," in Allen and Hill, eds., *British Essays*, pp. 123–125.

[21] Quoted in New York *World*, Dec. 7, 1861.

[22] Example quoted in Montreal *Witness*, Dec. 7, 1861.

[23] Saint John *Courier* and Montreal *Gazette*, both Dec. 7, 1861; Fredericton *Head Quarters*, Dec. 11, 1861.

[24] U.S. Congress, *House Reports*, 37th Cong., 2nd Sess., nos. 23 and 37; *The Times*, Jan. 7, 1862; FO 5, 776: Lyons to Russell, Dec. 13, 1861; G 8C, 10: Newcastle to Douglas, Jan. 7, 1862, 1–2.

The Finance Minister pointed out that the circular had caused uneasiness in the provinces, and Lincoln admitted that he had expected that it would. Galt also told Lincoln that the hostile New York press and the huge Northern army worried Canadians. Lincoln replied that the press did not reflect the views of the government, and he diplomatically omitted to point out that under the circumstances the size of the American army was natural and none of Canada's business. Lincoln did add that neither he nor his Cabinet entertained any aggressive designs against the provinces. Nevertheless, Galt was not comforted, for he feared that the American government was so subject to popular impulses as to make such assurances, no matter how honestly intended, virtually worthless. With respect to the *Trent* affair Lincoln had been quite conciliatory and had said that something would be said "to satisfy the people." Galt reported this conversation to his government, and Lincoln's statement was construed to mean that the democratic mob had to be placated.[25]

Galt interpreted Lincoln's remark that he would have to "say something to satisfy the people" as a covertly hostile statement. At least one recent historian also has viewed Lincoln's answer to Galt's query as a defense of the provocative action involved in Wilkes' seizure of Mason and Slidell "on the straight commercial grounds that there was a big demand for this in the home market of the United States . . . ."[26] This is unfair to Lincoln. He was not defending the "provocative action" itself, and he undoubtedly would have been happier had it not happened. Rather, he realistically saw that public opinion was so excited over the seizure that it would do much harm to Northern morale if he were to surrender Mason and Slidell without finding a means to do so that would not humiliate further an already humiliated nation. The implication was that Mason and Slidell would be surrendered as soon as a formula for doing so was found. Lincoln, as usual, was showing that politics was the art of the possible.

In the meantime, the news of the seizure of Mason and Slidell had reached England on November 27.[27] The Foreign Office was not unprepared for such news although it did come from an unexpected quarter, as Russell had feared that the captain of the Northern ship

---

[25] Skelton, *Galt*, p. 314: Galt's personal memo., Dec. 5, 1861; Edmond Fitzmaurice, *The Life of Granville: George Leveson Gower, Second Earl Granville, K.G., 1815–1891* (London, 1906), I, 401: Palmerston to Granville, Dec. 26, 1861.

[26] Creighton, *Macdonald*, p. 324.

[27] *The Times*, Nov. 28, 1861.

James Adger, which had lingered off the British coasts, was contemplating a similar maneuver against the Confederate commissioners.[28] Russell had asked the Lords Commissioners of the Admiralty to instruct Vice-Admiral Sir Alexander Milne, Commander of the British fleet in North America, which was stationed at Halifax, to keep in close contact with Lyons and to guard against sudden attacks from land batteries on the Maine coast.[29]

British North Americans who were on a railway mission to England were called together by Sir George Cornewall Lewis, the Minister of War, to discuss the possible threat to the province. These men, Howe, Watkin, Vankoughnet, and Samuel Leonard Tilley, the Prime Minister of New Brunswick, declared that the colonials would fight if and when the need arose, but that they could not do so with "jack-knives," and Vankoughnet charged Lewis with having failed to keep an adequate store of arms in the Canadas. Howe and Tilley remained in England to explain to the pro-Northern industrial workers why a Southern success would benefit Britain. This was, in Howe's case at least, a temporary change of heart, for until the *Trent* affair he had been pro-Northern.[30]

The Colonial Office decided to proceed with its preparation, in the words of the Under-Secretary for the Colonies, Frederick Rogers, "just as if war was declared." This decision was partially the result of a conference between Sir Edmund Head, who had just arrived in London from his former post at Quebec, the Colonial Secretary, the Duke of Newcastle, and the Under-Secretary, Rogers (later, Lord Blachford). It was possible, they thought, that Seward was trying a desperate

[28] The Law Officers of the Crown submitted a written statement to Russell on November 12 and again on November 28. On the position taken by the British law officers in the case, see J. P. Baxter, III, "The British Government and Neutral Rights, 1861–1865," *AHR,* XXXIV (Oct., 1928), 9–29, and Baxter, ed., "Papers relating to Belligerent and Neutral Rights, 1861–1865," *ibid.,* pp. 77–91. Baxter's article is an excellent summary of the legal questions involved in the *Trent* affair and revises the lengthy treatment in E. D. Adams, *Great Britain and the American Civil War,* pp. 203–243. For Palmerston's famous letter to Queen Victoria, and her reaction, see A. C. Benson and Viscount Esher, eds., *The Letters of Queen Victoria* (London, 1908), III, 466–467; and E. F. Benson, *Queen Victoria* (London, 1935), pp. 200–202.

[29] Horatio King, "The Trent Affair," *Magazine of American History,* XV (March, 1886), 285–286; S. J. Reid, *Lord John Russell* (London, 1895), pp. 310–312; and G. P. Gooch, ed., *The Later Correspondence of Lord John Russell, 1840–1878* (London, 1925), II, 321–325.

[30] Howe Papers: copy of Liverpool *Mercury,* Dec. 7, 1861.

gamble to establish himself above Lincoln. If Seward could get himself ejected from Lincoln's Cabinet because of some anti-British gesture, Rogers thought, he might be able to achieve the White House in the next election on the shoulders of an Anglophobic mob. Upon Newcastle's advice Lewis dispatched fresh troops and more arms to the provinces and sent Watkin, as President of the Grand Trunk Railway, to the Canadas to arrange for their transportation.[31]

The *Trent* crisis was timed badly in Seward's eyes. His defense circular had taken on a sinister meaning, as a stage in preparation for an "outrage" that might produce war. In Britain there were those who seemed convinced that Seward was trying to provoke a war in order to seize the Canadas, and at first it was rumored that he had ordered the *Trent* stopped.[32] The Duke of Newcastle reminded Russell of Seward's supposed threat in 1860 to find cause for war with England, adding that Seward had said that he would bombard Liverpool if he became President. This story was given to *The Times*, and later it was reprinted in British North American newspapers. Thurlow Weed, a leader of the Republican party in New York and Seward's political preceptor, then in Europe on a mission for the Secretary of State, went directly to Newcastle for an account of the story, believing that it could not be true. Weed learned that Seward indeed had told Newcastle that it was his intention to insult the British government. It now appeared to many in Britain that Seward was ready to make good his boasts.[33] Seward did not improve his position when he at first denied

---

[31] George E. Marinden, ed., *Letters of Frederick Lord Blachford, Under Secretary of State for the Colonies, 1860–1871* (London, 1896), p. 232: F. Rogers to K. Rogers, Nov., 1861; G. F. Lewis, ed., *Letters of the Right Hon. Sir George Cornewall Lewis, Bart., to Various Friends* (London, 1870), pp. 405–408; Watkins, p. 86.

[32] Some felt that Seward, "out of his senses with rage, fear, and helplessness," "intoxicated with his own boastfulness," and steeped in "moral and mental worthlessness," proposed to annex the Canadas by capitalizing on the *Trent* affair. See Seward Papers: Dublin *Daily Express*, enc. in M. B. Sims to Seward, both Nov. 29, 1861, and Weed to Seward, Dec. 2, 1861; E. R. Cameron, *Memoirs of Ralph Vansittart* (Toronto, 1924), which contains factual material in a fictional guise; Ernest H. Coleridge, *Life and Correspondence of John Duke Lord Coleridge, Lord Chief Justice of England* (London, 1904), II, 11–12: Coleridge to Ellis Yarnall, Dec. 8, 1861; S. M. Ellis, ed., *A Mid-Victorian Pepys: The Letters and Memoirs of Sir William Hardman, M.A., F.R.G.S.* (London, 1923), p. 52; John Bigelow, *Retrospections of an Active Life* (New York, 1909), I, 405.

[33] Albany *Evening Journal*, Dec. 27, 1861; Seward Papers: Weed to Seward, Dec. 7, 10, 22, 1861, Jan. 8, 1862; Watkin, p. 16; L.C., Zachariah Chandler Papers:

that he ever had made such a statement to Newcastle and then admitted that he might have done so, although only in jest.[34]

There is little doubt that Seward had said something of this nature to Newcastle during the latter's visit to America, but it also would seem clear that Seward spoke in badinage. According to Newcastle, Seward had said that either he or Lincoln would be the next President. The conversation was supposed to have taken place in September, 1860, but since Lincoln had received his party's nomination the preceding May, Seward already knew that he would not be the next President. Furthermore, Seward did not meet Newcastle until mid-October, a month later than the Duke recalled.

Seward may not have wanted to give the report the dignity of a public rebuttal, but his disinclination to contradict Newcastle permitted the story to add grist to the already active rumor mill. It also was rumored in diplomatic circles in Paris and London that General Winfield Scott, who was then on the continent, had been empowered to offer all of French Canada to France if she would support the United States in a war with Great Britain. An almost equally frightening rumor had it that the North meant to seize the vast fortune that British capitalists had invested in the United States.[35] The most common rumor, however, was that the North, realizing that it could not conquer the South, now was ready to take the Canadas as a replacement.[36]

Great Britain wanted "peace with honor." War was threatening in Europe, France appeared untrustworthy, Japan was making aggressive gestures in the Far East, and troops were needed in New Zealand. The British army was inadequate for dealing with a war on two fronts, and as a result both Britain's European and American policies were weakened. Britain would not be able to take a firm stand on the Continent for fear of an American war, and she could not pour her total

---

Weed to Chandler, Dec. 7, 1861 [incorrectly dated 1871]. Richard Cobden expressed the same thought in a letter to Sumner (Sumner Papers, cxxxvi: Dec. 19, 1861). See also Edward Younger, ed., *Inside the Confederate Government: The Diary of Robert Garlick Hill Kean* (New York, 1957), p. 17: Nov. 8, 1861.

[34] Univ. Rochester, Thurlow Weed Papers: Seward to Weed, Dec. 28, 30, 1861, Jan. 2, Feb. 19, March 7, 1862; Seward Papers: Weed to Seward, Jan. 16, 1862.

[35] Bigelow, I, 405; Toronto *Leader*, Dec. 23, 1861; Benson and Esher, eds., III, 468–469: Palmerston to Victoria, Nov. 29, 1861.

[36] Toronto's *Leader* and *Globe* frequently referred to this rumor during December, 1861. Historian John Lathrop Motley wrote to John Bigelow that the Canadas "would be a poor bargain" since the "frozen St. Lawrence . . . is a poor substitute for the Mississippi" (Bigelow, I, 416: Dec. 17, 1861).

resources into North America because of lowering clouds over Europe and in the Pacific. She virtually was forced into a policy of artificial isolation in Europe due to her North American commitments, and she was hampered by Europe's refusal to stay isolated.[37] But it was obvious that some troops must be sent to the North American provinces in order to encourage local defensive efforts and to demonstrate to the United States that Great Britain would fight if necessary. One of Lord Lyons first communications to Russell after learning of the *Trent* incident advised that the Northern government might be moved to give the commissioners up if the next news from England told of warlike preparations.[38]

The Colonial Secretary sent two sets of instructions to Monck. He made it clear that the Canadians were to defend their country and that Her Majesty's government would only second their operations, albeit vigorously. Newcastle warned that war was "too likely to be the result" of the crisis and advised Monck to take precautions to save the new Victoria Bridge on the St. Lawrence, to bring guns from Quebec if necessary, and to make the most of the winter until a strong British army could take the field in the spring. Newcastle promised to provide new uniforms and Enfield rifles for a Canadian militia of 100,000 men, and he implied that the Canadians would have to fight a holding action along the border for some time. Exportation from Great Britain or the provinces of ammunition, military stores, and saltpeter was prohibited.[39]

Newcastle tersely reminded Mulgrave in Nova Scotia to send all messages to Monck only by personal messenger through the provinces and not via the usual winter route through Maine. He also asked the Governor General to see to it that light ships on the St. Lawrence River were left in position until the full contingent of troops had arrived. This last order was not needed, for Monck, with his usual efficiency, already had made the necessary requests. However, he was unable to contact the lightkeeper on Anticosti Island, leaving at least

[37] See A. J. P. Taylor, *The Struggle for Mastery in Europe, 1848–1918* (Oxford, 1954), p. 129; Willoughby Verner, *Military Life of H.R.H. George, Duke of Cambridge* (London, 1905), I, 272; Harold Miller, *New Zealand* (New York, 1950), pp. 66–71.

[38] Theodore Martin, *The Life of His Royal Highness the Prince Consort* (London, 1880), v, 418–427.

[39] G 1, 154: Dec. 4, 1861, 395–401; Williams Papers: Monck to Williams, Dec. 30, 1861; N.S., Dispatches, 105: circular, Dec. 10, 1861, 431, 433; Martineau, *Newcastle*, pp. 304–305: Newcastle to Monck, Dec. 5, 1861.

one dangerously darkened passage through which the ships must slip. On Christmas day Monck ordered the telegraph offices kept open so that word of the arrival of the vessels could reach him quickly.[40]

The promised 100,000 rifles never were sent. Working throughout the last Sunday in November, the War Office had ordered that an initial shipment of 28,000 rifles should be ready to accompany the first troopships that were to sail at the end of the week. In all, the Colonial and War offices dispatched some 50,000 arms and two and a quarter million rounds of ammunition to North America. The size of the expeditionary force that the British government sent, however, would indicate that the administration took a serious view of the situation. The entire reinforcement, including those sent during the summer, consisted of sixteen batteries of Royal Artillery, four companies of Royal Engineers, eleven battalions of foot soldiers and two battalions of the Military Train, totaling 14,436 men. And 11,175 of these set out for North America aboard eighteen transports during the *Trent* crisis itself, while arrangements were made in the Canadas for calling out 38,000 members of the sedentary militia.[41]

In the first cold week of December, two men, in particular, rose very early to ride to St. James's Park to watch the British troops pass on their way to the docks. John Delane, editor of *The Times*, may have felt a thrill of expectation as he watched at length from his coach, for his newspaper often had indicated that the Yankee needed a good thrashing, but Thurlow Weed, thinking back almost fifty years to another war, was heartsick as he turned away from the scene.[42] Small boys mingled with the crowd in the park and near the dock, selling miniature Confederate flags, and the throng seemed united in its desire to see the Yankees chastised. Weed knew better than to base his

[40] G 2, 8: Newcastle to Monck, Dec. 5, 1861, 354; G 9, 38: Monck to Newcastle, Dec. 19, 1861, 309–313; Williams Papers: Monck to Williams, Dec. 25, 1861; N.S., Dispatches, 105: Newcastle to Mulgrave, Dec. 7, 1861, 394–396, and Dec. 14, 1861, 448.

[41] G.B., *Sessional Papers*, LXXII, 663; *Hansard's, 1862:* CLXV, col. 396, Feb. 17. The reinforcement figure is reported variously and incorrectly as eight thousand (Martin, v, 419 n.); ten thousand (W. L. Yancey to R. M. T. Hunter, Dec. 31, 1861, in *O.R.N.,* ser. II, III, 313); and twelve thousand (*The Times,* Feb. 10, 1862). Stacey, *Army,* p. 121, explains and accepts the figure given in *Hansard's.*

[42] Arthur I. Dasent, *John Thadeus Delane, Editor of 'The Times': His Life and Correspondence* (London, 1908), II, 37. Delane wrote to W. H. Russell that he hoped for war (*The Times, History of The Times* [London, 1939], II, 372–373: Dec. 11, 1861). See also Thurlow Weed Barnes and Harriet A. Weed, *Life of Thurlow Weed, including his Autobiography and a Memoir* (Boston, 1884), II, 368.

judgment of public opinion on a patriotic mob, however. He made a point to talk with Canadian businessmen and with British officers, and he was cheered slightly to find that not all of the officers favored war.[43] Many felt that the presence of several thousand British regulars along an already tense border was not likely to increase the prospects of harmony, while others agreed with Lyons that preparedness was linked intimately with peace. Many of the men sailed fully expecting war, and they were quick to recognize the precarious position in which they would be placed. Some, it was reported, even expected to be prisoners of war shortly, for the public disdain expressed for the Federal troops was shared by only a few of the British officers. Delane, on the other hand, expected that Portland would be seized with ease by British troops, and that the Americans barely would penetrate the provinces.[44]

In *Candide* Voltaire had referred to Canada as "a few acres of snow," and the arriving troops must have been in hearty agreement with him. The transports beat their way slowly across the Atlantic in the face of wintry storms, the seas running so high that the ships lost touch with their convoys. The first vessel to reach North America was the Cunard Line's *Persia*, commanded by one of the company's most noted captains, which rounded Cape Race at full speed, plunged past darkened Anticosti Island, and hove to off Bic, on the wagon road some fifty miles from the end of the railway line at Rivière du Loup. Keeping its screws turning to prevent ice from forming as the soldiers disembarked, the *Persia* had to dash for freedom so abruptly, as the ice stiffened, that a few of the soldiers and all of the baggage and heavy stores still were aboard. The slower ships, warned by the returning *Persia*, changed course for Halifax and Saint John. One vessel, the *Victoria*, never reached North America, putting back to England instead, and a second, the *Parana*, grounded on a sandbank in a snowstorm.[45]

---

[43] Seward Papers: James Lesley, Jr., to Seward, Dec. 4, and Weed to Seward, Dec. 7, 31, 1861; Ellice Papers, A-1, 2: Parkes to Ellice, Dec. 11, 1861.

[44] John Atkins, *The Life of Sir William Howard Russell, C.V.O., LL.D., The First Special Correspondent* (London, 1911), II, 88; H. Biddulph, ed., "Canada and the American Civil War: More Wolseley Letters," Soc. for Army Hist. Research, *Journal*, XIX (Summer, 1940), 113: Wolseley to Biddulph, Dec. 10, 1861; Frederick Maurice, *The 16th Foot: A History of the Bedfordshire and Hertfordshire Regiment* (London, 1931), p. 83; *History of The Times*, II, 371–373: Delane to W. H. Russell, Dec. 5, 1861.

[45] Williams Papers: Monck to Williams, Dec. 21, 1861; Montreal *Gazette*, Nov. 26, 1955. The voyage of the *Persia* is described in F. C. Bowen, *A Century of*

Lieutenant Governor Gordon of New Brunswick, who had proceeded to Saint John on Boxing Day, found no arrangements to receive the troops. The youthful Governor obtained the loan of a few buildings and called together the military authorities of the city to make emergency preparations. The townspeople worked for two days in the midst of a storm to convert eight school buildings into barracks. Religious leaders of all denominations called on their flocks to give aid to the arriving troops, and people from the back country came into Saint John with sleds and horses that they wished to lend to the soldiers without charge. As the late arrivals struggled through drifts along the Saint John River valley, the six hundred men who had landed at Bic, suffering from cold and lack of food and clothing, were transported by the local populace, who provided hundreds of carioles, to the railhead.[46]

The French-Canadian Bishop of Quebec urged all Roman Catholics in the provinces to welcome the British troops and to join, where possible, volunteer movements in defense of *le pays*. The curés of Bic, St. Simon, Trois-Pistoles, and l'Îsle-Verte prepared to receive the British troops as they descended from the New Brunswick highlands to the St. Lawrence River, and the French Canadians throughout the provinces, although formerly pro-Northern, now tended to unite in their opposition to the Northern enemy. The two leading French language newspapers of Canada East, *Le Pays* (Montreal) and *Le Courrier du Canada* (Quebec), championed the British, the latter declaring that a war would have a salutory effect on budding Canadian nationalism. The proprietor of *La Minerve* of Montreal pledged that he personally would raise five hundred men for the army. There was nothing, it was said by one such journal, "so much in horror as the thought of being conquered by the Yankees." [47]

Atlantic Travel, 1830–1930 (London, 1932), pp. 103–104; the *Parana's* trip is described in Frederick Maurice, *The History of the Scots Guards from the Creation of the Regiment to the Eve of the Great War* (London, 1934), II, 122–124. The latter dates the *Parana's* slow voyage in June rather than January, 1862. See also St. John's *Public Ledger and Newfoundland General Advertiser,* Jan. 7, 1862, and R. S. Prance, ed., "The Diary of John Ward of Clitheroe, Weaver, 1860–1864," Historic Soc. of Lancashire and Cheshire, *Transactions,* cv (1953), 170: Dec. 12, 19, 1861.

[46] G 8B, 62: Gordon to Newcastle, Jan. 4, 41–46, and Newcastle to Gordon, Jan. 24, 1862, 54–56; G 1, 155: Newcastle to Monck, Jan. 14, 1862, 15–18; H. C. Miles, "On the Winter March of Troops from Nova Scotia to Canada in 1861–62," *Lancet,* 1 (Feb. 15, March 22, 29, 1862), 180–181, 298–300, 322–324.

[47] Diocese of Quebec, *Mandements des Evêque de Québec,* IV, Baillargeon: cir-

If the North intended war, the British army felt that it would begin along the New Brunswick border. There the British troops, almost immobilized under heavy blankets on their eight-man sleighs, had to pass close to American communities. The greatest caution was taken at Lake Temiscouata because of a dangerous crossing at the Aroostook River, and it was feared that the American army would launch a surprise attack either at this point or at Woodstock, directly opposite Houlton in Maine, which had a good highway connection with Portland. The men pressed forward, following fir branches that had been set in ice to mark the road. Some became snowbound and others had to return to Saint John when snow obscured the branches, but most of the soldiers succeeded in reaching the railhead at Rivière du Loup.[48]

At the height of the crisis Sir Fenwick Williams proposed closing Toronto harbor by sinking offshore a few old vessels loaded with stones. The General may have forgotten momentarily that public opinion in Britain had declared that the North's sinking of a stone fleet across Charleston harbor was "barbaric," "the work of demons, not of *civilised* human beings . . . ." Williams twice renewed his suggestion, and it was referred by Monck to Macdonald, who reported that it would be best to wait until spring and see at that time whether such a drastic action was needed. Besides, Whitby, near Toronto, also had a good harbor where an invading force might land, and it would be impossible as well as pointless to plug all such potential landing spots. Monck felt that such a plan would attract too much notice, and he continued to advocate less obvious means of preparing for a possible war, directing British customs officials on the border to observe and report on American activities without taking any action on their own responsibility. The activity in the various provinces was anything but quiet, however, as nearly every move was reported in the Northern press.[49]

Many British North Americans took feverish but unco-ordinated steps to prepare for the possibility of invasion. In the Canadas most

culaire, Dec. 20, 1861; G 20, 87: Baillargeon to Monck, Jan. 11, 1862; G 9, 36: Monck to Newcastle, Feb. 2, 1862, 43–46; *Courrier de St. Hyacinthe,* quoted in Toronto *Leader,* Dec. 21, 24, 28, 1861; and *Gazette de Soie,* quoted in *ibid.,* also Dec. 28, 1861.
    [48] C 696: Confidential memo. for Col. H. D. Mackenzie, Dec. 5, 1861, pp. 167–173; C 1671: Doyle to Lewis, Nov., 1861, p. 2.
    [49] Williams Papers: Monck to Williams, Dec. 30, 1861; E 1, 85: Minutes, Dec. 28, 1861; G 20, 87: Ellis Yarnold to Monck, Dec. 17, 1861. See the well-informed Rochester *Evening Express,* Dec. 1861, *passim.*

border communities seemed to assume that they would bear the brunt of an attack. Chatham asked for a wall, Simcoe for Armstrong guns, Port Dover for a protective belt of forts, Dundas for fifty heavy batteries, and Caledonia, as the Hamilton *Times* put it, feared that the Yankees would "run up Grand River on skates during the winter or come down like grasshoppers on rail." [50] The University of Toronto organized a rifle corps, and the faculty of Upper Canada College entertained a similar project. To provide the new volunteers with arms, the Grand Trunk Railway's shops at Point St. Charles were engaged for the rifling of heavy ordnance. The barracks at Montreal already were full, so newly built stores along the hillside and old school buildings in the older town beneath the hill were requisitioned to house the arriving troops. Merchants throughout the Canadas had good reason to welcome the new men, for during the billeting emergency provisional barracks rents doubled. In Montreal the merchants closed their shops on three alternate afternoons so that their employees might drill, and on December 23 the Toronto *Leader* called upon that city's merchants to do the same. The previous May the people of Calais, Maine, and of St. Stephen, New Brunswick, had celebrated the Queen's birthday together, but now they bristled at each other across the St. Croix River bridge. At Christmastime one observer saw "every prospect of war" wherever he looked.[51]

Despite this activity the laboring class was slow to respond, and the Toronto *Leader* hopefully attributed this to the expense of uniforms. Although a public subscription was taken and benefit concerts were held to provide funds for the many-colored outfits, the response remained slight. Some onlookers began to wonder if it were not largely the upper class, at least in Canada West, that was willing to fight over "an English affair." Certainly many people in the upper province must

---

[50] Quoted in New York *Herald*, Dec. 13, 1861. St. Johns, C.E., and Collingwood, C.W., had feared invasion as early as June, and had petitioned Head for protection (C 696: June 27, pp. 67–70, and Aug. 2, 1861, pp. 99–100). Also see Galt Papers, I: H. S. Machim to Galt, Dec. 17, Sir John Young to Galt, Dec. 19, and J. H. Pope to Galt, Dec. 26, 1861, 680–687, 708–711; and Diary of H. C. R. Beecher, London *Advertiser*, Nov. 20, 1926: Jan. 3, 1862.

[51] Brown Diary: Dec. 16, 21, 24, 1861; Rochester *Daily Democrat and American*, Dec. 21, 1861; Stephen Leacock, *Montreal: Seaport and City* (Garden City, 1942), p. 181; Fred Landon, *Western Ontario and the American Frontier* (Toronto, 1941), p. 224. See also Calais *Advertiser*, May 30, Dec. 20, 1861; J. P. Edwards, "The Militia of Nova Scotia, 1749–1867," Nova Scotia Hist. Soc., *Colls.*, XVII (1913), 98–105.

have agreed with Marcus Gunn, who felt that Canadians had no
"voice, vote or veto" in the affair, although they probably did not
agree that the war, if it came, would be due largely to the "vile servile
Editors of Canada." The Irish of Canada East, under the guidance of
their fiery political leader, Thomas D'Arcy McGee, did meet to pledge
their support in case of war, and the Irish of Canada West, told by
their religious press that they were largely responsible for making the
province what it was, rallied to their adopted land. Farther east in
the Maritimes the laboring class continued to decline to contract war
fever. Nova Scotians, in particular, refused to be unduly alarmed, and
only five hundred men, most of them "quite old," were added to the
volunteer force in the province by Christmas.[52]

A second contingent of men was dispatched from Britain just before Christmas, and a group of "Nightingale nurses" and the Inspector
General of Hospitals followed shortly thereafter. Weed again rose
early to see the Fusilier Guards depart.[53] These campaigners began
to arrive on New Year's Day, when the original crisis was over, and
some progressed slowly along the Métis Route while four hundred
of them were stationed at St. Andrews, on the Maine border. At Woodstock, where the men were most exposed to an attack, the batteries became snowbound, and English-made sleighs brought expressly to transport the guns through the drifts proved to be useless. Upon hearing
of the difficulties that the men encountered, *The Times* tried to show
that such a march was healthful. "The Thunderer" clearly wanted
to counteract the fact that in September it had urged postponement
of intended troop movements on the grounds that they always could
reach the Canadas before the St. Lawrence froze over.[54]

During this time the North had not been idle. Winfield Scott, fully
expecting war, and hopeful that he might plan the defenses of New

[52] *Leader*, Dec. 23, 24, 1861; M. Gunn Diary, II: Dec. 17, 19, 1861, 321–322; Cleve-
land *Leader*, Dec. 23, 1861; Toronto *Canadian Freeman*, Dec. 19, 1861; Rochester
Evening Express, Dec. 27, 1861; N.S., Dispatches, 105: Mulgrave to Newcastle,
Dec. 24, 1861.

[53] *Ibid.*: Dec. 20, 1861; Seward Papers: Schuyler to Seward, Dec. 23, 1861;
Lancet, I (Jan. 4, 1862), 25; W. M. Muir, "Sherman's March," Army Medical
Dept., *Statistical, Sanitary and Medical Reports, 1864*, VI (1866), 507–510.

[54] Seward Papers: Weed to Seward, Dec. 20, 1861; N.B. Museum, Scrap Book
No. 6: MS. article, "The 'Trent Affair': The Part St. Andrews Played in it";
C 1671: Lewis to Doyle, Jan. 11, L. C. —— to —— Shadwell, Feb. 6, and Eardley-
Wilmot [?] to Williams, March 10, 1862; *The Times*, Dec. 24, 1861. See also
Brown Diary: Dec. 27, 1861.

York, had raced the British fleet back to North America, arriving four days ahead of the main body of troops. In the meantime Seward had sent Thomas Fitnam to the Gaspé basin, ostensibly to act as consul. There would be no trade with the Gaspé area during the winter, and Fitnam's real intent was shown when he pushed on for thirty-five days through severe blizzards to reach this vantage point from which most arriving British ships might be seen. He found, of course, that the *Persia* already had fled, that the river was closed, and that emotions were running high in the isolated little French village. Nevertheless, Fitnam used the same route that troops traveling from Halifax in winter were compelled to use, and he felt that in case of war his reconnoitering of the route would prove useful. An agent also was sent to Island Pond, Vermont, to report on traffic along the Grand Trunk Railway between Portland and Montreal.[55]

Other executive departments also showed concern over affairs on the frontier. During the height of the crisis an American postal official at Rouse's Point, on the Canadian border, took from the Montreal mail some letters that he felt Seward should see, and, following orders from the Post Office Department, forwarded them to the Secretary. Searching the mails during time of war is not uncommon, and since there were Southerners in the Canadas, it was possible that such letters would contain information of Southern activities there. But had the agent's action become known in Quebec, it could have added considerable fuel to the flames. Monck's letters were protected by diplomatic pouch, of course, but it is possible that one of the lesser colonial officials might have written something indiscreet. Certainly the agent's action, and Seward's or Montgomery Blair's failure to caution him, would indicate that Newcastle and Monck had been wise to specify the use of personal messengers for important communications.[56]

Municipal appeals in the Canadas for defense were paralleled in the North. After the Toronto *Leader* pointed out that in the event of war the British navy would be quick to occupy Portland, the mayor of that city complained of the defenseless condition of the harbor and of the weak nature of Forts Preble and Scannel, and on Christmas Eve heavy artillery was sent from Fortress Monroe, where Mason and Slidell were imprisoned, to the two forts. Two regiments that had been ordered to the front from Augusta were instructed to remain in the

[55] Weed Papers: Hughes to Weed, Dec. 11, 1861; CD, Gaspé, I: Fitnam to Seward, Jan. 15, 1862; CD, Montreal, IV: Howe to Seward, Jan. 6, 1862.

[56] MC: H. Dunn to Seward, Dec. 19, 1861.

state. A few hundred soldiers, who had been captured and released by Southern forces upon taking an oath that they would not bear arms against the Confederacy again, were hurried off to Sackett's Harbor, Rouse's Point, Oswego, and Fort Niagara, while twelve hundred raw recruits were moved into temporary barracks outside Buffalo.[57]

Something of a Canadian-Northern war of words was taking place in the press simultaneously with the military movement. Northern news commentaries on the rapidly developing situation arising from the *Trent* affair showed that there were those who still hoped for a foreign war to mend the nation. Dreams of Canadian conquests represented a strange myth that had continued to have wide acceptance in the North. In 1812 to capture the Canadas was said to be a "mere matter of marching." Despite the fact that such had not proved to be the case, many normally well-informed Americans, apparently having learned little from history and even less from recent Confederate strategy, continued to assume that American troops could walk almost unresisted through the Canadas, failing to realize the vast difficulties involved in capturing and holding any nearly continental area. People who should have known better wrote to Lincoln, to Seward, to Scott, or to anyone who would read, with plans of varying degrees of complexity and practicality on how to seize Sault Ste. Marie, the Red River, Montreal, Toronto, the Maritime Provinces, or Vancouver Island, most of them assuming that five to thirty thousand troops would be sufficient. The New York *World* thought that Canadian and British bluster was merely a "left-handed way" of bringing on annexation, while the New York *Herald* predicted that war with the North would cause Great Britain to lose not only British North America but the West Indies and Ireland as well. Fortunately, neither Lincoln nor Seward took such suggestions seriously. Nonetheless, the comparatively forthright response on the part of the Northern administration was partially lost in the popular clamor.[58]

The *Herald* had predicted that the English press would view the seizure moderately. Canadian pressmen, it said, would discover what fools they had been to become so agitated. Therefore, when the English press responded with an unexpected outburst of indignation, the *Herald* struck back. "Those who have the least authority for talking

---

[57] New York *World*, Dec. 20, and New York *Tribune*, Dec. 25, 1861; Rochester *Evening Express*, Dec. 1861, *passim*; C 1671: Doyle to Lewis, Dec. 26, 1861; FO 5, 777: Lyons to Russell, Dec. 26, 1861; G 20, 86: Donohoe to Monck, Dec. 23, 1861.
[58] *The Times*, Dec. 7, 21, 1861; *World*, Dec. 13, 1861; *Herald*, Dec. 11, 17, 26, 1861.

big and threatening are usually the very people who sound the loudest trumpet," Editor James Gordon Bennett philosophized, comparing the Canadians, in particular, to a noisy but toothless pack of yelping dogs. When the pack continued to yelp, the *Herald* increased what already was a crude campaign of villification of all things British and recommended the immediate repeal of the reciprocity agreement despite the fact that this would have violated the treaty.[59]

Each side goaded the other on, the *Herald* declaring that the North viewed an Anglo-American war with complacency and charging the Canadas, by now almost correctly, with being anti-Northern, while the normally judicious Toronto *Globe* reviled Wilkes as a "typical Yankee" who was unable to resist bravado and childish behavior.[60] The Detroit *Tribune* and the Albany *Evening Journal* violently attacked all things Canadian and the latter ran a "historical account" of the War of 1812 that implied that the British North Americans never had known how to fight. The Cleveland *Leader* compared the Canadians to a pack of puppies barking at a Newfoundland dog, and the *Evening Journal* maintained the canine metaphor by applying a blanket epithet, "the mangy pack," to all Canadian newspapers. To illustrate the depths to which the British had sunk, the *Evening Journal* also reprinted an advertisement allegedly authorized by a captain of a volunteer rifle corps at Dunnville, Canada West, calling on all male Negroes of Haldimand County to join the militia and make "War! War!! War!!!" on the North. The editor did not bother to point out that the appeal could have little practical importance since there were but twenty Negroes in the county.[61]

When the news that Britain was demanding the surrender of the Confederate commissioners arrived, and when it was learned that the English press supported this demand, even the more responsible and neutral newspapers in the British North American provinces devoted lead editorials to scathingly anti-Northern analyses of the affair. In particular *The Times* of London, which had begun to disturb even Foreign Secretary Russell with the intensity of its anti-Northern com-

    [59] Nov. 25, 1861. For an analysis of the *Herald*'s campaign, see Chapter Eleven.
    [60] *Herald*, Nov. 17–19, 21, Dec. 24, 26, 1861; *Globe*, Nov. 18, 23, 1861. See also Shippee, *Canadian-American Relations*, p. 128.
    [61] *Tribune*, Dec. 10, 1861; *Evening Journal*, Nov. 26, Dec. 6, 17, 24, Jan. 2, 1862; *Leader*, Dec. 30, 1861; New York *World*, Nov. 21, 1861; Rochester *Evening Express*, Nov. 18, 1861; Boston *Evening Traveller* and Rochester *Daily Democrat and American*, both Dec. 20, 1861; Bigelow, I, 416: J. L. Motley to Bigelow, Dec. 17, 1861; L.C., Salmon P. Chase Papers, LIV: B. R. Wood to Chase, Dec. 24, 1861.

ments,[62] was widely copied in the colonies. Many of the colonial newspapers followed the lead of *The Times* in deprecating the thought of war while inflaming their readers.[63] For every person who thought that the crisis would "end in talk," there was one who felt that war was unavoidable, and they tended to agree with the Montreal *Gazette* that Canadians would be "lily-livered, snivelling creatures" to flee from war if it were forced upon them.

The Toronto *Globe* was the clearest-eyed in its view of the international situation. The North was in no position to fight, Brown realized. The editor-politician noted that Captain Wilkes' "mid-summer madness" was "one of the most absurd and stupid acts which history records," since Mason and Slidell were on their way to Europe to obtain support for the South. In seizing them, Wilkes did more to accomplish their mission than anything they could have done themselves.[64]

The only other major Canadian daily newspapers to advocate a careful and lengthy appraisal of the legality of Wilkes' act were the generally anti-Northern Montreal *Gazette* and the consistently anti-Southern Montreal *Witness*. The *Gazette* was quick to see the anomaly in the situation, pointing out to its readers that it was "a coincidence of cross purposes," for if Britain complained of the capture of Mason and Slidell she would be denying a right she had long asserted, while if the United States defended the act she would be claiming a power she

[62] Desmond MacCarthy and Agatha Russell, *Lady John Russell: A Memoir with Selections from Her Diaries and Correspondence* (New York, 1911), p. 194.

[63] For examples see Montreal *Witness*, Nov. 23, 27, Dec. 4, 21, 25, 1861; Toronto *Globe*, Nov. 23, 1861; Charlottetown *Islander*, Dec. 13, 1861; Halifax *Morning Chronicle*, Nov. 30, 1861; Barrie *Northern Advance*, Dec. 11, 1861; Montreal *Evening Pilot*, Dec. 10, 1861; Montreal *Gazette*, Nov. 30, 1861; Toronto *British Herald and Protestant Intelligencer*, Nov. 20, 1861; Howe Papers, VIII: Howe to Mulgrave, Nov. 30, 1861, 150–161; Skelton, *Galt*, p. 340: Pope to Galt, Dec. 26, 1861; Duhamel, "La politique étrangère," p. 109; H. Macdonald, *Canadian Opinion*, p. 121.

[64] McNeilledge Diaries, M-113, 889, 2: Dec. 19, 1861; Landon, "Harris," art. 5: Nov. 19, Dec. 16, 1861; Montreal *Commercial Advertiser*, Nov. 20, 1861; Barrie *Northern Advance*, Dec. 19, 1861; *Gazette*, Dec. 14, 1861; *Globe*, Dec. 10, 1861. Nearly every account of nineteenth-century English history tells of the reaction to the *Trent* affair, as do most of the many volumes of Victorian reminiscence that nearly every British politician seemed constrained to write. The present writer has found comments on the seizure in nearly two hundred published diaries, collections of letters, and memoirs, and the opinions expressed by the authors were overwhelmingly pro-Southern and aggressive. The laboring class was less anti-American but also was less articulate.

had denied to others. The irony of this was lost on few Canadians, who recalled that one reason for the War of 1812 had been the impressment controversy. Within the month, however, the *Gazette* was demanding a militia of 100,000 men. The Montreal *Witness*, a liberal journal in the stronghold of Canadian conservatism, attacked the Liberal-Conservative administration in the Canadas for its handling of the crisis and asserted that hostility to America was the foolish product of war-mongering business interests, including the press itself.[65]

At least one editor, in fact, had written to John A. Macdonald to ask if the government would support the newspapers in time of war, and he had been informed that if war took place it probably would have a beneficial effect on the press. Certainly the Fourth Estate evinced a readiness for war, and accounts of defensive preparations, troop movements, war rumors, and forced marches were related in such a romantic and exaggerated manner as to elicit from at least one British officer the judgment that the reports were mere "twaddle." [66]

Certainly there were people in the provinces who would benefit from a war scare. If the imperial administration could be convinced that the provinces were in serious danger, several million pounds would be spent on defense, bringing prosperity to areas that, despite local "good times" induced by the nearby war, had not recovered from the depression of 1857. In addition, the *Trent* imbroglio came at a convenient moment to rescue the floundering Inter-colonial Railway project, as Joseph Howe clearly realized. Hamilton Merritt, a financier from Hamilton, Canada West, even tried to obtain government funds to establish a steamship line from Toledo to Liverpool via Quebec on the grounds that the line could be used for defense in time of war. While the Colonial Office might not give money directly to the Maritime Provinces or to the railway promoters to build a railway linking New Brunswick with Canada West, it might do so if it or the more powerful Foreign Office thought aid to be necessary for defense purposes.[67]

[65] *Gazette*, Nov. 22, 23, Dec. 14, 1861; *Witness*, Dec. 18, 1861; Montreal *Evening Pilot*, Dec. 28, 1861.
[66] Macdonald Papers, Private Letters, v: Macdonald to Joseph Blackburnkey [?], Dec. 21, 1861, 279; Biddulph, ed., p. 114: Wolseley to Biddulph, Jan. 26, 1862. See London *Canadian News*, Dec. 26, 1861, Jan. 3, 1862.
[67] E 1, 86: Merritt to Monck, March 7, 1862, 118–119; James Hannay, *The Life and Times of Sir Leonard Tilley, being a Political History of New Brunswick* (Saint John, 1897), pp. 234–257. On the other hand, it is interesting to note that at least one Southern newspaper reasoned that a cause of Britain's failure to recognize

The Toronto *Leader*, in particular, seemed intent on war. Second in circulation in British North America to the Toronto *Globe*, and edited with uncommon ability, it had the added prestige of being an unofficial organ of the provincial government. James Beaty, its proprietor, trumpeted that the *Globe* was a "Washington Organ" intent upon weakening the Canadas in case of war, while the *Globe* branded the *Leader* "Jeff. Davis's Agent." The *Leader* joined the *Montreal Gazette* in demanding a militia of 100,000 men and predicted that in case of war the North would be crushed.[68] In the midst of this crisis Beaty was trying to prove that George Brown was a swindler and a traitor who intrigued with a foreign government to betray his adopted country. Brown entered a libel suit against Beaty, but in order to keep from appearing to lend support to Beaty's wild charge Brown had to become less conciliatory toward the North at the very moment when a powerful voice for peace was needed most in the province.

The second-ranking editorial writer for the *Leader* was George Sheppard, the pro-Southern journalist who once had worked for the *Globe* and who had chosen to remain in Canada West when the war began rather than return to the South. Sheppard had meant to resign from the *Leader* in November, but Beaty prevailed upon him to remain when news of the *Trent* incident arrived. Charles Lindsey, the chief editorial writer, tended to excel in persuasion rather than diatribe, so Sheppard's presence apparently seemed essential to Beaty. The Toronto *Globe* attacked Sheppard personally for his war-mongering, and it intimated that Beaty retained him specifically for that purpose. The *Leader* went so far as to advocate censoring the press, for it feared that the *Globe*'s news and editorial comment pointed too clearly to the weak spots in Canadian defenses. The *Leader* also could be uncomfortably logical, as when it pointed out that the North could not invoke wartime international law if Lincoln insisted on regarding the conflict as a rebellion and had made no declaration of war.[69]

During the *Trent* crisis the Tory administration apparently made no move to muzzle the *Leader* or to contradict Beaty's repeated as-

---

the Confederacy was her desire to build a railroad to the Pacific through the Canadas and the northwestern United States. See S. D. Hoslett, "Southern Expectation of British Intervention in the Civil War, as Reflected in the Newspapers of Richmond, Virginia, Capital of the Confederacy," *Tyler's Quarterly Historical and Genealogical Magazine*, XXII (Jan., 1941), 142.

[68] Nov. 18, 20, Dec. 9, 1861.

[69] *Leader*, Dec. 7, 16, 25, 1861, Jan. 16, 1862; *Globe*, Dec. 18, 1861.

sertions that his views coincided with those of the government and of the business leaders of the community. After the crisis had passed, Sheppard was removed from the *Leader*'s staff, and the paper printed a disclaimer of any governmental responsibility for its editorials.[70] The Northern press reported that the disclaimer had been forced by the government in embarrassment over Sheppard's extreme views.

The press was partially successful in inducing the people to show their feelings through direct action. The *Leader*, and the Fredericton *Head Quarters*, the voice of the conservative party in New Brunswick, in particular, attempted to incite the Canadian people to some ill-defined course of action. The *Head Quarters* attacked the anti-Southern editor of the *St. Croix Herald*, which was published in St. Stephen, for being "rabid for Lincoln and the Union," and concluded that since he was a Yankee at heart his proper place was in Maine rather than in New Brunswick. Someone broke into the *Herald*'s office and damaged the presses, forcing the editor to move across the river to Calais in Maine. The *Leader* also launched a short-lived campaign against all Northern lecturers then present in the Canadas. Declaring that even a Northern temperance lecturer should not be allowed to pocket Canadian dollars, the paper implied that mob action to eject the unwanted Yankees would be proper. One Montreal newspaper warned that ten thousand bales of Canadian hay had been purchased by American agents and suggested that its shipment to the North be prevented. In Toronto a Federal officer who wore his uniform on the city's streets while visiting his wife's relatives caused "much indignation," and when he entered a saloon "Dixie" was played for his benefit and all present drove him away with shouts of "Bull Run." On the other hand, when a British officer appeared in Boston, he was subjected to repeated insults, and a Canadian was attacked in the streets of Buffalo. British North Americans who had booked passage for Europe through Portland feared that war might strand them in hostile territory, and Consul General Giddings found himself busy for once, quieting their fears.[71]

Popular indignation reached its height in the ten days before Christmas. When the Royal Mail Steamship *Europa* arrived at Halifax

[70] Jan. 9, 1862.

[71] *Head Quarters*, Dec. 4, 1861; Bangor *Jeffersonian*, Dec. 24, 1861; *Leader*, Nov. 20, Dec. 9, 10, 12, 1861; Montreal *Commercial Advertiser*, quoted in Rochester *Evening Express*, Dec. 27, 1861; Toronto *Globe*, Dec. 11, 1861; G 14, 26: Williams to Monck, Jan. 4, 1862; Seward Papers: Giddings to Seward, Nov. 20, 1861.

shortly before midnight on December 15, news reports were rushed to the Toronto *Globe* by direct telegraphic contact, and on the sixteenth the people of the Canadas read in their "AM extras" that Her Majesty's government was taking a firm stand. The news caused a great sensation, and on the following day, when a meteor passed over international Niagara Falls, many people felt that it was an omen of war. Business practically was suspended in the metropolitan centers, the "extras" sold as fast as they could be printed, and with a tense but almost cheerful feeling that doubt and suspense were nearly over, the people of the provinces waited to hear of Washington's reaction to this new development. The question of war in 1861, the Montreal *Gazette* thought, was "the most important decision that was ever laid before the people of Canada." This rising note of nationalism was echoed by such diverse sources as the French-language *Courrier du Canada* and *La Minerve* of Quebec and Montreal respectively, and in the Toronto *Leader*, which declared that a war would stimulate Canadian nationhood and force Britain to provide the provinces with a winter port. In one final, dazzling dream of Canada taking her place among the powers of the world, the *Leader* aped the expansionistic New York *Herald* and declared that the Canadas might annex Maine and the American West from the Mississippi River to the Pacific as far south as the forty-fifth parallel.[72]

Emotionally the response in the Atlantic Provinces was not unlike that in the Canadas, despite an earlier, less nationalistic reaction to the original news of the seizure. The first report of the British demand was read aloud to a large gathering in a news room in Saint John, the message passing by word of mouth out to the crowded street. Any warlike passage was received with applause. The Saint John (New Brunswick) *Courier, Reporter, Telegram,* and *New Brunswicker,* and the St. John's (Newfoundland) *Public Ledger* all attacked the North, while the Saint John *Globe* and *Colonial Presbyterian* urged moderation. "A war now would forever deliver us from all fear of our dangerous neighbour, and elevate us to a position of importance and influence," editorialized the *Christian Watchman* of Saint

[72] Montreal *Evening Pilot,* Dec. 16, 19, 1861; Montreal *Gazette,* Dec. 17, 1861; Montreal *Witness,* Dec. 17, 18, 1861, quotes a number of newspapers; Toronto *Leader,* Dec. 17, 26, 1861; Toronto *Globe,* Dec. 17, 1861, Jan. 2, 1862; O.P.A., William Kirby Notebook: Dec. 16, 1861; C 696: James Dougall to Sir Fenwick Williams, Dec. 27, 1861, printed in J. M. Hitsman, "Please Send Us a Garrison," *Ontario History,* L (Autumn, 1958), 189–192.

John, adding that, "We need some event which may stir the blood, unite us more closely together, provide for us the beginning of a noble history, and attach us more closely to Great Britain." But the influential Saint John *Morning Freeman* cautioned the people to remember that "taunts, and threats, and insults tarnish most deeply the character of those who use them," and enjoined the New Brunswickers to prepare for war while praying for peace.[73] Possibly the pithiest summary of how most British North Americans probably felt was written by an Englishman to a Canadian, and it never appeared in the newspapers: "God prevent a *War;* and with our own Bastards." [74]

One casualty of the emotion generated by the *Trent* affair was the New England Society of Montreal, founded a few years earlier by David Thurston to encourage Canadian-American harmony. At the annual Christmas meeting Giddings, John Cordner, an out-spoken champion of the North, and Thomas D'Arcy McGee were scheduled to speak, and the noted Gustav Schilling was to provide music. The Consul General in particular was placed in a delicate situation, for it would have been unwise to praise Wilkes at that juncture and equally unwise, as a well-known abolitionist, to urge moderation, since Giddings had no way of knowing whether such would be his government's policy. After three days' deliberation McGee withdrew from the program because such a gathering would be "out of season." In an open letter to the society, he said that it could perform a patriotic duty by informing Americans that the Irish would stand by the Canadas in the crisis so that Irish in the North would not presume that they would be welcomed as liberators. On the same day Schilling declined to take part, and the society's secretary, Jacob de Witt, thereupon postponed the meeting.[75]

Probably the most worried people during the crisis were the recent British North American emigrants to the United States. Thousands of former provincials now living in the North were faced with the prospect of fighting relatives who had remained in the provinces. The

---

[73] *Christian Watchman*, Dec. 26, 1861; *Public Ledger and Newfoundland General Advertiser*, Jan. 7, 1862; *Morning Freeman*, Dec. 17, 1861. The *Freeman* was not alone in preparing for war while praying for peace. Archbishop John Hughes of New York, then in Paris on a mission, took time to write a lengthy letter to Seward informing him that he prayed twice a day for peace between the two countries. With his letter the Archbishop enclosed a detailed account of how war might be made on the Canadas (Seward Papers: Jan. 3, 1862).

[74] Ellice Papers, 2: Parkes to Ellice, Dec. 26, 1861.

[75] CD, Toronto, 1: Thurston to Seward, Aug. 8, 1866; Montreal *Evening Pilot*, Dec. 20, 21, 23, 1861.

prospect was more fratricidal to many than was the Civil War itself. Anguished letters crossed the border during the height of the crisis, former Canadians expressing their loyalty to the United States, former Americans who had moved north proclaiming their loyalty to Britain. Some showed their feelings by public demonstration, as when a group of former Canadians tried to raise a subscription among Britishers living in New York City to prosecute Wilkes for violation of the Queen's neutrality, or when several hundred former Canadians resident in Chicago petitioned the British consul there to call on them if they were needed.[76]

The greatest quandary was reserved for British North Americans who had enlisted in the Northern army. Many had joined the Federal forces because of the high bounties, but at this time, still early in the war and before serious abuse of the bounty system had begun, many had enlisted from a sincere desire to show their hatred of slavery by some positive act. Now they found themselves presented with the possibility that they would be ordered to invade their own country.

A substantial group of Canadians decided that they should take some positive stand rather than simply resorting to desertion. Those who were in a position to do so met at Washington and named a small committee of fellow countrymen to interview President Lincoln himself. The committee was headed by one Newton Wolverton, one of three brothers from Walsingham, Canada West, who had enlisted in the Northern army the previous July. Although only seventeen, Wolverton already had shown qualities of leadership. He eventually was to become Principal of Woodstock College and Professor of Mathematics at the new McMaster University in Toronto. He presented his committee's petition to Lincoln in person, quite mistakenly but in good faith declaring that it spoke for fifty thousand Canadians fighting in the Northern armies.[77] "We wish to tell you in the most respectful way," Wolverton said, "that we did not enlist to fight against our Mother Country." He reported to his colleagues that Lincoln had promised that so long as he was President, the United States would not declare war on Great Britain.[78]

---

[76] O.P.A., A. N. Buell Papers: A. Thorp to Mrs. A. N. Buell, Dec. 22, 1861, Jan. 13, 1862; King, p. 280.

[77] For an analysis of this figure, see Chapter Ten. McMaster University later moved to Hamilton.

[78] A. N. Wolverton, *Dr. Newton Wolverton* (privately printed [Hamilton, Ont.?] n.d.), p. 28. The writer would like to thank Harold Wolverton of Hamilton for providing a copy of this scarce item.

Lincoln kept his promise. Before the British reinforcements had reached Quebec, the crisis had passed. On December 19 Lyons communicated to Seward the British demand for the release of Mason and Slidell. The first draft of Russell's instructions to Lyons was bare and sharp, and it might well have caused certain members of Lincoln's Cabinet to take offense. The version sent was softened somewhat by Albert, the Prince Consort, through the addition of an expression of hope that Wilkes had no authorization for his act, but it remained "coldly correct" in its tone.[79]

On Christmas morning Lincoln's Cabinet met to consider its answer. Sumner was present and read letters from the English reformer, John Bright, which eloquently pleaded for surrendering the envoys,[80] and Lincoln, although at first undecided, is said to have professed a preference for "one war at a time." On the following day the Cabinet, strongly led by Seward, agreed that war with Great Britain was to be averted at all costs, and the Confederate commissioners were duly placed upon a British vessel. In Lyons' words the British demand was "substantially complied with," and Lyons may have begun to see in Seward a diplomat of some ability who could be an agent for peace as well as for war.[81] Russell expressed his satisfaction through Lyons and declared the incident closed, although he did not agree with all of Seward's argument concerning the release of the commissioners. For the moment Russell seemed convinced that the wide-spread belief in Seward's enmity to all things British was false. The wisdom of Seward's

[79] Martin, v, 418–426, and John, pp. 220–241, contain the best accounts of Prince Albert's role. Slightly different versions appear in F. B. Chancellor, *Prince Consort* (Glasgow, 1931), pp. 273–276; E. E. P. Tisdall, *Queen Victoria's Mr. Brown* (New York, 1938), pp. 55–58; and Frank Eyck, *The Prince Consort: A Political Biography* (Boston, 1959), pp. 251–252. The settlement of the *Trent* affair is described by Russell in his *Recollections and Suggestions, 1813–1873* (2nd ed., London, 1875), pp. 315–318.

[80] Sumner Papers, CLXIX: Bright to Sumner, Dec. 14, 1861; R. A. J. Walling, ed., *The Diaries of John Bright* (New York, 1931), p. 255. The Duke of Argyll also kept Sumner informed of British opinion. See Duchess of Argyll, ed., *George Douglas, Eighth Duke of Argyll . . . Autobiography and Memoirs* (London, 1906), II, 169–213.

[81] P.P., *1862*, xxv, "Correspondence respecting the *Trent*": Lyons to Russell, Dec. 27, 1861; E. D. Adams, I, 232. Interestingly enough, a rumor soon was afloat in the provinces that Seward had capitulated only because Sir Alexander Milne, Commander of the British fleet in North American waters, who was a staunch advocate of Anglo-American harmony, had prevailed upon him to do so. See J. S. Trotter, *et al.*, "The Surrender of Mason and Slidell," *Spectator*, LXXXV (July 28, Aug. 11, 18, 25, 1900), 110, 173, 205, 239–240; and Anthony Trollope, *An Autobiography* (New York, 1935), p. 143.

decision—for in the final analysis it was his—was shown by the reaction in the South, where great disappointment over the release of
Mason and Slidell was generally voiced.[82]

Seward tried to turn the very act of surrendering the envoys into
a diplomatic victory. He argued that Britain now informally had ad-
hered to the American contention that impressment was illegal. He
made no apology and attempted to leave the impression that the entire
incident was of benefit to the North. Nonetheless, it was quite clear
that Great Britain had forced the North to retreat from an untenable
position, and in the North public opinion became increasingly hostile
to Britain.[83]

Upon news of the surrender the Northern newspaper attack increased. "The simple fact is that Canada hates us," [84] was one judgment, and a fortified frontier seemed to be the most effective reply.
That the war was only deferred, and that the postponement could be
used to prepare for a possible world war, was impressed upon Seward
and Thurlow Weed by John Hughes, Archbishop of New York, who
was in Paris on a mission for the Secretary of State. The Cleveland
Leader warned the British to beware, for at the end of the domestic
war "six hundred thousand men will want something more to do, and
in that day of our power, the insults and cowardly meanness of England
will be surely remembered and bitterly avenged." [85]

In the national House of Representatives Owen Lovejoy of Illinois,
a Congregational minister who was close to Lincoln, shouted that
Great Britain would pay for her arrogance when the domestic crisis
was over, for the United States would aid Irish rebels, inspire the
French Canadians to revolt, and encourage Chartist insurrection
throughout England.[86] The Senate Chaplain prayed that the United
States might soon be in a position to spread her glance "upon a broader

[82] Robert G. H. Kean, Head of the Confederate Bureau of War, noted that some
felt that from the Southern standpoint Seward had managed the *Trent* affair
"disastrously" (Younger, ed., p. 23). For another example, see Margaret M. Jones,
ed., *The Journal of Catherine Devereux Edmonston, 1860–1866* (Mebane, N.C.,
1955[?]), p. 36. Allan Nevins, in *The War for the Union* (New York, 1959), I,
394, describes the Cabinet meeting on the *Trent* affair as "perhaps the most perilous
moment of the Civil War . . . ."

[83] *O.R.*, ser. II, II, 1145–54: Seward to Lyons, Dec. 26, 1861.

[84] New York *World*, Dec. 28, 1861. See also Rochester *Daily Democrat and
American*, Dec. 31, 1861.

[85] Seward Papers: Hughes to Seward, Jan. 11, 1862; Weed Papers: Hughes to
Weed, Jan. 11, 1862; *Leader*, Dec. 30, 1861; Ottawa *Citizen*, Sept. 27, 1862.

[86] *Cong. Globe*, 37th Cong., 2nd Sess., 333. See also Pierce, *Sumner*, IV, 62:
Sumner to Bright, Jan. 9, 1862.

scale, with a vaster force," and Canadians read this as manifest destiny through revealed religion. However, it was the Buffalo *Express*, which was read widely along the Niagara frontier in Canada West, that stated the extreme of Northern resentment most eloquently:

> Out of this Trent affair has come one permanent good. The old, natural, instinctive and wise distrust and dislike for England is revived again in the American heart, and will outlive all the soft words and sniveling cant about international brotherhood and reciprocity. These are "our Canadian brethren," these suckling Britons to whom, like fools, we have opened our ports . . . . These reciprocal brethren of ours have been ready to fly at our throats from the moment when they felt it safe to be insolent.[87]

Others chose to scoff at colonial defensive efforts as the work of mere children who like to don fancy caps, beat tiny drums, snap popguns, and blow penny trumpets. "How silly, ashamed and foolish the provincials must feel, now that the whole matter is settled, without even the name of Canada being mentioned in the diplomatic correspondence," editorialized the New York *Herald*. "How will they dare to look an American in the face again . . . now that they find us laughing at their playing at soldier? . . ." It was fortunate, said the New York paper, that the militia had not been forced into action, for it was composed of "a lot of fellows who pay their military fines, are corpulent, short-winded and not muscularly developed . . . ." [88]

In British North America most of the Fourth Estate was satisfied that Mason and Slidell had been surrendered, but several editors found contemptible Seward's explanations to the Northern people of why he had bowed to Britain's demands.[89] With Biblical rhetoric one editor asked, "Was ever a proud people so humiliated? Was ever a great nation brought so low? . . ." Seward's surrender, the Toronto *Leader* opined, was "a solemn burlesque." The American eagle, "which soared, and soared, and soared almost out of sight, [had] descended like the stick of an exploded rocket." It was good, one of Macdonald's followers wrote, that "such a windbag as Mr. Seward should be thoroughly collapsed." But if one patriot had implored that, "If the Yankees mean to come, pray God they come this year while I can still hold a gun," and

[87] Quoted in Toronto *Leader*, Dec. 31, 1861.
[88] Dec. 30, 31, 1861.
[89] For example, see Toronto *Globe*, Dec. 30, 1861; Charlottetown *Examiner*, Jan. 10, 1862; Barrie *Northern Advance*, Jan. 15, 1862.

if a few Tories agreed with the wife of English historian George
Grote, who thanked God that she might yet live to see one Holy War,
most of the people of the provinces undoubtedly preferred to consider
the affair *"un drame série-comique,"* as one French Canadian judged it,
and relax.[90]

But the legacy of the *Trent* affair was to remain. The *San Jacinto*
helped unite the British North American provinces more closely than
ever before and brought forth no uncertain indication of their loyalty
to Great Britain. The French Canadians, thought in some Northern
circles to be annexationists, had demonstrated their loyalty to the
Crown, for they felt that their religious and ethnic traits would be in
danger of assimilation or complete submersion if they were incorporated into the Republic. The crisis had changed the several
provinces from generally neutral or even pro-Northern onlookers at
a foreign war into a generally anti-Northern land at the rear of the
Federal troops, for it had crystallized already wavering opinion.
Northern occupation of the Canadas, even if wanted, never would be
a "mere matter of marching," for imperial and local authorities now
realized the necessity for taking defensive measures, and British North
American defenses had been materially strengthened. Reasoning that
"Generals January and February" were their best strategists, the
Canadians were to continue to drill for the day when these generals
must retire from the field.[91]

The British North American press had treated the seizure of Mason
and Slidell as an affront to Britishers everywhere. It was chiefly an
imperial affair, they admitted, but one in which the provinces, as a
potential battlefield, were vitally interested. The *Trent* affair, as the
newspapers realized, was something of a border incident, for the
Atlantic Ocean constituted the only border between the United States

[90] Saint John *Morning Freeman,* Dec. 31, 1861; *Leader,* Dec. 30, 1861; Montreal
Evening Pilot, Dec. 30, 1861; Toronto *Globe,* Jan. 1, June 21, 1862; Macdonald
Papers, 161: E. P. Bouveril [?] to Macdonald, Jan. 4, 1862, 31–34; Ellice Papers,
A-1, 2: Parkes to Ellice, Jan. 2, 1862; Un Carabinier [N. Faucher], *Organisation
Militaire des Canadas: L'Ennemi! L'Ennemi!* (Quebec, 1862), p. v; Galt Papers, 1:
Galt to Senator W. P. Fessenden, Jan. 10, 1862, and John Young to Galt, Jan. 9,
1862, 749–758.
[91] MS. Group 10, 29, VI: Worthington to Rollo, Jan. 15, 1862; Montreal *Gazette,*
Dec. 18, 1861; Montreal *Witness,* Jan. 1, 1862; *The Times,* Jan 14, 16, 1862; Brown
Diary: Feb. 21, 1862; Louis-Phillippe Turcotte, *Le Canada sous l'union, 1841-1867*
(Quebec, 1882), p. 432; J. C. Weir, "The History of the Twenty-Fourth Regiment
of Canadian Militia," Kent. Hist. Soc., *Papers and Addresses,* II (1915), 39–40.

and Great Britain. Later, as the South made the sea more and more a battlefield, Great Britain became a neutral on the field of battle, and thus likely to be embroiled. British North Americans learned from the crisis that they must look seaward as well as southward.

In studies of Anglo-American relations during the Civil War it has become habitual to dwell on the emotion generated by the *Trent* affair.[92] To do so is to take the incident out of its context and to imply that relations after the crisis went more smoothly than before. This was not the case except for a brief interlude of fifteen months following the surrender of the Confederate envoys. From 1863 until early in 1865 one crisis was to follow another, and some of them were potentially as serious as was that of the *Trent* affair. Viewed realistically and with hindsight, it can be seen that the Lincoln administration was in no position in the winter of 1861 to fight Great Britain. The fact that the people clamored for war has been over-emphasized; whatever the people may have clamored, most of the statesmen of the North were aware of the weakness of their position both legally and strategically. On the other hand, the border raids of three years later [93] were to come at a time when the North was far more prepared militarily to fight a foreign war, if necessary, and when the South actively encouraged such a war. Had the St. Albans raid of 1864 been exploited by an inflammatory press as fully as was the *Trent* affair, the outcome might have been quite different.

Herein lies the basic difference between these two well-known events: in 1861 an irresponsible press in the United States and in the British provinces alike seemed willing to promote war, while by 1864 war-weariness apparently had tempered both presses. Other events during 1863–1865 could have been promoted into the crisis that the *Trent* affair was thought to be, but by then crises were commonplace, the dull nerve of border relations having continued to throb to major and minor irritations for so long as to make such events appear less important by contrast. The *Trent* affair was significant because it galvanized British North Americans into defensive action and because it demonstrated to any Northerners who may have had doubts that the provinces were loyal to Great Britain. But it is doubtful that within the

[92] Well over fifty additional works examined by the writer, too numerous and tangential to cite here, contain references to the *Trent* affair that either state or imply that it represented the sole period of strain in Anglo-American relations during the war.

[93] See Chapter Fourteen.

diplomatic chambers, away from the tumult of the people, the incident brought the two countries much closer to war or that it held any more potentially threatening aspects than did the several border or Fenian raids of subsequent years. Today it is the *Trent* affair that is remembered in Canada, although the St. Albans raid, which helped to win Colonial Office support for British North American confederation, is far more important in the history of the Dominion. When one Canadian chose to write the history of her country in sixty lines, she devoted an entire line to the *Trent* escapade, surely the highest of honors in this day of condensation.[94] Actually the affair of the *Trent* was a popular, but not necessarily a diplomatic, crisis.

Nonetheless, the incident renewed debate between the advocates of imperial and colonial responsibility for defense, and while this debate was to reveal a wide gap between these two positions, and was to create additional confusion over the best means of defense, there was little disagreement over the basic need. Wilkes set in motion a chain of events that gave meaning to the phrase "war in anticipation" for the border. During the less eventful months that immediately followed, all of the protagonists—North, South, Britain, and the provinces—reevaluated their positions *vis-à-vis* one another. The existing formalized diplomatic situation, as based on the Rush-Bagot agreement and the reciprocity treaty of 1854, was subjected to renewed pressures from Congress, and the stage was set for the climactic final two years of interchange in this quadrilateral complex.

[94] T. Chisholm, "The History of Canada in Sixty Lines," Women's Can. Hist. Soc. of Ottawa, *Transactions*, vii (1917). 59-60. The *Trent* affair was the only diplomatic incident of the Civil War to be included in Edmund Routledge, *Date-Book Recording the Principal Events of the World* (London, 1897), p. 52, an event that was ranked with the birth of the Duchess of Albany and making the Prince of Wales a bencher among the significant dates from the creation of the world in 4004 B.C. until 1897.

seven ⮂ INTERLUDE: *PETITES CHOSES*

> "Events have so crowded the last year that I am giddy in reviewing them."
>
> ELIZABETH LINDSAY LOMAX

AS THE NEWS OF POSSIBLE WAR CAME MORE QUICKLY TO BRITISH NORTH America than to Great Britain, so too did the news of continued peace. The Montreal *Gazette* managed to scoop the Toronto *Globe* for once inserting a few lines on the Northern Cabinet's decision in a late afternoon edition on December 28. In the churches on the following Sunday there was much giving of thanks. The sentries around the new fortifications at Toronto—who had become a common sight, beating their arms in order to keep warm—were to be seen no longer, and the people could tell that the army considered the immediate danger of invasion to have passed.

But a vocal portion of the British North American press was unwilling to allow the colonials to give up their renewed sense of awareness of the possible dangers that the Civil War posed for the provinces. In one sense, Captain Wilkes became a Father of Confederation, for the names of Mason and Slidell were not soon forgotten. The fear of American aggression, always present to some extent, had been made so palpable by the *Trent* affair as to create an armed border that in itself was a constant reminder to the several provinces of their collective weakness through political disunion. No major incident arose until late in 1863 to match the *Trent* affair as a warning to the colonists, but an intensified attack from the Northern press, problems arising from maritime blockade runners, heightened Congressional bluster, the fall of John A. Macdonald's ministry, the presence in the provinces of consuls who were thought to be Northern spies, and continued popular distrust of Seward, gave the imperial and colonial administrations, as well as the provincial press, sufficient reason to continue to advocate a policy of preparedness. By the time Lincoln issued his Emancipation Proclamation in September, 1862, a deed that probably would have won him substantial support in the provinces at the outbreak of the war, public opinion had so changed that the President received very little praise.

The great danger now, the press declared, was "apathy and carelessness." With the immediate threat gone the provincials might forget that the American eagle still was bent on continental conquest and be lulled into a false dream of security. To prevent this, George Denison and other Torontonians organized a mass meeting in which "Defense, not defiance," was adopted as a motto, and the members pledged to maintain defenses throughout the province. The people must realize that the day of security had passed; they would have to learn to live amidst the tensions of the modern world and be prepared at all times to meet the "American threat." Lincoln was "an honest but a very weak man," and he could not be trusted to control the *bêtes noires* of his Cabinet, Seward and Welles. Yet apparently very few British North Americans thought that this aggressive, distracted, unethical nation would destroy the reciprocity treaty, since its provisions called for its continuance until at least 1865. A nation that would not cavil at invasion, rapine, and Machiavellian diplomacy still would abide by its treaty agreements! [1]

Seward now issued a most peculiar order. The Secretary of State was adept at what Lincoln called "the horse-chestnut style of argument"—"a specious and fantastic arrangement of words, by which a man can prove a horse-chestnut to be a chestnut horse." [2] Seward

---

[1] FO 5, 827: April, 1862; London *Canadian News,* Jan. 30, Feb. 13, 1862; Montreal *Gazette,* Jan. 4, 18, 1862; Montreal *Witness,* Jan. 1, 1862; Fredericton *Head Quarters,* Jan. 22, 1862; Saint John *Courier,* April 12, 1862; Toronto *Leader,* Jan. 7, 1862, Dec. 19, 1864; Toronto *Globe,* Jan. 1, 2, 1862; Quebec *Morning Chronicle,* Jan. 3, March 6, 1862; Montreal *La Minerve,* Jan. 11, 1862; Ottawa *Citizen,* Dec. 20, 31, 1861; New York *Times,* Jan. 1, 1862; A. W. Tilby, *British North America, 1763–1867* (London, 1911), pp. 397, 416; An Upper Canadian [George T. Denison], *The Military Defences of Canada Considered* (Quebec, 1862), pp. 33–34; *Speeches of Edward Lord Lytton* (Edinburgh, 1874), II, 311–320; William Forsyth, *Letters from Lord Brougham to William Forsyth* (London, 1872), pp. 75–76: Jan. 29, 1862; Ellice Papers, A-12, 29A: Rose to Ellice, Jan. 10, Feb. 2, 1862; Reginald G. Trotter, "Some American Influences upon the Canadian Confederation Movement," *CHR,* v (Sept., 1924), 220–222.

[2] Nicolay and Hay, *Complete Works,* III, 229: Aug. 21, 1858, and IV, 212: Oct. 1,

offered to let the British troops that were coming to North America to fight the Northern states, if necessary, travel across Maine on their way to their posts in the Canadas. He may have intended to make a friendly gesture, to express disdain for the British, to send up a trial balloon to measure Northern public opinion, or to set a capstone to his supposed diplomatic victory in the *Trent* affair.

On January 4, 1862, the State Department received a telegram from the customs agent at Portland, Maine, advising Seward that the steamship *Bohemian* was off Cape Race with British troops for the Canadas and that it might come to Portland. The agent asked if any different course should be taken than what was "guessed." Seward also was asked whether the Canadian mail steamer *Hibernian* might enter the lower harbor to land mail and Portland passengers before taking the troops that she had on board on to Saint John.[3] Of greater importance was the fact that Edmonstone, Allan and Company, agents for and part owners of the Montreal Ocean Steamship Company, applied to Seward for permission to bring from Halifax, in one of their steamers, officers' personal baggage that had been left on board the *Persia* when she had dashed for the open sea from Bic. The baggage was to be sent by rail across Maine to Montreal.[4] Seward's permission on this last request probably was not necessary, for the transit-in-bond provision of the reciprocity treaty of 1854 provided for transit of nonwar materials across Maine via the Grand Trunk line.

Possibly by coincidence the New York *Herald* drew public attention to the presence of the British troop ships off Cape Race. It was rumored that the *Parana* had been lost with eleven hundred men on board while trying to navigate the St. Lawrence. While the rumor was false, it gave the *Herald* an opportunity to suggest that insofar as many of these troops were Irishmen who sympathized with the North in the war, the soldiers should be landed at Portland or New York City. If the British government would make a "respectful request," it would be granted, Bennett thought, thus giving the North an opportunity to

---

1858[?]; J. G. Randall, *Lincoln the President: Midstream* (New York, 1952), pp. 66–67.

[3] MC: E. L. O. Adams to Seward; Seward Papers: J. L. Farmer to Seward, Jan. 8, 1862.

[4] P.A.C., BMW to Lt. Gov. of N.B., xxiii: Edmonstone, Allan and Co. to Rollo, Jan. 13, enc. in Lyons to Gordon, Jan. 20, 1862; FO 5, 823: Monck to Lyons, Jan. 18, enc. in Lyons to Russell, Jan. 20, 1862.

return blessing for cursing and to heap "coals of fire upon an enemy's head."[5]

Possibly Seward saw the *Herald*'s editorial or possibly he conceived the plan independently. Whichever the case, he responded by giving permission for the British to transport across Maine all "baggage, military stores, arms, ammunition and all munitions of war of every kind without exception or reservation whatsoever and including troops also." Seward acted without contacting either Monck or Lyons. When the latter read in the newspaper that the Secretary had granted such permission, he concluded that it was a baseless rumor.[6] Two days later the British consul at Portland wired Lyons that such permission had been received by the American officials there and that great indignation already was being voiced in the Maine press. Lyons at once notified Monck, commenting that the grant looked like "a bravado or a sneer," and asked whether it should be accepted. That others viewed Seward's action in the same light is shown by one perceptive observer's interpretation of the grant as an "act of killing kindness" aimed at *The Times*.[7]

Lyons advised Monck, Doyle, and Gordon that the offer should be refused. He feared that if Seward's permission were accepted it would limit the effectiveness of the British troops transported through Maine since troops to which such courtesies were extended would be considered treacherous if they turned against their "benefactor." Lyons abstained from asking Seward about the situation because he feared that the Secretary would repeat his offer formally, forcing Lyons to be so rude as to reject it to Seward's face. He also feared that if the offer were accepted some incident might occur at Portland that would

[5] Jan. 5, 1862. The *Parana* safely reached Sydney, Nova Scotia, on January 6.

[6] GBI: Seward to Adams, Jan. 8, 1862, p. 96; New York *Herald*, Jan. 9, 1862; FO 5, 823: Lyons to Russell, Jan. 14, 1862. Apparently Lyons first saw the news in the Philadelphia *Press* of Jan. 8, 1862, at a time when the news could be rumor only, since Seward issued his instructions on the same day.

[7] G 13, 1, Telegraph Books: Lyons to Monck, Very Confidential, Jan. 17, 1862; Seward Papers: John Hughes to Seward, Jan. 24, 1862. A typical paean to the "century of peace" refers to Seward's offer as "a bright burst of international sunshine after a cloudy day" (J. L. Tryon, *The Century of Anglo-American Peace* [Washington, 1914], p. 7). Frederick B. Maurice, *History of the Scots Guards*, p. 123, states that Colonel Garnet (later Lord) Wolseley, who was among the officers, ascribed Seward's action to Lincoln's anxiety over a rising Fenian threat and mistakenly adds that the officers landed at Boston.

damage Anglo-American relations further. There also was the danger
that some of the British troops might desert while in Maine.[8]

Sir Fenwick Williams already had told W. Hugh Allan of the
Montreal Steamship Company that while he doubted the good faith
of Seward, the officers from the *Persia* were in great need of their
clothing and that the company could take the baggage from Halifax to
Maine if it would forward the material on its own responsibility.
Monck also was of the opinion that advantage should be taken of
Seward's offer to move to Montreal items that were not munitions of
war, and he thought that it would be unwise not to exercise the normal
transit privilege contained in the reciprocity treaty, for to ignore the
privilege would be to give undue emphasis to the war scare and would
weaken Britain in future negotiations over the transit question. Monck
added that no British officer should have anything to do with administering the move in any way. To this arrangement Lyons consented.[9]

The furor created in Maine by Seward's offer gave the Secretary of
State an additional opportunity to express his confidence that all was
well. The Bangor *Daily Whig and Courier* declared that the gesture
was pointless, and Governor Israel Washburn, Jr. was prompted by
the state legislature to ask for an official explanation. Seward replied that he had offered the British troops use of the Grand Trunk
Railway through Maine in order to save them from "risk and suffering
. . . in an inclement season." Knowing that his statement would be
made public, he added:

> The principle upon which this concession was made . . . is that,
> when humanity, or even convenience, renders it desirable for one
> nation to have a passage for its troops and munitions through the
> territory of another, it is a customary act of comity to grant it, if
> it can be done consistently with its own safety and welfare . . . .
> I shall not affect ignorance of the fact that popular asperities have
> recently appeared in [British North America]. . . . But the gov-
> ernment of Great Britain has, nevertheless, during all this time, held
> towards us its customary language of respect and friendship.

[8] Newton, *Lord Lyons*, I, 81; FO 5, 823: Lyons to Russell, nos. 34 [no. 39] and
40, Jan. 17, 1862.
[9] N.A., CO: J. Murray to Lyons, Jan. 16, enc. in Lyons to Gordon, Jan. 20,
1862; BMW to GCC, 10: Lyons to Murray, Jan. 18, 1862.

Seward thus was able to use the situation to indicate that the North had nothing to fear from Great Britain and that he felt that the British troops would not be used against the states. He ended his explanation by saying that if the Maine legislature wanted the orders to be changed, he would modify them, but he did not offer to rescind them. Seward then sent a copy of his explanation to Charles Francis Adams with the comment that it could be used to show Britain that the Northern states were friendly to her.[10]

In Maine the Chairman of the State Committee on Federal Relations took issue with Seward's explanation. He pointed out that four thousand American boys were enduring the rigors of the Northern winter because of the threat of war with Great Britain and concluded that the British troops should suffer too. In a short but heated debate this contention was answered effectively, and Maine's legislature resolved that Seward's explanation was entirely satisfactory.[11]

Despite the contention that Maine was "rancorous [with] animosity and ill-will," [12] the few officers who finally accompanied the baggage and stores, traveling with the military titles from their luggage removed, met with courtesy wherever they went. Newcastle approved Lyons' decision not to send any large body of troops through Maine, and he reprimanded the shipping company, which, he incorrectly assumed, had provoked the incident by having an unauthorized communication with a foreign government. The company, the Colonial Secretary noted, had produced "inconvenience, at a very anxious moment . . . ." A major portion of the British soldiers who remained in Halifax went on to Quebec via the sleigh route used previously, along which they were subjected to frequent visits by unofficial American recruiting agents who tried to induce them to desert.[13]

Seward's order respecting the British troops, whatever its purpose, served to lessen the tension that remained along the border. By showing

[10] *Courier,* Jan. 20, 1862; Augusta *Age,* Jan. 30, 1862; FO 115, 297–98 and FO 5, 824: Lyons to Russell, Feb. 2, 1862, draft and copy; GBI: Feb. 4, 1862, pp. 111–113; Louis C. Hatch, *Maine, A History* (New York, 1919), II, 444.

[11] FO 5, 825: Lyons to Russell, Feb. 21, 1862.

[12] P.A.C., CO 42: Gordon to Newcastle, Jan. 20, 1862.

[13] *Ibid.:* Feb. 3, 1862; FO 115, 285: Newcastle to Monck, Feb. 5, enc. in Hammond to Lyons, Feb. 15, 1862; Biddulph, ed., "American Civil War," p. 115: Wolseley to Biddulph, Jan. 26, 1862; Garnet J. Wolseley, *The Story of a Soldier's Life* (London, 1903), II, 109–110; Frederick B. Maurice and George Arthur, *The Life of Lord Wolseley* (London, 1924), pp. 34–36.

a nonchalant attitude toward the arrival of British reinforcements, Seward could hope to ease Maine's fear of war. Perhaps Seward was rising to the situation at last and, like Monck in Quebec, was attempting to underplay the war scare. It was typical of him that he would choose a dramatic and public means of doing so, however. Whatever Seward's motives, his relations with Lyons improved thereafter, and three weeks later even Russell warmly praised Seward in a letter to William E. Gladstone.[14]

Lyons continued to insist that the Canadas must prepare for war. Refining his military safety valve theory, he declared that, when demobilized, the vast Northern army would turn to the Northern frontier for employment, and that former soldiers, many of whom would be unable to find a congenial place in society after having been reared in the ways of war, would turn upon any defenseless neighbor for additional conquest, adventure, and plunder. Until the end of his Washington sojourn Lyons continued to advocate preparing "a warm reception" for the inevitable filibusterers. Russell also thought that war, possibly by summer, continued to be a factor that imperial policy should take into account.[15]

Even those who felt that war was inevitable were grateful for the respite, for it furnished more time to train native Canadian forces. Experts, both real and assumed, turned to devising schemes of defense. Those of the amateur variety showed a strange anomaly in logic, for when the newspapers opened their columns to street-corner strategists, a number based their assumptions on a Southern victory in the Civil War. How a subdued North, an army that could not defeat the outnumbered forces of the Confederacy, could fight a successful war with the imperial might of Great Britain was not explained, and the press paid many an unintended compliment to the North when it imagined that this defeated army would be so formidable as to make it almost impossible for Britain's finest troops to hold Canada West. The Niagara correspondent of the Toronto *Leader* reported to *The Times* that there was much to fear since the province would be overrun and plundered in case of war. "One month of American occupation," he wrote, "would involve the loss of more life and more destruction of property

---

[14] E. D. Adams, *Great Britain and the American Civil War*, I, 235–236: Jan. 26, 1862; Galt Papers, I: Ashmun to Galt, Jan. 8, 1862, 741–744.

[15] Newton, I, 72, 74–75: Lyons to Russell, Dec. 27, 31, 1861; G 19, 21: Williams to Monck, Feb. 13, 1862.

than would pay for our whole militia to be kept on a war footing for five years . . . ." [16]

Now an additional source of friction lay north of the border. Several thousand British regulars with nothing to do save guard the new Victoria Bridge might become restless for action. Soldiers rioted in Halifax, ostensibly over poor barracks conditions and late pay days and actually because of boredom. Frequent desertion and hostility between troops and civilians in London, Canada West, were thought to be symptoms of desire for action. "Nothing happened," wrote one. "We remained, and lived the lives of soldiers. We had good times; we had no care; we had our beer; we had a brisk time in Montreal." But some found beer and "a brisk time" the essence of boredom; they had come to North America to fight, and some were jubilant whenever rumor promised action. Even a young captain who had expected to be a Northern captive by March was "of a hopeful disposition" that the North might yet invade the Canadas, and there were those who had "longing desires" for war and who considered the averting of it to be "bad luck." On the other hand, the local militia was not so aggressive, and it was reported that in a regiment of eight hundred militia men queried, only twelve indicated any desire to fight the North.[17]

The question was not one of patriotism so much as one of divided responsibilities. Newcastle had written that an effective defense of the Canadas depended on a militia of one hundred thousand men. Most of the advisers close to Macdonald or Monck agreed. Nonetheless, although Captain Charles de Salaberry organized a French-Canadian rifle corps at Quebec, and although Newfoundland added two companies, little was done in the various provinces to provide the machinery for such a force on the grounds that any hypothetical war probably would be Britain's fault, not the provinces', and that Britain should shoulder the burden of defense. The imperial officials therefore continued to direct defensive measures at the military level and gave the measures what semblance of interprovincial unity they had. By

[16] Ellice Papers, A-2, 3: Parkes to Ellice, Jr., Jan. 9, 1862; Toronto *Globe,* Jan. 1, 4, 1862; Toronto *Leader,* Jan. 20, 1862; Montreal *Gazette,* Jan. 3, 1862; *The Times,* Jan. 2, 1862; Skelton, *Galt,* p. 345.

[17] Toronto *Leader,* Dec. 3, 1861, Jan. 25, 1862; William H. Atherton, *Montreal, 1534-1914* (Montreal, 1914), II, 211; George H. Ham, *Reminiscences of a Raconteur* (Toronto, 1921), pp. 75-76; Biddulph, pp. 116-117: Wolseley to Biddulph, March 17, 1862; Francis Duncan, *Our Garrisons in the West, or Sketches in British North America* (London, 1864), pp. 219-220.

early spring of 1862 Great Britain had 18,000 regular troops concentrated in the provinces, largely in Canada East, to meet a potential invader.[18]

Monck had several possible plans for defense drawn up. Additional troops were shifted to Gananoque and Kingston on the upper St. Lawrence River. The British consul at Buffalo studied the harbor defenses there, agents were sent to the small New York communities along the St. Lawrence, and Arthur Gordon sent an agent into Maine to procure military information before the spring thaw, for Maine was a "projecting incisor tooth," which, during the winter, separated the rich expanse of the two Canadas from access to the sea. Gordon's agent viewed the defenses of Augusta, Bangor, Houlton, Fort Fairfield, Fort Jarvis, and Fort Kent, traveled the principal roads, and learned the number of troops quartered in each place and the extent of their military experience, failing to obtain precise figures only at Portland and Eastport.[19]

In the meantime *The Times* reported that the North, under the guidance of elderly Winfield Scott and with the advice of General George B. McClellan, Commander of the Army of the Potomac, was planning an attack upon the Canadas along the old Champlain Valley route to Montreal.[20] Since *The Times* often spoke as a semi-official voice of the conservative ministry, the report undoubtedly was taken seriously in many quarters. It is difficult to find any immediate basis for *The Times*' report, however, unless one were to assume that President Lincoln's General War Order Number One, which directed McClellan to advance his armies on an unnamed target on February 22, and which was issued on January 27, was interpreted as a threat to the provinces. Since Lincoln had specified Manassas as a target in another war order on January 31, there was no basis for such an interpretation of Mc-

[18] Macdonald Papers: Memo., Jan. 1, 1862, pp. 22–29; G 26, 87: Williams to Lewis, enc. in Williams to Monck, both Jan. 3, 1862, and DeSalaberry to Monck, Dec. 26, 1861; R. L. Schuyler, *The Fall of the Old Colonial System: A Study in British Free Trade, 1770–1870* (New York, 1945), p. 228. It is interesting to note that this figure is nearly twice that of the number of troops kept in the seaboard colonies in 1776. Also see P.A.C., John Sandfield Macdonald Papers, II, 1009 C-D: H. G. Joly to Macdonald, Nov. 9, 1862, in reference to DeSalaberry, and 1005–1006; J. B. Dorion to Macdonald, Aug. 26, 1862.

[19] C 697: R. R. Lowell, Jan. 6, and Bouchier to Rollo, Jan. 11, 1862, pp. 29–31; G 8B, 62: Gordon to Newcastle, Jan. 20, and Newcastle to Gordon, Feb. 7, 1862, 65–68; W. B. Kerr, "Donohoe," p. 49.

[20] The first such report was on Feb. 19, 1862.

Clellan's activity. On the other hand, on Feburary 7 the state legislature of Maine had asked the Federal government for an appropriation to help defend the state, and the request came at a time when it may have been used to feed *The Times'* rumor.[21]

Throughout 1862–1863 the concept of an "unfortified frontier" was subjected to repeated re-evaluation both in the provinces and in the mother country. The British knew that any future war with the United States would be fought on two fronts—the Atlantic Ocean and the British North American borders. The strategists generally assumed that she would have to win such a war on the former while fighting a purely defensive battle on the continent. It would be impossible to place enough troops in North America to take the offensive, and it would be foolish to maintain large garrisons on the continent, for they might provoke like demonstrations on the American side of the border. Therefore in March the British House of Commons passed a resolution to the effect that colonies "exercising the rights of self-government ought to undertake the main responsibility of providing for their own internal order and security." [22] But Canadians were to continue to show that they considered defense to be largely the duty of the mother country and not their own. That Canada West could be had by conquest was evident, and perhaps as long as this were so the Americans would be content to wait for the Canadas to join the Union willingly. The best defense for the Canadas may have been their manifest lack of adequate defense. The Canadas continued to call on the Old World to redress the balance of the New.

If any effective delaying action within the Canadas was to be fought at all, some resistance would have to be made on the Great Lakes, which were the keys to the united Canadas. The Rush-Bagot agreement had not stated that the ships that were to be dismantled under its provisions need be destroyed, and they were not. The ships remained in the yards ready to be refitted if needed, although since the British vessels had remained uncovered at Kingston for thirty-five years, they ultimately were found to be unserviceable. And the British had continued to construct forts near the border, for the agreement never had applied to land fortifications. The most active fort-

---

[21] *OR,* ser. 1, v, 41: President's General War Order No. 1, Jan. 27, and President's Special War Order No. 1, Jan. 31, 1862, Toronto *Globe,* Feb. 7, 1862. See Warren W. Hassler, Jr., *General George B. McClellan: Shield of the Union* (Baton Rouge, 1957), pp. 52–60.
[22] *Hansard's, 1862:* CLXV, cols. 378–379, 1032–1060, Feb. 17, March 4.

building period in Canadian history had been between 1817 and 1862. As a result the British had a string of serviceable forts along or near the frontier, while at the beginning of the Civil War the United States had but two of equal size. The British fortifications generally were located so as to insure maximum concentration of troops outside Canada West, which was considered by some to be indefensible. A permanent citadel at Quebec had been constructed during 1820–1831, and a yet unfinished supply depot on St. Helen's Island, near Montreal, had been started in 1819. During the Oregon dispute Kingston had been strengthened with Martello towers.

The United States, on the other hand, had renovated only a few existing forts, with the exception of the newer forts Wayne at Detroit and Porter at Buffalo. Even Fort Montgomery at Rouse's Point was but half finished when the Civil War began. Now, with a new appropriation, construction on the fort was resumed. The United States had covered her vessels at Sackett's Harbor where for years they had stood ready for limited use. The navy yard had closed in 1826, but two ships remained with a sailing master in charge, and the U.S.S. *New Orleans* there was not dropped from the naval lists until 1868. However, during the *Trent* crisis the ship was found to have rotted away.

During the crisis states other than Maine had shown some concern over the weakly defended border. Oswego, Niagara, Buffalo, and Detroit were to have their fortifications repaired, and the smaller cities that were omitted protested loudly. Those who lived near the Genesee River were disturbed that they were not to have a stone fort, and a Committee of Harbor Defense was appointed at Rochester. A Canadian agent reported that the people of Sackett's Harbor wanted war despite having only forty-nine condemned cannon and four old mortars, two of which would not fire, for defense. Former President Millard Fillmore, who was living in Buffalo, issued a circular letter calling the people to meet to form a Committee of Defense that would petition the state legislature for an appropriation, and then adroitly cooled tempers at the meeting with an extremely conciliatory speech. The Montreal *Herald* reported that various small islands at the head of the St. Lawrence secretly were being fortified by the North and that ships were being built at Ogdensburg for offensive action on the Great Lakes in the spring.[23]

[23] B 29, VI: T. Worthington to Rollo, Jan. 15, 1862; Rochester *Evening Express*, Jan. 18, 1862; Montreal *Herald*, quoted in Toronto *Globe*, Jan. 4, 1862; *The Times*,

Despite the many reports concerning the "Yankee menace," as several newspapers put it, the colonials continued to drag their feet. The muddle over defense that occurred in the summer of 1862 was not due to indecisiveness about defense itself but to a basic disagreement between the mother country and her offspring over who should carry the burden of defense. This question of the delegation of responsibility was to intensify an already lengthy debate in the colonies and the mother country over defense, the nature of colonies, and the economics of empire. In the Canadas the debate was to result in the fall of the conservative government then in office.[24]

Canada's most important defensive step was to appoint a commission to report on the reorganization of the provincial forces. The committee included Macdonald, Galt, and Cartier as the government's representatives and had a War Office expert as its chief adviser. A new portfolio of Minister of Militia Affairs also was created, with Macdonald as the first minister.[25] On March 15 the commission presented its report,[26] recommending that an active force of fifty thousand men and a reserve of the same number be organized and that a gunboat flotilla within the limits of the Rush-Bagot agreement be placed on the Great Lakes.

John A. Macdonald introduced the government's Militia Bill, based on the committee's report, to the legislature on May 2, 1862. Despite the known aversion among Canadians, and especially the French, to compulsory military service, Macdonald was forced to state that conscription might be necessary and that a direct tax might be needed to finance the project. This was an unusual provision to bring before the House, and the cost was more than unusual, for a proposed twenty-eight-day training period was to require $1,110,000, or one-tenth of the provincial revenue. The Toronto *Globe* at once attacked the bill as economically unfeasible, declaring that the prospect of a fourth

April 1, 1862; F. H. Severance, ed., *Millard Fillmore Papers,* II, Buffalo Hist. Soc., *Pubs.,* XI (1907), 398: Jan. 2, 1862; FO 5, 823: Lyons to Russell, Jan. 9, 1862.

[24] This debate was not a new one. See Toronto *Leader,* May 7, 1861; Quebec *Morning Chronicle,* July 2, 23, 1861; Toronto *Globe,* Sept. 21, 1861. It became more heated in 1862: Quebec *Morning Chronicle,* Feb. 15; Toronto *Globe,* July 10, Sept. 15; Montreal *Le Canadien,* July 17, 18, Sept. 3; Perth *Courier,* July 18.

[25] Skelton, *Galt,* p. 340; Stacey, *Army,* p. 130; Creighton, *Macdonald,* pp. 324-325.

[26] *Report of the Commissioners Appointed to Report a Plan for the Better Organization of the Department of Adjutant General of Militia, and the Best Means of Reorganizing the Militia of this Province, and to Prepare a Bill Thereon* (Quebec, 1862).

increase in taxation in as many years, which the bill would necessitate, was too much. Macdonald asked Galt to steer the bill through the House, and the Finance Minister promptly staggered the French Canadians, in particular, by announcing that in the first year of the act's operation the Government proposed to call out thirty thousand men for fourteen days of training at an estimated cost of $480,000. While well below imperial desires, this bill represented the most advanced measure for self-defense that a Canadian ministry had put forward.[27]

The Liberal-Conservative government had been in power in the united Canadas since 1854. For some time Macdonald and Cartier had remained in office by hair-line margins, and it probably was evident to them that their administration could not survive much longer. To fall on a patriotic issue at least would provide a discredited government with a dignified exit. As Macdonald's most perceptive biographer has pointed out, the Militia Bill seemed to be the best escape.[28] Macdonald was drinking heavily during the debates on the bill, and he returned to the House only after a period of semi-alcoholic illness. On May 20 the Macdonald-Cartier Government fell on the second reading of the Militia Bill, following the defection of fifteen French Canadian members, and an administration characterized by the disappointed Governor General as "a wretched lot . . . of parish politicians," took office, retaining its position until May 6 of the following year.[29]

The government had fallen because it was discredited, and the Militia Bill merely had furnished the occasion.[30] This was not understood in either Great Britain or the United States, however, and the new ministry of John Sandfield Macdonald (who was not related to his predecessor) and Louis Sicotte was assailed by the British press for destroying the momentum of the Canadian defensive movement and was jeered by the Northern press as proof that Canadians would not

[27] Stacey, *Army*, pp. 130–136; Creighton, *Macdonald*, p. 330; G. P. deT. Glazebrook, "Permanent Factors in Canadian External Relations," in Ralph Flenley, ed., *Essays in Canadian History presented to George MacKinnon Wrong* (Toronto, 1939), p. 212.

[28] Creighton, *Macdonald*, pp. 329–334. See also Skelton, *Galt*, p. 342 n. 4.

[29] Martineau, *Newcastle*, p. 311: Monck to Newcastle, Aug. 4, 1862; P. G. Cornell, "The Alignment of Political Groups in the United Province of Canada, 1854–1864," *CHR*, xxx (March, 1949), 36.

[30] Ellice Papers, A-12, 29A: Rose to Ellice, May 28, 1862; Toronto *Globe*, May 21, 1862; Montreal *Transcript*, June 23, 1862; Quebec *Le Canadien*, Sept. 3, 1862; John Boyd, *Cartier* (Montreal, 1913), p. 128; Isabel Skelton, *Life and Times of Thomas D'Arcy McGee* (Gardenvale, Que., 1925), pp. 387–388.

fight. *The Times* lashed out at pampered colonials who lacked the intestinal fortitude to provide for themselves, and the New York *Herald* said the same thing without the euphemism. On the other hand, the *Tribune* hailed the new ministry, for Sandfield Macdonald was thought to be less sympathetic to the South, despite his having married the daughter of a Louisiana politician, and Thomas D'Arcy McGee, who was thought to be pro-Northern, was included in the new administration.[31]

Newcastle wrote to Monck with as much heat as his phlegmatic nature could generate. He reminded the Governor General of how patriotically the Canadas had responded during the *Trent* affair in December and pointed out that the English people, not understanding the problems of local provincial politics, would interpret the rejection of the Militia Bill wrongly. The Colonial Secretary suggested that Monck confer with Gordon and Doyle in order to organize a common defensive bond between the several provinces and warned that some substitute for the defeated bill should be found as soon as possible in order to counteract the effects of its rejection on London.[32]

The Secretary of State for War pithily summed up English indignation over Canada's failure to provide for her own defense. "During the American war," he said, "Parliament passed an Act by which it was declared illegal to tax the Colonies. I believe it would be very difficult to pass an Act declaring it illegal for the Colonies to tax us." [33] The Little Englanders and the Manchester school, who for various reasons felt that the Empire was an archaic burden, were supplied with new ammunition by the controversy.[34] The British North American provinces, they pointed out, were a major weakness to Britain for they created a constant danger of war with the United States, which fettered British policy in Europe. There were a few who wanted to exchange, sell, or give the Canadas to the United States,[35] and there were

[31] *The Times,* June 6, 1862; New York *Tribune,* May 29, 1862.

[32] G.B., *Sess. Papers, 1862,* XXXVI, col. 604: Newcastle to Monck, Aug. 21.

[33] *Hansard's, 1862:* CLXV, cols. 291–298, Feb, 14; J. W. Fortescue, *A History of the British Army* (London, 1930), XIII, 522–523.

[34] For the Militia Bill in the broader field of imperial relations, see John Morley, *The Life of Richard Cobden* (London, 1908), II, 470–471: Cobden to Gladstone, Feb. 13, 1865; Theodore Rogers, ed., *The Speeches of John Bright* (London, 1868), I, 153–154, 167; D. M. L. Farr, *The Colonial Office and Canada, 1867–1887* (Toronto, 1955), pp. 3, 9; C. A. Bodelson, *Studies in Mid-Victorian Imperialism* (Copenhagen, 1924), pp. 33–34, 38.

[35] Seward Papers: A. Alison to Seward, Jan. 7, 1862; London *Observer,* Dec. 8, 1861; J. A. Hobson, *Richard Cobden: The International Man* (New York, 1919), pp. 339–340.

many, including Lord John Russell, who professed to be willing to see the united provinces given their independence or to see them join the United States if they chose to do so of their own accord. This apparent willingness on the part of Britain to let the provinces fend for themselves gave new strength to the annexationist movement in the United States,[36] and one writer has concluded that the abusive tone adopted by the British press so damaged Canadian loyalty to the mother country as to increase anti-imperial sentiment in the provinces as well.[37]

The new Canadian ministry did amend the Militia Act of 1859 in order to augment the volunteer force. By the amended act the total paid corps were not to exceed ten thousand men, but the Governor General could accept unpaid volunteers in excess of this number. The final appropriation was $250,000, still three times that of the previous year, and this included monies for new drill instructors. In New Brunswick Lieutenant Governor Gordon reorganized the militia, and the legislature appropriated the niggardly sum of £2,000. Work was begun on a more defensible road from Saint John to Quebec via the Matapedia River, and Gordon attempted to establish telegraphic communications from Halifax to Quebec via the North Shore of New Brunswick. Nova Scotia also responded with a new Militia Act.

During the spring and summer of 1862 a group of British experts quietly surveyed provincial defenses, examining all possible avenues of attack. They concluded that a force of 150,000 men and permanent fortifications at nine key spots, costing an estimated £1,611,000, would be needed to defend the Canadas alone. Three officers from the British army were sent into the Northern states to observe artillery and ordnance in use by the Federal troops. Earl Russell, who was con-

[36] See a typical editorial in the Cleveland *Leader,* June 25, 1862.

[37] J. C. Dent, *The Last Forty Years* (Toronto, 1881), II, 426. The Canadian rejection of the Militia Bill served to bring forth Goldwin Smith's famous Manchester School letters on "The Empire" in the London *Daily News* which were reprinted in the *Leader* in 1863. Smith, then Regius Professor of Modern History at Oxford and later a professor at Cornell University and a journalist in Canada, wrote that the only way to make Canada impregnable was "to fence her round with the majesty of an independent nation." When it learned of Smith's views, the Toronto *Globe* re-affirmed Canadian loyalty and desire to remain within the Empire. See the *Globe,* Feb. 24, 1862; Alan Bullock and F. W. Deakin, eds., *The British Political Tradition,* VI: *The Concept of Empire: Burke to Attlee, 1774-1947* (London, 1953), 217-219; F. H. Underhill, "Canada's Relations with the Empire as seen by the 'Toronto Globe,'" *CHR,* X (June, 1929), 120-121. On Smith, see Elizabeth Wallace, *Goldwin Smith: Victorian Liberal* (Toronto, 1957), pp. 183-188; and Ronald McEachern, "Goldwin Smith," upubl. Ph.D. diss. (Toronto, 1934).

templating recognition of the Confederacy during this time, suggested that the British regulars be concentrated at the most defensible posts. At the end of the summer Lord Lyons returned to England to consult with Russell and to take a short rest, producing a flurry of rumors that he was to be recalled as a prelude to recognition of the Confederate government. As the summer of 1862 passed, it became evident that the Civil War would last another winter, so the spring of 1863 was set as the next possible invasion date.[38]

For three successive springs thereafter Sir Fenwick Williams prepared a revised plan for the disposition of forces in the event of war, and each summer the troops were drilled and paraded. Plans for new batteries near Saint John were drawn up, and Lieutenant Colonel W. F. D. Jervois, an extremely able engineer who later was to become Governor of New Zealand, visited nearly all of the provinces in the autumn of 1863 to reformulate defensive plans. He stated even more strongly than had his predecessors that Canada West could not be defended and that even a delaying action there or in Canada East south of Montreal would depend on naval superiority on Lake Ontario.[39]

John Sandfield Macdonald's government, now reorganized and supported by George Brown in Canada West and A. A. Dorion in Canada East, won Parliamentary approval in August, 1863, for two more acts that substantially improved the militia. A Service Militia was instituted with a view to making men on the volunteer rolls available quickly in case of an emergency, and a careful enrollment was to be taken the following year. The men might be ordered out for six days of annual drill, and they were to be officered by men who had attended a school of military instruction. The second act made it possible to increase the volunteer force to thirty-five thousand if necessary.

The Canadian militia was not called out. Two military schools did open in 1864 and in 1865 four more were added, and the effective force, while well below the legal limit, was five times greater at the end of the Civil War than at the beginning. The other provinces did not seem willing to prepare for war even on this scale, however, for in

[38] C 697: Lugard to Williams, Sept. 5, 1862, pp. 351-352; CFA, 80: Adams to Seward, Oct. 17, 1863; Toronto *Leader*, Sept. 26, 1862; N.S., Executive Council, *Journal, 1862*, p. 79; Hett, *Sibbald*, p. 320: June 18, 1862; Spencer Walpole, *Life of Lord John Russell* (London, 1889), II, 360: Russell to Palmerston, Sept. 17, 1862; Stacey, *Army*, pp. 143-147.
[39] P.A.C., War Office: "Report on the Defences of Canada and of the British Naval Stations in the Atlantic," Feb., 1864.

1863 New Brunswick trained but 1700 men, Nova Scotia but 2300, and Prince Edward Island but 750. Voices were raised to remind the people of the possibility of war but by 1863 there seemed to be little of the fervor that was present in 1861–1862.[40]

While addressing a gathering in Montreal in the summer of 1862 Monck again had warned the Canadians of the potential dangers that they faced. "The plain truth had better be told and at once recognized," he said, "there is but one quarter from which Canada can apprehend any serious attack; that quarter is the great Republic which lies along our extended frontier . . . ." [41] This speech had a somewhat different effect than he probably intended, for working against official anxieties were public apathy and the wide-spread hope that the prosperity that the Civil War now had brought would not be disturbed.[42] The Toronto *Globe* took the Governor General to task for being a disciple of that "statesman of fifty years ago," Palmerston: "We may not like the American people nor their institutions . . . but we need not call them a nation of scoundrels, for in the first place it is not true; and, in the second place, it would be neither wise nor prudent to say it if it were. They are our neighbors on this continent . . . ." To turn the province into an armed camp would be foolish, the *Globe* said, for it would drive away immigrants and impoverish the people. "Let him," Brown said of Monck, "take care that he does not convince the people of Canada that it is better to become part of the United States than to live the slave of a constant dread of invasion." Neutrality in word and deed was the only surety that Canadians had of the continued blessings of peace and prosperity. Canadian energies should be expended on building an empire in the west, not in tilting at American windmills. It was the West that the United States might attempt to annex, not the provinces, and while the North was disposed elsewhere, it would be wise to expand Canadian control over the defenseless Red

---

[40] Williams Papers: Monck to Williams, Jan. 26, Feb. 4, May 26, June 23, Aug. 11, 26, 1863; G 8B, 43: S. Westmacott to Doyle, July 23, enc. in Doyle to Gordon, July 24, 1863, 784–786; Macdonald Papers, 99: enc., *Canada and Invasion* (n.p., 1863); *The Times*, Jan. 14, June 25, 1863; Brantford *Courier*, Aug. 3, 1863; Montreal *Le Pays*, Oct. 11, 1864; O.P.A., J. T. Gilkison Family Papers: newspaper clippings on defense, 1863.

[41] Quebec *Morning Chronicle*, July 15, 1862.

[42] For a tentative analysis of the importance of the war to the economy of the provinces, see Robin W. Winks, "Some Notes on the Economic Impact of the Civil War on British North America," a paper read before the Nova Scotia Historical Society on March 7, 1958. A copy is on deposit at the P.A.N.S.

River territory, Brown concluded. In order to do so, peace and a strict neutrality would have to be the administration's goal.[43]

The defeat of the Militia Bill in 1862 had been followed by renewed vociferation in the American Congress that might pose a threat to British North American neutrality. In February, 1862, Representative Isaac Arnold of Illinois, who had promised vengeance on Britain, had reported for a select Committee on Lake and River Defenses that since recent events had revealed the Canadas to be anti-Northern the establishment of several depots on lakes Michigan, Ontario, and Erie, the construction of new forts, and the widening of the Illinois and Michigan Ship Canal were necessary defense measures.[44] Some also argued that Lake Michigan was not a "boundary lake," since it was separated from the boundary by the Straits of Mackinac and because it had not been named specifically in the Rush-Bagot convention.[45] If this were the case, an unlimited number of warships could be placed on the lake. Lyons took a copy of the report to Seward and asked if it were consistent with the agreement. Seward refused to resort to sophistry concerning Lake Michigan's status, and he told Lyons that he doubted whether a bill based on Arnold's report would pass either house. All the members from the select committee were from the lake states, and such a bill would be an obvious effort to dip into the "pork barrel" to obtain federal funds for local improvement.[46]

A small group of congressmen tried to give their schemes for local improvements an aura of patriotic necessity by citing the alleged danger that the Canadian canal system posed in case of war. The Rideau Canal, they said, gave the British an advantage on Lake Ontario, for it was beyond the range of Northern guns. During the *Trent* crisis *The Times* had declared that once the St. Lawrence River was open the canal system would make it possible to "pour into the lakes such a fleet of gunboats and other craft as will give us the complete and immediate command" of those waters. Selections from this article were read aloud to the House.[47]

[43] April 2, July 15, Nov. 20, 27, 1862.

[44] *House Reports*, 27th Cong., 2nd Sess., no. 23: Feb. 12, 1862.

[45] For most regulatory purposes Lake Michigan is considered a part of the boundary waters, as was made clear in the Boundary Waters Treaty of 1919. See C. G. Winter, "The Boundary Waters Treaty," *Historian*, xvii (Autumn, 1954), 76–96.

[46] MC: A. Penfield to Seward, May 27, 1862; FO 5, 829: Lyons to Russell, May 8, 1862; FO 5, 875: Lyons to Russell, Jan. 23, 1863; G 1, 230: Stuart to Monck, July 4, 1862, 140; NBL 10: Seward to Lyons, April 21, 1863, 563.

[47] *Cong. Globe*, 37th Cong., 3rd Sess., p. 772. See also H. W. Hill, "Historical

Congress now examined Northern defenses in the light of the canals, but this debate on defenses, unlike that in the Canadas, largely was fraudulent. Francis P. Blair, then a Representative from Missouri, undertook to report for the House Committee on Military Affairs on how to overcome the alleged British canal advantage. There was, in fact, no such advantage, for Britain's own military adviser saw that in case of war the entire Canadian canal system would have to be abandoned to the Northern armies after a token defense. Nonetheless, Blair ignored what was obvious even to the contemporary Northern press and reported that the only means of countering Britain's canal advantage was by constructing a ship canal for the passage of armed vessels from the Mississippi River to Lake Michigan. He couched his recommendation in the form of a bill and estimated that the cost would be $13,346,000. Blair did not explain how the fleet was to reach Lake Ontario by this canal in view of the fact that Niagara Falls was in the way.[48]

The Military Affairs Committee, to which Blair's bill was committed, reported on it on June 13, 1862. Blair and Arnold campaigned for the bill throughout the rest of the session, stressing the alleged military value of such a canal. Arnold attempted to demonstrate how one fleet, built in Ohio where labor and materials were then comparatively inexpensive, could serve on the Gulf of Mexico and on the Great Lakes.[49] This obvious effort to enlist support from Ohio's congressmen was not successful. As Seward had seen, the canal bill was an effort to get new dockyards at St. Louis and a waterway of great benefit to Illinois constructed at Federal expense.

New York's Representative Theodore M. Pomeroy professed to be won over by Blair's argument, but he and A. B. Olin, also from New York, suggested that an enlarged Erie Canal by which gunboats could pass from the Atlantic to Lake Ontario would accomplish the same purpose as would deepening the Illinois River. This plan would cost

---

Sketch of Niagara Ship Canal Project," Buffalo Hist. Soc., *Pubs.*, xxii (1918), 217–221.

[48] *Cong. Globe, op. cit.,* p. 903; *House Reports,* 37th Cong., 2nd Sess., no. 37: Feb. 20, 1862. A convenient summary of the early history of the canal system appears in Joseph R. Hartley, *The Effect of the St. Lawrence Seaway on Grain Movements* (Bloomington, Ind., 1957), pp. 42–50. See also Millington Synge, "The Lakes and Canals of Canada," Royal United Service Institute, *Journal,* x (1867), 183–208.

[49] *Cong. Globe,* 37th Cong., 2nd Sess., pp. 3023–24.

but $3,500,000, and it could be accomplished within a year, Olin thought, whereas the Illinois project would require five years, by which time its military need might well have passed. Thaddeus Stevens, Representative from Pennsylvania, jested at these pork-barreling schemes and suggested that the Susquehanna River be deepened from Chesapeake Bay to the river's source and a canal then cut to connect with the Erie Canal. This, he said, would cost a mere $100,000,000, a sum that Pennsylvania would be very pleased to receive.[50]

The efforts to obtain congressional consent to enlarge the canals canceled each other out. New York presented two rival schemes—to enlarge the Erie Canal or to match the Welland Canal on the American side of the Niagara River, while the old Northwest also had two plans —the canal from Lake Michigan via the Illinois River to the Mississippi River, and a canal via the Fox and Wisconsin rivers. Indiana, one of the few Northwestern states that would not benefit directly from any of the plans, resisted all of them. Sectional rivalries and the manifest nature of the canal schemes led to the tabling of Blair's bill in July.

In December the House passed a resolution that required the Committee on Naval Affairs to reconsider the means of getting gunboats onto the Great Lakes in case of emergency. The Chairman of the Committee, F. A. Conklin of New York, reported that such a need existed since the United States soon would be demanding redress of Great Britain. He concluded that the Canadian canals were of no danger to the North, however, since they could be captured easily, and that the Union could construct large vessels on the lake shores whereas Britain could pass only small gunboats through the Welland Canal.[51]

Various canal schemes continued to be brought before Congress throughout 1862–1863. While Blair's bill originally was treated as a defense measure against a British invasion, Arnold soon professed to see the bill as a step toward preventing European intervention in the war by sending more grain to the Great Powers and thus making them dependent on the American Northwest. Olin reported a composite bill to enlarge the Illinois, Erie, and Oswego canals, and Ohio and Indiana congressmen at once attacked him for trying to form a "log-rolling coalition." The House rejected the composite canal bill by a vote of 72 to 60 in February, 1863. Although Arnold introduced a

[50] *Ibid.,* pp. 3030–33, and App., pp. 312–314.
[51] *Ibid.,* p. 3056; *ibid.,* 3rd sess., p. 2; *House Reports,* 37th Cong., 3rd Sess., no. 4, Jan. 8, 1863.

similar bill in March, serious congressional discussion of canal-building
in the North during the war had ended.[52]

Illinois refused to be downed. The General Assembly instructed
Governor Richard Yates to appoint a delegation to call upon the
Governor General of British North America to confer on the pos-
sibilities of widening canals in the province or of constructing a new
canal from Georgian Bay to the Ottawa River route. Monck replied
that he could not receive the delegation officially, but he offered to
talk with the five delegates in an unofficial capacity.

In appointing this delegation, Yates demonstrated that the efforts to
obtain Federal support for enlarging canals for national defense were
insincere. In February Illinois needed a canal to help defend the nation
from Great Britain. In March Great Britain was asked to build a
canal to give Western merchants cheaper transport to the sea. It long
had been the dream of Chicago, Toronto, and Montreal mercantile
interests to tap the resources of the west and to make the Great Lakes
and St. Lawrence route the natural means of access to the sea. Now,
her fear of war with hostile Canadians suddenly a thing of the past,
Illinois declared that, "The commercial spirit of the age forbids that
international jealousy should interfere with great natural thorough-
fares . . . ."[53]

The border states also continued to petition for local fortifications,
but most of the petitions reflected a narrow conception of the national
interest. During the summer of 1862 and again in January of 1863, for
example, the Maine legislature petitioned the Secretary of War to
make Portland harbor into an impregnable naval station and recommended constructing an interior railroad line from Portland to Boston
with Federal funds. John A. Poor urged building a wide-gauge railroad from Portland to Madawaska, with branches to Houlton and to
the New Brunswick border opposite Saint Andrews. The following year
Governor Samuel Cony recommended Federal aid for a line from Portland to the St. Croix River settlements to protect them from possible
British attack. In Boston petitions from merchants to the Board of
Trade were so numerous that the mayor and Governor Andrew found

[52] *Cong. Globe*, 37th Cong., 3rd Sess., pp. 364, 539–541, 699, 769, 810–813, 827–828,
2903, and App., pp. 101, 156; Chicago *Tribune*, Feb. 16, 1863; Toronto *Globe*, Feb.
18, 1863.

[53] FO 5, 877: Lyons to Russell, Feb. 16, 1863, and W. B. Ogden to Monck, March
10, and Denis Godley to Ogden, April 6, enc. in Lyons to Russell, April 27, 1863;
Toronto *Globe*, Feb. 14, 1863.

it necessary to confer in Washington with the Secretaries of War and Navy, and Andrew appointed a committee to devise and execute a plan for harbor defense.[54]

The months from early summer of 1862 to late summer of 1863 represented the most tranquil period in British North American-Federal relations during the Civil War. Perhaps this merely was a reflection of general Anglo-American relations, for the danger of British intervention in favor of the South had passed by June of 1863,[55] and in September Earl Russell ordered the seizure of the rams that the Laird Brothers were building for the Confederacy.[56] Thereafter if intervention were to come, it probably would be as a by-product of some direct clash between the two nations, possibly along the British North American border. The very events that arose to disturb relations during the fifteen-month period were so minor, when viewed in perspective, as to represent a suspension of the "war in anticipation."

The major source of irritation was the Federal blockade and its effects, but for the provinces the blockade had less significance than for cotton-hungry England. President Lincoln had "set on foot" a

[54] Me. Legis., *Documents, 1864,* XII: 9–10; Augusta *Maine Farmer,* July 24, 1862; Calais *Advertiser,* Jan. 2, May 15, 1862; Eastport *Sentinel,* Jan. 1, Aug. 30, 1862; Fredericton *Head Quarters,* Oct. 8, 1862; Halifax *Morning Chronicle,* July 30, 1863; Boston Board of Trade, *Ninth Annual Report* (Boston, 1863), pp. 35–40, and *Tenth Annual Report* (Boston, 1864), pp. 42–51.

[55] There is disagreement between scholars as to the time when the possibility of British intervention in the Civil War had passed, but none of them places this date later than June, 1863. H. C. Allen, *Great Britain and the United States* (New York, 1955), is the most recent work on this subject. Allen implies that September, 1862, would be a more suitable date (p. 483). Earl Russell himself apparently felt that the time for intervention had passed by February, 1863, a date which E. D. Adams accepts (II, 71, 78). Even contemporary observers like Samuel G. Ward apparently saw that 1863 had been the year of decision for Great Britain (Baring Papers: Ward to Baring, Oct. 20, 1863).

[56] By contrast, also in September General Joseph Hooker, perhaps having heard that the Canadian Parliament had received the news of his defeat at Chancellorsville with scattered applause, predicted at an informal dinner party in Washington that the United States soon would be "the greatest military power on earth . . . greatest in number, in capacity, in dash, in spirit, in intelligence of the soldiery . . . ," and that thousands of men who had a taste of war would not be content to return to peaceful pursuits but would strike out against the Canadas. The Assistant Secretary of the Navy, Gustavus Vasa Fox, preferred to exact retribution from Britain by seizing Bermuda, for he felt that Canada would "fall of itself." See CD, Quebec, I: Ogden to Seward, May 9, 1863; Tyler Dennett, ed., *Lincoln and the Civil War in The Diaries and Letters of John Hay* (New York, 1939), pp. 87–88: Sept. 10, 1863.

blockade of the Southern coasts on April 19 and 27, 1861. A lucrative trade soon sprang up between the Maritime Provinces and the South, and the harbors of Halifax and Saint John often were filled with vessels suspected of blockade-running. A number of the vessels engaged in the practice were Confederate-owned, but there were many enterprising Maritimers who took advantage of the high prices and quick profits that running the blockade brought. As the North tightened the blockade, Federal ships frequently captured British North American vessels. For example, one Prince Edward Island and eight Nova Scotian vessels were brought into the New York Prize Court alone during the war.[57]

The first prize case noted in British North America was that of the *Labuan*. Early in 1862 this British steamer was seized at Matamoros, Mexico, by the United States' frigate *Portsmouth* for violation of the blockade. Great Britain protested the seizure, but before action could be taken, the judge of the New York Prize Court ordered the *Labuan* released, reserving the question of damages. Thereafter Lyons submitted repeated requests that damages be paid, and such was done in 1868. The *Labuan* was not a provincial ship, but the case received wide publicity in the Maritime Provinces, for a number of firms had legitimate trade with Mexico and still others were using Mexico as a way-station in shipping cargoes to the Confederacy.[58]

While the *Labuan* was being held, the seizure of a Nova Scotian ship created a furor in the Maritimes. A fast Halifax schooner, *Will o' the Wisp*, was seized by the U.S.S. *Montgomery* in the Rio Grande River off Matamoros and was sent to Key West for trial and adjudication. Captain Charles Hunter of the *Montgomery* contended that the *Will o' the Wisp*, which had gunpowder on board, was on the American side of the river illegally, but British witnesses insisted that it was in Texan waters with Hunter's permission. When news of the seizure reached Lunenburg in Nova Scotia, where the vessel was berthed, the "Bluenoses" declared Hunter's act an outrage almost equal to Captain Wilkes' stoppage of the *Trent*. At Key West the court adjudged the seizure illegal and released the ship. The Halifax merchants who had chartered the vessel then demanded compensation for their lost cargo of cotton and for damage done when Northern navy men who were

[57] Madaline R. Robinton, *An Introduction to the Papers of the New York Prize Court, 1861–1865* (New York, 1945), p. 151.
[58] F. L. Owsley, "America and the Freedom of the Seas, 1861–65," in Craven, ed., *William E. Dodd*, pp. 220–225.

taking the *Will o' the Wisp* to the prize court broke into the ship's liquor supply. While the merchants' demands were being presented by Lyons, the *Will o' the Wisp* slipped out of Halifax harbor with a cargo of contraband, and the following year she gained additional fame as a blockade runner before dropping out of sight.[59]

In addition to the Maritime blockade runners there were the usual number of petty annoyances calculated to try a diplomat's patience and occupy his time. One minor irritation would follow another almost as though they were organized. On the Great Lakes American ship owners required that all Canadian engineers take an oath of allegiance to the United States or forfeit their certificates, and in reprisal it was demanded that the Canadian Board of Railway Commissioners require oaths of allegiance to Her Majesty from American engineers passing through Canada West. In Washington John A. Kasson, the Assistant Postmaster General, ordered all postmasters to comply with an old but theretofore ignored ruling requiring postage on printed matter sent to the British North American provinces, thus decreasing the flow of free Northern newspapers across the border. In June, 1863, another Nova Scotian ship, the *Isabella Thompson,* was seized by the block-ading squadron, adding to Maritime annoyance, and the following month an officer from a Northern ship was threatened by a mob in Halifax.[60]

Following Lincoln's suspension of the habeas corpus in the North a great amount of time was consumed with correspondence over ar-

[59] CD, Halifax, IX: Jackson to Seward, Jan. 23, Feb. 3, July 21, 23, 1863; NFBL, 44: L. Brocker, deposition, June 7, and G. Tattran to Lyons, June 16, enc. in Stuart to Seward, July 19, 1862; NBL, 9: Seward to Lyons, June 16, Dec. 22, 1862, 200–202, 379–380; *ibid.,* 10: Jan. 28, 1864, 546; CFA, 85: Adams to Russell, Feb. 22, and Russell to Adams, Feb. 25, enc. in Adams to Seward, March 3, 1864; *ibid.,* 86: Russell to Adams, May 19, enc. in Adams to Seward, June 2, 1864; GBI, 19: Seward to Adams, Feb. 6, March 22, 1864, 179, 239; CO, and FO 97: Mulgrave to Newcastle, Nov. 26, 1863, Adams to Newcastle, Feb. 22, 1864, enc. in Newcastle to Doyle, n.d.; Halifax *Evening Express,* Jan. 28, 1863; Halifax *Acadian Recorder,* Aug. 1, 1863; *P.P., 1863,* LXXII, cols. 1–46; G.B., *Sess. Papers,* LXII: no. 12, cols. 513–560; Owsley, "Freedom of the Seas," pp. 225–226. See also Avila Larios, "Brownsville-Matamoras: Confederate Lifeline," *Mid-America,* n. s., XXIX (April, 1958), 77; M. P. Ursina, "Blockade Running in Confederate Times," Confederate Veterans' Assoc., *Addresses, 1895,* p. 36; and Hamilton Cochran, *Blockade Runners of the Confederacy* (Indianapolis, 1958), pp. 89–92.

[60] *Foreign Relations, 1864,* II, 385–387: Lyons to Seward, July 3, Welles to Seward, July 9, and Seward to Lyons, July 10, 1863; *Cong. Globe,* 38th Cong., 1st Sess., p. 2367; E 1, 90, AB: March 1, 1865, 131–132.

bitrary arrests of British North Americans who were charged with carrying letters to the Confederacy. One case, involving one Peter Needham, filled four volumes of Lyons' records, the most voluminous single subject with which he dealt during the Civil War. A typical case was that of John G. Shaver, imprisoned at Fort Warren without trial for allegedly carrying letters to Richmond. Apparently a Canadian by birth, Shaver was an employee of the Grand Trunk Railway and had been living temporarily in Louisville, Kentucky. He was jailed for three months and released only after he had taken an oath not to enter the Confederate states. Over a year later Lyons still was endeavoring to obtain compensation for Shaver because he had lost his job during his imprisonment, and Shaver was reviling the North throughout the Canadas.

Lyons was indignant over the arrest of British subjects but Earl Russell viewed such things more calmly, reminding his minister that Great Britain had acted in a similar manner in times of stress. In this, as with the question of the blockade, Russell showed farsightedness, for within three years the British were arresting American citizens in Ireland who were suspected of aiding the Fenian movement. Many of the arrest cases never were settled satisfactorily and many of those that were had to wait until as late as 1872.[61]

But if these fifteen months were relatively quiet on the North American diplomatic front, they brought an event of great domestic importance: the preliminary Emancipation Proclamation of September 23, 1862, which followed the battle of Antietam Creek in Maryland. The proclamation did not appreciably improve relations with British North America, however. The colonial press feared that the proclamation would stir up the horrors of a servile insurrection and that it would prolong the carnage by making the South fight more obstinately. It was viewed by many as done from military necessity or for its effect abroad, and those who already were predisposed to do so dismissed the proclamation as an incitement to a race war, a "piece of blotting paper . . . a demoniacal instrument." "Lincoln ought to be hung on a gibbet, with Seward on one side and Chase on the other . . . ," wrote one Britisher. "The Emancipation Proclamation after all," wrote

[61] G 1, 165: Monck to Newcastle, Nov. 10, 1861; *ibid.*, 168: Lyons to Seward, April 26, enc. in Newcastle to Monck, June 28, 1862; *ibid.*, 169: Lyons to Monck, Nov. 14, 1861, Newcastle to Monck, Jan. 31, 1863; Toronto *Globe*, March 7, 1862; Montreal *Advertiser*, Jan. 10, 1862; Ottawa *Citizen*, Sept. 27, 1862; New York *World*, Jan. 13, 1862; Rochester *Evening Express*, Jan. 15, 1862.

another, "is a piece of sheer humbug." It was a *petite chose*, a document of no importance that would be meaningful only to the antiquarian.[62]

Those who praised Lincoln's action also were predisposed to do so. The Toronto *Globe* admitted that it was a war measure but acclaimed the President for taking a "bold step" that was "right as well as politic . . . ." But only one influential, formerly anti-Northern, newspaper changed its views because of the proclamation. This paper, the Napanee *Standard*, considered that Lincoln had undertaken a "bold humanitarian act." On the other hand, many people seemed to think that emancipation would not be put into effect on the New Year as Lincoln had promised.[63]

Even when the Emancipation Proclamation of January 1, 1863, was announced, it caused no noticeable shift in public opinion. Most of the press declared that it was a barbaric act of which only Yankees were capable, a mistaken policy that, if announced eighteen months earlier, would have won universal praise in the provinces but which now, lacking even "a particle of principle," was hypocritical. The anti-Southern press repeated its words of praise from September, congratulated Lincoln for keeping his word, and used the proclamation as a weapon against rising efforts in Canada West to extend segregated schools for Negro children. Both factions agreed that Lincoln finally had rocked the boat, but the conservatives felt that he would sink only himself.[64] The people who had argued in 1861 that it was Lincoln's failure to declare a crusade against slavery that had led them to lose interest in the Northern cause did not manifest any sudden pro-Lincoln sentiments in 1863. A few ardent abolitionists may have felt that at last God was on the Northern side, but the proclamation appears to have had little practical effect in the provinces.[65]

The fifteen months of comparative quiet on the border were to be

[62] Fredericton *Head Quarters*, Sept. 24, 1862; Toronto *Leader*, Sept. 30, Oct. 17, 1862; Montreal *Gazette*, Sept. 26, 1862; Halifax *Christian Message*, Oct. 1, 8, 1862; *The Times*, Oct. 14, 1862; Ellice Papers, A-1, 2: Parkes to Ellice, Oct. 9, 1862.

[63] *Globe*, Sept. 23, 30, 1862; Montreal *Witness*, Sept. 27, 1862; *Standard*, Oct. 9, 1862.

[64] Barrie *Northern Advance*, Jan. 7, 1863; Saint John *New Brunswick Courier*, Jan. 3, 10, 1863; Sarnia *Observer*, Jan. 16, 1863; Toronto *Globe* and New York *Herald*, both Jan. 3, 1863; *The Times*, Jan. 19, 1863.

[65] The American Missionary Association reported that the proclamation had increased Canadian hostility to their own Negroes to an "exceedingly bitter" point. See A.M.A., *Seventeenth Annual Report* (Hopkinton, Mass., 1863), p. 27.

followed by nearly two years of increasingly deteriorating British North American-Federal relations. By the end of 1863 British neutrality was tested with respect to the provinces, and Governor General Monck was not found wanting. The Confederacy began to see how it might build "a fire in the rear" of the North that could embroil Great Britain in the Civil War, to the Confederacy's immense advantage, and before the end of the year the Confederate states were to send their first and only formal commission to the provinces. In response to increased Confederate activity in British North America Seward was to initiate a passport system, place restrictions on trade, and send new agents to the colonies as observers. These and other less visible means of controlling the border, while receiving belated cooperation from the imperial authorities, added to the growing anti-Northern sentiment. As Canada's leading military historian has noted, "The complacency of 1862 gave place to something like panic." [66]

[66] Charles P. Stacey, *The Military Problems of Canada* (Toronto, 1940), p. 60.

eight ⮂ CONTROLLING THE BORDER

"It is not necessary to be alarmists, but it is
wise to be ready."

LONDON *Canadian News*

BY 1863 IT WAS APPARENT FOR ALL TO SEE THAT THE AMERICAN CIVIL WAR
was not to be the short war anticipated in 1861. Realizing that it could
not win a victory on the battlefield alone, the Confederacy turned more
and more to what the Southern press sometimes described as "mere
diplomacy." Until 1864, efforts to help the South from within British
North America originated with unattached Confederates who used
the provinces as a rendezvous for escaped prisoners of war. By the
end of 1863, however, the Confederate administration was planning to
use this potentially destructive force against the North in hit-and-
run attacks originating in neutral territory. That the attacks, some of
them parts of grandiose schemes, might succeed in some limited ob-
jective was possible, but the more intelligent Southern leaders undoubtedly realized that a more likely effect of this channeling of latent
Southern strength in the colonies might be the winning of British intervention in the war.

Great Britain had observed her neutrality in her North American
colonies with care. During 1863 and thereafter the Canadian and Federal governments worked together to prevent the maturing of Confederate plots within the united provinces. The effect of this cooperation was detrimental to the South, but it hardly was an unneutral act,
as the Confederates contended, for Monck had every legal right to
report to Seward any information that he learned of Confederate plots.
When the plots had reached the stage of a clear and present danger to
the North, international usage held that the imperial and provincial

authorities could frustrate raids from British North American soil against a neighbor with whom Great Britain was at peace. Monck was acting not in the interests of the North but in the interests of British neutrality; that this hurt the South was true, but his was not an unneutral act. His intent was neutral, although the effect of his actions may not have been.

From 1862 the British North American provinces had been a rendezvous for Americans of many types. Southern emissaries on their way to Europe, dispatch-bearers returning from the continent's capitals, escaped Confederate soldiers, Northern observers, draft-dodgers, disgruntled Peace Democrats, and even the women spies necessary to all such cloak-and-dagger scenes met in the urban centers of the provinces. Consuls would report to Seward on the activities of known Confederates who were in their districts. The Secretary then would communicate with Lyons, asking that Monck take steps to frustrate any hostile expeditions. Canadian and Northern agents, paid informers, pro-Union Southerners, and even British civilians would supply the original information, would confirm it upon official request, and finally would conspire to trap Confederate plotters on the eve of their raid. The administration in the Canadas often preferred to avoid possible embarrassment and legal technicalities by allowing information to leak out that a plot had been discovered, thus forestalling the raid while permitting the plotters to remain free. In this way dozens of rumored raids failed to materialize, the plotters quietly slipping away from their rendezvous to begin designing another scheme.

Confederate agents who circulated throughout the free states obtaining military and political information would cross into the Canadas where they could travel to Halifax unmolested. At Halifax they boarded fast blockade-runners for Nassau and ultimately Wilmington. The North could intercept the agents only as they crossed the border into the provinces or when they ran the blockade. Success at either point was problematic, so the Federal War and State departments sent agents to the provinces to work their way into the confidence of the Confederates there. This, an early form of counterespionage, helped give British North America an air of wartime excitement upon which travelers frequently remarked.

The borderline was important because espionage work in the eighteen-sixties was intensely personal. Today the individual agent is not so important, for microfilm and electronics have made communication secret and rapid. An entire dispatch may be reduced to the size of a comma. To prevent communication by such means is extremely difficult, and the counterintelligence agent often must be content with making information difficult to obtain or with rendering it obsolete by delaying its transmittal rather than preventing its delivery once it has been obtained. But in 1863 information could be had for the asking. An efficient Southern agent could learn with comparative ease of troop movements, gun emplacements, or diplomatic squabbles. But the agent in 1863 had no rapid means of communication and no good means of duplication or reduction of records. He had to carry such records on his person or in his memory—and if he could be stopped or even delayed, his information might be made worthless. For this reason it was important for the North to guard the border and, at first despite Canadian disapproval and later with full approval, to send agents into the provinces.

Once within the provinces, Confederates found movement easy. The Great Western Railroad, running from Windsor, opposite Detroit, to Clifton, opposite Niagara Falls, afforded an opportunity for escape into the London district, where many Southerners congregated. Confederates found it more difficult to slip across the border at these two terminals, however, after Northern passport regulations were strengthened, and thereafter they traveled across Lake Ontario from Toronto or Hamilton on grain boats headed for ports in New York or slipped across the St. Lawrence River at night. During the winter the river was frozen over, making it possible to drive wagonloads of arms across the border. During the summer hundreds of skiffs passed up and down the river, making it difficult to detect an irregular river crossing. It was impossible, concluded Seward's trouble-shooting consul, David Thurston, to prevent documents from crossing the border. Southern dispatches were more likely to be intercepted at almost any point within British North America than at the border itself, for within the provinces the Confederates were not as cautious as they were when they attempted to pass the frontier line. Thereafter, border control could best be enforced from within the province.[1]

To watch and hinder Confederate activities, Seward, Stanton, Blair, and Chase sent special departmental agents into British North America to man listening posts. Monck was well aware of the nature of the North-South conflict within the provinces, and he felt that Seward's use of special agents to observe the Confederates was within legal

[1] NBL, 11: Seward to Lyons, May 31, June 24, 1864, 298–299, 393–394; CD, Montreal, v: Thurston to Seward, June 28, 1864.

bounds. The colonial and imperial administrations did not agitate themselves over such activities, and they were inclined to be tolerant of
the activities of both the blockade runners and those who made it
their business to stop them. Even occasional military activity near the
border on the part of the Union generally was understood in its correct light by 1863 by those in positions of responsibility. When two
new batteries were constructed near Eastport only a mile from Campobello Island, New Brunswick, Lieutenant Governor Gordon judged
their construction to be due to election promises and not to any intended threat. Rather than being alarmed by the fact that the new
Treat Island guns were so located as to make it impossible to fire them
without shot falling into the town of Welshpool on Campobello Island, he felt that the placement was another indication that the battery was not intended for use.[2]

However, when it appeared that Seward hoped to increase the number of consuls in Canada East, placing them at points where they were
needed for no apparent commercial purpose, Monck and Lyons objected, for they correctly suspected that the consuls had instructions
to report on British troop movements as well as on Confederate activities. Thomas Fitnam, who had been sent to the Gaspé basin, appeared to be more or less a free agent of Seward's, for he had operated
behind the lines in Virginia, and he now was cultivating the acquaintance of those residents of his area who drank heavily and talked loosely.
Beginning with a gala Washington's Birthday party in 1862, held despite the general cancellation of such parties elsewhere due to the
death of Lincoln's son, Willie, Fitnam gained a wide reputation for
his conviviality. It was to his type of consular agent that Lyons objected, and when submitting the State Department's annual estimate
in 1862 Seward had admitted to Congress that Fitnam and Charles
Ogden, consul at Quebec, were sent to Canada East to carry out "confidential agencies." Ogden, like Fitnam, therefore commonly was regarded by the Canadians as a spy.[3]

Fitnam and Ogden made use of every public occasion to praise
the North and to damn the Confederacy, but they were not spies,
for secrecy was not part of their equipment. Ogden, living in a single
Quebec hotel room with his wife and two sons, did employ the quiet
means of drinking with "low people" and talking with women of the

[2] CO 42: Gordon to Newcastle, Oct. 23, 1863.
[3] Toronto *Leader*, Jan. 16, 1862; Quebec *Morning Chronicle*, Jan. 17, 1862;
Watkin, *Recollections*, p. 454.

town to obtain information, but Fitnam preferred the more boisterous technique of the public spectacle to draw out opinion. During Fourth of July festivities in 1863 the latter presented no less than fourteen toasts to the celebrants, provocatively beginning with toasts to American independence and to the President of the United States before toasting Her Majesty, and following this tribute with spread-eagle oratory for the United States, its flag, its military might, and eventually, with a modicum of diplomacy, for the press and "Woman, dear Woman." He also engaged in frequent acrimonious public arguments with the agent for the government steamer that was berthed at Gaspé, especially after the agent and Joseph Howe, who had failed to win re-election to the premiership of Nova Scotia, gratuitously joined in offering three public cheers for "Jeff" Davis. Fitnam was not a spy, however, for despite his obvious superfluity as a consul, he still had to apply for funds and additional authority before he felt prepared to follow Southern agents to Quebec, and he was not paid from the "Secret Service fund." His chief service was in being situated at Gaspé, athwart the regular water route from Halifax to Quebec, so that he could report on new troop arrivals. Understandably the small beer diplomacy of Ogden and the champagne diplomacy of Fitnam created added resentment in the provinces.[4]

In 1862 Seward applied for exequaturs for new consulates at Coaticook, Kingston, Lacolle, and Morpeth, and for official recognition of Fitnam at Gaspé, all of which were in the united Canadas. The Canadian Minister of Finance reported to Monck that he did not consider that Lacolle and Morpeth, in particular, needed consuls, and Newcastle warned the Governor General that these appointments were not for commercial purposes. They were approved only with the accompanying condition that the United States station no more consular agents "at places where there is no trade," and when Seward made subsequent appointments, Lyons repeated the British request until Seward withdrew the new agents. However, Seward had other means of limiting Confederate activities in the provinces.[5]

In the summer of 1861 the State Department had issued a circular requiring that British North Americans must have passports before

---

[4] Seward Papers: J. McHugh to Seward, May 23, 1863; CD, Gaspé, 1: Fitnam to Seward, May 5, Dec. 26, 1863; Quebec *Morning Chronicle*, July 14, 1863.

[5] G 21, 441: Newcastle to Monck, Jan. 3, April 28, 1862, 311–313, 464, and Monck to Newcastle, March 1, 1862, 131; NFBL, 44: Lyons to Seward, May 10, 1862; *ibid.*, 63: May 11, 1863.

they could pass through the United States to embark from Portland or New York for Europe.[6] This was the first time that the northern boundary had been policed by the passport system, and in the Canadas the passport was regarded as a "badge of tyranny." The Maritime Provinces, which it affected less, apparently understood the necessity for it and complained very little.[7] The original order did not include people passing into the United States by railroad, however, and it generally was not applicable within the continent. The passport's original purpose was to prevent Southerners from traveling to Europe via Portland during the winter when the St. Lawrence River was closed, but forged documents were easy to obtain and the order failed to accomplish even its limited purpose.

The order served to confuse nearly everyone. The passport agents were confused as to how and to whom the directive should apply, and Canadians found it extremely inconvenient to apply within the United States for their passports. Monck therefore requested, through Lyons, that the American Consul General in Montreal be authorized to validate passports, and Seward consented. Later, Giddings himself unsuccessfully tried to secure a further mitigation of the passport system for Canadians.[8]

Mayors of the Canadian towns began to issue certificates of nationality in lieu of passports, hoping that they would be accepted in the United States. Seward complained of this practice, and with his consent it was arranged, in January, 1862, that the agents empowered to issue certificates of nationality over the signature of the Provincial Secretary should be appointed at various towns, and that the certificates would be given the force of passports by the Governor General or by State Department agents who were to be appointed to the Northern port cities for such a purpose. This system was open to abuse, however, for many reports reached Seward that agents demanded exorbitant sums to validate the certificates. In addition, the system, while possibly effective at such exposed and isolated places as Rouse's Point,

---

[6] Callahan, *Canadian Relations,* p. 279, incorrectly states that the first passport order was issued in 1864.

[7] Watkin, p. 520: Sept. 6, 1861; Ernest Gould, "Relations between the Maritime Provinces and the United States, 1854-67," unpubl. M.A. thesis (Univ. Toronto, 1934), p. 46.

[8] FO 5, 770: Lyons to Russell, Aug. 27, 1861; M.C.: E. L. D. Adams to Seward, Sept. 18, 1861; NBL, 9: Seward to Lyons, Nov. 27, 1861, 50-51; Albany *Evening Journal,* Dec. 7, 1861; CD, Saint John: Howard to Seward, Aug. 3, 1864; G 1, 166: Newcastle to Monck, Dec. 27, 1861, 501.

did not have the desired effect of policing Southerners who were crossing the border.[9]

Another such restriction on border traffic was the Federal government's wartime measures in relation to trade, and these were as unsuccessful in accomplishing their original purpose as was the passport
system. In April, 1862, exportation of anthracite coal was prohibited by
the Treasury Department at the instance of the Secretary of the Navy,
and in November it was forbidden to send arms or munitions out of
the country. In May, 1863, Lincoln extended the prohibition to horses,
mules, and other livestock.[10]

The exportation of livestock was prohibited in order to prepare for
an anticipated shortage of meat for the troops. The order of prohibition
was worded defectively, however, so that it applied to the entire animal, alive or slaughtered, but not to the flesh of the animals. The directive was ignored by the customs officials throughout 1863, at least
at Suspension Bridge, which was the chief point of entry into the
provinces for American livestock. When the order was enforced, beginning early in 1864, a number of Canadian packers appealed to Lyons
for help, since they had begun to find a market in England for Cana-
dian-cured but American-raised hogs. The prohibition never was effective anyway, for some customs official always could be persuaded
to ignore the directive and let live animals cross the frontier. These
violations, as well as the order itself, caused considerable irritation
in the Canadas, where those who obeyed it were placed at a disadvantage. After John F. Potter replaced Giddings as Consul General
in 1864, he suggested that the restriction either should be enforced
vigorously or removed altogether, but neither course was followed until President Andrew Johnson removed all of the wartime trade restrictions in June, 1865.[11]

The exportation of coal was prohibited because blockade-runners
were obtaining Northern anthracite, which made little smoke, from
British North American ports. It was this restriction that affected
Canadian merchants most adversely. From April, 1864, when Lyons
approached Seward concerning the prohibition, until the end of the

[9] NFBL, 43: Lyons to Seward, Jan. 24, 1862.
[10] NBL, 11: Seward to Lyons, March 18, 1864, 65–66; ITC, 36: Seward to Giddings, Feb. 19, 1864, 168–169; G 6, 232: Lyons to Monck, March 21, 1864.
[11] BMW to GCC, 11: memo., enc. in Lyons to Monck, March 18, 1864; G 6, 232:
Monck to Lyons, Jan. 9, enc. in Lyons to Monck, Feb. 24, 1864; CD, Montreal, v:
Potter to Seward, Aug. 23, 1864.

war, the two diplomats worked to find a solution. A firm in Trois-Rivières, Canada East, which manufactured railway wheels and which used large quantities of Lehigh coal, asked Lyons if it might replenish its supply by producing affidavits that the coal would not be sold. Seward refused, and the Governor General's Executive Council suggested that if the United States would withdraw its prohibition with respect to the interior line of the frontier, the Governor General might prohibit the exportation of any coal from any of the provinces, thus preserving a valuable trade and providing the factories and homes with much-needed fuel while preventing blockade-runners from making use of the anthracite. After some consideration Monck agreed that a proclamation to this effect would not be a violation of British neutrality, and Lyons presented the offer to Seward.[12]

While the Secretary of State was deliberating, a lengthy analysis of the problem, possibly prepared at Seward's request, arrived from Consul General Potter. The Montreal consul pointed out that Americans also were being harmed by the prohibition, for they often controlled the firms in the provinces that were being forced to curtail production for lack of coal. Welsh anthracite and English coke were being imported to keep the iron foundry business going, which cut into the American coal market in British North America. The use of American anthracite for domestic purposes had begun to take hold in the Canadas shortly before the war. Americans residing in the provinces had handled the coal business, and they and the ship-owners who had invested in special equipment for hauling coal were suffering unjustly, Potter argued. He then clinched his argument with two strong points: that a careful investigation on his part had revealed that only two small cargoes of anthracite had been re-exported from the Canadas, for anthracite was needed too much within the province, and that Canadians were delaying their coal purchases as long as they could in hope of obtaining American coal but that another winter without it might throw the Canadian market permanently open to Welsh coal, thus destroying this growing outlet for the American product. Blockade-runners were taking the new Welsh coal anyway, Potter noted, since it made no more smoke than American coal, and it could be obtained at Nassau and Halifax with ease, so that the prohibition on so-

---

[12] G 6, 232: Lyons to Monck, April 14, 1864; G 1, 465: Monck to Cardwell, May 6, 1864; NFBL, 65: Lyons to Seward, June 27, 1864; *Foreign Relations, 1864*, II, 667: Lyons to Seward, Aug. 4, 1864; Galt Papers, I: Fessenden to Galt, May 22, 1864, 845–846.

called smokeless anthracite was not having its desired effect. On behalf of the many American merchants residing in the provinces and, significantly, of the Clear Grit reformers who were thought to need some friendly gesture from the United States to use against the Liberal-Conservatives, the Consul General recommended that the restriction be removed.[13]

At Seward's suggestion Lincoln modified the prohibition on anthracite coal to permit its exportation to the Canadas except by sea, provided that the Governor General prevented re-exportation of the coal or its use in sea-going vessels. Monck issued such a proclamation even before the first shipment of coal reached the united provinces, and he asked Lyons to convey his "best thanks" to Seward. The Canadian order was enforced rigorously, even to preventing Welsh coal from being re-exported. In his proclamation Monck classified coal with arms, ammunition, gunpowder, and military and naval stores, on the grounds that coal could be used to increase the quantity and military effectiveness of such stores.[14] The Northern prohibition remained in effect for the Atlantic Provinces, however, and when, later in the year, the consul at St. John's, Newfoundland, reported that the Governor of that colony would issue a proclamation similar to Monck's if coal might be obtained to heat the city's homes during the winter, Seward informed him that the prohibition could not be rescinded because of the large number of blockade-runners operating from the maritime area.[15]

There were other Confederate activities than blockade-running originating in British North America. Assistant Secretary Frederick Seward kept the consuls in the provinces busy checking rumors. Some rumors had a basis in fact while others were utterly fantastic, but all had to be checked if control over Confederate activities was to be made even slightly effective. Rumors that Seward was coming to visit the provinces, that Jefferson Davis was dead, that ex-Confederate prisoners were gathering to raid New York, Buffalo, or Detroit were common-

[13] CD, Montreal, v: Potter to Seward, July 30, 1864.
[14] G 6, 233: Lyons to Monck, July 30, 1864; NFBL, 68: Lyons to Seward, Aug. 13, 1865; CD, Montreal, v: Potter to Seward, Aug. 13, and Proclamation of Governor General, enc. in Potter to Seward, Aug. 16, 1864.
[15] CD, St. John's, IV: C. O. Leach to Seward, Nov. 1, 1864. During the same months Seward and Lyons exchanged a coldly formal series of notes on the efficacy of the blockade, which touched upon trade with the Atlantic Provinces (NFBL, 67: Lyons to Seward, Aug. 4, 1864; NBL, 11: Seward to Lyons, Aug. 8, 1864, 573-575).

place. Rumors that the British were constructing sixty gunboats on the
Great Lakes or that they had forty gunboats at Bermuda, that Popish
French Canadians had thousands of guns and were ready to descend
on the Protestant states of the North, or that secret forts were being
built on Campobello Island were too wild for credence, but that Canadian and Maritime shipwrights were busy constructing vessels was
evident, and it was suspected that many of the ships had been financed
with Southern money. George N. Sanders, later to play a prominent
role in the St. Albans raid, entered Canada via the Suspension Bridge
disguised as a miner and passed on to England. Dozens of Morgan's
Raiders were showing up in Montreal. Young Southerners arrived in
Toronto, ostensibly to study law or religion at the university. Robert
E. Lee's body servant, Confederate bankers, personal messengers from
the Confederate Secretary of State, overrated woman spies like Rosa
"Rebel Rose" Greenhow and Belle Boyd—the movements of all were
reported by weary officers.[16]

It was rumored that Confederates planned to kidnap free Negroes
from Canada West by hiring squads of black workmen to go to the
oyster beds. A thousand rifles were shipped to Halifax, ostensibly for
Confederate use there, and a former Peace Democrat from Massachusetts who had become superintendent of a Toronto rolling mill tried
to send blueprints of what was thought to be a submarine torpedo to
the South via an employee, only to have his messenger captured and
his "model"—which turned out to be an alarm clock—confiscated.
Counterfeit Northern postage stamps from somewhere in Canada West
caused Detroit merchants considerable trouble, for in Michigan stamps
were used for small change in the absence of coins. It was reported,
doubtless with exaggeration, that there were one hundred thousand
Southerners in the provinces by 1863. A more circumspect estimate
was fifteen thousand. In either case it was impossible to check on them
all.[17]

[16] Cincinnati *Enquirer*, Dec. 29, 1862; John B. Brebner, *North Atlantic Triangle: The Interplay of Canada, The United States, and Great Britain* (New Haven, 1945), p. 163; Harold A. Davis, *An International Community on the St. Croix, 1604–1930*, Univ. of Maine, *Studies*, LII (Orono, 1950), 193–195; W. H. Rowe, *The Maritime History of Maine* (New York, 1948), pp. 188–206.

[17] ITC, 32: Seward to Jackson, Nov. 11, 1861, 114–115; ITC, 36: Seward to Gunnison, Dec. 22, 1863; CD, Montreal, IV: Giddings to Seward, Aug. 27, Oct. 30, Nov. 2, 1862, and April 13, 15, 1863; *ibid.*: F. B. Smith to Seward, March 26, 27 [in register only], Thurston to Giddings, Oct. 31, and W. P. Barton to Thurston, Dec. 14, 1862; *ibid.*, V: Potter to Seward, Sept. 21, and Thurston to Seward, June

In several of the cities of the provinces the Confederates established informal headquarters where they slept, drank, gathered to curse the North and to plot raids, and waited for someone with authority to show up to lead them. Across Nova Scotia and New Brunswick the Confederates had favorite stopping places—the Saverly House in Halifax, Hesslein's in Saint John, the Barker House in Fredericton, Renfrew's in Woodstock, Newcomb's in Tobique, the St. Louis Hotel and Russell House in Point Levi, the Clifton House at Niagara, and the American Hotel in Toronto. But it was to Montreal that most Confederates, with time hanging heavy on their hands, drifted.[18]

In Montreal the Confederate headquarters was St. Lawrence Hall, an imposing hotel with the only bar in the Canadas that served mint juleps. The Ottawa Hotel served as the Northern outpost in the city, while the lower-class Donegana Hotel, which stayed open during the winter for the first time in 1861 in order to cater to the Confederates, housed the escaped prisoners and those who had little money. A bachelor establishment, the Donegana was the only hotel in which Seward was unable to place an agent. During the war the North underwent the "guilt by association" phase of all efforts to combat "subversive activities." Anyone who stopped at St. Lawrence Hall was suspected of pro-Southern leanings, and if his name was obtainable, it was sent to Seward.[19]

28, 1864; *ibid.*, vɪ: Kimball to Thurston, July 21, 1864; CD, Quebec: Ogden to Seward, Aug. 24, Nov. 16, 1862; CD, Pictou, vɪɪ: B. H. Norton to Seward, May 5, 1862; CD, Saint John, ɪv: Howard to Seward, Nov. 8, 1862, Dec. 7, 1863, Aug. 11, 1864; CD, Halifax, ɪx: Vinton to Seward, July 2, Aug. 26, Nov. 11, 25, 1862; *ibid.*, x: Jackson to Seward, Feb. 20, 21, 1863, Feb. 27, Aug. 23, 1864; NBL, 9: Seward to Lyons, Nov. 29, 1862, 353; Seward Papers: J. Wier to Seward, March 18, 1862; N.A., War Records, 107, Letters Recd.: p. 224; Detroit *Advertiser and Tribune*, March 7, 1864; Detroit *Free Press*, Nov. 12, 14, 1863; Columbus (Ohio) *Crisis*, Nov. 18, 1863; Sarnia *Observer*, March 18, 1864; Halifax *British Colonist*, Nov. 11, 1862; Halifax *Chronicle*, Nov. 25, 1862; Fredericton *Head Quarters*, Oct. 22, 1862; Caleb Huse, *The Supplies for the Confederate Army: How they were Obtained in Europe and How Paid For* (Boston, 1904), p. 17; W. C. Borrett, *East Coast Port* (Halifax, 1944), pp. 97–101.

[18] Univ. of North Carolina, Edwin G. Lee Diary: Jan. 1–25, 1865.

[19] Lee Diary: Jan. 24, March 22, 1865; Montreal *Evening Pilot*, Nov. 19, 1861; *OR*, ser. ɪ, xxxɪx, 274–275: Hill to Fry; ITC, 38: Seward to Thurston, June 25, 1863, 3; CD, Montreal, ɪv: Giddings to Seward, April 8, 17, 20, 1863; *ibid.*, v: M. F. Chase to Thurston, June 22, 1864; Cleveland *Leader*, Aug. 14, 1863; J. Ross Robertson, *Robertson's Landmarks of Toronto* (Toronto, 1894), pp. 306–307; "A Run through Canada," *Hours at Home*, ɪ (July, 1865), 275; Newton, *Lord Lyons*, ɪ, 118. St. Lawrence Hall, Montreal, should not be confused with St. Law-

Nearby St. Johns, Canada East, was a major point of exchange for Confederate dispatches, which, according to consul Ogden, passed back and forth to Richmond more regularly than did official consular dispatches to Washington. Some of the British army officers stationed in the provinces who obtained the State Department's permission to visit the battlefront also carried Southern messages back with them. Money and arms arrived regularly from the South, so officials at Rouse's Point examined boxes and letters addressed to known Confederates, and agents rode the trains between Island Pond, Vermont, and Portland, Maine, the former place being the customs check-point for trains going to Montreal. When Southern plans for the forwarding of dispatches broke down late in the summer of 1863, Confederate Secretary of State Benjamin and his Assistant Secretary, L. Q. C. Washington, quickly made other arrangements, which apparently functioned well.[20]

During 1863 William "Colorado" Jewett, a mercurial Peace Democrat, was touring the provinces trying to persuade the British to mediate in the Civil War and acting as an effective propaganda instrument for the South. Jewett—who later was to act as the original messenger between Confederate Commissioner Jacob Thompson and Horace Greeley, editor of the New York *Tribune,* during the abortive "peace negotiations" at Niagara Falls—sent open letters to the provincial newspapers thanking the Canadians for extending to him the hospitality and shelter that his native land denied him, accusing Lincoln of lying about the feasibility of mediation, and declaring that an independent South would free her slaves, and the North, "united with the controlling power of Colorado," would renounce all intentions to annex the Canadas. The Toronto *Leader* and the Montreal *Herald* gladly reprinted Jewett's appeals, and the self-styled diplomatist was successful in obtaining noncommittal letters from Governor General Monck, and from Lieutenant Governors Gordon and Mulgrave that deplored the existence of the Civil War. Jewett unsuccessfully tried to submit these letters to Lord John Russell in England as proof that mediation would be received with official favor in North America.[21]

---

rence Hall, Cacouna, Canada East. For a picture of the former see C. W. Jefferys, *The Picture Gallery of Canadian History* (Toronto, 1950), III, 35.

[20] CD, Quebec: Ogden to Seward, Sept. 18, Nov. 16, 25, 1862; CD, Montreal, V: Thurston to Seward, June 21, 25, 28, 1864; M.C.: M. L. D. Adams to Seward, Dec. 2, 1861; C.S.A.: Benjamin to Mrs. Sanders, Oct. 6, 1863.

[21] Jewett, *Mediation Position of France* (London, 1863), with correspondence

The presence in Canada West of Clement Vallandigham, the "copperhead martyr," embarrassed the imperial administration, but the right of sanctuary for political exiles made it possible for him to remain. In June, 1863, Vallandigham had been nominated as the gubernatorial candidate on the Democratic ticket in Ohio, and he directed his unsuccessful campaign of protest against Lincoln from an unofficial headquarters in Windsor, opposite Detroit, from which his advisers virtually commuted. The formerly anti-British Vallandigham was fêted at a public dinner in Montreal, and he traveled to Niagara Falls in a special coach furnished by the Grand Trunk Railway. The railroad's President, William Walker, its Managing Director, C. J. Brydges, Governor Alexander Dallas of the Hudson's Bay territory, and John A. Macdonald all called upon him; Thomas D'Arcy McGee introduced him on the floor of Parliament, and the Stadacona Club of Quebec gave Vallandigham a private dinner at which British financier Edward Watkin presided. After this, Seward no longer answered Watkin's letters. The Toronto *Globe* was quick to remind these solicitous Canadians that Vallandigham had been among those Congressmen who had approved Captain Wilkes' action in the *Trent* affair, and by October, when he lost the election, Canadians apparently no longer were interested in him. Both Jewett and Vallandigham received considerable attention from Seward's consular agents.[22]

In Washington Seward had taken steps against possible Confederate agents in the State Department. During the spring of 1861 the State Department had been purged of known Confederate sympathizers. No one was proved to be disloyal, although consul Albert Catlin at Charlottetown, Prince Edward Island, had his salary withheld because of secessionist sentiments, and some customs officials along the Canadian border were thought to be pro-Southern. Catlin recanted his pro-Southern statements, took an oath of allegiance, had his salary restored, but lost the office anyway. Assistant Secretary Frederick Seward later declared that after the purge no state secrets ever were betrayed and

---

with C. L. Vallandigham, pp. 3–4; Toronto *Leader*, Oct. 6, 10, 20, 1863; Seward Papers: Jewett to Seward, Nov. 13, 1863; CD, Halifax, x: Jackson to Seward, May 7, 1863; *OR*, ser. I, XXXIX, 274–275: Hill to Fry; ITC, 38: Seward to Thurston, June 25, 1863, 3; CD, Montreal, IV: Giddings to Seward, April 8, 17, 20, 1863; *ibid.*, v: M. F. Chase to Thurston, June 22, 1864; Cleveland *Leader*, Aug. 14, 1863.

[22] CD, Quebec: Ogden to Seward, July 13, 15, Aug. 19, 22, 1863; CD, Halifax, x: Jackson to Seward, July 7, Aug. 21, 1863; Detroit *Advertiser and Tribune*, Aug. 1, 1863; Watkin, pp. 455–456.

no paper lost. There is considerable evidence to the contrary, however, and it was in affairs relating to British North America that the State Department had the most difficulty.[23]

Plagued with overwork, ill-trained clerks, a pusillanimous Congress, missing dispatches, and uncertain and slow contact with the consuls, Seward often had to allow consuls to act upon their own responsibility in times of emergency. Most of the consuls did their work well, and M. M. Jackson, in particular, sank himself into personal debt in order to finance the wide-ranging activities of his consulate. Through his almost daily reports two million dollars worth of Confederate-destined cargo was captured. On the other hand, Seward may have realized that Giddings was doing an inadequate job at Montreal, for the abolitionist was sounded out through his friend Sumner about accepting the mission to Haiti.[24]

Some dispatches were so slow in reaching their destinations as to be out of date when they arrived. Gloucester, Canada, was confused with Gloucester, England, by clerks; dispatches to Howard at Saint John were missent to St. John's, Newfoundland, and dispatches to Thurston at Toronto and later at Montreal were missent to London. From time to time important dispatches from Montreal would fail to reach Washington. As the Consul General noted, the loss of one dispatch could be attributed to accident, but several, mailed in person at the Montreal post office with official seals affixed, failed to reach their destinations. While representations were made to the Canadian postal authorities, the Consul General found that he had to turn to the local express agency to assure that his dispatches would not be tampered with, lost, or read by Southern agents in Canada East. It is especially significant that entire series of letters dealing with a par-

[23] CD, Halifax, IX: Vinton to Seward, Aug. 24, 1861; CD, Charlottetown, I: J. H. Sherman to Seward, Dec. 24, 1861, Jan. 8, 28, 1862, and Catlin to Seward, Feb. 3, 11, 1862; CD, Montreal, IV: J. Howe to Seward, May 14, and Giddings to Seward, June 19, 1862; M.C.: Howard to Seward, Feb. 15, 1862; Frederick Seward, *Seward at Washington* (New York, 1916), II, 633–634; H. M. Hyman, *Era of the Oath: Northern Loyalty Tests during the Civil War and Reconstruction* (Philadelphia, 1954), p. 9. Hyman seems to be in error in stating that Catlin retained his post.

[24] Giddings Papers: Sumner to Giddings, June 13, and Giddings to Giddings, Jr., June 19, 1862; D.L., 62: Seward to J. R. Doolittle, 1863, 533–534; Willshire Butterfield, "Mortimer Melville Jackson," *Magazine of Western History*, V (Jan., 1887), 426; *Our Representatives Abroad* (New York, 1874), p. 304. Jackson is the only consul to British North America to appear in Allen Johnson and Dumas Malone, eds., *Dictionary of American Biography* (22 vols., New York, 1928–44).

ticular subject might disappear, as when, at the end of the war, two dispatches and a telegram dealing with Southerners in the Canadas who might be implicated in the assassination of Lincoln dropped from sight.[25]

As Confederates began to use the provinces as a base for potential operations, it became more difficult for British North Americans to retain any pretense of personal neutrality. In the several provinces the various administrations gave little indication of official partiality until the Confederate plotters made some overt move that could compromise the British position. Monck tried to maintain his official neutrality in everything that he said or wrote, and although his sister-in-law sensed that he hoped for a Northern victory, he prudently did not make his wish explicit. On one occasion in a dispatch to Colonial Secretary Cardwell he absent-mindedly used the phrase "disloyal Citizens of the United States," an expression that he carefully changed to "persons described as 'disloyal Citizens . . .' " for his final draft. Gordon in New Brunswick and Mulgrave and Doyle in Nova Scotia disliked the North while the Governor of Newfoundland was pro-Northern but they too gave little indication of their sentiments in their official acts.[26]

Monck did not wait for an overt action, however. During the first week of November, 1863, Northern military authorities learned that Confederate agents in Montreal were trying to buy two vessels there and that a large sum of Confederate money had been sent by Confederate Secretary of the Treasury C. G. Memminger and Confederate Secretary of State Judah P. Benjamin to Canada West. This in-

[25] CD, Montreal, v: Potter to Seward, July 26, Sept. 16, 1864; *ibid.*, viii: Averill to Seward, Dec. 7, 1866. It also is possible that the various "lost" dispatches were received in Washington but were improperly filed before their contents were noted. Some support is given to this possibility by the large number of errors that the writer found in the official registers of the Department of State and by the fact that some instructions to the consuls contain acknowledgments of receipt of dispatches that later instructions declared had not been received. Perhaps some dispatches, sent to other executive departments for comment, were not returned.

[26] CD, St. John's, iii: W. S. H. Newman to Seward, Sept. 19, 1861; CD, Montreal, iv: Giddings to Seward, April 13, 1863; CD, Quebec, Ogden to Seward, March 19, 26, 1864; CFA, 82: Adams to Seward, March 13, 1863; G 9, 41: Monck to Cardwell, June 9, 1864, draft; Seward Papers: A. Russell to Seward, Sept. 21, 1864; L.C., Moran Diary, xiii: Jan. 1, 1864, and printed in Sarah A. Wallace and Frances E. Gillespie, eds., *The Journal of Benjamin Moran, 1857–1865* (Chicago, 1949), ii, 1252 (the writer used the original diary at the L.C. first and later checked it against the printed version in each case).

formation was sent to Consul General Giddings and apparently was reported to Monck as a matter of routine. On November 9 Lieutenant Colonel B. H. Hall, acting Assistant Provost Marshal General in Detroit, reported to his commanding officer, Colonel James B. Fry, that about two thousand Confederates were known to be in Canada West and that a former officer, who recently had returned from Toronto, supported Hill's belief that the Confederates intended to attack Johnson's Island. Lieutenant Colonel J. R. Smith, commanding officer at Detroit, also informed Brigadier General J. D. Cox, Commander for the District of Ohio, that an attack on the island was possible. Cox asked Giddings to investigate, thus reinforcing the original report that Giddings had received, and again Giddings apparently referred the matter to Monck. On November 10 Smith telegraphed Cox that a raid might be expected within forty-eight hours. Cox was skeptical but ordered a detachment of infantry to Sandusky. In the meantime Monck, who had learned of the plot against the island from another source, had been investigating the various reports.[27]

Johnson's Island was one of the most important Northern camps for Confederate prisoners of war. It lay a few thousand yards out into Lake Erie off Sandusky, Ohio. The island had been chosen because other islands on the lake were considered to be too close to Canada West to make imprisonment effective. Most of the more than two thousand Confederate prisoners on Johnson's Island were officers, and many of them were from John Morgan's famed band of raiders. Until the end of the war Confederates in the province plotted to cross Lake Erie, attack the prison camp while its defending ship, the U.S.S. *Michigan*—which no longer was used as a training vessel—was cruising on the lake, release the prisoners, and cut a swath through Ohio and Indiana to Kentucky. This basic plan took on more and more romantic elements as the possibility of success declined.[28]

As early as February, 1863, Stephen R. Mallory, the Confederate Secretary of the Navy, had been approached by a Lieutenant William Murdaugh with a scheme to seize the *Michigan* while it was docked at Erie, Pennsylvania, and to use it to destroy the aqueduct of the Erie

[27] Rochester *Evening Express,* Nov. 16, 1863; *OR,* ser. III, III, 1008, 1012-15: Cox to Col. W. Hoffman.
[28] William B. Hesseltine, *Civil War Prisons: A Study in War Psychology* (Columbus, Ohio, 1930), p. 38; Erie Mesnard, "Surveys on the Fire Lands so called . . . ," *Fire Lands Pioneer,* v (June, 1864), 97; Horace Carpenter, "Plain Living at Johnson's Island," *Century Illustrated Monthly Magazine,* XLI (March, 1891), 705-718.

Canal and to bombard Tonawanda, New York. This scheme apparently had been suggested by J. D. Bulloch, the Confederacy's naval agent in England. Mallory had agreed to the plan almost at once but much time was lost in persuading Jefferson Davis to support it. The Confederate President reasoned that the plot might arouse such protest in Great Britain as to halt the building of Confederate iron-clads then in progress there. Murdaugh thought that the Canadians might object when he asked to pass the captured ship through the Welland Canal, but otherwise he was not worried. From this scheme grew the abortive lake raid of 1863.[29]

On November 11 Governor General Monck finished his investigation and decided to take action before the anticipated raid could get under way. A late night telegram to Lyons authorized the minister to warn Seward of "a serious and mischievous plot" that had been originated in the Canadas by unidentified people who were "hostile to the United States." Monck ordered that the Welland Canal be watched and that any suspicious steamboat be stopped. Lyons at once sent a special messenger to Seward to warn him that an attack on Johnson's Island was imminent. The next day Michigan's Governor, Austin Blair, and one of her congressmen, Zachariah Chandler, notified Secretary of War Stanton that a raid was expected, and Chandler asked that heavy guns be rushed to Lake Erie from Pittsburgh, but the Secretary of War already had been informed.[30]

Shortly before midnight Seward took Stanton away from a nocturnal reading of Charles Dickens to tell him of Lyons' warning. Stanton dispatched telegrams to the governors of the lake states, to the mayors of potentially threatened cities, and to the military commanders of New York, Pennsylvania, and Ohio, and additional batteries and troops were sent to Sandusky. At first Port Stanley was thought to be the Confederate rendezvous, but an investigation there by Northern agents revealed nothing, so Lieutenant Colonel Smith sent the steamer *Forest Queen* around Lake Erie looking for the plotters. The captain searched the Canadian shore of the lake and, finding no raiders, declared that the reports were unfounded.[31]

[29] *ORN*, ser. 1, 11, 828–829: Murdaugh to Mallory, Feb. 7, 1863, and 823: Minor to Buchanan, Feb. 2, 1864; Joseph T. Durkin, *Stephen R. Mallory: Confederate Navy Chief* (Chapel Hill, 1954), pp. 286–288.
[30] NFBL, 56: Lyons to Seward, Nov. 11, 1863; *OR*, ser. 111, 111, 1019: Chandler to Stanton, Nov. 12, 1863.
[31] *Ibid.*, pp. 1022–23, 1032–1036: D. C. Judson to King, and Cox to Stanton, Nov.

This report to the contrary, Canadian and American officials remained active. John Sandfield Macdonald, the Canadian Prime Minister, went to Buffalo to confer with General John A. Dix and Mayor William Fargo. Monck asked Sir Fenwick Williams to keep men at Port Colborne and St. Catharines until navigation on the Great Lakes closed. Dix called out a regiment of New York militia, and Fort Porter at Buffalo was put in a state of defense. On the same day it was rumored that Confederates planned to attack Detroit, and a thousand laborers were sent to Belle Isle in the Detroit River where they felled trees near the shore and built a temporary barricade.[32]

Several Northern newspapers doubted that a raid had been planned at all and said that Monck had made a dramatic and empty gesture to win Northern friendship.[33] Another portion of the press believed that an attack was intended but discounted the importance of Monck's warning altogether on the grounds that it came after Northern officers had learned of the plot. It was implied by some that the Canadians were conniving with Vallandigham and the Confederates to let an armed steamer pass through the Welland Canal. A typical headline in the Rochester *Evening Express,* for example, "Canadian Gunboat on the Way to Burn Sandusky," was misleading, unfair, and inflammatory.[34]

Consul General Giddings lent some weight to the contention that Monck's warning was for publicity purposes by reporting that he had learned nothing that supported the existence of such a plot until he read of it in a newspaper. He added that Luther Holton, Canadian assemblyman from Châteauquay, who was his unofficial liaison with Monck, also knew nothing of any plots. When Preston King, a personal friend sent by Seward to inquire into the extent of the danger, arrived, Giddings said that he could discover no danger whatsoever.

12, Smith to L. Thomas, Nov. 13, and Cox to W. T. H. Brooks, Nov. 14, 1863, and pp. 1013-15: Stanton, tels., Nov. 11, 1863; Detroit *Advertiser and Tribune,* Nov. 14, 1863; Beale, ed., *Diary of Edward Bates,* IV, 314: Nov. 13, 1863; James Schouler, *History of the United States of America under the Constitution* (New York, 1899), VI, 411-412, n. 3.

[33] FO 5, 897: Donohoe to Lyons, Nov. 16, enc. in Lyons to Russell, Nov. 20, 1863; Williams Papers: Monck to Williams, Nov. 14, 1863; Detroit Public Library, N. W. Brooks Papers: Brooks to son, J. Wilson, Nov. 19, 1863; Buffalo *Express,* Nov. 16, 1863.

[33] Detroit *Free Press,* Nov. 13, 1863; Detroit *Advertiser and Tribune,* Nov. 12, 13, 1863; Rochester *Evening Express,* and Sandusky *Herald,* both Nov. 12, 1863.

[34] Nov. 13, 1863; New York *Times,* Nov. 13, 1863; Rochester *Union and Advertiser,* Nov. 12, 1863.

On the other hand, consul Thurston said that he had learned through an informant of general details concerning such a scheme. In view of Thurston's statement and of later developments, it seems probable that Giddings, who was none too efficient anyway, was trying to "save face" when the Governor General and the Northern military authorities uncovered a plot within his own territory.[35]

Preston King was commissioned to talk with Monck about the Governor General's warning. Lyons had telegraphed Monck that Seward wanted to send a special agent for this purpose, and Monck had replied that he would rather limit contacts with the Federal government to Lyons. However, King already had been commissioned and sent ahead, Seward's formal note of appointment having been delayed for a day, possibly in order to forestall just such a refusal on Monck's part. Using code, Lyons advised Monck to receive King and to "get rid of him as soon as is consistent with perfect courtesy," since greater embarrassment would result from trying to stop the mission than from letting it proceed.[36]

Although Monck did not reveal the ultimate source of his information, an informed guess is possible. It was rumored that one George P. Kane had instigated the plot. Kane was a former police officer from Baltimore who had been arrested in 1861 for alleged complicity in Confederate affairs in Maryland. He later had slipped into the Canadas via Halifax.[37] Some credence is given to this rumor by the fact that Monck had obtained his information through the British consul in Baltimore. The consul apparently was in Confederate confidences, for Lyons warned Monck by cipher that the consul must never be suspected of revealing any information. The consul never told the name of his informant, although it is probable that the informant did not serve Monck again, for Kane, at least, correctly guessed his identity and undoubtedly gave his name to the Confederate agents in the provinces.[38]

---

[35] CD, Montreal, IV: Giddings to Seward, Nov. 13, 21, 1863; Special Agents, 22: King to Seward, Nov. 21, 1863.

[36] G 13, 1: Lyons to Monck, Nov. 13, 1863, in cipher; Special Agents, 22: King to Seward, Nov. 14, 1863; FO 5, 896: Lyons to Russell, Nov. 13, and Seward to Lyons, Nov. 12, 13, 1863.

[37] CD, Halifax, X: Jackson to Seward, Jan. 25, 1864; Rochester *Evening Express,* Nov. 14, 1863; J. T. Scharf, *History of Baltimore City and County* (Philadelphia, 1881), pp. 133, 788–791.

[38] G 13, 1: Lyons to Monck, Nov. 16, and Monck to Lyons, Nov. 17, 24, 1863, all in cipher.

Here was an example of truly clever diplomacy. Lyons also had heard, presumably through the British consul in Baltimore, of the plot against Johnson's Island, but he had chosen to remain silent and to let Monck have credit for sending the warning to Seward, thus helping to allay anti-Canadian sentiment, which was becoming so vocal in the North. Monck, by a slip of the tongue, mentioned to Preston King that Lyons had told him of the plot sometime earlier, but Monck wrote Lyons that he was certain that the significance of the slip had escaped King, and apparently such was the case, since King evidently did not report the conversation to Seward.[39]

The effect was as Monck and Lyons must have hoped. On November 15 the plotters returned to Windsor publicly declaring that their plans, now postponed, had been frustrated by the British.[40] Some of the Northern press continued to comment that there had been no plot, but most of the Fourth Estate, including the New York *Herald*, praised the Canadian and imperial authorities for their prompt action. At least one pointed out that Canadian authorities actually could do very little to prevent such raids and prophesied that the North would have to contend with actual raids in due course, and the New York *Herald* soon added that the friendly act was "at the bottom" a selfish one. There was disagreement as to the probable effects of a successful raid, the New York *World* contending that it would embroil the United States in war with Great Britain while the Detroit *Advertiser and Tribune* argued that it would be the South that would be embroiled. Consul Donohoe at Buffalo reported to Lyons that "the best possible feeling towards the Canadian authorities" had been created by Monck's timely warning. Seward wrote to Adams praising Monck and the Canadian authorities while blaming the imperial authorities for having made such a plot possible by giving the Confederacy even that measure of recognition implied in Her Majesty's proclamation of neutrality.[41]

The response of the Canadian press was similar to that of the

[39] *Ibid.*: Lyons to Monck, Nov. 18, and Monck to Lyons, Nov. 19, 1863. A check of the Baltimore consul's dispatches has thrown no further light on the affair.

[40] *OR*, ser. III, III, 1043: Cox to Stanton, Nov. 15, 1863.

[41] *Herald*, Nov. 16, 17, 1863; Detroit *Free Press*, Nov. 13, 14, 1863; Rochester *Daily Union and Advertiser*, Nov. 12–17, 1863; *World*, Nov. 14, 1863; *Advertiser and Tribune*, Nov. 11, 1863; Williams Papers: Monck to Williams, Nov. 20, 24, 1863; Special Agents, 22: King to Seymour, Dec. 22, enc. in King to Seward, Dec. 23, 1863; Toronto *Globe*, Nov. 18, 1863; *Foreign Relations, 1863*, II, 1274: Nov. 18; FO 5, 897: Donohoe to Lyons, Nov. 16, enc. in Lyons to Russell, Nov. 20, 1863.

Northern. At first the news of the plot was thought to be a hoax. However, when Monck warned Seward, the newspapers generally agreed that he acted wisely and from necessity.[42] The Barrie *Northern Advance* was angered by Sandfield Macdonald's visit to Buffalo, "that most anti-British of all frontier towns," and called the premier a man of "weakness and vacillation" because he had interfered in the Confederates' activities. It lashed out at the North with a *non sequitur*: "If these people mean war let them have it." The Toronto *Leader* also refused to believe that refugees from Northern tyranny would abuse the laws of their hosts, for Southerners were too "manly and honorable." [43]

For several weeks doubt that a raid had been planned grew in people's minds. Finally Monck was vindicated, for in London the Confederate *Index* admitted that there had been an abortive plot against Johnson's Island. Defending the intended raiders, the *Index* said that British neutrality was in no way compromised, for the raid had been organized, with a gentle touch of irony, through the personal column of the New York *Herald;* that every item to be used in the raid had been purchased in New York state, not in Canada West, and that although Canadians had asked to participate in the raid, their help had been refused.[44] It also was reported that the ultimate leader of the plot, one R. D. Minor, had obtained accurate maps that showed the location of every grain elevator and warehouse from Chicago to Oswego. According to one report, thirty-six officers and three hundred men had planned to convey the Confederate prisoners from Johnson's Island across the provinces to Halifax.[45]

Temporarily further support was lent to Monck's position when the Washington *Morning Chronicle* published what appeared to be a copy of the Confederate Secretary of the Navy's Annual Report for 1863.

[42] See, for example, Toronto *Globe*, Nov. 16, 18, and Sarnia *Observer*, Nov. 20, 1863.

[43] *Northern Advance*, Nov. 25, 1863; *Leader*, Nov. 13, 1863; CD, Quebec: Ogden to Seward, Jan. 7, 1864.

[44] "The Canadian Expedition," *The Index*, IV (Feb. 18, 1864), 107; G 1, 159: Adams to Russell, Feb. 22, enc. in Newcastle to Monck, March 1, 1864, 156–160; CFA, 85: Russell to Adams, Feb. 24, enc. in Adams to Seward, Feb. 25, and Moran to Seward, Feb. 20, 1864.

[45] Buffalo *Courier*, Dec. 12, 1863; New York *World*, Dec. 16, 1863; Rochester *Evening Express*, Nov. 17, 1863. Minor's report on the abortive raid was printed in the Richmond *Dispatch*, Dec. 15, 1895, and reprinted as "The Plan to Rescue the Johnson's Island Prisoners," in Southern Historical Soc., *Papers*, XXIII (1895), 283–290.

The report stated that Secretary Mallory had sent twenty-seven com-missioned officers and forty petty officers to British North America to organize an expedition against Johnson's Island. The original of this report had appeared on December 15 in the New York *Sun* together with an undoubtedly genuine report by the Confederate Secretary of the Treasury. Apparently neither Seward nor Lyons noticed the reports in the *Sun* or when they were reprinted in the New York *Times* and *Herald* and the Washington *Star*. It was not until Mallory's report was printed in the *Morning Chronicle* that either Seward or Lyons learned of it. Seward sent an extract from the report to Charles Francis Adams, declaring that he had no doubts about its authenticity and suggesting that it be used to show how the Confederacy had violated British neutrality. Lyons inquired as to the validity of the report and then sent extracts from it to Monck with the opinion that it was genuine. Monck chortled that no one could sneer at his "gul-libility" any longer.[46]

That Seward would accept the "Mallory Report" as genuine was natural, for it supplied moral ammunition for his complaints about British neutrality, but that Lyons did so reveals how his anti-Southern views led him astray. A careful reading of the report would have shown that it was a fake. It bore no date, was irregularly addressed to the Speaker of the House rather than to the President of the Con-federate States, and it was too damaging to the Southern cause. No Secretary of the Navy would have expressed himself with such candor.

Adams did read the extracts closely, and he wisely decided to wait until the next ship brought a full copy. While he waited, Matthew Fontaine Maury, the famed Southern oceanographer, denounced the report in a letter to the London *Herald*. As late as February 25 Seward continued to insist that the report was genuine, but on March 10 Mal-lory broke his strange silence with a letter to the Richmond *Sentinel* that branded the report a complete forgery. Seward then began the investigation that he should have made originally.[47]

The original "Mallory Report" had been concocted by Moses G. Beach, an editor of the New York *Sun*, in two hours one December afternoon. Beach had given no thought to its consequences and, like

[46] GBI, 19: Seward to Adams, Dec. 20, 1863, 103–106, and Jan. 4, 1863 [*sic* for 1864], 114–122; CFA, 85: Adams to Russell, Jan. 19, enc. in Adams to Seward, Jan. 21, 1864; Williams Papers: Monck to Williams, Dec. 28, 1863; BMW to GCC, 11: Lyons to Monck, Dec. 22, 1863; Sarnia *Observer*, Jan. 15, 1864; Ernest Baldwin, "The 'Mallory Report' and Its Consequences," *National Magazine*, xi (March, 1899), 556–557.
[47] *Ibid.*, pp. 558–559; London *Herald*, Jan. 29, 1864.

James Gordon Bennett of the *Herald*, only seemed interested in attacking the British North American provinces, for he had implicated certain Canadians in the Johnson's Island plot. Now frightened, Beach wrote to Seward that he had something to say about the report, and Thurlow Weed was sent to talk with the editor. Beach confessed his authorship, and Seward wrote to Adams that the report was spurious. He did not act gracefully in admitting his mistake, however, for he did not want information concerning the falsity of the report communicated to Russell unless it was found to be absolutely necessary, and he continued, in the face of all contrary evidence, to insist that Beach had taken the substance of his ideas from an actual report and that the editor was denying the fact in order to protect some anonymous informant in Richmond.[48]

Despite Seward's wish, Adams felt it best to inform Russell of the spurious nature of the report. The minister confided to his diary that it seemed Seward did not understand the need for less aggressive tactics in dealing with Britain and that the Secretary of State erroneously expected a policy of agitation to produce results. Adams shared Seward's conviction that Beach was attempting to protect the guilty, for Adams apparently believed that the Mallory report, while fictitious in form, was based on facts passed on to Beach by an informant.[49]

The Confederates were angry with Lyons in particular for having been taken in by the report. John Slidell wrote from Paris that the article had been accepted because Lyons had wished to be deceived and that the minister had "rendered himself fairly obnoxious" by his "servile submission to the dictates of Seward . . . ." The New York *Times* rationalized its acceptance of Beach's fabrications and defended the administration on the grounds that the report had said what everyone knew to be true and that the British officials would not have accepted it had they not felt this to be so.[50]

Raids and rumors of raids came not single spies but in battalions thereafter. The Governor of Vermont feared an attack from Canada East and asked for five thousand rifled muskets for defense. General Dix asked if the Canadian authorities should not be called on through Lyons to prevent such a raid, for border warfare might result. Confederates in Montreal reportedly meant to plunder Plattsburgh and Burlington and to seize Fort Montgomery. General John Morgan was

---

[48] CFA, 85: Adams to Russell, April 4, enc. in Adams to Seward, April 7, 1864; GBI, 19: Seward to Adams, March 21, 1864, 240; New York *Times*, May 16, 1864.
[49] CFA, Diary: March 28, April 4, 1864.
[50] *ORN*, ser. II, III, 1107: Slidell to Benjamin, May 2, 1864.

thought to be in Toronto to organize a raiding party, and a hundred British soldiers were ordered to Windsor to prevent the departure of a band of three thousand Confederates said to be there. The most interesting report was that the same three thousand Confederates intended to raid Sandusky by walking across the ice of Lake Erie from Point Pelee, a distance of some thirty miles.[51]

The abortive raid had been exploited by the British in such a manner as to mitigate much of the anti-Canadian feeling on the American side of Lake Erie. Seward made use of the episode to suggest that Her Majesty's Government should make more effective provision for enforcing her neutrality laws while thanking Russell for the cooperation shown by Lyons and Monck. Canadians who openly had fraternized with Southerners were impressed by Monck's actions and realized, perhaps for the first time, the seriousness of their position. As a result, relations between the North and the provinces were improved by Monck's timely warning. However, this improvement was short-lived, for the next organized Confederate plot was to prove more successful. Both North and South were soon to damn the united provinces. The South felt that the imperial authorities were far too strict in preventing border raids, while the North felt that the same authorities were too lax in preventing incursions because they refused to act against the Confederates until it was evident that aggression across the border was intended.[52]

But before considering the more successful Confederate plots of the last eighteen months of the war, and the effect of those plots and Seward's countermeasures on British North American neutrality, imperial policy, and Canadian affairs, it would be well to pause to examine certain long-range factors involved in the shaping of British North American opinion, to consider the problems of "crimping" within the provinces and provincial enlistments in the American armies, and to consider the role of the British North American West in diplomatic relations during the war.

[51] *OR*, ser. III, III, 1091–92: Stanton to Dix, Nov. 24, 1863, and 1096: Dix to Stanton, Nov. 25, 1864; CD, Quebec: Ogden to Seward, Jan. 20, 1864; Quebec *Gazette*, Nov. 25, 1863; Toronto *Leader*, Dec. 1, 1863; Sarnia *Observer*, Jan. 22, 1864; Rochester *Union and Advertiser*, Dec. 14, 1863.

[52] FO 5, 897: W. T. H. Brooks to Stanton, and Cox to Stanton, both Nov. 13, enc. in Lyons to Russell, Nov. 17, 1863; CFA, 84: Adams to Seward, Dec. 10, 1863; CD, Quebec: Ogden to Seward, Nov. 17, 1863; Special Agents, 22: Thaddeus Stevens to King, Dec. 16, 1863.

nine ϨϿ THE BRITISH NORTH AMERICAN WEST AND THE CIVIL WAR

> "Events of great consequence take place before our eyes, but their significance is not at first apparent."
>
> SAMUEL G. WARD, *1862*

THE CIVIL WAR HAD LITTLE IMMEDIATE EFFECT UPON THE PEOPLE OF the Hudson's Bay Company's territory or of the Far Western colonies of British Columbia and Vancouver Island. At the individual level the inhabitants of the vast reaches beyond the Great Lakes and the Mississippi River hardly knew that such a thing as Anglo-American relations existed. From Lake Superior to Puget Sound the long international boundary was at its most artificial, as the Dakotas merged imperceptibly with Montana and both merged with Rupert's Land. Those who chose to dwell in this high, lonesome country generally were content to have anyone's company, and the trappings of civilization and of civilization's sometime pacifier, diplomacy, had not reached the plains. No passports, no border raids, and no enforceable trading restrictions were present. American plainsmen could sweep into Fort Garry with the speed of a mountain spring, and Her Majesty's Indian wards often descended upon the border with a tribal internationalism induced by factors that diplomacy could not control—grazing conditions, the caprice of water courses, the migration of the buffalo, or the harshness of the paralyzing winter.

Only in Britain's two colonies on the Pacific Coast, British Columbia and Vancouver Island, was there diplomatic activity of the usual nature. On the whole, relations between these colonies and the North were friendly during the Civil War, and the colonial administration there was successful in maintaining neutrality, since no great strain was placed upon it.[1] Northerners and Southerners alike had swarmed into the colony late in 1861 to take part in the new gold rush to the Fraser River and in a copper rush to the Cowichan district, and in general they were more interested in fighting for gold than in fighting for ideologies. According to Allan Francis, the American consul at Victoria, Vancouver Island, whose district included British Columbia as well, there were twelve thousand adventurers from the United States in the colony by 1862 searching for gold or working on new wagon roads. Francis pointed out that no more than two thousand of the prospectors were successful and suggested that many would join the Northern army if furnished transportation to an enlistment point. But for every one who dejectedly drifted out of the colony, he stated that six stayed. By 1864 the number of American miners in British Columbia had not diminished and Americans had gained control of half of the colony's business houses.[2]

Governor (after 1863 Sir) James Douglas feared the unsuccessful American gold seekers who remained in the colony. One of the pioneers of the West who had worked with James McLaughlin in opening up the region to the fur trade, Douglas was an administrator of exceptional ability, wide knowledge of Western affairs, and nearly despotic power. He worried that the disgruntled Americans who brought prosperity to the colony would demand local government and would attempt to erode away his powers until the time when they could invite annexation to the United States. Douglas was fully as much the geopolitician as Thomas D'Arcy McGee or John A. Macdonald. In 1865, looking to the West for the source of potential Canadian greatness, Macdonald was to declare that the United States must not be permitted to intercept the British route to the Pacific. Douglas voiced the same sentiment five years earlier, and in 1861, partially to counteract American influence and without receiving prior authority to do so, he began the building of the Fraser River road to Barkerville, thus economically attaching the entire river valley to the rest of the colony

[1] Willard E. Ireland, "British Columbia, the United States, and British American Union," unpubl. M.A. thesis (Univ. of Toronto, 1935), p. 139.

[2] Victoria *British Colonist*, Oct. 22, 1861; Victoria *Daily Press*, Oct. 15, 1861; CD, Victoria, 1: Francis to Seward, Oct. 1, 1862; William C. Hazlitt, *The Great Gold Fields of Cariboo* (London, 1862), pp. 130–135; Bruce Hutchison, *The Struggle for the Border* (Toronto, 1955), p. 323; Marcus L. Hansen and John B. Brebner, *The Mingling of the Canadian and American Peoples* (New Haven, 1940), p. 155.

and forestalling attempts to unite the area with Oregon. By 1863 the road, 385 miles long and 18 feet wide, was finished.[3]

Two interrelated diplomatic disputes involving the British colonies remained unsettled in 1861. The San Juan boundary controversy, which had become heated during the "Pig War" in 1859, had cooled, and once the Civil War began, the possibility of using the controversy to prevent a domestic war evaporated. The second problem, that of the sum that was to be paid to the Hudson's Bay Company to liquidate the claims of its subsidiary organization in the Washington Territory, the Puget Sound Agricultural and Improvement Company, was settled in part in 1863.

The field operations of the boundary survey commission, which in 1857 had begun to run the boundary line under the Treaty of 1846 across the Northwest, continued throughout 1861. Only once did disagreement arise. It was found that when the original lines were run the environing mass distribution of the mountains had caused the line to vary as much as a quarter of a mile, so on March 4 the British and American commissioners, Colonel J. S. Hawkins and Archibald Campbell, respectively, adopted a mean parallel along the ninety-six-mile strip that was in error between Similkameen and Statapoosten. But the boundary channels between the San Juan Islands in Puget Sound remained in dispute.[4]

One historian has written that during the Civil War Great Britain "magnanimously" left the question of the San Juan Islands in abeyance.[5] The fact is correct but the adverb is badly chosen. At Lyons' urging, Great Britain left the question in abeyance only because she feared that the position of the Hudson's Bay Company would suffer if a settlement were reached during the war, not wanting the delicate question to become entangled in problems that arose from the war itself. There was nothing magnanimous in this, for as has been seen, in 1861 Lyons feared that if Britain agitated for a settlement in the Northwest, the San Juan question might be used by Seward as a *casus belli* for an international war to avert a domestic conflict.[6]

---

[3] Macdonald Papers, Letterbook VIII: Macdonald to Watkin, March 27, 1865, 9–10; Hutchison, p. 324; F. W. Howay, "The Attitude of Governor Seymour toward Confederation," Royal Soc. of Canada, *Trans.*, 3rd Ser., XIV (1920), 31.

[4] FO 5, 811: Hawkins to Russell, Nov. 27, 1861; Otto Klotz, "The Forty-ninth Parallel," *The University Magazine*, XVI (Oct., 1917), 425–428.

[5] F. W. Howay, *British Columbia: The Making of a Province* (Toronto, 1928), p. 187. See Ellice Papers, A-2, 4A: Ellice, Jr. to Sr., Jan. 25, 1860.

[6] For a definitive treatment of the controversy, see John W. Long, Jr., "The

During the Civil War the joint occupation continued, and the two
hostile camps became neighborly to the point of taking their meals
together. In 1861 orders that the American troops on the island should
embark for San Francisco were revoked because of hostile Indian
activity in the territory. The troops still were on San Juan Island
at the end of the war.

Colonial Secretary Newcastle asked the British War Office to send
a regiment of troops to Vancouver Island early in 1861, but his request
was declined on the grounds that the troops could not be spared from
China and that a single regiment would be inadequate to protect the
colony in case of war. Foreign Secretary Russell also asked that troops
be sent to the island to guard British interests there from the squatter
population that was coming in from the United States. When it was
reported again that the American forces were to be withdrawn from
San Juan Island, Newcastle insisted that the British Marines nevertheless should remain. Governor Douglas planned to carry any Anglo-
American war south to the Columbia River and asked that two regiments be sent to his aid, but he received no support. The British forces
on the Pacific slope remained unchanged during the Civil War—Royal
Marines on San Juan Island, a detachment of Royal Engineers on the
mainland, and three vessels.[7]

Before the war Russell had sent the United States a draft convention
providing for arbitration of the water boundary. The convention
would provide that a compromise line could be chosen, if necessary,
and that the United States would pay half a million dollars to the
Puget Sound Company. The general question of arbitration had been
submitted to the Senate by President Buchanan on March 3, too
late for any decision before Lincoln took office. Lyons then approached Seward, who declared that the evaluation of the company's
claims was far too high. Lincoln resubmitted the question, but the

---

San Juan Island Boundary Controversy: A Phase of Nineteenth Century Anglo-
American Relations," unpubl. Ph.D. diss. (Duke Univ., 1949). See also Alfred
Tunem, "The Dispute over the San Juan Island Water Boundary," *Washington
Hist. Quart.*, XXIII (Jan., 1932), 38–46; (April, 1932), 133–137; (July, 1932), 196–
204; (Oct., 1932), 296–300; E. C. Towey, "San Juan Island Water Boundary Con-
troversy, 1846–1872," unpubl. M.A. thesis (Fordham Univ., 1941); and J. N. Barry,
"San Juan Island in the Civil War," *Washington Hist. Quart.*, XX (April, 1929),
134–136.

[7] FO 5, 816A: T. F. Elliott to B. Hawes, Jan. 4, and Hawes to Elliott, Jan. 7,
enc. in Newcastle to Hammond, Jan. 14, and Russell to Newcastle, Jan. 21, 1861;
ibid., Special order No. 13, June 21, 1861; G 8C, 2: Lyons to Russell, Aug. 5, enc.
in Newcastle to Douglas, Aug. 24, 1861, 557–561.

Senate adjourned without dealing with it. In the meantime, Russell had sent Lyons a second draft convention that specified that the water boundary question should be submitted to the President of the Federal Council of the Swiss Confederation, and the power to indicate a compromise line was omitted. By the time of the *Trent* affair, when Anglo-American relations became strained, Lyons had decided to drop the issue altogether, and he did not mention it to Seward again until March, 1863, when evaluation of the Puget Sound Company's property was separated from the boundary line controversy.

Seward preferred to delay settlement of the boundary until after the war, and Lyons agreed. However, in 1863 in his Annual Message Lincoln referred to an arbitration entered into with Spain, and Russell suggested that since Anglo-American relations had improved during the year the United States might reconsider arbitration. Seward thought that if the King of Italy or the Emperor of Russia would act as arbiter the Senate might agree, but the latter was unacceptable to Great Britain. Early in 1864 negotiations again lapsed and were not resumed until after the war. During this time American squatters continued to move into the San Juan Islands, further complicating the settlement.[8]

The details of the final settlement of the San Juan boundary controversy need not be repeated here. Essentially the dispute was one of semantics, for the wording of the Treaty of 1846 had been vague. Due to the wording, the United States claimed that the Canal de Haro was the main channel to the Straits of Fuca while the British claimed that Rosario Strait was the proper line. This problem was not settled until 1872, when the joint occupation ended. Until well into the twentieth century Hudson's Bay Company employees continued to make pilgrimages to a little graveyard on the island where twelve men who had died during the occupation were buried, and a blockhouse still stands as a reminder of one joint occupation that was settled without bloodshed.[9]

Seward did prove amenable to a settlement of the claims of the Puget Sound Agricultural and Improvement Company. In the counties of Pierce and Lewis at the time of the Treaty of 1846 the company

[8] FO 5, 740: Lyons to Russell, Dec. 31, 1860; *ibid.*, 816A: Russell to Lyons, Jan. 25, March 21, Dec. 14, 1861, April 9, Dec. 24, 1863, Jan. 31, 1864, and Lyons to Russell, Aug. 5, 1861, March 24, 1863, Jan. 18, 1864; *ibid.*: Head to A. M. Layard, Dec. 3, 1863; *ibid.*, 1342: Lyons to Russell, Feb. 18, 1861; *ibid.*, 816: Lyons to Russell, Feb. 25, March 3, 4, 1861, and Russell to Lyons, March 16, 1861; FO 115, 300: Lyons to Russell, May 8, 1862.
[9] E. H. Wilson, "San Juan Island," *Beaver* (Sept., 1927), pp. 70–71.

was cultivating large tracts of land and was running cattle and sheep on uninclosed, widely separated areas. When the office of Surveyor General was created for Oregon, which then embraced the Washington Territory, the company filed claims for the plats. Settlers moved in over most of these tracts, fencing and cultivating the usual quota of land allowed under American law. By 1861 the company was maintaining its claims to a large tract of land but was in actual occupancy of less than a thousand acres. Pierce County continued to levy taxes on the entire tract that the company claimed despite the fact that the company was obtaining no benefit from it and was not exercising the rights of ownership, and the personal property of the company was seized for taxes on land that was the company's in name only. In addition, the United States military authorities who leased company property at Fort Steilacoom ceased making rent payments. The company objected to these tactics, and the entire question of liquidating the company's claims within United States territory was submitted to Seward. The company placed an evaluation of half a million dollars on its claims, and some American expansionists suggested that the United States seize the opportunity to buy the entire Hudson's Bay Company's territory for twenty million dollars.[10]

Seward realistically saw that as long as the Civil War continued Congress would not agree to a complete settlement that Great Britain would accept. In order to create the machinery for a solution, therefore, he suggested to Lyons that a convention be made that dealt with the company's evaluation only. From this suggestion grew a treaty, negotiated on July 1, 1863, and signed by the President on June 29, 1864, which Lyons signed on his own responsibility, not wanting to delay the negotiations long enough to give Seward an opportunity to change his mind. The treaty provided for the creation of a joint commission to review the claims of the Hudson's Bay Company and of its subsidiary, the Puget Sound Company.[11] Alexander S. Johnston and

---

[10] M.C.: B. F. Kendall to Seward, Oct. 13, 1862, and William Barnes to Seward, March 11, 1866; NBL, 14: Seward to Bruce, Feb. 6, 1867, 145; C. M. Gates, ed., *Messages of the Governors of the Territory of Washington to the Legislative Assembly, 1854–1889*, Univ. of Washington, *Publications in the Social Sciences*, xii (Seattle, 1940), 154–155, 174–175.

[11] NBL, 10: Seward to Lyons, June 22, 1863, Jan. 21, 1864, 114–115, 508; *ibid.*, 11: Seward to Lyons, March 2, 1864; Seward Papers: R. B. Minturn to Seward, Nov. 30, 1863; and Adams to Seward and C. M. Lampson to Seward, both Dec. 7, 1863; FO 115, 364: Lyons to Russell, June 30, 1863; *Cong. Globe*, 38th Cong., 1st Sess.: June 24, 26, 29, pp. 3222, 3266, 3360.

Sir John Rose were appointed American and British commissioners, respectively, and they met in Washington in January, 1865. The settlement again was delayed when consul Francis wrote from Victoria that a document existed that would prove that the Puget Sound Company never had any legal rights in Washington [Oregon] Territory, and the United States requested that Caleb Cushing, who was presenting the American case, be given permission to investigate the archives of the Hudson's Bay Company in London. Permission was refused, and the commission did not reach a settlement until 1869.[12]

But neither the problems of the boundary nor those of the company's claims were direct products of the Civil War. The war's distinctive effect on the two Far Western British colonies was to divide opinion as it did in the Eastern provinces and to give rise to the usual rumors of border raids and Confederate privateering. For the most part the authorities in the colonies were friendly to the North, but not necessarily from conviction and possibly only because of the thousands of Northerners already within the two colonies, and because the colonies were linked economically to San Francisco. The colonies were over-burdened with debt, and each year's recurring deficit reminded the permanent settlers of how dependent they were on the smelting companies in California. The older British population of Vancouver Island tended to favor a Southern victory, possibly because they resented the fact that so many Northern "birds of passage" drained the colonies of gold. On the other hand, the ladies of Victoria gave donations to the Freedman's Association and apparently disagreed with their pro-Southern spouses. News from the Atlantic coast was very slow in coming, but military events that had long passed still excited great interest in both colonies. The Victoria press generally was conciliatory toward Northern sensibilities, and at the conclusion of the *Trent* affair the *British Colonist* praised the United States for being a great nation that knew how to make amends.[13]

The two colonies were not untouched by the war: Occasional draft-

---

[12] R. R. Martig, "Hudson's Bay Company Claims, 1846-69," *Oregon Historical Quarterly*, XXVI (March, 1935), 69-70; NBL, 12: Seward to Lyons, Aug. 20, 1864, 32-33; CD, Victoria, VI: Francis to Seward, April 8, June 15, 1864; M.C.: Cushing to Seward, Jan. 16, 1865, June 28, 1866.

[13] CD, Victoria, I: Francis to Seward, Oct. 1, 1862; *ibid.*, VI: H. Hamlin to Francis, Dec. 11, 1863, and Francis to Seward, March 4, 1865; *Colonist*, Dec. 23, 1861, Jan. 13, 1862. See the excellent study by James W. Pilton, "Negro Settlement in British Columbia, 1858-1871," unpubl. M.A. thesis (Univ. of British Columbia, 1951).

dodgers and bounty-jumpers appeared, and the presence of several Confederates led to rumors that British Columbia would be used as a base for raids into California and Nevada. Possible danger from Confederate privateers in the Pacific led to an increase in insurance for the gold bars that were shipped from the colonial government's assay office in New Westminster to San Francisco. In 1862, when it was thought that war with the United States was possible, insurance for war risk also was required, and in 1863–1864 two volunteer rifle corps were formed to defend the colonies,[14] although their chief concern was the supposed Indian menace.

Considerable excitement was created in Vancouver Island in February, 1863, when the Victoria *Chronicle* declared that a Confederate naval commander had arrived in the colony to buy an English vessel, the *Thames*, which was to be converted into a privateer for preying on the gold and silver shipments. The effort had failed only because of lack of funds, according to the *Chronicle*, which warned California to prepare for Confederate attacks. The rival newspaper in Victoria, the *British Colonist*, labeled the story "bosh" and declared that the supposed Confederate was an agent who had been sent to Victoria by a company in San Francisco to purchase a vessel for use in the Mexican trade. The *British Colonist* and the *Chronicle* continued to attack each other, the former decrying David W. Higgins, editor of the *Chronicle*, for his efforts to convince Americans in the colony that the administration was pro-Southern. The *Chronicle* printed a letter supposedly written by a Confederate, which admitted that privateering was intended, and Higgins announced that Southerners in the vicinity, with the aid of a young Englishman, hoped to seize the United States' revenue cutter *Shubrick* when it next visited Victoria. The *British Colonist* denied Higgins' story.[15] Later, in an apocryphal autobiography, Higgins embellished the tale of how he had learned of the Confederate plot with duels, women spies, secret confidences, perfumed clues, and other characteristics of the old *police romancier*.[16]

[14] CD, Victoria, 1: Francis to Seward, Oct. 1, 1862; Victor Ross, *A History of the Canadian Bank of Commerce* (Toronto, 1920), 1, 295–296.

[15] *Chronicle*, Feb. 4, 6, 7, 10, 12, 14, 1863; *British Colonist*, Feb. 5, 7, 9, 13, 1863. See B. F. Gilbert, "Kentucky Privateers in California," Kentucky Hist. Soc., *Register*, xxxviii (1940), 256–266, for a somewhat different account of this episode, and Gilbert, "Previews of Confederate Privateers Operating in Victoria, Vancouver Island," *British Columbia Hist. Quart.*, xviii (Oct., 1954), 240–241.

[16] *The Mystic Spring and Other Tales of Western Life* (Toronto, 1904), pp. 108–123. See also another apocryphal book, James H. Wilkins, ed., *The Great Dia-*

Apparently there was at least some truth in editor Higgins' reports. With the aid of two "detectives" consul Francis learned that an unsuccessful effort had been made to purchase the *Thames* and to enlist a crew. When the steamer left for Barcley Sound, ostensibly to undergo extensive repairs, Francis was convinced that it was destined for Confederate use since there were no facilities for making such repairs at the sound. He therefore accepted Higgins' version of the plot, reporting its existence as fact to Seward. The Secretary brought the report to Lyons' attention and asked that steps be taken to prevent such plots from bearing fruit. Lyons telegraphed the British consul in San Francisco, William L. Booker, who was the minister's quickest contact with the Pacific colonies, and the consul replied that the *British Colonist*'s version of the so-called plot was the correct one. To protect the *Shubrick* from possible seizure most of her officers and crew, who were suspected of being Southern sympathizers, were discharged by the Collector of Customs for Puget Sound. Brigadier General Benjamin Alvord, Commander of the District of Oregon, attempted to prosecute Higgins' Confederate informer on the basis of the *Chronicle*'s report but apparently was unable to do so.[17]

Despite the fact that the first rumor of Confederate privateering was highly dubious, and that evidence showed that it may well have been an effort on the part of the Victoria *Chronicle* to create a sensational story for circulation purposes, Francis continued to believe such rumors. The consul, who had been subjected to the indignity of seeing a Confederate flag raised in Victoria and lowered only upon protest to Governor Douglas, did not have a subtle mind. He had protested the flag incident by ostentatiously staying away from an official dinner, and he was equally direct in reporting nearly every rumor he heard as though it were true. As a result, he continued to worry about non-existent and potential Confederate activities in the two colonies.[18]

---

mond Hoax and Other Stirring Incidents in the Life of Asbury Harpending (San Francisco, 1913), p. 73, and as reprinted (Norman, 1958), p. 48.

[17] CD, Victoria, VI: Francis to Seward, Feb. 14, 1863; NBL, 9: Seward to Lyons, March 31, 1863, 502–503; NFBL, 51: Lyons to Seward, May 15, and Douglas to Lyons, May 14, enc. in Lyons to Seward, May 21, 1863; *ibid.*, 52: Newcastle to Hammond, May 11, enc. in Lyons to Seward, June 1, 1863; M.C.: Ira Rankin to Seward, April 14, 1863; OR, ser. I, L: Alvord to Francis, Feb. 25, 1863, Jan. 1, 1864, 322–323, 714–715. See also *Foreign Relations, 1863:* Seward to Lyons, March 31, April 15, and Lyons to Seward, April 2, 16, May 21, pp. 478, 507, 542, 549.

[18] CD, Victoria, VI: Francis to Seward, Nov. 13, 1862; ORN, ser. I, II: Francis to T. O. Selfridge, May 13, Selfridge to Hopkins, April 23, Selfridge to Welles,

Activities there were, although not of an incendiary nature. Southerners sat around the bar in the St. Nicholas Hotel in Victoria to drink beer and apollinaris water and to concoct plots against the North, but nothing came of their ruminations. When steamers were overdue, their tardiness frequently was ascribed to Confederates, and the U.S.S. *Saginaw* cruised the waters of Puget Sound and San Juan de Fuca Strait to check on possible privateers, calling periodically at Victoria and Esquimalt on Vancouver Island.[19]

A secondary privateering scare took place in October, 1863. Some of the Southerners, unsuccessful at prospecting, had formed a Southern Association, which drew members from the two colonies, and its President, Jules David, was in contact with James M. Mason in London. At Mason's advice David wrote to Judah P. Benjamin to obtain a letter of marque for use by a yet-unprocured vessel. Francis noted the arrival of two English ships, one carrying a thousand barrels of powder and shell and the other a peculiar vessel made almost entirely of iron, and he concluded that the two might be destined for Confederate use. He requested that a ship be sent to patrol the waters around Vancouver Island, and in January, 1864, the U.S.S. *Narragansett* was sent to Victoria. However, no privateer ever was obtained by the Southern Association, despite Francis' continued fears and despite a number of table-thumping meetings at the newly dubbed Confederate Saloon.[20]

By the end of the Civil War Francis had turned his attention to the possibility of annexing both colonies to the United States, and he felt convinced that a majority of the people within the colonies favored such a step.[21] For the major international issue in the West during the Civil War was not Confederate privateering but the political future

---

June 3, 1863, and Bell to Welles, Jan. 9, 1864, 165–166, 259–261, 583, 2619. On the basis of the published correspondence Brainerd Dyer, in "Confederate Naval and Privateering Activities in the Pacific," *Pacific Historical Review*, III (Sept., 1934), 437, writes that "it seems certain that Confederate attempts to that end [to obtain a privateer] continued throughout the war . . . ."

[19] *ORN*, ser. I, II: Selfridge to Welles, April 28, June 3, 1863, 173, 259–260; CD, Victoria, VI: Francis to Seward, April 14, 1863. Some of the pro-Confederates in Victoria did attempt to obtain the release of a small group of Southern privateers who had been captured by the San Francisco Police (Gilbert, "Kentucky Privateers," pp. 261–266).

[20] *ORN*, ser. II, III: David to Benjamin, Oct. 16, 1863, 933–934; *OR*, ser. I, L: A. Francis to S. Francis, Oct. 20, Alvord to Francis, Nov. 20, Francis to Alvord, Nov. 23, 1863, and Francis to Irvin McDowell, Nov. 18, 1864, 678–680, 682, 1061.

[21] CD, Victoria, VI: Francis to Seward, Sept. 15, 1866.

of the colonies and of the Hudson's Bay Company's northern holdings. The United States had coveted this vast region since well before the Civil War. Men like Senator William McKendree Gwin of California had dreamed of a world empire with the United States at its center, and when he, and later Seward, embraced the plan of purchasing Alaska from Russia, they acted partially because the acquisition of Alaska would sandwich British Columbia in between American territory, making that valuable mineral region's annexation more probable.[22]

Many Canadians were concerned over American expansion, for they felt that the provinces' chances of greatness lay with a British West. British Columbians were well aware of Senator Gwin's aspirations, and they realized that the Civil War had only delayed their fruition unless the mother country acted first. It would be a "masterstroke" on Seward's part if Alaska went to the United States, the *British Colonist* argued, thus placing the British Pacific colonies in a position where they might be "devoured at a single bite."[23] But Canada had ignored the Alaskan question, and when she began her drive for hegemony in the British provinces by agitating for the annexation of the Hudson's Bay Company's area to the slowly forming dominion, she ignored the strategic position of the Alaskan corridor. That most expansionistic of newspapers, the Toronto *Globe*, was to call Seward's purchase of Alaska "ridiculous." But after 1867 Canadians came to realize why, when the United States was distracted during the Civil War, the British colonists in the Far West had urged that strong ties with Great Britain should be forged through granting provincial status to the settlements in the Red River valley as well.

There was no singleness of purpose in America's interest in the British Northwest, however, and the sporadic talk of annexation often was insincere.[24] In 1864 the Republican party used annexationism to

[22] H. M. McPherson, "The Interest of William McKendree Gwin in the Purchase of Alaska, 1854–1861," *Pacific Hist. Rev.*, III (March, 1934), 31; Thomas A. Bailey, "Why the United States Purchased Alaska," *ibid.*, p. 49, n. 30; Robert MacG. Dawson, *The Government of Canada* (Toronto, 1954), p. 25.

[23] *British Colonist*, May 16, 1867, quoted in Virginia H. Reid, *The Purchase of Alaska: Contemporary Opinion* (Long Beach, 1940), pp. 38–39; McInnis, *Unguarded Frontier*, p. 219.

[24] Since full documentation for the material that follows is available in Robin W. Winks, "The British North American West and the Civil War," *North Dakota History*, XXIV (July, 1957), 139–152, footnotes have been reduced to a minimum here. The argument that much of American annexationism at this time was

secure the Irish vote, and in 1865–1866 annexationism was a means of reconciling the West and New England to the abrogation, engineered by the protectionist Middle Atlantic states, of the reciprocity treaty. In 1864 former Postmaster General Montgomery Blair wrote a public statement to the Irish National Fair that as soon as the Confederacy was defeated, British America would be invaded by Union troops. Throughout the Civil War the Chicago *Tribune* and New York *Herald* consistently advocated annexing all of Britain's possessions on the continent up to Hudson Bay. On the day that the platform was announced at the Republican Convention of 1864, Henry J. Raymond of the New York *Times* declared that all monarchical governments should be driven from the proximity of the United States. Such tactics undoubtedly won many votes for the Republican party, especially among the Irish Fenians.

But in reality there were two annexationist movements. One, which embraced the united Canadas, was a convenient political device on both sides of the border for winning votes, a phantom with which Northern politicians vied for Anglophobe support at election time and a "bogey" that the Liberal-Conservative party in the Canadas used to defeat the allegedly pro-American Clear Grits. This annexationist movement was a useful political device in the northern United States, for it appealed not only to the Irish but to the land-hungry, and those of spread-eagle mentality in the Republican party, as well. As Seward himself once voiced it, and as the New York *Herald* limned it, the Canadas would join the United States voluntarily when the time was ripe, and unless it was necessary to invade the provinces at the end of the war in order to pacify the voracious Northern army, the Canadas probably had several years of suffering under a monarchy before they could be made free. Despite electioneering gasconade and rumors of sudden invasion and infiltration, of economic warfare and strangulation, there was no sense of urgency in the eighteen-sixties about annexing the Canadas. Goldwin Smith thought that the manufacturing population "would annex Hell as a market," but the manufacturers

---

"window dressing" to win the votes of anti-British ethnic groups is most forcefully presented by Joe Patterson Smith in *Republican Expansionists of the Early Reconstruction Period* (Chicago, 1933). Alvin C. Gluek, Jr. in "The Struggle for the British Northwest: A Study in Canadian-American Relations," unpubl. diss. (Univ. Minnesota, 1953), takes issue with Smith and concludes that annexationism was very real. There would seem to be considerable evidence in support of both views.

seemed willing to wait until "the course of history" made force unnecessary.[25]

But there was a second annexation movement, and it was no phantom. This was the drive to the Northwest, the frequently expressed hope of burgeoning Minnesota that what is today Manitoba, Saskatchewan, and Alberta might be attached to the American orbit, first economically and later politically. It was upon this annexationist movement that the Civil War had its most obvious effect. The drive to the Northwest had begun well before the Civil War, and the American frontier now had marched up to the Hudson's Bay Company's territory and temporarily stopped.[26]

In 1860 Seward had made his famous speech in which he forecast a great future for the Northwest and declared to loud applause that the ultimate seat of power in North America would be found in St. Paul. He had praised the people of Rupert's Land for conquering their wilderness because they were creating an excellent state for the American Union. Even sedate Charles Francis Adams, who listened to the oration, had felt that the vision of power that Seward expressed produced an effect "much like intoxication"—a feeling not entirely accounted for by the fact that Adams had been downing glasses of German lager a few days earlier in order not to offend Republican voters.[27] And the people of St. Paul also felt intoxicated by the vision.

It must be kept in mind that in 1861 the Canadian frontier also lay within the United States. Canadian movement toward the West was

[25] Arnold Haultain, ed., *A Selection from Goldwin Smith's Correspondence* (New York, 1913), p. 290: Nov. 16, 1864. See L. O. David, *L'Union des deux Canadas, 1841–1867* (Montreal, 1898), p. 220.

[26] See Baring Papers: Ward to Baring Bros., Feb. 25, 1862; Alfred L. Burt, *A Short History of Canada for Americans* (2nd ed., Minneapolis, 1944), p. 173; Vernon C. Fowke, "National Policy and Western Development in North America," *Journal of Economic History*, xvi (Dec., 1956), 470; J. S. Galbraith, "The Hudson's Bay Company under Fire, 1847–62," *CHR*, xxx (Dec., 1949), 335. John B. Brebner, "The Survival of Canada," in Flenley, ed., *Essays in Canadian History*, pp. 262–263, disagrees with the above and says that Canada West, not the Hudson's Bay Company's area, was most threatened by American expansionism. An epitome of the traditional view may be found in the twentieth century's finest example of nineteenth-century scholarship, Winston S. Churchill, *A History of the English Speaking Peoples: iv, The Great Democracies* (New York, 1958), p. 104.

[27] CFA, Diary: Sept. 14, 18, 1860. The full text of Seward's speech appears in the St. Paul *Daily Times*, Sept. 22, 1860. See also the unpublished "Political History of Minnesota from 1847 to 1862," by John P. Owens (pp. 570–571), at the Minnesota Historical Society.

blocked by the vast pre-Cambrian shield that came down to meet the Great Lakes at Thunder Rock on Lake Superior. Canadians moved westward only through the United States, through Chicago, St. Paul, and Pembina, to Fort Garry. As long as Canadians could continue to immigrate to the United States and could use the North as a way-station on the road to the Red River, the people of the Hudson's Bay Company's territory were likely to be nearly as American as British in outlook. The coming of the Civil War curtailed both this immigration and the steady flow of Americans across the border, and while the merchants of St. Paul continued to dream of the potential empire to the northwest, the Eastern interests that could have financed the railroads and the forts that might have been forerunners of eventual annexation turned to financing the Civil War instead.

But the coming of the Civil War did not mean that the Northwest need be lost to the United States. The inhabitants of the Red River-Assiniboia district still were tied closely to the North and they themselves might have voted for annexation, as the territory's only newspaper, the Fort Garry *Nor'wester*, frequently pointed out. Discontent over lack of a proper system of representative government was growing in the old Selkirk settlement, especially as a continuing, although decimated, flow of Americans pressed into the Fort Garry area, and in 1863 the people of the Red River district asked British and Canadian officials to grant them some measure of self-government.[28] The Canadian conservatives turned their backs on the demand for colonial status along the Red River. The Toronto *Leader* declared that it was not Canada's business to follow the Western settlers with British political institutions. Cartier and Macdonald did talk of a separate crown colony for the Northwest, but they apparently did nothing to urge their views upon Great Britain until they became aware, late in the Civil War, of the power vacuum that existed along the Red River.

The area was becoming increasingly Americanized, and nearly fifteen thousand people lived within British territory along the banks of the river. Many Americans and Britishers felt that, except for the symbol of British authority in the British and Hudson's Bay Company's flags that flew over Fort Garry, they were a part of the United States. The *Nor'wester*, edited from 1860 to 1864 by James Ross, a liberal, did not hesitate to point out to the administration that the area was being driven into the arms of the Republic. The district's business relations

[28] Canada, *Sess. Papers, 1863*, xxi: no. 83, "Memorial of the People of Red River to the British and Canadian Governments," 6.

were almost exclusively with the United States, and the only regular mail communication that the people of the Red River had with the outside world was established in 1853 by and through the United States and was kept up at considerable expense by the American government to benefit people who lived in British territory. The only steamboat line on the Red River originated in the interior of Minnesota. As the *Nor'wester* noted, "It is surely no matter of surprise that public sentiment is in favor of annexation to the United States . . . [since] connection [with Britain] is nominal and fruitless."[29] Even the Governor of the Hudson's Bay Company's territory, who was a company, not an imperial, appointee, admitted that unless the system of government were changed, the people themselves might form a provisional government and request annexation to the United States. By 1863 *The Times* belatedly and sporadically began to take some interest in the area, but it had lingered long behind such men as Thomas D'Arcy McGee. That it was not too long was largely the fault of the United States.[30]

For if the Red River valley still looked to Washington despite the Civil War and if it was clearly pro-Northern, as it was, then annexation still was possible. But the Civil War induced the United States itself to lose the Northwest. A Sioux uprising in 1862, which cut off communication to St. Paul, and the withdrawal of American troops from the Pembina region in 1864 created a sense of insecurity in the region that led to a revival of interest in the British connection, and when repeal of the Bonding Act was threatened in 1864, which would have curtailed commercial transportation into Minnesota, the people of the northwestern settlements were forced for the first time to look to an all-British route as a means of transport from England. These events coincided with the reawakening of at least some vocal Canadian interest in the West, and despite the energetic activities of a group of American annexationists at Fort Garry, the events aided the creation of the Dominion of Canada and its extension to the Pacific.

Throughout the Civil War and until well after, the annexationists at Fort Garry and St. Paul were led by an exceptional American expansionist, James Wickes Taylor. In the summer of 1859, at his own request, Taylor had been appointed a special agent of the Treasury

[29] Oct. 1, 15, 1861.

[30] Since the present author wrote his article on this subject, additional light on the Red River situation has been provided by W. L. Morton, *Manitoba: A History* (Toronto, 1957), pp. 101, 106–110.

Department to make a report for the House of Representatives on the Red River district, and he became America's expert on northwestern affairs. A preliminary report in 1860 was followed by a fuller report in 1862. In both, Taylor wrote that forcible annexation was not necessary in order to gain the district for the United States, although in case of war he felt that Minnesota could "hold, occupy, and possess" the entire Red River to Lake Winnipeg. He hoped to use the more statesmanlike machinery of treaties and concurrent legislation in working out "the mutual destiny" of the region.[31] Taylor kept in close contact with C. J. Brydges, General Manager of the Grand Trunk Railway who doubled as an agent for the Hudson's Bay Company, in order to learn of any plans for an all-British road to the Red River, and he frequently wrote to Seward concerning annexationist sentiment in the district, after having arranged for a talk between Seward and the Reverend David Anderson, the Bishop of Rupert's Land, during the former's visit to St. Paul. When his commission from the Treasury Department expired Taylor was made United States consul at Fort Garry, and he continued to serve the interests of both his country and the "Assiniboians" in the international manner peculiar to so many residents of the great plains, eventually winning the nickname of "Saskatchewan" Taylor.[32]

According to Edward Watkin, who was a close friend of Colonial Secretary Newcastle, the latter even gave some thought to selling or exchanging part of the Northwestern territory. Watkin wanted to see responsible government established in the Red River settlement, and he suggested that a small portion of the land might be sold or leased to the United States to finance the colony, which he hoped to name "Hysperia." Newcastle and Watkin apparently agreed that an exchange of land would be better, however, and in his memoirs—which are not an entirely reliable source—Watkin states that in 1862 they decided that "rectification of the boundary" was in order. He adds that the negotiations were "very hopeful" at one time, but there is no evidence that there ever were any formal negotiations of the type that Watkin suggested.[33]

[31] Taylor, *Relations between the United States and Northwest British America* (Washington, 1862), in U.S. Congress, *House Executive Documents*, no. 196, pp. 43–45.

[32] Minn. Hist. Soc., Taylor Papers: Brydges to Taylor, Feb. 22, March 26, 1864; M.C.: Taylor to Seward, Nov. 15, 1861.

[33] Watkin, *Recollections*, pp. 122–129, 205.

The only incident along the northwestern frontier which actually led to formal negotiations arose from the Sioux rebellion in Minnesota in 1862. On August 18 a small band of Sioux attacked a farmer and his family, and within the next six weeks the attack grew into a full scale uprising caused, according to the Indians, by dishonest governmental agents. Governor William Mactavish of Assiniboia, realizing that once the American army mounted a successful offensive the Sioux would be forced to cross the border, informed the Governor of Rupert's Land, Alexander Dallas, that British troops would be needed to keep the peace. At the same time Consul General Giddings in Montreal offered the rather fantastic suggestion that the Indians had been sent on the rampage as part of a great Secession Plot and implied that the people of the British North American provinces were implicated. Apparently Seward chose not to take Gidding's suggestion seriously.[34]

During the fall and winter of 1862 the intensity of the war with the Indians mounted, eclipsed in magnitude by the greater struggle to the southeast but nonetheless one of the most destructive Indian uprisings of all time. The route from the Red River to St. Paul was closed temporarily, and it was opened once again only when two thousand troops garrisoned the many sod forts that dotted the plains. The people of stricken Minnesota reacted violently against everyone with a red skin, and it was suggested that all of the Indian remnants of the old Northwest should be banished to a penal colony on Isle Royale in Lake Superior or should be forced to flee across the border. Taylor attacked both the Indians and the army's handling of the problem in frequent letters to the St. Paul *Daily Press,* while the officials of the Hudson's Bay Company prepared for the inevitable influx of retreating Sioux.

In 1863 Chief Little Crow of the Sioux wrote to the English residents of Pembina, in Dakota Territory, reminding them that the Indians had been allies of the Crown in previous wars with the Americans and asking for the return of an old cannon that his grandfather had captured and given to the British. The Sioux were said to be obtaining guns and ammunition from métis traders in Rupert's Land, and it was evident to the Americans that the Indians were extending special consideration to the British, for a party could cross in safety from St. Paul to Fort Garry only if it carried a British flag.

[34] CD, Montreal, IV: Giddings to Seward, Aug. 29, 1862.

Seward brought to Lyons' attention the fact that the Sioux were committing outrages, possibly with British rifles, and were escaping into the Hudson's Bay Company's territory. Shortly afterwards Governor General Monck issued a circular to the Indian superintendents in Canada West forbidding the sale of arms to the rebellious Sioux, but he had no authority at Fort Garry. Nevertheless he sent a request to Governor Dallas that the sale of supplies be restricted within the company's territory. In February Dallas rejected an offer from Little Crow of a present of women and mules, letting it be known that "the mules would be more acceptable than the women," and the Bishop of Rupert's Land added his name to those who were writing to Newcastle for troops.[35]

Late in the winter six hundred half-starved Sioux appeared at Fort Garry and as Dallas had feared requested guns and ammunition. Anticipating an order that arrived early in the summer prohibiting the sale of guns to Indians from the United States, Dallas sent orders to all of the Hudson's Bay Company's agents that they must not trade in arms or munitions with the Sioux. After some petty thievery, Little Crow's band eventually left Fort Garry with a grant of £250, food, and clothing, in exchange for some white women and children whom they held prisoner. In May the American War Department requested permission through Lyons to pursue the Sioux Indians beyond the international boundary if necessary, and Lyons referred the question to Monck for advice. Monck declared that he could not take the responsibility for granting such permission, and Lyons wrote to Russell. In July permission was refused.[36]

In the meantime Little Crow, with a party of eighty, returned to Fort Garry. Reminding Dallas that they always had been told that they could turn to "the red flag in the north" when in trouble, wearing George III medals and parading with British flags, the Sioux asked Dallas to intercede with Brigadier General H. H. Sibley, who was in charge of the campaign against them. Dallas gave them food and declined their repeated requests for ammunition, which Little Crow insisted was necessary for hunting game. The Governor told the Indians that the President of the United States was interested in their

[35] NFBL, 48: Lyons to Seward, Jan. 12, 1862 [*sic* for 1863], Jan. 26, Feb. 7, 1863; Ellice Papers, A-2, 4A: Dallas to Ellice, Feb. 7, 1863.

[36] NFBL, 51: Lyons to Seward, May 18, 27, 1863; NBL, 10: Seward to Lyons, May 23, 1863, 40–41; BMW to GCC, 10: Lyons to Monck, May 26, June 4, 1863; *ibid.*, 11: Lyons to Monck, July 25, 1863.

welfare and that if they had been treated badly it was due to subordinates and not to Lincoln. He then wrote to Sibley outlining Sioux complaints and advising the General that while the security of the frontier and retribution for the deaths of innocent Americans were matters of importance, the Sioux probably would fight until exterminated unless given an immediate opportunity to make peace. Sibley personally felt that the Sioux nation should be wiped out "man, woman and child as the Israelites destroyed the Canaanites of old." [37]

Four hundred American cavalry under Major Edwin Hatch arrived at Pembina in December, 1863. Faced with the prospect of a second winter without peaceful communication with St. Paul and with the growing possibility of a Sioux attack on Hudson's Bay Company settlements, the people of the Red River began urging Dallas to permit the American troops to enter British territory. Outlying settlers were drifting into Fort Garry demanding that since Britain had supplied no troops, and since the United States appeared willing, Hatch should be asked to act. Some of the settlers appealed directly to Hatch, who promptly replied that he could not cross the border without permission from Dallas. Seward therefore conveyed the War Department's request to Lyons once again. [38]

Both Dallas at Fort Garry and Sir Edmund Head, the former Governor General of British North America who now was the Governor at Hudson's Bay House, London, feared that pro-American Red River settlers might use the Sioux threat as an occasion for appealing to the United States for annexation. Since it was rumored that gold had been discovered on the Bow River to the west, both also anticipated a rush of prospectors from Minnesota in the spring. The conjunction of these two events might well end British rule on the Red River. On the other hand, to invite American troops into the area would be to encourage the district's dependence on the United States. [39]

In the meantime, General Sibley had written to Major General John Pope, Commander of the Department of the Northwest, that along the Red River nearly a thousand Sioux were subsisting off the British government. He hinted that Great Britain should be held accountable if the Indians whom they succored renewed their depredations in the

[37] FO 5, 890: Dallas to Sibley, and Dallas to Monck, both June 3, enc. in Lyons to Russell, July 3, 1863.

[38] NBL, 10: Seward to Lyons, Jan. 21, 1864, 516.

[39] GB, *Sess. Papers, 1864*, XLII: no. 1, Head to Sir Frederick Rogers, Feb. 5, col. 599; *Nor'wester*, Dec. 8, 1863.

spring. Sibley again declared that he wanted to exterminate all of the Minnesota Sioux who were in the Hudson's Bay Company's territory.[40]

Probably because of pressure from Sibley and from the local residents, and possibly because he shared Head's fear that annexationism might be strengthened by his refusal, Governor Dallas persuaded the Sioux to remove themselves to the Turtle Mountains, well away from Fort Garry. Acting on his own responsibility, Monck now gave Hatch permission to cross the border, despite Lord John Russell's previous refusal to grant such permission, with the stipulation that there was to be no bloodshed in the houses of any settlers where the Indians might seek refuge. Monck could point out, of course, that Russell's refusal had been based on a hypothetical situation, whereas the renewed requests were based upon an evident need. Impressed by the destitution of the Indians, who were attempting to sell their own children rather than see them starve, Dallas had given the Sioux the ammunition for which they had asked, on their solemn promise that it would be used only to replenish their food supply. Due to deep snowdrifts, Hatch was unable to cross the border, however, and in April, when he learned that Chief Standing Buffalo and two thousand braves were on their way north, the Major and his men retired to Fort Abercrombie. They left behind an unofficial local force that had been raised at Pembina by an American, which consisted of both American and British subjects, the latter chiefly métis, who wished to prepare an international group to operate against the Sioux.[41]

Before Hatch withdrew from Pembina one of his officers violated the international boundary. Anxious to capture two of the main Sioux leaders, Little Six and Medicine Bottle, who were known to be in the vicinity, Hatch sent a lieutenant from his battalion to call on an American citizen living at Fort Garry with instructions to obtain the surrender of the two Indians. Hatch apparently did not receive prior approval from General Pope. The officer encountered the two Sioux on the road to the fort and asked them to surrender to him, which they refused to do. They accepted his offer of a ride to the trading post, however, and that night and the following day the two Indians visited various bars in the company of the officer. While they were in

[40] FO 5, 943: Pope to J. C. Kelton, Jan. 12, and Seward to Lyons, Jan. 21, enc. in Lyons to Russell, Jan. 22, 1864.

[41] GB, *Sess. Papers, 1864,* XLII: no. 2, Dallas to Thomas Fraser, Dec. 11, and no. 3, Mactavish to Fraser, Dec. 25, 1863, enc. in no. 1, Head to Rogers, Feb. 5, 1864, cols. 599–600.

a private home, a drug was added to their drinks and Little Six was chloroformed. With their hands and feet tied, strapped to a dog sled, the two Indians were taken to Pembina and delivered by the lieutenant to Major Hatch.[42]

When the news of the kidnapping of Little Six and Medicine Bottle became known, the people of the Red River were indignant. Possibly fearing retaliation by the Sioux when summer came, they denounced Hatch for permitting one of his men to violate the border, but they also redoubled their efforts to obtain American troops to protect the settlements along the river. The *Nor'wester* probably spoke for most of the inhabitants when it noted that the people of the region paid no attention to the "niceties" of international law.[43] It was true that Monck had given Hatch permission to cross the border, but his injunction against bloodshed in the homes of settlers was violated in spirit if not by the letter when the two Indians were kidnapped from a private home.

When the news reached the Canadas, portions of the press disapproved of the violation of British sovereignty involved, and in London the *Canadian News*, a financial sheet, declared that Great Britain must not pass over so flagrant an outrage against the flag. Apparently neither Dallas nor Monck protested, however, and since he had acted without authority, the latter was in no position to do so. There is no evidence that Lyons ever took the matter up with Seward. When Confederates were taken from a British ship, a crisis was the result, but when Indians were removed from British territory, there was no protest. The kidnapping probably was viewed by all concerned in the same light as were numerous minor violations of the British North American border by American and Canadian law enforcement officers that took place throughout the war,[44] and possibly because the two Indians allegedly were guilty of murder the *fait accompli* was accepted.

No one bothered to go through the formalities of an inquiry, an exchange of notes, or an explanation of the incident. Actually the two Indians were political refugees illegally removed from their asylum, but even when Medicine Bottle protested during his trial that the proceeding was illegal, the military commission decided, by inverse

[42] C. M. Oehler, *The Great Sioux Uprising* (New York, 1959), pp. 233, 266 n. 13, corrects an error in the present writer's article.

[43] May 20, 1864. For example, see Montreal *Telegraph*, April 13, 1864, March 3, 1864.

[44] See Chapter Ten for an account of several such incidents.

logic, that since Hatch's orders to his lieutenant had been unauthorized, the defendants did not have to be returned to British soil. Medicine Bottle and Little Six were found guilty of murder by a military commission in November, 1864, but in 1865, upon the appeal of the Bishop of St. Paul, President Andrew Johnson ordered Secretary of War Stanton to suspend their execution. A re-examination of the case by Judge Advocate General Joseph Holt confirmed the original judgment, and on November 11, 1865, both Sioux were executed, unquestionably guilty of murder but also the victims of a lapse in the judicial process.[45]

The Sioux rebellion served to stir British interest in the fate of the Hudson's Bay Company's outposts in the Northwest. For two years, from 1862 to 1864, communication from Fort Garry to St. Paul had been made precarious by Sioux activities, and in 1864 a local withdrawal of the bonding privilege further interrupted trade. The people of the Red River district had looked to Great Britain and the Canadas for help during this time. Early in 1865 the British North America Association in London, led by Lords Shaftesbury and Wharncliffe, urged upon the new Colonial Secretary, Edward T. Cardwell, some action with respect to the Northwestern territory, so that American occupation might be prevented. Watkin, who worked with the Association, wrote to John A. Macdonald that Cardwell had given him the impression that he hoped Macdonald would champion a recommendation through Canada's Liberal-Conservative party that the area be made a Crown Colony.[46]

This suggestion already had been made by Cartier and Macdonald in 1863. In July of that year the Duke of Newcastle had told the House of Lords that some action would be taken to colonize the Hudson's Bay Company's territory, and in the same month of the following year Cardwell repeated this promise. Lord Wharncliffe, who had visited the Red River valley, was particularly outspoken in expressing the fears of Big Englanders and expansive Canadians alike that American squatters, métis internationalism, the need for some form of government in the region, and the Indian menace might combine to produce an irresistible outburst of American annexationism. The *Canadian News* in London continued to impress upon the Colonial Office the financial value of the area, adding that as soon as the United

---

[45] WR, Office of the Judge Advocate General: March 25, and Nov. 17 [*sic* for 7], 1865.

[46] Macdonald Papers, 339: Watkin to Macdonald, Feb. 18, 1865, 42–47; *Canadian News*, Feb. 23, 1865.

States no longer was distracted by a civil war she would be free to expand.[47]

The métis of the region were as international as the Indian. Having forged a rude democracy of their own, passionately filiopietistic, pro-Northern or pro-British only when left alone, the métis wandered across the rim of the then-known world. Most of the métis lived in the territory of the Hudson's Bay Company, but they were a group united by blood, not by a flag. Some people, British and American alike, hoped that the métis might provide the key to a new empire. If the métis could be persuaded to want union with the United States, the forces of American annexation might continue, a possibility of which Fort Garry's British residents were aware. That they were not so persuaded is one of the manifold intriguing stories of American expansionism.[48]

But the problem of the Northwest had been merged by 1864 with an even greater one—whether the North would seize upon a series of attempted Confederate border raids, which originated in the British provinces, and upon the manifest anti-Northern sentiment there, as an excuse for attempting to annex all of British North America. The events of 1864 on the Canadian border produced a second war scare and kept public attention directed to the East. The sometimes stumbling efforts of the provinces to maintain British neutrality in the face of an influx of thousands of Southerners now would occupy the center of the Canadian-American stage until the end of the war, and in the long run would spell success or failure for the efforts of those Britishers in the Hudson's Bay Company's territory, British Columbia, or Vancouver Island who envisioned a continental nation that would stretch from the Atlantic to the Pacific to give Great Britain a single swath of red from London to the Orient. It is the British North American provinces and the strength and sources of anti-Northern sentiment there that must be considered now, as well as the problems arising from crimping and enlistment practices during the war.

[47] *Hansard's, 1863:* CLXXII, cols. 47–54, July 2; and *1864:* CLXXVI, col. 1709, July 19; *News,* Feb. 23, April 13, 1865.
[48] See Marcel Giraud, *Le métis canadien: Son rôle dans l'histoire de province de l'ouest,* Univ. de Paris, *Travaux et Mémoires de l'institute d'ethnologie,* XLIV (Paris, 1945), p. 946 n. 3: F. G. Johnson to G. Simpson, April 9, 1857; and Joseph K. Howard, *Strange Empire* (New York, 1952). The best study of this postwar period is George F. G. Stanley, *The Birth of Western Canada: A History of the Riel Rebellion* (London, 1936). The classic account of Rupert's Land in the 1860's, Joseph J. Hargrave, *Red River* (Montreal, 1871), has been re-issued with an introduction by Robin W. Winks (New York, 1960).

ten ଚ THE BRITISH NORTH AMERICAN

AND THE NORTHERN ARMIES

> "I love this Country with all my soul and heart, and I will
> offer all the assistance in my power to sustain it in its hour
> of trial. I hope and pray England will not meddle with us
> not that *I am afraid of her* . . . you can imagine me under
> the starry banner and fighting against my land of birth . . . .
> Oh Could you see and know or realize the love of country
> that abounds in this loved land."
>
> J. R. COTTER *of Buffalo, a former Canadian,*
> *to* JOHN TWIGG *of the Bay of Quinté, August 12, 1862*

DURING THE AMERICAN CIVIL WAR THE USUAL FLOW OF HUMAN TRAFFIC
back and forth across the Canadian-American border was increased
by the military situation that prevailed in the United States. An unknown number of British North Americans crossed the frontier to
fight with the Union forces. Another substantial but unnumbered
group of colonials were crimped, i.e. forced by military procurers,
into the Northern armies. British soldiers were induced to desert their
flag for the better pay of the Federal uniform. After 1862 thousands
of Northern "copperheads," draft-dodgers, and deserters reversed the
direction of travel by fleeing to the provinces for sanctuary. It is
this artificially stimulated wartime border traffic that shall now be
considered.

I

Textbooks often tell us that British North Americans were pro-
Northern during the Civil War. Almost invariably the chief means of

178

supporting this generalization is to cite the commonly accepted statement that several thousand "Canadians" served with the armies of the North. This figure generally has been placed between thirty-eight and one hundred thousand, but the two most frequently cited figures are forty and fifty-three thousand. If even the smallest of these figures were accepted, it would provide strong support for the contention that the provinces were pro-Northern in sentiment. At least three historians have used these figures as the chief or even sole means of arriving at precisely such a conclusion. Given the importance of the figures as the core of any argument concerning British North American public opinion during the war, it would have seemed advisable to have submitted the original sources to investigation. Yet no one did so.

Recently the present writer attempted to provide documentation for the enlistment figures. After tracing the figures back through a series of articles and books, each of which cited another undocumented article or book as its source, the writer concluded that the commonly accepted enlistment figures had no basis in fact. They are inflated, confused by improper terminology, and undermined by emotionalism. The writer presented his findings—which remained largely negative in nature, concluding only that a truly accurate enlistment figure does not and probably could not exist--in an article. The reader who wishes to follow the entire argument concerning the mythical figures and how they grew, or who would like to consult the documentation for the summary that follows, is directed to this more detailed study.[1]

The statistic of the mythical forty thousand rests solely upon an undocumented speech given on an emotional occasion before the war was over and upon a statement remembered in old age of what a shrewd and publicity-conscious politician had said. In February, 1865, *l'abbé* Hercule Beaudry, parish priest of Saint-Constant, Canada East, delivered a funeral oration at the dedication of a memorial in Montreal to French Canadians who had died while serving in the Northern armies. In his address he declared that forty thousand "Canadiens-français" had fought under the American flag and that fourteen thou-

---

[1] See Robin W. Winks, "The Creation of a Myth: 'Canadian' Enlistments in the Northern Armies during the American Civil War," *CHR*, xxxix (March, 1958), 24–40. This article examines other enlistment figures not included in the present summary and provides extensive documentation. A portion has been translated by Adolphe Robert as "Un point d'histoire controversé," *Le Canado-Américain*, i (March, 1960), 33–43.

sand were buried in that foreign land. He did not give any source for the figure that he cited nor did he distinguish between residents of the British North American provinces and long-time residents or even citizens, of French descent, of the United States.[2]

Almost at once confusion arises over the use of the term "Canadian." Beaudry's original reference undoubtedly was to the French Canadians *in toto*. He almost certainly did not refer exclusively to residents of British North America. Determined to maintain *survivance* whether they lived in the United States or in Canada East, French Canadians tended to view themselves as an international unit. Cultural survival rather than assimilation has been their goal. As a rule the French Canadian who came to live in the United States during the nineteenth century did not take out American citizenship. Thus, although many of the French Canadians had been living in New England for several years, they still were viewed as "French Canadian" rather than as "American" both by themselves and by their recruiting officers.

Most of the French Canadians who enlisted probably were from New England, not from British North America. Canada East generally was pro-Southern in its outlook, and while many young Canadians undoubtedly did come to the United States specifically to enlist in the armies, most of the alleged forty thousand or more "Canadians" who enlisted probably were third- and even fourth-generation French-Canadian Americans. No accurate figures on French-Canadian, or "Franco-American," enlistments are available, and a close study of the enlistment records themselves does not help the researcher. Often the officers who made the lists were ill-educated in English and knew nothing of French, so that spellings on the forms do not reveal whether a recruit was of French descent or not. "Vertefeuille" was recorded as "Greenleaf," "Courtemanche" as "Shortsleeve," "Larivière" as "Rivers," and "Lucier" as "Lucia." On occasion French-Canadian, Belgian, and Swiss recruits were mixed in the same battalion, making an accurate designation of names almost impossible.

That French-Canadian historians have spread their nets wide in order to support *abbé* Beaudry may be seen by a glance at some of the names that they have gathered to bolster the number. For example, six brothers who had lived in New York since 1853, and many who came to the United States after the rebellion of 1837—who considered themselves more American than British certainly—are included in the

[2] The speech was reported first in *L'Echo du Cabinet de lecture paroissial* of Montreal, Feb. 15, 1865, and later in *La Minerve* of Montreal, Nov. 16, 1865.

calculations.[3] The French-Canadian press even speculated on whether Confederate General P. G. T. Beauregard might be a French Canadian.[4] Edmond Mallet, the most famous French Canadian to serve the North, who was a major in the New York Volunteers and after the war became a local historian and a leader of the French-Canadian nationalist movement, had lived in New York since he was five and hardly could speak French.[5] The *abbé's* figure may accurately apply to Franco-Americans living in the United States and French Canadians living in Canada East combined, but not exclusively to French Canadians from the British provinces. Historians since have forgotten that Beaudry could have had no firm foundation upon which to base what undoubtedly was an estimate, for it was not until 1869 that even a preliminary detailed analysis of enlistment in the Northern armies was released. Nevertheless, Beaudry's speech was given wide publicity, and through its repetition in the Canadian press it eventually was transmuted into something different: a popular legend that forty thousand "Canadians," taken to mean all British North Americans, had served in the Northern armies.

Beaudry's statistic apparently was appropriated by John A. Macdonald, possibly because of its propaganda value. In 1904 Goldwin Smith, the British and Canadian historian, wrote that Macdonald had told him at an unspecified time that he had ascertained the extent of British North American enlistment in the Northern armies. According to Smith's recollection Macdonald had said that forty thousand British Canadians had served the North.[6] However, Macdonald did not tell

[3] Emile Falardeau, "Les Canadiens-Français et la guerre de Sécession," *BRH*, xxxii (Sept., 1926), 566; Adrien Verrette, "Les Acadiens aux Etats-Unis," *Bulletin de la Société Historique Franco-Américaine*, n.s., 1 (1955), 79. See also the list compiled by Robert Prévost, "Les Canadiens-Français à la guerre de sécession," Fall River *Indépendant*, Feb. 19, 1939, and reprinted in *Bulletin de la Société Historique*, n.s., 11 (1956), 143–155. From this list, which also appeared in *L'Avenir National* of Manchester (N.H.), it is apparent that most of the French Canadians who enlisted were residents of the Northern states.

[4] Quebec *Courrier de Canada*, quoted in Barrie *Northern Advance*, Sept. 4, 1861. Beauregard was not: see T. Harry Williams, *P. G. T. Beauregard: Napoleon in Gray* (Baton Rouge, 1955), pp. 2–4.

[5] Among the Mallet papers in the library of l'Union Saint-Jean-Baptiste d'Amérique, Woonsocket, Rhode Island, there are some eighteen letters concerning French Canadians from Canada East who served in the Northern army. These letters deal with but three men, however.

[6] Haultain, ed., *Goldwin Smith's Correspondence*, p. 414: Smith to [Charles Frederic] Moberly Bell, Sept. 2, 1904; Bodleian Library, Oxford, James Bryce Papers: Smith to Bryce, Oct. 22, 1904, xvii, folio 20.

Smith how he obtained his figure, and he apparently cited the number
to the historian during the negotiations for the Treaty of Washington
in 1871, a time when he had reason to want to discount his known anti-
American views. Whence came Macdonald's guess?—for a guess it most
certainly was. Even yet no accurate nationality statistics concerning
enlistments in the Northern armies have been compiled, and the best
general figures, which were released in 1898, came after Macdonald's
death. Clearly there was no method by which any records in the provinces could have been kept, for all who enlisted with the North were
violating the British Foreign Enlistment Act, and they were unlikely
to publicize their enlistment beyond the extent that gossip would naturally and inaccurately provide.[7]

The second commonly cited statistic, rather than Beaudry's estimate,
may have been Macdonald's source, however. At first glance this figure
would appear to have official support, and it has the virtue of an exactness that will win credence where an obvious estimate will not. The
supposed total, 53,532, is derived from the work of a prominent mathe-
matician and astronomer, Benjamin Apthorp Gould, the younger,
who served as actuary to the Sanitary Commission from July, 1864, to
the end of the war. In his *Investigations in the Military and Anthro-
pological Statistics of American Soldiers*, published in New York by
the Commission in 1869, Gould presented this figure in terms of "British Americans" who served in the Federal armies.

Although Gould's statistic has been cited frequently in the standard
secondary works, his estimates are of little value. No records of birthplace or parentage were kept when men first enlisted in the armies. Not
until the war was well along was information concerning the state of
one's birth requested on enlistment forms. When such information at
last was asked for, many recruiting agents filled in the forms with hap-
hazard guesses of their own. In order to fill state or town quotas or
in connection with state and county aid, this information sometimes
was changed or falsified by the recruiter. Gould could have obtained
little accurate information concerning nativity from such records.
In addition, interdepartmental rivalry led to the closing to Gould of

---

[7] It is typical of most English accounts of the Civil War that the British North
American aspect is ignored. For example, in a lengthy inquiry into the operation
of the Foreign Enlistment Act, Roundell Palmer, Earl of Selborne (*Memorials:
Part I, Family and Personal, 1766–1865* [London, 1896], II, 376–452), shows no
awareness of the provincial phase of the problem.

the records of the Surgeon General's office and later of those of the Adjutant General as well.[8]

To overcome these handicaps, Gould sent questionnaires to one thousand officers, asking them to estimate the nativities of their respective regiments. The questionnaires were answered by such generalizations as, "¾ American, other ¼ Irish, and German, and a few English and Scotch." Only three hundred and fifty of the officers answered, and on the basis of these vague replies Gould established a ratio for all regiments upon the obviously false assumption that it would remain constant. Applying his ratio to total enlistments, Gould arrived at the interesting statistic that 2.65 per cent of the Northern forces were from the British North American provinces. This, he said, indicated 53,532 men. The lack of scientific accuracy in this method needs no further comment.

When he released his figures Gould added that they were based on "inferences" and called attention to their many inaccuracies. However, the encyclopaedias, almanacs, after-dinner speeches, newspapers, and articles in which these statistics were quoted apparently omitted Gould's lines of caution. This was true despite the fact that when Frederick Phisterer, who had far more data available than did Gould, published his *Statistical Record of the Armies of the United States* in 1883, he declared that, "To give the number of individual persons who served in the army during the war is not practicable" and that it was "not practicable to ascertain" the total number of deaths.[9] In 1896 the United States Record and Pension Office issued two brief memoranda, both of which generally have been overlooked by historians. One, relating to deserters, declared that published statements showing the percentage of deserters by nativity were entitled to no credence whatever. The second, relating to the nativity of soldiers, added that, "No compilation has ever been made by this [War] Department showing the nativity of the whole number of men accepted for military service during the late civil war." [10]

[8] See J. D. O'Connell, "Bogus Statistics Regarding the Union Troops," letter to the editor, New York *Sun*, Dec. 13, 1896, for an account by one of Gould's assistants, and G. C. Comstock, "Benjamin Apthorp Gould," National Academy of Sciences, *Memoirs*, XVII (1924), 162.

[9] (New York), pp. 11, 70.

[10] "Memorandum Relative to the Nativity of Deserters in the United States Army during the War of the Rebellion," and "Memorandum Relative to the Nativity of Soldiers in the United States Army during the War of the Rebellion,"

In any case, even if one were to assume that half the number of alleged British North American enlistments took place, one would be
unwise to conclude from such an assumption that the provinces, as a
whole, were pro-Northern during the Civil War. It must be remembered that many of the British North Americans who were in the
Northern armies had been the victims of crimping and that many
others served only because of the high bounties involved and not because they favored the Northern cause as such. So many French Canadians joined the Union army because of the bounties that the three
leading Roman Catholic bishops of Canada East—the Bishops of Trois-
Rivières, Saint-Hyacinthe, and Quebec—were forced to issue letters
to the parish priests instructing them to warn their followers against
enlistment. General H. B. Carrington, at one time in command of the
Great Lakes' frontier, reported that many British Canadians would enlist, desert, and enlist again, and that to stop this practice he had court
martialed and shot Canadians who had collected three bounties apiece.

Even among those who had entered service willingly, there were
many cases, especially as it became evident that the war was real and
not romantic, of efforts to revive forgotten claims to British citizenship in order to invoke Queen Victoria's proclamation of neutrality
and thus to obtain release from the army. Some were not released in
time and died in the field while others were seriously wounded. Those
who returned to British North America, disillusioned with harsh army
life, were not likely to carry back pro-Northern sentiments. The families of British North Americans who died in action probably felt no
great warmth for the North.[11]

The myth of thousands of British North American enlistments in
the Northern army lacks any basis outside the realm of wishful thinking, and the conclusions that in the past have been based on this ethe-
real structure must be submitted to re-examination. Such considerations,
however, should not overshadow the fact that many British and French
Canadians from the provinces did serve with the Federal troops. Some
undoubtedly fought for the love of adventure, some fought as a private

---

in War Records, Record Group 94, Statistics, Gen'l. Info. Recs., "Nationality of
Soldiers," no. 1362.

[11] Another myth of interest is the report that many boys at Upper Canada College in Toronto left school to join the armies of both North and South. There
was, in fact, no falling off of enrollment at the college during the war that would
justify such a belief (H. E. Orr, Archivist of Upper Canada College, to writer,
July 30, 1956).

crusade against slavery, some fought because they originally had enlisted for the bounty and found that they liked the life, some fought because they had nothing else to do, and a few probably fought because they had too much else to do, but they nonetheless did fight. It is certainly true that many colonials served the North, and their contribution should not be ignored nor their sincerity impugned. While the "myth of the forty thousand" may quantitatively be wrong, the exploits of a handful of brave men can lend qualitative support to the figures.

II

Throughout the war years Lyons and Seward exchanged hundreds of notes on British North American enlistments, voluntary and forced, in the Northern armies. Those enlistments that were voluntary often were a matter of as much diplomatic correspondence as were those that involved coercion. Enlisting in the armed forces of another country was illegal and unwise, since Great Britain might one day be at war with that country. Frequently a minor, seeking adventure, would slip off from home to enlist with the North or South, and Lyons eventually would receive requests from frantic parents to get the boy out of the service. Many parents made long and expensive trips from the provinces to Washington to see the British minister. In some cases the parents originally had given their consent; in others, the boys had run away from home and did not want to be discharged. Often a boy of fourteen or fifteen would discover, after his first battle, that he wanted no red badge of courage, and he would ask his father to apply for his release.

Such requests were voluminous, but they fell easily into patterns. A few parents tried to achieve their purpose through American consuls, who might point out that the supplicants were liberals who supported George Brown and that a discharge would be good diplomacy. Most went directly to Monck or to Lyons and straightforwardly petitioned for the release of their sons. Others, upon learning that a son who had served with the South—and about one in fifty of the British North Americans who enlisted did so—was a Northern captive, would petition for his release on the grounds that he was forced into Confederate service. Some merely requested that their sons be given a position higher than that of ordinary seaman or private. There were fathers who offered to supply substitutes, to repay bounties, and to furnish additional funds, if needed, to secure release. Each case eventually reached Lyons, who then transmitted the requests to Seward. From Seward they went to the Secretary of War, who ordered that an investigation be made at the front. By the time Seward was in a position to reply on a particular appeal, the person in question often was dead, had deserted, or was missing.[12]

There was a great increase in the number of appeals in 1864, probably due to increased crimping activities and the fact that the battles were becoming deadlier. Many of these appeals received the personal attention of Lincoln himself. Boys who had enlisted in 1861 or 1862, when they expected the war to be a short one, had accepted a bounty, which they had sent home. When the war dragged on into a third year, parents who had forgotten for two years that their sons were under age suddenly remembered and petitioned for discharges.[13]

Many of the individual accounts read like melancholy Victorian novels. One such case is that of George S. Grange, who, his affections spurned, gave up his law studies to enlist in the United States Navy. Shortly after he left home, his sister died, and on the day following her burial news of his enlistment arrived, deranging his mother's mind. When word of these occurrences reached him two months later, the son deserted ship and was captured, confined in double irons, and sent to Fortress Monroe for court martial. His mother was not informed, and each day she watched for her son's return. The boy's father carried his appeals one by one to Monck, Lyons, Brown, McDougall, Potter, Thurston, and Seward.[14]

In 1862 the War Department refused to consider any more applications for the discharge of soldiers who had enlisted as minors. Seward

[12] CD, Montreal, VI: Ferguson Blair to Thurston, Nov. 2, and Thurston to Seward, Nov. 7, 1864; and Potter to Seward [error in register], Jan. 9, 1865; *ibid.,* V: Thurston to Seward, July 19, Nov. 7, and Potter to Seward, Sept. 19, 1864; CD, Quebec, II: Thurston to Seward, Oct. 8, 1864; G 17A, 15: Monck to Lyons, Nov. 22, 1861, 17, and May 10, 1862, 114; G 21, 86: McLaughlin to C. J. Coursol, Sept. 13, and Coursol to E. Parent, Sept. 14, 1864, and O. J. Devlin to Monck, July 22, 1865; *ibid.:* Anne Cunningham to Monck, Sept. 23, Nov. 16, 1868; BMW to GCC, 12: Lyons to Monck, Aug. 22, 1864. These G 21 citations deal with a typical appeals case, that of one Andrew Cunningham.

[13] Randall, *Midstream,* p. 44; NFBL, 66: Lyons to Seward, July 19, 1864.

[14] Seward Papers: G. J. Grange to Seward, Nov. 3, 1864; John Sandfield Macdonald Papers, II: J. A. Islin to Macdonald, July 9, 1862, and Macdonald to Sumner, Jan. 5, 1863, 998–1000, 1012–1013.

already had told Lyons that discharges for such enlistees probably should not be considered, and in October of 1861 in anticipation of a change in the Enlistment Act, the Secretary himself had declined to consider any further applications. In April, 1862, Congress passed the expected modification, which provided that the War Department could accept as binding an oath as to age taken by the enlistee and that no further consideration need be given to whether he actually was the required eighteen years of age when he took it. Lyons despaired of getting any new cases before the department, although he submitted those that had been brought to his attention between October and April.[15]

The War Department did modify its policy in 1864 and took under consideration discharges for men who had been recruited illegally, provided that they would refund their bounties. The machinery for this transaction was cumbersome, however, and a recruit was likely to be killed before his discharge reached him. Commutation money was to be given by the parent to the Governor General, who sent it to Her Majesty's legation. Lyons then would show the receipt to Seward, and Seward would ask the War Department to grant the discharge.[16]

There undoubtedly were several thousand British North Americans who enlisted in the Northern army because of a desire to help put down slavery, who gave no thought to a discharge, and who served honorably and sometimes with exceptional bravery and skill throughout their term of enlistment or throughout the war. Among them were some who returned to the provinces to win fame. Some, like Newton Wolverton, who presented the Canadians' petition to Lincoln during the *Trent* affair, or like H. C. Saint-Pierre, who became judge and jurist in the Cour Supérieure of Montreal, continued to look back upon their service as their most vital formative experience.[17] Edward W. Thomson, later a Canadian poet of some ability, enlisted at sixteen and

[15] NBL, 9: Seward to Lyons, Oct. 5, Dec. 11, 1861, 12–13, 65–67; BMW to GCC, 22: Lyons to Manners–Sutton, Nov. 9, 1861; Newton, *Lord Lyons*, 1, 51.

[16] G 6, 235: Burnley to Monck, Jan. 6, 10, 1865; G 14, 44: Monck to Thurston, Dec. 29, 1864, 125–126.

[17] Toronto *Globe*, Feb. 2, 1932; Jean Jacques Lefebvre, Chief Archivist of the Cour Supérieure, Montreal, to writer, April 12, 1956; Lois Darroch Milani, "Four Went to the Civil War," *Ont. Hist.*, LI (Autumn, 1959), 259–272. The writer would like to thank Mrs. Milani for letting him read an advance copy of her article.

served until the end of the war. He saw Lincoln and later produced several poems with a Civil War theme, including at least one, "When Lincoln Died," which is moving to this day. William Canniff, a physician from Canada West, returned from medical service in the Northern army to write his famous history of Ontario. Others, like Augustus Yeomans and Francis M. Wafer, young Canadian doctors, crossed the border on humanitarian missions, and several, like Yeomans, remained after the war.

Some represented British North America during a moment of ceremony, as did John McEachern, who was among sixteen privates attending General U. S. Grant as guard of honor at Appomattox Court House.[18] Some died, with only long-delayed obituaries in home-town newspapers as their last testament. Some returned to the provinces crippled, local reminders for younger generations of what modern warfare meant for the continent. Some enlisted in groups for company, as when Essex and Lambton Counties, Canada West, sent hundreds of men to the Michigan regiments, or when a number of Nova Scotians helped fill quotas in Maine and Vermont. One regiment raised in Boston was filled with so many Nova Scotians that it was dubbed the "Highlanders." [19]

A few British officers serving in the provinces attempted to obtain release from their service so that they might fight in the Civil War. These men chose not to desert despite the higher pay south of the border, but they raised a delicate question of neutrality because of their obvious desire to participate in the conflict. Most of them merely pe-

---

[18] G. S. Ryerson, *Looking Backward* (Toronto, 1924), p. 19; Thomson, *When Lincoln Died, and Other Poems* (Boston, 1909), pp. 24-30; T. G. Marquis, "English-Canadian Literature," in Adam Shortt and A. G. Doughty, eds., *Canada and Its Provinces* (Toronto, 1914), XII, 499; "Frater," "Un Oublie, Joseph-Caleb Paradis," *BRH*, XLIV (March, 1938), 79; Constance Kerr Sissons to writer, Whitby, Ont., April 20, 1956; H. Pearson Gundy, "A Queen's Medical Student in the Army of the Potomac, 1863-4," *Douglas Library Notes*, VI (Dec., 1957), 3-8, and Gundy, "A Kingston Surgeon in the American Civil War," *Historic Kingston*, VII (1958), 43-52. See also Doris Fleming, ed., "Letters from a Canadian Recruit in the Union Army," *Tennessee Historical Quarterly*, XVI (June, 1957), 159-166; and Hector W. Charlesworth, *Candid Chronicles: Leaves from the Note Book of a Canadian Journalist* (Toronto, 1925), p. 11.

[19] New York *World*, Jan. 9, 1864; Me., Legislature, *Report of the Adjutant-General, 1864-65;* Thomas H. Raddall, *Halifax: Warden of the North* (London, 1950), p. 204; James A. Roy, *Joseph Howe: A Study in Achievement and Frustration* (Toronto, 1935), p. 248. The Ottawa *Journal*, March 31, 1951, tells of Samuel Chapleau, a veteran of the war.

titioned Seward for a commission, but others set about their purpose with greater publicity.[20] The case of Colonel Arthur Rankin was the most prominent, for it served to stimulate a Canadian debate on the nature of neutrality.

Colonel Rankin, who was a member of the Canadian Parliament, set out in 1861 to raise a regiment of sixteen hundred lancers for service with the North. After setting his program afoot, Rankin requested and was refused a leave of absence as Commander of the Ninth Military District of Canada. The Toronto *Leader* promptly attacked him for violating Her Majesty's neutrality, and Rankin contended in the press that the Queen's proclamation applied to governments only, leaving individuals free to do as they chose. On the following day he was arrested for violation of the Foreign Enlistment Act on a warrant issued on information furnished by a confectioner called Sugar John, who in turn had obtained his information from George Sheppard of the *Leader*. The Toronto *Globe* and the *Leader* immediately took the floor to debate Rankin's actions and the regiment of lancers was all but forgotten amidst a libelous newspaper battle.[21]

In England, Lord Stanley, a former Colonial Secretary under Palmerston, asked Lord John Russell whether newspaper reports that a regiment of Canadian volunteer militia had been accepted by the United States were true. Russell made inquiries, learned of the Rankin episode, and asked Lyons to discuss the matter with Seward. The Secretary instructed Adams to assure Russell that the United States had not authorized any recruiting in British territory, although, as Seward pointed out, immigration could not be stopped, and many of the *bona fide* immigrants from Ireland or from the provinces naturally entered military service.[22]

During this time a member of Rankin's regiment distributed some eight hundred handbills throughout Hamilton. The bills advertised for five hundred men to come to Detroit for work as farm laborers and ostlers. It was evident that this was a plan to recruit men for Rankin's lancers, for fraudulent certificates that declared that the Ca-

[20] CD, Quebec, 1: Ogden to Seward, Dec. 26, 1863; CD, Halifax, 1: Jackson to Seward, Jan. 19, 1864. *British and Foreign State Papers* (London, 1868), LI, 243–247, includes documents on cases not cited or discussed here.

[21] G 20, 85: Retallack to Rankin, Sept. 14, 1861; Toronto *Globe*, Sept. 13, 1861; Toronto *Leader*, Sept. 13, Oct. 5, 11, 1861; New York *Tribune*, Sept. 12, Oct. 8, 1861; Frank Moore, ed., *The Rebellion Record: A Diary of American Events* (New York, 1862), III, 187–189.

[22] GBI, 18: Dec. 13, 1862, 368–369; *Hansard's, 1861:* CLXIII, col. 632, June 6, 1861.

nadian recruits came from Milwaukee already had been prepared. In addition, an American styling himself "Lieutenant-Colonel Davies" openly was seeking recruits in Hamilton, and the commanding officer there concluded that both men were helping Rankin.[23]

Rankin was bound over to the Assizes on a charge of accepting a commission in the United States Army. In the meantime, three other officers had enlisted in the Northern armies, and the Governor General had cancelled their militia rank. When the Assizes rose without considering Rankin's case, the Toronto *Leader* explained that his crime, being against an imperial statute and having been committed in a foreign country, could be tried only before the Court of Queen's Bench in England. Rankin was deprived of his Canadian commission and during the *Trent* affair he resigned his American commission as well. In an open letter to the Detroit *Free Press* he explained that he had offered his services in friendship and that in view of the possibility of war between the United States and Great Britain he must return to his first loyalty.[24]

Lyons, Monck, and Seward labored to solve the many such problems that enlistment produced, and for the most part they worked in harmony. In the provinces the civil administrations matched the ecclesiastical in warning British North Americans not to enlist in the American armies. In May, 1861, Governor General Head issued a notice to British North Americans that explained the Foreign Enlistment Act. In New Brunswick Lieutenant Governor Gordon issued two proclamations the following December reminding the inhabitants that enlistment in foreign armies was illegal.[25]

Seward was personally careful in his observation of British neutrality in the matter of enlistments. To requests from British North Americans for commissions he consistently replied that he could give no encouragement. Offers were made by civilians who promised to raise full regiments, but Seward even found it possible to discourage men who promised that they alone were worth a regiment of ordinary men. He occasionally received a request from some Canadian couched in terms

[23] NFBL, 42: Booker to Monck, Oct. 7, and Monck to Lyons, Oct. 10, enc. in Lyons to Seward, Oct. 15, 1861; *OR*, ser. III, I, 734, 750.

[24] Macdonald Papers: Head to Macdonald, Oct. 12, 1861, 33–36; E 14, 38: H. Duncan to W. A. Himsworth, Oct. 7, 1861, 255; G 1, 38: Head to Newcastle, Oct. 21, 1861, 254–255; Toronto *Globe*, Oct. 7, 14, 1861, Jan. 1, 28, 1862; Toronto *Leader*, Oct. 7–11, 1861; Montreal *Gazette*, Oct. 19, 1861, Jan. 7, 1862.

[25] G 1, 165: Newcastle to Head, June 27, 1861; CO 189: Gordon to Newcastle, Dec. 9, 1861.

sufficiently provocative to raise the suspicion that it had been sent by a Southerner who hoped to get the Secretary of State to accept an enlistment that would violate British North American neutrality. Seward's response remained unchanged.[26]

The War Department was equally scrupulous about observing the letter of the law but far less strict about the spirit. When offers to enlist were received from individual Canadians early in 1861, Secretary Simon Cameron declined them because he felt that the North's "great material resources" would be sufficient to fill her needs. Following Queen Victoria's proclamation of neutrality in May the War Department insisted that the mustering officers should not muster in any regiment until satisfied that all of its recruits were enlisted within the limits of the United States, but it was quite impossible to enforce such a rule. And in 1864 Secretary of War Stanton showed that he had a rather simple and unrealistic concept of the status of a neutral when he gave permission to a recruiter to raise a regiment of Negroes, partially to be filled with men smuggled from the Canadas "with due regard to 'Queen's neutrality.'" Yet Stanton continued to feel that the War Department was doing its best to prevent crimping.[27]

In June, 1864, the Northern Senate asked whether authority had been given to anyone to obtain recruits in Ireland or British North America and was answered in the negative. Secretary of War Stanton's reply was scarcely the whole truth, showing that he either had his own definition of foreign recruits or that he was willing to overlook lapses from the recruiting law as though they did not come within the meaning of the Senate's question. Stanton informed Lincoln that no recruits had been obtained in "Canada" with his knowledge or consent and that to the best of his information none had been obtained at all nor had any efforts to obtain them been made. Therefore, Stanton concluded, "no measures have been adopted . . . to arrest any such conduct, because no information of any such conduct has reached the Department . . . ." Nonetheless, Seward and Stanton were quick

---

[26] Seward Papers: Yale to Seward, July 2, H. J. Morgan to Seward, Nov. 5, and R. V. Montague to Seward, Feb. 22, 1863; M. Cameron to Seward, Nov. 20, 1865; ITC, 36: Seward to Ogden, Jan. 5, 1864, 80; Marguerite B. Hamer, "Luring Canadian Soldiers into Union Lines during the War between the States," *CHR*, xxvii (June, 1946), 151.

[27] *OR*, ser. iii, i, 137: Cameron to Giddings, April 30, and Cameron to J. H. Dickson, May 8, 1861, 175–176; Seward Papers: E. D. Townsend to E. Backus, Dec. 17, 1861; H. G. Pearson, *The Life of John A. Andrew, Governor of Massachusetts, 1861–1865* (Boston, 1904), ii, 91.

to complain when they learned that British subjects were serving in Confederate ranks. Russell quietly pointed out that as long as thousands of British subjects fought for the North it was no breach of neutrality if hundreds served the South.[28]

III

There were many "enlistments" that were the result of crimping, and these served to muddy Anglo-American diplomatic relations and to counteract any evidence of a common cause between the North and the provinces that voluntary enlistments may have indicated. The practice of crimping was not peculiar to the Civil War. It had long existed in the great port cities of the world, and New York had earned a reputation for crimping from the days when shipping merchants sent out crimps to obtain crews for the merchantmen. Whether a man was on a ship because he was paid or because he was shanghaied had mattered little to the agent or the ship's master, as long as the crew was complete. It was natural that such means of impressment would be resorted to in time of war.

The trade in illegal enlistments did not cross the British North American border all in one direction. During and after the Crimean War there had been attempts made by colonials or by British officers stationed in the provinces to recruit Americans for the British army, and Joseph Howe, in particular, had been involved in a controversy over recruiting. There was nothing approaching the magnitude of the crimping problem that arose during the Civil War, however, a problem that one historian has called "the worst scandal of the war period." [29] With large bounties being offered to both the enlistee and the recruiting officer, it was natural that there would be many abuses. In retrospect the number of injustices done to individual British North Americans in the name of union is appalling.

[28] *OR*, ser. III, IV, 455–458: Seward to Lincoln, June 8, Stanton to Lincoln, June 27, and Welles to Lincoln, June 27, enc. in Lincoln to Senate, June 28, 1864; *Cong. Globe*, 38th Cong., 1st Sess., IV, 3219; GBI, 19: Seward to Adams, Sept. 20, 1864, 458–459; CFA, 83: Russell to Adams, May 1, enc. in Adams to Seward, May 7, 1863; NBL, 10: Seward to Lyons, Aug. 1, 1863, 180.
[29] NFBL, 43: Lyons to Seward, Dec. 9, 1861; Ella Lonn, *Foreigners in the Union Army and Navy* (Baton Rouge, 1951), p. 451. See John B. Brebner, "Joseph Howe and the Crimean War Enlistment Controversy between Great Britain and the United States," *CHR*, XI (Dec., 1930), 300–327.

The more skillful crimps made a point of doing no actual enlisting within the provinces, thus subverting the War Department's order relating to place of enlistment. They would find a likely recruit, advance him a small sum of money and some clothing, and transport him to the United States, where he was enlisted officially. For his trouble the agent would receive a fifteen- to twenty-five-dollar fee plus as much of the recruit's bounty as he could fleece from him. Despite Stanton's disclaimers, higher officials in Washington and in the field knew of the crimping practices and considered that obtaining recruits from British North America was a "dangerous experiment" that would threaten the peace with Great Britain. But they virtually were powerless to stop the practice, especially from 1863 when fresh troops were in constant demand. And when the American War Department made an effort, in 1864, to control crimping in the New York City area by enlisting the support of Simeon Draper, Collector of the Port of New York, the New York police failed to cooperate.[30]

In the face of Northern willingness to enhance the letter of the enlistment laws but disinclination to enforce their spirit, the imperial and colonial governments did what they could to stop crimping. While Lyons was absent in England in 1864 *chargé* J. Hume Burnley privately wrote to Seward with some asperity:

> I can assure you nothing will tend to facilitate matters more than a little harmonious action between our Legation and the U.S. Govt. It will do more good than all the Desp[atch] writing. . . . It would be a source of great satisfaction to me to be enabled to report that something has been done to aid the Canadian Authorities in bringing to justice the [recruiting agents] . . . .[31]

Seward replied archly that the United States Government had used "all diligence in preventing and when discovered in severely punishing such transactions" and that crimping was "practically arrested." Burnley correctly considered that crimping had not been arrested, and shortly thereafter John A. Macdonald, who already had issued a circular asking all county attorneys in the Canadas to help in detecting crimps, began to organize a body of detectives to patrol the border

[30] *OR*, ser. III, I, 734: Backus to L. Thomas, Dec. 9, 1861; MC: William Ludlow to John A. Dix, Dec. 5, 1864, enc. in C. A. Dana, Assistant Secretary of War, to Seward, Dec. 12, 1864; Lonn, pp. 451, 466–469.

[31] Seward Papers: Sept. 17, 1864. Consul Donohoe also tried to get some action (G 6, 233: Donohoe to Lyons, May 25, enc. in Lyons to Monck, Aug. 8, 1864).

towns. Loyal British soldiers were encouraged to appear to be ready to desert so that they might attract crimps whom they could then deliver to the authorities.[32]

The suppression of crimping was especially difficult because convictions were hard to obtain and sentences were not severe.[33] Not until March, 1865, when the war nearly was over, was the American fine for crimping increased to $160. In the provinces the reward in 1861 for the apprehension of crimps was $50 and it was not until 1864 that it was raised to $200 for the capture of each crimp and $50 for the capture of each deserter. Abetting desertion carried an original penalty of six months' imprisonment and $100 fine. In some cases deserters had the letter "D" tattooed across their chests, and in 1864 two soldiers were condemned to death for desertion, although Sir Fenwick Williams commuted the sentence to life imprisonment. Crimps themselves generally were sentenced to six months' hard labor, and on at least one occasion to as much as five years' imprisonment. Such punishments did not stop crimping, and Seward's repeated declaration that the United States would not countenance any of its subordinate officers in holding out inducements to foreign soldiers to desert fell on deaf ears.[34]

Prevention of crimping ultimately depended upon the local recruiting and mustering officers, and the former could be bribed while the latter were too busy to check every instance of alleged misconduct. So many long-time residents of the United States suddenly remembered that they were, in fact, British citizens and appealed to Lyons that even he was inclined to view their claims to protection skeptically, and

[32] NBL, 12: Sept. 19, 1864, 159; G 1, 172: Cardwell to Monck, Nov. 1, 1864; CD, Montreal, VI: Thurston to Seward, Nov. 4, 1864; FO 5, 943, IV: Burnley to Russell, Sept. 23, 1864; G 20, 94: Circular, Feb. 1, 1864; E 1, 89: Dec. 16, 1864, 516–517; C 699: March 10, 1865; Macdonald Papers, 234: Order no. 1, Dec. 31, 1864, 49–51. On the border police, see pp. 322–326.

[33] A. R. Hassard, *Not Guilty and Other Trials* (Toronto, 1926), pp. 164–180, describes several typical cases. See also G 1, 465: Monck to Cardwell, Sept. 23, 1864; G 14, 44: Oct. 14, 1864, 99–103; NFBL, 48: Lyons to Seward, Feb. 3, 1863.

[34] C 693: Hall, April 6, 1864; Toronto *Globe*, March 2, 1864; E, AA: p. 2; Toronto *Leader*, Sept. 9, 1864; CFA, 83: Adams to Seward, July 16, 1863; ITC, 36: Seward to Ogden, Jan. 5, 1864, 80; *ibid.*, 38: Seward to Thurston, July 18, 1864, 63–64; C 179, 180: *passim;* W. F. Raney, "Recruiting and Crimping in Canada for the Northern Forces, 1861–5," *MVHR*, x (June, 1923), 24–25. It is interesting to note that in the period 1843–1861 desertion fills two-thirds of a volume of the Canadian "C" series, while in the period 1861–1865 the subject fills one and a third volumes of the series.

army officers, anxious to get their men to the front, looked with disdain upon anyone claiming release from the army because of British citizenship. Illegal enlistments continued throughout the war, all efforts to the contrary notwithstanding.[35]

At first the crimps concentrated on British soldiers stationed in the provinces rather than on civilians. The troops already had chosen a military life and did not need initial persuasion to shoulder a gun. They also were more highly prized than civilians, for they knew something of war. They were fairly easy targets, for life in the British army was hard, discipline exacting, and pay poor. Even before the first battle of the war Rear Admiral Sir Alexander Milne had to place H.M.S. *Pyramus* off Halifax with orders to search every merchant vessel, British or foreign, leaving the harbor thereafter, in order to retard "systematic desertion." This order was inspired by the desertion of nineteen crew members of H.M.S. *St. George,* who had slipped away on three American merchantmen. The consul at Halifax, then Albert Pillsbury, objected to stopping the ships for a search once they had started from the harbor, and Milne agreed to inspect them while they still were in port and then to have his ship accompany them from the harbor to make certain that no one boarded them later. This method—sometimes referred to as the "*Aldanah* plan" after the first vessel to which it was applied—apparently was successful. Desertion of this type, while aggravated by the Civil War, was not caused by it, however, for Milne had reported similar organized desertion at Sydney on Cape Breton in 1860.[36]

Recruiting agents from Maine poured into New Brunswick during 1861 to promote desertion there. In Woodstock, Saint John, and St. Stephen, they tried to persuade members of the voluntary militia to bring their new Enfield rifles into Maine with them. Under such circumstances the desertion of army men was not uncommon. Officers apparently did not desert as readily as did enlisted men, for they often were allowed to go to Maine or elsewhere to watch Union forces train,

[35] MS. Group 10, 29, 6: Worthington to Rollo, Jan. 15, 1862; CD, Clifton, 1: Jones to Seward, Aug. 8, 1866; Toronto *Globe,* Jan. 2, 1862; Detroit *Advertiser and Tribune,* Sept. 3, 1863, March 8, 1864; Detroit *Free Press,* July 10, Nov. 19, 1863; Halifax *Reporter,* Jan. 14, 1864; Goderich *Huron Signal,* April 23, 1861; Landon, "Harris," art. 10: Aug. 6, 9, 1862; Newton, 1, 87.

[36] G 8B, 62: Gordon to Newcastle, Nov. 25, 1861, 10–11; CD, Halifax, ix: Pillsbury to Milne, June 17–19, and reply, June 19, all enc. in Pillsbury to Seward, June 20, 1861; G 8A, 1: Milne to Mulgrave, Aug. 5, 1861, 279–283; Halifax *Morning Chronicle,* June 15, 1861.

and despite meeting with a friendly reception they apparently returned to the provinces. But even this activity had to be curtailed as
crimps became more aggressive. In February, 1862, military and civil
authorities at Woodstock established patrols on the roads leading to
the American border and thus limited desertions to a single case during the following month. Tobique remained famous as a center of
crimping, however, and desertion at St. Andrews and Saint John continued with small groups of six to ten soldiers slipping across to Calais
in Maine every now and then to enlist.[37]

Desertion from the British army was better organized along the upper New York border. By May of 1861 recruiting agents already had
appeared in Montreal and Toronto. At Watertown, New York, deserters were welcomed with no questions asked. Citizens would wait
along the shore of the St. Lawrence to hear the firing of the evening
curfew gun at Kingston, across the river in Canada West. Fired once
additionally for each deserter, it gave ample warning of how many
British soldiers might be expected to arrive in some crimp's rowboat in
quest of a change of clothes, hot food, and a recruiting officer. Clothes
were especially important and an entire new wardrobe had to be furnished the deserter, for everything he wore bore his regimental in-
signia. In the lower peninsula of Canada West trains were carefully
watched for deserters, and it was reported that any detachment of
troops stationed near Detroit would melt away. Orders were given
to British soldiers on lookout duty at Sandwich to arrest any soldiers
found over one mile from camp and to apprehend anyone with them.[38]

The crimps at first advertised for recruits in the British North American press. Later the newspapers were forced to stop accepting such
advertisements when the Colonial Office gave permission to the imperial administrators to threaten them with loss of government advertising if they continued. Agents turned to posting placards in border
towns or to distributing handbills that offered handsome inducements

[37] G 8B, 62: Gordon to Newcastle, Dec. 9, 1861, Feb. 3, March 17, 1862 and
Monck to Newcastle, June 21, 1862; Calais *Advertiser*, April 24, 1862; Eastport
Sentinel, Sept. 7, 1864; Fredericton *Head Quarters*, Oct. 8, 1862; Francis Duncan,
Our Garrisons in the West; or, Sketches on British North America (London,
1863), p. 238.

[38] CD, Montreal, IV: Giddings to Seward, March 17, 1863; *ibid.*, V: Giddings to
Seward, Feb. 27, 1864; C 698: Lugard, Jan. 30, 1861, p. 1, and March 29, 1864, p. 8,
and Hall, April 6, Aug. 16, 1864, reports; Toronto *Leader*, May 2, 4, 1861, Aug.
7, 1862, Jan. 30, 1863; G. G. Heiner, Jr., *From Saints to Red Legs: Madison Barracks, the History of a Border Post* (Watertown, 1938), p. 49.

to enlist. One recruit was offered $113 a month plus clothing and medical attention, $100 as a bounty at the end of the war, and 120 acres of land upon honorable discharge. Another potential recruit was offered $250 upon passing a surgeon's examination, $1250 more upon entering service, and 160 acres of land at the end of the war. British soldiers often were promised pay of eighty-five cents per day. When one realizes that British privates received only six pence a day, the magnitude of the temptation is clear. Sergeants, who received four times this, were offered up to three dollars per day.[39]

The crimps had to turn to the civilian population of the provinces by late in 1862, and they obtained their victims by unlimited variations of set patterns. Crimps came from British North America as well as from the United States, and the most famous crimp of all, F. B. Bonter, was a British Canadian. There also were many highly successful French-Canadian crimps, especially in Montreal, and several women also were able to make use of their knowledge of local conditions in this way. Methods did not differ greatly, except that to render their victims unconscious the women used drugged tea while the men used several rounds of perfectly normal local whiskey. Crimps often worked in league with boardinghouse keepers, making it possible to drug prospective victims with sleeping potions or to chloroform them before turning them over to substitute brokers. The cleverest means of obtaining men was to buy army horses in the provinces and to have three or four boys accompany the stock to work in livery stables. The boys then could be recruited as wranglers. Covered wagons were sent to Quebec for supplies and returned with new and inductible drivers, and young men also accompanied carloads of wheat across the border. Some men were abducted from their homes along the Canadian side of the shore, while several on visits to New York state were arrested for alleged desertion from the American army to which they had never belonged and were forced to enlist in order to win their freedom. The Collector of Customs at Coaticook, Canada West, reported that crimps made it unsafe for townspeople to be out at night and that their sleep was disturbed by the "hideous noises" of those crying for help while they were being kidnapped. One vain young man who foolishly took his Canadian militia uniform with him on a visit to Memphis was arrested on suspicion of trying to join the Southern forces. Men were taken to Detroit, ostensibly to work in

[39] G 8B, 62: Gordon to Newcastle, Dec. 9, 1861, 32–34; C 696: Wynne to Bouchier, July 15, 1861; C 698: R 26,470, Oct. 27, 1864; *The Times*, Feb. 19, 1862.

a cotton mill, and were asked to enlist, while others were taken to some point near the border to chop wood, made drunk, carried across the frontier, and enrolled.[40] It was said that potential settlers in the American West were frightened to enter the United States, and when a male visitor to the Republic failed to write or was overdue in his return, crimping often was suspected. By 1864 at least one guide book for prospective immigrants to the Canadas saw fit to warn its readers of the dangers of crimping.[41]

As a result of crimping practices, legitimate requests from American businessmen for British North American laborers often had to be rejected from fear that they were disguised recruiting schemes. The Michigan lumbering interests, in particular, suffered from lack of men but could not get them despite paying high wages. The British consul at Boston often received appeals for laborers, but most of the appeals clearly were illegitimate. One crimp bluntly asked what would happen if an agent raised troops by inviting Canadians across the line to work on farms, and another rather transparently asked whether certificates of citizenship could be obtained for Welshmen to work in the Vermont quarries. With justification the consul read "Canadians" for "Welshmen." [42]

Even the supposed prototype of Uncle Tom, Josiah Henson, who was living in Canada West, violated the enlistment laws. As soon as

[40] Macdonald Papers, 339: Thomas Moody to Macdonald, March 22, 1865, 86–89; Mulgrave Letter Book: Howe to Mulgrave, Sept. 17, and Mulgrave to Lyons, Sept. 18, 1861; C 698: May 23, Aug. 6, Nov. 21, 1864, and H. Salvin to Hall, Aug. 8, 1864; C 699: April 10, 11, 1865; NFBL, 62: Lyons to Seward, March 31, April 2, 1864; *ibid.*, 67: Lyons to Seward, Aug. 4, 1864; *ibid.*, 68: Burnley to Seward, August 25, 1864; *ibid.*, 70: Burnley to Seward, Oct. 1, 1864; *ibid.*, 76: Burnley to Seward, Feb. 22, 1865; NBL, 9: Seward to Lyons, Aug. 21, 1862, March 19, 1863, 249, 485–486; Seward Papers: C. Calahan to Seward, Nov. 17, and E. H. Goff to Seward, Dec. 28, 1863, and M. J. Ferguson to Father Proulx, Sept. 22, enc. in J. G. Moylan to Seward, Sept. 27, 1864; Toronto *Leader*, July 28, 1862; Sherbrooke *Freeman*, Feb. 20, 1865. See Lonn, *Foreigners in the Union Army and Navy*, pp. 455–468, for several cases not discussed here.

[41] Sarnia *Observer*, March 10, 1865; Quebec *Gazette*, Feb. 22, 1865; MC: Rev. E. Strowbridge to Seward, Jan. 19, 1865; Lady Frances Elizabeth Owen Monck, *My Canadian Leaves: An Account of a Visit to Canada in 1864–65* (London, 1891), p. 194; H. T. N. Chesshyre, *Canada in 1864: A Hand-Book for Settlers* (London, 1864), App. B.

[42] CD, Montreal, IV: David Munger to Seward, Sept. 4, 1862; FO 5, 899: Lousada to Lyons, Dec. 15, 1863; BMW to GCC, 11: Lyons to Monck, Dec. 8, 1863; G 6, 231: Memo., Dec. 5, and C. F. Dunbar to Lousada, enc. in Lyons to Monck, Dec. 8, 1863; *ibid.*, 232: Lousada to Lyons, April 5, 1864; *OR*, ser. I, XLIII, 930: Harper to Rowley, Aug. 26, 1864.

Lincoln issued a proclamation permitting Negro enlistment in the army, forty young Negroes from the Elgin Settlement in Canada West volunteered to join a Negro regiment being organized in Detroit. In all, seventy Negroes from the Buxton district enlisted. Late in 1862, Governor Andrew of Massachusetts appointed George L. Stearns, who had been a friend of John Brown, to the chairmanship of a committee to raise a Bay State Negro regiment, and Stearns sought out recruits in the Canadas. He apparently was successful in obtaining enlistments, for among the thousand Negroes who were sent to camp at Readville, Massachusetts, in 1863, were several from Canada West.[43]

As the patriarch of the expatriate group, Henson advised all ablebodied Negroes to enlist in the Northern armies, and as encouragement he offered to advance small sums to the families of those who did so. Fearing that the Negroes would have their bounty money stolen, he accompanied them to obtain the bounties and to return them to the families concerned personally. As a result, Henson was charged with inducing enlistments, and he escaped trial only because the informer's character was judged unacceptable for testimony in court.[44]

Impressed by the extent of the crimper's trade, some historians have concluded that British North Americans lived in a state of constant fear of Northern abduction and death before a Confederate charge. Whether many British North Americans actually were frightened by crimping is difficult to judge, especially since no accurate figures on the number of victims can be compiled. Despite their fear for loved ones visiting in the United States and despite increased reports from 1864 of kidnapping in the North the provincials did not hesitate to visit across the border. Significantly, those who could do so continued to send their children to universities in the United States. It is rather surprising to learn, for example, that despite the fact that boys of college and university age would have been ideal targets for crimps, the number of British North Americans attending Harvard University and Columbia College actually increased during the war.[45] Thousands of

[43] P.A.C., William King Papers: MS. autobiography; P.A.C., microfilm collection of King's newspaper holdings; Annie S. Jamieson, *William King, Friend and Champion of Slaves* (Toronto, 1925), pp. 174-175; Benjamin Quarles, *The Negro in the Civil War* (Boston, 1953), p. 9; Pearson, *John A. Andrew*, II, 82.

[44] Brion Gysin, *To Master—A Long Goodnight: The Story of Uncle Tom, A Historical Narrative* (New York, 1946), pp. 170-176.

[45] *Catalogues of the Officers and Students of Harvard University*, 1858-66 (8 vols.), *passim*; *Annual Catalogues of the Officers and Students of Columbia College*, 1860-66 (6 vols.), *passim*. British North American enrollment at Harvard rose from twenty-seven in 1860 to forty-eight in 1865 and at Columbia such enroll-

British North Americans took employment in Northern factories, mills, and mines, or on the Western railroads, apparently unafraid of being crimped, and dozens of upper-class Canadians continued to take their holidays along the coast of Maine.

Nonetheless, the crimping problem was a serious one, and it ended only with the end of the war itself. In July, 1865, the Orders in Council concerning rewards were repealed.[46] Throughout the Civil War the British evinced a fair attitude toward the various problems relating to enlistments and showed great patience in unraveling the confused and conflicting claims that arose.

IV

During the Civil War there were many violations of the international frontier by individual law officers, violations that grew out of the atmosphere that crimping produced. A general breakdown in legal procedures threatened, for American and Canadian law enforcement officers frequently violated the boundary to pursue escaped criminals, suspects, crimps, and deserters, and the officers even resorted to some of the crimper's techniques. Seward, in particular, often took a nonchalant attitude toward law enforcement along the border.

That the nature of British neutrality had not been made sufficiently clear to the Northern soldiers is evident, for they showed incredible naiveté in assuming that they had any powers on Canadian soil. In 1863 a sergeant from the Northern army took it upon himself to go to Bradford, Canada West, to recover a deserter, forcing him to return to his regiment. While apologizing for this violation of the border, Seward partially defended the sergeant on the revealing grounds that he was ignorant of the importance of his offense. The following year another sergeant was arrested in Canada for attempting to recruit soldiers, and Giddings, who paid his bail, defended him on identical grounds.[47]

---

ment rose from seven to thirty-one during the same years. Canadian students did disappear from the student catalog of the University of Wisconsin after 1862 (*Catalogue of the Officers and Students of the University of Wisconsin*, 1861–67 [7 vols.], *passim*), and one student was crimped from Oberlin College in Ohio (NFBL, 47: Doherty to Lyons, Nov. 7, enc. in Lyons to Seward, Nov. 20, 1862).

[46] E 1, 90, AB: July 27, 1865, 503–504.

[47] NBL, 9: Seward to Lyons, Jan. 3, 1863, 392–393; CD, Montreal, v: Potter to

The case that received the most publicity at the time concerned one Ebenezer Tyler, a Canadian deserter from the Northern army. In January, 1863, a party of armed Union soldiers forcibly entered Tyler's house on Wolfe Island, Canada West, and carried him back to New York. When Lyons complained with somewhat more force than usual, Seward partially excused the abductors because of their "earnest zeal," but he disavowed their act, promised that the officer who led the expedition would be discharged, and ordered Tyler returned to his home.[48]

Many of the cases of abduction involved criminal offenses at which both Monck and Seward were willing to wink. In most instances Seward would offer regrets, but the abducted criminal would remain in jail. Occasionally American and British North American police cooperated in some extralegal activity, as when a thief was arrested by the constabulary in St. Catharines at the suggestion of New York police and returned to the scene of her crime without recourse to the usual procedures of extradition. Canadians later were hired to kidnap a criminal who had escaped to the province and to deliver him to an American officer at the border, thus preventing a violation of the letter of the law. Abductions were none too gentle, and little regard for individual rights was shown. One man—the subject of Lyons' second most extensive wartime correspondence—was kidnapped from his home in Canada West, charged with aiding the South and with theft, and was imprisoned by being gagged and chained to the floor of his cell.[49]

Abduction did not run all in one direction, however. An armed party from a Canadian gunboat landed within the jurisdiction of the United States on the River St. Clair and captured a British deserter, an action of which Seward only mildly complained, and with the assent of the police of Port Huron, Michigan, two Canadian constables forcibly

Seward, Sept. 12, 14, 1864; ITC, 36: Seward to Giddings, May 27, 1864, 448–449; DL, 64: Seward to Stanton, May 28, 1864, 398. See G 6, 299: Lyons to Monck, Nov. 4, 1861, and G 1, 166: Newcastle to Monck, Nov. 10, 1861, for a similar case in which a Michigan Infantry captain tried to force several deserters to return to the United States and was stopped by a Canadian magistrate.

[48] G 6, 231: Lyons to Seward, March 19, enc. in Lyons to Monck, March 21, 1863, and Seward to Lyons, April 15, enc. in Lyons to Monck, April 25, 1863, 121; Ottawa *Citizen*, Jan. 23, 1863.

[49] NBL, 13: Hunter to Bruce, Jan. 16, 1866, 496–497; *ibid.*, 14: Seward to Bruce, June 5, 1867, 188–191; NFBL, 57: Lyons to Seward, Dec. 31, 1863; MC: Dart to Seward, Jan. 11, 1866; FO 5, 833: H. Murray to Lyons, June 20, enc. in Lyons to Russell, July 6, 1862.

conveyed two thieves to Canada West. Again Seward did not require that the men be returned. One Canadian wanted in Ottawa for seduction was arrested in Ogdensburg. As his was not an extraditable offense, it apparently did not come to Seward's attention, but the Ogdensburg police transferred the prisoner to Canadian authorities nonetheless. Seward's general attitude toward all such cases was that if the men involved were proved guilty, the abduction or illegal transfer of the prisoner from one country to another was a *fait accompli* best ignored. Monck felt the same way, but the new Colonial Secretary, Edward Cardwell—who replaced Newcastle after the latter's death in 1864—felt that such laxity concerning the formalities of extradition might lead to serious international complications. Thereafter, only a few such cases arose.[50]

Other abnormal wartime border traffic grew out of the Northern draft. By the autumn of 1862 the presence of draft-dodgers in British North America had become quite obvious. The provincials formed a bad impression of Northern troops and patriotism when hundreds of "skedaddlers," as they were called, streamed into the colonies. Desertion and "skedaddling" were as serious a problem in the Confederacy as in the Union, but few Southern deserters went so far north. As a result, some Canadians refused to believe that Southerners ever deserted.[51]

Lincoln had anticipated that there would be many attempts to evade the draft, and on August 8, 1862, the President issued an order prohibiting citizens subject to military duty from going to a foreign country without permission. Later that day Secretary of War Stanton was informed that men were fleeing to the Canadas, and four days later four hundred draft-dodgers were reported to have crossed into Canada West at Niagara Falls within a twenty-four-hour period. No exact figures can be obtained, but contemporary sources estimated the number of draft-dodgers and deserters in the united Canadas alone by 1865 at ten to fifteen thousand.[52]

[50] CD, Montreal, IV: McMullan to Giddings, April 17, enc. in Giddings to Seward, April 21, 1863; NFBL, 51: Monck to Lyons, May 22, enc. in Lyons to Seward, May 30, 1863; NBL, 14: Seward to Bruce, July 12, 1866, 32–33, and Aug. 1, 1866, 49; G 1, 172: Cardwell to Monck, July 23, 1864; Toronto *Globe*, March 20, 1863.

[51] Toronto *Weekly Leader*, Feb. 19, 1864.

[52] OR, ser. II, II, 370; *ibid.*, ser. III, II, 320, 527; G 6, 230: Stuart to Monck, Sept. 14, 1862; Toronto *Globe*, Aug. 22, 25, 1862; Toronto *Leader*, Aug. 12, 1862; New

If for no other than economic reasons, the draft-dodgers were un-popular in British North America. While it is true that the skedaddlers —sometimes referred to by the farmers with earthy humor as "breeding hogs"—ended the prewar labor shortage in the countryside, they also formed roaming bands who indulged in petty thievery as they drifted from county to county. Available at ten dollars a month, the draft-dodger made it possible for the farmer to step up production to take advantage of inflated wartime prices. But the skedaddler was untrustworthy, and he was likely to leave the farmer in the midst of harvest season or to raid the farmer's barn upon leaving his job.[53]

The Civil War also affected the urban labor market in British North America. Early 1861 was a period of urban unemployment in the provinces as well as in the United States, and colonials were advised not to go south of the border for work, so that migration declined until autumn. However, following the Battle of Bull Run and the mustering of thousands of Americans into the armies, Canadians, especially from Canada East, poured into the United States looking for work and simultaneously adding to the labor shortage on Canadian farms while eliminating unemployment in the larger centers for a few months. New Brunswickers and Nova Scotians also joined in the exodus, although they began to return the following year to take part in the shipbuilding boom, which was induced partially by blockade-running. By 1863 draft-dodgers had spread throughout the provinces, lowering wages in the country and once again creating unemployment in the cities. The flow of skilled mechanics from the Canadas to the United States also continued, and in 1864 the Canadian government actively began to encourage European emigrants, who had been passing through the provinces on their way to the North, to remain, using the dangers of crimping as a talking point.[54]

Although the evaders went to the cities at first, they later spread throughout the smaller towns of most of the provinces, a reproach to their nation wherever they went. Facetiously it was said that the young ladies of the border communities had to look under their beds at night

---

York *Tribune*, March 7, 1864; *Cong. Globe*, 38th Cong., 1st Sess., II, 1249; Ella Lonn, *Desertion during the Civil War* (New York, 1928), pp. 201–202.

[53] Toronto *Globe*, Oct. 9, 1863; Sarnia *Observer*, Sept. 23, 1864; Detroit *Adver-tiser and Tribune*, July 24, 1863; Detroit *Free Press*, Nov. 20, 1863.

[54] Charlottetown *Islander*, July 5, 1861; G. B., *Sess. Papers, 1863*, III, no. 5; Giddings Papers: Giddings to A. Coleman, Sept. 27, 1861; London *Canadian News*,

for skedaddlers.[55] In New Brunswick, for example, so many draft-dodgers settled around Mapleton that the area was named Skedaddle Ridge, and there also was a Skedaddler's Reach on Campobello Island. Entire settlements of draft-dodgers appeared along Golden and Parent ridges and at American Lodge on the Restigouche River. When the draft of 1862 went into effect, Aroostook County, Maine, failed to supply its quota of men, and fifty potential draftees fled from Penobscot to St. Stephen. By 1863 the international Madawaska-Aroostook region was said to be a haven for copperheads and deserters, who were helped across the border whenever the law began to search out draft-evaders.[56]

The skedaddlers also helped to poison provincial opinion of the North. British North Americans sometimes seemed ready to view the draft-dodgers as typical Northerners. Some apparently formed their opinions of the Northerner almost exclusively on the basis of the many itinerants, forgetting that most Northerners obeyed the laws regardless of their dislike for the draft and conveniently ignoring French Canada's well-known antipathy for conscription. Draft-dodgers often spread the view that the war had been whipped up by Lincoln in order to establish a dictatorship, and the provincials seldom came into contact with a Northerner who understood why he was fighting, for those who did know generally were at the front. The colonial press commented frequently and unfavorably on the ske-daddlers and on the country that produced them and pointed out that had they served as was required crimps would not have been so active. The Toronto *Leader*, for example, defended the draft-dodgers as victims of Northern persecution, and the *Berliner Journal* saw them as

---

March 30, 1865; CD, Montreal, IV: Thurston to G. J. Abbott, Oct. 26, 1863, 29; CD, Halifax, X: Jackson to Seward, Aug. 15, 1863; Hansen and Brebner, *Mingling of the Canadian and American Peoples*, pp. 140, 153-154; D. N. Panabaker, "The Town of Hespeler," Waterloo Hist. Soc., *Tenth Annual Report* (1922), 214-221.

[55] Saint John *Courier*, May 4, 1861; Portland *Progressive Age*, Oct. 20, 1864; Calais *Advertiser*, July 17, 1862; Machias *Union*, June 30, 1863; Presque Isle *Loyal Sunrise*, Oct. 14, 1863; N.B., House of Assembly, *Journals, 1862*, 14; W. F. Ganong, *A Monograph on the Origins of the Settlements in New Brunswick* (Ottawa, 1904), pp. 99, 135, 157; T. C. L. Ketchum, *A Short History of Carleton County, New Brunswick* (Woodstock, 1922), p. 69; Esther C. Wright, *The Miramichi* (Sackville, N.B., 1944), p. 61.

[56] CD, Halifax, X: Jackson to Seward, Aug. 23, 1864; OR, ser. III, III, 425-426; N. F. Morrison, *Garden Gateway to Canada: One Hundred Years of Windsor and Essex County, 1854-1954* (Toronto, 1954), p. 52.

another *Einwanderung*, but the Barrie *Northern Advance*, one of the more independent journals in Canada West, declared that no hospitality should be shown men who deserted their country in its time of need. To the draft-dodgers it applied the lines usually reserved, far more unjustly, for the Botany Bay convicts: "True patriots we, for be it understood,/We leave our country for our country's good." [57]

At the end of the war, as the draft-dodgers drifted back into the Northern states, the British North Americans began to return to the provinces, attracted by the wages that rose as the cheap skedaddler labor supply dwindled. The border did not return to its old patterns of migration, however, for thousands of French Canadians who had worked in the New England textile mills or in Northern mines either returned to or remained in the United States, and in 1865 the great period of French-Canadian immigration was to begin. [58]

That crimping and draft-dodging would have an adverse effect on Canadian-American relations during the Civil War was to be expected. Crimping and enlistments were trying problems for Lyons and Monck, and they, together with the tensions created by the draft-dodgers, contributed to the growth of anti-Northern public opinion in British North America during the war. It would not be unreasonable to conclude that crimping practices, in particular, did much to counteract the friendlier feeling manifest in the thousands, albeit popularly inflated thousands, of voluntary British North American enlistments. The skedaddlers were cited as evidence of wide-spread Northern dislike even for the cause of union, of violations of an individual's rights—for many British North Americans strongly resisted conscription within their own provinces—of Yankee cowardice, or of a Lincolnian dictatorship. Little of this border traffic in manpower during the Civil War was ennobling, and it undoubtedly served to stain both maple leaf and eagle with a touch of avarice.

[57] Albany *Evening Journal*, Nov. 25, 1861; *Advance*, Aug. 26, 1862; *Berliner Journal*, Dec. 5, 1861, Jan. 15, 1863. Berlin, Canada West, is now Kitchener, Ontario.
[58] CD, Quebec: Ogden to Seward, Dec. 16, 1863, May 17, 1864; Saint John *Courier*, May 20, June 24, 1865; Chicago *Tribune*, July 30, 1865; Hansen and Brebner, p. 141; Mason Wade, "The French Parish and *Survivance* in Nineteenth Century New England," *Catholic Historical Review*, xxxvi (July, 1950), 173.

eleven ൠ PUBLIC OPINION IN BRITISH

NORTH AMERICA ON THE CIVIL WAR

"We live under a government of men and morning newspapers."
WENDELL PHILLIPS

SOME DIPLOMATIC HISTORIANS QUESTION THE VALUE OF STUDIES OF PUBLIC
opinion. After all, one may ask, before the day of universal suffrage,
when the franchise was limited to tax-paying males, what difference
did it make what the mass of people thought? Yet this is to ignore the
proper function of *public* opinion and to confuse it with *popular*
opinion. "The public" in 1860 embraced only those who could play an
effective public role: the electorate, mature, male, and interested, at
least slightly, in public events. However, to pretend that the average
British North American voter or politician was interested in Anglo-
American relations, as such, during the Civil War would be to forget
that most important truism of politics: Elections generally are won or
lost on domestic, not foreign, issues. Since foreign policy was controlled from Westminster, it mattered less what "the people" thought
of the Civil War than what Her Majesty's government chose to do
about it.

Apparently the intelligent British North American was avidly
interested in the battles of the Civil War, for many-columned battle
reports appeared in his local newspapers. It is reasonable to assume that
it was the color and the drama of the conflict that fascinated him, just
as the color and drama have lost none of their ability to enthrall the
present generation of armchair strategists, and that it was not the
foreign policy of the United States, of Great Britain, or, through the
latter, of the provinces, that excited him. That no British North

American newspaper printed more than an occasional letter to the editor on the *issues* of the Civil War as distinct from the *events* would seem to indicate that few people were sufficiently aroused, except during the *Trent* affair, to make the newspaper the public forum that, in theory, it should be. And as the *Trent* affair illustrated, the governments of Great Britain and the United States were not inclined to support aggressive actions simply because the populace made belligerent noises. A daring cavalry raid by J. E. B. Stuart was exciting; what one chancery clerk said to another chancery clerk was not.

Of course, if a provincial government grossly mishandled the increasingly dangerous border situation, it might receive a reprimand at the polls. But the war was not likely to have any profound influence on the delicately balanced political situation that existed in most of the provinces, for the major issues during the war years remained the issues that always have gripped Canada—land, race, and religion. Representation by population, or "Rep. by Pop.," as George Brown's rather irreverent followers called their program, was made an important issue, as were the ever-present questions of depression in the Maritime Provinces, tax increases in the Canadas, in this case to finance the defense program, and the fisheries off the Atlantic coast. Each of these issues was altered somewhat by the Civil War, but they remained largely domestic or imperial questions. It was on issues such as these that elections turned, and except for the defeat of the Militia Bill, which earned more historical prominence than it deserved because Macdonald's government chose to fall on it, little of importance stemming from the Civil War was discussed at any length in any of the provincial assemblies until 1864. Confederation, which held the rostrum from 1864 to 1867, was given a vital stimulus by the Civil War, but it, too, reflected a political and imperial problem that began long before the war.

But all of these considerations do not remove the necessity for the historian to make some attempt to understand what the people of British North America thought about the Civil War. Public opinion remains important because it is partially through his opinion made vocal that the human being exercises that human dignity and worth of which philosophers teach. In one sense, popular history itself is but public opinion narrowly drawn. Less abstractly, it is important to know what opinions were held in the provinces because these opinions inevitably colored local border relations and created situations that required delicate diplomacy to unravel. The diplomatic history of the last two years of the Civil War, in particular, was influenced by public opinion, for the climate of that opinion made the growth of Confederate plots within British North America possible. After 1863 public opinion also was important because of the climate that it created within the United States for the reception of those plots. Finally, through its didactic qualities the Civil War had a profound influence upon the thought of the Fathers of Canadian Confederation. The Dominion of Canada's present form of government stems, in part, from the Canadian conviction partially induced by the Civil War that a nation must have a strong central government in which ultimate power is vested and that to it, and not to its component states or provinces, should go all residual powers.

It is impossible to declare with any exactness how much public opinion in the British North American provinces favored either the North or the South during the Civil War. There is general agreement that the North had the sympathy of the provinces during the secession crisis and for the first months of Lincoln's administration, and most sources, contemporary and scholarly, agree that public opinion began to change by early summer due to Lincoln's failure to declare a war on slavery.[1] The Northern loss at Bull Run quickened the current and, as has been shown, the *Trent* affair crystallized opinion into a generally anti-Northern form. There is considerable disagreement as to whether public opinion, always highly mercurial, returned to its original pro-Northern position by 1863, following the enunciation of the Emancipation Proclamation, and therefore there is a difference of opinion among writers as to how British North American public opinion should be classified for the war period as a whole. Some students of the subject have concluded that, for the most part, public opinion was pro-Northern.[2] However, a number of writers contend that British North

[1] See Raddall, *Halifax*, p. 204, and W. C. Barrett, *Down to the Sea Again* (Halifax, 1947), p. 28, for Nova Scotia; Callahan, *Canadian Relations*, p. 270, for the Canadas; G. Gunn, "Maine-New Brunswick Relations," pp. 184–186, for New Brunswick; Oscar Skelton, *Galt*, p. 307; L. E. F. English, Curator of The Newfoundland Museum, St. John's, to writer, Feb. 17, 1956; Brebner, *North Atlantic Triangle*, p. 161; Edward W. Thomson, *Old Man Savarin and Other Stories: Tales of Canada and Canadians* (New York, 1917), p. 197; Richard Cartwright, *Reminiscences* (Toronto, 1911), p. 24.

[2] Helen G. Macdonald, *Canadian Public Opinion on the American Civil War* (New York, 1926), makes use of some two dozen British North American newspapers as its chief source. Most of the official British, Canadian, and American

America was "almost universally with the south," [3] and at least one writer has professed to find that the intensity of this feeling varied according to proximity to the American border.[4]

The human desire to find a label and even a statistic for every sentiment conspires against impartiality. From the sources now available, newspapers, diaries, private letters, and public speeches, the best that the present writer can say is that contrary to previous findings public opinion probably was somewhat more anti-Northern than has been thought, that a major portion of the British North American press was outspokenly anti-Northern, and that to the residents of the Northern states at the time the people of British North America must have seemed predominantly pro-Southern, since the conservative press was more vocal than was the liberal press. The last conclusion is more im-

---

correspondence and many of the collections of the letters of statesmen apparently were not available to Miss Macdonald. Most of the articles of Fred Landon, cited elsewhere, conclude that the Canadas were pro-Northern, usually basing this conclusion on the alleged enlistment of forty thousand or more British North Americans in the Northern armies (see Chapter Ten, above). One recent study of this same period, David Fred Hill, "Some Aspects of the Rise of Canadian Nationalism, 1858–1865: A Study of Public Opinion with Special Reference to the Influence of the United States," unpubl. Ph.D. diss. (Univ. of Southern California, 1955), accepts Macdonald's conclusions as "established" (p. 175, n. 7), and on the basis of some two dozen Canadian (not Maritime) newspapers supports her conclusions. See also D. H. Gillis, *Democracy in the Canadas, 1795–1867* (Toronto, 1951), p. 204; and A. P. Cockburn, *Political Annals of Canada* (Toronto, 1905), p. 378.

[3] The wording is J. W. Bailey's, in *Loring Woart Bailey: The Story of a Man of Science* (Saint John, 1925), p. 38. Others who support this contention, without the judgment of intensity, include Charlesworth, *Candid Chronicles*, p. 10; Atherton, *Montreal*, II, 210; Alexander M. Ross, *Recollections and Experiences of an Abolitionist, from 1855 to 1865* (Toronto, 1875), p. 125; John Buchan, ed., *British America* (Boston, 1923), p. 109; C.-P. Choquette, *Histoire de la Ville de Saint-Hyacinthe* (St.-Hyacinthe, 1930), p. 278; W. P. M. Kennedy, *The Constitution of Canada, 1534–1937: An Introduction to Its Development, Law, and Custom* (2nd ed., London, 1938), p. 291; F. B. Tracy, *The Tercentenary History of Canada, from Champlain to Laurier* (Toronto, 1908), III, 910; J. L. Morison, *British Supremacy and Canadian Self-Government, 1839–1854* (Glasgow, 1919), pp. 288–289. In 1864 Samuel Medary, editor of the anti-Lincoln Columbus (O.) *Crisis*, claimed that seventy-five per cent of all Canadians sympathized with the South (Nov. 23, 1864). At the same time George Brown hopefully felt that at least half the Canadian press was pro-Northern (Skelton, *Galt*, p. 311).

[4] Mabel Burkholder, *The Story of Hamilton* (Hamilton, 1938), p. 143.

portant than the first, since what the American people believed was true of the provinces was of greater practical importance at the time at the popular level than what may have been the truth. If only the dress circle of British society was pro-Southern while the gallery favored the North, it must be remembered that "the children of the gods" do not hold the socially influential tickets.

The British North American press expressed itself on the Civil War in negative terms. The writer has found only two newspapers that actually defended the South and slavery.[5] On the other hand, the pressman's dislike for the North often was so great that he hoped for Southern success on grounds of self-interest. Nor did many of the editors who tended to favor the North have any love for Northern institutions; their hatred of slavery or of rebellion led them to hope for a Northern victory. It is significant that very few papers argued the merits of the Civil War on either moral or legal principles after the *Trent* affair; nearly all viewed it in terms of the war's effect on the British connection and on the problems of British North American unity. Therefore, it is more accurate to speak in terms of "anti-Northern" or "anti-Southern" newspapers rather than to use the prefix *pro* in either case.

I

To a certain extent British North American opinion reflected the levels of opinion in England. While the laboring class generally tended to favor the North in the Civil War, the major newspapers, many of the governing officials, and the foreign service—the most effectively vocal element of society—generally appeared to favor the South.[6] The conservatives in power in the provinces tended to echo conservative opinion from England. This opinion denigrated the North on four almost incompatible grounds: because of hatred for a mobocracy and the conviction that in the North the mob did rule; because the North

[5] These were the Montreal and Ottawa *Gazettes*. Until Beaty removed Sheppard in 1862 the Toronto *Leader* also defended slavery.

[6] W. D. Jones's article, "The British Conservatives and the American Civil War," *AHR*, LVIII (April, 1953), 527–543, is an attempt to refute this generalization. The argument is not entirely convincing, and it would seem best to rely on the usual generalization until further evidence to the contrary is produced. Recent research also has shown that the British working class was by no means solidly pro-Northern.

dashed the hopes of upper class humanitarianism, which hoped for a gradual rather than a violent end to slavery; because the North was held responsible for fighting that most horrible of wars, one of brother against brother; and for reasons of *Realpolitik*, especially in relation to the Canadas.[7]

The chief organs for the expression of intelligent conservative opinion in Great Britain were *The Times, The Saturday Review,* and *The Quarterly Review.* Each was quoted widely in the colonial press. While all three purported to speak the truth of America, they often were badly informed. Just as Karl Marx wrote in 1848 of a world that was dying as though it were the strongest fruit of the vine, conservatives wrote of 1860 in the terms of 1830. *The Times* had admitted ignorance of America and of the details of the slavery question,[8] and a single American correspondent, located in New York, had been considered sufficient to keep the British well informed until 1858 when a correspondent was placed at San Francisco as well. American news was irregular, and a weekly column was the best England's greatest and most circumspect newspaper could muster. On a typical day before the war three column inches were devoted to American affairs while thirty-three column inches were given over to "Sporting Intelli-

---

[7] There is a vast literature on newspaper opinion in Great Britain. The author found the following especially helpful in formulating his generalizations for this chapter: M. M. Bevington, *The Saturday Review, 1855–1868: Representative Educated Opinion in Victorian England* (New York, 1941); C. L. Graves, *Mr. Punch's History of Modern England* (London, 1921), II, 3–22; Oscar Maurer, "'Punch' on Slavery and Civil War in America, 1841–1865," *Victorian Studies,* I (Sept., 1957), 5–28; P. M. Wheeler, *America through British Eyes: A Study of the Attitude of the* Edinburgh Review *toward the United States of America from 1802 until 1861* (Rock Hill, S.C., 1935); G. H. Putnam, "The London 'Times' and the American Civil War," *Putnam's,* v (Nov., 1908), 183–191; Leslie Stephen, "The *Times* and the American War," *Mag. of Hist., with Notes and Queries,* x (1915), extra no. 37; Raymond Postgate and Aylmer Vallance, *England Goes to Press: The English People's Opinion on Foreign Affairs as Reflected in their Newspapers since Waterloo (1815–1937)* (Indianapolis, 1937), pp. 113–123; J. H. Park, "Lincoln and Contemporary English Periodicals," *Dalhousie Rev.,* vi (Oct., 1926), 297–311; Herbert Maxwell, *A Century of Empire, 1801–1900* (London, 1910), II, 304–316; A. A. W. Ramsay, *Idealism and Foreign Policy: A Study of the Relations of Great Britain with Germany and France, 1860–1878* (London, 1925), pp. 1–60; A. G. Gardiner, *The Life of Sir William Harcourt* (London, 1923), I, 125–148, 162–169; H. D. Jordan, "The Daily and Weekly Press of England in 1861," *South Atlantic Quarterly,* xxviii (July, 1929), 302–317; and Jordan and E. J. Pratt, *European Opinion on the American Civil War* (London, 1931), pp. 3–189.

[8] Feb. 17, 1858.

gence." [9] From the basis of such comprehensiveness of knowledge did the conservatives draw their conclusions.[10]

The Saturday Review had the answer: "The indifference of England to American politics forms a curious illustration of the enormous influence of newspapers. The managers of the *Times* in a great measure create or suppress the public interest . . . ." [11] *The Saturday Review* admitted that the English were ill informed on things American and attempted to rectify the laxity of *The Times*. However, the *Saturday* had no correspondent in the United States; *The Times* furnished the basic news releases, so to speak, and *The Saturday Review*'s writers based their articles largely upon this inadequate source. A comparison, by similar dates, of the "American Intelligence" column of *The Times* with the leaders and "middles" of the *Saturday* quickly reveals that the longer articles of the latter consist of *The Times'* factual base interlarded with certain intelligent speculations. London's *Quarterly Review* also was of little use to the Britisher interested in American affairs, for its American space was devoted to book reviews that afforded a point of departure for a generally vague discussion of America as a carrier of the "fatal germ of democracy" without any particular reference to current events.[12]

The Englishman was left ignorant of most of the details of the American scene just as the Bible leaves the fundamentalist ignorant of most of the details of Hell. Obscurity lent fear to either view. Georgia was pictured as populated by a peasantry, tropical flowers grew in the Wyoming Valley of Pennsylvania, and a Cambridge prize poet was allowed to place Labrador in the United States without correction,

---

[9] Based on averages computed from one hundred issues of *The Times* for 1858. (The Ottawa *Citizen* noted that *The Times* seldom touched upon a trans-Atlantic subject "in which it does not make itself ridiculous" [Sept. 3, 1863]. Even conservative Philip Vankoughnet of Canada West admitted that the English were in no position to understand the American problem or American politicians [Moran Diary, x: Feb. 1, 1862, printed in Wallace and Gillespie, eds., *Moran*, ii, 948].)

[10] The naiveté of the Englishman with respect to the Civil War often was incredible. One example may be cited merely to illustrate this point: John Ruskin, the English aesthete, wrote to President Charles Eliot Norton of Harvard University that the Civil War was of no more interest "than a squabble between black and red ants" and that "fighting will be good for [the Americans], and I suppose when they're tired, they'll stop" (C. E. Norton, ed., *Letters of John Ruskin to Charles Eliot Norton* [Boston, 1904], i, 120: Aug. 26, 1861, and 121–122: Jan. 6, 1862).

[11] x (Oct. 13, 1860), 413.

[12] For example, see cx (July, 1861), 249.

surely the most peaceful annexation in history.[13] When first reporting
the news of Lincoln's election, *The Times* stated that a "Mr. Hamlyn"
had been elected Vice-President and thereafter not infrequently mis-
quoted Lincoln's speeches.[14]

The North American Review took impish delight in documenting
inaccuracies concerning the United States that appeared in the British
press, and the editor had no difficulty in satiating himself. Errors in
forecasting were even more common although far more excusable, for
there was no atlas at hand for guidance in prophecy. The *Saturday*'s
observation, hardly an astute one through the most charitable eyes,
that the Republican party had melted away due to its defeat by the
Democrats in New York in 1857, was typical of the conclusions that
were based on incomplete news reports, inaccurate information, and a
certain inability to read the admittedly confusing American political
weather.[15] When all conservative organs alike predicted that the Union
was split irretrievably in 1861, there was greater apparent cause for
trusting the prophecies. The moralizing tone of the conservative press
was conducive of such divination. Value judgments thereby became
facts, as when the *Quarterly* declared that with Americans "passion is
not the exception, but the rule." In the United States the mob was the
ultimate arbiter of power.[16]

Especially in the North independence and originality of mind had
been swept away, according to conservative thought, for church,
state, and society were dependent upon the caprice of untutored public
opinion. "Americanism" or "Red Republicanism" were vast and creeping dangers for Europe. The "quaint figment called 'the rights of
man' " had been the basic premise that had perverted the American
people. As an abstract theory it had its rightful place, but the Ameri-

---

[13] Henry T. Tuckerman, *America and Her Commentators* (New York, 1864),
p. 273. How well-informed on American matters the rising university generation in
Britain was would be an interesting question to explore. Matthew Arnold thought
that ninety-nine per cent of the students at training college in London were pro-
Southern (G. W. E. Russell, *Letters of Matthew Arnold, 1848–1888* [London,
1895], I, 245: Arnold to Mrs. Forster, Jan. 6, 1865, and I, 157: Arnold to his mother,
Dec. 18, 1861) while Frederic W. Maitland felt that students may have affected
such sympathies in order to "get a rise" out of their more liberal teachers (*The
Life and Letters of Leslie Stephen* [London, 1906], p. 66).
[14] For a typical example, note how *The Times* changed a word in Lincoln's
First Inaugural to give it a more aggressive tenor (March 18, 1861).
[15] IV (Dec. 26, 1857), 577.
[16] cx (July, 1861), 268.

cans had made it their article of faith, "that though men or bodies of
men might err, and though statesmen of character and education were
peculiarly liable to frailties, intellectual and moral, the mob in the
state, starving, violent, and unwashed, were exempt from this human
weakness." [17]

The Civil War seemed to bring the word of truth to these judgments. The idea that evil was wiped from the face of the earth, that
"commerce had triumphed where Christianity had failed," and that it
was "heresy to distrust anybody, or to act as if any evil still remained
in human nature," had been thoroughly shattered. Democratic institutions had failed; no longer would Americans write "homilies to corrupt, extravagant old England . . . ." The result of democracy had
been a "poverty of greatness" and a gradual degeneration of the body
politic. Democratic government had proved to be a success only under
"conditions of absolute sunshine . . . ." [18]

Lincoln's suspension of the writ of habeas corpus was proof that the
American people never were free, just as the Irish were not free.
Whether this admission regarding Ireland was inadvertent is not clear,
but the comparison can easily be made: the American people always
were subject to a "resident garrison" of political manipulators and the
South, in particular, had been subject to the domination of the industrial North. That the South acted in partnership with a democracy
for seventy years was unfortunate, but the South had learned a valuable lesson and had "deliberately decided that civil war, with all its
horrors . . . was a lighter evil than to be surrendered to the justice or
the clemency of a victorious Democracy." Thus spoke the *Quarterly
Review*.[19]

Nor was the mobocracy to be trusted in foreign affairs. The United
States was greedy for expansion, Machiavellian in dealing with
other nations, and unconcerned with the international welfare of the
Negro. Conservatives had been annoyed that the United States sneer-
ingly had called efforts to suppress the slave trade a "crusade," a rather
strange term of opprobrium for an American to employ. *The Saturday
Review* considered American foreign policy "too much . . . for the
stomach of the English nation." [20] America was a nation of "vulgarity
of thought and violence of expression," an "aggressive and unscrupu-

[17] *Sat. Rev.*, vi (Aug. 28, 1858), 216; *Quart. Rev.*, cx (July, 1861), 251.
[18] *Quart. Rev.*, cxii (Oct., 1862), 538, 542–544, 547, 563.
[19] *Ibid.*, cx (July, 1861), 274.
[20] v (June 12, 1858), 606.

lous empire," which tried through bluff and bluster to "live by bunkum alone." [21] As Edward FitzGerald, the translator of "The Rubáiyát of Omar Khayyám," wrote, Americans were "a bad set—really, a Continent of Pirates." [22]

The United States had reached the ultimate irony: The American Government had reversed the colonial argument of 1776 and was asserting a philosophy of legitimacy against one of revolution. Conservatives professed to be shocked. They read the Civil War as a lesson for their times, a parable upon the root of all evil, man uncontrolled. John Locke had proved to be a false god and the Northern mob his Judas. The only hope left was that the South might prove a regenerate Barabbas. The new Confederacy should be recognized, its ambassadors received, and the British North American provinces made ready for the Northern attack that surely would follow.[23]

Much of the conservative opposition to the North stemmed from the fact that the English Radicals often had pointed to the United States as an example of the success of a democracy. It is well known that the current agitation for an extension of the franchise in Britain was thought to be tied closely to "democracy's trial" in North America, and although recent scholarship has somewhat modified the traditional interpretation, it still is correct to say that the Lost Cause was being lost in Great Britain as well as in the South as the Civil War came to a close. Within two years after the end of the war Britain had taken not one, but two, "leaps in the dark," through the Reform Bill and the British North America Act of 1867. While it is not entirely correct to say that the Reform Bill transformed Great Britain from an aristocracy to a democracy, the bill made the erosion of the aristocratic code apparent for all to see. An awareness of this erosion added to the conservatives' harsh judgments of the North throughout the war.[24]

[21] *The Times*, June 15, 1858; *Quart. Rev.*, cxi (Jan., 1862), 279; *ibid.*, cxii (Oct., 1862), 570; *Sat. Rev.*, v (Jan. 30, 1858), 108; *ibid.*, ix (Jan. 15, 1860), 35; G. W. E. Russell, i, 155: Arnold to his mother, Dec. 8, 1861.

[22] A. McK. Terhune, *The Life of Edward FitzGerald, Translator of the Rubáiyát of Omar Khayyám* (New Haven, 1947), pp. 260–261: FitzGerald to Spring Rice, Dec. 12, 1861.

[23] *Quart. Rev.*, cxi (Jan., 1862), 279.

[24] J. G. Randall, *Midstream*, pp. 339–347; E. D. Adams, *Great Britain and the American Civil War*, ii, 274–305: R. J. Zorn, "John Bright and the British Attitude to the American Civil War," *Mid-America*, xxxviii (July, 1956), 131–145. For a recent account see Asa Briggs, *The Age of Improvement* (London, 1959), pp. 489–503.

II

Conservative opinion in the provinces consistently echoed conservative opinion in the mother country and considered that democracy
was on trial during the Civil War. Thomas Chandler Haliburton of
Nova Scotia, who is known to Canadian literary history as the author
of the sometimes amusing "Sam Slick" tales, may not have been typical
of the provincial Tories, since he had left North America for England
in 1856, but he unquestionably spoke for one, perhaps extreme, wing
of colonial opinion. Despite the fact that he once had regarded the
American constitution as a "masterpiece of wisdom," by 1863 he was
convinced of the inevitability of war between the North and Great
Britain. Like so many humanitarian abolitionists, he disapproved of
slavery in the abstract but felt that the Northern mob went too far in
not considering the property rights of the planters. Like so many
British North Americans who never had visited the Southern states,
he freely refuted the anti-slave stories related by travelers who had
been there, by putting faith in Southern chivalry.[25]

The British North American had no reason to love the Northerner.
He could look back upon the War of 1812 and unofficial American
support of the rebellion of 1837 as sufficient proof of what the con-
servate press of England had to say about "grasping Yankee ways." It
was considered a sign of cultural attainment in some segments of
Canadian society to show disgust over the "low Americans" who
visited the provinces in the summer, and Canadians felt that the culture
of the wealthy of New York and Boston could be improved if they
would take their manners from the drawing rooms of Toronto and
Montreal. Northern leadership seemed to reflect the worst qualities of
the American, and Lincoln was an "incarnation of Yankeedom," while
Jefferson Davis obviously was a man of dignity. Even among those
who felt no sympathy for the South there was a desire to see the
"braggarts" of the North taught a lesson.[26]

[25] V. L. O. Chittick, *Thomas Chandler Haliburton ("Sam Slick"): A Study in
Provincial Toryism* (New York, 1924), pp. 519, 559–561, 586, 609, 637.

[26] Fredericton *Head Quarters*, July 17, 1861; Pictou *Colonial Standard*, Nov. 11,
1862; Halifax *Reporter*, Jan. 4, 1862, Jan. 14, 1864; Halifax *Morning Chronicle*,
Jan. 21, 1862, July 25, 1864; Halifax *British Colonist*, Jan. 31, 1865; Napanee *Standard*, Dec. 17, 1863; E. L. Godkin, *Reflections and Comments* (New York, 1895),
p. 270; J. A. Stevenson, "The Canadian Press in the Nineteenth Century," in H. F.
Angus, ed., *Canada and Her Great Neighbor: Sociological Surveys of Opinions
and Attitudes in Canada concerning the United States* (Toronto, 1938), pp. 71–72.

The Canadian's birthright and duty was to hate the Yankee, wrote one editor, just as the Englishman once had hated the Frenchman.[27] The presence of the Irish in the Northern population helped cause Orange Canada West to prefer the "English-stock" Southerners, and the French-Canadian Catholic had little use for the non-French Catholics in America or for the Protestant commonalty of the North. The Northerner also indulged in a systematic attempt to teach everyone to hate Great Britain and her colonies. The greatest crime of the North, said Joseph Howe, was against the minds of men, for the Northern dictatorship was trying to establish a complete mastery over man's thought "for which a parallel will be sought in vain among the despotisms of the old world." [28] Was it any wonder that the provincial Tory disliked the aggressive American, who, everyone knew, wanted to conquer the world and spread dangerous ideas of democracy?

As we have seen, the people of Britain and of the provinces alike at first had viewed the Civil War in terms of slavery. *Uncle Tom's Cabin* had been read from Halifax to Victoria, and in the year before the war a cyclorama of Eliza crossing the ice, already embellished with the bloodhounds that Mrs. Stowe never mentioned, had toured the Canadas. When John Brown was executed, British North American newspapers had printed long accounts of the events at Charles Town, his name had been heard along the St. Lawrence as part of a work song, and editorial opinion clearly had been anti-Southern. When the Civil War came, the press, assuming that it would be a war on slavery, had continued to deride the South. Within a few months, however, all this had changed. Conquest, not slavery, was said to be the issue of the war, and even the Emancipation Proclamation had failed to change opinion. When Northern whites rioted against Negroes, when a free Canadian Negro nearly was sold as a slave in Delaware during the war, when reports were circulated in the anti-Northern press that Northern generals were hanging liberated Southern Negroes by the thumbs, many British North Americans felt they had proof that no American, North or South, was interested in aiding the Negro. However, when the British and the provincial press, and scholars subsequently, declared that it was this lack of a crusade against slavery that turned public opinion, they generally rejected the possibility that this alleged lack supplied an occasion but not a cause.[29]

[27] Montreal *Evening Pilot*, Dec. 28, 1861.
[28] Howe Papers, VI: Howe to Miss Burdett Coutts, undated; see also *Quart. Rev.*, CX (July, 1861), 265–266.
[29] Thomas Carlyle at first called the war the "Nigger-Agony" (D. A. Wilson,

When the North had the support of the colonials, they thought that the war would be short and almost bloodless. But when, following the Northern debâcle at Bull Run, it became apparent that the war might well be long and sanguinary, and when Southern declarations that they would lay down their arms and stop the bloodshed whenever the North would permit them to do so reached the provincial press, the North began to be blamed for continuing a senseless war for a senseless cause. Soon blame for continuing the war was metamorphosed into blame for beginning it. As the British North American press attempted to fasten war guilt onto the Northern statesmen, it underscored the particular horrors of a fratricidal war with the usual dramatic stories of fathers being forced to fire upon their sons.[30] As the people of the provinces dug into their pockets late in 1862 to raise funds for relief of sufferers from the cotton famine in England, they thought of the Federal blockade of the Southern coast that was responsible for the famine.[31] Human life, editorialized *The Quarterly Review*, had never been so cheap in any Christian country.[32] "When will this horrible expenditure of human life end?," Governor General Monck asked Sir Fenwick Williams when he learned of another "frightfully bloody battle without any decisive result . . . ." "It is a fearfully cruel war," said the Earl of Malmesbury in one breath, and with the next noted that if the war

---

Carlyle at His Zenith [London, 1927], p. 53). Charles Kingsley, who had been a strong abolitionist before the war, as his three volume novel, *Two Years Ago* (London, 1857), shows, came to feel that the North had exaggerated the slave case against the South (M. F. Thorp, *Charles Kingsley, 1819–1875* [Princeton, 1937], p. 150). Like many of the sentimental abolitionists of Britain, Kingsley also used the term "nigger" rather than "Negro." As John Dollard has pointed out in *Caste and Class in a Southern Town* (3rd. ed., Garden City, 1957), p. 46, even today many people who want to "liberate" the Negro still mouth this term, for they cannot bring themselves to use a word that would imply equality within their own minds. The term "nigger" was used freely in the British North American provinces as well.

[30] G 6, 233: Lyons to Russell, June 24, enc. in Lyons to Monck, Aug. 2, 1864; CD, Halifax, XI: Jackson to Hunter, June 30, 1865; Sarnia *Observer*, Nov. 13, 1861; Pictou *Eastern Chronicle*, Dec. 1, 1859, Halifax *Reporter*, Jan. 17, 1863, Jan. 2, 1864; Halifax *Morning Sun*, March 17, July 9, 16, August 29, 1862; *Quart. Rev.*, CXI (Jan., 1862), 240; Monck, *Leaves*, p. 141; E. C. Guillet, *Toronto from Trading Post to Great City* (Toronto, 1934), pp. 402–403.

[31] For examples see Fredericton *Head Quarters*, Oct. 22, 1862; Pictou *Colonial Standard*, Nov. 11, 1862; *The Times*, Nov. 20, 1862; Cleveland *Leader*, July 15, 1862; Landon, "Harris," Dec. 4, 1862.

[32] CX (July, 1861), 268.

continued the North would have a fine army that might conquer the Canadas. It was just such a combination of sentiment and *Realpolitik* that distinguished the British and Canadian statesmen from the theoretical man in the street.[33]

Several of the British North American newspapers published atrocity stories, and whether anti-Northern or anti-Southern they tended to employ a fairly uniform vocabulary. "Noble Southerners" suffered terrible "barbarities" at the hands of Northern forces. The Southern troops generally were "gallant" whether in victory or defeat. Anti-Southern newspapers in the provinces were "subsidized by Washington." When the Toronto *Leader* reported outrages against "gentle Southern womanhood," the Sarnia *Observer* replied with equally salacious stories of Southerners who lusted after their slaves, but the *Leader* had the second greatest circulation of any newspaper in the province while the *Observer* was read only locally. The best that some of the anti-Southern papers could do was to reprint sections of *Uncle Tom's Cabin* or, rather inappropriately, chapters from Mrs. Stowe's new book, *The Pearl of Orr's Island*, the locale of which was Maine, not the South. One newspaper delighted in running its editorial comments on the Civil War under the standing title, "Affairs in the Model Republic," while another used the rubric, "The Great Split Nation." [34] The British North American press, Thurlow Weed concluded, was nothing less than incendiary.[35]

[33] Williams Papers: Monck to Williams, Jan. 6, 1863; Quebec *Morning Chronicle*, June 4, 1861; Halifax *Morning Journal*, Jan. 2, 1865; James H. Harris, Third Earl of Malmesbury, *Memoirs of an Ex-Minister: An Autobiography* (London, 1885), pp. 547-548; Earl of Lytton, *The Life of Edward Bulwer, First Lord Lytton* (London, 1913), II, 353: Bulwer-Lytton to John Foster, Sept. 1, 1862.

[34] See Barrie *Northern Advance*, 1864, *passim*.

[35] Seward Papers: Weed to Seward, May 15, 1862; Halifax *British Colonist*, Jan. 2, 3, 1865; Halifax *Acadian Recorder*, Jan. 9, 1864; Halifax *Morning Journal*, July 29, 1863, Jan. 2, 1865; Toronto *Weekly Leader*, Sept. 16, 1864. The reader may wonder about the influence on press opinion of three factors not discussed in the text: the presence of Negroes in the community, the proximity of the American border, and the amount of United States advertising that the newspapers carried. Communities that had a substantial Negro population had either a neutral press or one that tended to view the war issues in terms of Northern aggression rather than in terms of slavery. The proximity of the American border as a factor is much more difficult to evaluate, for proximity also meant that a substantial American merchant population was resident in the community, thus promoting, as a general rule, a press that was less overtly anti-Northern. On the other hand, such communities received a greater number of draft-dodgers (see Woodstock [N.B.] *Colonial News*, Feb. 3, 1864). However, during the two serious war scares

Journalism was a thriving and noisy business in British North America during the war years. It was at its most scurrilous in Toronto, where the *Leader* and *Globe* fought the Civil War with far less chivalry than the war itself, according to popular legend, was fought. In Montreal, on the other hand, the *Gazette* and *Witness* were well conducted, sane, and careful, using persuasion in place of invective. There were over three hundred newspapers being published in the provinces, over half of them in Canada West. Shortly before the Civil War began, at least twenty dailies were flourishing, and it was these that set the tone for the rest of the press. The journalist was of equal stature to the lawyer in politics and some journalists, like Brown, Howe, and McGee, commanded substantial political followings.

The age of personal journalism was one of lively reading, and circulations were growing during the war years, partially due to the desire for war news. In 1861 the major dailies averaged 42 columns of American news space and 6 columns of editorial opinion on American issues per week in an average of 228 columns of total newspaper space, and the weeklies averaged two columns of American news and one column of editorial opinion on American issues each week in an average of thirty-six columns of space. Although frequently in error, the news was at least as accurate as that which appeared in Northern newspapers and possibly more so, since the time required for transmission of it also permitted corrections on overhasty dispatches. That the average British North American reader, unlike the English, was in a position to be relatively well informed on Civil War events, if not issues, would seem evident.

The majority of the British North American press was somewhat anti-Northern. Of eighty-four British North American newspapers upon which the writer could secure sufficient information for a tentative judgment,[36] forty-three tended to be consistently anti-Northern,

---

of the Civil War the towns that were close to the border tended, quite naturally, to be more conciliatory, and from the outset they tended to view the Northern position in a more favorable light. American newspaper advertising played practically no role in the formation of opinion, for each paper carried but a few American advertisements, and these generally were for the *Atlantic Monthly* or Beadle's Dime Novels. The possible threat of withdrawal of American advertising could have had little effect on the British North American press.

[36] The reader will want to know the method used in compiling these statistics. The writer selected, on the basis of importance and availability, a group of twenty-five representative British North American newspapers for detailed use. These were searched on an issue-to-issue basis, and consisted of the following: on microfilm, Barrie *Northern Advance*, [Kitchener] *Berliner Journal*, Charlottetown

thirty-three tended to be consistently anti-Southern, and eight were neutral or varied from time to time according to changing circumstances.[37] New Brunswick's press was predominantly anti-Northern,

Examiner, Fort Garry *Nor'Wester*, Goderich *Huron Signal*, Halifax *Morning Chronicle*, Saint John *New Brunswick Courier*, Saint John *Morning Freeman*, St. John's *Public Ledger and Newfoundland General Advertiser*, Sarnia *Observer*, Victoria *British Colonist*, Victoria *Chronicle*, and Yarmouth *Herald;* and in their original form, files of the Fredericton *Head Quarters*, Halifax *Evening Express*, Halifax *Novascotian* (sometimes referred to as the *Nova Scotian*) London *Free Press*, Montreal *Evening Pilot*, Montreal *Gazette*, Montreal *Herald*, Montreal *La Minerve*, Montreal *Witness*, Quebec *Gazette*, Toronto *Globe*, and Toronto *Leader*. These files were used at the L.C., P.A.C., O.P.A., P.A.N.S., T.P.L., and the Parliamentary Library of Ontario.

A second group of newspapers was searched upon the basis of editorial commentary during a three-week period following twenty-one key dates which ranged from the election of Lincoln to his assassination. The writer established these dates upon the basis of a noticeable bulge in editorial commentary during these times in the newspapers in the first group. Several of the files of the lesser journals are incomplete, and only a few of the key dates could, at times, be checked against them. If commentary on seven of the events represented by the dates was available (provided, the seven dates bridged a minimum span of three of the war years) the writer ventured a judgment on the paper's opinion for the entire period, and seventeen newspapers of some thirty used filled these requirements. He recognizes the weakness of this method and realizes that he will have misjudged some of the newspapers. He therefore cautions the reader that the statistics represent a general trend, not an exact fact. More study of this nature is needed, and it well may be that future researchers will totally disprove the generalizations drawn from these papers.

A number of people made it possible to add additional newspapers to the forty-two that the writer effectively consulted. Ronald Grantham of the Ottawa *Citizen* sent extracts from that paper. Gertrude Tratt of Mount Allison University furnished extracts from six Nova Scotian newspapers that the writer was unable to consult under the definitions of either group one or group two. Gertrude Gunn of the University of New Brunswick gave permission to use her conclusions on two newspapers from that province that the writer could not examine. Although he consulted a file of *Le Canadien* of Quebec under group two, his findings were confirmed by Robert Toupin, "*Le Canadien* and Confederation, 1857–1867," unpubl. M.A. thesis (Toronto, 1956). Two newspapers now available on microfilm—the Chatham *Planet* and St. John's *Newfoundlander*—were not ready in time for use in this study. The writer also would like to thank the following for their assistance in supplying extracts—some of which he ultimately did not use— from other newspapers that he was unable to consult: Dorothy L. Dixon of the Ottawa Public Library, Grace Schmidt of the Kitchener Public Library, W. K. Wall of the Barrie *Examiner*, Antonio Drôlet of l'Université Laval, and H. C. Hazen of the Saint John Free Public Library. The writer alone, of course, is responsible for the judgments drawn from these extracts.

[37] In 1861 John A. Macdonald prepared a list of Canadian newspapers, of which there were 162, and found that 77 could be counted on to support the admin-

with nine newspapers opposing three anti-Southern publications; only one apparently truly neutral newspaper existed. In Canada East, four of five important French-language papers and four of six important English-language papers were anti-Northern. Nova Scotians appeared to make a greater effort to maintain neutrality of thought, for five of their newspapers appeared to be neutral while nine were anti-Northern and four were anti-Southern. Prince Edward Island's two leading newspapers divided their opinions, as did Vancouver Island's two newspapers. The only newspaper published in the Hudson's Bay Company's territory was strongly pro-Northern. In Canada West twenty of the newspapers examined were anti-Southern and fourteen were anti-Northern while one was neutral. Of the anti-Southern newspapers, however, many were small local weeklies. If the ten most important Canada West daily journals are considered, six were anti-Northern, one neutral, and three anti-Southern. These divisions are only approximate, for the generally negative nature of press response means that while a particular newspaper might hope for a Northern victory, it did not do so out of regard for the North. The consistently anti-Southern Napanee and Newburgh *North American* was typical in denouncing the South while declaring that the North also had helped the United States win the title, "Nation without God." [38] Even most of the clearly anti-Northern newspapers made a point of declaring that they did not favor slavery even though they favored the people who did.[39]

Because the most important British North American newspapers appeared to be anti-Northern, with the notable exceptions of the Toronto *Globe* and the Montreal *Witness*, the press of the Northern states assumed that the colonials were even more antagonistic to the North than they actually were. Northern newspapers exaggerated the anti-

---

istration, that 68 were in opposition, and that 12 were "independent." The conservative press tended to be anti-Northern, although by no means in all cases. See Macdonald Papers, 298: 262–268.

[38] [Newburgh], Sept. 10, 1862.

[39] See Toronto *Globe*, Oct. 15, 1861. For other revealing comments, see *Globe*, Oct. 7, 1861, Jan. 6, 1864; Toronto *Leader*, Sept. 21, 1861; Montreal *Gazette*, July 25, Aug. 24, Nov. 21, 1861; Napanee *Standard*, Dec. 17, 1863; Sarnia *Observer*, Feb. 17, 1865; Montreal *Witness*, Nov. 16, 1861; Halifax *Acadian Recorder*, July 11, 1863; Halifax *Novascotian*, Sept. 3, 1863; Halifax *Morning Journal*, Aug. 10, 1862, March 4, 1864; Yarmouth *Tribune*, April 15, Aug. 5, Oct. 28, 1862; Fredericton *Head Quarters*, Aug. 28, 1861; London *Canadian News*, Jan. 3, 1862; and Saint John *Morning Freeman*, Dec. 12, 1863.

Northern temper in the press of British North America and, disappointed over provincial editorial policies that waxed anti-Northern where once abolitionist voices had been heard, demanded an explanation from the provincial press. Following upon the reply that opinion had changed because the North was not fighting the expected war against slavery, the commonest answer given was that the change from a pro- to an anti-Northern position was caused by abusive and scurrilous Northern editors in general and by the New York *Herald* in particular.[40]

Many considered that the *Herald* and *The Times* of London were attempting to create a war. Pro-Northern Britishers like Joseph Parkes, John Bright, and Goldwin Smith blamed both newspapers for the tense atmosphere, but most Englishmen laid the blame squarely at the feet of the Northern press as a whole.[41] Some pointed out that newspapers like the New York *Times*, the Buffalo *Commercial Advertiser*, the Albany *Evening Journal*, and the Boston *Traveler* had joined the *Herald* in campaigns of abuse against Great Britain following her proclamation of neutrality. That some papers, like the New York *Tribune* and the Philadelphia *Inquirer*, had done what they could to cultivate friendly relations generally was conceded, but even the Toronto *Globe* at one time supported this interpretation of changed Canadian opinion, scourging "the insolent bravado of the Northern press" in general and declaring that the New York *Herald* was "chiefly to blame" for bad feeling along the border. Many colonial editors omitted the qualification and settled the onus directly upon James Gordon Bennett.[42]

[40] Ellice Papers, A-1, 2: Parkes to Ellice, Nov. 10, 1861; Hamilton *Spectator*, July 12, 1862; *The Times*, Jan. 2, 1862; Rochester *Evening Express*, Nov. 22, 1861; W. D. Bowman, *The Story of 'The Times'* (New York, 1931), p. 336; H. R. F. Bourne, *English Newspapers, Chapters in the History of Journalism* (London, 1887), II, 263; R. G. G. Price, *A History of Punch* (London, 1957), p. 83.

[41] Haultain, ed., *Goldwin Smith's Correspondence*, p. 11: Smith to E. S. Beesly, Jan. 23, 1863; *John Bright on America* (New York, 1891), pp. 37-38: Rochdale Speech, Dec. 4, 1861; James Ford Rhodes, *Lectures on the American Civil War* (New York, 1913), p. 159; Edward Cook, *Delane of The Times* (London, 1916), p. 131.

[42] CO 189: Gordon to Newcastle, Dec. 31, 1862; Quebec *Daily News*, July 30, 1862; Quebec *Morning Chronicle*, April 10, 1863; Montreal *Gazette*, Nov. 29, 1861; Saint John *New Brunswick Courier*, Jan. 18, 1862; Ottawa *Citizen*, Feb. 8, 1861; Halifax *Unionist*, quoted in Sarnia *Observer*, Feb. 17, 1865; Toronto *Globe*, June 3, July 29, Aug. 7, 1861; Pictou *Eastern Chronicle*, Jan. 7, 1863; *The Times*, Jan. 21, 1862; London *Post*, Nov. 9, 1861; New York *Times*, Nov.

Indeed, the Union was served so badly by Bennett that the Toronto *Globe* contended he was working secretly for the South. In an irresponsible effort to build his paper's circulation among the Irish of New York, Bennett heightened tensions at a time when a foreign war might have brought the destruction of the United States. Even Charles Francis Adams feared that the *Herald* would bring about war if it could, and he felt that his and Lyons' duty was to counteract the invidious influence of the *Herald* and *The Times*.[43]

Just how important and how anti-British North American was the *Herald?* For factual news of the "American War" far in advance of that which *The Times* would bring, the colonial press invariably turned to the *Herald*'s pages. Bennett had introduced the "war map" to the United States in 1838, and during the Civil War he spread half-page maps across the front sheet, dramatically pinpointing each battle. Long before hostilities began he had told his editorial staff to study European history and military tactics and personally had pored over the campaigns of Napoleon, Wellington, Caesar, and Hannibal.[44] Factually Bennett's war coverage was the finest on the continent, and even the Cabinet and Mrs. Lincoln turned to the pages of his newspaper for the news.[45] The *Herald* proclaimed that it was, by general consensus of its friends and enemies, "the greatest intellectual and electric moving paper of the age."[46] Whether its editorial page was taken seriously by its more intelligent readers is a moot point, however.

There is no question that the *Herald* often spoke from the gutter against the British provinces. On June 1, 1861, the *Herald* launched a campaign against Great Britain with an attack on Lord Lyons. For each day thereafter for sixteen days a lengthy editorial reviled John Bull, branded his minister a secessionist, his neutrality dishonest, and his intentions warlike. Bennett predicted that when the cotton crop was ready for export in October Great Britain would declare war on the United States, and he urged that the coastal defenses be put on a war footing four months before Seward actually did so. The editor

---

25, 1861; Portland *Eastern Argus*, Jan. 11, 1862; Cameron, *Vansittart*, pp. 44–46; Charles Mackay, *Forty Years' Recollections* (London, 1877), II, 418.

[43] CFA, 83: Adams to Seward, May 1, 1863.

[44] Carlson, *Bennett*, pp. 191, 321. The map was of Navy Island during the Canadian rebellion.

[45] Possibly Lincoln also read the *Herald*, although Carl Sandburg insists that he would not have done so.

[46] Feb. 14, 1862.

predicted a Puritan revolt in England in which "the people" would institute a second Reign of Terror, destroy the "aristocracy," and win the war with Britain for the United States from within. On June 10 Bennett asked Congress to authorize the President to issue a declaration of war against Britain upon her first overtly hostile act.[47]

Originally Bennett had predicted that British North America would rush to the aid of the North because economically the provinces were an appendage to the United States. He undoubtedly was chagrined when this did not prove to be the case. The editor then suggested that the North and South should join hands and seize Santo Domingo and the Canadas. Geographically, he claimed, the Canadas belonged to the United States, and Bennett felt that if the North could send enough troops there to protect the Canadians from British retaliation, the Canadians at once would declare their independence of Great Britain. The Canadas would be overrun in a fortnight, and the Atlantic Provinces, including Newfoundland, would follow without a blow. Bennett, who once had lived in Halifax, also implied that the reinforcements that were sent to the provinces during the summer of 1861 were to police the colonials in order to assure their loyalty to the Crown. When the inevitable annexation of the provinces to the Republic came, they at last would be shown how to "act an independent part, and to assert the dignity and freedom of the Anglo-Saxon race." In the final analysis England was the cause of the Civil War because she had been the first to introduce abolitionist dissension.[48]

However, the British newspapers were not wholly sincere in arguing that they genuinely favored the North until the *Herald* began abusing the mother country. The *Herald*'s abuse furnished a convenient excuse, a basis for rationalization, and a bridge by which the transition in opinion could be made. There is an anomaly in the idea of quoting the *Herald* so often to prove that the Lincoln administration was belligerent. True, it had the greatest circulation of any American newspaper, but this partially was due to the fact that it published long casualty lists, that it was written in a lively manner, and that its extracts from Southern newspapers, its war maps, and its feature articles made it "required" reading, especially for the masses. On the other hand, time and again it attacked the "Blunders of the Navy Depart-

---

[47] June 2-4, 7, 8, 10, 1861, Oct. 10, 1863.
[48] May 21, June 30, July 1, 9, 14, 23, 1861, Sept. 5, 1863. See also Halifax *Morning Sun*, Sept. 3, 1862; Halifax *Reporter*, Jan. 4, 1862; W. R. Houghton, *Kings of Fortune* (Chicago, 1888), p. 408.

ment," the "Unparalleled Corruption of the Administration," and Lincoln personally.[49]

Had the British pressmen thought logically, one would think that prior to the election of 1864 they would have concluded that the administration was unlikely to follow the *Herald's* foreign policy since Bennett opposed both Lincoln and Seward and could not possibly be considered a spokesman for the party in power. One also would think that after the triumphant re-election of Lincoln despite an electorate that had been fed on Bennett's venom for four years, the provincial press would have concluded that since the people themselves did not follow the *Herald's* policy with respect to Lincoln, they would not follow the *Herald's* policy with respect to Great Britain, and that the administration now would be even less likely to listen to Bennett. Had the colonials thought in terms of quality rather than quantity, they might have concluded that the *Herald* did not speak for those who led America. That they did not do so would seem to be because they too firmly believed their own analysis of the American political system and felt that the mob to which the *Herald* catered did, indeed, rule. The *Herald* was apt for once when, describing *The Times'* American policy, it applied to her the slightly altered epithet, "The Blunderer."

The British on both sides of the Atlantic continued to blame the New York *Herald* for strained international relations despite the fact that they frequently admitted that the *Herald* did not speak for those in power, or even for the majority of the people in the North. In England *The Saturday Review* long had refused to accept news dispatches from the *Herald* on the grounds that it did not "address a class which exercis[ed] any serious influence on public opinion." In Canada West the Toronto *Globe* noted that journals that claimed to have become anti-Northern because of the insults of the American press were resting their conversions on a weak base: "If there are fools who contribute to Northern journals, there is no reason for us answering them according to their folly . . . . [T]he *Herald* writes against England, and the *Herald* is read by thousands says somebody. Very true, but it is not followed by tens . . . ." Brown declared that the vituperation of Bennett and his ilk was of little importance since they had but slight influence in Washington. Ellis Yarnall, American correspondent for Britain's leading religious newspaper, the London

[49] See W. G. Bleyer, *Main Currents in the History of American Journalism* (Boston, 1927), p. 205.

Guardian, wrote that the *Herald* had "no weight or influence" in the United States.[50] The *Herald* and *The Times* were engaging in "a grand paper duello" that was representative of governmental opinion in neither nation, said others. When asked why *The Times* quoted the nonrepresentative *Herald* almost exclusively for American news, William H. Russell, *The Times'* own American correspondent, confessed that he did not know. Even *The Times'* editor, Mowbray Morris, privately admitted that, "We don't believe one single word that appears in the American journals . . . ."[51] One of the American representatives of the Baring brothers, Samuel G. Ward, told them that the *Herald* was not typical, while reform advocate Richard Cobden wrote to Sumner that the English were "accustomed to disregard the Herald as an Ishmaelite organ . . . ."[52] Perhaps Bradford Wood, the American Minister to Denmark, most heatedly testified to Bennett's lack of credentials in attempting to speak for the North: "I have never beleived [*sic*] in Lynch Law, but I will beleive [*sic*] in it, if it will send Bennett and his press into the sea, or send him to the Devil, his master."[53]

Despite these admissions, despite the fact that the *Herald* was in obvious disagreement with the administration on so many points, despite its constant attacks on "nigger worshipers" and despite the fact that it had, at first, favored the very policy to which the British North American press itself was changing—that of letting the South go in peace—the provincial pressmen accepted Bennett's editorials as though they were representative of American opinion. That they chose to do so is significant. The colonial press was too ready to follow the lead of *The Times* in believing that the North was a mobocracy. It was not the New York *Herald* that was the primary cause of the shift in

[50] *Saturday,* III (June 13, 1857), 542; *Globe,* Oct. 26, Nov. 30, 1861, Feb. 20, March 5, June 21, 1862; Yarnall, *Forty Years of Friendship as Recorded in the Correspondence of John Duke Lord Coleridge and Ellis Yarnall during the Years 1856 to 1895* (London, 1911), 78: Yarnall to Coleridge, Sept. 19, 1861.

[51] Sarah Forbes Hughes, *Letters and Recollections of John Murray Forbes* (Boston, 1899), I, 254: to Nassau W. Senior, Dec. 10, 1861; Gordon S. Haight, ed., *The George Eliot Letters* (New Haven, 1954-55), IV, 52: George H. Lewes to Silas W. Mitchell, Aug. 30, 1862; Atkins, *William Howard Russell,* II, 75: Russell to Delane, Sept. 13, 1861; *History of The Times,* II, 384: Morris to Antonio Gallenga, July 30, 1863.

[52] Baring Papers: Ward to Baring Brothers, March 10, 1864; E. L. Pierce, ed., "Letters of Richard Cobden to Charles Sumner, 1862-65," *AHR,* II (Jan., 1897), 316: Jan. 11, 1865.

[53] L. C., Salmon Chase Papers, 54: Wood to Chase, Dec. 24, 1861.

opinion, just as it was not the failure of the North to crusade against slavery that caused the change. Both were occasions, even reasons, for change, but they were not basic causes.

The British North American press and the provincial leaders showed a peculiar disjunction of thought that actually was a combination of an emerging nationalism and continental isolationism. The press declared that any war generated by the *Trent* affair was Britain's concern, not the provinces', and that if a war resulted from an insult to the British flag, Britain must assume the responsibility of defending her colonies. Yet, the same press took offense at Northern taunts of Great Britain and wrote as though an insult to England were a slap at her colonies as well. When war threatened, the Canadian press in particular loudly declared that it was not the province's fault and tried to isolate it from all responsibility for war. But when war did not seem imminent, the same press could bait the hot-headed New York newspapers as regularly as *The Times*.

The conclusion is difficult to escape that fear as expressed through latent anti-Americanism, nationalism as expressed in the growing Canadian desire to take advantage of the Civil War for expansion to the west and to confederate for defense and for nationhood, and a narrow continentalism as expressed in a desire to avoid a British-oriented war were the basic causes of the change in public opinion. The colonials tended to be anti-Northern not because of the New York *Herald* but because an inchoate sense of geopolitics made it evident that a Southern victory might re-establish the North American balance of power that had been eroded away during the two previous decades. The *Herald* was the scapegoat for nearly a century of "war in anticipation."

III

Although the conservatives, under various party names, were in power in most of British North America, they were not of the landed class that comprised much of the Tory party in England. Many of them had been born in Great Britain of middle-class parents and had migrated to North America. For the most part they had gained their wealth through trade or the law, and many of them, like John A. Macdonald, were not men of wealth. Other than controlling a substantial portion of the provincial press, they were not in a position to make their views the views of the provinces. Canada West, in particular, was still on the edge of the frontier, and the commonalty, the great middle class with which Canada's economic and political future rested, was not necessarily predisposed to accept the tenets of Burkean conservatism or to conclude that democracy had failed. Democracy as practiced in the United States might be a failure, but perhaps the Canadas could apply democratic principles in a different manner. The doctrinaire conservative in the provinces may have accepted the English conservative's views of the Civil War, and even the middle-class merchant probably agreed with the humanitarian impulse that reacted against the North after union became the paramount issue, but the bourgeois Canadian was not prepared to damn the North solely on matters of theory. The average British North American was open to persuasion, for, being a pragmatist of the variety often bred by frontier societies, he would not attempt to fit every American action into a framework, however flexible, of the far right or of the far left. Propaganda would, and did, move him. If he shared the beliefs of England's Tory press, this was due in part to effective Confederate and conservative propaganda and ineffective if not nonexistent Northern propaganda.

To the present-day Canada has complained that the United States has tended to ignore her, and such was the case during the Civil War. Seward and Lincoln sent a number of special agents to Europe to serve their propaganda purposes.[54] Since accredited diplomatic and consular officials were prevented by protocol from indulging in propaganda activities, such special agents were needed. American consuls in British North America similarly were limited in the extent to which they could engage in public debate from the podium or the press, and yet after the failure of Ashmun's journey in May, 1861, the North sent no missions, hired no speakers, and supplied no literature to present the Northern case to the British North American people. In England the Confederacy published its own newspaper, *The Index* and supported the energetic Henry Hotze as chief propaganda agent. To British North America the Confederacy sent three commissioners and a num-

---

[54] For a discussion of Northern missions abroad, see J. H. Kiger, "Federal Governmental Propaganda in Great Britain during the American Civil War," *Historical Outlook*, XIX (May, 1928), 204–209; and A. C. Miller, Jr., "Lincoln's Good-Will Ambassadors," *Lincoln Herald*, L (June, 1948), 17–27, 42. The standard authority on Southern activities abroad, which omits British North America, is Frank L. and Harriet C. Owsley, *King Cotton Diplomacy: Foreign Relations of the Confederate States of America* (2nd ed., Chicago, 1959).

ber of propaganda agents who operated out of headquarters established
in Toronto and Montreal.[55] The North had no propaganda system at
work in the provinces or in England, and any person whom the North
could call upon as truly expert in British North American matters was
as mythical as Sherlock Holmes's famous brother Mycroft, the Foreign Office's fictitious expert on Canada.

It was not only the Northern government that failed to match the
Confederacy on the propaganda front. Private agencies such as The
Loyal Publication Society followed the State Department's lead. In
1864, in conjunction with the Union League of New York, the
Society sent sets of *The Rebellion Record*, edited by Frank Moore,
and bound volumes of the Society's first forty-four pamphlets to fifty
European monarchs, libraries, and editors. Not a set went to the
provinces.[56] During the same year, when printed copies of diplomatic
correspondence were sent to a long list of pro-Northern politicians
abroad, the librarian of the Canadian Parliament had to write twice to
the State Department to obtain the same volume, and then it was sent
with the remark that copies were very scarce and that it should be
cherished. Seward had no one but himself to blame if Confederate
propaganda proved more effective in British North America.

For Southern propaganda there was. The *American Union*, a
history of the United States written by an Englishman, James Spence,
almost became a manual for Southern propagandists, for it had an air
of impartiality, and not having been written by a Southerner, it could
convince where other similarly slanted books would annoy. Both it
and a series of Spence's letters to *The Times*, reprinted as *On the
Recognition of the Southern Confederacy* (London, 1862), were sent
to the Canadas. Other pro-Southern books were in substantial circulation in the provinces, including Thomas Grattan's *England and the
Disrupted States of America* (London, 1861). Provincial printers issued
dozens of booklets on the war, and they published Canadian and Nova
Scotian editions of such works as Charles Hallack's *Sketches of 'Stonewall Jackson'*, rushed into print from an English edition of 1863, and
Edward Pollard's *Southern History of the Great Civil War in the*

---

[55] See Chapter Thirteen, below.
[56] Frank Freidel, "The Loyal Publication Society: A Pro-Union Propaganda
Agency," *MVHR*, xxvi (Dec. 1939), 359-376, contains a list of recipients. See
also G. W. Smith, "Broadsides for Freedom: Civil War Propaganda in New
England," *New England Quarterly*, xxi (Sept., 1948), 291-312.

United States, which appeared the same year. The North did nothing to counteract these books, and British North American publishers apparently did not find it profitable to print even pirated editions of pro-Northern material. While a certain number of Northern books undoubtedly circulated in the provinces, and while the recently-founded *Atlantic Monthly* had a small readership there, the State Department even considered cutting off the flow of Northern publications to the provinces altogether at one point.[57]

Perhaps the most effective propaganda agents for the South were not formal or official but were the informal and unofficial Southern tourists. Since well before the war, Southerners had made Niagara Falls one of their chief summer resorts, and earlier than usual in 1861 they had begun to flock in, quickly convincing many who lived in the Niagara peninsula of the righteousness of their cause. After 1862 wealthy Northerners began to use Toronto as a summer resort, for due to high war prices it was cheaper to spend the season in Canada West than to stay at home, and the Northern visitors did not contrast favorably with the aristocratic Southerners, already well entrenched in the higher society of Toronto and Montreal.[58]

While the Southerner who visited the provinces tended to be a man of refinement, the Northerner often was a draft-dodger, a crimp, a *nouveau riche* merchant, or a Yankee trader in a hurry to finish his business and return to the States. English and British North American travelers who met Southerners in the provinces agreed that they found them more refined than the Northerner. From the particular they reasoned to the general, forgetting that Southerners who could travel in the Canadas on business represented a wealthier group, while the Northerner met by the British traveler so much closer to his home ground often was of a lower class economically. People of other nations often create their own image of the typical American on the basis of the American abroad, a person who scarcely is typical by virtue

[57] See Monaghan, *Carpet Slippers,* p. 159; Canada, Emigration Agent, Quebec, *Canada: for the Information of Intending Emigrants* (Quebec, 1864), p. 72. Perhaps the Consul General was to disseminate the Northern interpretation of history, for he alone of American consuls in the provinces received a copy of *The Political History of the United States . . . during the Great Rebellion* by Edward McPherson (CD, Montreal, v: Potter to Seward, Oct. 6, 1864).

[58] Bancroft, *Seward,* ii, 82; Lloyd Graham, *Niagara Country* (New York, 1949) p. 153; Henry Scadding and J. C. Dent, *Toronto: Past and Present, Historical and Descriptive* (Toronto, 1884), p. 233.

of the very fact that he is abroad, and a person who may act quite differently when he is at home.[59]

Of course, the Southern flow did not go unanswered. Northern newspapers were readily available in the provinces. The New York *Tribune* was widely read in Montreal, the New York *News* was popular in Toronto, and Chicago, Buffalo, and Detroit papers were plentiful in Canada West. The New York *Herald* generally was available in both Canadas. But papers such as the *Herald* did not help the Northern cause, and the impact of lukewarm endorsements of the war, as in the *Tribune*'s case, was lessened even further by the fact that *The Index*, Atlanta *Intelligencer*, and Richmond newspapers were brought into the Canadas.[60]

Nor did Northern business enterprise ignore the provinces as the State Department did. *Uncle Tom's Cabin* continued to circulate throughout the provinces during the war, as did a "shocker" by Mrs. Metta V. Victor, *Maum Guinea and Her Plantation 'Children'; or, Holiday-Week on a Louisiana Estate: A Slave Romance*, which contained a particularly gruesome description of Nat Turner's rebellion and the South's retaliation. During the war Erastus Beadle seized upon the demand for inexpensive reading material and sent great quantities of anti-slavery books to the front lines. In 1861 Beadle opened a branch office in London and distributed his books to the working class in England. Hundreds of the books were sold in the British North American provinces as well, particularly in the Maritimes.[61]

There were unofficial propagandists at work for both causes. The most active of these was Alexander M. Ross, an ornithologist and doctor whom Seward and Lincoln had asked to propagandize for the North in the Canadas shortly after the failure of Ashmun's mission. Ross received neither pay nor commission, but he apparently felt that

[59] Macdonald Papers: J. R. Gowan to Macdonald, Sept. 24, 1864, 137–150; FO 5, 827: Jan., 1862; "T.D.L.," *Western World*, p. 110; H. Macdonald, *Canadian Opinion*, p. 144.

[60] Quebec *Gazette*, Jan. 16, Feb. 22, 1865; *The Times*, Feb. 19, 1862; John W. Headley, *Confederate Operations in Canada and New York* (Cincinnati, 1906), p. 216.

[61] The standard work on Beadle is Albert Johannsen, *The House of Beadle and Adams and Its Dime and Nickel Novels: The Story of a Vanished Literature* (2 vols., Norman, 1950). See also C. M. Harvey, "The Dime Novel in American Life," *Atlantic Monthly*, c (July, 1907), 37–45; and A. J. Crockett, "George Munro, 'The Publisher'," *Dalhousie Rev.*, xxxvi (Spring, 1956), 81–83. Mr. Crockett has supplied the writer with an advertisement for Beadle's books that appeared in the New Glasgow (N.S.) *Eastern Chronicle*, June 10, 1868.

he could serve in a semi-official capacity and he frequently presented himself at the Toronto consulate and officiously interfered with the work there. Ross also tried to establish a branch of the United States Sanitary Commission at Montreal without first asking the Commission. When he began to call himself an agent for the Commission, its Secretary, Reverend F. N. Knapp, was asked to investigate, and Knapp denounced him. Later, Ross unsuccessfully tried to obtain a consulate-ship at Kingston, but because of Ross's tactics he was *persona non grata* to Seward, to the Consul General at Montreal, and to the American residents of the city.[62]

Nevertheless, Ross did work hard for the North, publishing many letters and pamphlets throughout the Canadas. His chief tract was *The Slaveholder's Rebellion: Its Internal Causes*, but probably his best was not written until it was too late to have much effect—*Slavery in the Southern States*, which appeared in February, 1865. While he was called a "nigger thief" and "damned Yankee" by the anti-Northern press, especially because of his declaration that a slave had the right to kill all those who sought to "prevent his enjoyment of liberty," Ross continued to write of Southern atrocities against Negro women and children until well after the end of the war.[63]

Ross served his most useful purpose unwittingly. Lincoln, knowing that Ross's activities were reported in the Canadian press, sent him to Richmond with the request that he arrange to have Negro soldiers included in the exchange of prisoners of war. Receiving a pass from

[62] DL, 65: Seward to Knapp, July 5, 1864, 116; ITC, 36: Seward to Thurston, June 13, 14, 1864, and Seward to Giddings, April 11, 1864; *ibid.*, 38: Seward to Thurston, June 29, 30, July 9, 1864; *ibid.*, 64: Seward to Stanton, June 14, 1864, 543; NBL, 11: Seward to Lyons, July 8, 1864, 433; CD, Montreal, V: J. Cordner to C. Brown, enc. in Brown to Thurston, both June 30, 1864; Ross, *Memoirs of a Reformer*, pp. 119–125, 143.

[63] Ross, *Experiences of an Abolitionist*, pp. 180–206; T. E. Champion, "The Underground Railway and One of Its Operators," *Canadian Mag.*, V (May, 1895), 9–16; W. H. Withrow, "The Underground Railway," Royal Soc. of Canada, *Transactions*, n.s., VIII (1902), sec. 2, 54; Fred Landon, "A Daring Canadian Abolitionist," *Michigan History Magazine*, V (Oct., 1921), 364–373. The American Missionary Association continued its work in the Canadas until July, 1864. The previous year Samuel Gridley Howe visited Amherstburg, Canada West, at Lincoln's request to investigate the condition of Negro refugees there. See Fred Landon, "Over Lake Erie to Freedom," *Northwest Ohio Quarterly*, XVII (Oct., 1945), 132–138; Landon, "The Work of The American Missionary Association among the Negro Refugees in Canada West, 1848–1864," Ont. Hist. Soc., *Papers and Records*, XXI (1924), 198–205; the organ of the society, *The American Missionary*, for 1861–64; and the *Fifteenth Annual Report* of the Association.

Robert E. Lee, Ross was ushered into the "purring presence" of Judah P. Benjamin and Jefferson Davis. Both refused to accede to the request, and Benjamin told Ross that Lincoln had known that they would refuse. When Ross returned to Lincoln the President admitted that he had expected just such an answer. Ross seems to have missed the point of his trip and of Benjamin's remark—Lincoln probably wanted this "red-hot abolitionist" to experience the Confederacy's refusal to treat Negroes as prisoners of war so that he would carry the story back to the Canadas.[64]

Other British North Americans were touring the provinces and speaking on the Civil War. Some of them did so because they sincerely felt that the North needed a defender in the provinces. Others, who knew nothing of the United States except what they had gleaned from the newspapers or learned from a few days of travel in the states, posed as experts on the American problem, charged admission to their talks, and argued for both factions with equal felicity when the occasion arose. John Charlton, later to be an outspoken exponent in the Canadian Parliament of closer ties with the United States, was one of the more effective propagandists. Born in New York but now a Canadian merchant, Charlton had prepared an anti-slavery lecture in 1860, "Does the Bible Sanction Slavery?," which brought him into prominence, and he continued to give this lecture throughout the war. He prepared a second lecture on the "Political Aspects of American Slavery," but it was not as successful as was his Biblical approach. In opposition to Charlton, the scriptural basis for the pro-slavery argument was presented by the Reverend Stuart Robinson in a sermon on "The Slavery Feature in the Civil Code of Moses," and upon receiving the stamp of approval from pro-Southern Episcopalians in the Canadas, Robinson made arrangements to publish his talk.[65]

Two of the most persistent speakers, John Cordner and William Sommerville, were outspokenly for the North. Two able French journalists, L. R. Cortambert and F. de Tranaltos, gave a series of sparkling lectures at Montreal in 1863 in favor of the North, and the following year L.-A. Dessaulles presented six more talks of the same

[64] Ross, *Memoirs of a Reformer*, pp. 136–138.

[65] Thomas H. Hines [and J. B. Castleman], "The Northwestern Conspiracy," *Southern Bivouac*, II (April, 1887), 701: Hines to Thompson, March 2, 1865; Toronto *Leader*, Jan. 14, 1862. On Charlton see Lorne J. Curnoe, "John Charlton and Canadian-American Relations," unpubl. M.A. thesis (Univ. Toronto, 1939), and Charlton's MS. autobiography, University of Toronto Library.

type. On the other hand, other French-Canadian journalists delivered a number of intensely anti-Northern lectures throughout Canada East. Some speakers, like the popular Charles Bass, propagandized on the basis of Gladstone's remark that the Confederate States of America were an accomplished fact and declared that it was Canada's duty to seize the opportunity for her own advancement, and the Roman Catholic Archbishop of Halifax seldom missed an opportunity to praise the Confederacy, once offering to travel throughout the North as a peace-with-separation advocate.[66]

In Nova Scotia the Yarmouth Y.M.C.A. sponsored lectures on "The Present Struggle in the States" which were pro-Northern in content, and it is significant that the speaker found it necessary to ask people to hear him through since he knew that he was taking the unpopular side of the question. Speaking for two and a half hours, he declared that many people were favoring the South because they disliked "Yankee bluster" and not because of any reasoned, rational basis. The typical Nova Scotian, he said, was like a sea captain to whom he spoke who originally had favored the North and who now favored the South. The captain could account for his "Southernism" only by saying that he had "ate it, drank it, or slept it into him." [67]

The North apparently extended little aid, moral or financial, to the numerous speakers in the provinces who willingly argued the Federal cause. Aside from a few decorous postprandial speeches by American consuls, Jackson, Francis, and Fitnam in particular, nothing was done by the State Department. When agents were sent to England to point out that some of the Southern states had a history of repudiating their debts, no one was sent to the colonies. While Count Agénor de Gasparin's effective *Un Grand Peuple qui se releve—Les*

---

[66] Cordner, *The American Conflict* (Halifax, 1864); Sommerville, *Southern Slavery Not Founded on Scripture Warrant* (Saint John, 1864); Bass, *Lectures on Canada, Illustrating Its Present Position, and Shewing Forth Its Onward Progress, and Predictive of Its Future Destiny* (Hamilton, 1863), pp. 14–20; Cortambert and de Tranaltos, *Etats-Unis D'Amérique: Histoire de la Guerre Civile Américaine, 1860–1865* (2 vols., Paris, 1867); Dessaulles, *La Guerre Américaine, son Origine et ses vraies causes* (Montreal, 1865); *Boston Journal*, Nov. 2, 1863; *New York Herald*, Oct. 26, 1861; Duke Univ., Clement C. Clay Papers: Connelly to Clay, May 20, 1864, Jan. 2, 4, 1865, Clay to Benjamin, June 14, and Clay to J. P. Holcombe, May 27, 1864.

[67] Yarmouth *Herald*, Jan. 23, 1862. See also James Young, *Public Men and Public Life in Canada, being Recollections of Parliament and the Press* (Toronto, 1902), p. 238.

Etats-Unis en 1861 was made available in translation in Great Britain, no one thought to have it published for French Canadians. When it was reported that Alexander H. Stephens, Vice-President of the Confederacy, had declared that slavery would be the chief cornerstone of the new nation, the speech—later proved to be based on an erroneous report—was printed by a London publisher and sold for sixpence but it apparently was not distributed in the provinces.

True, there were local volunteer societies in Canada that could serve a propaganda purpose, but there is little evidence that they did. In Montreal four such groups met throughout the war. The New England Society, with an American-born resident of wealth, Champion Brown, as its President, recovered from the *Trent* affair and continued to function, and Mrs. Brown organized a local Soldier's Aid Society to provide funds and clothing for hospitalized Northern troops. An American Ladies' Society was active socially, and a Society for the Abolition of Human Slavery enjoyed evenings of oratory, but none of these groups could serve as an effective cynosure for pro-Northern propaganda.[68]

It is possible, but not likely, that toward the end of the war the Northern State Department gave small sums of money to a few British North American newspapers that were truly pro-Northern. Seward had a vaguely defined "Secret Service fund" at his disposal over which he apparently exercised sole control. The fund was used for sending agents to the provinces to report on Confederate activities there but whether it was used for other purposes is not known, although occasionally someone from the provinces would ask for help to keep a failing newspaper going on the grounds that it was defending the North's position. J. F. Cotton of the Halifax *Sun and Advertiser* asked the Massachusetts Republican State Committee for aid and the Committee referred the editor to Seward. Whether the Secretary helped Cotton or not cannot be determined. He did not help the editor of the Toronto *Daily Evening Journal*, A. Hyacinthe St. Germain, however, who had a greater claim than Cotton upon the Secretary's patronage, and it is not likely that he provided a subsidy for any newspaper. In not doing so, Seward again failed to recognize the importance of a friendly public opinion. His chief Canadian agent, Ashmun, championed St. Germain and had the editor prepare a set of clippings to show how he had defended the North, probably in the hope that Sew-

[68] CD, Montreal, v: Thurston to Seward, June 24, 1864; Ross, *Experiences of an Abolitionist*, p. 180.

ard might subsidize the newspaper. Instead, the journalist received a copy of the treasured diplomatic correspondence and three months of paid telegraphic dispatches from Americans living in Toronto. The Confederacy won the war of words in British North America by default.[69]

IV

The role of leadership, as social scientists have demonstrated, often is vital to the formulation of a coherent public opinion. It therefore is fortunate that most of the important British North American leaders attempted to remain outwardly neutral throughout the war. A few, like George Brown, were outspoken on foreign affairs, but at the time most gave only slight public indication of preference for either the North or the South. There was an occasional anti-Northern manifestation in the Canadian Parliament, as when light applause greeted the announcement of Hooker's defeat at Chancellorsville, but even then a member spoke out against such unneutral behavior. Whichever party was in power, it had been good politics to accuse the other of imbibing "Americanism," and consequently few politicians cared openly to praise the North despite what they may personally have felt.[70]

On the other hand, few people in prominent positions openly favored the South. There were those like Colonel George T. Denison who were unconcealed friends of Confederate agents, but for each Colonel

[69] Seward Papers: Dix to Sumner, Nov. 29, 1864, and St. Germain to Seward, March 3, 7, 8, 15, 31, Nov. 2, 1865, May 9, 1866; Rochester *Evening Express*, Feb. 25, 1865; Toronto *Leader*, Dec. 11, 1861. Frederick Seward promised to get private aid from New York sources for the journalist but eventually St. Germain went to work for George Brown.

Seward also received a request to furnish a thousand dollars so that a "Northern Light, or *Aurora Borealis*," might be published in Quebec that would promote: (1) Seward for President; (2) "Action, Action, Action"; (3) "a Rule of Action" based on the teachings of George Washington, Andrew Jackson, and the Bible; (4) "The Lion roar[ing] in the forest" to herald the Kingdom of God upon Earth; and (5) "The Annexation at all events of all British North America to the United States of America, as Providential . . . While, *Ad Interim*, The U.S. is making gigantic efforts, Day and Night, to be prepared to war with all the World!" "We are the Men, like Gods," the request concluded, "of the present Age . . ." (Seward Papers: Rev. John C. Nazro to Seward, Jan. 20, 1865).

[70] CD, Quebec: Ogden to Seward, May 9, 1863, April 9, 1864.

Denison there was also an Arthur Rankin who had championed the North. Some, like Edward Watkin, declared that the Civil War was only "to find out which brother shall rule the house and run away with the dying old man's goods," but for each Watkin there was a politician like the aged John Le Boutillier, member of Parliament from the Gaspé basin, who was a faithful friend of the North. John Sandfield Macdonald was warmly pro-Northern, and late in 1863, after his fall from office, he visited New York City and talked with Seward. William McDougall, Commissioner of Crown Lands for the united Canadas, kept in touch with Seward, was at Gettysburg when Lincoln spoke, and near the end of the war went so far as to offer to send to Washington a Canadian who had invented a highly destructive shell that might aid the Northern armies. When Britishers actually talked with individual Northern leaders, they often were surprised to find them likeable and intelligent. David Glass, the Mayor of London, Canada West, for example, was struck by Lincoln's "manifest honesty, sincerity and common sense," and Goldwin Smith, upon meeting General Grant, reported that he was "rather taken with the beast." [71]

But John A. Macdonald dominated the political scene in Canada West. A bundle of anti-American prejudices who had not yet developed any self-conscious theory of society or government, Macdonald nevertheless had a hard core of fundamental beliefs, nearly all of which tended to reflect against the American system of government. He disliked the wartime suspension of the habeas corpus and suppression of newspapers in the United States and considered both acts to be symbolic of American contempt for the orderly processes of the law. As a modified Burkean conservative he felt that class and property should be represented in government, agreeing that unless property were protected and made one of the principles on which representation was based, the Americans "might perhaps have a people altogether equal, but they would soon cease to have a people altogether free." [72] Mac-

---

[71] MC: Fitnam to Seward, May 22, 1862; CD, Gaspe, 1: Fitnam to Seward, May 5, 1863; CD, Quebec: Ogden to Seward, Dec. 17, 1863; Sumner Papers, CXL: Macdonald to Sumner, Jan. 16, 1864; Seward Papers: Ogden to Seward, Nov. 13, Macdonald to Seward, Dec. 31, 1863, and McDougall to Seward, Dec. 8, 1864; Watkin, *Recollections*, p. 518: Sept. 1, 1861; F. S. Glass, "Biographical Sketch of the Life and Times of the Hon. David Glass," London and Middlesex Hist. Soc., *Transactions*, x (1919), 40–41; A. J. Clark, "When Jefferson Davis Visited Niagara," Ont. Hist. Soc., *Papers and Records*, XIX (1922), 88 n.

[72] Quoted in T. W. L. MacDermot, "The Political Ideas of John A. Macdonald," *CHR*, XIV (Sept., 1933), 250–252. In 1939 the leading biographer of Macdonald,

donald wanted to save the provinces for British civilization, and he felt a "lingering anxiety for the problem of British North American defense." [73] He had been quick to grasp the drift of the times and resisted the creeping continentalism of the United States throughout his career. His tolerance for other views promoted his dislike for the North, for he felt that Lincoln and Seward had not attempted to see the Southern viewpoint. Throughout his political career he was in office only by virtue of the art of compromise, an art that the North apparently had ignored, and he was constantly aware of the importance of the individual in society, an awareness that the mechanized warfare to the south apparently had stamped out. Essentially unreflective in character, predisposed to dislike Americans, and with little interest in the development of world-wide movements such as abolitionism, Macdonald was unable to sympathize with the Federal government. His finest speech had been on "the failure of the American system," given a week after Fort Sumter was fired upon, long before that system had been or could be proved a success or failure. To Macdonald the Civil War was a lesson in constitution-making, and as he studied the debates of the Philadelphia Convention of 1787 and *The Federalist* papers he underscored those passages that emphasized a strong central government.[74]

Cartier, Macdonald's French-Canadian counterpart in the administration, felt that the United States was a menace to the monarchical system. He often pointed out that his people were more inclined to be royalists than the "Yankeefied" people of Canada West, and in the manner of Walter Bagehot he felt that the Crown stabilized and dignified government and produced a decent gradation in provincial society that did not exist across the border. The Roman Catholic Church was the great stabilizing force, a force badly needed in the Protestant United States, he said. *The Federalist* papers also had a prominent place in Cartier's library, and he worked with Macdonald for a union with a powerful central government. He fully realized that a Southern vic-

---

D. G. Creighton, felt that his subject entertained a "jealous suspicion of the United States" ("Conservatism and National Unity," in Flenley, ed., *Essays in Canadian History*, p. 162), but by 1952 Creighton felt that Macdonald had "little prejudice against the United States" (*Macdonald*, p. 319). More recently see Creighton, "'Old Tomorrow'," *Beaver* (Winter, 1956), pp. 6–10, and Creighton and Paul Fox, "A Long View of Canadian History," *Script* (June, 1959), pp. 2–10.

[73] Creighton, *Macdonald*, p. 49.

[74] *Ibid.*, p. 308; Trotter, "American Influences," p. 215 n. 2. Macdonald's underscored copy of the debates is in the P.A.C.

tory in the Civil War might release the Canadas from the danger of an American invasion, and he looked back romantically to the days when he too had been a rebel. On the other hand, Cartier's intense insistence on adhering to the letter of the law made him a particularly strong advocate of strict neutrality.[75]

There were other leaders than Macdonald and Cartier, of course. Joseph Howe, once Prime Minister of Nova Scotia, could argue with equal facility either side of a question. When in England he sometimes appeared to be anti-Northern, at other times anti-Southern. In general, he insisted that while he was not in favor of annexation Nova Scotians should be the "fast friends and firm allies" of the United States. He placed great reliance on the ability of the Northern people, once the passions of war had subsided, to realize that they had abused the Maritime Provinces unjustly. Part of his feeling was merely practical, for Halifax's trading connections with Boston and Portland were close; part of it was due to the fact that he had a son serving in the Northern army; part of it was due to his desire to prevent the creation of a union of the British North American provinces from unnecessary fear of Northern aggression.[76]

Thomas D'Arcy McGee, on the other hand, was an outspoken Canadian nationalist who preached his message in eloquent terms, never varying it, announcing again and again that the first shot fired at Fort Sumter contained a warning to all Canadians. Only three courses were open to Canada: annexation, a closer connection with the Empire, or a "guaranteed neutrality" similar to that of Belgium under the joint protection of the United States and Great Britain.[77] The choice was obvious to McGee: a closer connection with Britain and a closer union of the several provinces. He propounded a law, that "Enthusiasm is to war, as the water to the millwheel . . . ," and he found that his law forecast an American invasion. In order to prepare the British

[75] John I. Cooper, "The Political Ideas of George Etienne Cartier," *CHR*, XXIII (Sept., 1942), 286–293; Watkin, p. 497.

[76] Howe Papers, 28/4, A: Howe to his wife, Dec. 10, 1865; Howe Diary, LV: Dec., 1864; D. C. Harvey, ed., *The Heart of Howe: Selections from the Letters and Speeches of Joseph Howe* (Toronto, 1939), p. 152; Roy, *Howe*, pp. 255–256. Among Seward's pamphlet collection is an oration by Howe on Shakespeare, delivered in Halifax in 1864, which the Nova Scotian sent to the Secretary of State.

[77] Quebec *Morning Chronicle*, Jan. 16, 1862; Toronto *Leader*, April 30, Dec. 26, 1861; Toronto *Globe*, Aug. 19, 1863, Jan. 2, 1865; London *Canadian News*, Jan. 16, 1862, all expressed the same sentiment in other words.

provinces for a century of living with the possibility of an American war, when troops might be expected to invade at any moment, or when the dangerous new weapon of ironclad boats might steam up the St. Lawrence, the unsettled heartland of the Hudson's Bay Company's territory must be united with the provinces so that a single nation, stretching from sea to sea and working from a position of united strength, could confront the danger by actively promoting continental peace.[78]

McGee favored the North during the Civil War. Before the *Trent* affair he had declared his belief that "all that is most liberal, most intelligent, and most magnanimous in Canada and the Empire are for continental peace, for constitutional arbitration, for universal, if gradual emancipation, for free intercourse, for justice, mercy, civilisation, and the North." [79] Even after the *Trent* affair he testified to "a feeling of deep and sincere sympathy and friendliness towards the United States." [80] Nevertheless, he was typical of those who quite naturally hoped to see Canada take advantage of her opportunities. He toured the British North American provinces, warning that they must unite to prevent annexation. He also stated that the Canadas should think independently and not wait to see what the London press said about the war, for wherever he went he preached an ardent nationalism, the product of which, as consul Ogden pointed out, was a bitter feeling against the North despite the speaker's professed pro-Northern sentiments.[81]

[78] McGee, "A Plea for British American Nationality," *British American Magazine*, 1 (Aug., 1863), 338–340; McGee, "A Further Plea for British American Nationality," *ibid.*, 1 (Oct., 1863), 562–564.

[79] McGee, *Speeches and Addresses on the Subject of British-American Union* (London, 1865), p. 31: Sept. 26, 1861. *Per contra*, see McGee's "Speech on Motion for an Address to Her Majesty in Favour of Confederation," *ibid.*, pp. 261–308: Feb. 9, 1865. McGee's September speech is analyzed in W. K. Thomas, "Canadian Political Oratory in the Nineteenth Century, I," *Dalhousie Rev.*, xxxix (Spring, 1959), 19–30.

[80] In a speech at Fort Popham, Maine, Sept. 29, 1862.

[81] CD, Quebec: Ogden to Seward, Sept. 16, 1863, July 8, 1864; Ottawa *Citizen*, Jan. 18, 1861; Toronto *Leader*, Jan. 16, 22, 1861; Barrie *Northern Advance*, Nov. 20, 1861; Halifax *Novascotian*, July 27, 1863; Alexander Brady, *Thomas D'Arcy McGee* (Toronto, 1925), pp. 76–77; John Heisler, "The Halifax Press and British North American Union, 1856–1864," *Dalhousie Rev.*, xxx (July, 1950), 192: July 26, 1863. It is interesting to note that John A. Roebuck, chief exponent of Southern recognition in the British House of Commons, may have been thinking along the same lines of *Realpolitik* as McGee, for he had grown to early manhood in British North America and knew something of the provinces' potential (Justin McCarthy, *Portraits of the Sixties* [New York, 1903], p. 204).

George Brown was the only Canadian leader of importance who was strongly anti-Southern, but he, too, was fascinated by the strides toward nationhood that the provinces might take while the United States was preoccupied. Brown advocated a strict official neutrality during the war, for the Canadas must cling "to the principle of monarchial and liberal institutions," he wrote, but they could sympathize with the yeomanry of the North. He did not like the North, he said, for he disliked its corruption, its finances, and its monopolies, but he hated slavery more, for he was an intense abolitionist of many years standing. Because of this he tried, as he wrote to Seward in 1862, to "keep public opinion . . . right" in Canada West.[82] He openly propagandized for the North, ignoring the black spots on the Federal record just as his rivals ignored those on the Confederate standard. Unlike his colleagues, he made no pretense to personal neutrality. In this he was far more the man in the street than the circumspect statesman.[83]

But it was Lord Monck's brother, Richard, who expressed his feelings in the direct manner most closely associated with the man in the street. In 1864, when relations between the British provinces and the North once again were tense, Richard Monck bought a new horse, one which proved to be erratic and difficult to handle, for his coach. He named it "Bill Seward," taught it to eat sugar from his hand, and gave it to the Governor General to ride whenever he wished.[84]

Throughout the Civil War the British North Americans waited to see which of McGee's three alternatives would be thrust upon them.

[82] Seward Papers: June 30, 1862. See also *ibid.*: Thomas Nelson to Seward, Jan., 1863; A.N. Buell Papers: Addie Thorpe to Mrs. Buell, March 4, 1863; Moran Diary, xiv: Dec. 16, 1864, printed in Wallace and Gillespie, eds., *Moran*, ii, 1358; Toronto *Globe*, April 10, 1863; P.A.C., George Brown Papers, vii: L. H. Holton to Brown, Feb. 24, 1862, 643–647.

[83] For various expressions of personal feeling in the provinces by merchants and farmers, see: M. Gunn Papers, i: Jan., 1863, 36–37, June 8, 1863, 51; Buell Papers: J. Van Doren to Mrs. Buell, Jan. 29, 1861, and Addie Thorpe to Mrs. Buell, Sept. 9, Oct. 10, 21, 1861; CD, Toronto, i: Thurston to Seward, Dec. 5, 1866; Seward Papers: Howard to Seward, Oct. 17, 1864, and Potter to Seward, April 5, 1865; O.P.A., William Kirby Papers: Jane Fuller to William Kirby, May 3, 1861, and Josephine W— to Kirby, May 7, 1863. See also London *News*, June 2, 1863; Monck, *Leaves*, p. 71: July 17, 1864; and C. O. Paullin, "Early British Diplomats in Washington," The Columbia Hist. Soc., *Records*, xlv (1943), 241–262.

[84] Monck, *Leaves*, p. 186.

For the moment, Northern complaints were aimed only at the anti-Northern attitude of the more vocal colonials. The situation would become considerably more serious when these complaints could be directed against some specific and apparently unfriendly act. Advocacy always was less important than acts, and the autumn of 1863 was to bring renewed tension to border relations. British North America was maintaining a state of semi-armed neutrality, an "impression of preparedness," and the Confederacy set out to test that neutrality.

twelve ᘒᑈ **THE SECOND**

CHESAPEAKE **AFFAIR**

> "To be beneath the protection of the old Lion
> and hear his roar and see the shaking of his
> shaggy mane . . . is not that enough to fill the
> heart of a *loyal* subject with thankfulness?"
>
> A. N. BUELL, *1862*

LESS THAN A MONTH AFTER THE CANADIAN BORDER WAS AROUSED BY THE
abortive raid on Johnson's Island, New England and the Maritime Provinces were electrified by a second Confederate plot, one which created
a situation potentially as explosive as the *Trent* affair. It is strange that
this, the "second *Chesapeake* affair"—as Haligonians who recalled the
earlier and storied U.S.S. *Chesapeake* and its battle with H.M.S. *Shan-
non* named it—has received but scant attention from historians. The
affair was one of the most colorful and significant events to occur
in British North American–United States relations during the war.
It destroyed much of the good-will created by Monck's warning of
three weeks earlier, and it was one of the first of a series of severe tests
of British neutrality laws.[1]

[1] The only secondary material on the *Chesapeake* affair is George Cox, "Side-
lights on the Chesapeake Affair, 1863-4," Nova Scotia Hist. Soc., *Collections*,
XXIX (1951), 124-137, which is totally inadequate; W. C. Borrett, *Down to the Sea
Again*, pp. 27-36, the text of a radio talk; and F. L. Littlefield, "The Capture of
the Chesapeake," Maine Hist. Soc., *Collections*, 3rd ser., II (1906), 285-309.
The last contains such excessive statements as the one that Halifax and Saint
John were greater centers of secession than was Richmond (p. 288) and concludes that Providence was responsible, through the creation of a gale that
prevented the *Chesapeake*'s escape, for the final capture (p. 308). The writer has

The chief protagonist in the *Chesapeake* drama was one John C. Braine, a twenty-three-year-old professional artist who claimed to have been born in London. Arrested at Michigan City, Indiana, in 1861 and charged with membership in a seditious organization, the Knights of the Golden Circle, Braine had spent six months in prison without trial, emphatically denying the while that he had committed any act of hostility against the North and demanding British protection as a native of New Brunswick.[2] Ill and penniless he was released in March of 1862. Whether he was innocent of the original charge or not— and he apparently was, or he would not have been released—Braine now evinced considerable hatred for the North. Over a year later, possibly in revenge for unjust imprisonment or possibly as indirect evidence of his original guilt, Braine engineered the capture of the *Chesapeake*, despite having taken the usual oath that he would do nothing that was hostile to the United States during the war.[3]

Braine's principal help came from Vernon Locke, a Canadian citizen who was a long-time resident of South Carolina. Confederate Secretary of State Judah P. Benjamin had issued a letter of marque to one Thomas B. Power of the C.S.S. *Retribution,* who had transferred his name and letter to Locke after the latter had appropriated the name of a steamship captain, John Parker, who recently had died in Richmond. Locke, alias Parker, alias Power, used the *Retribution* to capture a Northern ship, the *Hanover,* and sold her cargo in the Bahamas, where he was arrested and released on his own recognizance, which he forfeited. Locke kept the *Retribution*'s letter of marque in hope of fraudulently using it for another ship. His opportunity came when, on a trip to New Jersey in 1863, he became acquainted with Braine.[4]

expanded the present chapter as an article, which appeared in *American Neptune,* XIX (Jan., 1959), 51–72.

[2] The writer has been unable to ascertain the truth about Braine's nativity. At one time he claimed to be a Kentuckian, the son of a colonel in the Mississippi cavalry. During his imprisonment someone claiming to be his father wrote to the British minister, but the "father's" claims seemed fraudulent.

[3] NFBL, 43: Lyons to Seward, Feb. 4, March 1, 1862; NBL, 9: Seward to Lyons, Oct. 26, 1861, 333–334, March 4, 1862, 128; FO 115, 330–331: Lyons to Russell, May 15, 1862; CD, Saint John, v: Howard to Seward, Dec. 11, 1863, and copy of oath, dated Feb., 1862.

[4] CSA, 52: Power to N. Levin, Feb. 22, 1864, and Levin to Benjamin, Feb. 25, 1864; CFA, 89: Russell to Adams, May 19, enc. in Adams to Seward, May 25, 1865; CD, Saint John, v: Howard to Seward, Dec. 9, 1863, Feb. 25, 1864; *The Times,* Dec. 30, 1863; *Register of Officers of the Confederate States Navy, 1861–1865* (Washington, 1931), p. 20.

During the summer of 1863 Braine lived in Halifax, posing as a Montreal book publisher who was collecting subscriptions and advertisements for a book that he styled "Braine's Mercantile Statistical Work, and Business Directory of Canada and the Provinces." He obtained sums ranging from twenty-five shillings to twenty-five dollars for the publication, which he promised to deliver free to each advertiser within eight months.[5] The merchants of Halifax thus unwittingly financed Braine's attack on the *Chesapeake*. In the autumn Braine was persuaded by the Reverend David Kinyou of Halifax, an Englishman in whom he had confided, that Saint John was a better point from which to launch a raid on a Northern steamer. Thereafter, over tall bottles of Allsopp's India Pale Ale, Braine, Locke, and a resident of Canada West who had become a Confederate, John H. Parr, discussed the best means of obtaining a privateer. These meetings were held in Lower Cove, Carleton, opposite Saint John, and an undetermined number of British subjects attended the meetings.

In June the coasting steamer, the *Chesapeake*, which plied the route between New York and Portland, had won some local fame for being chartered temporarily in a successful effort to capture a Confederate privateer that had attacked the revenue cutter *Caleb Cushing*.[6] The *Chesapeake* had performed well during the chase, and it seemed to Parr to be one of the fastest nonmilitary vessels left on the New England coast. The conspirators decided to seize the *Chesapeake* and discharge her passengers on Grand Manan Island, to sell the cargo along the New Brunswick coast, purchasing arms with the proceeds, and to convert the steamer into a Confederate privateer that could prey on Northern shipping. The New Brunswickers who participated were to be paid from the subscription and advertising money Braine had collected and from shares of the proceeds from the sale of the steamer's cargo. Despite the Foreign Enlistment Act, those British subjects who wished to remain with the rechristened ship were to be permitted to do so, and they were promised $500 when the ship ran the blockade at Wilmington. Locke contended that the letter of marque issued to the *Retribution* would make all of this "an act of war," provided that the *Chesapeake* were given the name of the former vessel.[7]

[5] CD, Halifax, x: Jackson to Seward, Feb. 3, 1864.

[6] Clarence Hall, "The Capture of the Caleb Cushing," Maine Hist. Soc., *Collections*, 1 (1904), 197–198.

[7] Saint John *Globe*, Dec. 10, 12, 1863; *The Times*, Dec. 22, 1863; CD, Saint John, v: Howard to Seward, Feb. 25, 1864; CD, Halifax, x: Jackson to Seward, Feb. 3, 1864.

Late in November, 1863, sixteen of the conspirators sailed to Boston on the *Chesapeake's* sister ship, the *New England*. On the first lap of the journey from Saint John to Eastport, Maine, the editor of the Saint John *Colonial Presbyterian* noticed that a young man whom he knew had purchased his ticket under an assumed name, and when he confronted the latter, he was told that an attack on some steamer was intended. Strangely, the anti-Southern editor did not pass this information on to the Federal authorities.[8]

The *Chesapeake* set out from New York for Portland on December 5 with a crew of seventeen and a full load of passengers, including sixteen young men who had brought a heavy trunk aboard with them. A New York detective searched for Braine while the ship was taking on cargo, for a rumor that a plot of an unknown nature was underfoot had reached him, but he failed to find his quarry. Shortly after midnight on Monday, December 7, while the steamer was on the high seas off Cape Cod, the sixteen young men, led by Braine, threw open their trunk to reveal a cache of arms. They seized the watch, killed the second engineer without warning and wounded the first, disabled the first mate, and surprised the captain and crew, confining the captain in irons. Since none of the raiders could navigate the ship, the wounded engineer had to man the engine while a passenger was forced to pilot the vessel. Braine and Parr took the captain's money, the ship's papers, and the cargo permits.

In order to find their bearings the conspirators first made a landfall off Mount Desert Island, then turned to Grand Manan Island, where a few members of the group went ashore at Seal Cove. When Braine fired a distress signal, Locke joined the *Chesapeake* in a pilot boat into which the passengers and most of the crew were forced. This vessel was towed to within six miles of the Saint John shore, where it was cast off. After the dead engineer's body was weighted with iron and thrown overboard, the *Chesapeake* was taken north to within the three-mile limit, where a small and insufficient supply of coal was brought to her by a cohort who had obtained the fuel illegally in small lots from New Brunswick merchants. Before the *Chesapeake* could finish coaling, however, the passengers had rowed to Saint John.[9]

The captain of the *Chesapeake* roused consul Howard at Saint John

[8] CD, Quebec: Ogden to Seward, and Saint John *Morning Freeman*, both Dec. 12, 1863.
[9] NBL, 10: Seward to Lyons, Dec. 18, 1863, 415–417; CD, Saint John, v: Howard to Seward, Dec. 9, 13, 30, 1863, Feb. 25, 1864; Quebec *Gazette*, Dec. 16, 1863.

at four in the morning, just as the vessel put out to sea once again, leaving British waters without enough coal to reach the intended haven in Bermuda. Howard arranged to have the passengers taken to Portland on the *New England,* and the International Steamship Company paid the charges as a gesture of good will. The consul telegraphed the *Chesapeake*'s owner, Emory and Fox and Company of Portland, about the seizure, spent the day trying to ascertain how the *Chesapeake* got its coal supply, and settled down with the crew to await the steamer's capture.

The deputy collector of the port at Portland notified the Secretary of the Treasury of the incident, asking for authority to use the gunboat *Agawan,* then being fitted out at the Portsmouth Navy Yard, in pursuit of the *Chesapeake.* All Northern government ships near the Maritime Provinces were ordered in pursuit of the steamer and consuls and their agents were instructed to report on her movements from St. Pierre and Miquelon to Eastport. At the same time the Saint John *News* obtained the story from the *Chesapeake*'s captain.[10]

The owner of the ship also gave the news to the press. The New York *Herald* branded the "piracy" the "most daring and atrocious on record." The New York *World* castigated "Sir Forcible Feeble" and other British and American symbols of official negligence, while the Portland *Advertiser* warned that British North America must not be permitted to become a base for such Confederate operations. In Saint John the general feeling, according to the *New Brunswick Courier,* was regret that the city was in any way connected with the affair. In Quebec there was consternation among the merchants, for the *Chesapeake* had carried goods consigned to them and some illegal liquor as well. In New York merchant George Templeton Strong summed up the Confederate raid with enthusiasm: ". . . its audacity is wonderful," he wrote on the day the news arrived, and he predicted that the *Chesapeake* would not be caught.[11]

But caught she was. Braine and Locke took the *Chesapeake* across the Bay of Fundy to Nova Scotia, where they unsuccessfully tried to get coal along St. Mary Bay, and they finally sold most of the ship's

[10] CD, Saint John, v: Howard to Seward, Dec. 14, 1863; Saint John *New Brunswick Courier,* Dec. 12, 1863.

[11] *Herald,* Dec. 16, 1863; *World* and *Telegram,* both Dec. 14, 1863; *Courier,* Dec. 12, 1863; CD, Quebec: Ogden to Seward, Dec. 12, 1863; Allan Nevins and M. H. Thomas, eds., *Diary of George Templeton Strong* (New York, 1952), III, 379: Dec. 11, 1863.

cargo at Shelburne, New Dublin, and Mahone Bay. At Shelburne they were able to bring the *Chesapeake* to within two miles of shore and to obtain an additional small supply of coal. The United States' Consular Agent there, Cornelius White, learned of the ship's presence but acted too late to stop it. On December 14 the *Chesapeake*, now bearing the name *Retribution*, anchored off Petite Rivière, and Braine went ashore. The vice-consul at Liverpool, Nova Scotia, tried to arrest him, but interference by a group of anti-Northern citizens made it possible for Braine to escape by land to Halifax. John Parr then fled with the ship to La Have River.

Two Northern warships closed in on the *Chesapeake* the following day, the U.S.S. *Ella and Annie* moving south from Halifax and the U.S.S. *Dacotah* [12] moving north from Shelburne. Ironically, Lieutenant S. F. Nichols of the *Ella and Annie* seemed to have been something of a special nemesis to the *Retribution*, for as commander of another Northern ship he had pursued the original *Retribution* when it was under Captain Power. Hopeful of obtaining more coal, Parr went to Lunenburg, where he saw the *Ella and Annie* approaching. Ordering that the lights be turned out, Parr slipped the *Chesapeake* behind the Spectacle Islands at the mouth of La Have River, and the Northern gunboat went on to Lunenburg, cleared for action, but found nothing. Lieutenant Nichols then went ashore to the post office to send a telegram, where he nearly encountered Parr, who had hurried ashore for the same purpose. The postmistress hid Parr in another room. Nichols obtained a supply of coal from Cunard and Company to continue the pursuit. The following day Parr took the *Chesapeake* to St. Margaret Bay where a few of the conspirators left the ship. Parr's telegram, which apparently had been to Vernon Locke, who had gone on to Halifax to join Braine, asked that coal be brought to Sambro harbor, and it was answered when a small Nova Scotian vessel, the *Investigat* ;[13] met the *Chesapeake* at Sambro.

Before the coal could be transferred to the *Chesapeake*, the *Ella and Annie* was sighted. Since the Northern vessel controlled the entrance to the harbor, escape appeared impossible, and Parr and the conspirators abandoned the ship to the few remaining crew members. Parr's final departure was so rapid that he apparently failed to warn

[12] At one time the *Dacotah*, which had been serving in the East Indies when the war began, was suspected of harboring Southern sympathizers (MC: Isaac Taylor to Seward, Dec. 5, 1861).

[13] This vessel is referred to as the *Intendant* in some reports.

all of his band, for two Nova Scotians, Alexander and William Henry, were captured while sleeping below decks. Captain John Holt of the *Investigator* took his boat to within two hundred yards of shore and waited. During the confusion someone, presumably one of the five original captured crew members who had been held on board, raised the international distress signal of an inverted flag over the *Chesapeake*, and Lieutenant Nichols took advantage of it to seize the ship within British waters.

An hour later six armed men from the Northern gunboat boarded the *Investigator* while her captain and crew were below decks. An armed officer demanded to know whether any of the conspirators were on board, and despite Holt's denial, and his warning that the Americans were in British waters, the ship was searched and one raider, John Wade of Nova Scotia, was found asleep in the captain's cabin. Over Holt's protests that they had no authority to do so, the Northerners took Wade and some baggage belonging to the conspirators back to the *Ella and Annie* with them.[14]

In the meantime the vice-consul, Nathaniel Gunnison, a Congregational minister who temporarily was replacing consul Jackson at Halifax, had asked the Provincial Secretary and the Attorney General of Nova Scotia to seize the *Chesapeake*. They refused to do so without more evidence, and after Gunnison hired an agent to investigate Braine's activities, Chief Justice William Young issued a warrant for the latter but not for the rest of the conspirators. But when three officers tried to serve the warrant on Braine, who still was in Halifax, a group of armed Haligonians helped him to escape.

The U.S.S. *Dacotah* now entered Halifax harbor with the *Chesapeake* in tow. Lieutenant Nichols had intended to take his prize directly to Portland, but Captain A. G. Clary of the *Dacotah*, who had some understanding of international law, and who fell in with Nichols at Sambro harbor following the capture, ordered that the prisoners and the ship be taken first to Halifax and thence to Portland after British approval had been given. In the meantime Secretary of the

[14] CD, St. John's, IV: Leach to G. Hughes, Dec. 11, enc. in Leach to Seward, Dec. 14, 1863; CD, Halifax, X: Jackson to Seward, Jan. 14, 15, 19, Feb. 3, March 9, 1864, Gunnison to Jackson, Dec. 11, and Gunnison to Seward, Dec. 14, 1863; CD, Saint John, V: White to Seward, Dec. 15, 1863; ITC, 36: Seward to Jackson, Dec. 31, 1863, 76; MC: Sanford to Fox, Dec. 16, and Sanford to Welles, Dec. 17, 1863; NBL, 10: Affidavit of Holt, enc. in Seward to Lyons, Jan. 9, 1864, 471–473; Saint John *New Brunswick Evening Globe*, Dec. 10, 1863; *The Times*, Dec. 22, 1863; *Hansard's, 1863:* CLXV, 1270–73.

Navy Gideon Welles had sent word that the *Chesapeake* must be delivered to the colonial authorities, since she had been captured in British waters. To compound their injury to Nova Scotian pride, the American naval officers towed the *Chesapeake* well into the inner harbor and remained there for nearly three hours without communicating with the shore. The Northern gunboat *Acacia* arrived soon after with prisoners, including one Canadian, taken from the coaling vessel that originally had tried to supply the *Chesapeake*.[15]

The situation was tense. Lieutenant Governor Doyle sent for the Provincial Secretary, Charles Tupper, who advised him to send his private secretary to the *Dacotah* to demand the release of the one Nova Scotian whose name was known, Wade. When Doyle asked what to do if Clary refused to release him, Tupper is said to have replied, "In that case, you must sink his vessel from the batteries." [16] An angry, pro-Southern mob milled about on Queen's Wharf, waiting to see whether the prisoners would be freed. Five Federal vessels rode at anchor in the harbor with two more nearby. A shot from the shore, accidental or planned, might have drawn return fire that would have wrought havoc in Halifax, a flimsy city of wood. Had Doyle acted as Tupper advised, or had Clary given him a reason to do so, the Anglo-American war that the Confederacy wanted so badly might well have begun.[17]

Tupper declared that the provincial authorities would take the prisoners. He advised Gunnison and Clary that a county official would receive the prisoners on the following day at one o'clock and that a revenue schooner would take possession of the *Chesapeake* an hour later. Tupper added that the American naval officers had committed "a great infraction of the international law" by making a forcible entry on board the Nova Scotian schooner *Investigator*. Doyle considered that this "flagrant violation of neutral rights" rendered it imperative that he demand the unconditional surrender of the vessel and prisoners, and that because of his illegal arrest Wade should be discharged from custody until a proper warrant could be sworn out against him.[18]

[15] *Diary of Gideon Welles*, I, 490; CD, Halifax, x: Jackson to Seward, Sept. 30, Oct. 21, 1863, and Gunnison to Seward, Dec. 21, 1863.

[16] E. M. Saunders, *The Life and Letters of the Right Honorable Sir Charles Tupper, Bart., K.C.M.G.* (London, 1916), I, 90–91.

[17] See *Yarmouth Herald*, Dec. 24, 1863; *The Times*, Jan. 6, 1864.

[18] CD, Halifax, x: Gunnison to Seward, Dec. 21, 1863. See also NBL, 10: Seward to Burnley, Oct. 11, 1864, 123; Doyle Letter Book: Doyle to Newcastle, Dec. 23, 1863.

Then followed "one of the most unfortunate occurrences of the day . . . ."[19] When the time for Wade's release drew near, a large crowd of Haligonians and Southerners gathered on the Queen's Wharf. The crowd grew restive when it was rumored that the prisoners had been kept in irons in the *Dacotah*'s hold. The irons were visible as the boat conveying Wade to the shore came closer, and a strongly pro-Southern colonial, Dr. W. J. Almon, declared that as a Nova Scotian he would not allow a British subject to be dealt with by Yankees in such a manner. In the meantime Gunnison had succeeded in getting a last-minute warrant, which was good only in the city limits, against Wade. The city sheriff told Constable Lewis Hutt, who was to serve the warrant, not to be in a hurry about it, so Hutt arrived at the wharf just in time to see Wade unchained and turned over to the county marshal. The crowd pressed about the marshal, cutting him off from Wade, who, at Almon's suggestion, jumped into a rowboat that had just entered the slip, and Wade was pulled to safety. Hutt, who was not in uniform, rushed forward, brandished a revolver, and commanded that the rowboat stop, whereupon Dr. Almon grasped his arm. As it appeared that Hutt might fire upon Almon, a Dr. P. H. Smith also wrestled with him while the crowd cheered the oarsmen on, drowning out the marshal's demands that Wade be returned. Both officers attempted to procure a boat for pursuit, but one Alexander Keith forcibly stopped the marshal while Hutt was unable to obtain a boat.

Gunnison rushed back to the consulate and in the heat of the moment dashed off a letter to Tupper, declaring that the citizens of Nova Scotia had violated the extradition clause of the Webster-Ashburton Treaty. Some of Halifax's most prominent citizens, including wealthy merchant John Y. Payzant, the Solicitor General, W. A. Henry, and the Lieutenant Governor's *aide-de-camp*, had been among the crowd, estimated at one hundred and fifty men, on the Queen's Wharf. Gunnison demanded that the provincial authorities arrest Wade, Keith, and Almon. That evening Gunnison wrote Seward that justice could not be obtained in Halifax and that Braine had returned to the city boasting that he was perfectly safe there, walking about with the three policemen who were charged with arresting him. Justice would have to be obtained, if at all, through Lord Lyons, Gunnison concluded.[20]

When the news of Wade's escape arrived, the New York *Herald* lashed out at the "Blue Noses—men with the cold blood and feeble circulation of reptiles," and condemned the "Halifax Riot." [21] Doyle took exception to this type of reporting and protested to Colonial Secretary Newcastle that he could not have anticipated Wade's escape. There had been no "mob," he insisted, for he estimated that only fifty men were on the wharf and that only eighteen were on the slip when Wade escaped.

When news of the *Chesapeake*'s capture reached Washington, Seward informed Lyons that the United States had not authorized and would not attempt to justify any violation of Nova Scotian authority. In striking contrast to his initially belligerent attitude during the *Trent* affair, Seward expressed his "profound regret" even before he was certain that the *Ella and Annie* had violated British waters. He declared himself certain that Lyons would "adopt all proper measures," but he did not fail to cite the *Chesapeake* affair as another example of the bad effects of Britain's proclamation of neutrality. Seward requested that the United States be allowed to keep the *Chesapeake* and the "pirates" so that the authorities at Halifax would not be "embarrassed." Lyons expressed his complete satisfaction with Seward's disavowal of Lieutenant Nichols' act and promised that Doyle would consider the Secretary's suggestion with "good neighborhood." He wired both Mulgrave and Doyle to apprehend Braine and Parr if circumstances warranted such action.[22]

When news of Wade's escape reached Washington, Seward told Lyons that he feared that some expression of popular resentment against the British province might take place. The Secretary reported that the Chairman of the House Ways and Means Committee already had notified the Department that the Committee was going to ask Lincoln to terminate the reciprocity treaty. If the provinces would act in some manner to inspire friendship, Seward said, he was confident that he could keep the reciprocity question from being introduced on the floor of the House of Representatives, and he felt that the best

---

19, 1863, Jan. 22, 1864; Halifax *Morning Journal*, Jan. 13, 1864; Halifax *Reporter*, Jan. 19, 1864.

[21] Dec. 21, 1863.

[22] ITC, 36: Seward to Gunnison, Dec. 12, 1863, 45; NBL, 10: Seward to Lyons, Dec. 16, and Seward to Adams, Dec. 18, 1863, 412, 415–417; *Foreign Relations, 1864*, I, 45: Seward to Adams, Dec. 17, 1863; GBI, 19: Seward to Adams, Dec. 19, 1863, 103; NFBL, 57: Lyons to Seward, Dec. 16, 18, 1863.

way for Great Britain to show this friendship would be to withdraw the proclamation of neutrality that had accorded belligerent rights to the South, thus indirectly causing the. *Chesapeake* affair. In writing to Russell, Lyons declared that his powers of arguing with Seward on the subject of neutrality "were long ago exhausted." [23]

Shortly thereafter Doyle's report of the events at Sambro and Halifax reached Lyons, and he cast aside his diplomatic aplomb for the moment. From the report, Lyons was convinced that the Northern ships had violated British territorial rights so flagrantly as to render a strong protest mandatory. Happily, Seward was absent from Washington, and by the time he had returned, Lyons was learning that Doyle's report had not told everything. When Seward returned, Lyons conveyed his annoyance unofficially, and Seward replied that Lincoln regretted the incident and that the officers concerned would be censured. Lyons indicated that Her Majesty's government would accept this as a full apology.[24]

Despite the fact that the *Chesapeake* affair potentially was as explosive as that of the *Trent*, Northern, colonial, and imperial statesmen did not permit it to become so. That Lyons and Seward handled the incident so well and so quietly that it virtually is forgotten today, that they maintained amicable relations while Gunnison and Jackson, Tupper and Doyle, were firing verbal salvos at each other, shows that Seward had grown in statesmanship and after three years of bloodshed had realized that Lincoln was right when he advocated "one war at a time." Great Britain was preoccupied with rumors of war on the Continent, where Prussia was preparing to launch her drive for hegemony, and public opinion in the North and in the provinces was less inflammatory after Monck's open cooperation with Seward over the abortive raid on Johnson's Island. Minister Adams also deserves praise for his role in the affair, for Seward did send him one rather heated dispatch in which the Secretary suggested that Adams should make representations to Earl Russell over the conduct of the colonial authorities in Nova Scotia and New Brunswick. Exercising the elasticity of his position, Adams decided not to make such representations, since he received news from the North that the colonial authorities in New Brunswick were cooperating with the Federal government.[25]

[23] FO 5, 900: Dec. 24, 1863.
[24] FO 115, 356: Lyons to Russell, Dec. 29, 1863, 920; NBL, 10: Seward to Lyons, Jan. 9, 1864, 471–473; NFBL, 60: Lyons to Seward, Feb. 29, 1864.
[25] Seward Papers: A. F. Farrar to Seward, Oct. 22, Dec. 8, 1863; CFA, 85: Adams to Seward, Jan. 28, 1864; *Diary of Gideon Welles*, I, 508–509.

The British North American and Federal newspapers did not seem as ready to whip up emotionalism over the *Chesapeake* affair as they had been during the *Trent* crisis. The New Brunswick press condemned Braine and his men and seemed willing to condone the violation of Nova Scotian waters. They were a bit pleased, perhaps, that Nova Scotia's smug attitude that New Brunswick was in a more precarious position had proved illusory. In Saint John the *Globe* regretted that the Confederates had been given shelter in New Brunswick while the *Courier* called the raiders "deluded men" who should return to the South. Nova Scotian newspapers scolded those who aided Wade's escape and condemned Braine as an "adventurer of the worst type." Even the anti-Northern Halifax *Citizen* attacked the adventurer, albeit for behaving like a Yankee.[26]

The New York press also was restrained in dealing with the affair. For four days during the previous July the city had been the scene of serious draft riots. By their failure to quell the riots New Yorkers had forfeited any right to criticize Nova Scotia for the Queen's Wharf mob. The New York *Times* declared itself satisfied that the conspirators were not captured, for had they been captured and not extradited, the North would have had another quarrel with Britain, while if they were surrendered to the North, the provincial member of the group would have complicated the prohibitions on prisoner exchange. The New York *World* grew whimsical and was content to compare the entire affair to medieval times when, according to the *World*, peasants slipped into hostile castles disguised as meal bags or bundles of hay. Only the New York *Herald* and *Tribune* recommended countermeasures against Nova Scotia. Outside New York the Cleveland *Leader* was more abusive, noting that Nova Scotia never would be annexed to the United States because it was not "fit for decent society."[27]

But if Great Britain and the United States took the matter calmly and soon forgot it, Nova Scotia, and to a certain extent New Brunswick, could not. From December until March the two provinces were the scene of no less than three trials growing out of the *Chesapeake* affair, each of which was attended with excoriations of the North, condemnation of the South, and some self-searching by provincials.

[26] *Globe*, Dec. 12, 1863; *Courier*, March 12, 1864; Halifax *Sun*, Dec. 21, 1863; Yarmouth *Herald*, Oct. 27, 1864; *Citizen*, editorial enc. in CD, Halifax, x: Jackson to Seward, Feb. 3, 1864; Toronto *Globe*, Dec. 22, 1863; Toronto *Leader*, Jan. 4, 1864.

[27] *Times*, Jan. 6, 7, 13, 1864; Ottawa *Citizen*, July 18, 1863; *Tribune*, Dec. 31, 1863; *Leader*, Dec. 21, 1863; *World*, Dec. 18, 1863.

Court action was slow and halting, giving time for colonial opinion to become calmer.

Consul Howard had been successful in getting a warrant issued in New Brunswick for the arrest of eleven of the conspirators, including Braine, Locke, Parr, and another Canadian, Linus Seely. On the following day Locke and Parr were arrested, but Braine again escaped. The provincial officials gave every assistance, night and day, to help capture the remaining fugitives, and in sharp contrast to the Halifax constabulary, the Chief of Police of Saint John personally conducted the search for Braine. Seward promptly thanked Lyons for New Brunswick's cooperation.[28]

The preliminary examination began on January 4, with a third conspirator, Seely, in the dock. New Brunswickers showed great interest in the proceedings, crowding the courtroom and overflowing into the streets. The proceedings went slowly, but the popular interest was held when it was disclosed that at least nine of the original conspirators were British subjects. Some of New Brunswick's desire to capture those who were still at large probably was dampened during this time when a portion of the New York press falsely accused the provincial authorities of conniving to permit Locke's continued freedom and began to publish pointed articles recounting questionable American victories over the British during the War of 1812, a war that British North Americans always considered they had won.[29]

On February 24 the court sustained all of the charges made by the prosecution and committed the prisoners to jail to await a requisition for extradition to the United States. The police magistrate called the raid "the work . . . of a coward and a villain, which ought to be considered as against all law—Human or Divine," and declared that the letter of marque made out to the *Retribution* could not be transferred to the *Chesapeake*. The raid on the *Chesapeake* was judged to be piracy, not a lawful act of war.

The prisoners were not turned over to the United States, however. The defense attorneys carried the case to a higher court on the contention that if the capture of the *Chesapeake* were piracy, the trial for that crime also would have to take place in New Brunswick, whose

[28] CD, Saint John, v: Howard to Seward, Dec. 30, 1863, Jan. 4, 1864; NBL, 10: Seward to Lyons, Jan. 5, 1864, 456.
[29] CD, Saint John, v: Howard to Seward, Jan. 14, 20, 1864; CD, Halifax, x: Jackson to Seward, Jan. 21, 1864; Saint John *New Brunswick Courier*, Jan. 23, 1864.

waters the vessel first had entered after the seizure. J. W. Ritchie,[30] a Nova Scotian attorney, also had taken up the case, and he wrote to Benjamin Wier, the Confederacy's unofficial consul at Halifax, broadly hinting that the *Chesapeake*'s captors, if Confederates acting under Southern orders, could be freed. Ritchie advised Wier that the capture of the vessel was piracy only if non-Southerners comprised a majority of the body of conspirators. Wier at once wrote to Secretary Benjamin asking for a copy of Locke's commission and a Confederate affidavit that would show that Parr was acting with proper authority. This would end the "Billingsgate" that Northern papers were heaping upon "our devoted heads," he felt. At the same time a Southerner in Saint John wrote to the Confederacy suggesting that a commission for Braine or Locke be obtained that would validate their act. While he did not suggest that the commission be antedated, the implication was clear.[31]

Locke presented his own defense at the trial, using the commission originally given to Captain Power of the *Retribution*. Southerners testified as "expert witnesses" that the commission was authentic and that Braine had authority to give orders to Locke under general Confederate usage. A Nova Scotian identified Locke as a lost brother who had left the province some twenty years before. On March 10 Judge W. J. Ritchie upset the police magistrate's decision, declaring that the prisoners should be discharged because the warrant for their arrest had been processed incorrectly, and that since piracy appeared to be the offense, the proceedings should have begun before a court in the United States. Overcome with annoyance, consul Howard wrote to Seward that the "stupidly bad" British subjects involved, the "rotten rubbish . . . of the dregs of society," had to be punished, or "any notorious offender may murder the Governor . . . of Massachusetts, may take the steamer to this province, and walk the streets of St. John . . . with impunity, there being no power to arrest him for an offense within the Extradition Treaty."[32]

[30] Not to be confused with W. J. Ritchie, Judge of the Supreme Court of New Brunswick. See J. W. Lawrence, *The Judges of New Brunswick and Their Times* (Saint John, 1907), p. 494.

[31] CSA, 52: Ritchie to Wier, Jan. 5, 1864, and Walker to Benjamin, Jan. 15, 1864; *ibid.*, 54: Wier to Walker, Confederate consul at Bermuda, Jan. 5, 1864 [not in CSA catalog], and W. H. Turlington to George Davis, Jan. 4, 1864. Littlefield, pp. 299–300, writes of a "Turlington" and a "Turlingham" without realizing that they were the same person.

[32] CD, Halifax, x: Jackson to Seward, Feb. 3, 1864; MC: J. H. Drum to Lincoln,

Seward did not protest the decision, for, if extradited, the prisoners would have been white elephants. As the majority of the conspirators proved to be British subjects, to execute them for murder or piracy would have created an additional furor in the provinces, while not to administer some severe punishment would have been to encourage repetition of the *Chesapeake* incident. The New York *World*, an anti-Lincoln paper, recognized this fact and expressed the opinion that Judge Ritchie had saved the government from "a serious and embarrassing dilemma." [33]

A second trial took place in Halifax. Drs. W. J. Almon and P. H. Smith, and Alexander Keith, were arrested for helping Wade to escape. During the trial it was learned that the North had captured Dr. Almon's son, who had a commission in the Confederate service, on board a blockade-runner. Attorney J. W. Ritchie, who defended the three men, praised Almon for preventing murder, alleging that Hutt intended to kill Wade. The mayor and an alderman spoke in defense of Almon, and the doctor confessed that he could not stand by and see a Nova Scotian sent to trial in the United States where everyone knew that "law was a mockery." [34]

Keith's position was compromised when it was learned that he had been acting as a relay agent for Confederate messages to and from Richmond. The postmaster of New York intercepted two envelopes addressed to Keith. One contained a coded letter to Judah Benjamin and the second, addressed through Keith to the Confederate Secretary of War, told of twelve thousand muskets that had been shipped to Halifax and hinted darkly of plans to seize two more steamers. Assistant Secretary of War Charles A. Dana hurried to New York where he conferred with General John A. Dix, who was in command of border defense in the East, and the conspirators involved were captured within the city. Despite this evidence against Keith, the three Haligonians were released with a mild reprimand and Almon was given a light fine. [35]

Jan. 14, 1864; DL, 63: Seward to Drumm [*sic*], Jan. 22, 1864, 73; CD, Saint John, v: Howard to Seward, Dec. 9, 1863, March 3, 10, 14, with copy of Ritchie's decision, March 31, May 7, July 7, 1864; CFA, 85: Adams to Seward, April 1, 1864; Halifax *Express*, Feb. 3, 1864; Canada, *Sess. Papers*, 1877, no. 17, pp. 8–60; *Judgement of the Honorable Judge Ritchie* (Halifax, 1864), a microfilm copy of which is in the Yale University Library.

[33] March 12, 1864.

[34] CD, Halifax, x: Jackson to Seward, Jan. 22, 1864; Halifax *Morning Journal*, Jan. 13, 1864.

[35] See the sometimes unreliable work of David H. Bates, *Lincoln in the*

In New Brunswick, the imperial officials, conscious of the province's role in the *Chesapeake* affair, continued to cooperate with Howard and Seward. New warrants, properly processed in the United States, were sworn out, and Lieutenant Governor Gordon suggested that the British conspirators should be tried for violation of the Foreign Enlistment Act if all else failed. Newcastle submitted Gordon's plan to the Law Officers of the Crown, Roundell Palmer, R. P. Collins, and Robert Phillimore, and they replied that if the conspirators escaped from the charge of piracy, they were, by their own admission, automatically guilty of violating Her Majesty's neutrality. Newcastle therefore advised Gordon to prosecute the men under the Foreign Enlistment Act. However, due to confusion among the provincial authorities, the conspirators were released three days before new British warrants were issued against them. The youthful Lieutenant Governor, plagued with incompetent aids, wrote Lyons that if Seward were to broach the subject, the minister should convey Gordon's sincere regrets that the conspirators had escaped once again.[36]

The *Chesapeake*'s fate was yet to be decided. The goods from the steamer, except for a church bell, which apparently was overlooked, were impounded and returned to their owners. Adjudication on ownership of the vessel itself came before Judge Alexander Stewart of the Vice-Admiralty Court in Halifax, and on February 15 the ship was given up to her lawful owners as the victim of piracy. In the provincial assembly a member declared that Stewart had acted too quickly and said that had he waited until a messenger could arrive from Richmond the *Chesapeake* seizure would have been shown to be an act of war, but Tupper replied that the House of Assembly could not interfere with the courts. Stewart's decision created much recrimination in Halifax, and the judge was upbraided publicly in the chambers of the Halifax Club by a fellow member for his "anti-Southern decision." [37]

Telegraph Office: Recollections of the United States Military Telegraph Corps during the Civil War (New York, 1907), pp. 71–76; Callahan, *Canadian Relations,* p. 276.

[36] G 8B, 62: Gordon to Newcastle, Jan. 4, 1864, 438; *ibid.,* 64: Newcastle to Gordon, Feb. 19, 1864, 568–583; CO, 189: Gordon to Lyons, March 16, 1864; CD, Saint John, vi: Howard to Seward, Jan. 16, 1865. On Gordon's unhappy period in New Brunswick, see Paul Knaplund, "Sir Arthur Gordon and New Zealand, 1880–1882," *Pac. Hist. Rev.,* xxviii (May, 1959), 155–172.

[37] CD, Halifax, x: Jackson to Seward, Jan. 7, 13, 14, Feb. 17, 19, 1863; ITC, 36: Seward to Jackson, Feb. 24, 1864, 191–192; GBI, 19: Seward to Adams, Feb. 24, 1864, 199–200; *Foreign Relations, 1864,* i, 196–200: Seward to Adams, Feb. 24,

The owners of the *Chesapeake* feared that Confederate privateers would attempt to seize her again. While the vessel's final disposition was still in doubt, a regular officer in the Confederate navy, Lieutenant R. D. Minor, who had helped to plan the abortive Johnson's Island raid, inspected the ship and applied for command of her if she were awarded to the Confederacy. During the same months a London newspaper correspondent arrived in Halifax and began a series of sensational reports that seemed intended to whip up war sentiment. The situation concerning the *Chesapeake* raiders, he said, was getting "more ugly and more complicated in its ugliness every day." [38] Consul Howard asked the State Department to have a gunboat sent when possession of the steamer was taken, for he feared repetition of the Queen's Wharf incident. Seward asked Gideon Welles for the gunboat, and the Secretary of the Navy refused, ascribing the request to Seward's desire to glorify the State Department. However, because the owners of the *Chesapeake* also feared for the safety of the ship, Welles sent a revenue cutter as convoy. It was not until March 19, three and a half months after her capture, that the steamer returned to Portland. [39]

The aftermath of the *Chesapeake* affair extended over the following year. It produced a series of rumors, a diplomatic *faux pas*, and a final trial for one of the conspirators. During December all male passengers boarding the steamer *New England* were searched by the captain with the aid of a squad of police before the ship left Boston. Rumor had it that a group of Confederates intended to seize the vessel, set fire to the St. Croix River towns, and rob Maine's banks. On Christmas eve the people of Calais and Eastport spent a cold night guarding the bridge to New Brunswick. During the night a fire broke out, and while the townspeople refused to fight it, feeling certain that it was a decoy to lure them from the river bank, a building burned to the ground. [40]

1864; Halifax *British Colonist*, Feb. 14, 16, 1864; Raddall, *Halifax*, p. 213; C. J. Townshend, "Life of Alexander Stewart," Nova Scotia Hist. Soc., *Collections*, xv (1914), 1–15.

[38] Howe Papers, 27: June, 1865, 214; Saint John *Morning Journal*, Feb. 10, 1864.

[39] CD, Saint John, v: Howard to Seward, Feb. 24, 25, 1864; CD, Halifax, x: Jackson to Seward, Jan. 15, 20, Feb. 27, March 3, 14, 29, and Gunnison to S. Perkan, March 28, 1864; Doyle Letter Book: Doyle to Newcastle, Dec. 23, 1863, Doyle to Lyons, Jan. 20, 1864; NFBL, 59: Johnstone to Doyle, Jan. 13, 1864; N.S., Council Minutes, 202: Dec. 31, 1864, 70; *Diary of Gideon Welles*, I, 545.

[40] Saint John *Morning Freeman*, Dec. 22, 1863; Saint John *New Brunswick Courier*, Dec. 26, 1863.

For the protection of Northern vessels leaving New York harbor, passengers were required to obtain special passports. Warships were stationed at Sandy Hook and at Thragg's Neck to examine the ships in order to detain anyone who did not have the proper credentials, a precaution that was ended in the new year. Seward warned Lyons that continued Confederate activity in the provinces would create an increasingly strained border condition. The Secretary also used the *Chesapeake* case and the discovery of the coded letters addressed to Keith as an occasion to exact from export merchants new bonds of security that provisions sent to the Maritime Provinces were not destined for the Confederacy. The colonial administration, determined that another incident should not occur, vigorously protested the removal from Halifax of the flagship of Admiral Sir Alexander Milne, H.M.S. *Styx*, for its presence was thought to help prevent violation of the harbor by the belligerents. The Governor of Maine demanded protection against border raiders, and it was reported that Locke had returned to Nova Scotia and was trying to obtain a ship for privateering, while Braine was supposed to be in Canada West plotting a raid on Detroit.[41]

The New York Chamber of Commerce passed a resolution that praised Judge Stewart and commended Cunard and Company for having sold coal to the *Ella and Annie*. This well-intended *faux pas* angered the new Colonial Secretary, Edward Cardwell, who refused to convey the resolution on the grounds that praise was not due for an impartial act. He pointed out that everyone concerned in the adjudication of the *Chesapeake* case had acted according to law, showing no favoritism to the North. When *chargé* Burnley explained this to Seward, the Secretary of State returned the resolution to the Chamber of Commerce.[42]

The old warrants were enforced against a number of the conspira-

[41] *The Times*, Jan. 6, 1864; ITC, 38: Seward to Howard, Aug. 9, 1864, 146–147; NBL, 10: Seward to Lyons, Jan. 25, 1864, 525–529; GBI, 19: Seward to Adams, Jan. 7, March 2, 1864, 214–218, 461–464; CD, Halifax, x: Jackson to Seward, Feb. 18, 1864; CD, Montreal, v: Giddings to Seward, Jan. 12, 1864, Potter to Seward, Aug. 24, 1864; FO 5, 943: Lyons to Russell, Jan. 12, 1864; G 13, 1: Lyons to Monck, Jan. 12, 25, 1864, and Monck to Lyons, Jan. 26, 1864, all in cipher; *OR*, ser. III, IV, 36: Stanton to Dix, Jan. 18, 1864; Doyle Letter Book: Doyle to Vice-Admiral Sir James Hope, March 29, 1864. Hope succeeded Milne on March 15, 1864.

[42] NFBL, 69: Cardwell to Hammond, July 16, enc. in Burnley to Seward, Sept. 9, 1864.

tors involved in the seizure of the *Chesapeake* when they returned to New Brunswick in January, 1865. Linus Seely again was arrested, but in the preceding year he had contracted syphilis and by this time was nearly an imbecile. Annoyed with the slowness of the High Sheriff, consul Howard tried to get the warrants placed in the hands of the Chief of Police of Saint John. Lieutenant Governor Gordon acted with particular alacrity, instructing the sheriffs of each county to arrest the plotters. A watch was put on the homes of Wade's wife and father, but the Nova Scotian made good his escape to Halifax.

Prosecution of the *Chesapeake* raiders was not important by 1865. Had it been accomplished earlier, it might have deterred repetition of the scheme, but by the end of the war the matter seemed to be of little urgency. Nonetheless, despite Seely's condition Seward insisted that he be brought to trial, and in June, 1865, after the Civil War had ended, the syphilitic Seely was tried in the Court of Admiralty with Judge Ritchie presiding. Ritchie charged the jury to find the defendant not guilty if they found that he had joined the raiders with the impression that he was acting under proper authority from the Confederate government. Colonial Secretary Cardwell also reminded Gordon that Ritchie's former adjudication in the *Chesapeake* matter had been strengthened by the decision of the Court of Queen's Bench in England in the *Joseph L. Garrity* case in which it had been determined that piratical acts committed on the high seas on board a United States vessel over which British Criminal and Admiralty Courts could exercise jurisdiction were not automatically extraditable. Seely was acquitted, only to be killed in a brawl a few months later. Locke on the other hand, eventually was extradited on a charge of being engaged in the slave trade.[43]

---

[43] NBL, 13: Seward to Burnley, Jan. 25, March 3, 6, 7, 13, 1865, 44–46, 140, 145, 148–149, 163–164; NFBL, 76: Gordon to Burnley, Feb. 7, enc. in Burnley to Seward, Feb. 15, 1865, Gordon to Burnley, Feb. 8, 18, both enc. in Burnley to Seward, Feb. 25, 1865, and Burnley to Seward, March 9, 1865; CD, Saint John, VI: Howard to Seward, Jan. 16, Feb. 20, June 9, 1865; CD, Halifax, X: Jackson to Seward, Oct. 19, 1864; MC: G. F. Talbor to Seward, March 29, 1865, T. K. Lothrop to Seward, April 4, 1865, Henry Stanbery to Seward, Sept. 25, 1866, and B. D. Silliman to Seward, Sept. 22, 28, 1866; CFA, 89: Russell to Adams, May 19, enc. in Adams to Seward, May 25, 1865; GBI, 20: Seward to Adams, July 20, 1865, 246–247; G 8B, 45: Cardwell to Gordon, March 31, 1865, 91–94; CO 189: Gordon to Cardwell, June 6, and Gordon to Bruce, June 13, 1865; *Register of Officers*, p. 20. For a fragment of the decision see Norman Mackenzie and L. H. Laing, eds., *Canada and the Law of Nations* (Toronto, 1938), pp. 528–529.

Braine continued his daring exploits. In September, 1864, Braine, Parr, and seven conspirators repeated the *Chesapeake* seizure by taking control of the New York to Havana steamship. Taking the steamer into Burmuda, where he discharged her forty passengers, Braine burned the vessel. Apprehended, he escaped once again, but in February, 1865, he was arrested in Nassau for having forfeited his recognizance in the *Hanover* case of 1862. Seward requested that Braine be extradited to stand trial for piracy and murder, but before a decision was reached the artful Braine again escaped. In March and April he seized the schooners *Spafford* and *St. Mary's*, taking the latter to Jamaica. John Camp, American vice-consul there, tried to obtain Braine's arrest, but as in British North America, the authorities acted too slowly and Braine escaped to Liverpool. Thereafter he dropped from sight, only to be captured in September, 1866, in New York City. Papers that he had in his possession at the time showed that he had spent the intervening year organizing the "Knights of Arabia," of which he was the Grand Commander, and that he was planning to use this organization for a filibustering expedition to Santo Domingo. He was released without trial, and he dropped from sight once again, outliving the *Chesapeake* itself, which ran aground in 1881 on Fishers Island, off New London, Connecticut, in a heavy fog.[44] Braine apparently continued his roguish career, for he was again heard of in 1903, languishing in a Baltimore jail for attempting to defraud one of that city's leading hostelries,[45] and he died in 1906, while posing as the president of a nonexistent fertilizer company in Birmingham, Alabama. Of such people are historical novels made.

[44] The writer visited Fishers Island and attempted to locate the hull of the *Chesapeake* but was unable to do so. Nor could the secretary of the New London Historical Society supply any information. Information on salvage operations for the *Chesapeake* appears in the New York Maritime Register, May 4, 11, 21, July 27, 1881.

[45] Saint John *Globe*, March 9, 1903, Dec. 4, 1906. An obituary notice for one of the raiders appears in the *Globe*, Nov. 29, 1909. See Baltimore *Sun*, Jan. 29, 30, Feb. 14, 27, 1903, Dec. 11, 1906.

thirteen ॐ CONFEDERATE COMMISSIONERS

IN BRITISH NORTH AMERICA

> "The English characteristic is to hasten to the discovery of truth very slowly. I doubt if the governments of either country will care to play into the hands of the rebels."
>
> CHARLES FRANCIS ADAMS' *Diary, December 30, 1864*

ALTHOUGH THE CHAIRMAN OF THE CONFEDERACY'S HOUSE COMMITTEE ON Foreign Relations insisted that the Confederate states never had a foreign policy,[1] the South did pursue a somewhat unco-ordinated program that constituted at least a *modus operandi* for diplomacy. This diplomacy originally was based on the conviction that Great Britain, because of the power of King Cotton, because of a desire to strike at the North, or because of fear for the future safety of her colonial possessions, would aid the Confederacy if given an opportunity to do so. One possible approach was to obtain that aid by embroiling Her Majesty's subjects in the war. By the end of 1863 it was evident that Great Britain would enter the war only if she or her empire were threatened, for the persuasive powers of King Cotton had proved illusory. If an incident or a series of incidents were to provoke a Northern attack on Britain, a world war might be produced from which the South probably would emerge as an independent nation.

Southern resentment against British North America began to grow by late 1863. Monck had exposed the plot against Johnson's Island, and the *Chesapeake* raid had failed. That neither failure was the fault of the people of the provinces generally was ignored in the South.

[1] James Morton Callahan, *The Diplomatic History of the Southern Confederacy* (Baltimore, 1901), p. 66.

Resentment over Earl Russell's seizure of the Laird rams helped gain official Confederate approval for raids from neutral territory, raids that hitherto had been largely independent of official sanction.[2] In his message of December 7, 1863, President Jefferson Davis contended that the Confederacy no longer was bound by any treaties with foreign nations because they had been signed for her by the Federal government. Treaties with Great Britain might be considered void. The door was open to lighting a "fire in the rear" of the North.

One historian has viewed 1864 as the year when the Confederacy made "desperate attempts to create a diversion by opening up a new front" in the British North American provinces.[3] This is an overstatement of the case because of the modern connotations of such terms as "new" or "second front," for the Confederacy intended, at least at first, to observe the Queen's neutrality while operating on British soil, and the "new front" was intended to have little direct military significance. Later, the Confederacy was less careful about British neutrality, and the fire in the rear did appear to be capable of creating a second diplomatic front, a second area in addition to the palaces and chanceries of Europe where the South might be able to find the key to intervention or European mediation. As Alfred Russell, the United States District Attorney for Eastern Michigan, wrote to Seward in 1864, the best hope of the South was "to embroil [the North] in war with England."[4]

The first Confederate mission to British North America was an outgrowth of the *Chesapeake* affair. When Wier wrote from Halifax that the steamer might be considered lawful Confederate prize if a legal commission for Vernon Locke could be obtained, Judah Benjamin asked a professor of law at the University of Virginia, J. P. Holcombe, to investigate the original commission for the *Retribution* and to go to Halifax to assess how the Confederacy might best turn the *Chesapeake* incident to her advantage. He also was charged with a second mission: to organize some means of transport to the South for stranded Confederate soldiers who, having escaped from Northern prisons, were said to be anxious to return to battle.[5] In Wilmington Holcombe ob-

---

[2] J. G. Randall, *Lincoln the President* (New York, 1945), II, 51 n. 1.

[3] G. P. de T. Glazebrook, *A History of Canadian External Relations* (London, 1950), p. 76.

[4] MC: Sept. 28.

[5] CSA, 59–67: Holcombe to Benjamin, Feb. 29, March 12, 1864; *Times*, Feb. 29, 1864.

tained the names of witnesses who were willing to swear that Locke
had resided in South Carolina for many years. He then ran the blockade to Bermuda, where he learned that adjudication of the *Chesapeake*
case had been completed. Noting that the New York *Times* was demanding the death penalty for Locke if he were extradited, Holcombe
decided to go on to Halifax to investigate the incident in order to see
what could be done for the prisoners and to test Nova Scotian feeling.

Soon after reaching Halifax, Holcombe reported to Benjamin that
the Confederacy should not forsake the conspirators, for he was convinced that they had risked their lives out of sincere sympathy for the
Southern cause. He considered that Judge Stewart's surrender of the
Chesapeake to her owners discredited British justice, but he felt that
it would be unwise for the Confederate government to interfere, for
to obtain the *Chesapeake* the South would have to approve the raiders'
actions, which were "doubtful in law and equivocal in morals," since
only one of them—Parr, who was said to have lived in Tennessee for
eight years—could claim to have been a *bona fide* resident of the Confederacy. After a lengthy visit to the provincial law library to refresh
his memory, Holcombe decided that neither Braine nor Locke had any
lawful claim to Confederate citizenship and that Parr's presence was
not sufficient to stamp the seizure of the *Chesapeake* with legality.
Holcombe added that the North was correct in contending that letters
of marque attached only to a vessel and that they did not confer upon
a commander any personal authority that could survive the destruction
of the original ship. Thus, Locke had violated both Confederate and
British law, and any claim the Confederacy advanced would be defeated in the courts. Holcombe concluded that attorney Ritchie, and
perhaps Keith, Wier, and Almon, should be rewarded for their help.[6]

During the same week Holcombe conferred with Wier to arrange
transportation for escaped Confederate prisoners. Wier undertook to
contact parties in Montreal, Kingston, and Toronto who would act as
forwarding agents for the Confederacy, gathering the soldiers together
in the respective cities and sending them on to Halifax when navigation on the St. Lawrence River opened. Each applicant for aid was to
furnish an affidavit concerning his Confederate service and a declaration that he wished to return to active duty. Holcombe approved the
plan and told the provincial authorities of it, promising to observe the
Queen's neutrality and asking for their suggestions as to any pre-

[6] CSA, 59–67: Holcombe to Benjamin, April 1, 26, 1864.

cautions that they thought he should take. Apparently the authorities did no more than acknowledge Holcombe's message. Six Confederates then in Halifax thereupon were sent to Wilmington.[7]

Holcombe also wrote to Governor General Monck to inform him that he was in British North America to fulfill, "amongst other duties," the Confederacy's desire to facilitate the movement of Southern army men out of the provinces. He outlined the arrangements made for this purpose. Monck acknowledged receipt of the message without comment, cautiously debating whether even to mention the "so-called President of the Confederacy" in the note. The Governor General communicated the information to Lyons, who also acknowledged it without comment.[8]

Holcombe remained in Halifax for two months, arranging transportation for the Confederates and testing public opinion, and he frequently reported to Benjamin that the local authorities were strongly pro-Southern. To win further support Holcombe used the same rather arrogant argument that Mason and Slidell had used in Europe: that an independent Confederacy would be indifferent to any future struggles between Britain and the North if the British continued to remain aloof from the South's struggle for freedom. He was entertained by Lieutenant Governor Doyle and by the Roman Catholic Archbishop of Halifax, the Right Reverend Dr. Thomas L. Connelly, both of whom made no secret of their desire for a Southern victory, and he had the unhappy duty of transmitting to the wife of "Stonewall" Jackson a copy of a poem written on the occasion of Jackson's death. Dr. Almon, who received the letter of commendation from President Davis that Holcombe recommended, had offered a prize to a member of the graduating class of Windsor University for a Latin ode to the Confederate general, and the son of the Attorney General of Newfoundland had responded with a lengthy dithyramb.[9]

By the end of his stay in Halifax the professor realized that it would

[7] *Ibid.*, April 1, 1864; *ORN*, ser. II, III, 1103-104: Holcombe to Benjamin, April 26, 1864.

[8] CSA, 59–67: Holcombe to Benjamin, May 27, 1864; FO 5, 950: Holcombe to Monck, n.d., and Monck to Holcombe, May 14, enc. in Lyons to Russell, May 31, 1864; BMW to GCC, 12: Lyons to Monck, May 30, 1864; G 20, 100, contains Monck's reply in draft form.

[9] *ORN*, ser. II, III, 1101-103: Holcombe to Benjamin, April 26, 1864; CSA, 59–67: Holcombe to Benjamin, April 26, 1864, and Almon to Holcombe, May 26, 1864.

be better if the returning Confederate soldiers sailed directly from Quebec and that the response to his offer of transportation to the South was not going to be overwhelming. Disappointed that expectations had been too high, and predicting that not more than a hundred men would be sent from Halifax, he left for Windsor where he hoped to find a larger group of soldiers.[10] Giving five thousand dollars to Wier in order to finance the operation in Nova Scotia, Holcombe traveled through the border towns of Canada West, finding men at Montreal, Toronto, Hamilton, St. Catherines, Niagara, and Windsor who would act as forwarding agents without pay. He expressed his desire to leave the provinces by August, but a second tour of the border towns during that month convinced him that he should remain, and he reported that he hoped a large number of escaped prisoners soon would be in the Canadas. A second plan was being devised to free the Confederates on Johnson's Island.[11]

Apparently few Confederates availed themselves of Holcombe's machinery to aid their return to the South. While a number of them did return via the sea to fight again, a greater number probably made their way overland to the Confederate states, and several hundred chose to remain in the British North American provinces. Consul Jackson kept a careful check on the number of the escaped prisoners who passed through Halifax, and by July only seventy had done so. Holcombe was removed at the end of the summer, having accomplished what he could, and was sent to England, where it was hoped that his legal knowledge would be of use in the growing debate there over the *Alabama* case.[12]

In the meantime another unofficial Confederate attempt to harry the North was more successful, but it undoubtedly was of little real aid to the South. Consul General Giddings, who had turned his attention to submitting reports on how and when the Canadas might be an-

[10] *Ibid.*, April 28, May 27, 1864; *ORN*, ser. II, III, 1120-121: Holcombe to Benjamin, May 27, and 1103-104: April 26, 1864. It may be to this estimate of Holcombe's that Edward Channing and Marion F. Lansing refer in *The Story of the Great Lakes* (New York, 1909), p. 318, when they say that there were a hundred escaped Confederate prisoners in the Canadas in 1864. The figure for escaped prisoners who remained in the provinces must have been much higher.

[11] CSA, 59–67: Holcombe to Benjamin, June 16, 18, Aug. 11, 1864; *ORN*, ser. II, III, 1187-188: Holcombe to Benjamin, Aug. 11, 1864.

[12] CD, Halifax, x: Jackson to Seward, June 8, 17, July 21, 22, 1864; James D. Horan, *Confederate Agent: A Discovery in History* (New York, 1954), p. 111.

nexed to the Union and to suggesting that the reciprocity treaty be terminated so that "the British Element may understand the value of American Commercial friendship," [13] was tricked into compromising his official position. In November, 1863, two men representing themselves as Montreal and New York detectives obtained from the guileless Giddings a note authorizing payments by the New York police to the latter detective for expenses incurred in assisting the Montreal detective to arrest one James L. Redpath, allegedly charged with arson and murder in New York. The so-called Montreal detective took Redpath to New York City, where he was told that there was no charge against him and was set free. Redpath returned to Montreal and commenced civil action against Giddings for complicity in an unlawful arrest. If a plaintiff who sued for damages could satisfy a judge that the defendant was about to leave the jurisdiction of the court, he could obtain an order for the defendant's arrest. Since it was known that Giddings intended to visit the United States shortly, the Consul General was arrested when he appeared at the railway station in Montreal. His bail was set at thirty thousand dollars, which was furnished by two wealthy Canadians, Harrison Stephens and Ira Gould. Continuing his journeys, Giddings reported his arrest to Seward from his home in Jefferson, Ohio, and requested that extraterritorial privileges be extended to him. Seward refused to defend Giddings' claim to diplomatic immunity, for the Consul General clearly had acted foolishly in not ascertaining whether there was a lawful warrant out against Redpath, and Seward did not consider that a consular official was a diplomat.[14]

Canadians were intensely annoyed by Giddings' indiscretion. A similar attempt to enmesh consul Charles Ogden in a false arrest charge at Quebec had failed when Ogden insisted on proper affidavits, and Giddings' behavior contrasted badly with his subordinate's correct action. The Consul General also compounded his error by writing an open letter to the press explaining that he had felt that it would have been indelicate of him to question an officer of the Canadian govern-

---

[13] W. D. Overman, ed., "Some Letters of Joshua R. Giddings on Reciprocity," *CHR*, xvi (Sept., 1935), 291–292: Giddings to Seward, Oct. 13, 1863.

[14] CD, Montreal, v [incorrectly filed; should appear in iv]: Nov. 28, 1863; G 6, 232: Lyons to Monck, Feb. 24, 1864; Toronto *Globe*, Nov. 20, 1863; New York *Evening Post*, quoted in Rochester *Evening Express*, Nov. 19, 1863; Saint John *New Brunswick Courier*, Dec. 12, 1863; Ross, *Memoirs of a Reformer*, pp. 140–141.

ment. This act only made Giddings' naiveté more evident, especially when Redpath at length admitted that the entire affair had been instigated by Confederate agents in Montreal.[15]

Representative James A. Garfield of Ohio introduced a resolution to the House requesting information on Giddings' arrest, and Senator Benjamin F. Wade, also of Ohio, offered a resolution to repeal the bonding privilege that the Canadas enjoyed in retaliation for the indignity. Giddings' Congressional friend and biographer, George W. Julian of Indiana, introduced a similar resolution to the House. Lyons asked Seward to do what he could to prevent the fruition of either resolution, and neither was reported back from the committee to which it was sent. Seward admitted that the measures had been prompted by irritation over Giddings' arrest. When Lyons spoke to Seward about Wade's resolution, the Secretary partially defended the action on the grounds that Giddings had reported that bonded supplies were being sent, with Lyons' permission, from the Canadas to the South. Lyons denied that he had given such permission, and Seward said that if the Canadian government would "remain perfectly quiet" with regard to Wade's bill, it might be stifled. On the other hand, Seward recommended that Canada should do something to appease Giddings personally.[16]

Although the charges against him were dropped,[17] Giddings launched a campaign against the reciprocity treaty as a means of personal vengeance upon the Canadian people. His son took over the consulate while Giddings, ostensibly too ill to return to Montreal, journeyed to Washington to express his indignation. Although he frequently insisted that there was nothing personal in his now open attacks on reciprocity, and although he once reversed himself to declare, on the floor of the House, that abrogation would not be wise, he wrote to his son that the United States must teach the Canadians a lesson for "imprisoning our Consul General at the instance of skedadlers [*sic*] from our States. Now you may understand," he promised,

[15] Toronto *Globe*, Nov. 20, Dec. 11, 1863, Jan. 12, 1864; Toronto *Leader*, Nov. 19, 1863; Rochester *Evening Express*, Nov. 19, 1863; G 6, 232: Giddings to Seward, Jan. 14, enc. in Lyons to Monck, Feb. 24, 1864; CD, Montreal, v [incorrectly filed; should appear in iv]: Giddings to Seward, Jan. 14, 1864.

[16] G 6, 232: Lyons to Monck, Feb. 24, 1864; Giddings Papers: Jan. 8, 1864; FO 5, 945: Lyons to Seward, Feb. 19, and Giddings to Seward, Feb. 8, enc. in Lyons to Russell, Feb. 23, 1864; *Cong. Globe*, 38th Cong., 1st Sess., pp. 460, 526, 2622.

[17] "Redpath vs. Giddings: Capias—Unliquidated Damages," *The Lower Canada Jurist: Collection de Décisions du Bas-Canada*, ix (1866), 226–234.

"that I shall make the Canadian government feel the insult offered ours by my arrest." [18]

Seward also noted that British sympathy with the South was giving new strength to those who opposed the treaty. Early in 1864 Cartier and other Canadians visited Washington to discuss reciprocity, talked with Seward and Sumner, the latter the only important Senator who could speak French, and returned to Quebec discouraged. Giddings jubilantly wrote, "You may set down the reciprocity treaty as defunct" and predicted that American consuls in the Canadas would be recalled. He instructed his son to be "very cool" in his dealings with Canadians, for he wanted the people of the provinces to know that Congress had more respect "for an old and long tried Servant who has full knowledge of our national offices" than it had for the Canadian Parliament. Thus spoke the tired old man who had taken no interest in international law, who could not spell *extraterritoriality* even when he hoped to invoke it, who in righteous indignation and egoism magnified the original Confederate plot against him into a personal grievance against the Canadas.[19]

The Confederate attempt to exacerbate Canadian-American relations through the Consul General of the United States was successful only as long as Giddings continued to exert almost all of his waning energy in denouncing the reciprocity treaty, in promoting annexation, and in declaring that there were no statesmen in all of Canada: ". . . when Earl Russell takes snuff, they sneeze," he wrote.[20] Giddings personally quarreled with Seward, who had not given him the support of a formally lodged complaint about his arrest, and on the floor of the House he denounced Seward's renewed efforts to place more consuls in Canada. In his final letter to his son, Giddings implied that Governor General Monck was a weak and biased administrator. As a diplomat, consul, and prophet, Giddings proved to be single-minded, humorless, and ineffective. On May 27 he died of apoplexy brought on partially by his arrest and partially by exertion while speaking at St. Lawrence Hall in Montreal.[21]

[18] Toronto *Globe*, April 1, 1864; Overman, ed., pp. 292–293.

[19] *Ibid.*, pp. 293–294: Jan. 23, 1864; GBI, 19: Seward to Adams, Feb. 8, 1864, 186–187.

[20] Julian, *Giddings*, pp. 392–394: Giddings to Sumner, April 5, 1864.

[21] Toronto *Globe*, April 1, 1864; G 20, 465: Monck to Cardwell, Dec. 9, 1864, 215, Jan. 4, 1865, 241; CD, Montreal, v: C. S. DeWitt to Seward, May 30, 1864; Overman, ed., pp. 295–296: April 29, 1864; Gerritt Smith Miller Collection: Giddings to Smith, April 15, 1864. Giddings wrote Smith: "Unfortunately

Giddings' removal hurt rather than helped the Southern cause. Giddings alive was an instrument for nurturing anti-Northernism in the Canadas. Giddings dead was a loyal servant to the cause of human freedom, a garrulous but upright old man who had suffered at the hands of secessionists in the provinces. The Toronto *Globe* lamented his passing, and as death "doth clothe the man in sunlight," even the anti-Northern Montreal papers praised him. There was an immediate scramble for his vacant office, but Seward probably was relieved to be able to appoint the energetic and well-informed David Thurston temporarily to the post. In July John F. Potter of Wisconsin was appointed Consul General, and Thurston was retained as his assistant until made consul at Toronto.[22]

By the time the new Consul General had taken office Holcombe had been followed by a second official Confederate commission to British North America. Early in 1864 Beverley Tucker wrote through a Halifax intermediary to President Davis and R. M. T. Hunter, former Confederate Secretary of State, that an agent should be sent to the Canadas to promote additional Northern opposition to Lincoln in the coming presidential election. Such an agent easily could be used "to create diversion and disaffection in the North and to promote war with England via Canada," as an astute consul recognized.[23] But the mission already was planned by the time Tucker suggested it.

Late in 1863, just before Holcombe had left on his mission, Davis summoned Jacob Thompson to Richmond. Thompson was one of Mississippi's most powerful politicians, a former Senator and Secretary of the Interior in Buchanan's Cabinet. He was a personal friend of Vallandigham, who was then in Canada West, and of President Lincoln. While the Confederacy made a number of diplomatic ap-

Mr[.] Seward differs so widely from me, or rather I differ so widely from him, that my relations with his department are not pleasant." See also J. G. Randall, *The Civil War and Reconstruction* (Boston, 1937), p. 147, who refers to Giddings as the prototype of abolitionists, and Galt Papers, 1: Ashmun to Galt, May 28, 1864, 847–49.

[22] *Globe*, May 28, June 3, 1864; ITC, 36: Seward to Thurston, June 4, 1864, 479–480; CD, Montreal, v: Potter to Seward, July 29, 1864; *ibid.*, vi: Thurston to Seward, Jan. 2, 1865; Seward Papers: McDougall to Seward, April 8, 1864. Originally Lincoln approved the appointment of P. Frazer Smith of Pennsylvania as Consul General (Basler, ed., *Works of Abraham Lincoln*, vii, 375: Lincoln to Seward, June 4, 1864, and note).

[23] Halifax *Journal*, June 12, 1865; CD, Halifax, xi: Jackson to Seward, June 27, 1864.

pointments that were unwise, Thompson's was not among these. Davis asked Thompson to serve as one of three "Confederate commissioners" in (not to) British North America, and after some hesitation Thompson accepted. After verbally giving Thompson secret instructions, Davis provided him with a commission that left much to the Mississippian's discretion.[24] Years later Assistant Secretary of State Washington, who was present, declared that although Davis's instructions did not specifically enjoin Thompson to observe Her Majesty's neutrality, "not a word or a thought that looked to any violation of the rules of war" passed between them.[25] A second commissioner, Clement C. Clay, a former Senator from Alabama, also was chosen at the same time, and Holcombe, who already had left for the provinces, was appointed as the third commissioner. The three men, as one of their closest assistants wrote, were to "crystallize anti-Northern feeling in Canada and to mould it into some form of hostile expression."[26]

Traveling under false names, Thompson, Clay, and a secretary left Wilmington for Bermuda via the blockade-runner *Thistle.* Thompson arrived alone in Halifax in May and hurried on to Toronto while Clay, who was taken ill, followed two weeks later.[27] The commissioners established a "headquarters" in the Queen's Hotel in Toronto, where

[24] *ORN*, ser. II, III, 174: Davis to Thompson, April 27, 1864; CSA: Benjamin to Thompson, April 28, 1864; J. F. H. Claiborne, *Mississippi as a Province, Territory, and State* (Jackson, 1880), pp. 460–465; J. F. Bivins, "Life and Character of Jacob Thompson," Hist. Soc. of Trinity Col. [Duke University], *Annual Publication of Historical Papers*, II (1898), 90. T. M. Harris, *Assassination of Lincoln: A History of the Great Conspiracy* (Boston, 1892), quite incorrectly refers to the commissioners as "Davis's Canada Cabinet" (pp. 118–146, 182–191).

[25] Butler, *Benjamin*, p. 348.

[26] J. B. Castleman, *On Active Service in Peace and War* (Louisville, 1917), p. 134. See also B. M. Smith, "Civil War Subversives," Illinois Hist. Soc., *Journal*, XLV (Autumn, 1952), 231. The men also were to strengthen the anti-Lincoln movement in the North before the election of 1864. It is upon this phase of their activities that all other studies have concentrated. See CSA: Benjamin to Slidell, April 30, 1864; CD, Montreal, V: Thurston to Seward, June 14, 15, 25, 1864; CD, Saint John, V: Howard to Seward, June 17, 22, 1864, and J. P. Hill to J. S. Hill, Nov. 22, 1863, enc. in Howard to Seward, Aug. 31, 1864; CD, Halifax, X: Howard to Jackson, June 18, 1864; Seward Papers: Levi Beardsley to Seward, Oct. 29, 1864; Rochester *Union and Advertiser*, Nov. 12, Dec. 14, 1863, Nov. 7, 10, 30, 1864.

[27] CD, Saint John: Howard to Seward, June 2, 3, 1864; Castleman, p. 132. See also Ruth K. Nuermberger, *The Clays of Alabama: A Planter-Lawyer-Politician Family* (Lexington, Ky., 1958), pp. 234–235, and the highly erroneous Wilfrid Bovey, "Confederate Agents in Canada during the American Civil War," *CHR*, II (March, 1921), 1–11.

nearly a hundred Confederates were staying. Thompson opened an account with the Montreal branch of the Bank of Ontario before going on to Toronto, and as Holcombe had done, he informed Monck of his arrival. The mission was abundantly financed, for Thompson reportedly had nearly a million dollars at his disposal, and he spent it lavishly.[28]

As one of Thompson's chief assistants later admitted, many of the steps taken by the commission were not practical, and in the long run the mission was a failure. Its lack of success may be ascribed partly to the fact that all three commissioners were as ardent Confederates as Giddings was an ardent abolitionist and thus were blind to the realities of their situation. While an able man, Thompson was inclined to believe that nearly everyone in the provinces favored the South in the war, and he entrusted a number of acquaintances whom he had known before the war under entirely different circumstances with dispatches or with the execution of matters pertaining to his activities in the Canadas. Unable to see any failings in the South, unable to believe that the North could win the war, he blamed the world for every Southern defeat, writing to Mason and Slidell that "the Confederate States have had to fight all the world, Ireland, Germany, Switzerland, Sweden, the Indian Territories having also sent forward thousands, and uniting them with our own slaves and renegades . . . ." [29]

Clay was a sick and lonely man who was little concerned with British neutrality and who showed the same blind spot as his compatriot. He sincerely was surprised that anyone would consider the *Index* a propaganda sheet and refused to believe news of Northern

[28] CD, Montreal, vi: Potter to Hunter, May 29, 1865; CD, Quebec, ii: Thurston to Seward, Oct. 14, 1864, 16; Clay Papers: fragments of diary, April 30, 1864–March, n.d., 1865; Headley, *Confederate Operations*, p. 309. The highly unreliable Felix Stidger also reported that an additional two million dollars in gold had been sent to the Canadas to aid the Sons of Liberty (F. A. Stidger, ed., *Treason History of the Order of Sons of Liberty* [Chicago, 1903], p. 117). Benjamin did have an undefined amount of "secret service" money available. See John B. Jones, *A Rebel War Clerk's Diary at the Confederate Capital* (Philadelphia, 1866; reissued, Howard Swiggert, ed., New York, 1935, with identical pagination), ii, 153: Feb. 20, 1864.

[29] G 10, 1: Burnley to Monck, Dec. 31, 1864, 34–40; American Art Assoc., *The Political Correspondence of the Late Hon. George N. Sanders, Confederate Commissioner to Europe during the Civil War* (New York, 1914), a sale catalog with selections from Sanders' correspondence, in the Yale University Library; Hines [and Castleman], "Northwestern Conspiracy," pp. 509–510: Thompson to Mason and Slidell, Aug. 23, 1864; Castleman, *On Active Service*, pp. 129–133.

victories because he felt that all Northerners were liars. He was as concerned for his wife, who remained in the South, as he was for his mission, and he wrote to her weekly complaining that he never heard from her, while almost every week he sent his "darling Ginie" fans, gloves, stockings, or shoes. When he did hear from Mrs. Clay, it was only to receive a list of twenty-five items that she wanted him to buy for her, to read of the shade of purple silk dress that she required, or to learn of her desire for a set of Hudson Bay sables. Clay carried his fashion-conscious wife's list with him, checking off each item as he obtained it, wearing it thin with repeated readings. It was a touching relationship, but as bachelor Lyons knew, the egotism of bachelorhood frequently is more productive of efficient diplomats than is a sentimental loneliness. Other than giving permission for and financing the St. Albans raid, which reacted against the Confederacy, Clay's only fruitful service in the Canadas was to recover Robert E. Lee's favorite dog, a Newfoundlander, and to return it to the General.[30]

Clay and Holcombe, in particular, soon were under the influence of a Confederate who was almost a fourth, but unofficial, member of the commission—George Sanders. Holcombe was the most learned of the four men, but he lacked experience and tact, and he was wanting in the boldness necessary to carry out his duties. For solace he frequently turned to a book of inspirational poems that he carried, and for advice he too often turned to the ebullient Sanders. Sanders was a menace to British North American neutrality, for he had liberal views of the legitimacy of Confederate retaliation against the North from Canadian soil. He had been United States consul in London under President Franklin Pierce, and it was he who had helped goad James Buchanan into signing the Ostend Manifesto. A drinking companion in Germany of Victor Hugo, an early leader of the fiery "Young America" movement, Sanders also was the self-proclaimed inventor of "a perfect self-protecting freight transport and war vessel" for blockade-running. Now he was at the Queen's Hotel constantly unkempt and unshaven, but living affluently in a room overlooking the bay, working to obtain the release of his son from a Northern prison and trying to convince Thompson that robbing the banks of Buffalo would be a legal act of

---

[30] CSA, 68–71: Clay to Benjamin, June 17, 1864; G 10, 2: Clay to Mrs. Clay, intercepted letter, enc. in Monck to Cardwell, Jan. 9, 1865, 152, 156–157; Virginia Clay-Clopton, *A Belle of the Fifties* (New York, 1905), pp. 255–256: Mrs. Clay to Clay, Nov. 18, 1864, and p. 227 n.; Clay Papers: Clay to ——, Sept. 2, 1864 (mutilated).

war. Sanders organized peace meetings in Niagara, clashed with Thompson's closest subordinates, and finally forced Clay to wish him, euphemistically, in Asia. In addition to Sanders' interference, the mission was prejudiced by the incompatibility of Clay and Thompson, and the former eventually established his own headquarters in Montreal and persuaded Thompson, who handled the finances, to place $93,000 at his disposal for independent use.[31]

A fifth member of the Confederate group was Thomas Hines, a young Kentuckian who had won a reputation for daring exploits and who now was ordered by Confederate Secretary of War James A. Seddon to go to Toronto to organize a band of Southern soldiers who could strike against the North. In particular many of the prisoners at Johnson's Island, with a not uncommon military ignorance of diplomatic problems, dreamed of escaping to Canada West and of using the province as a base for an attack. Hines was given a free hand to organize any operation he saw fit, but he was instructed to observe the neutrality of the British provinces. When he arrived in Toronto, he was placed under Thompson's orders, and the commissioner again reminded him of the neutrality proclamation.[32]

It is possible that Benjamin also sent female agents to the British North American provinces. In the retelling of the Confederates' exploits in the colonies, various women have come to embellish the proceedings, and they flit in and out of the secondary accounts with just the persistence that salable fiction demands. Apparently the Confederate Secretary of State did give a thousand dollars to a married woman, a Roman Catholic whose only son was in a Northern prison, to go to Canada East to enlist Catholic sympathy for the Southern cause. There is no evidence that she completed this mission, however.[33]

---

[31] CSA, 68–71: Clay to Benjamin, June 17, 1864; Hines [and Castleman], "Northwestern Conspiracy," p. 502; Castleman, *On Active Service*, pp. 135–136; Merle E. Curti, "George N. Sanders—American Patriot of the Fifties," *South Atlantic Quart.*, XXVII (Jan., 1928), 80. Much of the Thompson correspondence has been printed, among other places, in U.S. Cong., 39th Cong., 1st Sess., House Judiciary Committee *Report*, no. 104 (July, 1868), and P. L. Rainwater, ed., "Letters to and from Jacob Thompson," *Jour. of So. Hist.*, VI (Feb., 1940), 95–111.

[32] CSA, 68–71: Benjamin to Hines, March 16, 1864; John B. Jones, II, 175 n. 2, and 180: April 1, 1864; Horan, pp. 36, 68, 71–73, 79–81, 86; "The Chicago Conspiracy," *Atlantic Monthly*, XVI (July, 1865), 108–120. For Hines' earlier reputation, see E. M. Coffman, "Captain Thomas Henry Hines and His February, 1863, Raid," Kentucky Hist. Soc., *Register*, LV (April, 1957), 105–108.

[33] John B. Jones, II, 175: March 21, 1864.

Thompson found it very difficult to organize any plots in the Canadas. He reported to Benjamin that, "The bane and curse of carrying out anything in this country is the surveillance under which we act. Detectives, or those ready to give information, stand on every street corner. Two or three cannot interchange ideas without a reporter." The relatively simple cipher that the Confederates used soon was broken by the United States Telegraph Office, and Hines, who was responsible for much of the Confederate activity in the Northwest, added to the breakdown in secrecy by making numerous errors in his messages, foolishly marking the notes with symbols to indicate the beginning of new encryption cycles, inserting plain text words, and using a straight alphabet based on a simple movable wheel.[34] In addition, Clay's messages often were intercepted, and in order to prevent his discovery of this fact, duplicates of his dispatches were prepared on matching paper especially brought from England for the purpose. Clay's idea of a baffling variation of his name was to move a letter and write as "T. E. Lacy," and when he learned, months too late, that Wier's mail was being intercepted, Clay proposed no one more unknown to Seward's agents than Dr. Almon as a substitute. Seward also obtained information on the activities of the commission from intercepted telegrams and letters that were written to other known Confederate sympathizers, especially in Halifax. As a result, many of the commission's moves were known to Seward, who could limit Thompson's activities merely by reporting them to the Northern press. Thereafter the spotlight of publicity would be useful in turning potential raids into mere rumors of raids.[35]

Whether Thompson violated British neutrality or not is a moot point. He apparently thought that he had, for portions of his official journal have been blotted out. He wrote to Clay that the various schemes hatched by his subordinates, J. B. Castleman and T. H. Hines, most of which were directed against Camp Douglas near Chicago, or against New York City, and which were planned in the Canadas but neither launched nor executed there, were likely to place the commissioners in an awkward position if the United States demanded their

[34] M. N. Macdonald, U.S.A.F. cryptographer, to writer, May 31, 1956. See CFA, 72: E. G. Lee to Benjamin, Dec. 15, 1864, intercepted letter, for an example of this system.

[35] New York *Herald*, Aug. 19, 1864; Seward Papers: Wier to Seward, Sept. 23, 1864; Clay Papers: T. E. Lacy [Clay] to Holcombe, Sept. 14, 1864; Headley, pp. 215, 294.

extradition. When he gave Castleman and Hines money to finance a cooperative movement with a subversive Northern organization, the Sons of Liberty—which Thompson also joined at Vallandigham's behest—to work for a Democratic victory in the coming election, he worried that he was endangering his position. Thompson was careful to remain within the letter of the law, however, even when his activities finally succeeded in producing a second attempt on Johnson's Island. The far more provocative St. Albans raid in October, on the other hand, was the sole responsibility of Clay and Sanders, for Thompson had advised against it, and after the raid Clay mutilated his letters to prevent implicating Canadian correspondents in his violation of British neutrality.[36]

The most famous of Thompson's activities was the "peace offensive" that he launched in the summer. From this came the Niagara Peace Conference with Horace Greeley, the details of which need not be repeated here.[37] The so-called conference was of importance chiefly on the domestic scene, for through it Lincoln showed his willingness to talk with any *bona fide* peace negotiators from the South, but in British North America the affair tended to react against Lincoln. The Confederates spread the word that the President had acted in bad faith by promising William "Colorado" Jewett, their medium of communication, to talk with them and then refusing to do so when it was learned that they did not have what he deemed to be proper credentials. Seward failed to furnish any evidence that the Confederate charge of insincerity on Lincoln's part was incorrect, again failing when an obvious propaganda counter-gesture was needed, and many Canadians believed that Lincoln had changed his policy unfairly during the course of the "negotiations." The fiasco also was important in that it furnished the first nation-wide publicity for the Confederate commissioners, making many Northerners aware of their presence in the Canadas for the first time.[38]

The renewed Northern moves to tighten controls along the frontier in the face of growing Confederate activity in British North America were viewed in the provinces as an implication that the Northern administration feared that the British could not or would not preserve

---

[36] Toronto *Globe*, Sept. 8, 1864; Chicago *Tribune*, Aug. 27, 1864; Filson Club, Hines Papers: notebook 1, 7.

[37] See E. C. Kirkland, *The Peacemakers of 1864* (New York, 1927).

[38] J. G. Randall and R. N. Current, *Lincoln the President: The Last Full Measure* (New York, 1955), p. 163; J. P. Jones, "Abraham Lincoln and the Newspaper Press during the Civil War," *Americana*, xxxv (July, 1941), 465.

their own neutrality. Monck showed his good faith by running down every lead concerning the operations of the Confederates on the lakes, and in March he went so far as to ask Newcastle to put five gunboats on the Great Lakes to protect the commerce of the United States from raids that might be organized in British territory. The Governor General contended that anti-Canadian uneasiness in the United States over potential Confederate raids could be checked by the "moral effect" of even one small British vessel, intended to prevent illegal Confederate activity, on each lake. Monck's suggestion was a wise one, for five months later a raid across Lake Erie proved him right in his prediction that Britain could not prevent such expeditions without a naval force. Nevertheless, the suggestion did not meet with favorable response, and Colonial Secretary Cardwell, who replaced Newcastle in April, unimaginatively suggested that coasting steamers be hired to observe shore activity instead, for he feared that if Britain put ships on the lakes the United States might do so as well, thus nullifying the Rush-Bagot agreement.[39]

It appeared that the North already was preparing to nullify the convention. Stimulated by the Giddings incident and by the abortive Johnson's Island raid of the previous year, the House was discussing a resolution to abrogate the agreement, and Seward already had mentioned to Lyons that such a step might be necessary. Furthermore, rumor had it that an ironclad ram was being built at Black Rock Harbor near Buffalo, and certainly smaller vessels were in progress. When Lyons inquired about the newly laid keels at Black Rock, the Secretary of State answered that they were for revenue cutters of an experimental design and promised that they would form no part of the naval force on the lakes, since they were intended solely for prevention of smuggling by the Treasury Department. Lyons replied that it made little difference which department the vessels served if their presence violated the convention, and Seward gave his assurance that the revenue cutters never would be used for any other purpose, adding that smuggling was so frequent on the lakes that the United States might have to abrogate the convention if Lyons would not permit a

[39] G 20, 465: Monck to Newcastle, March 19, 1864, 45; G 9, 41: copy of same, 63–67, and Monck to Newcastle, March 31, 1864, 97–100; G 1, 159: Newcastle to Monck, Feb. 1, 1864, 77–79, and Cardwell to Monck, April 30, 1864, 311–314; Quebec *Gazette*, Aug. 29, 1864; Ottawa *Citizen*, May 16, Dec. 15, 1864; New York *World*, Nov. 26, 1864. On Cardwell's Canadian policy, see A. B. Erickson, *Edward T. Cardwell: Peelite* (Philadelphia, 1959), pp. 33–40.

modus vivendi. Seward then asked the Secretary of the Navy, Gideon Welles, whether another revenue cutter, the *Hector,* could be transferred to the lakes, and Welles, who unlike Secretary of War Stanton was aware of the Rush-Bagot agreement, correctly refused to permit the transfer, since the force on the lakes already was larger than the convention permitted. But whether the North was going to abrogate or disregard the agreement or not, the Canadians also were beginning to give more serious consideration to their defenses than they previously had done.[40]

Between March and June, 1864, the Liberal-Conservative party in the united Canadas was returned to power, with a coalition formed by John A. Macdonald and Etienne Taché replacing that of A. A. Dorion and Sandfield Macdonald. The new government represented a party that had learned how to use the charge of "looking to America" to political advantage and how to broadcast the fear of American expansionism to win continued imperial support. The new administration, as Seward knew, was not likely to be as cooperative as the group that it replaced. And during this period of political maneuvering the debate over how the provinces might best be defended was renewed. Since the defeat of the Militia Bill *The Times* had ridiculed the Canadas and had attacked "Canadian complacency." The British must never forget, *The Times* warned, that the Americans hated them. Fearful of seeming afraid, many Canadian pressmen echoed the bluster of the London newspaper, while others defended the Canadian position.[41]

Partially because of *The Times'* obvious suspicion of Canadian intentions with respect to their own defense, partially because of the changing nature of the war to the south—increasingly obvious since the Union victory at Gettysburg in July of the previous year—and

[40] G 20, 99: H. W. Price to Monck, April 4, 1864; G 1, 172: Lyons to Russell, May 13, enc. in Cardwell to Monck, June 4, 1864; BMW to GCC, 12: Donohoe to Lyons, April 9, 14, 15, enc. in Lyons to Monck, April 19, 1864; NFBL, 67: Lyons to Seward, Aug. 4, 1864; *ibid.,* 70: Burnley to Seward, Sept. 28, 1864; NBL, 11: Seward to Lyons, May 11, 1864, 222; *ibid.,* 13: Seward to Burnley, Nov. 4, 1864, 438–439; DL, 64: Seward to Chase, May 7, 1864; *Foreign Relations, 1864,* II, 668: Lyons to Seward, Aug. 4, 1864; *The Times,* Feb. 10, 1865; *Cong. Globe,* LVIII, 38th Cong., 1st Sess.: 9, 19, 1387, 2233–238, 2364–371, 2454–456, 2476–483, 2502–509, 2909, 3084; *House Reports,* 38th Cong., 1st Sess., I, no. 39.

[41] Seward Papers: McDougall to Seward, April 8, 1864; G 9, 41: A. C. Walshe to Monck, April 12, 1864, 153–165, and Monck to Newcastle, Jan. 27, 1864, 14–21; G 20, 172: Cardwell to Monck, Aug. 6, 1864, 210–212; *The Times,* Aug. 2, 13, Sept. 15, 17, 21, 1864; Quebec *Morning Chronicle,* July 16, 1864; Quebec *Daily News,* Aug. 5, 1864; Montreal *La Minerve,* Oct. 4, 1864.

partially because of the Liberal-Conservatives' renewed drive for confederation with defense as an aspect of that drive, the entire question of the colonies' relation with the Federal Union was in a state of almost constant reconsideration for the remainder of the war. And because of the new administration's alleged anti-Northern leanings, Seward felt that Macdonald's victory, coming as it did when the Confederate commissioners were just beginning their activities, would be followed by a renewed period of border tension. Seward was to prove correct, although Macdonald could not be blamed for this, for in the months following his re-election he was preoccupied with the confederation movement and quite naturally emphasized the "American menace" to dramatize the need for union.

The new coalition government that took office in June was unlike the immediately previous governments in several ways. It was not dedicated to the status quo, to "deadlock" and "double majority," to the ineffective system of administration that slowly had been binding the Canadas since 1858 at least. The coalition, which brought together such old opponents as Macdonald and Brown, took office dedicated to securing a union of the British North American provinces. This union obviously was needed, they felt, not only because of the crippled and insecure governments that the preceding months had produced, but because of the manifest danger from the United States. The months after Gettysburg and Vicksburg were months in which the Canadians came to regard the Northern army—an army that they once thought could so easily be defeated in an Anglo-American war—with awe. In size, in spirit, in armaments, in leadership the Northern army clearly was a new and destructive machine, a machine that well might be turned against the British provinces. Confederation seemed necessary to defense.

And defense seemed necessary to confederation. A union of the several provinces could not be achieved quickly, and in the interim, while local, provincial, and imperial approval was to be won, wooed, or bought, the Canadas must be capable of defense. Already the Little Englanders in the mother country were declaring with Goldwin Smith that the Canadas were indefensible. "It would be just as possible for the United States to sustain Yorkshire in a war with England, as for us to enable Canada to contend against the United States," wrote Richard Cobden, and the strong voice of John Bright seconded him throughout the isles. Many in Britain who opposed the high cost of maintaining a defensive posture in the Canadas had done so long before the Civil War, but the war and the North's now-evident superiority in that war had swelled the ranks of those who refused to fight to defend colonies that they considered to be of little or no benefit to Britain. The "withdrawal of the legions" had begun well before the war, and while a temporary reverse had occurred during the *Trent* affair, many voices in the imperial Parliament made it clear that as soon as the war was over the Canadas must expect to shoulder the major burden of their own defense.

Or even before the war was over if certain outspoken critics of the Canadas were to have their way. While the British force in North America had grown from some seven thousand in 1861 to nearly nineteen thousand in 1862, the force would be down to 8,200 by the spring of 1865. The imperial government clearly implied that the Canadas would have to make up the difference. Thus, the new coalition government turned not only to confederation but once again to a reconsideration of provincial defense in the summer of 1864. When first begun, the reconsideration was oblivious of the presence of the Confederate commissioners, but by November their presence would have been so felt as to become an additional major factor in the ultimate Canadian reevaluation.[42]

At the end of August, Lyons went to Quebec at Lord Russell's suggestion, partially to recover from the excessive heat of Washington but chiefly to confer with Monck on questions of defense. He remained in the Canadas until October. Considerable data was available to him for study, and little of it was encouraging. The North could pour half a million troops across the border almost at will, and clearly neither the imperial troops nor the growing but still weak Canadian militia could stop their progress. Certain Canadian proposals then under discussion—such as the construction of a ship canal between Georgian

---

[42] Montreal *Le Pays*, Oct. 11, 1864; Rochester *Evening Express*, Jan. 18, 1864; New York *World*, Feb. 2, 1864; Sumner Papers, CXL: Parkes to Sumner, Oct. 13, 1864; *ibid.*, LXXII: Moran to Sumner, March 6, 1865; Baring Papers, 44: Ward to Baring, Sept. 5, 1864; G. T. Borrett, *Letters from Canada and the United States* (London, 1865), p. 40; Richard Cartwright, *Remarks on the Militia of Canada* (Kingston, C. W., 1864), p. 6; Wolf, *Ripon* I, 200–201; John Morley, *The Life of Richard Cobden* (London, 1881), II, 470–471; G. B. Smith, *The Life and Speeches of The Right Honourable John Bright, M.P.* (New York, 1881), II, 93–94; G. F. G. Stanley, *Canada's Soldiers, 1604–1954* (Toronto, 1954), p. 221; Stacey, *Army*, pp. 153–164. Compare the attitude of 1864 with that of 1860 as expressed in G. B., *P.P.*, *1860*, XLI, "Report of the Committee on Expense of Military Defences in the Colonies," 2–18.

Bay and Lake Ontario to facilitate naval defense, or a theoretically sound but practically slow program for the training of militia officers and the raising of nearly a hundred thousand men—were too long range to be of benefit should the Civil War end within the next twelve months. Many officers attached to the British army in the Canadas had visited the battlefronts, and these observers were impressed with what they saw.[43] In the spring civilian investigators had quietly been sent from the Maritime Provinces to view the defenses of Maine, and an officer had prepared—at Lyons' personal request—a detailed report on the probable operations of American troops in case of war.[44]

A pessimistic report on Canadian defenses had been prepared in 1862 by five commissioners, and, as we have seen, a second report, equally unhappy from the Canadian point of view, had been drawn up in 1863 by Lieutenant Colonel W. F. D. Jervois, then Deputy Director of Fortifications and ultimately Governor of New Zealand. Jervois had visited Bermuda, British North America, and the United States, and he had concluded that Great Britain could fight a victorious war in North America only by attacking the American coastline with fleets based at Halifax and Bermuda. In the Canadas action would be purely defensive, and Canada West would have to be surrendered entirely. The imperial government had not hurried to transmit this report to the colonial administrations, but when the coalition government took office Cardwell apparently felt that the time had come for another attempt to discuss cooperative defense between colony and

[43] G 172: Cardwell to Monck, Aug. 6, 31, Sept. 2, 1864, 205, 259, 267; C 482: 185; FO 5, 954: Lieutenant Colonel T. L. Gallway to Lyons, May 27, 1864; *Report of the Commissioners Appointed to Consider the Defences of Canada* (London, 1862), with an appendix by Sir John Burgoyne, Inspector General of Fortifications; William Bross, *The Toronto and Georgian Bay Ship Canal* (Chicago, 1864); *Report of the Select Committee appointed to Consider the Practicability and Propriety of Constructing a Ship Canal between the Georgian Bay and Lake Ontario via Lake Simcoe* (Quebec, 1864); R. A. Preston, "A Letter from a British Military Observer of the American Civil War," *Military Affairs*, xvi (Summer, 1952), 49–60; Preston, "Military Lessons of the American Civil War: The Influence of Observers from the British Army in Canada on Training the British Army," *Army Quarterly*, lxv (Jan., 1953), 229–237; Jay Luvaas, *The Military Legacy of the Civil War: The European Inheritance* (Chicago, 1959), pp. 29–32.

[44] Newton, *Lord Lyons*, i, 132–134; NBL, 13: Seward to Burnley, Jan. 14, 1865, 13; *The Times*, June 28, 1864; *Hansard's, 1864*: clxxvi, cols. 373–382; Gzowski Papers: Memorial, July 23, 1864, to Monck. On Gzowski, see Wiktor Turek, *Sir Casimir S. Gzowski* (Toronto, 1957), in Polish with an introduction and resumé in English.

mother country. In August the Colonial Secretary sent Jervois' 1863 report to Monck, and the War Department dispatched its author to Quebec to advise the government there.[45]

The coalition government was not overwhelmingly eager to hear Jervois' advice, for he already had threatened to leave Canada West and even the portion of Canada East south of Montreal to the invader. But his 1863 report had not been acted upon, in part because of a well-directed memorial against such proposals to withdraw troops from the colonies, authored by some seventy Toronto dignitaries, and in part because the Commander-in-Chief, the Duke of Cambridge, recommended that Monck and Sir Fenwick Williams should distribute the troops in British North America as they saw fit; perhaps Jervois would change his mind, especially if he saw how actively the Canadian leaders were moving toward defense by another path, that of confederation. There was no time to take the defense issue up before his arrival, for the problems of confederation had precedence.[46]

By the fall several events, some directly attributable to the presence of the Confederate commissioners and others to more informal groups of Southerners, increased the urgency of the problem of defense but also changed its nature and gave colonial and imperial administrators in the provinces several opportunities to act in such a way as to win at least begrudging thanks and even praise from influential portions of the Northern administration. Strangely, while the Confederate commissioners' actions, combined with evident Canadian nervousness over defense, were to increase international tension at the popular level, the same actions of the Confederate commissioners were to create situations in which Monck and Macdonald, in particular, could respond in a way that would attract Seward's support. In July a small party of Confederates in New Brunswick launched a stupid and badly handled attack upon Maine, in September the long-planned second attempt against Johnson's Island was made, and in October a party of raiders from Montreal successfully attacked the village of St. Albans in Vermont while another group attempted to purchase a steamer to use for offensive action on the Great Lakes.

In Toronto a group of Confederates were planning another im-

---

[45] P.A.C., Jervois, "Report on the Defences of Canada and of the British Naval Stations in the Atlantic . . . Part 1"; *Memorandum of the Defence Committee on the Report of Lieutenant-Colonel Jervois on Defence of Canada* (Quebec, 1864); Richard Harrison, *Recollections of a Life in the British Army during the Latter Half of the Nineteenth Century* (London, 1908), p. 107. See above, p. 119.

[46] See Stacey, *Army*, pp. 158–160.

practical raid as a "major diversionary move." An army of five thousand men was to be brought to New Brunswick in eight blockade-
runners and was to move through Maine in five columns while subsisting off the land, burning the countryside as it went.[47] Needless to
say, this plan remained a schoolboy dream, although it indirectly produced a raid on Calais on July 16. One Captain William Collins, an
Irish-born, New Brunswick-bred, Southerner-by-adoption, arrived in
Toronto, possibly expecting to lead one of the five columns. Jacob
Thompson told Collins to go to St. Johns, Canada East, and to wait
there for further orders. Collins apparently was little interested in the
Southern cause, for he quickly attracted attention to himself and his
plans by killing two men at St. Johns. With the aid of three Confederates, one of whom—Francis Jones—was the son of the President
of St. Louis University, Collins decided on a "reconnaissance raid"
into Maine. He boasted of his intention, word reached consul Howard
in New Brunswick, and the townspeople of Calais were waiting for
Collins and his cohorts when they descended upon the bank there.
All four were captured after a short struggle.[48]

The men were taken to the county jail at Machias. There, over
chess with the sheriff, Jones unfolded the wild tale of the army that
was to capture Maine. The sheriff reported to Seward and Stanton, and
Assistant Secretary of War Dana sent the Assistant Judge Advocate
General to Maine to get a full confession from Jones and to inquire into
his story. During the investigation the Confederate ship *Tallahassee*
showed up off the Maine coast, leading him to conclude that Jones'
tale was correct. Howard, however, declared that no such plot existed.[49]

---

[47] Horan, p. 114. Horan tells how fifteen hundred seamen ᵕ fifty engineers and
topographers were sent from Richmond to cooperate with Thompson in an attack
on Maine. He writes (p. 115) that the topographers posed as artists in order to
sketch the Maine coastline and that by July finished charts hung on the walls of
a hideout in Halifax. The present writer has found little of reliability in support
of this. This report also appears in Philip van Doren Stern, *Secret Missions of the
Civil War* (Chicago, 1959), pp. 219–220. The very evidence contained in their
chief source would seem to disprove the story, however. See J. T. Wood, "The
'Tallahassee's' Dash into New York Waters," *The Century Illustrated Mo. Mag.*,
n.s., xxxiv (July, 1898), 408–417.

[48] CD, Saint John: Howard to Seward, July 14, 20, Aug. 25, 1864; NFBL, 66:
J. Cole to Lyons, July 19, enc. in Lyons to Seward, July 20, 1864; G 10, 1:
Deposition of M. Langhorne, Feb. 25, enc. in Burnley to Monck, March 13, 1865,
53, 56–59.

[49] CD, Saint John: Howard to Seward, July 27, 1864; CD, Halifax, x: Howard
to Seward, July 16, 1864; BMW to Lt. Gov. N.B., 23: Lyons to Cole, July 19,

The raid itself was so patently a private attempt at bank robbery by Southerners posing as commissioned Confederate raiders that it excited no particular interest in diplomatic circles. On the other hand, in Saint John the anti-Northern City Council showed its feelings by passing a resolution censoring Howard for warning Calais of Collins' activities, and the council demanded that Howard explain his statement that the raid had been planned in Saint John. The council especially was aroused by reports in the Maine press that a number of Northern gunboats had been sent to the St. Croix River area. The Mayor of Saint John, embarrassed by the council's ridiculous resolution, apologized to Howard, who acidly responded to the council, "It should be remembered that in the United States service the editors of the daily papers do not have charge or control of the gunboats . . . ." The Saint John *Evening Globe* confessed that New Brunswickers were humiliated to learn that Collins had believed they would give him sanctuary if he could escape to the province.[50]

Well into August the Maine press continued to give currency to the usual flurry of wild rumors. The three bank robbers were magnified into an invading army, and it was reported that President Lincoln would call out half a million men to protect the state. At Belfast and Rockland an invasion from New Brunswick was thought to be imminent, the battery at Castine was considered to be a prime target, and an attacking force that turned out to be fog was seen off the mouth of the Little River at Cutler. In Portland it was rumored that the *Chesapeake* again had been seized by Confederates.

In the meantime the *Tallahassee* had caused a brief sensation in Nova Scotia. After destroying a number of Northern fishing vessels near Cape Sable and burning three Northern schooners, Captain J. T. Wood put in at Halifax for coal. This he obtained through Wier and Company from a Prussian brig that was not under the Governor General's jurisdiction. Wood called on the local authorities and was given an additional twelve hours to remain in the harbor for repairs. Consul Jackson spent the time attempting to have Wood arrested, with no

---

Aug. 11, 1864; Adjutant General of Maine, *Report, 1864,* 5; Saint John *Daily Evening Globe,* July 26, 1864.

[50] CD, Saint John: Howard to Seward, July 27, 1864, July 7, 1865; NBL, 11: Seward to Lyons, Aug. 9, 1864, 579; *OR,* ser. ii, iv, 702-703: J. T. Sprague to E. G. Morgan, Aug. 15, enc. in Morgan to Stanton, Sept. 8, 1864; Bangor *Times* and Portland *Advertiser,* both July 17, 1864; Saint John *Evening Globe,* July 20, 1864; Calais *Weekly Times,* Dec. 10, 1902; Saint John *Globe,* Oct. 14, 1903.

success, and after obtaining a new spar, apparently from Dr. Almon, Wood made a dramatic escape to the open sea with the aid of a local pilot furnished by Wier.[51]

The Calais raid did legitimate Confederate raiders a disservice. It branded attacks aimed at banks as robbery rather than as acts of war, and it caused Lyons to depart from his usual position to suggest that Howard be permitted to communicate directly with the provincial authorities if he learned of any further plots. The raid also revived Maine's efforts to obtain Federal aid for building railroads to New Brunswick's border and for improving Portland's harbor defense. The House appointed a Committee on Defense of the North East Frontier, with John H. Rice of Maine as Chairman, and he and its members were invited to tour the Maine coastline with Seward and Blair. At the Governor's direction this group was enlarged to a party of nearly a hundred, which spent more time touring the St. Lawrence River and Gaspé peninsula, creating additional animosity wherever the group went, than viewing the defensive situation on the St. Croix.[52]

However, such minor sensations as those at Calais and Halifax soon were overshadowed by the second major Confederate plot along the Great Lakes. In September the famous "Lake Erie raid," the first of two important raids during the autumn of 1864, took place.[53] One John

[51] NFBL, 67: Lyons to Seward, Aug. 11, 1864; NBL, 12: Seward to Lyons, Aug. 17, 1864, 19; Halifax *Novascotian*, Aug. 22, 1864; Halifax *Acadian Recorder*, Aug. 27, 1864. The escape of *Tallahassee* is an important part of Nova Scotia's local folklore. A display concerning her voyage is in the Maritime Museum in Halifax, and Andrew Merkel has written a 103-page ballad (which was given a radio performance): *Tallahassee, A Ballad of Nova Scotia in the Sixties* (Halifax, 1945). On Almon and his son, see K. A. MacKenzie, "The Almons," *Nova Scotia Medical Bulletin*, xxx (Feb., 1951), 31–36.

[52] FO 5, 959: H. J. Murray, H.M. consul at Portland, to Lyons, Aug. 16, enc. in Lyons to Russell, Aug. 19, 1864; Boston *Journal*, Aug. 9, 1864.

[53] Unlike other incidents in Canadian-American relations during the war, the "Lake Erie raid" has received full attention from both scholarly and popular writers, and it seems unnecessary to recount the initial plotting of the episode in any detail here. For full, sometimes conflicting, accounts, see W. F. Zornow, "Confederate Raiders on Lake Erie: Their Propaganda Value in 1864," *Inland Seas*, v (Spring, Summer, 1949), 42–47, 101–105; F. J. Shepard, "The Johnson Island Plot," Buffalo Hist. Soc., *Publications*, ix (1906), 1–52; Shepard, *Burleigh—and Johnson's Island* (Buffalo, 1905); M. M. Bigelow, " 'Piracy on Lake Erie,' or The Confederate Attempt to Capture Johnson's Island in Sandusky Bay, Ohio, September 19, 1864," Detroit Hist. Soc., *Bulletin*, xiv (Oct., 1957), 6–17; F. B. Stevenson, "The Johnson Island Conspiracy—An Episode of the Civil War," *Frank Leslie's Popular Monthly*, xlvi (Sept., 1898), 257–266; L. J. Ryall, *Sketches*

Yates Beall, a Virginian with a degree in political economy from his state's university, had organized a group of Confederates at Windsor to try to liberate the Southern prisoners on Johnson's Island off Sandusky, Ohio. Beall's plan was daring, simple and desperate. Desperation clearly was necessary, for Gettysburg and Vicksburg were history, and on September 2 Sherman had marched into Atlanta. The Virginian planned that he, Bennett Burley—his second in command— and a group of Southerners would seize a coasting steamer on Lake Erie. In the meantime a third leader of the conspirators, Charles Cole, a Canadian who had been living in the South, was to have won the confidence of the captain and crew of the U.S.S. *Michigan*, then at Sandusky, so that he might drug them in order to make it possible for Beall and his men to board the ship from the captured lake steamer. With the *Michigan*'s guns trained on Johnson's Island the prisoners could be freed. Some of them would use the captured steamer to attack Detroit, while the *Michigan* would be used to bombard Sandusky, Erie, and Buffalo. Grandiose as the scheme was, it had a certain chance of limited success, and in July Thompson, who endorsed the plan, with the proviso that British neutrality was to be observed, sent Cole around the lake as a passenger on a coasting steamer to familiarize himself with the area.

On Sunday evening, September 18, Burley boarded the lake steamer *Philo Parsons* at Detroit and asked the ship's clerk and co-owner, Walter Ashley, to make an unscheduled stop at Sandwich to pick up three passengers. At Sandwich the following day Beall and two others jumped on board before the vessel touched the dock. They later contended that by boarding the *Philo Parsons* before it touched the Canadian shore they had avoided violating British neutrality. However, at Amherstburg sixteen Confederates, posing as draft-dodgers and carrying a battered trunk filled with guns, boarded the vessel, and it was fast to the dock at the time.[54]

---

and Stories of the Lake Erie Islands (Norwalk, O., 1913), pp. 344–356, which contains the reminiscences of the master of *Island Queen;* D. T. Bowen, *Memories of the Lakes* (Daytona Beach, 1946), pp. 38–43; D. B. Lucas, *Memoir of John Yates Beall* (Montreal, 1865); John Robertson, comp., *Michigan in the War* (Lansing, 1882), pp. 145–154; and W. H. Knauss, *The Story of Camp Chase* (Nashville, 1906), pp. 207–224. The most recent account is C. E. Frohman, "Piracy on Lake Erie," *Inland Seas*, xiv (Fall, 1958), 172–180.

[54] Buffalo *Express*, quoted in Toronto *Globe*, Aug. 11, 1864; Toronto *Leader*, Aug. 12, 1864; Buffalo *Courier* and Rochester *Daily Union and Advertiser*, both Sept. 21, 1864; Chicago *Tribune*, Oct. 25, 1864; Montreal *Gazette*, March 26, 1864; FO 115, 460: Lyons to Russell, Feb. 29, 1864; OR, ser. III, IV, 201: Morgan to Stan-

Shortly after the *Philo Parsons* left Kelley's Island, on the American side of Lake Erie, Beall took control of the vessel, stepping into the wheelhouse with a drawn Navy Colt to proclaim that the ship was a Confederate prize. At Middle Bass Island the women passengers were put ashore, accompanied by the clerk and mate who were pledged to silence for twenty-four hours, and the male passengers were locked in the hold of the ship. Learning that the fuel supply was very low, Beall turned toward Middle Bass Island to get wood. The coasting steamer *Island Queen,* her deck swarming with unarmed Union soldiers who were on an unauthorized holiday, also stopped at the island for wood. Beall's men seized and scuttled the *Island Queen,* wounding one crew member in the process, in order to prevent her crew from warning the mainland of the Confederate plot. Beall paroled the captured soldiers on their promise not to bear arms against the Confederacy and took the *Philo Parsons* to a position off Sandusky where he waited for a signal from the *Michigan* which would indicate that Cole had control of the ship and that the Confederates could board her.

However, Cole, who had posed as a Northern oil man who wished to give the gallant crew of the *Michigan* a champagne dinner, had been captured. Although he had won the confidence of the captain of the warship, and although the dinner had been scheduled for that evening, Cole indiscreetly had revealed his identity to a woman—variously described as a prostitute, a Federal spy, and an innocent maid of chaste and patriotic ways—while overindulging in his own champagne, and he was arrested in his hotel room while preparing for the dinner. Word of Cole's true nature was sent at once to the *Michigan*'s captain.[55]

---

ton, Sept. 8, 1864; Headley, p. 291, and p. 310: Mallory to Thompson, Dec. 19, 1864; Hines [and Castleman], "Northwestern Conspiracy," pp. 567–570.

[55] Western Reserve Hist. Soc., Misc. MS. no. 1481: Statement by D. K. Huntington, "The Capture of the Philo-Parsons and the Island Queen on Lake Erie 1864, and Events Leading up to the Capture." The Philadelphia *Press,* June 29, 1882, contains Cole's statement, which is reprinted in T. A. Burr, "A Romance of the Great Rebellion," *The Fire Lands Pioneer,* n.s., 1 (June, 1882), 78–91. Cole's account was a fantastic exercise in self-aggrandizement. He declared that Beall was his second in command, that Thompson had $86,000,000 available for his work, and that Thompson visited the *Michigan* disguised as a woman. Cole insisted that he was able to warn the men on the *Philo Parsons* of his capture. Most fantastic of all, Cole (or Carter, as he then was called) told of a British woman who romantically rescued him from Federal agents by posing as his wife and claimed that they plotted to take the *Michigan* in June of 1865, after the war was over. Actually Cole was in prison from 1864 until 1866.

The news of the seizure of the *Philo Parsons* and the *Island Queen* was made known while the former lay off Sandusky. Ashley, no better than he should have been, broke his pledge of silence and rowed to Kelley's Island, where he warned John Brown, Jr., a resident and son of the Harper's Ferry protagonist, and together they alerted the islands and then the mainland. Brown was placed in charge of an improvised militia, which he supplied with his private arsenal, part of which he had acquired from his father's militant forays, and an old cannon commemorative of Oliver H. Perry's naval victory over the British at Put-in-Bay in 1813 was hauled into position. Captain Jack Carter of the *Michigan* set out to find the raiders but was unsuccessful in doing so. He then returned to Sandusky to forestall any attack on Johnson's Island during the *Michigan*'s absence.[56]

By then the *Philo Parsons* was gone. Sensing that something was wrong when the *Michigan* had failed to display a light, the Confederates on the captured steamer had demanded that Beall and Burley return the vessel to Canada West. Beall had refused to do so until he had realized that his crew would mutiny. Extracting a written statement from them that he was giving up his plans at their request, Beall raced the *Philo Parsons* up the Detroit River, a Confederate flag flying from her masthead, set his men ashore at various points, and sank the steamer off Windsor by boring holes in her. Canadian authorities at Windsor neutrally and properly stood by and watched Beall carry out his act of destruction. Many of the men unthinkingly carried the baggage of some of the passengers ashore with them, as well as a cache of arms and the ship's piano, and Beall appropriated one hundred dollars belonging to the captain, thus throwing themselves open to the extraditable charge of robbery. Desperate from frustration, Beall later defiantly took fifteen Confederates out onto Lake Erie in small open boats to launch an attack upon Cleveland and was driven back by a storm.[57]

The Northern press was outraged, and the Toronto *Globe* called

[56] Horan, p. 164, incorrectly states that the engine room of the *Michigan* was wrecked by an engineer whom Cole bribed.

[57] MC: H. H. Emmons to Seward, Oct. 26, 1864, 248; G 13, 1: Burnley to Monck, in cipher, n.d., rec'd. Sept. 21, 1864; *OR*, ser. I, XLIII, 930–936: Thompson to Benjamin, Dec. 3, and Dix to Stanton, Sept. 30, 1864, 225–247; C. S. Van Tassel, *Story of the Maumee Valley, Toledo, and the Sandusky Region* (Chicago, 1929), I, 432–435. Horan, p. 162, imaginatively tells of how Beall watched the *Philo Parsons* sink, saw her boilers explode, and noted how the ship went through her "death agony." This is impossible since she was surfaced and was in service on the lakes within four days.

the raid "naked piracy." Even the Toronto *Leader* felt that the Southerners had abused Canadian hospitality, especially when at first it was reported that Beall had stolen eighty thousand dollars. From Canada West Beall publicly wrote to defend his actions, falsely denied that he had stolen any money, and declared that since the *Michigan* carried thirteen more guns than the Rush-Bagot agreement permitted, he had sufficient reason for attacking her. After thus defending himself on the peculiar grounds that he was protecting British rights in North America, he fled into the northern forests. Beall was arrested on the New York side of the Suspension Bridge in December after having failed to carry out an amateurish scheme of Thompson's to derail an express train near Buffalo in order to free several Confederate officers. After being tried before a military commission for sabotage and treason, he was executed, defiant to the end.[58]

More fortunate, Burley lived to continue an exciting career. Like John C. Braine, he was a professional adventurer. Born in Glasgow, he had served under Garibaldi, had switched his allegiance to the Papal Guards, and had cast his lot with the South during the Civil War. He had been arrested while running the blockade and had been imprisoned in Castle Thunder. As he had with him a drawing of a submarine battery that his father had invented, he had been taken before Captain John Brooke, inventor of the Brooke cannon, and had been set free for reasons which are not clear. He then had gone to the Canadas to join Thompson, who by then was hiring incendiaries to burn ships on the Mississippi River and hotels in New York. After the St. Albans raid later in 1864 Burley was arrested, and while cleared of any part in that raid, he was charged with robbery during the *Philo Parsons* affair. He managed to escape, returned to Canada West, and was arrested at Guelph.[59]

[58] *Globe*, Sept. 22, 1864; *Leader*, Sept. 23, 1864; New York *Times*, Feb. 25, 1865; Quebec *Gazette*, March 3, 1865; FO 115, 432: Russell to Burnley, March 18, 1865; John B. Jones, *Diary*, II, 436: March 1, 1865. A rumor that John Wilkes Booth assassinated Lincoln to avenge the death of Beall, who was Booth's friend, was given some currency after the war. According to this story Booth went to Lincoln and on bended knee and in tears begged for his friend's life. The President agreed, the tale goes, only to change his mind the next day when Seward convinced him that Northern sentiment demanded blood. See Isaac Markens, *President Lincoln and the Case of John Y. Beall* (New York, 1911), which refutes the story. For a brief account of Beall's career, see J. T. Dorris, *Pardon and Amnesty Under Lincoln and Johnson* (Chapel Hill, 1953), pp. 76–79.

[59] New York *Tribune*, Jan. 24, 1865; Headley, p. 253; W. D. Foulke, *Life of Oliver P. Morton* (Indianapolis, 1899), I, 412–414.

Burley was tried before Chief Justice William Draper of the united province of Canada in January, 1865. Draper asked justices from the Courts of Queen's Bench and Common Pleas to sit with him as advisers. By unanimous decision Burley was found extraditable for theft, and in February, to foil an expected Confederate attempt to free him, Burley was delivered to American officials at the Suspension Bridge in a closed train guarded by twenty British regulars and a police force of ten. Taken to Port Clinton, Ohio, on the *Philo Parsons*, he was tried for robbery. He gave the court a duplicate of his Confederate commission and a letter from President Davis that maintained that the Lake Erie raid was a legitimate belligerent action. The prosecution declared that Burley had disobeyed his instructions by violating British neutrality and that this deviation from duty had deprived him of belligerent rights. The jury disagreed and Burley was recommitted. While his lawyer was working to obtain his release on a technicality, Burley escaped to Detroit and then to Canada West with the aid of friends who bribed a jailer. He then wrote to the sheriff at Port Clinton asking that the books that he had left in his cell be sent to him. After the war Burley joined the Houston *Telegram* as a reporter and later returned to England to become a war correspondent in the Sudan for the London *Daily Telegram*. He lived to become one of Britain's most respected newspaper men, having covered the Moroccan, Greco-Turkish, Somali, Tripolitan, and Russo-Japanese wars.[60]

In the meantime the Northern port cities had responded to the Lake Erie raid with demands that Canada West be chastised for permitting the plot to originate on her soil. The Solicitor General of Canada felt it necessary to ask that two companies of soldiers be placed at Windsor to forestall retaliation from Detroit. Monck wrote to the Colonial Secretary that peaceable Anglo-American relations would be jeopardized if Southern refugees continued to use the provinces as a rendezvous as they had in the *Philo Parsons* affair. He repeated his desire for a strong British force on the Great Lakes to prevent such raids and indirectly agreed for the first time with Seward's contention that Canada's neutrality law was not strong or explicit enough. With a touch of sarcasm Monck sharply told his superior that he had not

[60] CD, Toronto, 1: Thurston to Seward, Feb. 4, 1865; MC: A. Russell to Seward, Jan. 27, 28, Feb. 2, 11, 1865; Montreal *Herald*, Feb. 11, 1865; Toronto *Leader*, Sept. 30, 1864; Toronto *Globe*, Jan. 28, 1865; NFBL, 77: Burnley to Seward, March 15, 1865; C. S. Blue, "The Case of Bennett Burley, The Lake Erie Pirate," *Canadian Mag.*, XLV (June, 1915), 190–196. Burley also spelled his name "Burleigh."

wanted the force for carrying on war against the United States, as the Secretary apparently thought, but to maintain Canada's own municipal laws. Monck concluded that the season was too far advanced to take any measures before the closing of navigation, but he earnestly pressed upon Cardwell the necessity for vesting the Governor General with additional powers before the opening of navigation in the spring. Monck was urging a lethargic and economy-minded Colonial Office, in the grip of anti-imperialism, to take some steps before Great Britain, through the colonies, drifted into war with a nation that the Governor General had grown to respect militarily.[61]

On the same day that Monck wrote to the Colonial Secretary, Seward informed *chargé* Burnley that in view of the situation on the Great Lakes the United States probably would have to discontinue temporarily the armaments limitation, but that any American warships placed on the lakes would be instructed to respect British rights in every case. Seward advised Charles Francis Adams that the Canadian authorities had acted in a friendly and honorable manner in dealing with the Lake Erie episode. General Dix thereupon investigated the lake defenses and recommended that five tug boats be armed and placed at harbor entrances. Construction of one of the revenue cutters being built at Black Rock was hurried, for it could carry six guns. At General Hooker's recommendation an additional regiment was sent to Detroit and Buffalo, where troops already were patrolling the Canadian border. By early autumn the Canadian-American border was an armed frontier in nearly every sense of the word, and to all intents and purposes the Rush-Bagot agreement had been suspended, as Canadians had feared.[62]

The Lake Erie raid was important in Anglo-American relations because it stirred Monck to make his most vigorous statements yet to the Colonial Office and because it brought on an unofficial suspension of the arms agreement. The imperial authorities redoubled their watchfulness, and the Canadian administration gave additional attention to the defense situation. While border tension increased as a result of the

[61] Macdonald Papers, 56: James Cockburn to Macdonald, Sept. 23, 1864, 1–4; G 10, 12: Monck to Cardwell, Sept. 26, 1864, 136–138; Toronto *Globe*, Sept. 22, 1864; Detroit *Free Press*, Jan. 29, 1865.

[62] NBL, 12: Seward to Burnley, Sept. 26, 1864, 185; GBI, 19: Seward to Adams, Oct. 4, 1864, 470–471; BMW to GCC, 12: Donohoe to Burnley, Sept. 26, enc. in Burnley to Monck, Sept. 30, 1864; OR, ser. III, IV, 918: Hooker to Stanton, Nov. 3, and Stanton to Hooker, Nov. 4, 1864, Hooker to Blair, Nov. 4, 1864, 919, and J. B. Fry to A. S. Diven, Nov. 6, Fry, Circular no. 41, Dec. 8, 1864, 920, 988–989.

affair, thus heightening the danger from the inflammatory effects of future border raids, the imperial and local authorities in British North America were aroused sufficiently by the violation of British neutrality involved in the *Philo Parsons* incident to be prepared to take vigorous action should another such raid occur. And while Seward continued to complain that the Canadian neutrality act was too weak, machinery was put into operation to give it strength to assure British neutrality in the event of further raids.

Nonetheless, the early activities of the Confederate commissioners had not tested British North American neutrality to the utmost, for in both the Calais and the Lake Erie raids the men involved easily could be extradited on a simple charge of robbery. It was not necessary, therefore, for the British courts to take up the delicate question of extradition where the raiders had been more successful in branding their activities as an act of war. But such a raid soon was to come. On October 19, while the action on Lake Erie still was being discussed, one month to the day after the capture of the *Philo Parsons* and *Island Queen*, a group of Confederates sponsored by commissioner Clay launched the most famous raid of the war.

fourteen ๑๑ TESTING CANADIAN NEUTRALITY: THE ST. ALBANS RAID AND ITS AFTERMATH

> "The Country has passed through so many of these critical periods in the present struggle without missing its foothold, that there is reason to hope it will now be able to march with a firm step to the end of it."
>
> CHARLES FRANCIS ADAMS, *1864*

THE AUTUMN OF 1864 BROUGHT A SERIES OF EVENTS COLLECTIVELY KNOWN to history as the St. Albans raid, events in which there was all the pretext for an Anglo-American war that either nation could want. As their fear for the Southern cause grew, Confederate leaders in British North America began to show less regard for British neutrality. By 1864 the Confederate commissioners were allowing British North Americans to enter the ranks of the conspirators not only in planning the raids, as in the *Chesapeake* affair, but in executing the plans as well.[1] The *Philo Parsons* incident, in particular, had created a populace that would magnify every report of Confederate movements. Rumors had been so numerous during the preceding summer that the saturation point had been reached by autumn, and summer's vigilance had turned to autumn's carelessness. But Seward's actions indicated that he expected rumor to be made reality shortly.

[1] This shift in practice coincides with the period in which some scholars have professed to find a distinct disintegration in Southern morale. See Charles H. Wesley, *The Collapse of the Confederacy* (Washington, 1937), and Bell I. Wiley, *The Road to Appomattox* (Memphis, 1956).

There had been a particularly heavy spate of rumors concerning the forthcoming presidential election. After Lincoln's renomination in May, Jacob Thompson had financed various anti-Republican schemes, and as the election neared he increased his payments. The Republican party leadership charged that the Democratic party was pro-Southern, since the latter's platform did not condemn "the rebellion," and a few Republicans maintained that the platform was the work of Confederates residing in the Canadas, an interpretation that won Seward's spoken approval. The Peace Democrats' nominee for Lieutenant Governor of Ohio declared that if Vallandigham were elected fifty thousand armed Ohioans would march to the Canadian border and escort him to the state house. In August a rumor that anti-Lincolnians intended to raid Vermont or eastern New York from Montreal led the Canadian authorities to place the area south of the city under military patrol. A series of messages, photographed on paper that was pasted to the insides of metal buttons, had passed successfully between Richmond and Toronto, and questionable boxes labeled "mineral specimens" had been arriving in Canada West from time to time. One Confederate agent promised that as Lincoln's election approached Southerners in Canada would "do such deeds . . . as shall make European civilization shudder." [2]

Seward's men found it increasingly difficult to keep up with the various Confederate movements, and they had to neglect many rumors for known activities of higher priority.[3] Thompson was busy helping

[2] *OR*, ser. I, XLIII, 929–931: A. M. Harper to T. A. Rowley, Aug. 26, 1864; CD, Montreal, v: Potter to Seward, Aug. 19, 1864; *The Times*, Aug. 30, 1864; CD, Toronto, I: R. J. Kimball to Seward, Jan. 3, 1865; New York *Tribune*, Sept. 22, 1864; New York *Times*, Sept. 7, 1864; Cordner, *American Conflict*, p. 44 n.; W. F. Zornow, "Treason as a Campaign Issue in the Re-election of Lincoln," *Abraham Lincoln Quarterly*, v (June, 1949), 348–363; E. H. Roseboom, *The History of the State of Ohio* (Columbus, 1944), IV, 419–420.

[3] The writer has made no effort to deal with the many rumors concerning the provinces that arose during the Civil War, but he has attempted to mention several that occurred frequently enough to be more than the fancy of a single mind. "Rumor" influences "public opinion" and "public opinion" influences "local attitudes," as seen in Chapter Eleven. These words have certain precise meanings to social psychologists, and while the present writer has not attempted to maintain scientific controls over the misinformation that he reports as "rumored," it would be interesting to apply to any of the more prominent rumors some of the criteria (rumor as "a specific proposition" passed "by word of mouth, without secure standards of evidence," reflecting "hate and hostility" in wartime) used by G. W. Allport and Leo Postman in their excellent primer, *The Psychology of Rumor* (New York, 1947).

Beverley Tucker negotiate a contract for the Confederacy to exchange Southern cotton for Union bacon through the Canadas on a pound for pound basis. Tucker, a Virginian and former consul to Liverpool under Buchanan, had gone to British North America at the request of Jefferson Davis to arrange for the bacon exchange, and although he tried to disengage himself from Thompson's other activities by refusing to take part in Confederate plotting in the provinces, Seward's agents had no way of knowing this. In Nova Scotia it was stated that the Confederacy had secured thirty thousand soldiers from Poland and that fifty swift steamers were to be built in England to bring these troops through the blockade. The embellishments that this footless report soon acquired were typical of such rumors. And when Judah Benjamin sent a special agent, Canadian-born George Dewson, to the provinces to test sentiment, Dewson overenthusiastically reported that nearly all British North Americans privately wished "God Speed" to the Southern cause. Even George Brown, personally pro-Lincoln, was beginning to believe that the United States might attack the Canadas if Lincoln were re-elected, while others feared that a victory for General George B. McClellan, the Democratic candidate, would place the provinces in even greater danger.[4]

Even in the British provinces it was apparent that the Confederacy was being worn down by the North's "anaconda policy." In September John A. Macdonald for the first time referred to the "gallant defence" made by the South in the past tense. The Confederate Commissioners in British North America would have to authorize some new and desperate measure if they were to further the goal of "embroilment," a goal that was obvious by this time. To prevent such a step Seward dispatched yet another group of agents to the Canadian border to check on the many rumors and on October 16 a man was

[4] CD, Halifax, x: Jackson to Seward, Oct. 7, 1864; Clay Papers: check stub no. 35, Oct. 10, 1864, to Tucker; CSA, 73: Dewson to Benjamin, Aug. 26, 1864; CD, Saint John: Howard to Seward, July 6, 1864; CD, Montreal, v: Thurston to Seward, June 22, 1864, and Potter to Seward, July 25, Sept. 6, 1864; CD, St. John's, iv: Leach to Seward, June 4, July 26, 1864; G 9, 41: Monck to Cardwell, June 21, 1864, 232; ITC, 36: Seward to Thurston, June 13, 1864; Halifax *Acadian Recorder*, Oct. 7, 1864; Toronto *Globe*, June 2, 1864; Toronto *Leader*, Aug. 18, 1864; John B. Jones, *Diary*, ii, 280, 319–320; Haultain, ed., *Goldwin Smith's Correspondence*, pp. 281, 284: Sept. 28, 1864; Jane E. Tucker, *Beverley Tucker: A Memoir by His Wife* (Richmond, 1893), p. 23; Beverley R. Tucker, *Tales of the Tuckers: Descendants of the Male Line of St. George Tucker of Bermuda and Virginia* (Richmond, 1942), pp. 37–42.

sent to Swanton, Vermont, hard upon the railroad town of St. Albans. He arrived one day too late to learn of a strange young American with a Southern accent, apparently a student of theology from the University of Toronto, who had just completed his third round trip on the new railroad between Montreal and St. Albans.[5]

Three weeks before election day the rumor-fed tension was broken and a situation of considerable gravity was created by a group of some twenty young Kentuckians. Early in the morning of October 20 Lord Monck rose from a hurried breakfast to deal with a disturbing telegram that had arrived during the night from the Governor of Vermont. The Governor reported that a large body of Confederates had used Canada East as a base for a raid upon St. Albans, where they had robbed the banks, killed a number of civilians, and put the town to the torch.[6]

Over the space of several days a group of men posing as Canadians had arrived in St. Albans. They had stayed at separate hotels and, when queried, had explained that they belonged to a Montreal hunting and fishing club that had selected Lake Champlain as the site for its annual outing. Their fishing was of a different kind, however. They spent their time talking to the stable masters and shopkeepers, learning of the relative merits of the various horses at the stables, and of the number of arms available in the town, and one of the young men, later identified as Lieutenant Bennett H. Young, reportedly called upon the Governor's wife to inspect his stable as well.

[5] Toronto *Globe*, Sept. 21, 1864; CSA, 73: Dewson to Benjamin, Sept. 24, Oct. 27, 1864; MC: T. H. Canfield to Seward, Oct. 16, 1864; Creighton, *Macdonald*, pp. 368–369.

[6] G 13, 1: Smith to Monck, Oct. 19, and Monck to Smith, Oct. 20, 1864; Headley, *Confederate Operations*, pp. 257–260; Monck, *Leaves*, pp. 183–185. The writer has been unable to determine whether there were twenty, twenty-one, or twenty-two raiders. Young's commission called for twenty, but he apparently exceeded that number, for Clay wrote checks to provide transportation for Young and twenty-two men. Many of the details of the raid remain unclear. Some writers state that it took place on a cold and rainy day (see J. L. Heaton, *The Story of Vermont* [Boston, 1889], p. 264, and Maria J. B. Tuttle, ed., *Three Centuries in Champlain Valley* [Plattsburg, 1909], pp. 343–344), while others report that the Indian summer sun made the day warm and clear (Horan, *Confederate Agent*, p. 169). Some report that the raiders wore their uniforms or parts of them, while others testify that they were dressed in civilian attire. However, the details of the raid itself are not important to the present study. For an extensive bibliography of St. Albans raid material, see Robin W. Winks, "The St. Albans Raid—A Bibliography," *Vermont History*, xxvi (Jan., 1958), 44–51, and xxvii (April, 1959), 168–169.

On the stroke of three on the afternoon of October 19, at the same hour that General Philip Sheridan was ordering his Vermont troops to make a general advance in the Battle of Cedar Creek, in Virginia, Bennett Young, a twenty-one-year-old Kentuckian, stepped onto the porch of his hotel, brandished a Navy Colt revolver, and declared loudly, "In the name of the Confederate States, I take possession of St. Albans!" As a group of his men herded a small band of surprised townspeople, caught in the midst of their weekly shopping, onto the town green, teams of raiders went to St. Albans' three banks, which were closing, while a fourth team obtained choice horses from a nearby livery stable and from farmers' wagons. All three banks were robbed successfully, although one team overlooked a chest of money in its hurry to escape. In the Franklin County Bank the raiders whimsically presented themselves as purchasers and sellers of gold and a local financier bought some of the gold from them which, unknown to him, they had just stolen.

Young had instructed his men clearly to stamp the raid as an act of war, but despite his own announcement from the hotel porch, his followers left themselves open to serious charges by the way in which they identified themselves. In the months to come the exact nature and timing of their declarations was to assume considerable importance for the raiders. At the Franklin County Bank the Confederates foolishly robbed a private citizen of nearly $400, and only while in the midst of the robbery did one think to state: "We are Confederate soldiers. There are one hundred of us in town. We have come to rob the banks and burn the town, and we are going to do it." At the First National Bank the leader of the looting team gave a greater appearance of legality to his act by declaring, "We represent the Confederate States of America, and we come here to retaliate for acts committed against our people by General Sherman." This was said only after the cashier was held up, however.[7]

The Confederates assembled on the town green with over two hundred thousand dollars as their "prize of war."[8] By then a young captain who was on leave from the Northern army, George Conger, had

---

[7] Testimony is conflicting as to the exact wording of these statements.

[8] Sources disagree as to the total amount taken from the banks. The commonly accepted figure is Bennett Young's own estimate of $208,000. In a short manuscript on the raid, which the present writer has read, E. B. Wilcox of Denver has recomputed the various amounts and submits the figure of $186,133. Both figures involve a certain degree of guess work.

escaped from a raider and was organizing a posse of some forty men in another section of town. On a hill above the village the Governor's wife, Mrs. J. Gregory Smith, having observed the events below, had barricaded her house to await an expected attack, rifle in hand, apparently unfrightened by the knowledge that she had no ammunition.

But Young and his men had no time for secondary attacks. The raiders formed a line on the green and dashed from the town, throwing bottles of Greek fire—a mixture of sulphur, naphtha, quick lime, and water—against the frame buildings as they fled in an unsuccessful effort to put St. Albans to the torch. Townspeople fired upon the Southerners from nearby buildings, and the Confederates returned the fire at random, wounding two men, killing one—ironically, the only copperhead in town—and causing slight injuries to others, including a young girl, from flying splinters. Conger's men, mounted on horses that they had unhitched from farmers' wagons, and spurred on by Mrs. Smith, who is said to have cried, "Kill them! Kill them!," set out in close pursuit, following a trail of bills dropped from a raider's pocket. At Swanton the Confederates had planned to rob the bank but Conger's posse had drawn into view, so Young paused only long enough to fire a barn in an unsuccessful attempt to distract the pursuers. On a covered bridge near the border a wagon loaded with hay also was fired, temporarily blocking the bridge and delaying pursuit until the frontier was reached.

While the raiders were on the town green, word of the attack was wired to Governor Smith in Montpelier, and he in turn sent news of the event to Seward, Dix, and Monck. The first messages had it that the city was in flames and that five unarmed civilians, including the child, had been killed by a band of nearly a hundred Confederates, and the raiders' final volleys had put an end to telegraph service before these reports could be corrected. Smith, who was also President of the Central Vermont Railroad, recalled a St. Albans-bound train to Montpelier and sent it on its way again with seventy-five invalid veterans aboard, while a number of armed civilians hurried north from Burlington. The Governor assumed that the raiders at St. Albans were precursors of a host of Confederate forays into Vermont, and the frontier was placed under military guard. Cadets from Norwich University in Northfield were sent to border points, and by morning thirteen hundred men were in arms. Realizing the seriousness of the situation, Monck set out to confer with the provincial administration, and he ordered Judge Charles J. Coursol, Police Magistrate at Montreal, to arrest any raider found on Canadian soil.

Thinking themselves safe in Canada East, the raiders made no particular effort to hide. However, after a slight delay the American posse chose to ignore the boundary line and continued in close pursuit to Frelighsburg and Phillipsburg, both of which were well over the border. During the night the Americans succeeded in capturing a few of the Southerners, including Bennett Young, whose presence had been reported by a Canadian farmer with whom Young had sought shelter. As Young made an attempt to escape from his captors, a British major providentially appeared, saving the Kentuckian from being beaten to death by the enraged posse. The Britisher warned the Americans to turn their prisoner over to the Canadian militia or to be guilty of further violations of British neutrality. At this point one Vermonter stepped forward to face the officer, drew a gun, and shouted, "We don't give a damn for your neutrality." Fortunately calmer heads prevailed and the badly beaten Young was delivered to the Canadian authorities. Monck also had ordered the local militia commander and magistrate, Colonel Edward Ermatinger, to apprehend the raiders. Ermatinger acted quickly, and by October 23 fourteen of the Confederates were in custody. Nineteen thousand dollars was surrendered to the sheriff at St. Johns, Canada East, and some of the money dropped on the road by the raiders was brought in later by Canadian farmers.

The border towns were thrown into a state of turmoil that lasted until the following spring. That blank commissions for almost any desperate act were being issued to Confederates in Canada, and that two thousand raiders were to descend upon Plattsburg, Malone, and Ogdensburg in New York, were among the commonly accepted rumors. In St. Albans a curfew was established and the streets were patrolled at night. A group of industrialists from the Great Lakes petitioned the Governor of Michigan to give added protection to the canals and locks at such far away places as Sault Ste. Marie. Another raid on election day was expected, and when an order was issued to place troops at the polling stations, the prevention of Confederate interference was one of the reasons given.[9]

[9] Good general accounts of the raid include: R. C. Muir, "A Cause Célèbre," Brant Hist. Soc., *Papers and Records* (1930), 9–19; E. A. Sowles, "The St. Albans Raid," Vermont Hist. Soc., *Proceedings,* LIV (Oct., 1876), 7–48, which is a detailed account by an eye-witness; R. F. Andrews, "How 'Unpreparedness' Undid St. Albans: A Forgotten Chapter of Civil War History that has Its Timely Lesson for the Nation To-Day," *Outlook,* CXIV (Nov., 1916), 673–684; and H. W. Crocker, "The St. Alban's Raid," unpubl. M.A. thesis (Queen's Univ., 1938). The raid has became a part of American folklore, as is seen in a book for children, Robert

Violation of British neutrality again was threatened through an order issued by General John A. Dix, Commander of the Military District of the East. News of the raid reached Dix at a dinner party where
the British Minister, recently returned from Quebec, was among the
guests. The General ordered the commanding officer at Burlington,
Vermont, to send troops to St. Albans, to find the raiders, and to "pursue them into Canada if necessary and destroy them." Dix informed
his fellow diners that such a course was justified by international law,
presumably referring to the ambiguous concept of "hot pursuit." Seriously worried, Lyons pointedly asked whether Washington had authorized the order, and Dix admitted that he was issuing it on his own
responsibility. The directive was received in St. Albans during the
night while Captain Conger was searching the Canadian countryside
for Young and his men. It was sent on to him by special messenger,
only to be received a few minutes after he had surrendered the last
of his prisoners to the Canadian authorities.[10]

Through an order such as Dix's the Confederate policy might have

---

Ashley, *Rebel Raiders* (Philadelphia, 1956). Oscar A. Kinchen, *Daredevils of the
Confederate Army: The Story of the St. Albans Raiders* (Boston, 1959), is the
fullest account yet of the raid and its aftermath. The present writer had completed his chapter on the raid before the book was published. Kinchen has been
too ready to accept the word of Sowles and of the highly biased *abbé* H.-R. Casgrain, in "David Têtu et les Raiders de Saint-Alban: Épisode de la Guerre Américaine, 1864-65," *L'Opinion publique*, XIII (Oct. 5-Dec. 21, 1882), variously between
pp. 472 and 604. Many aspects of the latter are contradicted by Guillaume Lamothe's unpublished MS. "Autobiographical Sketch" in the P.A.C. The author also
appears to take Bennett Young's word at face value. Throughout Kinchen has
tended to combine evidence from conflicting sources rather than to resolve the
conflicts, and he has allowed a number of errors to creep into his account. However, he has written a useful work on the raid, and his treatment of the various
legal proceedings that followed, while very literal, is exhaustive. The best contemporary accounts of the attack are: CD, Montreal, v: Thurston to Seward,
Oct. 20, 1864, and Cartier to Coursol, Oct. 20, enc. in Potter to Seward, Oct. 24,
1864; Toronto *Globe*, Oct. 21, 22, 1864; Montreal *Gazette*, Oct. 20, 1864; Toronto
Leader, Oct. 27, 1864; Montreal *Herald*, Dec. 24, 1864; Montreal *Witness*, Nov. 9-
11, 1864; St. Albans *Messenger*, Oct. 19-21, 1864; Burlington (Vt.) *Free Press*,
Oct. 26, 1864; Chicago *Tribune*, Dec. 12, 1864; *The American* [Appleton's] *Annual Cyclopaedia and Register of Important Events* (New York, 1865-66), IV,
178, 796, 807, and v, 797; and E. L. de Bellefeuille, "L'Incursion de St. Albans,"
Revue Canadienne, II (June, 1865), 361-375.

[10] G 11, 233: Monck to Burnley, Oct. 26, 1864, 335-337; G 17, 6: 87-90; Newton,
Lord Lyons, I, 135; Vermont, Adjutant and Inspector General, *Report from Oct. 1,
1864, to Oct. 1, 1865* (Montpelier, 1865), p. 99.

been successful, for a group of vengeance-bound Northern troops roaming Canada East might well have ignited an Anglo-American war. In Richmond, news of Dix's move brought satisfaction. "A war with England would be our peace," wrote a clerk in the Confederate War Department, and he looked to the Canadas for "light." In the North, George Templeton Strong astutely noted that the order would be an inducement for Confederates to repeat the raid, for another foray might attract pursuit across the border by a military rather than an irregular force. Samuel G. Ward wrote to the Barings that the Confederacy finally had discovered "a very weak place" in the North's foreign relations, and he suggested that if the South had exploited this weakness systematically the war that the Confederacy now openly hoped to generate might well have been created earlier.[11]

Seward was aware of the danger from Dix's order, but he also wanted to press home the diplomatic advantage that the raid had given him. A greatly changed man from his "foreign war panacea" days of 1861, the Secretary told *chargé* Burnley that the raid was a deliberate effort to create a border war, and he asked for extradition of the captured men. But for Adams he blamed the raid primarily on the weakness of the British neutrality act rather than on Confederate policy. Revising a message that he originally had based on the Lake Erie raid and had not yet dispatched, Seward offered the two attacks as sufficient reason for arming the lake frontier and on October 24 instructed Adams to tell Lord Russell that the United States would feel at liberty at the end of six months, the required time limit under treaty provisions for such a warning, to increase naval arms on the lakes if affairs at that time required such a step. The people of the Canadas, Seward felt, were not displaying "good neighborhood" in permitting such raids to be planned in their midst. Adams thereupon submitted a long notice to Russell informing him of the United States' desire to terminate the Rush-Bagot agreement in six months' time.[12]

Seward wished to preserve the agreement, and apparently he hoped that Britain would accept its "temporary suspension." To have terminated the arms limitation altogether would have been to play directly into the Confederacy's hands, and Seward was well aware of the desired end for "the fire in the rear." However, he had reason

---

[11] John B. Jones, *Diary*, II, 359: Dec. 19, 1864; Nevins and Thomas, eds., *Strong*, III, 528: Dec. 14, 1865; Baring Papers: Ward to Baring, Jan. 16, 1865.

[12] NBL, 12: Seward to Burnley, Oct. 21, 25, 1864, 295–296, 307–308, and Seward to Lyons, Oct. 29, 1864, 328–329; GBI, 19: Seward to Adams, Oct. 24, 1864, 491–503.

to know that Congress would clamor for abrogation of the convention, and the St. Albans raiders had provided him with a far more persuasive argument to use in urging a stricter Canadian neutrality law than Seward possibly could have devised. Thus he went through the motions of setting termination on foot, conscious of the large reservation he had entered in his instructions to Adams, which permitted him to review the border situation at the time abrogation was to take effect.

The House of Representatives had been considering terminating the Rush-Bagot agreement since the previous June. That body had passed a resolution condemning the convention, because, it said, the agreement had been designed as a temporary arrangement at a time when both nations concerned had equality on the Great Lakes, but by the construction of a number of ship canals Britain had placed the United States at a disadvantage. The Senate had failed to act on the resolution, however. The St. Albans raid now provided the impetus needed to push abrogation through the upper house, and in December John Sherman of Ohio introduced a new bill to the Senate to augment the revenue cutters already on the lakes. The bill was passed on the day following the unexpected discharge of the raiders, with a provision for the construction of six new cutters, each to be armed with a light pivot gun. The following month Senator Sumner reported an amendment to a House resolution that, in effect, gave Congressional approval to Seward's actions, and this was accepted on January 18. What Seward undoubtedly had hoped would be a temporary hiatus in the operation of the convention now was given a more rigid interpretation by Congress, for it is clear that while most members hoped that the "unarmed border" could be restored, they felt that new negotiations would be necessary. They considered that their action had killed the Rush-Bagot agreement by giving formal Congressional assent to Seward's temporary arrangement. The convention apparently had but six months to live.[13]

To control the situation, Seward took Dix's inflammatory order to Lincoln. The order had been condemned in the provinces, and it was threatening to obscure the essentially anti-Southern response within the Canadas to the raid itself. Dix had telegraphed Seward the fact but

[13] For a summary of Congressional activity, see John W. Foster, *Limitation of Armament on the Great Lakes* (Washington, 1914), pp. 37–44. Consult *Cong. Globe*, 38th Cong., 1st Sess., 2809, and *ibid.*, 2nd Sess., 1, 9, 25, 37, 44, 57, 292, 311–315, 348; Detroit *Free Press*, March 11, 1865; E. H. Scammell, "The Rush-Bagot Agreement of 1817," Ontario Hist. Soc., *Papers and Records*, XIII (1915), 58–66.

not the contents of his order the day following its issuance, and he had justified it as a means of preventing further raids by forcing Canadian authorities to forestall them. The order had received support from the New York press, and especially from the *Herald*, which demanded that all raiders be followed into the Canadas and shot on the spot. If such raids continued, the newspaper noted, the provinces should be treated as a dangerous enemy. Even the more circumspect New York *Times* warned the Canadian authorities to avoid "humbug" about the matter. In the meantime Monck had asked Burnley to call Seward's attention to the order, and it was rumored that Secretary of War Stanton was prepared to resign if it were disavowed.[14]

Seward did not send an explanation of Dix's order to Quebec until November 12. Asserting that the prisoners were yet to be extradited and that his requests for their extradition and for a stronger neutrality law had gone unanswered, Seward impatiently concluded, "It is not the Government nor is it the people of the United States that are delinquent in the fulfillment of fraternal national obligations." In writing to Lyons he warned that "spirited, hasty, popular proceedings for self-defence and retaliation" were to be expected if raids continued. Bridling at Seward's implication that the Canadian authorities were delaying the extradition proceedings, Monck wrote to the British minister detailing the dates of his receipt of and reply to each extradition request.

Late in November, with the dangerous order still standing, Seward promised to give it "due consideration." He sent Preston King to Quebec to confer with the Governor General. The New Yorker reported that Monck was most eager "to maintain the friendly relations now existing," and King agreed with consul Ogden that Canada at last was showing considerable indignation over Confederate misuse of her hospitality. Lyons wrote to Lord Russell that if the raiders were treated as belligerents by the Canadian courts, "a very serious outburst of feeling" in the North against Great Britain probably would result. The Confederate foray had given Seward an opportunity to show "demonstrations of a *'spirited foreign policy'* . . . for electioneering purposes," Lyons predicted.[15]

There is little question but that the raid itself was an actual vio-

[14] Toronto *Leader*, Oct. 24, 1864; Toronto *Globe*, Oct. 25, 26, 1864; New York *Herald*, Oct. 24, Nov. 1, 1864; New York *Times*, Oct. 20, 1864; G 11, 233: Monck to Burnley, Oct. 26, 1864, 335–337; MC: Dix to Seward, Oct. 20, 1864.

[15] FO 5, 963: Lyons to Russell, Nov. 21, 1864; Creighton, *Macdonald*, p. 385: Lyons to Russell, Oct. 24, 1864.

lation of British neutrality. Thompson had been enjoined to observe that neutrality, to "neither command nor permit destruction of private property, nor injury or annoyance to non-combatants." In adhering to these orders he specifically had rejected George Sanders' plan for robbing the banks of Buffalo. Sanders, whose son had died a Northern prisoner, had approached the more naive Clement Clay, who still had several thousand dollars at his disposal, and had convinced Clay that attacks against Northern banks would be legitimate acts of war in retaliation for the campaigns of William T. Sherman and Philip Sheridan in the South. Clay had authorized Bennett Young to organize a raiding party—which was to be the first of a series of such raids, if successful—to strike initially at St. Albans, selected because of its proximity to the border, its size, and its importance as a railway junction, and Clay advanced nearly two thousand dollars to the raiders. He did not have Confederate authority to authorize such a raid, for he technically still was a subordinate of Thompson's, but Young accepted Clay's spoken approval of the plan and personally selected his followers without taking the precaution of obtaining a written order. As this fact was unknown until the trial of the raiders, general opinion in the North was aimed at Thompson, who, it was assumed, had authorized the raid, and the Confederate Commissioner soon implicated himself by writing to Benjamin to ask for an official statement sanctioning the attack, a statement that obviously would have to be predated. Thompson clearly disapproved of the raid and of Clay's activities, but he declared that he could not desert the men who had risked their lives while thinking that they had approval for their exploit.[16]

The raid hurt rather than helped the Southern cause. Any satisfaction gained in the South by the daring that the raiders displayed was more than offset by the feeling created in the Canadas that the Confederates had abused British hospitality. Seward's observers reported that a strong reaction in favor of the North had taken place among formerly anti-Northern merchants and bankers. Even papers that had been highly sympathetic to the South, like the Montreal *Evening Telegram* and the Toronto *Leader,* deplored the acts of "the brigands."

[16] G 6, 234: intercepted letter, Young to Benjamin, Nov. 1, enc. in Burnley to Monck, Dec. 21, 1864, 177–200; MC: B. J. Sweet to Seward, Dec. 22, 1864; L.C., Jacob Thompson, *Letters* (N.p., but printed, n.d.): Thompson to Benjamin, Jan. 8, 1865; New York *Tribune,* Sept. 6, 1864; *A Leaf from History: Report of J. Thompson* . . . (Washington [1868?]); Bennett H. Young [and C. S. Forbes], "Secret History of the St. Albans Raid," *Vermonter,* VII (Jan., 1902), 22–27.

The reaction of the Saint John *Morning Telegraph* to the raiders' "abuse of British hospitality" probably was fairly typical of the anti-Northern press. This journal had warmly supported the concept of Southern chivalry. In 1864 a number of transient Southerners had tricked New Brunswickers out of various sums of money to aid "The Cause," and the newspaper had attempted to write them off as Northerners posing as Confederates in order to give the South a bad name. No Southerner, the *Telegraph* had assured its readers, would "stoop to schemes of imposture." Such attempts at rationalization were quieted by the St. Albans raid and its aftermath. The *Telegraph* now felt compelled to denounce the raiders, and as nearly everyone else already had acknowledged, it discovered that the Confederacy was abusing provincial hospitality in order to embroil Great Britain in war with the United States. This was a remarkable change of opinion, and especially so since the *Telegraph*'s office had served as a Confederate rendezvous during Holcombe's stay in the Maritime Provinces. Such near reversals of opinion were not uncommon after the raid.[17]

From the day of the raid Monck went out of his way to avoid any further contact with Confederates, and he refused an audience to Thompson and Clay. Even in the South Robert E. Lee advised Jefferson Davis that he was opposed to any illegal actions along the border or the use of men needed at the front for wild and generally fruitless schemes. And in Washington the thought was beginning to be made vocal by a few that the Confederate activities in the Canadas could continue only with the active connivance of members of the Canadian government. In the words of the Anglican General Confession, the Canadian officials had, it seemed, "left undone those things which [they] ought to have done; And . . . done those things which [they] ought not to have done . . . ."[18]

[17] *Morning Telegraph*, Jan. 16, Feb. 2, Oct. 27, 29, Nov. 3, 1864; Toronto *Globe*, Oct. 21–26, 1864; Montreal *Gazette*, Oct. 10, 21, 1864; Sarnia *Observer*, Nov. 18, 1864; Barrie *Northern Advance*, Oct. 26, 1864; [Kitchener] *Berliner Journal*, Nov. 3, 1864; St. Albans *Messenger*, Oct. 22, 29, Nov. 11, 16, 1864; Chicago *Tribune*, Oct. 22, 27, 1864; G 20, 103: John McDowell to Monck, Dec. 2, 1864; MC: G. F. Edmunds to Seward, Dec. 16, and Alfred Russell to Seward, Dec. 21, 1864; CD, Montreal, v: Thurston to Seward, Oct. 22, 1864. John Branch, ed., *The St. Albans Raid* (St. Albans, 1935), presents further selections from several Canadian newspapers.
[18] G. Gunn, "New Brunswick Opinion," p. 165; Monck, *Leaves*, p. 146; D. S. Freeman and Grady McWhiney, eds., *Lee's Despatches, Unpublished Letters of General Robert E. Lee, C.S.A., to Jefferson Davis and the War Department of the Confederate States of America, 1862–65* (New York, 1957), pp. 302–304: Oct. 25, 1864.

To offset such thoughts, George-Etienne Cartier called a meeting in David Thurston's Montreal office between the consul, Cartier, McGee, and McDougall, to plan some means of preventing further attacks from the Canadas. These men told Thurston that they hoped the trial would favor the United States, and Cartier promised his full support in the future. The French-Canadian leader's reaction is interesting to note, since in the meetings of the Washington Claims Commission in 1872 Cartier was accused of having had prior knowledge of the raid, an accusation that his actions both at the time and afterwards would seem to disprove.[19]

Monck was even more eager to block further Confederate attempts to compromise British neutrality from the provinces, and he was able to demonstrate this in a minor affair, that of the steamer *Georgian*. Certainly the *Georgian* incident was significant only in that it brought forth Monck's most energetic effort to comply with Northern requests. Before the St. Albans raid Jacob Thompson had arranged for a Kentuckian, Dr. James P. Bates, to purchase a lake steamer, the *Georgian*,[20] through young Colonel George T. Denison with $18,000 of Thompson's money, and to turn the vessel over to the Confederates as a raider for use on the Great Lakes. The ship was delivered to John Y. Beall (who had not been captured yet) at Port Colborne, Canada West, on November 1. It was Beall's intention to arm the steamer and to shell and capture Buffalo. He also had the constant hope that he yet might seize the U.S.S. *Michigan* and free the prisoners on Johnson's Island. However, on November 5 an informer told the United States consul at Toronto of the sale of the *Georgian*. Consul General Potter in turn warned Monck and Stanton, the latter wired Dix, and the general replied that he might take steps independently of the Canadian authorities. Fearing just such a contingency, Monck asked revenue collectors at the lake ports to examine the *Georgian* when it docked. The vessel put in at Sarnia on November 12, was searched, and was given clearance when nothing suspicious was found. According to those on

[19] CD, Quebec, II: J. S. Bowen to Seward, Dec. 22, 1864, 23–24; CD, Montreal, VI: Thurston to Seward, Nov. 8, 10, 1864; Macdonald Papers, 203: Pemmell to Cartier, Nov. 15, 1872, 220–221, 224–226, Cartier to Kimberley, Nov. 18, 1872, 233–237, Wodehouse to Cartier, Nov. 12, 1872, 215–216, and Enfield to Pemmell, Nov. 22, Howard to Granville, Nov. 12, both enc. in J. P. Deane to Gray, Dec. 26, 1872, with enclosures, 240–241, 248–251, 259–261; Moran Diary, XIV: Nov. 22, 30, 1864, and printed in Wallace and Gillespie, eds., *Moran*, II, 1350, 1354.

[20] This ship should not be confused with the privateer *Georgiana*, or with the Confederate cruiser *Georgia*.

board, the ship was going to be used in the Saginaw lumber trade.

Under the watchful eyes of an American gunboat, which lingered near the opposite shore, *Georgian* put out for Collingwood with the Kentucky doctor in command. During the week an old cannon disappeared from a yard in Guelph, Canada West, and the consul at Toronto suggested that it was destined for use on the steamer. The gun was taken apart and sent to Collingwood in two crates, but it was found before the *Georgian* reached Owen Sound. A few crude bombs also were transported to Guelph to await some means of conveyance to Collingwood, and these, too, were intercepted. Despite the apparent innocence of the vessel, the North armed two more lake tugs with cannons, and Canadian detectives apparently succeeded in preventing a rendezvous between Beall, Bates, and an intended crew of ten. As a result, the ship put in at Collingwood without a crew and without any armaments for her readily obtainable.[21]

Seward took the unusual step of wiring Monck in a private capacity on November 7 when the mayor of Buffalo indicated his fear that the *Georgian* might be used against that city. In sending such a telegram Seward departed from the correct procedure, for he often had been told that his proper line of communication with the Governor General was through the British minister in Washington. However, the St. Albans raid had so lessened Monck's insistence on the normal triangular communications that he not only acted upon Seward's suggestion that the *Georgian* be investigated, but he did not add the usual reminder that the Governor General could not receive messages directly from the Secretary of State.[22]

The Canadian government took the matter seriously enough to keep the vessel under almost constant observation and to investigate young Denison's role in the sale. And when two boxes, shipped from Sarnia and marked "potatoes," were found to contain ammunition, the authorities assumed that efforts to arm the *Georgian* were continuing and again had the steamer detained. An injunction was issued to keep Denison from completing formal transfer of the ship's title to Bates, and the vessel remained at Collingwood, ostensibly undergoing repairs, while the case was considered by the government. Not

[21] G 6, 234: Humball to Potter, Nov. 5, enc. in Burnley to Monck, Nov. 12, 1864; G 9, 465: Monck to Cardwell, Nov. 14, 1865; *OR*, ser. 1, XLIII, 557: Dix to Stanton, Nov. 6, 1864; Toronto *Globe*, Nov. 10, 21, 1865.

[22] G 13, 1: Seward to Monck and reply, both Nov. 7, 1864, and Fargo to Monck, Nov. 8, 1864; BMW to GCC, 13: Burnley to Monck, Nov. 12, 1864.

long thereafter George Dewson, the personal agent of Judah P. Benjamin, let it be known that he was in Canada West to purchase a boat for the Confederacy, and the authorities assumed that he intended to make another attempt to convert the *Georgian* to wartime use. In the investigation that followed Denison inadvertently revealed that he had paid an inflated price for the vessel, and this was taken as a final indication that it was wanted for Thompson's service.[23]

The incident dragged on well after the end of the war. In April, 1865, a confidant of Thompson and Denison, now a paid Northern informer, told David Thurston that the ship had, in fact, been intended as a raider for the Confederacy. When this news was made public, the Toronto *Globe* attacked Denison for violating the neutrality proclamation, and in May he was tried on that count. Eventually acquitted, Denison recovered his boat in November and sued for damages. The court decided that the government had acted correctly in seizing the ship, but Denison did not drop his charges until late in 1866.[24]

In the meantime the captured raiders, with the exception of one who had been arrested in Montreal, had been taken to St. Johns, Canada East, for preliminary examination. They had telegraphed George Sanders tersely, "We are captured. Do what you can for us," and Sanders was on hand with six thousand dollars for their defense when the examination began before police magistrate Coursol. The raiders originally had tried to secure a hasty examination at Frelighsburg, but through the insistence of consul Thurston, Governor Smith, and Governor General Monck, they were placed before the magistrate, who came from Montreal for the purpose. Monck telegraphed Governor Smith that he was certain that Seward would find Coursol completely satisfactory, and Seward expressed his pleasure over the prompt Canadian action.[25]

[23] CD, Toronto, 1: Thurston to Seward, Nov. 25, 1864, Dec. 1, 2, 6, 9, Feb. 6, 1865, and McDonald to Murphy, Dec. 20, 1864; CD, Montreal, VI: Thurston to Seward, Dec. 10, 1864; NBL, 12: Seward to Burnley, Dec. 29, 31, 1864, 555–556, 656–658; G 6, 235: Seward to Burnley, Dec. 29, 1864, enc. in Burnley to Monck, Jan. 1, 1865; Sarnia *Observer*, Nov. 18, 1864; Toronto *Globe*, Dec. 5, 1864; *OR*, ser. I, XLV, 1076: Hill to Hooker, Nov. 26, 1864.
[24] CD, Toronto, 1: Thurston to Seward, April 7, Oct. 7, Nov. 4, 1865, March 9, 1866; Ottawa *Times*, May 19, 1868.
[25] CD, Montreal, V: Thurston to Seward, and Smith to Thurston, both Oct. 21, 1864; Clay Papers: check stub nos. 26, 27, 29, 30, 38, 39, 44, 45, Sept. 28–Nov. 1, 1864; G 13, 1: Monck to Smith, Oct. 21, 1864; G 17, 6: Seward to Burnley, Oct. 21, enc. in Burnley to Monck, Oct. 23, 1864, p. 92, and printed in *Correspondence*

Coursol had opened the preliminary examination in the last week of October. A rising Montreal criminal lawyer, Bernard Devlin, who later was to fight against Americans in the Fenian invasion of 1866, represented the United States, while Sanders retained three prominent Montreal attorneys to defend the raiders. Soon the proceedings were transferred to Montreal, as Coursol felt that tension was too great so near the border for a fair examination. Shortly before the examination began, Bennett Young penned an eloquent open letter to an anti-Northern Montreal newspaper, explaining that the raid was undertaken in retaliation for Sheridan's activities in the Shenandoah Valley. He declared that he was commissioned to act as he did and that the raiders had violated no Canadian laws. Young pointed out that he was captured by Vermonters who had violated the Canadian border. "Surely the people of Vermont must have forgotten that you are not in the midst of war, and ruled by a man despotic in his actions, and supreme in his infamy," he wrote.[26]

The proceedings were slow, for evidence was to be taken on each of six potentially extraditable charges: assault, murder, attempted murder, robbery, attempted arson, and horse-stealing. The prisoners were housed in the jailer's own home and were well fed on expensive delicacies supplied by Sanders. He provided wine at each meal, and it was said that those who felt the need had the solace of feminine company at night. Young carried on friendly chess games with the jailer and read of his exploits in the St. Albans *Messenger*, to which he had subscribed. The prisoners were carefully guarded, but not so much to prevent escape as to forestall possible kidnappers from the United States. Outside, tight little knots of noisy Southerners and their sympathizers milled about, singing. The law's slow course and the favorable treatment that the prisoners received soon turned Northern gratification at the speed of the original arrest to annoyance and exasperation. By November the New York *Herald* had resumed its anti-Canadian stance, declaring that the Canadas had no government at all, only "a muddle," and that the North must show that "the strong hand is the only law that we can recognize."[27]

Relating to the Fenian Invasion and the Rebellion of the Southern States (Ottawa, 1869), pp. 136–137; ITC, 38: Seward to Thurston, Oct. 24, 1864, 317–318; Montreal *Witness*, Oct. 29, 1864.

[26] Montreal *Evening Telegram*, Oct. 22, 1864; Montreal *Witness*, Oct. 26, 1864.

[27] *Ibid.*, Oct. 29, 1864; Montreal *Gazette*, Nov. 3, 1864; Cobourg *World*, Nov. 25, 1864; New York *Times*, Nov. 1, 1864; New York *Herald*, Nov. 9, 1864; CD,

The examination proved to be long and tedious. The Canadian government indicated its desire to be rid of the unwanted raiders by appointing the Clerk of the Crown to aid the prosecution. Overflowing crowds were present at the court to listen to the defense, led by the dogged and very able John J. Abbott, former Solicitor General for Canada East, contend that the raid was a legitimate act of war that was not extraditable. Abbott insisted that each charge be examined separately, for he wanted to allow time for public temper to cool and for the ever-changing military situation to the south to have some influence on popular opinion. The defense presented the prisoners' statements, and Young submitted to the court copies of his vague commission from Confederate Secretary of War Seddon, which authorized him to organize a company of twenty men for an unstated purpose. Young further declared that the particular expedition was neither organized nor projected in the Canadas, and in this he appears to have been less than honest. He added, for emotional effect and apparently with some truth, that he also was avenging his fiancée, who had been criminally attacked by a Northern soldier, a point which impressed the pro-Southern crowd in the courtroom. The defense requested a thirty-day delay so that messengers might go to Richmond to obtain copies of commissions and other documents that would prove that the expedition had been an act of war, and Coursol suspended the charges until December 13.[28]

When the defense appealed to Lincoln to grant the messengers safe conduct to Richmond, the President refused. The prisoners petitioned Monck to help them by sending a British governmental courier to the Confederate capital, and he also adamantly declined. Clay wrote

---

Montreal, vi: Thurston to Seward, Nov. 2, 7, 1864; John D. Borthwick, *History of the Montreal Prison* (Montreal, 1886), p. 184; Morgan Dix, *Memoirs of John Adams Dix* (New York, 1883), I, 353. The writer would like to thank Edna L. Jacobsen of The New York State Library for examining the John A. Dix letters for pertinent material.

[28] CD, Montreal, vi: Thurston to Seward, Nov. 17, 1864; CD, Toronto, i: Thurston to Seward, Oct. 20, 1864; Montreal *Witness*, Nov. 5–9, 1864; Toronto *Leader*, Nov. 17, Dec. 10, 1864; Toronto *Globe*, Oct. 22, 1864. A transcript of the entire examination and subsequent trial appears in L. N. Benjamin, comp., *The St. Albans Raid; or, Investigation into the Charges against Lieut. Bennett H. Young and Command, for their Acts at St. Albans, Vt., on the 19th October, 1864: being a Complete and Authentic Report of all the Proceedings on the Demand of the United States for their Extradition, under the Ashburton Treaty* . . . (Montreal, 1865).

Benjamin asking for a commission to justify the specific acts involved in the raid, and with his usual impetuousness he made it clear that he alone had authorized the venture. Clay's letter was intercepted and a copy of it was sent to Adams, who showed it to Russell. However, Sanders also sent a personal appeal to Richmond and it was this which at last was answered. The same clerk who rejoiced over Dix's order cynically noted in his diary, "I doubt if such written orders are in existence—but no matter." Sanders hinted broadly that the commission should be dated and written in such a way as to afford the raiders some measure of retroactive protection. Young passed the interim by penning open letters to the local press and by paying his St. Albans hotel bill with a check drawn on a bank that he had helped to rob. The raiders frequently were visited by Thompson, Dewson, and Colonel Denison, and a few were allowed to visit with Denison in his home, where he devised new schemes for getting Confederate messages through Northern lines to Richmond.

By now Clay had tried to wash his hands of the raiders, for he insisted that he had not anticipated the bank robberies. At his behest Beverley Tucker prepared a statement declaring that he had heard Clay tell Young to "burn and destroy, but don't rob . . . ." Clay and the leader of the raiders exchanged harsh words when the commissioner asserted that the stolen money should go to the Confederate government, for apparently many of the raiders—although probably not Young himself—considered some of the money to be their own. During the examination they insisted that all of the money was intended for the Confederate treasury, possibly on advice from counsel, in particular Abbot, who had no particular liking for some of the raiders or what they had done but who consistently fought to prevent their extradition.[29]

When Coursol resumed the St. Albans case on December 13, counsel for the defense challenged the magistrate's jurisdiction. The defense pointed out that in the extradition clause of the Webster-Ashburton Treaty no machinery for extraditing was created. To give the

[29] Montreal *Gazette*, Nov. 18, Dec. 1, 1864; CD, Montreal, vi: Thurston to Seward, Nov. 17, Dec. 5, 1864; FO 115, vi: Law Officers to Russell, enc. in Russell to Monck, both Dec. 22, 1864; G 21, 1: intercepted correspondence, enc. in Cardwell to Monck, Dec. 31, 1864; John B. Jones, *Diary*, ii, 355: Dec. 15, 1864; Nicolay and Hay, *Complete Works*, viii, 23–27; Clay Papers: Tucker to Clay, Dec. 9, 1864, and Young[?] to Clay[?], Nov. 21, 1864; O.P.A., Denison Diary, xxiv: Nov., 1864, *passim*; George T. Denison, *Soldiering in Canada* (Toronto, 1901), p. 60.

treaty its desired effect the British Parliament had passed an act that provided that previous to the arrest of any offender a warrant signifying that a proper requisition had been made by the United States had to be issued by the Governor General or by a Lieutenant Governor. This imperial act further contained a self-liquidating clause, in that it ceased to function within a specific colony when that colony had passed a statute of its own to carry into effect the purpose of the treaty. The Canadian Parliament had done precisely this, and it had broadened the possibility of extradition by giving any judge or justice of the peace throughout the province authority to issue the necessary warrant. The colonial act had been repealed, however, only to be re-enacted in a modified form, taking jurisdiction of extradition cases away from justices of the peace. The defense contended that when the original Canadian act was repealed it brought the original British act back into force, and that subsequent Canadian acts were without authority. Since the Governor General had issued no warrant, the defense argued that the presiding magistrate had no jurisdiction in the case, for the prisoners had been arrested illegally.[30]

Coursol suspended the examination to consider this involved argument, and on the same afternoon he delivered himself of an elaborate declaration that he had no jurisdiction in the case. Coursol also argued that the Canadian extradition act of 1861 was not in force because it had not been proclaimed, clearly an error on his part since an Order-in-Council had been passed in England that expressly recognized the act. Thereupon Coursol, without binding the prisoners over to a higher court, as was the usual procedure in such cases, ordered that the raiders be discharged. Bernard Devlin protested that Coursol could discharge the prisoners with respect to the first charge only, since the other five had not been presented, thereby preventing the magistrate from taking recognition of them. Overriding Devlin's protest, Coursol declared that he would hear no more of the matter and discharged the prisoners from all six warrants.[31]

As soon as Coursol's intent became apparent, two Vermont attorneys who were present hurried from the court room to draw up a new complaint. Obtaining a warrant, they applied to the Chief of Police of Montreal, Guillaume Lamothe, who earlier had received a substantial reward from the United States government—at his own

---

[30] Benjamin, pp. 117–122, 146–148.
[31] *Ibid.*, pp. 122–128; Toronto *Leader*, Dec. 16, 1864; Toronto *Globe*, Dec. 17, 1864.

request—for apprehending an escaped criminal from Detroit. The lawyers asked that the raiders be rearrested, but the thousand dollar reward that Giddings had passed on to Lamothe, "to secure prompt and efficient disposition in . . . cases in future," apparently had done little good. Lamothe, who had just surrendered to Thompson's banking agent friend a receipt that had been entrusted to his care for eighty-four thousand dollars of the stolen St. Albans money, demanded three-quarters of an hour for consideration, sufficient time to permit the Confederates to escape on the evening train from Montreal. He had acted without any authorization from Coursol, making his decision to surrender the receipt on the basis of an informal tête-à-tête that he had had with the magistrate some days before on the then-hypothetical question of what Lamothe would have to do in case the Southerners were freed. Thompson's agent had rushed to the bank after closing time with the receipt and had received the money through the back door, all within an hour after Coursol's decision that he had no jurisdiction in the case.

The Vermont attorneys next sought out the High Constable, and he directed the Montreal Water Police to execute the warrant, but the delay had given the raiders ample time to escape with the money.[32] Lawyers pointed out that Coursol had delivered an opinion on the defense counsel's long and involved argument in so short a time as to raise suspicions that he had expected just such a move and already had prepared his answer. There were ugly rumors that the magistrate had been influenced by stolen bank money, and Cartier suspended him until an investigation could be made, and disavowed Coursol's act. The magistrate had had earlier contacts with Confederates, for during the week of the St. Albans raid he had told David Thurston that he knew of a man who would reveal the nature of future Confederate plots for pay. Others observed that Lamothe had acted as though he expected that the Confederates would be freed that day. Certainly, it was argued, the Bank of Ontario had shown unusual and unnecessary courtesy in carrying out a back-door business transaction after closing hours.[33] Having vouched for Coursol, Monck felt

[32] CD, Montreal, v: Giddings to Seward, April 26, May 20, 1864, Thurston to Seward, June 6, 28, 1864; G 13, 1: Monck to Burnley, in cipher, Dec. 19, 1864; Montreal *Witness*, Dec. 24, 1864; Toronto *Globe*, Dec. 15, 20, 1864.
[33] CD, Montreal, v: Thurston to Seward, Oct. 20, 1864; G 13, 1: Monck to Burnley, in cipher, Dec. 14, 1864; Montreal *Gazette*, Dec. 16, 1864; Detroit *Free Press*, Dec. 18, 1864; *Diary of Gideon Welles*, II, 198: Dec. 16, 1864.

particularly chagrined, and he wrote Burnley that the magistrate's actions were absurd.

Late in November Monck had conferred with Macdonald and Cartier on means of stiffening the Canadian neutrality law, but up to this point nothing had been done to augment the Governor General's powers. Seward repeatedly had pointed to the American neutrality act of 1838—which was to suppress and prevent hostile invasions of Canadian territory launched from American soil—as an example of the type of law that the province needed, and Cardwell had given Monck permission to apply to the legislature for increased power of a purely temporary nature. The Governor General now set out to act on Cardwell's suggestion.[34]

The Canadian newspapers also deprecated the outcome of the examination, the Montreal *Gazette* expressing the feeling of many: "We feel, and we believe that the great body of the public feel, that the Federal applicants at our door had a right to expect different treatment from us than they have received." The consensus of responsible opinion was that Coursol's action had been unwise and would worsen relations with the Federal government. According to the Quebec *Daily News*, affairs with the United States occupied "men's minds to the almost exclusion of ordinary affairs." A group of Montreal businessmen petitioned Monck to launch an inquiry into the affair, and the Montreal City Council established a committee to investigate Lamothe's curious behavior. The people of Brantford voted an appropriation of $650 to equip a volunteer company to help maintain the neutrality laws, and the Windsor Town Council passed a resolution condemning Coursol.[35]

[34] G 9, 455: Monck to Cardwell, Nov. 25, 1864, 205, Jan. 26, 1865, 259; FO 115, 409: Cardwell to Monck, Dec. 3, 1864; NBL, 12: Seward to Lyons, Dec. 4, 1864; OR, ser. I, XLIII, 789–790: Smith to Stanton, Dec. 14, 1864. There is an incredible story that Lincoln sent for Lyons and said, "Now look here Lord Lyons, I want to keep peace with England but I can't stand this. You just write to the Queen and tell her that I don't want to go to war but I can't stand this sort of thing." An account of it appears in one of Henry Cabot Lodge's journals (J. A. Garraty, "Lincoln and the Diplomats," *Indiana Mag. of Hist.*, XLVI [June, 1950], 202).

[35] *Gazette*, Dec. 15, 23, 1864; *Daily News*, Jan. 4, 1865; Toronto *Globe*, Dec. 23, 1864, Jan. 12, 1865; Toronto *Leader*, Dec. 26, 1864, Jan. 23, 1865; *The Times*, Dec. 16, 1864, Jan. 9, June 4, 1865; Detroit *Free Press*, Dec. 17, 1864; Montreal *Transcript*, Dec. 21, 1864; Montreal *Morning Chronicle*, Jan. 18, 1865; Montreal *Witness*, Dec. 21, 1864, Jan. 4, 1865; Quebec *Gazette*, Jan. 16, 1865; Quebec *Le Canadienne*, Nov. 7, 1864; St. Albans *Messenger*, Dec. 15, 1864, April 5, 1865; CD, Montreal, VI: Potter to Seward, Jan. 6, 1865.

As soon as he heard of the release of the raiders General Dix issued a second order. He instructed his troops to pursue raiders wherever they took refuge and under no circumstances to surrender prisoners to anyone before returning with them to the United States, where they could be tried by martial law. When Lord Russell learned of this order, he warned Charles Francis Adams that the North would be falling into a Southern trap if Dix crossed the border, and the minister replied that Dix was a man of "sense and moderation." Applying pressure as Seward had done, Adams said that he knew General Dix too well to believe that he would magnify the seriousness of the situation and that his order indicated how agitated the populace was becoming. Russell concluded the interview by acknowledging that the Confederacy was attempting to create an Anglo-American rupture and expressing the hope that neither the Confederates nor Dix's order would produce such a result.[36]

Despite his defense of Dix, Adams privately hoped that the order would be withdrawn. The existence of two standing directives to Northern troops that invited violation of the Canadian frontier was an obvious threat to Anglo-American peace, the *The Times* referred to Dix's second order as "a declaration of war against Canada." Charles Sumner also correctly saw that the real danger in the St. Albans raid lay in the renewed tension on the border. "The whole proceeding was a trap in which to catch the government of our country," he warned. "It was hoped that in this way the rebellion would gain the powerful British intervention which would restore its falling fortunes . . . ."[37]

The day following Coursol's decision Senator Zachariah Chandler of Michigan arose on the floor of the Senate, a news item concerning the raiders clutched in his hand, and presented a resolution asking the Committee on Military Affairs to organize an army corps to defend the border. Although the motion was laid over, Chandler had made his point: that war with Great Britain could result over the "protection" that Canadian authorities were giving the raiders. Demands that the reciprocity treaty be ended were repeated more vociferously than ever, and it was evident that before the session was over Con-

---

[36] New York *World*, Dec. 15, 1864; *OR*, ser. i, XLIII, 784, 789–790; CFA, 88: Russell to Adams, Dec. 16, enc. in Adams to Seward, Dec. 22, 1864; CFA, Diary: Dec. 28, 1864, Jan. 2, 1865; FO 115, 405: Russell to Burnley, Dec. 29, 1864.

[37] *The Times*, Dec. 29, 1864, Jan. 4, 1865; CFA, Diary: Dec. 28, 1864, Jan. 2, 1865; *Foreign Relations, 1864*, p. 1.

gress might promote the St. Albans affair into a first-class diplomatic crisis. Then, too, in his fourth Annual Message to Congress, following the raid, Lincoln had referred to the "insecurity of life and property" that existed along the Canadian border and had confirmed the fact that notice had been given to end the Rush-Bagot agreement. He had added that the Canadian authorities were not thought to be intentionally unjust, but he felt that more rigid measures to protect the border might be necessary, and he had hinted that these would include terminating the Canadian transit privilege through Maine.[38]

Northern annoyance, which had been building up during Coursol's examination, now turned to anger, and the Canadas found themselves bearing the brunt of a newspaper attack nearly as intense as that during the *Trent* affair. Part of the American press predicted war while another group called for a complete nonintercourse policy against the Canadas and openly accused the Canadian officials of conniving with the raiders.[39] The Chicago *Tribune* hysterically shouted that the North should take Canada by the throat and throttle her "as a St. Bernard would throttle a poodle pup . . . ," while one New Yorker blamed "thousands of *worthless* Canadian Sympathisers" for untold deeds of villainy yet to come. The New York *Times* felt that henceforth Canadian territory was entitled to no more respect than was that of Virginia or South Carolina. "It may be said that this will lead to a war with England," the *Times* admitted, and added, "But if it must come, let it come. Not ours the guilt . . . . We were never in better condition for a war with England." "The next raid is likely to be avenged upon the nearest Canadian village which gives refuge to the marauders," concluded the New York *Herald*.[40]

To prevent another border incident some action on Dix's orders had to be taken. Gideon Welles and Edwin Stanton favored the di-

[38] FO 115, 409: Burnley to Russell, Dec. 23, 1864; Baring Papers: Ward to Baring, Dec. 20, 23, 1864; Seward Papers: "Man at the Helm" to Seward, Dec. 2, 1864; New York *Herald*, Dec. 17, 1864; New York *Times*, Dec. 29, 1864; Detroit *Free Press*, Dec. 15, 1864; *The Times*, Dec. 30, 1864; *Cong. Globe*, 38th Cong., 2nd Sess., 33-34, 58, 65; Richardson, *Papers of the Presidents*, VI, 246.

[39] For example, see Detroit *Free Press*, Dec. 14-20, 1864; Buffalo Morning *Express*, Dec. 17, 1864; New York *Tribune*, Dec. 14-17, 1864; Chicago *Tribune*, Dec. 16, 17, 1864; New York *Herald*, Dec. 17, 1864; New York *Times*, Dec. 16, 29, 1864; St. Albans *Messenger*, Dec. 15, 1864; Toronto *Globe*, Dec. 15-17, 19, 21, 23, 1864.

[40] Seward Papers: J. K. Hartwell to L. A. Spalding, Dec. 20, 1864; *Tribune*, Dec. 16, 20, 1864; *Herald*, Dec. 17, 1864; *Times*, Dec. 16, 1864.

rective, and Seward was presented with a grave and delicate problem. To disavow the orders would create serious public feeling against him, jeopardizing his future political ambitions, while not to disavow them would be to risk war and to miss an opportunity to ingratiate himself with the Canadian and British authorities. But Seward was losing many of his earlier demogogic traits. Upon his advice Lincoln revoked the orders on December 17. The President declared that in the future all commanders were to report by telegram to Washington and await orders before crossing the boundary. Thus he did not specifically deny the possibility of pursuit into the provinces, but he did remove the immediate threat. General U. S. Grant also gave the revocation his official endorsement.[41]

Lincoln was acting in accord with the United States's own interpretation of international law when he revoked Dix's orders. During the *Caroline* affair in 1837–1840, which had involved a British violation of the American boundary, Secretary of State Daniel Webster had argued in a note to Great Britain that exception to the principle of national inviolability could be made only when the necessity to violate a border was "instant, overwhelming, leaving no choice of means and no moment of deliberation." By international law a border may be crossed under some circumstances when in "hot pursuit" of an enemy, but there must be unbroken continuity in the pursuit. By requiring his commanders to obtain permission from Washington before crossing the frontier, Lincoln had destroyed any possibility of the exercise of "continuity" in pursuit. Lincoln also saw that to have allowed Dix's orders to stand would have been to encourage the very policy that the Confederacy was promoting.

Dix's acceptance of Lincoln's countermanding order clearly was reluctant, and he was not the only fiery and unwise general on the Northern border. A few days after the President revoked Dix's second order, General Joseph Hooker wrote from his Cincinnati headquarters to Senator Chandler that he himself had wanted to issue such instruction but was restrained "by the conscious weakness of our Govt. in its foreign policy. . . . I assure, Senator," Hooker added, "in case a raid should be attempted from Canada I intend that some-

[41] *Diary of Gideon Welles*, II, 198: Dec. 16, 1864; *OR*, ser. I, XLIII, 800: Dec. 17, 18, 1864; Sumner Papers, CXL: John Sandfield Macdonald to Sumner, Dec. 27, 1864; *ibid.*, LXXII: H. J. Parker to Sumner, Jan. 20, 1865; John B. Jones, *Diary*, II, 361: Dec. 21, 1864; *The Times*, Jan. 2, 1865; Nicolay and Hay, VIII, 25; Pierce, *Sumner*, IV, 204–205: Sumner to Lieber, Dec. 27, 1864.

body shall be hurt if I have to go into Canada to do it. Then if exception is taken it can be adjusted by negociation [*sic*] afterward." [42] Hooker, who was angered that Philip Sheridan and George G. Meade, his juniors in the army, had been promoted over his head, was ready to do something rash in order to regain his lost glory and vindicate his generalship.

Nor were Dix and Hooker alone among men of some intelligence who were ready to march into the Canadas. From England even youthful Henry Adams wrote to his brother, Charles Francis, that "The Canadian business is suddenly found to be serious, and the prospect of Sherman marching down the St. Lawrence, and Farragut sailing up it, doesn't seem just agreeable. They are annoyed at Dix's order. If they are not sharp they will find annoyance a totally inadequate expression for it." As Samuel G. Ward observed, so long as it was "in the power of a petty Canadian judge, or an obscure U.S. Commander" to raise diplomatic questions that, given the irritated state of public feeling that existed, required all of the "wisdom and strength of the Govt. to avoid making [a] question of war or peace," it was impossible to feel safe. [43]

Monck expressed his gratification over Lincoln's decision and promised to do all that he could to "remedy the effect" of Coursol's proceedings. Between December 16 and New Year's a number of steps were taken to increase Canada's ability to deal with the border situation and, in part, to pacify the North. On December 20 the Canadian government offered a reward of two hundred dollars for information leading to the capture of any of the raiders, and Seward announced a reward of five hundred, and later of a thousand, dollars. On the same day Bennett Young and four of his men were re-arrested near Quebec. Eventually five more, who tried to hide by the ingenious method of enlisting in the Northern army, were arrested in Maine. Others, aided by Lamothe, who had resigned his position, and by a famous guide, David Têtu, made good their escape via the St. Lawrence River. Lamothe, using a portion of the raiders' loot, purchased a whaling

[42] Chandler Papers: Hooker to Chandler, Dec. 19, 1864; New York *Herald*, Dec. 21, 1864, Jan. 1, 1865. Alexander Hamilton wrote Seward that his father's writings supported Dix's interpretation of the "right of entry" (Seward Papers: Oct. 29, 1864), but while Seward consulted the published works of the senior Hamilton, he did not act upon them.

[43] W. C. Ford, ed., *A Cycle of Adams Letters, 1861–1865* (Boston, 1920), II, 238–239: Dec. 30, 1864; Baring Papers: Ward to Baring, Jan. 16, 1865.

ship, the *Canadian Eagle,* and succeeded in getting a few of the Southerners to Newfoundland despite exceptionally active police efforts in
Canada East.[44]

Cartier had ordered a further investigation, which revealed that
the police chief's action had stemmed from political motives. As a
liberal he had wanted to embarrass the Macdonald-Cartier government. Nonetheless, the Montreal City Council, with its French-Canadian members unanimously supporting Lamothe, cleared him *in
absentia* of charges of complicity in the foray itself, and in May both
Coursol and Lamothe were exonerated of illegally aiding the St. Albans raiders. The latter was found to have committed "an improper
act" in surrendering the receipt for the St. Albans bank money, and
Coursol was said to have laid himself open "to the imputation of a
grave dereliction of duty . . . ." Eventually Lamothe was to return
to Canada East and become an ardent advocate of Canadian annexation
to the United States.[45]

Governor General Monck took the first opportunity to ask the
legislature for the temporary powers that Cardwell had suggested,
including the power to eject undesirable aliens from the provinces.
Although New Brunswick was not involved in the St. Albans affair,
Lieutenant Governor Gordon demonstrated his good faith by issuing
a warrant for the arrest of the raiders should they take refuge there.
Monck's Executive Council also responded by recommending that a
stipendiary magistrate be appointed for Canada West to co-ordinate
existing border patrols in the peninsula and by authorizing a call for
fifteen hundred volunteer militia to guard the frontier. When two

[44] G 21, 1: Monck to Cardwell, Dec. 16, 1864, 197; Macdonald Papers, 1: Monck
to Macdonald, n.d., 113; Sumner Papers, cxxxix: J. W. Newman to Sumner,
March 20, 1865; St. Albans *Messenger,* Dec. 29, 1864; *The Times,* Jan. 9, 1865;
Quebec *Gazette,* Jan. 6, 1865; E 1, 89: Dec. 19, 1864, 532; G 20, 106: A. Comeau to
Monck, April 15, 1865; P.A.C., Lamothe Papers: MS. account by Lamothe of his
aid to the Confederates, and copy, Lamothe to Senator S. C. Pomeroy, May, 1870,
with sworn statement, Jan. 6, 1872. Arthur Buies, who later became a well-known
French-Canadian writer, helped Lamothe at one point. On the escape see H.-R.
Casgrain's articles, reprinted by Henri Têtu, *David Têtu et les Raiders de Saint-
Alban, Episode de la Guerre Américaine* (Montreal, 1893); Têtu, "David Têtu et
les Raiders de St.-Alban," *BRH,* XVII (Aug., 1911), 225-233; Montreal *Soleil,* Dec.
10, 1910; Montreal *La Patrie,* Jan. 12, 1924.

[45] G 21, 57: Frederick W. Torrance Report; Montreal City Council, *The St.
Albans Raid: Investigation . . . into the Charges Preferred by Councillor B. Devlin against Guillaume Lamothe* (Montreal, 1865). Reprinted, 1865, with a slight
change in title.

thousand men offered their services, military commanders from London, Toronto, and Montreal met in Quebec to receive personal instructions from Monck on frontier protection.[46]

Macdonald announced the appointment of an additional secret detective force to operate among the Confederates along the Niagara and Detroit frontiers, and on December 19, in keeping with the previous recommendation, he chose an energetic and respected stipendiary magistrate from the border town of Windsor, Gilbert McMicken, to supervise and co-ordinate border patrols. Shortly thereafter a similar body of detectives was established for Canada East under Colonel Ermatinger. The Conservative leader received considerable praise from the press of the Northern border communities for his action, and the United States District Attorney in Detroit, Alfred Russell, expressed high regard for his selection of McMicken.

Some of the credit that went to Macdonald at the time, and that has since been accorded to him by historians, for establishing a police force along the frontier might have been modified had the full nature of the force been known. Presumably Macdonald was in a position to know who the Confederate leaders in the united Canadas were and to know their leading agents as well, although it is entirely possible that he did not, of course. In any case, he chose Gilbert McMicken to supervise the detective force. Actually, McMicken had been working with the Confederacy, for he was Holcombe's unpaid agent in Windsor for sending Confederate soldiers on to Halifax for return to the battlefront. In addition, McMicken's men quite naturally did not concentrate all their attention on the danger of Confederate raids into the United States, for they were at least as interested in the possibility of a Northern invasion of Canada West and in stopping the activities of crimps along the border. There was no reason why McMicken's men should have restricted their activities to Confederates, and to have done so would have been unneutral, but Macdonald wisely failed to correct the impression, which was wide-spread in the North, that his police force was intended to control Southern activities exclusively.[47]

[46] E, AA: 516; Toronto *Globe*, Dec. 19–21, 1864; G 1, 172: Cardwell to Monck, Dec. 3, 1864, and Russell to Burnley, Dec. 29, enc. in Cardwell to Monck, Dec. 31, 1864, 477; G 1, 173: Cardwell to Monck, Jan. 7, 1865, 11.

[47] CD, Quebec: Thurston to Seward, Oct. 14, 1864, 14–15; *ORN*, ser. 11, 111, 1239: Holcombe to Benjamín, Nov. 16, 1864; CD, Montreal, vi: Potter to Seward, March 15, 1865; Seward Papers: G. W. Brega to Seward, March 25, 1865; Macdonald Papers, 56: R. A. Harrison to Macdonald, Dec. 15, 1864, 19; *ibid.*, 253: J. C. Mor-

Macdonald also had become increasingly worried over the activities of the Fenian Brotherhood in the North.[48] The Fenians were a group of Irish-Americans who looked upon their experiences in the Northern army during the war as valuable training for an intended invasion of British North America. *Fianna*, the name of an ancient Celtic body of warriors, was to them a symbol of the rebirth of Ireland through deliverance from Great Britain, and despite their oft-repeated patriotic sentiments concerning the United States they were quite willing to embroil their adopted country in a war with England in order to achieve their purpose.

In retrospect the Fenians appear a bit ridiculous. They "oft declared their intentions and little acted," and their marching song, which was bad poetry and worse sense, ended with the rather revealing line, "And we'll go and capture Canada, for we've nothing else to do." With a monomania deserving of a leader more like Captain Ahab than their own incompetent "General" John O'Neill, the Fenians saw the British behind every misfortune of either the United States or Ireland: "This rebellion is England, but it is not England open armed, but England in her own masked, assassin, slimy, serpentine character," one wrote of the Civil War. The movement was condemned by the Roman Catholic Church, but one of the Fenian leaders had written with unblinking pragmatism, "Waste no time in attempting to gain the priests. Their one idea is the good of the Mother Church. Let the revolution only succeed; Mother Church always knows how to adapt herself to accomplished facts." The restraining force of their religion was not likely to prevent the Fenians from making Hamilton their capital, as they vowed to do.[49]

---

rison to Macdonald, n.d., 24–29; E 1, 89: 516–517; E 1 90AB: 470–472; Pope, ed., *Correspondence*, pp. 18–20: Macdonald to Swinyard, Dec. 19, 1864. McMicken ultimately became Speaker of the House in Manitoba.

[48] The best and most complete account of Fenian activities during this time is William D'Arcy, *The Fenian Movement in the United States: 1858–1886* (Washington, 1947). See also Charles P. Stacey, "Fenianism and the Rise of National Feeling in Canada at the Time of Confederation," *CHR*, xii (Sept., 1931), 238–262; S. D. Hoslett, "The Fenian Brotherhood," *Americana*, xxxiv (Oct., 1940), 596–603; and Clyde King, "The Fenian Movement," Univ. of Colorado, *Studies*, vi (1909), 187–213, which remains of value.

[49] Chicago *Tribune*, Oct. 7, 8, 1864; John Macdonald, *Troublous Times in Canada* (Toronto, 1873), p. 15; B. J. Blied, *Catholics and the Civil War* (Milwaukee, 1945), p. 106; Milwaukee *Sentinel*, Aug. 12, 1862, quoted in M. J. McDonald, *History of the Irish in Wisconsin in the Nineteenth Century* (Washington, 1954),

Macdonald feared that this group of adventurers was preparing an invasion of the provinces that would not be long delayed. He also was determined that the Fenian movement would gain no foothold within the Canadas. The acknowledged leader of the Irish in the provinces, Thomas D'Arcy McGee, who once had toyed with Fenianism himself, repeatedly had said that no Canadian would support the movement, and in general he was correct, for the Fenians had only a small following in Montreal and Toronto. But across the border the Fenians were talking about fleshing their bayonets in corpulent John Bull, and shortly before Christmas a small band of members from Detroit had crossed to Malden and senselessly attacked a group of Canadians there. The Fenians had offered to patrol the borders, ostensibly to prevent invasions from Canada West, but Lincoln wisely had turned their suggestion down. Early in January a Fenian convention met in Chicago to plan their campaign against British North America, and the delegates declared themselves willing to avenge the North for the Confederate raids by carrying on guerilla warfare along the frontier, subjecting the Canadas to the same fear of incendiarism as that to which the North had been subjected by "Canadian-harbored" Southerners. For some time the British Consul General in New York City had been obtaining information on Fenian movements through a paid informant, and in Albany he had been able to obtain a set of the organization's newspaper, *The Fenian Spirit*. Most ominous of all, it was learned that General Dix had been present at a pro-Fenian meeting. That the Fenians would invade the Canadas at the earliest opportunity following their mustering-out from the Northern army seemed likely.[50]

On December 17 Macdonald drew up a memorandum based in part upon Consul General Archibald's reports and in part on what he could piece together from his own informants. The mayor of Ottawa had warned that the Fenians were preparing for a possible attack

p. 141; *The Times,* April 6, 1865; John Rutherford, *The Secret History of the Fenian Conspiracy* (London, 1877), I, 59; Burkholder, *Hamilton,* p. 147; J. G. Harkness, *Stormont, Dundas, and Glengarry* (Oshawa, 1946), p. 231.

[50] New York *Herald,* Dec. 19, 1864; Chicago *Tribune,* Dec. 22, 29, 1864, Jan. 12, 26, 1865; Toronto *Globe,* Jan. 4, 1865; Barrie *Northern Advance,* Nov. 30, 1864; FO 5, 1014: Burnley to Russell, secret, Feb. 7, 1865; *ibid.,* 1013: Burnley to Archibald, secret, enc. in Burnley to Russell, both Jan. 16, 1864; *ibid.,* 962: Lyons to Russell, secret, Nov. 1, 1864, Archibald to Burnley, secret, Oct. 27, 1864; CFA, 88: Adams to Seward, Dec. 16, 1864; *The Fenian Raid at Fort Erie* (Toronto, 1866), p. 14.

in mid-January, since they had a rumored sixty thousand armed men available who already were out of the army, and from New Jersey had come word that the Fenians would invade the Canadas on January 15. In Buffalo a Roman Catholic servant had been heard to declare that the Protestants "should not be so stiff for they would soon be begging their lives of their servant girls." A check on a rumor that Confederates were drilling in Prince Edward County, Canada West, had revealed a company of armed Fenians instead. The Chief of Police of Toronto had reported that the Fenians had three thousand pikes hidden in that city. The extent and nature of Macdonald's memorandum indicate that he was taking the Fenian movement seriously. And it was on the basis of this memorandum that Macdonald prepared instructions for McMicken.[51]

The first paragraph of the instructions was devoted to the Confederates, but the second and longer paragraph enjoined McMicken to watch in particular for Fenian activities. In this manner Macdonald had accomplished two purposes: He had convinced the North that he earnestly was seeking out Confederates with an energetic police force, and he quietly had set out to block the potential Fenian threat. Gilbert McMicken's special body of twelve agents continued to guard the border region well into the summer, long after Confederate raids had stopped, by which time the death of President Lincoln had altered relations between the provinces and the United States sufficiently to provide a brief respite from Fenian scares as well. While considerably reduced, the force was not completely disbanded. It was called into action again late in 1865 when the Fenian threat reappeared.

By the end of the first week of January McMicken had his agents distributed throughout the peninsula of Canada West and could collate their reports on "Rebbles" and "Hibernians." Apparently he originally intended to employ two dozen men, a number of whom were to be recommended by the mayors of Detroit and Buffalo, but there is no evidence that this was done, although both cities cooperated with the magistrate. McMicken conferred with the mayor of Detroit over the danger that Confederates might attempt to use air guns to hurl Greek fire at the city from some point on the frozen Detroit River; the possibility of a raid on Lexington, Michigan, was unearthed; Fenian meetings were discovered in Thorold; and unlawful drilling was detected at

---

[51] Macdonald Papers, 56: "Memorandum in re. Fenians, 1864," Dec. 17, 1864, with W. A. Alger to Macdonald, Dec. 11, Philip Low to Macdonald, Dec. 10, and Prince and Cockburn to Macdonald, both Dec. 20, 1864, 57–78.

Maidstone. It was reported that three hundred Yankees meant to raid Kingston, free the men in the penitentiary there, and attack the town, and although no such raid materialized, twelve extra guards were stationed at the penitentiary at the warden's request. McMicken's agents kept an eye on iron works capable of manufacturing guns or chemical plants where Greek fire might be made, checked on suspicious vessels at the docks, watched the incoming trains, attempted to apprehend recruiting agents and crimps, and traced some of the stolen St. Albans bank money, in addition to watching those who spoke with a Southern drawl or with an Irish brogue.[52]

In the meantime, the Canadian authorities had set about repairing the damage to their status as a neutral. After lengthy debate the Executive Council recommended that the Canadian Government should assume liability to the sum of fifty thousand dollars for the money that the Bank of Ontario had returned to the raiders, and Monck submitted an appropriation request to Parliament. The Governor General began to prepare a case against one of the Confederate commissioners for violation of the British neutrality act, and when some of Clay's revealing correspondence was intercepted, it seemed evident that the Crown held a strong position against the five re-captured raiders if they were not extradited on one of the original counts against them. The Canadian telegraph lines even volunteered to accept orders from the American government to communicate Confederate telegrams directly to Washington, but Seward wisely rejected this offer as "incompatible with the self respect of the U.S."[53]

Lincoln promulgated a new passport order on December 17. He stipulated that no one was to enter the United States from any foreign territory after that date without a passport. In the Canadas his ex-

[52] *Ibid.*, 234: E. P. Dorr to McMicken, Dec. 28, 1864, 36–37, McMicken to Macdonald, Dec. 20, 22, 29, 1864, Jan. 7, Feb. 11, 1865, 11–13, 15–17, 30–32, 137–143, 473–475, and Charles Clarke to McMicken, n.d., 63–65; *ibid.*, 233: McMicken to Macdonald, Jan. 14, 16, 1865, 212–214, 228–230, James Redfern to McMicken, Jan. 6, 1865, 4, Samuel Allan to McMicken, Feb. 2, 24, 1865, 26, 38, A. D. Fraser to McMicken, Feb. 18, 1865, 34, William Black to McMicken, Jan. 4, 18, 1865, 3, 16; *ibid.*, 510: Letter Book no. 7, Macdonald to McMicken, Feb. 15, 1865, 325–327; C 699: Anon. to Creighton, Jan. 8, 1865, 91–94, and A. Burrows to Rollo, Feb. 21, 1865, 97–98; E 1, 90AB: March 6, June 30, 1865, 145–146, 470–472.

[53] Seward Papers: Rose to Ashmun, Jan. 24, 1865, Potter to Seward, Jan. 25, 1865, and Burnley to Seward, Dec. 29, 1864; NFBL, 74: Burnley to Seward, Dec. 30, 1864; *ibid.*, 76: Burnley to Seward, March 2, 1865; CD, Montreal, VI: Emmons to Thurston, Dec. 19, enc. in Thurston to Seward, Dec. 23, and Dec. 21, 24, 1864; Macdonald Papers, 56: J. H. Cameron to Macdonald, Dec. 14, 1864, 17a–b.

tension of the area of passport control west of the Maritimes was viewed solely as additional retaliation for Coursol's misguided decision, coming as it did a day after the Executive Council had taken action to augment Canada's border patrol. Already the Rush-Bagot agreement was expiring and the reciprocity treaty was under heavy fire. Seward, who had advised Lincoln to issue the order, either thought that the danger of further raids from the Canadas was serious or at least wanted to convince the Canadian authorities that he thought so. In explaining the order to Charles Francis Adams, he wrote, "a crisis has been reached . . . [for our] treasure is not safe in [our] mouths, and [our] sleep is disturbed by well-founded apprehensions of midnight fire, robbery, and murderous aggressions from the British border premises." [54]

A passport system applied to the Canadian-American frontier could never be anything but a means for showing displeasure, for it manifestly was ineffective. The Toronto *Globe* pointed out that the system would not hinder the activities of potential raiders and recommended that the provinces retaliate with a passport system of their own, while the Toronto *Leader* considered the order to be a "vindictive expedient." The Detroit press also opposed the passport system, for it created difficulties for hundreds of Canadians who resided in Windsor and worked in Detroit, and it also interfered with many trade ties that Detroit enjoyed. The *Free Press* argued, correctly, that the border was too long, the nature of water traffic on the Great Lakes too complicated and too abundant, and the people of the two areas too interrelated, for a passport system to have any beneficial effect. The Detroit newspapers agreed with the Canadian press: that Seward was motivated by a desire to retaliate.[55]

That the passport order caused discomfiture is plain, but it also brought results of a kind. Complaints ranged from the specious, that the order was holding up an international curling match at Buffalo, or that it was creating havoc with attendance at a private girls' school in Detroit, to the serious, that it was destroying the cooler feeling toward the South that the St. Albans raid had provoked, that it was limiting immigration, or that the passport agents abused their power to line their own pockets. But it was at this time that Lord Russell re-

[54] GBI, 19: Seward to Adams, Dec. 27, 1864, 549–554; *Foreign Relations, 1864,* p. 54; *Hansard's, 1865:* CLXXVII, cols. 660–661.
[55] *Globe,* Dec. 20, 1864, Jan. 7, 1865; *Leader,* Jan. 5, 6, 1865; *Free Press,* Dec. 23, 1864, Jan. 4, 5, 10, 11, 18, 1865; Cleveland *Leader,* Jan. 9, 1865.

marked, after expressing his regret that passports were introduced, that "if the effect should be to check the Canadian tendency to favor the insurgents, there would be little harm in that." Adams felt this was the closest to an expression in favor of the North that Russell had come.[56]

Seward's own informants told him that passports were harmful. Alfred Russell wrote from Detroit that Coursol's decision had caused a "revolution" in Canadian thought and that the passport order should be rescinded, and the mayor of Buffalo agreed. Seeing their traffic with the United States threatened, both the Great Western and the Grand Trunk railroads put their own men on guard at border points, and Thomas Swinyard, manager of the Great Western, sent his personal agent to confer with Seward. For Macdonald, Swinyard estimated that the Grand Trunk Railway would lose eighty thousand dollars a month because of the order, and a number of men had to be laid off from both lines. Macdonald gave Swinyard little encouragement, said that Canada could not go on its knees to Washington, and advised assuming an indifferent tone so that the Western states, which transported goods from Buffalo across Canada West, could bring pressure to bear on Seward.[57]

Aware that a passport system would have little effect on Confederate activities in the provinces, Seward had a more positive goal in mind than mere retaliation. Eager to see the Canadian government pass a rigorous neutrality act, he used the passport as a means of helping

---

[56] CFA, Diary: Jan. 28, 1865; MC: E. G. Spaulding to Seward, Dec. 30, 1864, A. Russell to Seward, Jan. 9, 1865, Emmons to Seward, Jan. 27, 1865, Smith to Seward, Feb. 9, 1865; Seward Papers: Ross to Seward, Jan. 12, 1865, William Cornell to Seward, Jan. 25, 1865; Macdonald Papers, 233: W. Blick to McMicken, Jan. 2, 1865, 1, and A. Fraser to McMicken, Jan. 4, 1865, 2; CD, Montreal, VI: Thurston to Seward, Dec. 29, 1864, and Potter to Seward, Jan. 14, 1865; BMW to GCC, 13: Burnley to Monck, Feb. 21, 1865; Toronto *Globe*, Feb. 25, 1865.

[57] MC: A. Russell to Seward, and W. A. Howard to Seward, both Dec. 21, and W. G. Fargo and Edward Beach to Seward, both Dec. 31, 1864; Macdonald Papers, 510: Macdonald to Brydges, Jan. 1, 1865, 187–190, and Macdonald to Swinyard, Jan. 1, 1864 [*sic* for 1865], 174–177; *ibid.*, Fenians, 1: Swinyard to Macdonald, Dec. 31, 1864; G 8B, 45: Cardwell to Gordon, April 7, 1865, 664–680; FO 5, 1013: Burnley to Russell, Jan. 20, 1865; NFBL, 74: Burnley to Seward, Jan. 20, 1865; NBL, 13: Seward to Burnley, Jan. 25, 1865, 46–47; Seward Papers: J. H. Whiteside to Seward, Jan. 28, 1865, and St. Germain to Seward, March 15, 1865; CD, Toronto, 1: Thurston to Seward, March 31, 1865; John Sandfield Macdonald Papers, II: Ogden to Macdonald, Jan. 27, 1865, 1067–1068; Galt Papers, 1: Fessenden to Galt, Dec. 31, 1864, 925–928.

Monck to apply pressure on reluctant colonial authorities. Late in December Adams again conferred with Lord Russell on the question of the Canadian neutrality act, and the Foreign Secretary told him that the home government had recommended that Canada should pass a stronger act. Adams therefore chose to exercise his discretion not to convey to Russell Seward's statement that "a crisis" had been reached. Early in January Burnley informed Seward of the steps taken by both the imperial and colonial governments to rectify the border situation.[58]

Acting upon Cardwell's permission, Monck convened the Canadian Parliament on January 19, nearly a month earlier than it was scheduled to meet, and presented his request for augmented powers. The following day Seward wrote Adams that the North would refrain from retaliation "at present" and gave a copy of his note to Burnley, who had been acting in Lyons' place since the latter sailed for England early in December, with the apparent expectation that the message would be sent to Monck. With Macdonald leading the way the "frontier outrages bill" passed its second reading on February 1 by a vote of 104 to 4. On February 6 the new law was promulgated, Monck forcing his brother's horse, "Bill Seward," through heavy snow drifts in order to give the act his official approval at the earliest possible moment. The Alien Act, as it ultimately was called, provided for expulsion from the united Canadas of any foreign nationals suspected of engaging in hostile acts against any friendly nation, for a three thousand dollar fine against such aliens, and for the seizure of arms or vessels intended for use by such foreigners. The act was to remain in force for one year. Canadian opinion appeared to support the bill, although the conservative press felt that it was the result of American dictation and demanded similar legislation at Washington with respect to Fenian activities.[59]

Seward acknowledged that the Federal government was pleased with the Alien Act, but the passport system remained in effect for another month. It now could be used for a second purpose: upon advice

[58] CFA, 78: Adams to Seward, Dec. 30, 1864, Jan. 5, 1865; GBI, 20: Seward to Adams, Jan. 26, 1865, 26–27; NFBL, 75: Burnley to Seward, Jan. 3, 1865.

[59] G 8B, 45: Cardwell to Gordon, Jan. 21, 1865, 617–631; G 1, 173: Cardwell to Monck, Jan. 7, 1865, 11–16; G 10, 1: Seward to Adams, Jan. 20, enc. in Burnley to Monck, Jan. 22, 1865, 47–51; MC: Ross to Ashmun, Jan. 23, Feb. 1, and Emmons to Seward, Feb. 1, 1865; Sumner Papers: Emmons to Sumner, Feb. 2, 1865; Seward Papers: McDougall to Seward, Feb. 6, 1865; Detroit *Free Press*, Jan. 24, 1865; Toronto *Leader*, Feb. 1, 1865; Toronto *Globe*, Jan. 27, 1865; Canada, Legis. Assembly, *Journal, 1865*, XXIV: 8, 31, 54, 63, 67, 77; Canada, Legis. Council, *Journal, 1865*, p. 76; *Statutes of the Province of Canada*, 8th Parl., 3rd Sess., 1–9.

from Thurlow Weed, Seward let it be known that he would have the order rescinded when the Canadian Parliament had appropriated, as the Executive Council had recommended, fifty thousand dollars for the St. Albans banks. At Lincoln's second inauguration on March 4, Seward took Burnley aside and promised that once the money was paid the passport system would be abolished. After short but heated debate, and despite a public meeting of protest in Toronto, the required sum was added to the province's supplementary estimate, and although actual payment had not been completed, the passport system was removed insofar as it applied to the Canadas on March 8. On the following day Seward also withdrew the notice concerning armaments on the Great Lakes and stated that the Rush-Bagot agreement should remain in force. Canadians and Americans mingled happily on the Suspension Bridge and the Great Western Railroad promptly added two extra through trains. In September the Canadian authorities paid to the St. Albans banks $30,010 in bank notes and $39,512.75 in gold, since the bankers of St. Albans argued that Canadian bank notes were not on par with American notes. No restitution was made for the stolen money which had not passed through Lamothe's hands.[60]

The old passport order remained in effect for the rest of British North America, however, and Lieutenant Governor Gordon in New Brunswick complained of this. The Colonial Secretary instructed the imperial administrators of the Maritime Provinces to employ every possible means to prevent the maturing of Confederate plans within their jurisdiction, and he recommended to Gordon that New Brunswick should pass a law similar to the Alien Act if he wished to win removal of the passport order. Cardwell added that if public opinion in the province was opposed to such an act, the people of the province must expect unfriendliness and suspicion to be shown by the United States. Gordon felt that a bill could not be obtained from the legislature, but he attempted to show Washington that at least the imperial administration in the province was not sympathetic to the St. Albans raiders by letting it be known once again that he was willing to issue

⁶⁰ ITC, 38: Seward to Potter, Feb. 9, 1865, 565; Seward Papers: Weed to Seward, March 4, 1865; G 13, 2: Burnley to Monck, in cipher, March 4, 1865; Baring Papers: Ward to Baring, Feb. 7, 14, 1865; E, AB: April 4, 1865, 247–251; Macdonald Papers, 56: E. H. King to Macdonald, Dec. 27, 1872, 48a–f; G 1, 173: Burnley to Russell, March 9, 1865, 308; Montreal *Transcript*, Feb. 8, 1865; Denison Papers: Scrapbook, clipping from *The Pick* of Montreal; Quebec *Gazette*, Feb. 8, 1865; *The Times*, March 6, 1865.

warrants for their extradition if they were apprehended within his jurisdiction.[61]

Nova Scotia also expressed annoyance, especially when consul Jackson refused passports to Alexander Keith and to a member of Wier's company because of their known pro-Southern sympathies. However, when the administrator of Nova Scotia approached his Executive Council for the same powers that had been given to Monck for the Canadas, he was told that there was no real need for such powers and was advised that it would be best if the province did not draw attention to popular sentiment by holding a public debate. Late in May Prince Edward Island still was complaining that the passport system was "confusing, objectionable, and anomalous." It was not until June 2 that the passport order finally was revoked for the Maritime Provinces, and extralegal arresting of Confederates residing in New Brunswick who attempted to cross the frontier even continued under the order for a short period thereafter.[62]

Four days following Monck's promulgation of the Alien Act, the examination of the recaptured St. Albans raiders was resumed in Montreal, this time on the single charge of robbery. In January the proceedings, which had been instituted late in December, had been suspended so that messengers again might go to Richmond to obtain a copy of Bennett Young's commission. One of the messengers was drowned while crossing the ice on the Potomac River and a second messenger was captured, but a former chaplain from Morgan's cavalry succeeded in returning with a series of formal and rather unprecise commissions. It is probable that these were drawn up for the occasion, for there seems to be abundant evidence that Young never was issued any formal written orders of the type needed. However, on the basis of the commissions, and possibly because of the execution of John Y. Beall in February, which was accompanied by loud cries that the same fate awaited the Confederate raiders if they were extradited, the judge quashed the charge of robbery in March on grounds that made it clear that each subsequent charge also would be dismissed.

[61] G 8D, 299: Cardwell to Dundas, Feb. 4, 1865, 26; G 8B, 45: Cardwell to Gordon, May 19, 1865, 682–684; NBL, 13: Seward to Bruce, Sept. 19, 1865, 417–418; Sumner Papers, cxxxix: Gordon to Sumner, April 12, 1865.
[62] Seward Papers: Burnley to Seward, March 22, 1865; NBL, 13: Seward to Burnley, Feb. 27, 1865, 132; NFBL, 75: Gordon to Burnley, Jan. 7, 21, enc. in Burnley to Seward, Jan. 31, 1865; GBI, 20: Seward to Adams, Jan. 16, 1865, 15–19; G 8B, 46: Bruce to Gordon, June 3, 1865, 301–302; CD, Halifax, xi: Jackson to Seward, March 13, 1865; CD, Charlottetown, ii: Sherman to Seward, May 22, 1865.

Upon instructions from Washington the prosecution therefore withdrew the remaining charges so that the raiders could be prosecuted
for violating Canadian neutrality.[63]

The imperial authorities did not permit the St. Albans raiders to go
free. Sometime earlier Cardwell had suggested to Monck that the
Southerners might be charged with a breach of Her Majesty's neutrality act, and if they were found guilty the North still would have
the satisfaction of seeing the raiders punished. Seward had been forwarding copies of intercepted Confederate correspondence to Russell
and Monck, and the latter saw that if proof of the writers' identities
could be established, they too could be charged with violating Canadian
laws. The writers were Thompson and Clay, and Monck could strike
at the source of the Confederate activities by arresting the two commissioners. Seward provided depositions, signed by two Southerners
who had been captured in Chicago in connection with a plot to free
Confederate prisoners at Camp Douglas, which showed a *prima facie*
case against the commissioners. The Governor General asked if Seward
would send his informants to Quebec where they might help the
government institute proceedings against the writers of the letters, and
the Secretary of State replied that he could not do so because the
informants' names had to be kept confidential. Thus Monck was unable to proceed against the instigator of the St. Albans raid, Clement
Clay. However, it seemed apparent that at least some of the raiders
had violated the neutrality law, and therefore a new warrant was enforced against them on the day of their dismissal.[64]

[63] MC: Devlin to Seward, Feb. 8, 1865; FO 115, 437: Burnley to Russell, Feb. 24,
1865; Benjamin, pp. 178–191; Univ. North Carolina, Edwin G. Lee Diary (microfilm): March 24, 29, 31, April 5, 1865; CD, Montreal, vi: Devlin to Seward, March
28, 1865, and Potter to Seward, March 29, 30, 1865; Montreal *Witness*, March 4,
April 1, 1865; Montreal *Telegraph*, Feb. 15, 1865; *The Times*, March 3, 13, 1865;
Toronto *Leader*, March 31, April 1, 1865; New York *Tribune*, quoted in Toronto
Globe, April 3, 1865. The British Parliament continued to labor under a surprising
lack of information concerning American affairs, as may be seen in the excitement
shown by Lord Robert Cecil and George M. W. Peacocke in the Lords and
Commons, respectively, over the news of Beall's execution. Thinking that Beall
had been extradited from Canada West, they were in high dudgeon over the
supposed Northern violation of British courtesy, until they were informed that
Beall had been captured quite legally in New York state (*The Times*, March 15,
1865; *Hansard's, 1865:* CLXXVII, col. 1536).

[64] G 11, 234: Monck to Burnley, Dec. 27, 1864; BMW to GCC, 180A: Seward
to Burnley, Dec. 30, enc. in Burnley to Monck, Dec. 31, 1864; *ibid.*, 180B: Monck
to Burnley, Jan. 6, 1865.

The St. Albans raiders were taken from Montreal to Toronto, where a preliminary examination was held on the new charge, and Young was committed for trial. The Alien Act that had been passed in February did not apply to his case, and it generally was assumed that Young would escape under the less strenuous neutrality law that was in effect at the time of the raid. Nonetheless, the news of Young's committal was greeted by the Confederates in Montreal and Toronto with expressions of outrage. Again, mobs milled about in both cities, singing Confederate songs, and the Toronto *Leader* excitedly urged "the people" to prevent such a travesty of justice. But in England *The Times* showed how sentiment had changed by asking for the raider's conviction. In October the Kentuckian finally was discharged because of imperfect evidence. In 1872 the claims commission established under the Treaty of Washington disallowed American demands against Great Britain on behalf of the citizens of St. Albans, and the United States, to Canadian surprise, did not continue to press its claims.[65]

In the years that followed, the St. Albans raid grew in magnitude until some reports had expanded the affair into an attack upon five banks, the taking of three hundred prisoners, and the imaginative notion that twenty-five thousand men were hunting for the raiders on the night following the incident. In 1911 a reunion was held in Montreal between Bennett Young and four residents of St. Albans after an attempted reunion in 1909 at the village itself had been rebuffed by members of the Grand Army of the Republic. Five aging minds added to the general confusion over the event by remembering it rather differently than the way in which it actually happened. At this time Young, who remained convinced that the raid was of material benefit to the Confederacy, said that he delivered all of the money taken from the St. Albans banks to the Confederate government at Richmond, but there is no documentary evidence that he did so, and it is extremely unlikely since Lamothe and others spent much of it. In 1915 Young visited Colonel George T. Denison at his Toronto

[65] CD, Toronto, I: Thurston to Seward, April 10, 28, 1865; CD, Montreal, VI: Potter to Seward, April 13, 1865; *ibid.*, VIII: Potter to Seward, Oct. 29, Nov. 13, 1865; G 9, 465: Monck to Cardwell, April 21, May 19, 1865, and Michael to Cardwell, Oct. 27, 1865; Macdonald Papers, 234: McMicken to Macdonald, Feb. 11, March 15, 1865, 473-475, 784; *ibid.*, Fenians, I: Monck to Macdonald, April 4, 1865, 48; FO 5, 948: Lyons to Russell, April 18, 1865; Montreal *Gazette*, April 13, 1865; Toronto *Leader*, April 1, 14, May 5, 1865; Montreal *Transcript*, April 11, 1865; *The Times*, April 14, June 4, 1865; "Regina vs. Bennet [*sic*] Young et al.," *Lower Canada Jurist*, IX (1866), 29-52.

home to extend his personal thanks for Denison's moral support during the preliminary examination, and the following year Denison was a guest of honor at a reunion of Confederate veterans in Birmingham, Alabama, where he received a standing ovation.[66]

Clearly the St. Albans raid did not benefit the Confederacy as Young hoped and continued to insist until his death. The raiders turned many formerly pro-Southern Canadians against the South. A noticeable shift in public opinion coincided with a noticeable shift in official attitude. To offset the feeling in the North that, as one of Seward's friends expressed it, the raid had been "purely Canadian— that it was a missile hurled from Canada . . . ," the united province had passed a stringent neutrality act that practically ended further Confederate activities there, had made restitution for some of the stolen bank money, had acted with considerable vigor in the *Georgian* incident, and had instituted a series of border patrols. Abroad, the raid so angered Lord Russell that he let James Mason know of his displeasure, and both Russell and Palmerston clearly disapproved of the Confederacy's policy in the provinces, thus helping bring to an end the Confederate commission in British North America. When Adams showed Russell one of Clay's intercepted dispatches, which revealed how the Kentuckian had authorized the raid, Russell declared that if Judah Benjamin lent support to Clay's argument the Confederate Secretary of State would be acknowledging that the South deliberately was violating neutral territory and was guilty of "a high misdemeanor." [67]

That the St. Albans affair did not become the full-scale crisis that Burnley feared was due to several factors. Seward clearly did not want

[66] Montreal *Gazette*, July 29, 1911; Mrs. A. Woodburn Langmuir to writer, Feb. 22, March 3, 1958; Birmingham *News*, May 18, 1916 (photostat). As Young reminisced about the raid he assumed the responsibility for the shooting of the three casualties. Conflicting reports on the circumstances of the copperhead's death added to the confusion. At the 1958 anniversary observance of the raid, George P. Anderson, a former newspaperman and lawyer, then 85, entertained a substantial St. Albans audience by telling of an interview that he had with Young in Boston in 1908 (elsewhere reported as 1909). At this meeting Young concluded that the Greek fire failed to ignite because it was prepared by a pro-Northern Canadian. This is certainly rationalization after the fact, and there is no evidence to support such a view. See Burlington (Vt.) *Free Press*, Oct. 20, 1958; St. Albans *Sunday News*, Sept. 22, 1957.

[67] MC: George Edmunds to Seward, Jan. 28, 1865; *The Times*, Jan. 12, March 6, 1865; L.C., James Mason Papers, Dispatch Book: Russell to Mason, Feb. 13, and Mason to Russell, Feb. 28, 1865; CFA, Diary: Dec. 28, 1864.

war, for he saw that it was precisely for such an outcome that the Confederacy hoped. The outward appearance of crisis—tension that he, in reality, could control—was what the Secretary wanted, so that he might bring pressure to bear to achieve his purpose, the new Canadian neutrality law. In 1861–1862 during the *Trent* affair Seward had not been in control of the situation but had thought that he was; now, in 1864, he commanded the situation, he knew it, and he knew what to do about it. Fortunately the end of autumn was too late for an invasion of the Canadas and therefore even those who mistakenly favored active rather than apparent retaliation realized that they would have to wait until spring. Prompt action taken by the Canadians in October to apprehend the raiders helped smooth over the early weeks of the incipient crisis, and when Coursol freed Young and his men in December the colonial and imperial authorities at last responded with the measures that Seward had wanted from the outset. Monck's quick action in every case that was presented to him in the winter of 1864–1865, combined with evidence of considerable activity—even if it were undefined or misunderstood activity—on the part of McMicken and Ermatinger, undoubtedly did much to mollify the North. Then, too, the major battles raging in the South during the height of the St. Albans affair kept popular attention from the skirmish in Vermont. The day Coursol released the raiders, Confederate General J. B. Hood was ready to clash with General George H. Thomas at Nashville and Sherman was at Savannah. And the Northern, English, and provincial presses that had spilled forth belligerent crys for war in 1861–1862 during the height of the *Trent* affair remained comparatively quiet, awed perhaps by the long months of war already fought in North America and unwilling to add to the months that clearly remained by indulging in low campaigns of villification.

Seward extracted from the St. Albans affair a diplomatic victory for the North, one of the few real ones gained on the British North American frontier, by using Canadian apprehensions to force the united province to strengthen her neutrality law. This law effectively ended any further Confederate efforts to embroil Great Britain in the American war through her colonies. In turn, the Canadian officials, through their display of activity along the border and by their swift action against Coursol and Lamothe, succeeded in turning much of the Northern anger against the two individuals rather than against the provinces.

The St. Albans raid had other more far-reaching and less tangible results. It was thought to be in retaliation against the Canadas that Congress abrogated the reciprocity treaty of 1854. Insofar as the North wished to end reciprocity the raid furnished an opportunity, striking a blow at what many considered óne of Canada's most needed assets. And the affair played a role of some importance in the Canadian confederation movement, coming as it did in the midst of deliberations on forming a regional or continental union, federal or legislative. Voluntary British North American confederation was thought by some to be racing against forceful annexationism in the North. When Lady Monck asked her brother-in-law whether there was going to be a war with the United States, he refused to answer her. With womanly and perhaps misplaced intuition she wrote in her diary, "They hope it won't come till summer is over." Four years of tension already were nearing their resolution. It is to that resolution that we now must turn.

fifteen 𝕡𝕠 DAYS OF DECISION:

CONFEDERATION, RECIPROCITY,

AND DEFENSE

> "Our American cousins of the North having had their
> waiting, whining and scolding time, have now come
> to the crowing, swelling, and bullying time."
>
> QUEBEC *Gazette, April 7, 1865*

THE FIRST FOUR MONTHS OF 1865 WERE DECISIVE ONES IN THE HISTORY
of North America. Between January and March the Canadian Parliament met to consider among other things the desirability of confederation and the means of protecting the Canadas from the dangers of the
"American menace." In April a delegation left for London to discuss
the entire question of maintaining the British connection. In the
troubled nation to the south the same months witnessed the collapse of
the Confederacy, the abrogation of America's first attempt at reciprocal
trade, and the death of a revered leader. In these four months one
nation—the Confederacy—died and two were born.

Canadian historians have focused an intensive scholarship upon the
confederation period and especially upon the several months between
June, 1864, when a coalition government dedicated to the establishment
of a federal union of the provinces took office in the Canadas, and July,
1867, when the British North America Act, which signified the creation
of that union, became effective. While much still can be done for this
period, especially at the local level, the scholarly deluge has been of a
high order, and the present writer can hope to add little of value to
the history of the confederation movement.

Yet if the position of British North America vis-à-vis the United States during the period of the Civil War is to be understood, the confederation movement also must be viewed in the light of that war. A narrow interpretation of confederation, based upon Goldwin Smith's famous explanation that the movement arose out of a need to resolve the political deadlock that gripped the united Canadas in the spring of 1864, has given way to an international interpretation that includes among the causal factors to which confederation may be attributed British fears of potential American annexationism, especially in the West, and the felt need for some form of alliance as a protective measure against the possibility of an American invasion in the East. Canadian scholars generally recognize that the American Civil War had a profound influence upon the provinces by helping to promote confederation, and that while some Canadian leaders did not actually expect a Northern invasion, they were quite willing to use the fear entertained by their colleagues to promote union.

The war also helped shape the potential Dominion's constitution, for John A. Macdonald and the rest of the Fathers of Confederation insisted that the conflict in the United States demonstrated that federations of the American variety were divisive and that the new nation should have a stronger central government, one built upon British parliamentary principles. As one Canadian historian has expressed it, Anglo-American relations on the Canadian border helped supply "the temperature and the pressure" to bring the "reagents at last into re-action," while events south of the border helped determine the nature of that reaction. The invasion that never came, whether as a potential reality or as a "bogey" used for internal propaganda purposes, played an important role in shaping the Canadian nation.[1]

[1] Chester Martin, "British Policy in Canadian Confederation," *CHR*, XIII (March, 1932), 19. Among the many discussions of confederation, the writer found the following most useful in preparing the summary that follows: A. R. M. Lower, *et al., Evolving Canadian Federalism* (Durham, 1958); D. G. Creighton, *British North America at Confederation* (Ottawa, 1939), and "The United States and Canadian Confederation," *CHR*, XXXIX (Sept., 1958), 209–222; Fred Landon, "The American Civil War and Canadian Confederation," Royal Soc. of Can., *Transactions*, 3rd ser., XXI (1927), 55–62; W. B. Munro, *American Influences on Canadian Government* (Toronto, 1929); H. A. Smith, *Federalism in North America: A Comparative Study of Institutions in The United States and Canada* (Boston, 1923); Chester Martin, *Foundations of Canadian Nationhood* (Toronto, 1955), pp. 275–404; Edgar McInnis, "Two North American Federations: A Comparison," in Flenley, ed., *Essays in Canadian History*, pp. 97–103; M. A. Pope, "Confederation: Defence or Deadlock?," *Canadian Defence Quarterly*, XV (April, 1938),

It was during the interval of Coursol's suspension of his examination of the St. Albans raiders that the Colonial Secretary, Cardwell, indicated his conversion to support for the British North American confederation movement. On September 1, 1864, a delegation from the Maritime Provinces had assembled at Charlottetown for a conference on maritime union, a regional union based on a legislative rather than a federative plan. The atmosphere at the conference had been leisurely, with the people of Prince Edward Island far more interested in a local circus than in the meetings. Delegates from the Canadas had been present only on the sufferance of the Maritime men who had permitted them to present their counterproposal in an unofficial capacity. The Maritimers jokingly had referred to the ship in which the Canadians had arrived as a "Confederate cruiser," for they well knew, and some bitterly resented, the fact that the Canadians hoped to capture the Maritime Provinces in a broader federal union that the Canadas ultimately would dominate. Earlier Cardwell's predecessor, Newcastle, had pointed out to Monck that colonial and imperial ob-

---

274–281; G. F. G. Stanley, "Act or Pact? Another Look at Confederation," *C.H.A.*, *Annual Report* (1956), pp. 1–25; Reginald G. Trotter, "Why Confederation Came," *Queen's Quart.*, XLV (Spring, 1938), 22–28, and "Canada as a Factor in Anglo-American Relations in the 1860's," *CHR*, XVI (March, 1935), 19–26. Brebner, *North Atlantic Triangle*, p. 169, says that fear of the United States was "the principal cause of the germinal federation."

However, some recent students of Canadian government have relegated the war to a highly secondary position as a causal factor in confederation: H. McD. Clokie, *Canadian Government and Politics* (Toronto, 1944), pp. 26–27; Kenneth McNaught, "American-Canadian Relations," *India Quarterly*, XII (Sept., 1956), 282–290; and D. F. Hill, "Rise of Canadian Nationality," p. 217. It is interesting that in the same year that doctoral-candidate-in-history Hill found that fear of the United States was not important to confederation, a doctoral candidate in political science at the same institution concluded that confederation largely was the product of such fear: F. B. Sheeran, "Federalism in the United States, Canada, and Australia, with Particular Reference to Selected Institutional and Functional Aspects," unpubl. Ph.D. diss. (Univ. of Southern California, 1956), both summarized in U.S.C., *Abstracts of Dissertations* (Los Angeles, 1956), pp. 154–157, 177–180. However, Mr. J. R. Turnbull, who is writing an M.A. thesis at the University of Toronto on "grass roots" public opinion in Canada West concerning confederation, on the basis of an examination of the local press of eighteen communities, has concluded that defense against the North was "a catalyst and the sole factor present to all protagonists . . ." (Turnbull to writer, Dec. 1, 12, 30, 31, 1957). The present writer would agree with the last analysis. Toupin ("*Le Canadien* and Confederation," p. 107) says that the defense question was "the foremost topic of public discussion during the spring of 1865."

jections to confederation as a political move did not prevent a temporary union for defensive purposes. But the Canadians repeatedly asserted that the only effective means of preventing piecemeal absorption by the United States was a permanent confederation.[2]

The perambulating intercolonial meeting moved on to Halifax and eventually reassembled in Quebec in October. The plenary conference adjourned on October 29, in the midst of an angry fusillade of invective from across the border because of the St. Albans raid, and the future for confederation still did not look promising, partially because the Colonial Office continued to withhold its full approval. But during the critical early days of November Great Britain shifted her position. Monck had warned Cardwell again and again of the possibility of an attack from the United States, and in the light of the impending termination of the Rush-Bagot agreement and of Dix's then unrevoked order, together with the passport requirements and Congressional attacks on the reciprocity treaty, Monck advised that confederation was the safest means of forestalling war or the absorption of the colonies. The Governor General felt that no fundamental change in policy was involved—only a change in the implementation of established policy—since Britain clearly wanted the provinces increasingly to become able to stand on their own feet. On December 3 Cardwell wrote to Monck, approving a broader plan for federation in place of the plan for regional union. Significantly, as we have seen, it was in this same dispatch that the Colonial Secretary advised Monck to consult his legal advisers on the latent powers of his office for suppressing border raids.

The confederation movement by no means met with Maritime approval. The Maritimers feared American invasion less than the seasonally landlocked Canadians did, and they suspected that confederation would mean absorption in an expanded Canada. In Nova Scotia Joseph Howe dubbed the plan the "Botheration Scheme" and set out to defeat it. Maritimers also knew that George Brown, that representative of Canadian expansionism, had sailed for London on November 16 to discuss the wider union, and they thought that it was he who had persuaded Cardwell to change his mind. Brown had not done so directly or on that occasion, for Cardwell wrote his dispatch to Monck three days before Brown talked with him, but certainly Brown, Macdonald, Galt, and the Governor General himself had influenced the

[2] Macdonald Papers, 228: Bishop J. J. Lynch to Macdonald, Dec. 13, 1864, 3–6; *Imperial Blue Books on Affairs Relating to Canada*, xix, 42: Newcastle to Monck, Aug. 21, 1862.

Colonial Secretary, and many suspected that they had exaggerated the admittedly tense border situation to him. As Howe wrote to Lord Russell, Nova Scotians had little to fear from the United States, but Canadians did, and perhaps deservedly so.[3]

But between October 29, when the intercolonial Quebec Conference adjourned, and January 19, when Monck called the Canadian Parliament to order, the events connected with the aftermath of the St. Albans raid, together with the imminent collapse of the Confederacy, growing awareness of the parlous state of British North American defenses, and Congressional abrogation of the reciprocity treaty contributed to a sense of greater urgency. There seemed to be abundant evidence of the vindictiveness of the United States in the passport orders and the termination of the Rush-Bagot agreement, and the fall of the reciprocity treaty not unnaturally was regarded as another example of Northern retaliation for the St. Albans raid and as a possible prelude to war. Thus the treaty frequently is referred to as a victim of the Civil War. This was and is an oversimplification, however, for the raid merely furnished the opportunity for abrogating the treaty. It was the occasion, not the cause, for Congressional action. For this reason, and because the history of the reciprocity treaty has been dealt with at length by many competent writers,[4] a detailed examination of its

[3] Halifax *Morning Chronicle*, Jan. 11, 1865; W. M. Whitelaw, "Reconstructing the Quebec Conference," *CHR*, XIX (June, 1938), 123–137; Martin, *Foundations*, p. 340; Alexander Mackenzie, *Life and Speeches of George Brown* (Toronto, 1882), pp. 228–230. Howe also prepared an extensive memorandum for Sir Frederick Bruce in an attempt to demonstrate that Nova Scotia was not anti-Northern (Howe Papers, 27: memo., draft, June, 1865, 210–217).

[4] The best volume on the treaty is D. C. Masters, *The Reciprocity Treaty of 1854: Its History, Its Relation to British Colonial and Foreign Policy and to the Development of Canadian Fiscal Autonomy* (London, 1936), while the most valuable articles are Masters, "Reciprocity and the Genesis of a Canadian Commercial Policy," *CHR*, XIII (Dec., 1932), 418–428; and S. A. Saunders, "The Reciprocity Treaty of 1854: A Regional Study," *Can. Jour. of Econ. and Pol. Sci.*, II (Feb., 1936), 41–53, and "The Maritime Provinces and the Reciprocity Treaty," *Dalhouse Rev.*, XIV (Oct., 1934), 355–371. Saunders has brought several of his articles together in *Studies in the Economy of the Maritime Provinces* (Toronto, 1939). See also C. D. Allin and G. M. Jones, *Annexation, Preferential Trade and Reciprocity* (Toronto, 1911); F. E. Haynes, "The Reciprocity Treaty with Canada of 1854," Amer. Econ. Assoc., *Publications*, VII (1892), 417–486; W. E. M. Corbett, "Nova Scotia under the Reciprocity Treaty of 1854," unpubl. M.A. thesis (Acadia, 1941); Eleanor Poland, "Reciprocity Negotiations between Canada and the United States, 1866–1911," unpubl. Ph.D. diss. (Radcliffe College, 1932); C. C. Tansill, *The Canadian Reciprocity Treaty of 1854* (Baltimore, 1922); and Sidney Webster,

demise has no place in the present study. Nevertheless, a brief indication of the causes for and nature of that demise is necessary if this additional reason for Canadian anxiety over "the American question"
late in 1864 and early in 1865 is to be understood.

From the outset reciprocal trade with the provinces was unpopular
in the Middle Atlantic protectionist states. For the most part such trade
was supported by the Middle Western states and, especially before the
Civil War, by certain Eastern manufacturing interests. The extent to
which the treaty initially benefited either the United States or British
North America still is a matter of debate among economic historians,
but the Civil War largely ended any benefit that the treaty had given
the former. The wartime North consumed its own manufactured goods
at such a rate as to preclude a need for the provincial market. On the
other hand, the war brought new prosperity to British North America,
for it created a demand for Canadian livestock, grain and hops, for
New Brunswick lumber, and briefly for Nova Scotian coal. Therefore,
the war increased colonial desire to maintain the treaty while decreasing the American desire. One of the principal strengths of any
reciprocal trade agreement thus was undermined, and during the war
the opinion that the treaty was of benefit only to the provinces frequently was expressed.[5]

To a certain extent reciprocity was a marriage of convenience. The
principal items imported by the provinces under the treaty were not
manufactured goods anyway, and Canada took agricultural and raw

"Franklin Pierce and the Canadian Reciprocity Treaty of 1854," Grafton and
Coös (N.H.) Bar Assoc., *Proceedings*, IV (1893), 358–385. An important con-
temporary statistical estimate of the treaty is Joseph Royal, "Le Traité de Réc-
iprocité," *Revue Canadienne*, I (Feb., 1864), 89–103. A recent summary is Donald
F. Warner, *The Idea of Continental Union: Agitation for the Annexation of
Canada to the United States, 1849–1893* (Lexington, Ky., 1960), pp. 33–59.

[5] For examples among many, see Howe Papers, 8: Howe to Mulgrave, March
21, 1862, 261, and Howe to Lyons, March 2, 1864, 546–548; CD, Montreal, IV:
Giddings to Seward, Nov. 20, 1862, Sept. 30, 1863; CD, Halifax, X: Jackson to
Seward, Jan. 20, 1864; CD, St. John's, IV: Leach to Seward, March 9, 1864; CD,
Saint John, IV: Howard to Seward, Oct. 20, 1862, Jan. 30, 1863; *ibid.*, V: Howard
to Seward, Oct. 10, 1864; CD, Charlottetown, II: Sherman to Seward, Jan. 10,
1864; Saint John *New Brunswick Courier*, Jan. 16, 1864; Halifax *Morning Chroni-
cle*, March 26, April 8, 1865; Victoria *British Colonist*, April 15, 1862; Rochester
Evening Express, Dec. 31, 1861; Arthur Harvey, *The Reciprocity Treaty: Its
Advantages to the United States and to Canada* (Quebec, 1865); Watkin, *Recollections*, pp. 374, 414–421, 430; R. C. Johnson, "Logs for Saginaw: An Episode in
Canadian-American Tariff Relations," *Mich. Hist.*, XXXIV (Sept., 1950), 213–214.

materials not unlike those she herself exported. In effect, the treaty reduced long hauls and high transportation costs by making it possible for local merchants and farmers along the border to trade with the nearest substantial centers of population. Canadian wheat was made into flour in the United States and then sold in the Maritime Provinces. Nova Scotian coal was used in Boston while Pennsylvania and West Virginia filled the market at Montreal and Toronto. When this trade was interrupted by the Civil War, the element of convenience was removed for the North.

Then, too, the Northern protectionists had rather strong grounds for arguing that the provinces had failed to observe the spirit of the agreement. Two successive Canadian Ministers of Finance, William Cayley in 1858 and Alexander Galt in 1859, raised the provincial tariff, and in 1860 Galt tried to induce additional trade to follow the St. Lawrence route from the American West by introducing a ninety per cent refund on tolls charged at the Welland Canal for any vessel that proceeded all the way down the river. By late 1860, therefore, New York's canal interests joined the already considerable opposition to continuation of the Marcy-Elgin Treaty. In 1859 New Brunswick also raised her tariff, and she did so again in 1863. Israel Hatch, a special agent of the Treasury Department, concluded in a lengthy report to Congress in 1860 that the provinces reaped most of the benefits from reciprocal trade. When the Republican party, which had espoused the cause of protection, won the election of that year, Hatch was given added support. Thus reciprocity was under heavy fire in Congress from 1860 or earlier.[6]

There were defenders of the treaty, of course. The Northwestern grain states, in particular, wanted to maintain it because they often

[6] See Select Comm. of the Chamber of Commerce of N.Y., *Report . . . on the Reciprocity Treaty* (New York, 1865), pp. 30–36; *Statements Concerning the Trade and Commerce of the City of Montreal for 1862* (Montreal, 1863); "Our Destiny," *Trade Review*, 1 (Aug. 4, 1865), 265, and "Shall We Have It? [reciprocity]," *ibid.*, p. 364; Joseph Howe, *The Reciprocity Treaty, Its History, General Features, and Commercial Results* (Hamilton, 1865); Oswego Board of Trade, "Reciprocity: United States and Canada," *Merchant's Magazine*, XLIV (Feb., 1861), 160–173; [G. D. Griffin], "The 'Globe' and Protection," *Canadian Quarterly Review and Family Magazine*, 1 (April, 1864), 52–66; *Canadian Farmer*, 1 (Feb. 15, 1864); *Cong. Globe*, 36th Cong., 1st Sess., 1357, 1414–417; *ibid.*, 2nd Sess., 1065; *House Misc. Docs.*, 36th Cong., 1st Sess., XIII, no. 96; and Edward Porritt, *Sixty Years of Protection in Canada, 1846–1907* (London, 1908), pp. 125–145. For the New Brunswick tariff, consult *Acts Imposing Duties for Raising a Tariff, or Rates of Duty of the Province of New Brunswick* (Saint John, 1863).

used the Great Lakes route, and Chicago, and to a lesser degree Detroit, which had favorable balances of trade with the Canadas, were centers of treaty support. The chief voices in this support were those of James Wickes Taylor, then representing the St. Paul Chamber of Commerce, who proposed a customs union modeled on the German *Zollverein* as a prelude to annexation, and Israel D. Andrews, who had helped negotiate the original agreement. They pointed out that the United States had derived at least some benefit from reciprocal trade, and many historians agree that the North, if not actually benefited by the treaty, was not directly harmed by it. There also were those who openly argued that the treaty should continue in operation because it would speed annexation by placing the provinces more firmly within the American economic orbit.[7]

The Civil War did cut into the waning support that the treaty had, because Congress was angered by the provinces' apparent anti-Northern attitude. In 1862 F. A. Pike, Representative from Maine, launched an offensive against the agreement—which he continued until victorious—by citing examples of anti-Northern opinion in the Maritime Provinces. When the Canadas refused to place agricultural machinery on the free list in 1861, Eastern support for reciprocity declined further. The New York *Herald* undertook a campaign against the agreement with the emotional argument that as long as Great Britain aided the South by her neutrality proclamation, the North should not aid the colonies with reciprocity. During the war Eastern lumbermen attacked the trade arrangements because under certain conditions they provided free entry for timber, and in April, 1862, an abortive resolution to abrogate the treaty was introduced in the House. In 1863 another such resolution was introduced, and during this time Consul General Giddings began his personal campaign against reciprocity.[8]

[7] *Senate Exec. Docs.*, 62nd Cong., 1st Sess., XIII, no. 80; *House Misc. Docs.*, 36th Cong., 2nd Sess., no. 92; *ibid.*, 61st Cong., 3rd Sess., no. 1350; *Senate Misc. Docs.*, 37th Cong., 2nd Sess., no. 26; E 1, 86, x: March 14, 1862, 109–110; E 1, 87, Y: March 14, 1863, 343–346; FO 5, 765: Lyons to Russell, secret, June 3, 1861; Macdonald Papers, 137: Poor to Macdonald, Dec. 6, 1860; Toronto *Globe*, July 4, 1860; Chicago *Tribune*, Oct. 18, 1863, Dec. 21, 1864; Elias Colbert, *Chicago: Historical and Statistical Sketch of the Garden City* (Chicago, 1868), pp. 52–53.

[8] *Cong. Globe*, 37th Cong., 2nd Sess., 1847, and App. 291; *ibid.*, 38th Cong., 1st Sess., 9, 377; *Senate Misc. Docs.*, 37th Cong., 2nd Sess., no. 74; CD, Montreal, VII: Potter to Seward, June 26, 1865; BMW to GCC, 7: Head to Lyons, March 6, 1861; Newton, *Lord Lyons*, I, 50–51: Lyons to Head, Aug. 2, 1861; Toronto *Globe*,

The final and successful campaign against the treaty was begun by Elijah Ward, Chairman of the House Committee on Commerce, in April, 1864. The New Yorker did not wish to end reciprocal trade, and his resolution included a provision for negotiating a new treaty. Ward even asked that provincial ill-will for the North be forgotten, but this hardly was possible. The United States already had endorsed a policy of high protection in Justin S. Morrill's tariff of February, 1861. Now Morrill, Chairman of the House Ways and Means Committee, attempted to amend Ward's resolution in order to eliminate future negotiations. Both resolutions were defeated, in part because an election was approaching in which the proreciprocity West was thought to be ready to defect to a peace party, and in part because of effective speeches and cloakroom work by Isaac Arnold of Illinois and to a lesser extent by John Pruyn of New York. It also was during this time that Seward failed to give his support to the antireciprocity drive and that Lyons, acting upon his advice, did what he could to conciliate Northern feelings.[9]

But when Congress reconvened in December, 1864, the St. Albans raid had occurred. On the day that Coursol released the raiders Ward's resolution again was brought before the House, and through the efforts of Morrill and E. B. Washburne of Illinois an amended resolution, which called for unconditional abrogation, was passed eighty-five to fifty-seven. The following day Zachariah Chandler began his campaign in the Senate by reading the report on Coursol's decision, and Senator James W. Grimes of Iowa delivered himself of a long and impassioned argument in which he contended that repeal would eliminate the necessity for border defenses by forcing annexation upon the Canadas. Since it was on this day, December 14, that Congress provided for the placing of new cutters on the Great Lakes, and only three days later that Lincoln issued his order extending the passport to the interior provinces, the context of the renewed reciprocity debate

---

March 6, 1861; "A.A.B.," "The Reciprocity Treaty," *Br. Amer. Mag.*, II (March, 1864), 522–532.

[9] *Cong. Globe*, 38th Cong., 1st Sess., 1387, 2298, 2333–234, 2364–371, 2455–456, 2482–484, 2502–509; FO 115, 470: Lyons to Russell, May 31, 1864; W. B. Parker, *The Life and Public Services of Justin Smith Morrill* (Boston, 1924), pp. 149–151; Robert Hadfield, *Elijah Ward* (New York, 1875), pp. 26–35. A search for material on the reciprocity treaty in the Henry Winter Davis and Reverdy Johnson papers at the Maryland Historical Society in Baltimore yielded little that was of use.

inevitably implied Northern retaliation. In January, while Seward was putting additional pressure on Monck to push a neutrality bill through the Canadian legislature, the antireciprocity movement received the invaluable support of Charles Sumner.[10]

The Senate hastily passed its resolution calling for abrogation of the treaty by a vote of thirty-eight to eight on January 12. According to some historians haste was necessary because the Civil War was nearing its close and the Northern senators feared the return of Southern representatives to Congress. However, the Republicans were aware that it would be some time before the South had senators in Washington, and their haste probably was due more to the fact that British North America was removing any excuse for an appearance of retaliation, having established special border patrols, re-arrested several of the St. Albans raiders, and provided for an early session of Parliament to deal, in part, with the question of a neutrality act. Seward sent Adams a copy of the Congressional resolution and instructed him to notify Lord Russell on March 17—ten years and one day after the effective date of reciprocal trade—that in twelve months the United States would consider the treaty null and void. This Adams did, although he personally had hoped that Congress would not abrogate the treaty at the time since inevitably it would appear that the basic motive was revenge.[11]

Lyons and Monck had done what they could to stay the execution, but they were prepared for it. In March, 1864, the Executive Council had sent a Montreal businessman, John Young, to discuss reciprocity with Seward. Sandfield Macdonald had wanted to send George Brown as early as January of that year, but while Brown and Alexander Galt had unofficial talks with the Secretary of State, Monck had been unwilling to appear too eager. The Governor General had opposed any agitation on Canada's part to defend the treaty, for he and Lyons reasoned that if the provinces appeared anxious to retain reciprocity

[10] *Cong. Globe*, 38th Cong., 2nd Sess., 35, 57–61, 96; G 20, 104: Archibald to Monck, Dec. 21, 1864; CD, Montreal, IV: Giddings to Seward, Sept. 30, 1863; Howe Papers, 27: memo. for Bruce, May, 1865, 202–209; Sumner Papers, LXXII: Sumner to Lieber, Jan. 20, and N. C. Keep to Sumner, March 25, 1865; Sumner, *Works*, IX, 184: Dec. 20, 1864; Boston Board of Trade, *Annual Report*, I (1865), 103; Chicago *Tribune*, Dec. 21, 1864; Lorenzo Sabine, *et al.*, *The Reciprocity Treaty between the United States and Great Britain, of June 5, 1854* (Boston, 1865); William Salter, *The Life of James W. Grimes* (New York, 1876), p. 266.

[11] CFA, 88: Adams to Seward, Feb. 23, 1865; CFA, Diary: Dec. 16, 1864, Feb. 23, Dec. 22, 1865.

the North would be convinced that the Canadas had an especially fine bargain and might repeal the treaty even more rapidly. Young had reported that while the Secretary of State was not opposed to the agreement, it appeared that those who wished to abrogate it would be successful. Thus, Monck was aware even before the St. Albans raid that reciprocity was on its way out, and he must have realized that the joint resolution in January of 1865 was not in direct retaliation against the Canadas for the raid, although its timing may deliberately have made it appear so.[12]

When the Canadian Parliament was convened on January 19 to consider the Alien Act, it was in an atmosphere laden with somber expectancy, an atmosphere conducive to the promotion of confederation on the basis of the real or imagined "American menace." Although a few voices spoke of years of continued warfare in the United States, most observers correctly foresaw but a few months at most. The long-anticipated spring when Northern troops and demobbed Fenians would be free to look northward appeared to be at hand. This knowledge acted as an additional spur to the men who sought British North American union, weakened their opponents, and contributed to another lengthy season of rumor and war scare. While the Governor General and the imperial administration professed to consider the danger of an Anglo-American war nearly over, there were those both in England and British North America who felt otherwise, and Lady Monck was told as late as April that there was going to be a *"bloody war."* Whether as epithet or adjective, the expression would have found at least substantial popular support in the Canadas and in the mother country as well, in February and March during the short but intense period of renewed popular apprehension.

---

[12] John Sandfield Macdonald Papers, II: Brown to Macdonald, Jan. 25, 1864, 1041–1043; FO 5, 403: Monck to Newcastle, March 15, 1864; *ibid.*, 409: Lyons to Russell, March 23, 1864; CFA, 85: Seward to Adams, Jan. 28, 1864; NBL, 9: Seward to Lyons, Feb. 4, 1862, 114; *ibid.*, 12: Seward to Burnley, Oct. 13, 1863, 259; ITC, 34: Seward to Giddings, Dec. 19, 1863, 58–59; G 10, 2: Young to Holton, March 8, enc. in Monck to Newcastle, March 15, 1864, 107–115; Seward Papers: J. H. Moore to Seward, Jan. 12, 1865, Buchanan to Seward, Feb. 20, 1865, and William Wilkison to Seward, March 19, 1865; Sumner Papers, LXXII: S. D. Bloodgood to Sumner, Feb. 6, 1865; *Foreign Relations, 1865*, I, 92: Seward to Adams, Jan. 18, 1865; *ibid., 1867–68*, II, 1182: Adams to Russell, March 17, 1865; Mackenzie, pp. 206, 208: Brown to Holton, June 26, 1863; Newton, I, 123–126: Lyons to Monck, Jan. 28, and Lyons to Russell, Feb. 9, 1864; Brown Papers, VIII: Brown to Sandfield Macdonald, Jan. 25, 1864, 843–846.

From February 3 until March 10 the Canadian Parliament discussed confederation. During this time no less than sixty members of the Legislative Council and Assembly spoke to the point of the dangers that the United States held for the united Canadas. On the first day Etienne-Pascal Taché, then Minister of Militia, moved his address to the Crown for a union based on the resolution made at Quebec, and he provided what virtually became a slogan for the confederationists. Taché predicted that if the present opportunity were allowed to pass, the provinces would be forced into the American Union either by violence or by being "placed upon an inclined plain [*sic*] which would carry [the Canadas] there insensibly." Time and again speakers who followed after Taché referred to this inclined plane as an ever-present danger to the Canadas. Each touched upon a particular way in which he felt that the United States inexorably was drawing the provinces into the Union, politically, economically, and culturally.[13]

Those who used the United States as a *deus ex machina* to prove the necessity of confederation either insisted that the Republic was performing a service for the provinces in warning them of the need to unite or resignedly stated that confederation was being forced upon a reluctant people by the manifest needs of defense and self-preservation. Another group argued that confederation would not save the provinces if the United States truly intended to annex them by force. An even smaller body insisted that confederation actually would promote annexation rather than retard or prevent it by making it possible for the United States to obtain all of the provinces at a single stroke.[14]

Thomas D'Arcy McGee shouted that the United States was driven by the triple demons of "Tax! Blood! Gold!" Everything that the United States had coveted, he warned, the United States had obtained, and now she coveted the provinces. Citing the notice of the abrogation of the reciprocity treaty and the growth of the Northern army, McGee declared that a change had taken place in the spirit of the

[13] Canada, Parliament, *Parliamentary Debates on the Subject of the Confederation of the British North American Provinces* (Quebec, 1865), usually and hereafter referred to as *Confederation Debates*, pp. 6–7, 82, 326, 343, 397, 667; Quebec *Le Canadien*, Jan., 1865; *The Times*, Jan. 21, 1865; Brown Papers, XII: Brown to Anne, his wife, Feb. 6, 1865, 1144–1145.

[14] *Confederation Debates*, pp. 7, 32–34, 44, 180. John A. Macdonald's key speech is reprinted in W. P. M. Kennedy, ed., *Statutes, Treaties and Documents of the Canadian Constitution, 1793–1929* (2nd ed., Toronto, 1930), pp. 550–569, and in A. P. Newton, *Federal and Unified Constitutions* (New York, 1923), pp. 177–190.

American people. "Mushroom *millionaires,* well named a shoddy aristocracy," performed the remarkable feat of shouting in a "chuckling undertone" about American expansion. To prevent the "universal democracy doctrine" from "gobbling up" British North America, the provinces would have to stand shoulder to shoulder as a single nation. The Irish orator reinvoked his original concept of the "three warnings" that the provinces had been given—the warning shown in the attitude of the Little Englanders in Britain toward the colonies, the warning of the Civil War, and the warning of deteriorating politics, deadlock, and "double majority" in the Canadas—and the message of these "three warnings" was spread throughout the provinces by the press. If Taché furnished a slogan, McGee furnished an emotional summation in behalf of confederation.[15]

It was Cartier who argued that confederation was necessary despite the fact that it was being forced upon a reluctant people. Like Rousseau, he felt certain that he could read the "general will," and his readings told him that Canada must preserve the purity of its monarchical spirit against the American mob. There were but two alternatives according to Cartier—confederation or annexation. For *survivance* the French Canadians must bind themselves to the British flag, for then their language, religion, and law would not be assimilated into an indiscriminate melting pot.[16]

In retrospect, one of the most thorough attacks upon these positions came from Christopher Dunkin, an outspoken member from Brome, who insisted that an artificial dread of the United States—"a bogey"— was being used to force an otherwise unpopular and unnecessary measure upon the several provinces. Dunkin pointed out that New York state alone was more than a match for Canada West militarily, and he argued that confederation would not strengthen the winter-locked united provinces and would give the Canadas a longer frontier to defend in time of war. Dunkin also felt that any attempt to construct a unified nation to the north of the United States might be construed in Washington as a hostile effort to re-establish the lost balance of power in North America or even as a violation of the Monroe Doctrine. The United States, which is "not very fond of us," he

---

[15] *Confederation Debates,* pp. 107, 129-146; Watkin, pp. 282-319, quotes the speech. See also Montreal *Weekly Herald,* Feb. 11, 1865; [McGee], "A Monarchy, or a Republic! Which?," *Br. Amer. Mag.,* II (Dec., 1863), 114; and [P. I. Tickle], *The Future of British America* (Toronto, 1865).

[16] *Confederation Debates,* pp. 55-62, 338-339, 366, 391, 437, 827-841, 902-904.

thought, would not be frightened "by our taking upon ourselves great aims." Jesting not too slyly at the nation-builders of Canada, Dunkin concluded that the United States had politicians "quite as bold, shrewd and astute as any we have," and the result well could be that they would swoop up the would-be fathers of confederation into the American Union. But Dunkin spoke neither well nor briefly, and his comprehensive replies and pessimistic timidity were no match for men such as Macdonald, McGee, and Cartier.[17]

While the Canadians debated confederation and while apprehension over a Northern invasion was expressed in the British Parliament, New Brunswick held an election in which the province rejected the proposed plan of union. Led by the Saint John *Globe* and *Freeman*, which advocated John A. Poor's Western Extension program for the European and North American Railway and closer commercial ties with the United States, anticonfederationists launched a temporarily successful attack upon the union movement. Many in the province feared that the merchants of Saint John would so aid Poor's railroad schemes as to permit the port and the entire Saint John River valley to be sucked into the American economic orbit even more closely than already was the case, and the conservative Fredericton *Head Quarters* had been advocating closer railway connections with the Canadas as an antidote. The Halifax press also had viewed the so-called Americanization of New Brunswick with alarm, for that province could cut Nova Scotia off from union with the Canadas should confederation prove desirable in the future. Now the election in New Brunswick could be read as an indication that the province had turned toward a pro-American economic policy.[18]

The news that Conservative leader Samuel L. Tilley had been defeated in New Brunswick reached Canada on March 6. A portion of the Quebec press at once opined that American money had prevented the victory of the proconfederation group. Tilley, of course, had no desire to lessen this impression, and there can be little question that some American money had been used against him. However, the decisive factors in the election had been its prematurity, popular dis-

---

[17] *Ibid.*, pp. 528–532. See also pp. 46, 180, 257, 284, 296, 621, 658–659, 668, 714, 960, 988; and Halifax *Novascotian*, Jan. 16, 1865.

[18] See A. G. Bailey, "Railways and the Confederation Issue in New Brunswick, 1863–1865," *CHR*, xxi (Dec., 1940), 367–383, and "The Basis and Persistence of Opposition to Confederation in New Brunswick," *CHR*, xxiii (March, 1942), 375–397.

trust of the Canadas, and the feeling that the Canadian leaders were not sincere in their promises to promote the intercolonial railway. But despite—or perhaps because of—the debâcle in New Brunswick, Macdonald and the confederationists pressed their cause home with a vote of ninety-one to thirty-three on March 10 and then set out to win the final imprimatur from London.[19]

Many issues were involved in the mission to England. The delegates —Galt, Cartier, Macdonald, and Brown—were to confer with the British ministry on confederation, the problems arising from the abrogation of the reciprocity treaty, questions concerning the eventual disposition of the Hudson's Bay Company's lands, and "the arrangements necessary for the defence of Canada, in the event of war arising with the United States, and the extent to which the same should be shared between Great Britain and Canada." [20] For the months of the St. Albans raid and its aftermath, of the confederation conferences and the Canadian parliamentary debates, and of the growing hostility of the American Congress were months that saw an important shift in the expressed Canadian attitude toward defense.[21]

At the request of the Canadian government Lieutenant Colonel Jervois had submitted his second detailed report on the defenses of the Canadas on November 9.[22] This report was more in keeping with the provinces' capacity for self-help than were the previous ones, and it realistically took advantage of the Canadian climate as an important defensive factor. Nor did Jervois surrender quite so much to a potential invader. He envisaged fortifications that would furnish not a temporary but a permanent basis for defense, provided gunboats could be placed on the Great Lakes and the provincials could continue to count on the support of Her Majesty's navy. Jervois suggested that an elaborate ring of fortresses be constructed for Quebec, Montreal, and Kingston, with lesser works for Toronto and Hamilton. The forts

[19] Quebec *Chronicle*, March 6, 1865; Quebec *Le Canadien*, March 29, 1865. See also *Confederation Debates*, pp. 863–876, 879, 1015–1016.

[20] E, AB: March 24, 1865, 197.

[21] See the excellent work by Charles P. Stacey on the Canadian defense question in his two articles, "British Military Policy in Canada in the Era of Federation," C.H.A., *Annual Report* (1934), pp. 20–29, and "Britain's Withdrawal from North America, 1864–1867," CHR, xxvi (Sept., 1955), 185–198, and in his book, *Army*, pp. 165–188. The writer has followed Stacey's works on defense throughout this chapter.

[22] Macdonald Papers, 100: Jervois to McDougall, Nov. 9, 1864, 5–9. The report is dated November 10.

could protect their respective cities, he reasoned, and the new gun-boats should make it possible to keep the waterways above the Welland Canal open. Each fort would occupy the full efforts of a potential American siege force so that a smaller number of troops could stand off a force superior in numbers and efficiency each year until winter broke the siege. Planned retreats to a second line of defense might then follow, until Britain had won her victory at sea.[23]

But the total cost would be a staggering £1,754,000, and Jervois admitted that Canada from Toronto west and ultimately all of Canada West up to Kingston might be lost despite the siege method. He hoped for successive retreats from the Niagara and Detroit frontiers, troops falling back upon London, Guelph, Hamilton, and Toronto in orderly stages. Canada East would make its principal stand at the St. Lawrence River, abandoning the Eastern Townships. If Canada made concentration rather than dispersion its principle of defense, Jervois concluded, and if no energy were wasted in defending exposed positions, it might withstand an invasion until the British fleet could win the war. While scarcely optimistic, this report clearly was more acceptable to the Canadians than Jervois' first effort. The main question was, who was to man and to pay for the forts?

Upon receiving Jervois' report, the Canadian government responded to Cardwell's original request for an exchange of opinion. The border situation had changed since Cardwell had written in August. The passport order and the abrogation of the reciprocity treaty were yet to come, but already Seward had announced the North's desire to end the Rush-Bagot agreement and had sent his wire concerning the *Georgian*, while General Dix's orders still stood. The Canadian leaders placed confederation first in their reply to Cardwell, however, pointing out that union would make British North America's ability to contribute to her own defense much greater in the future. They proposed to construct the necessary fortifications at Montreal if Great Britain would pay for those at Quebec and arm both. Perhaps most important, they promised to ask the Canadian Parliament for one mil-

---

[23] [Jervois], *Report on the Defence of Canada, Made to the Provincial Government on the 10th November 1864 and of the British Naval Stations in the North Atlantic: Together with Observations on the Defence of New Brunswick . . .* (London, 1865); R. L. Way, "The Topographical Aspects of Canadian Defence, (1783–1871)," *Can. Defence Quart.*, XIV (April, 1937), 275, 287; Martin, *Foundations*, pp. 341, 356–357. See also G 19, 28.

lion dollars for the militia, a sum that nearly all had opposed in 1862. Since Jervois had estimated that the fortifications at Montreal would cost twice this, the Canadians were prepared to undertake a considerable expense.[24]

The British response was not what the Canadians hoped it would be. In Parliament some failed to support such measures because they no longer feared invasion, while others failed to respond precisely because they did fear invasion and did not want British purses to pay for a war involving a colony that they no longer desired. The Colonial and War offices refused to commit themselves on how expenses should be apportioned, and while Britain promised to build the necessary fortifications at Quebec, the new structures were to be used to concentrate the imperial forces there, leaving Canada West virtually undefended.

Four days after the Canadian Parliament began to discuss Taché's motion on confederation, the British House of Commons received Jervois' second report together with the government's request for £50,000—one quarter of the proposed total cost—for the fortifications at Quebec. While the money was voted, the accompanying debate led to what Charles Francis Adams regarded as one of the sharpest war scares of the period. John A. Macdonald also considered that the publication of the Jervois report was indiscreet, for news of its contents ultimately created what he described as "a panic in Western Canada," and unquestionably the report disturbed the British Parliament and certain vocal segments of the British public. During the debates the government promised that the mother country would go to the defense of her colonies if the Canadas were attacked, but this affirmation scarcely was inclined to put Canadian minds at ease, for they considered that such declarations should not be necessary.[25]

Macdonald agreed that Canadian defense truly was hopeless if Britain could do no better than vote for that purpose, as she had just done, £200,000 to be expended over four years. He predicted that any war with the United States would have to occur within two years and

[24] E, AA: Nov. 16, 1864, 427.
[25] CFA, 88: Adams to Seward, Feb. 10, 1865; CFA, Diary: Feb. 7, 10, 1865; E, AB: Feb. 1, 1865, 74; G 1, 173: Cardwell to Monck, Jan. 21, 1865, 69; *Hansard's, 1865:* CLXXVII, cols. 416–422, 430–438, 1539–1637; *The Times,* Feb. 15, April 12, 1865; Chicago *Tribune,* April 12, 1865; New York *Tribune,* April 8, 1865; Watkin, pp. 432–441, 445–450: March 23, 1865; John Bigelow, *Retrospections,* II, 436: W. H. Russell to Bigelow, March 28, 1865; Buckle, *Letters of Queen Victoria: Second Series,* I, 248–249: Palmerston to Victoria, Jan. 20, 1865.

sarcastically wrote that "by that time a hole may be made in the mud opposite Quebec, and the foundation of a single redoubt laid." [26] Therefore in March the coalition government passed a special supply bill for a million dollars, a sum equal to the entire proposed British appropriation, despite the fact that many Canadians continued to view defense as an imperial rather than a colonial task, and to back up this gesture, which italicized Canadian anxieties concerning the British connection, the ministry decided to send its mission to London to obtain, among other goals, an understanding on the future of colonial defense. By the time the last members of the delegation sailed, on April 12, General Robert E. Lee had delivered his sword to General Grant at Appomattox and President Lincoln appeared ready to lead his victorious nation, now the world's foremost military power, into the years of recovery and reconstruction.

Throughout the winter and spring Charles Francis Adams closely followed public opinion, and he repeatedly urged Seward to make allowances for British tempers, especially because of concern for Canadian safety and "mortification" in some quarters over the now-evident outcome of the Civil War. Adams confirmed that the measures that Congress apparently had directed against the Canadas were being cited in London as proof of Northern enmity. "Thus it is that conscience works," he noted in his diary, for he thought that the British anticipated further Federal retaliation against the Canadas because of their failure to prevent Confederate activities there. Adams momentarily feared that Britain might even resort to a form of preventive war, rushing to the aid of the Confederacy at the last moment in order to forestall a reconciliation between the two sections. Several times he cautioned Seward that there must be no error in American policy that could give Britain a *casus belli*, and he advised restricting any policy decisions to those of "immediate exigency" so that the Whig Party might not be weakened in England due to some American action. Benjamin Moran wrote that the Tories were exerting themselves to convince everyone that the North meant to attack Britain or the provinces, and one English writer declared that it was "only crying peace, peace, when there is no peace, to say that there is no danger of war." To his son the minister added that he feared that the anxiety Parliament had shown concerning the Canadas was likely to strengthen

[26] Macdonald Papers, 511: Macdonald to Watkin and to J. H. Gray, both March 27, 1865—the latter is quoted in Pope, *Macdonald*, 1, 280–281; Toronto *Globe*, March 17, 1865.

the annexationists in the North and perhaps lead to an attack upon the colonies. On one occasion Adams reported that the impression was "very general" that peace in the United States meant war with Great Britain. The period was one of "extraordinary uneasiness and indefinite apprehension as to the future." The North, he repeatedly warned, must not play into the hands of "the mischief makers" of the Tory Party or of the Confederacy.[27]

Seward accepted most of Adams' suggestions and replied that the United States would not press its claims against Great Britain in the *Alabama* case until after the forthcoming Parliamentary elections. The Northern Secretary privately summarized the grievances that the North entertained against the Crown, adding for the first time the charge that the group of Confederates who had attempted to put the hotels of New York City to the torch had been given protection in the North American provinces. "It is thus seen that we have had not one but many just causes of war against Great Britain," Seward concluded,[28] leaving the door open to a number of possible approaches with respect to future negotiations, for by now the Secretary knew that he could achieve his goals through diplomatic rather than military channels. Adams need not have feared that his chief still was looking for an excuse for war.

The imperial administration also thought that Seward no longer wanted war with Britain, but it could not be certain. The Northern Secretary still had not removed the various "retaliatory measures" passed against the provinces when two new and especially strong rumors arose to add to British concern. In February, aboard a Northern ship in the harbor of Hampton Roads, Virginia, Abraham Lincoln and

[27] CFA 88: Adams to Seward, Feb. 2, 16, 17, 23, March 9, 1865; CFA, Diary: Jan. 1, 28, 31, Feb. 14, 23, March 9, 1865; Sumner Papers, LXXII: James Phalen to Sumner, Feb. 13, and Moran to Sumner, March 6, 1865; Ford, ed., *Adams*, II, 253–254, 258–259: Adams to C. F. Adams, Jr., Feb. 10, March 24, 1865. Had Lord Russell, as distinct from the British Cabinet or Parliament, truly feared war at this time, he might have given favorable reception to an American's offer to reveal the plans for the harbor defenses of Boston and New York. Late in January an assistant in the office of the Chief Engineer to the Commonwealth of Massachusetts wrote *chargé* Burnley that he would furnish copies of the plans of both harbors and of secret coastal defenses for £1200. Russell replied that while Her Majesty's government would be very happy to receive such information, it would not be proper to obtain it in this manner (FO 5, 1014: W. G. Chase to Burnley, Jan. 16, 21, enc. in Burnley to Russell, Jan. 24, 1865; FO 115, 432: Russell to Burnley, secret, Feb. 18, 1865, 176).

[28] GBI, 20: Seward to Adams, Feb. 21, 1865.

Alexander Stephens, Vice-President of the Confederate States, had conducted abortive peace negotiations. Stephens apparently had gone as far as to suggest that the North and South should unite against a third party in defense of the Monroe Doctrine, and word of this proposal leaked out. Britain not unnaturally assumed that she might be the third party, although Stephens probably had French activities in Mexico in mind.

Early in March Robert Walker, a former Senator from Mississippi and former Governor of Kansas Territory, visited the provinces at Seward's request, probably to confer with his former friends, Thompson and Sanders, but possibly to learn whether the Canadian business community felt that without reciprocity the colonies would join the United States. Both the New York *Times* and the Montreal *Gazette* reported that Walker was sent as a spearhead for annexationism, which he denied in a public letter. Seward considered the allegations serious enough to ask Adams to tell Russell that Walker's visit was in no way unfriendly to the Canadas, and Walker promptly returned to the North.[29]

Frequently Adams advised that something positive should be done to soothe the rising British fears, for, as he pointed out, the British government had removed one of the chief causes of Northern complaint by requesting an end to all Confederate activities in her North American provinces. As he had told Adams he would do, Russell had informed Mason and Slidell by letter on February 13 that the "so-called Confederate States" had disregarded Her Majesty's position as a neutral and had asked them to stop attempting to foment an Anglo-American war. A copy of Russell's letter had been sent to Washington, and Lincoln had forwarded it to General Lee without comment. Lee had refused to receive the copy of Russell's note officially, but he had sent it on to Confederate Secretary of State Benjamin. After much consultation the letter was returned, the Confederacy declining to acknowledge it. However, Russell's request already had been met.[30]

On March 2 Benjamin had recalled the mission that had been sent to the provinces, before Russell's note had reached Richmond and in accord

---

[29] Seward Papers: Potter to Seward, Jan. 31, 1865; CFA, 88: Adams to Seward, March 2, 1865; New York *Herald*, March 29, 1865; Ford, ed., II, 256–257: Adams to Adams, Jr., Feb. 17, 1865; Stephens, *A Constitutional View of the Late War between the States* (Philadelphia, 1870), II, 600–601.

[30] John B. Jones, *Diary*, II, 449: March 14, 21, 1865; Moran Diary, XIV: Feb. 15, 1865, and printed in Wallace and Gillespie, eds., *Moran*, II, 1378.

with Jacob Thompson's own recommendation. Thompson had served no useful purpose in the Canadas following the St. Albans raid, and he realized this. Benjamin instructed him to give a sum of money to someone whom he could trust in order to continue the program of aid for escaped prisoners of war, to withdraw all support from anyone who might cause a complaint regarding the neutrality laws of the provinces, and after keeping enough money for the return trip home to remit the rest to London. By mid-March all organized Confederate activities against the North from within British North America had ceased.[31]

As seen in the previous chapter, Seward made the gestures for which Adams hoped on March 8 and 9, immediately following his receipt of the news that the Confederate commissioners had been recalled from British North America and that the Canadian Parliament had appropriated money for the St. Albans banks. Declaring that existing circumstances made any further raids from the Canadas unlikely, the Secretary said that the United States was "willing that the Convention [of 1817] should remain practically in force . . . ," and he also removed the passport order as it applied to the Canadas. By these acts Seward wiped away much of the fear in Britain that the North intended war, although because of the ambiguous wording of Seward's dispatch further correspondence was necessary before the British government felt satisfied that the Rush-Bagot agreement was unimpaired. In June Seward was to restate his instructions to Adams for the benefit of the new British minister to the United States, Sir Frederick Bruce, who replaced Lyons in April, and again in August Seward declared that the notice of abrogation was "absolutely withdrawn," using the words urged upon him by the British ministry itself. On March 30 Adams was able to report that Cardwell's announcement to Parliament that the Convention of 1817 would remain in force had given "the final blow" to British alarmists, but he again cautioned Seward to show "prudence and moderation in tone not less than in action for some time to come." [32]

[31] D. S. Freeman, ed., *A Calendar of Confederate Papers* (Richmond, 1908), pp. 190–191: Benjamin to Thompson, March 2, 1865, and notes 57, 58; Younger, ed., *Confederate Government*, p. 205: March 23, 1865; Lee Diary: March 10, 23, 1865.

[32] GBI, 20: Seward to Adams, March 8, 1865; G 6, 173: Russell to Bruce, April 21, 1865, 391; NBL, 13: Seward to Bruce, June 18, Aug. 22, 1865, 358, 411–412; CFA, 88: Adams to Seward, March 16, 1865; CFA, 89: Adams to Seward, March 24, 30, 1865; Seward Papers: W. H. Russell to Bigelow, copy, March 8, 1865, and Seward

Popular fears remained, of course, even though the successful carrying of the confederation resolution in Quebec and Seward's actions early in March did much to decrease such fears. Continued fear found its most obvious expression in continued rumor. Just before Lincoln's second inauguration the Montreal *Gazette* had reported that Great Britain and France might acknowledge him as President of only the states in which he was elected, thus indirectly recognizing the Confederacy, and Southern mobs staged noisy demonstrations in Montreal during the first two weeks of March. During this time two ships being fitted out ostensibly for use as passenger vessels in the tropics were investigated, at the request of the consul in Quebec, and cleared. One D. Campbell McNab, principal of a classical academy at Richmond, Canada West, wrote Consul General Potter and Secretary of War Stanton that Confederates were planning a raid from Canada West upon New York state. As a reward for detailed information McNab wanted a Master's degree from Yale College, "as it is the most renowned university on this side of the Atlantic." Stanton and Seward, neither one a Yale man, turned the letter over to Monck, who learned that the plot was a creature of McNab's imagination. In Halifax consul Jackson persuaded the provincial authorities to seize a Confederate-bound quantity of arms and ammunition which arrived in a schooner from Boston, and he wired Seward that an attack by six hundred Southerners was expected at any moment, although an investigation by both provincial and state authorities revealed no raid in prospect. Jackson also warned Seward that the famous Laird rams, which had been constructed in England, were on their way via Nassau to attack New York City. Five vessels had left Saint John to cooperate with the ironclads in their raid, he reported. This was too much for Seward to accept from even so diligent a consul as Jackson, for Britain had seized the rams in October of 1863. The Secretary informed Adams of Jackson's warning, and the minister replied that the dispatch from Jackson was "a pure invention." Adams, who had kept Seward calmed throughout the delicate negotiations over the seizure of the Laird rams, gave the Secretary of State a number of suggestions as to how he should word his next dispatch so that Adams might use it, when advisable, to indicate that the wild rumors that even American consuls accepted at

---

to Bigelow, March 28, 1865; P.A.C., Isaac Buchanan Papers: Joseph Gilkinsin to Buchanan, April 29, 1865; London *Canadian News*, March 30, 1865; Montreal *L'Ordre*, March 29, 1865; Toronto *Globe*, April 7, 1865.

face value were not believed by the State Department, thus emphasizing Seward's peaceful intentions.[33]

Unfortunately during the final months of the war Lord Lyons had not been present in Washington and had been unable to bring the full force of his own restraining influence to bear. On March 4 he wrote to Seward privately that, due to ill health, he was retiring from public service and would remain in England. Exhausted by four years of delicate and tense negotiations in a war-torn capital, worn by the heat of some of Washington's hottest summers on record, Lyons at last had asked to be recalled. In his letter to Seward he showed that mutual respect if not actual affection had grown between the two men since the early months of 1861, when Lyons feared that Seward would catapult the world into war to further his political career, for by 1865 the British minister was among those who considered the Auburn lawyer a force for world peace. Seward replied in a spirit of sincere friendship, reminding Lyons that much of the future progress of the world would depend on Anglo-American cooperation and suggesting that the parting should not be a final one.

Sir Frederick Bruce, an unknown quantity in Anglo-American relations, was sent to fill Lyons' post. There were those who felt that Bruce would not be equal to the task of dealing with the United States during its period of reconstruction. William Howard Russell, for example—who had not held Lyons in particularly high regard either—doubted that Bruce could deal with the imagined American animus against Britain, and Sir Edward Watkin wrote in London that the new minister was inexperienced in North American matters. On the other hand, Adams had been favorably impressed with Bruce's friendliness and ability.[34]

[33] CD, Montreal, vi: Potter to Seward, Feb. 16, March 15, 31, April 7, 1865; CD, Halifax, xi: Jackson to Seward, Feb. 1, 3, 4, 13, 1865; *ibid.*, x: Jackson to Seward [misfiled in March, 1864], March 1, 1865; CD, Toronto, i: Thurston to Seward, Feb. 23, 1865, and Kimball to Thurston, March 28, 1865; BMW to GCC, 235: McNab to Stanton, March 12, enc. in Burnley to Monck, March 22, 1865, 186; Seward Papers: Donald Ross to Seward, March 13, 1865, and Brega to Seward, March 25, 1865; CFA, 88: Russell to Adams, March 11, enc. in Adams to Seward, March 16, and 17, 1865; Baring Papers: Ward to Baring Bros., March 7, 21, April 6, 1865; *Foreign Relations, 1864*, pp. 550–585; Boston *Daily Advertiser*, March 13, 1865; Chicago *Tribune*, March 28, 31, June 14, 1865; Halifax *Morning Advertiser*, April 11, 1865.

[34] Seward Papers: Lyons to Seward, March 4, 1865; NBL, 13: Seward to Lyons, March 20, 1865, 190; CFA, 88: Adams to Seward, March 2, 1865; Watkin, pp. 443–444.

As it happened, Bruce never had an opportunity to deal with the Lincoln administration. By the time he reached Washington on April 18 the President of the United States had been assassinated and the Secretary of State lay near death. While the new ambassador hurriedly looked for someone to whom he could present his credentials, the people of British North America responded with an emotional outburst as strong, and perhaps as unreasoning, as their essentially emotional response after 1861 in favor of the South. In 1861 the chivalrous Southerner was an underdog battling the North; in 1865 an increasingly respected President had been struck down, as the orators repeatedly declaimed, in the hour of his triumph. The Chicago *Tribune*'s recent prediction, intended for another context, that the force of argument was to be replaced with "the argument of force," had proved true.[35]

[35] April 12, 1865.

sixteen ꝏ   "CHOSEN BY ANGELS"

> "It is clear that the homage which was refused to justice
> and humanity will be freely given to success."
>
> RICHARD COBDEN

THE LAST WEEKS OF MARCH AND THE FIRST WEEKS OF APRIL, 1865, WERE
filled with news of the final defeat of the Confederacy, news which
the provincial press recorded "factually and stoically" but seldom with
jubilation. Word of the evacuation of Richmond arrived on April 3.
From across the river Canadians could watch Detroiters celebrate
through the night with torch parades, and the waters of Lake St. Clair
carried the insistently punctuated sound of a hundred-gun salute. On
April 10 came the news of Lee's surrender at an unpronounceable Virginian crossroads. The war was over and spring, the season for invasions, was at hand. Lady Monck confided to her journal that she was
in despair, for "All the nicest and bravest men belong to the South,"
but Lord Monck was exultant. The Toronto *Leader*, for so long so
certain of an ultimate Confederate victory, reminded its readers that
the cause of the South had been a just one and prayed that peace could
now be achieved even if only through restoration of the Union. The
President of the United States, who, according to the *Quarterly Review*, would have to be "chosen by angels" to keep the Union together, had succeeded.[1]

In Canada West Jacob Thompson hurried the preparations for his
departure. During the summer of 1864 he and some of his friends had
declared publicly that they would resort to any means of saving the
South, even to having the tyrannical Lincoln "put out of the way,"

[1] G. Gunn, "New Brunswick Opinion," p. 177; Monck, *Leaves*, pp. 225, 240:
April 11, 1865; *Leader*, April 11, 13, 14, 1865; *Quarterly*, CXII (Oct., 1862), 551–552.

but now such a step seemed pointless. Lincoln had sent word to Thompson through a mutual acquaintance that he would welcome an opportunity to see him, for these two men once had been friends, but Seward had side-tracked the President. Now, belatedly acting upon his instructions from Judah Benjamin, Thompson set out for Europe. Midway to Portland he was recognized, and the Provost Marshal of that city telegraphed Secretary of War Stanton that the Confederate commissioner would be in town shortly.[2]

On April 14 Lincoln permitted Thompson to escape. Assistant Secretary of War Charles A. Dana brought a request from Stanton to authorize Thompson's arrest, and Lincoln replied with one of his aphorisms: "When you have got an elephant by the hind leg, and he's trying to run away, it's best to let him run." When Dana told Stanton of Lincoln's advice, the Secretary of War decided to send no reply to Portland. Thus, if in the absence of instructions the Provost Marshal had arrested Thompson, Stanton would have had his prisoner without having disobeyed orders. The marshal allowed Thompson to escape, however. The ex-Confederate commissioner arrived in Halifax in the private carriage of Benjamin Wier and eventually made his way to the English lakes, where he consoled himself by reading the Lake Poets.[3]

Also on April 14 Mrs. Lincoln was reading a copy of *Julius Caesar*, that account of a famous assassination. And on this day Lincoln penned a note, the last he was to write, asking that his unofficial emissary to the Canadas, George Ashmun, be allowed to see him the following morning. This note he gave to Ashmun at half past eight in the evening just as the Lincolns were leaving for Ford's Theatre. That evening John Ross Robertson, one day to be city editor of the Toronto

[2] MC: Emmons to Seward, Aug. 4, 1865; Claiborne, *Mississippi*, pp. 464–465.

[3] CD, Toronto, 1: Emmons to Thurston, n.d., enc. in Thurston to Hunter, May 20, 1865; Carl Sandburg, *Abraham Lincoln: The War Years* (New York, 1939), IV, 268–269. According to one of Thompson's biographers, J. F. Bivins ("Life and Character," p. 89), there is a telegram in the History Collection of The Johns Hopkins University Library that, over Stanton's signature, says, "Arrest Jacob Thompson," but the present writer could find no record of such a telegram, and all of the sources contradict Bivins. Judah Benjamin also escaped to England, where he became an English citizen and a leading barrister, and where, in 1881, with gentle irony, a friend found him arguing a case on Canadian constitutional law. See Castleman, *On Active Service*, pp. 199–202; and Gustavus Wald, "Judah P. Benjamin," *Harvard Graduates' Magazine*, XXXVI (June, 1928), 539.

Globe, hurried to the home of George Brown with the news that the President of the United States had been assassinated, waited until Brown wrote an editorial, and in the small hours of the morning hurried back to the *Globe* office to prepare the first black-bordered memorial edition that the *Globe* ever had printed.[4]

There can be little question that a profound wave of sympathy for Lincoln, for the North, and for the American people as a whole swept the provinces as the full meaning of the news of Lincoln's death was grasped. From Toronto David Thurston wrote that in twelve years' residence in the Canadas he never had seen the community so emotional over any subject. From as far away as Victoria consul Francis remarked upon the same profound sensation that was observed by consuls throughout the provinces. Even General Edwin Lee, Judah Benjamin's personal courier, reported "universal horror." In Toronto the streets were choked with men and women who thronged the newspaper offices to hear the latest news. A meeting at the American Hotel was crowded with Canadians who wished to pay homage to a leader whom they had never known. Canadians streamed into Detroit to attend mourning services and to watch a huge catafalque hauled through the street behind bands playing funeral dirges. Within a day the merchants' stock of crepe was sold out.[5]

As with the outset of the Civil War, the provincial reaction was largely emotional. Wilfrid Laurier, then a schoolboy, found that he had a "perpetual interest" in the life and words of Lincoln from the President's death onward, and in the years to come he filled his library with Lincoln items. Several Canadians responded with poetry, and Edward W. Thomson, the soldier in the Northern army who later became one of the Dominion's minor poets, expressed the continental feel-

[4] Basler, ed., *Works of Abraham Lincoln,* VIII, 413: April 14, 1865; Sumner Papers, LXIII: Mary Lincoln to Sumner, April 13, 1865; Careless, "The Toronto *Globe*," pp. 109, 555.

[5] CD, Toronto, I: Thurston to Hunter, April 24, 1865; CD, Victoria, VI: Francis to Seward, April 22, 1865; CD, Quebec, II: Bowen to Seward, April 25, 1865; J. S. Near, consul at Sarnia, to M. R. Mackenzie, in Sarnia *Observer,* April 28, 1865; G 17, 8, Letter Book: Monck to Bruce, April 17, 1865, 170; NFBL, 78: Monck to Bruce, April 17, enc. in Bruce to Hunter, April 22, 1865; M. Gunn Diary, III, 34: April 15, 1865; Lee Diary: April 15, 30, 1865; Landon, "Harris," art. 7, p. 13: April 15, 1865; Monck, *Leaves,* p. 340; Galt Papers, III: Gzowski to Galt, April 17, 961–964, Tilley to Galt, April 22, 975–978, Galt to Taché, April 27, 980–987, and Galt to Cartier, April 27, 1865, 988–991.

ing of loss, recounting hours around the campfire when Canadians who
owed no allegiance to Lincoln or to his flag paid homage to him in
their own way:

> We talked of Abraham Lincoln in the night:
> Oh sweet and strange to hear the hard-hand men
> Old-Abeing him, like half the world of yore . . .
> And strange and sweet to hear their voices call
> Him 'Father Abraham,' though no man of all
> Was born within the Nation of his birth.

"Not in my time," wrote James Young, already an active man-about-
town and later a leading Canadian politician, writer, and raconteur,
"did I ever know Canada so profoundly stirred." [6]

There were a scattered few, of course, who felt differently about
the death of the Northern leader. In a barroom of the Queen's Hotel
in Toronto two of the St. Albans raiders were overheard praising
John Wilkes Booth, and a group of Southerners held a champagne sup-
per at St. Lawrence Hall to celebrate Lincoln's death. A preacher informed his congregation that Lincoln had gone to Hell, while Lady
Monck found it necessary to explain to a group of nuns that dissenters
went about on Good Friday like any other day, for she suspected that
they felt that Lincoln had been given just retribution for attending the
theater on a holy day. In the Toronto City Council unsuccessful but
highly vocal opposition was offered to a motion that business be suspended during the hours of Lincoln's funeral because there was "plenty
of government business of our own without attending to that of another." [7]

[6] Boston *Daily Evening Traveller*, May 10, 1865, reprinted in *Mag. of Hist.,
with Notes and Querries*, XLIII (1931), 48–49; Oscar D. Skelton, *The Day of Sir
Wilfrid Laurier* (Toronto, 1916), p. 16; Thomson, *Many-Mansioned House and
Other Poems* (Toronto, 1909), p. 334. At least three other Canadian poems were
written at this time on Lincoln themes. J. D. Trayes, who was living at Cam-
bridgeport, Massachusetts, wrote "Abraham Lincoln," a photostatic copy of which
was sent to the present writer through the kindness of Trayes' grandson, A. Ross
Trayes of Hamilton, Ontario. Evan MacCall, in *Poems and Songs* (Kingston,
Ont., 1888), and Mrs. J. C. Yule, in *Poems of the Heart and Home* (Toronto,
1881), also presented works dedicated to Lincoln.

[7] L. C. Baker, *History of the United States Secret Service* (Philadelphia, 1867),
pp. 544–545; G.S.C. to Stanton, April 18, 1865; Monck, *Leaves*, p. 350: April 24,
1865; CD, Montreal, VI: Potter to Seward, April 27, 1865; Toronto *Globe*, April
19, 1865.

The response of the provincial press was striking. Now the Sarnia *Observer* discovered that Lincoln had shown more prudence, courage, and tact than any American leader since Washington, and the *Berliner Journal* responded with a black-bordered edition that praised Lincoln for his patience and humility and wept with Canada West over his death. For those who attempted to defend the assassins, Toronto's *Canadian Freeman* had the single epithet, "depraved." In fact, the Toronto *Leader* was the only major newspaper that did not extend sympathy to the fallen President or to his family. The *Freeman* of Saint John asserted that "the chivalrous gentlemen of the South could not be accomplices in so foul a crime," and without comment it published a prayer for conquered Southerners by William G. "Parson" Brownlow, Tennessee's Unionist governor: "Let them be punished! Let them be impoverished! Let them be slain! And after slain, let them be damned!" The Barrie *Northern Advance* deprecated the deed but pointed out that, considering the character of the people of the United States, just such an outcome of the war was to be expected.[8]

It was the official response throughout British North America that was particularly gratifying to the Northern administration. The Toronto City Council appointed three of its members to represent the city at Lincoln's funeral in Washington, and when the funeral train passed through Buffalo on its way to Illinois many Canadians were present. The Nova Scotia Legislature adjourned upon hearing of Lincoln's death and sent words of sympathy to Mrs. Lincoln. Messages of condolence were received by the Department of State from the Municipal Councils of nearly all the leading British North American communities. On April 19, the day of the funeral, flags on public buildings throughout the provinces were at half-mast, stores were closed, and special services were held in churches in nearly every community, the service in London being the largest of its kind in the history of that city. Toronto's churches, Protestant and Roman Catholic alike, tolled

[8] *Observer*, April 21, 28, 1865; [Kitchener] *Berliner Journal*, April 20, 1865; *Canadian Freeman*, April 17, 1865; *Leader*, April 15, 21, 1865; *Freeman*, April 15, 19, 1865; *Advance*, April 17, 1865. For other expressions in Lincoln's favor see Montreal *L'Echo du Cabinet de lecture paroissial*, VII (May 1, 1865), 129–132; Montreal *Witness*, April 21, 1865; Yarmouth *Herald*, April 21, 27, 1865; Charlottetown *Islander*, April 20, 21, 1865; St. John's *Public Ledger and Newfoundland General Advertiser*, April 18, 1865; Halifax *Morning Freeman*, April 20, 1865; Saint John *New Brunswick Courier*, April 15, 1865; Saint John *Morning Journal* and Saint John *Evening Globe*, both June 2, 1865; Halifax *Sun and Advertiser*, April 19, 1865; *The Times*, April 27, 1865.

their bells for the entire period of the two-hour funeral, and in the ports flags were at half-mast on all of the ships, except where a few blockade-runners raised festive bunting in reply. Negro churches throughout Canada West also held their own special commemorative meetings.[9]

In buildings of worship throughout the land ministers of all faiths reminded their listeners that Lincoln's death must be the beginning of a period of true peace between British North America and the United States. In St. Catharines the Reverend J. B. Howard of the Wesleyan Methodist Church argued that this response in favor of Lincoln should prove to the North that Canadians were not anti-Northern, anticipating the arguments of dozens of writers since. In New York City the Reverend Henry Ward Beecher told his congregation that America must now live in peace with all of her neighbors, including the Canadas, and must renounce any claims to additional territory. John Greenleaf Whittier, who had not hesitated to express anti-British sentiments in verse, sent copies of two poems he had written to abolitionist Alexander Ross in Toronto with the comment that "the tears which both nations are shedding over the grave of our beloved President, are washing out all bitter memories of misconception and estrangement between them. So good comes of the evil." Actually, the response of sympathy at the time of Lincoln's assassination proves only that Lincoln, in death, had captured the imagination of British North Americans just as he was to capture the imagination of the world. But as Samuel Ward noted in his weekly report to the Barings, these expressions of public sympathy were bound to have a beneficial effect on foreign relations.[10]

[9] T.P.L., Larrett Williams Smith Diary: April 19, 1865; CD, Halifax, XI: Howard to Hunter, April 19, 1865; CD, Montreal, VI: Potter to Seward, April 24, 25, 28, June 9, Aug. 11, 1865; ITC, 47: Seward to Potter, June 22, 1864, 374; CD, Saint John, VI: Howard to Hunter, April 16, 18, May 5, June 3, 1865; N.S., House of Assembly, *Debates and Proceedings, 1865*, 245–246: April 15, 1865; David Savage, ed., *Life and Labours of the Rev. William McClure, for More than Forty Years a Minister of the Methodist New Connexion: Chiefly an Autobiography* (Toronto, 1872), p. 307. Many of the memorials are printed in U.S., Dept. of State, *The Assassination of Abraham Lincoln, Late President of the United States of America . . . on the Evening of the Fourteenth of April, 1865* (Washington, 1867), pp. 227–461.

[10] Baring Papers: April 18, May 16, 1865; Sumner Papers, CXXXIX: Gladstone to Sumner, June 11, 1865; Seward Papers: Taché to Seward, April 25, 1865; Detroit *Free Press*, April 29, 1865; Chicago *Tribune*, May 4, 1865; Whittier to Ross, May 22, quoted in Toronto *Globe*, June 1, 1865; Charles M. Ellis, *The Memorial Address on Abraham Lincoln Delivered at the Hall of the Mechanic's Institute,*

The death of Lincoln did more than create for the North a well of sympathy within the provinces. It brought to the presidency Andrew Johnson, a man whom British North Americans feared as an unknown quantity, and Johnson in turn quickly offended a vocal portion of the Canadian public by an inept choice of terminology. Upon evidence offered by one Sanford Conover to the military tribunal concerned with the John Wilkes Booth case, Johnson proclaimed that Jacob Thompson, Clement Clay, Beverley Tucker, and George Sanders had been involved in the assassination plot and that they were being "harbored" in the Canadas. Later Conover's testimony was shown to be perjured, but by then both the Montreal *Evening Telegram* and the *Gazette* had run an identical editorial that caused considerable comment throughout the provinces. The editorial insinuated that since Johnson was the only person who had profited directly from Lincoln's death, and since Booth was known to have left a note in Johnson's hotel box on the night of the assassination, perhaps the new President had been involved. Both papers printed open letters from Sanders and Tucker to Johnson that branded the presidential proclamation "a living, burning lie." In an "Address to the People of Canada" Tucker denied any knowledge of the plot against Lincoln. To bolster his public argument, he added that he was sending copies of his denials to Monck and Bruce, but there is no evidence that they ever received them.[11]

Lincoln's death also set off a man hunt in the Canadas for the supposed killer—for it was thought by many that Booth had escaped via rail into the provinces—which gave Governor General Monck another opportunity to demonstrate cooperation. When Bernard Devlin wired him that some of the persons who had planned the assassination of Lincoln were on their way to Quebec, Monck promised his full assistance. Booth had visited Montreal briefly in 1864, and it was thought that he might now return.[12] Along the border citizens took it upon

---

Saint John, N.B., June 1, 1865, at the Invitation of the Citizens (Saint John, 1865); Robert Norton and R. F. Burns, *Maple Leaves from Canada, for the Grave of Abraham Lincoln* (St. Catharines, 1865). The two pamphlets have been reprinted in *Mag. of Hist., with Notes and Queries*, XVII (1919), and XXII (1924), respectively.

[11] Montreal *Gazette*, May 6, 20, 1865; Montreal *Evening Telegraph and Daily Commercial Advertiser*, May 5, 1865; *Address of Beverley Tucker, Esq., to the People of the United States, 1865* (Montreal, 1865), pp. 3–33, a portion of which is quoted in *ibid.*, and in the New York *Press*, Sept. 17, 1898, and the whole of which is reprinted in J. H. Young, ed., Emory Univ. Publications, *Sources and Reprints*, V (1948), 3–32.

[12] For the highly fanciful and contradictory story of intrigue in Montreal on the part of Booth, see Clayton Gray, *Montreal Story*, pp. 46–48, and *Conspiracy*

themselves to patrol crossing points, and at Malone, in New York state, an emergency company was formed that scouted the border eastward to Rouse's Point, not being overly careful to keep south of the Canadian boundary line. Police hurried to Trois Rivières on information that the guilty parties were hiding there, and although news soon arrived of Booth's death in Virginia, reports of his presence in the British provinces continued to circulate for years thereafter. A pocket handkerchief marked with J. H. Surratt's initials was found in the depot at Burlington, Vermont, and this intensified the search, for Surratt had acted as the Confederacy's messenger to Benjamin's courier, Edwin Lee, early in April and was suspected of being involved in Booth's activities. At the end of May Potter reported to the State Department that Surratt was hiding in some Roman Catholic institution in Montreal —actually the rectory of St. Liboire—and the Consul General also was kept busy tracing down two trunks, which presumably had belonged to Booth and which eventually appeared in Rimouski in Canada East. The new consul at Quebec, W. H. Y. Gurley, was dispatched to obtain the trunks, which he ultimately forwarded to Stanton. Despite all precautions, Surratt made good his escape to Rome, however.[13]

Late in April one Doctor L. P. Blackburn, with forty to fifty men, was said to be leaving Montreal for Bermuda, each of his men reportedly carrying shirts, underclothing, coats, and army trousers "im-

---

in Canada (Montreal, 1959). See also Theodore Roscoe, *Web of Conspiracy* (Englewood Cliffs, N.J., 1959).

[13] CD, Halifax, xi: Howard to Hunter, April 19, 1865; CD, Montreal, vi: Potter to Seward, April 24, and Potter to Hunter, May 22, 30, 1865; *ibid.*, viii: Potter to Seward, Oct. 23, 25, 27, 1865; CD, Gaspé, i: Fitnam to Seward, Oct. 20, 1865; CD, Quebec, ii: Gurley to Seward, June 3, 8, 1865; G 13, 2, Tel. Bk.: Devlin to Monck, April 21, 1865, and reply; Quebec *Morning Chronicle*, July 19, 1865; GBI, 21: Seward to Adams, Dec. 3, 1866, 102; Alfred Isacsson, "John Surratt and the Lincoln Assassination Plot," *Maryland Hist. Mag.*, lii (Dec., 1957), 323-328, which contains several errors. The trunks proved not to be Booth's, and twenty-six years later a local historian claimed to have traced the actual trunks to a wreck at Bic. See New York *Herald*, Nov. 15, 1891.

For some time a number of rumors centered on Surratt and Booth. One rumor that was aired in a Canadian parliamentary committee had it that international bankers, desiring "establishment of the gold standard," hired Booth. It commonly was asserted that Booth worked with the Confederate commissioners in British North America. G. S. Bryan, in *The Great American Myth* (New York, 1940), has shown that there is no evidence that Booth worked with the Confederates. For an example of contemporary propaganda that implicates Canadians, see Dion Haco, *J. Wilkes Booth, The Assassinator of President Lincoln* (New York, 1865).

pregnated" with the virus of yellow fever—it was not yet known that the mosquito was the carrier of the disease—which were to be shipped into the United States from Saint John, Halifax, Montreal, Quebec, Toronto, and St. Catharines. The clothing, Consul General Potter's informant said, was to be distributed through the Sanitary and Christian commissions to Northern hospitals and out-patients so that it would reach sick and wounded soldiers who were too weak to resist the virus. Blackburn had attempted to carry out the same scheme a few months earlier from Bermuda without success. Potter advised Seward to request that the men involved be expelled from the provinces, and that if Monck refused to comply all intercourse between British North America and the United States should cease.

Again Monck was most cooperative. Because of Monck's evident willingness to help the Federal government, Lady Monck even came to fear for her brother-in-law's life and begged him not to go to the theater because some Southerner might attempt to assassinate him. Dr. Blackburn was arrested in Montreal on a warrant charging him with a breach of the neutrality law. At the hearing Potter's informant made public his story. Blackburn was brought to trial in October and eventually was discharged because of insufficient evidence, but the incident had given Monck an opportunity to make his position abundantly clear.[14]

In the first two weeks following Lincoln's death there was some fear on the part of the consuls that Southerners like Sanders or Tucker might attempt a final raid from the provinces, which, considering heightened emotions in the North because of the assassination plot, could create serious repercussions. From Saint John, Howard notified Acting Secretary of State William Hunter that a naval vessel was needed to protect northeastern Maine, and Stanton warned Dix to take special precautions along the frontier. A report from the Canadas that a band of Confederates had sworn to murder Johnson and Stanton within the month, and the dispersal into the border townships of Canada East of many of the Southerners who had been in Montreal, added to the watchfulness of those on guard. Well into the summer rumors

[14] Sumner Papers, LXXIII: Emmons to Sumner, April 14, 1865; CD, Montreal, VI: Potter to Seward, April 27, 1865; G 9, 44: James Corstman to Godley, June 1, enc. in Monck to Cardwell, June 2, 1865, 21–26; CD, Toronto, I: Thurston to Hunter, May 23, 1865; Monck, *Leaves*, pp. 347, 353: April 19, 28, 1865; Toronto *Globe*, May 19, 1865; Canada, *Correspondence Relating to the Rebellion*: Cockburn to Godley, June 1, enc. in Monck to Cardwell, June 2, 1865, 112.

that the Confederates would strike a dying blow against New York City continued to circulate, and it was not until June that the frontier police in Canada East under Colonel Ermatinger was reduced to a skeleton force, and the passport order as it applied to the Maritime Provinces was rescinded.[15]

But the cessation of Confederate activities and the emotional bridge created by Lincoln's death did not remove the realities of the situation. There were still a number of Northern newspapers preaching a doctrine of expansion, agreeing with the New York *Tribune* that it was time to stride "in the majesty of newly asserted strength . . . toward a dazzling destiny." Canadians feared that their province might be the first goal of this dazzling destiny, and it was pointed out that the North had continued to enlist troops throughout April when it was evident they would not be needed in the South. Portions of the Canadian press continued to call Seward a master plotter who would recover to capture the provinces by stealth. The press also reported, with some truth, that a senatorial plan to promote annexationism was in preparation.[16]

And there still was the Fenian threat, against which the reduced border patrols continued to guard. Early in May news arrived of efforts to recruit an expedition to march against the provinces from New York City. British Consul General Archibald, who had continued to observe Fenian activities throughout the war, answered an advertisement in the Brooklyn *Daily Eagle* and learned that an invasion of the Canadas was being planned. Archibald presented his information to Bruce, who in turn submitted it to Hunter, and the Acting Secretary promised to prevent filibustering along the border, but Archibald repeatedly warned the British authorities that discharged soldiers who no longer had jobs and who had learned the art of war, combined with professional recruiters who understood the science of organizing such expeditions, could seize upon the slightest excuse to harry the Canadas. Later Archi-

[15] CD, Saint John, VI: Howard to Hunter, April 24, 1865; *OR*, ser. I, XLVI, 952: Stanton to Dix, April 26, 1865, and 967: D. T. Van-Buren to General Robinson, n.d.; L. C. Baker, p. 546: J. P. H. Hall to Johnson, April 20, 1865; Quebec *Gazette*, June 9, 1865; Macdonald Papers, 233: Black, Carr, and Dallas to McMicken, May 13, 1865; *ibid.*, 339: Chamberlin to Macdonald, March 22, 1865; E 1, 90AB: March 24, June 27, 30, 1865, 465, 470–472; CD, Montreal, V: Thurston to Seward, July 20, 1865.

[16] [G. D. Griffin?], "The Trumpet Sounded," *Can. Quart. Rev. and Family Mag.*, II (July, 1865), 284–452; G. R. Brown, ed., *Reminiscences of Senator William M. Stewart of Nevada* (New York, 1908), pp. 177–178.

bald's correspondent informed him that he had gathered three thousand ex-soldiers who desired "a little more active occupation," and while nothing came of this particular plan, it was just such schemes that posed the greatest threat for the future, as was to be demonstrated at Fort Erie in 1866.[17]

There also was an entire host of problems that would form a legacy of the Civil War for years to come, and Macdonald continued to impress his two-year time-table on the Colonial Office. The victorious North, too exhausted to retaliate against the provinces even had it wanted to, might one day turn upon British North America for "harboring" Confederates or for displaying anti-Northern sentiment during the war. The threat of the annexation of Canada was to be used during the next decade by astute Republican politicians to win votes from the increasingly important Irish bloc, just as the threat was used in the provinces to hasten the culmination of British North American confederation in 1867.[18] Most of the diplomatic questions that had been raised during the war with respect to the provinces had been settled by the end of the conflict, and the work of Monck and even of Seward, together with Lincoln's death, had produced another momentary period of apparent Canadian-American harmony, but there still were outstanding problems with Great Britain, the foremost of which were categorized under the generic term *"Alabama* claims," and in the ultimate settlement of such problems British North America would be the hostage of the United States. Such would be the case in 1871 when the Dominion of Canada was to see itself "sold on the block" of Anglo-American harmony at Washington.

At the end of the Civil War two important issues between the United States and the British provinces themselves remained unresolved. The

[17] G 8B, 45: Archibald to Bruce, May 18, and Bruce to Russell, May 19, both enc. in Cardwell to Gordon, June 10, 1865, 692-699; NFBL, 78: "K.Y." to G. W. Gibbons, May 8, 13, Gibbons to "K.Y.," May 10, 16, and "E.M.A." to Bruce, n.d., all enc. in Bruce to Hunter, May 19, 1865; G 1, 174: Cardwell to Monck, June 3, 1865.

[18] See Joe Patterson Smith's two articles, "American Republican Leadership and the Movement for the Annexation of Canada in the Eighteen-Sixties," C.H.A., *Annual Report* (1935), pp. 67-75; and "A United States of North America—Shadow or Substance? 1815-1915," *CHR*, xxvi (June, 1945), 109-118; Barnard Fensterwald, Jr., "The Anatomy of American 'Isolationism' and Expansionism. Part I," *Journal of Conflict Resolution*, II (June, 1958), 111-139; and the stimulating final chapter in Norman A. Graebner, *Empire on the Pacific: A Study in American Continental Expansion* (New York, 1955).

abrogation of the reciprocity treaty, which would take effect in March of 1866, was to be a bone of contention between the two countries until well into the next century. The perennial fisheries question also had been re-opened, for in abrogating reciprocal trade, the United States threw the fisheries settlement back upon the principles of the unsatisfactory Convention of 1818, principles that New England's fishing interest refused to accept. Thus, as Canada maneuvered in the future to regain the reciprocity treaty, she was to use the fisheries as an enticing bait.

But perhaps the most important legacy of the war was a catalogue of fears, an awareness that the "war in anticipation" was not yet over, and an awareness that as Britain completed her withdrawal from the continent the survival of a separate Canadian nation would become more, not less, difficult. As Canadians came to discover that the common North American environment they shared with the United States helped produce similar social patterns, they learned that the battle against annexation was neither solely political nor solely economic, for the cultural achievements of the American Republic, together with her great material success, might lead to annexation by gravitation. Less than a century later Canadians would ask whether they had achieved political independence only to lose their souls, to have their wants and desires, the system of values that helps denote a true nation, shaped by the United States.

But the Civil War was over at last and the continent rejoiced. The usual border traffic, legal and illegal, which marks nations at peace, slowly began to recover its peacetime nature. A great increase in trade followed British North American efforts to take advantage of the final year of the reciprocity treaty. Joseph Howe hurried to Washington to view the last of the Northern troops marching through the city's streets, and the skedaddlers drifted back into the North. The British North Americans who had served in the armies of the blue and the gray hurried home to enjoy the short northern summer, while junketing Northern generals Sherman and Grant, potential invaders, were entertained royally at Canadian banquets dedicated to renewed "Anglo-American harmony." [19] A number of Confederates drifted in from

[19] CD, Toronto, I: Thurston to Hunter, June 27, 1865; CD, Montreal, VII: Potter to N. Sargent, Aug. 1, 1865; *ibid.*, VIII: Potter to Seward, Aug. 8, Nov. 2, 1865; CD, Fort Erie, I: F. N. Blake to Seward, Nov. 28, 1865; NFBL, 77: Brydges to Monck, March 9, and Monck to Burnley, March 13, both enc. in Burnley to Seward, March 21, 1865; Montreal *Witness* and Quebec *Gazette*, both Aug. 9,

the defeated South, unwilling to live under Federal surveillance, while many of those already in the provinces waited until they could present themselves to the crepe-decked consulates to apply for a pardon under Johnson's general proclamation of amnesty in 1866. The diplomats set about preparing the hundreds of pages of briefs that would be necessary in the negotiations that were to come, and on June 3, 1865, Cardwell transmitted to Governor General Monck a letter from Lord Russell announcing that Her Majesty's government officially recognized that after four years and two months peace had been restored in the United States.[20]

The Civil War had ended—but not without malice toward some.

1865; *The Times,* Aug. 19, 1865; Kirby Papers: Kirby to Eliza, Aug. 7, 1865; Fred Landon, "Joseph Howe Visits Civil War Sites," London *Free Press,* Aug. 29, 1955; Lloyd Lewis, *Sherman: Fighting Prophet* (New York, 1932), p. 631.

[20] G 1, 174: Cardwell to Monck; CD, Quebec, II: Bowen to Seward, April 24, 1865; CD, Charlottetown, II: Sherman to Seward, May 25, 1865; CD, Saint John, VI: Howard to Seward, Dec. 5, 1865; CD, Toronto, I: Thurston to Seward, Oct. 11, 1865; CD, Montreal, VIII: C. G. B. Drummond to Seward, July 31, 1866; Seward Papers: Tucker to Seward, April 13, 1865; Lee Diary: May 12, 20, 29, June 6, 18, July 4, 6, 1865; Denison Papers, I: Lee to Denison, April 30, 1868, 128–138, and Early to Denison, Oct. 27, 1868, 161–164; Saint John *New Brunswick Courier,* June 24, 1865; A. J. Clarks, "When Jefferson Davis Visited Niagara," Ontario Hist. Soc., *Papers and Records,* XIX (1922), 87–89; Ishbel Ross, *First Lady of the South: The Life of Mrs. Jefferson Davis* (New York, 1958), pp. 301–304; W. B. Hesseltine, *Confederate Leaders in the New South* (Baton Rouge, 1950), pp. 7, 11, 35.

seventeen ❧ TOWARD CONTINENTAL

SECURITY?

> "Not much satisfied with myself, but hope what
> I said will tend to good."
> JOHN BRIGHT, *speaking to the Jervois Report*

AT THE END OF THE AMERICAN REVOLUTION IN 1783 DAVID HARTLEY, THEN
the personal emissary of Charles James Fox, Great Britain's Secretary for Foreign Affairs, called Benjamin Franklin's attention to an
"awful and important truth." "Our respective territories are in vicinity," he said, "and therefore we must be inseparable . . . . Political
intercourse and interests will obtrude themselves between our two
countries because they are the two great powers dividing the Continent
of North America." Hartley was premature in bestowing the accolade
of "Great Power" on the United States, but he was wise before the
event. Certainly by the mid-nineteenth century the "awful and important truth" was abundantly apparent to the United States and to the
British North American provinces alike. These provinces seemed destined for one of two alternatives: gradual absorption into the American Republic by peaceful means induced by economic necessity, or
sudden envelopment through force during a general Anglo-American
war. To prevent the former, British North Americans had to protect
their ties with the mother country while they promoted their own
unity. To prevent the latter, they could attempt to see to it that no
Anglo-American war would be fought over causes generated by or
within the provinces. Both they did, but clearly they did not always
counter their rather neutral view of their position as a North Atlantic
country with the more positive concept of actively encouraging Anglo-American harmony.

As long as Great Britain had made some effort to maintain a balance of power in North America by garrisoning her provinces and controlling the seas, the colonies had enjoyed a degree of safety. But in 1854, for the first time in her history, Britain negotiated a reciprocity treaty for the sole benefit of a colonial area, and she gave every sign of expecting the North American provinces to help themselves thereafter. As she recalled her legions, the Mother Country gave tacit recognition to the fact that a military, land-based balance of power no longer was possible in North America. Britain's position on the continent was recognized as a secondary one, and where her needs in Europe came into conflict with the reality of her position in North America, the strategy of European diplomacy was to be given precedence. Thus, at times Great Britain felt the need to sacrifice British North America's more local interests for the sake of Anglo-American harmony, a goal often considered to be for the good of the Empire as a whole. In so doing she angered the provinces, but they were at least as annoyed with the United States for placing Britain in such a position as they were with Britain for using the position as a basis for action. The Northern victory in the American Civil War destroyed any remaining possibility of a restoration of the balance of power in North America. Thereafter, Canadian-American relations and British policy with respect to the New World were posited upon the assumption that the United States had the preponderance of power on the continent. The provinces became a hostage to a subjective American judgment on the "good behavior" of the British throughout the world.

With the passing of the Confederate States and the destruction of any lingering British hope of maintaining a parity of power within North America, Great Britain was forced to recognize the ultimate meaning of her withdrawal of the legions. When the Colonial Office agreed, in the autumn of 1864, to transfer support for regional union to support for a broader confederation, she was acknowledging that in the long run a united and increasingly independent British North America had the greatest chance of remaining outside the burgeoning and reunited republic. Little Englanders also would be happy to be free of the colonies, not only because they seemed economically burdensome but because they seemed to be an obvious enticement for an American war with Britain.

British North Americans knew that relations with the United States were at their worst since the War of 1812, and driven by compelling domestic as well as external causes they cautiously pushed ahead with their plans. In 1867 the title "Kingdom" was rejected for the new confederation because it might offend the United States, and Leonard Tilley seized upon the encouraging Psalm, less accurate but also less emotional, "he shall have dominion also from sea to sea" (72:8), for the rubric by which the new nation might be described. It can be, and has been, argued that Canada became the first Dominion not only because Britain saw a need to shape a new imperial policy, but because both found in Dominion status a partial answer to the alleged dangers of American expansionism.

That a war did not come should be a lesson to those who would read inevitability into the course of history. Canada was and remained "an almost defenseless prize"—yet, she was neither absorbed nor made a battleground in a new Anglo-American war. By assuring the victory of Republican capitalism and middle-class ethics in North America, the Civil War created a nation which chose to expand where she could economically but hardly at all militarily except as an emotional crusade, thereby decreasing the immediate pressure on the provinces. If we are to accept the sociology of a Quincy Wright or the economics of a Joseph Schumpeter, a bourgeois and nonmilitant nation seldom indulges in calculated imperialism. To some extent Canada may have become an economic appendage to the United States, but if so, she was becoming this before 1861 anyway.[1] The Civil War at least helped evoke the new British policy that contributed so much to Canadian preservation and blunted the force of American spatial, as distinct from ideological, expansionism. In effect the war had helped create not one but two nations.

During the war, Great Britain and the provinces looked down opposite ends of the same telescope. The mother country felt that one of her greatest dangers of conflict with the United States lay in her connection with the provinces, and this produced a willingness on the part of many Victorians to sever such connections. On the other hand, the British North Americans felt that war would come to them only over imperial matters and not over provincial errors. Because of this short-sightedness, the provinces were slow to correct their mistakes, were slow to enforce their own neutrality, and despite repeated warnings

---

[1] See H. A. Innis, *Great Britain, The United States and Canada: The Cust Foundation Lectures* (Nottingham, 1948), and Schumpeter, *Social Classes and Imperialism: Two Essays* (New York, 1955), p. 73. See also Robin W. Winks, "A Nineteenth-Century Cold War," *Dalhousie Rev.*, XXXIX (Winter, 1959), 464–470.

by homegrown geopoliticians, failed to prepare adequately for the possibility of continental war. The colonists also realized that Great Britain was more than willing to let them depart in peace so long as the British flag lost no prestige in the parting. Many provincial statesmen felt that they had to walk between the two mythical monsters whom it would be trite to mention in order to prevent rejection by the one which would lead to absorption by the other. That they were able to do so was a success story worthy of the North American continent, where success and manifest destiny often have been taken as synonymous, for had they wished, the re-United States might well have fought a victorious war for the provinces.

Another source of danger to Great Britain lay within the colonies. The Confederate government early realized that if Britain could be drawn into the war on the side of the South, a Southern victory might be assured. Yet it failed to see that diplomacy could be at least as important as military victories. Led by a President who considered himself something of an expert on military matters, the Confederacy found itself with strong generals and weak diplomats. By 1863 it was apparent that London was not the only way to British hearts, and the Confederacy attempted to precipitate an Anglo-Northern war along the Canadian frontier. But by then Britain had seen that she had little to gain from recognition of the Confederacy, and Britain and the North were aware that Confederate raids were meant to create a war that both wanted to avoid.

The Southern attempts to produce "embroilment" were weakened by not being pursued with sufficient tenacity. Even today historians commonly view the Confederate missions to British North America as little more than an effort to divert Federal attention to the northern flank during the election of 1864. Certainly the number of attempts were so few and so poorly conducted as to give superficial support to this interpretation, and yet the Confederates had a weapon that the St. Albans raid, in particular, demonstrated to be capable of creating an atmosphere that might have induced Northern retaliation. The Confederate policy was reckless in its conception, weak in its implementation, and obviously devoid of the desired results.

The Confederacy also failed because of the sanity of leadership in the provinces, Great Britain, and the North. Monck, who fought for the neutrality act; Macdonald, who planned for defense through union; Lincoln, who wanted but one war at a time, and none at all if possible; and Seward, who—with Charles Francis Adams' restraining advice—learned to gauge just how far he could push the colonial and imperial authorities to achieve his ends, were the architects of peace amidst war. The Civil War demonstrated the fact that effective leadership could do much to counteract bitter public opinion and uncontrolled emotionalism and could help to avoid the use of force as an arbiter of international problems. That Nova Scotians constructed a drill hall that never was used, and that the only extensive military loss of life within the provinces was the result of an explosion in an ammunitions laboratory, and not to the misplaced braveries of the battlefield, were homely and pathetic testimony to the men and forces that maintained peace.[2]

Many factors have been cited to account for Britain's failure to recognize or to aid the Confederate states. British need for American wheat and the influence of the working class in Britain are traditionally noted. British preoccupation with the Schleswig-Holstein dispute on the continent was a significant factor, as were the profits that certain Lancashire manufacturers realized over the scarcity of cotton, and the fact that the linen and woolen industries were booming. A repugnance for slavery among the royal family had its effect, as did Northern propaganda. But while each of these was important, the possibility of losing the British North American provinces through force, with a resulting loss of prestige, and Confederate abuse of British neutrality in North America, were at least equal parts in the mosaic that finally shaped Britain's policy during the war. The provinces, Great Britain's "hostages to fortune," simply were too great a price to pay for intervention.

But if Confederate diplomacy ended in failure, Northern foreign policy with respect to British North America was at best a negative success. The North's only substantial diplomatic victory was in securing the passage of the Canadian Alien Act of 1865, and this was but the reverse side to the Confederate coin, a Canadian response to Southern abuse of their hospitality as much as to Seward's maneuvering. Because the Federal government ignored the provinces as a field for propaganda activity, the British North Americans tended to discount even abolitionism as a point in common between the North and the colonies. By pushing to the fore the question of preserving the Union, President Lincoln won the border states to his cause and lost the provinces.

[2] D. G. Whidden, *The History of the Town of Antigonish* (Wolfville[?], 1934), p. 137; Gale, *Twixt Old and New*, p. 203. In March, 1864, an explosion in Quebec led to eleven deaths.

A growing sense of moral distance between the provinces and the North added to the serious strain upon the gossamer webs of peace. One proudly boasted a monarchical system, the other a democracy, which, when viewed from afar, appeared to some a mobocracy. Two ways of life seemed in conflict. The moral alliance which Canadian and Northern abolitionists might have forged through their common humanitarian goal never became a reality, partially because of a disagreement on means, partially because of a confusion over the way in which ends should be expressed, and primarily because the Canadian abolitionists, never having the responsibility of devising a rhetoric by which they could make their moral crusade politically palatable, had little understanding of that group of Northern abolitionists who had to combine their moral slogans with the more practical language of a political party. This misunderstanding may have broadened rather than narrowed the gap in the crucial months of 1861. Certainly the failure of Canadian abolitionists to lend their support to the war to preserve the Union surprised and angered American abolitionists.

Some have argued that the Civil War obscured the Anglo-American harmony that had been reached by the time the Prince of Wales visited the United States in 1860. Actually, the Civil War demonstrated that Anglo-American harmony had not been attained at all, and rather than obscuring the general trend, the war threw the actual trend into bold relief. The war helped illustrate to the Colonial Office that some other form of government for the series of disconnected North American colonies was essential, and it revealed the hostility that existed between those colonies and the Northern states. The "century of peace" was still a phrase waiting to be coined by some future after-dinner speaker, and the so-called undefended or unfortified frontier was patrolled closely throughout the conflict, so closely as to destroy any meaning, contemporary or historical, for the word "undefended."

But the Civil War was beneficial to Canada, for it promoted British North American unity in at least four ways. The possibility of an American invasion made union a means to a more effective defense. With the loss of reciprocal trade with the United States the colonies needed to band together to develop complementary markets. The war furnished a respite from American expansionism, which gave the counterexpansionism of Canada West an opportunity to move toward eventual absorption of the Red River district. And the spectacle of war provided a potent object lesson in statecraft and constitution-making that Canadian leaders did not ignore.

The influence of the Civil War on the form ultimately taken by both the Canadian government and economic system was of great importance. But the war also was decisive in Anglo-American and in Canadian-American relations, for as much as any event in the nineteenth century it demonstrated, to Canada most strongly, the ultimate need for Anglo-American harmony. Born in fear, deadlock, and confusion, Canada grew into a nation that could not afford to exhibit the rampant nationalism usually associated with young countries, and even today, due to her mother, the nature of her gestation, and the continuing pressures from her large, pragmatic, and restless neighbor, Canada remains a nation in search of a national culture.

Ultimately the Civil War was a shared experience. American heroes became Canadian heroes, and if during the war the outstanding figure was Robert E. Lee, after the war Abraham Lincoln assumed the role of the continent's mythic giant. If the century of peace technically was a myth, the undefended frontier is a reality today because men and human institutions were sufficiently flexible in the 1860's to stand the stresses that were placed upon them. Myths, if allowed to endure long enough, sometimes become folk truths.

Such has become the case in the twentieth century. Continentalism, for good or ill, is triumphant, and Canada willingly, if on occasion nervously, joins in a system of continental security with the nation against which she inveighed in the 1860's. In the last century the move from continental insecurity to continental security has been complete. The United States and Canada are inextricably bound to each other in a system of defense and in a pattern of economic interchange so that neither can do without the other.

Yet tensions continue, less dramatic perhaps but more basic for being at the level of ideas, not things. Today Canadians fear that annexation is an accomplished fact, that "continental security" may represent a form of insecurity for things distinctively Canadian, for the United States controls Canadian defense and large portions of Canadian industry, dominates the Canadian popular mind with its songs, its motion pictures, its books and magazines. With a small population and a vast territory, the former aggravated by a constant drift of Canadian intellectuals to the United States and the latter yet to be developed, Canada has been living beyond her intellectual income. Having no large metropolitan center of her own, with the possible exception of internally directed Montreal to which French Canada looks, the Dominion has developed in a provincial pattern, if not "looking to Washington" as Macdonald charged the Clear Grits, then looking alternately, inconsistently, and unhappily to London and New York. And if, as seems to be the case, Canadians acquire American tastes, pursue American goals, come to accept the American value system, direct their lives according to the motives usually associated with another nation, how are they to remain a nation a part, a people at once North American and Canadian, with their own symbols, value system, and national image? Today the hopes of Canada are tied to the United States. Is this a subtle form of annexation? some ask. Were confederation and independence won only to be lost in the counting houses and at the television studios? In the jargon of the sociologist, can an other-directed nation survive?

From Civil War to Collective Security the two nations have remained separate. But Canada remains a nation in search of a soul, a country unknown to itself. What is needed is a new Crèvecoeur who may ask, in modified form, as the author of the famous Letter III in *Letters from an American Farmer* did over a century and a half ago, "What then is the Canadian, this new man?"

A NOTE ON SOURCES

FOR THE MOST PART THIS BOOK IS BASED ON MANUSCRIPT MATERIALS. FORtunately almost all of the official papers of any importance for a study of Canadian-American relations during the Civil War are available to the researcher at various repositories in the United States and Canada. Several significant collections of private papers also were used, as were numerous files of newspapers, nineteenth-century pamphlets of a promotional or polemical nature, and other primary sources. The following essay will deal with contemporary materials only. The notes will readily lead the reader to the most important of the secondary works, including printed documents not discussed here.

Documentation has been substantially reduced for the present volume. Anyone who might wish additional references to a given point is directed to the notes in the writer's dissertation, entitled "Maple Leaf and Eagle: Canadian-American Relations during the American Civil War," on deposit in the library of The Johns Hopkins University. The second volume contains a lengthy bibliography of printed materials.

Official Papers

The most important collections of official papers used in this study are the State Department Diplomatic and Consular Correspondence at the National Archives, the "C," "E," and "G" series at the Public Archives of Canada, and the British Colonial and Foreign Office records, on deposit at the Public Record Office in London and available by photoduplication for the period of the Civil War at the Library of Congress and the Public Archives.

The Diplomatic Correspondence consists of thousands of documents organized chronologically by content or by nation concerned. The instructions to and from the minister to Great Britain, together with the notes to and from the British Legation, are voluminous and extremely valuable. This material, used in conjunction with the many volumes of interdepartmental Domestic Letters, appointment books, special collections of correspondence relating to reciprocity and extradition, and various miscellaneous records, were the most obvious although not the most significant sources.

Of far greater importance were the dozens of bound volumes of Consular Correspondence. While it would be improper to say that consular records are an untapped source, especially since those relating to Latin America have been exploited for some time, one is quite correct in saying that they remain little used and that, while a few of the volumes relating to British North America have been consulted by others, the writer apparently was the first to search most of them. The consuls were in a position to observe at first hand provincial attitudes toward the United States, and Secretary Seward and his son were fortunate to have a relatively astute and literate group in the provinces. On occasion the volumes are difficult to read, for pages have become blurred and words have been transferred from one page to another, and documents often have been filed incorrectly. Dispatches appear in invoice books, are misdated, and on occasion are missing altogether. Contemporary registers for the material have been preserved, but they often are incomplete or inaccurate.

Nonetheless, the many consular volumes were invaluable. In their reports the consuls wrote of the contemporary scene at length, showing considerable talent for balancing street corner gossip with the latest editorials—carefully clipped and forwarded with their dispatches— and for balancing both against official or declared policy. While they knew that what they wrote should justify themselves, their remarks stand the test of subsequent research surprisingly well. Used judiciously, the consuls' many essays on British North American affairs are useful for domestic as well as for international history. The writer used all of the material that was available for 1860–1867 from the following posts: Victoria, Vancouver Island; Newcastle, St. George, and Saint John, New Brunswick; St. John's, Newfoundland; Halifax, Nova Scotia; Fort Erie, Hamilton, Kingston, Johnstown (now Prescott), Sarnia, Toronto, and Windsor, Canada West; Charlottetown, Prince Edward Island; Coaticook, Gaspé, Montreal, Quebec, and St. Johns,

Canada East; and Kingston and Nassau for the Caribbean region. In addition departmental instructions to the consuls and to Consuls General Giddings and Potter were of great importance.

Other official State Department papers used at the National Archives include the various Special Agents Reports, especially those relating to George Ashmun, William M. Evarts, and Preston King, and material relating to foreign service posts in Record Group 84. From the papers of the Office of the Adjutant General in the War Records came the Books and Letters Received relating to the Department of the East, which deal with defense along the British North American frontier; incoming telegrams; certain general information records on Canada; the individual packets of war records for specific participants in the border incidents, such as Bennet G. Burley; and the rather overrated Baker-Turner Papers, which have not proved to be as revealing as many had hoped. From the records of the Treasury Department the writer used the domestic letters and outgoing telegrams for the years 1861–1865, and from the records of the Post Office Department the letterbooks of the Postmaster General for 1861–1864 were consulted on various matters of detail.

Additional official or semi-official American papers used include the Confederate State Papers—once known as the "Pickett Papers" —at the Library of Congress. This collection contains much of the correspondence between Holcombe, Thompson, and Judah P. Benjamin, as well as one of Benjamin's diaries. The writer attempted to discover other Benjamin papers, but it is known that he destroyed most of the Confederate records before he fled from Richmond. An effort to trace certain papers through the son of one of Benjamin's biographers, Pierce Butler, was unsuccessful. The Confederate State Papers contain a very few letters written by Clement Clay and other Southerners while in the British provinces, and these were supplemented by the Clay papers at Duke University and the diary of Edwin G. Lee at the University of North Carolina.

The Canadian "G" series (or, more correctly, Record Group 7) at the Public Archives of Canada was the most valuable and largest collection of documents used. The series consists of the thousands of dispatches and related records pertinent to the office of the governor general. The record group is divided into twenty-three numbered series; the working titles of these series and the volumes consulted within the series are:

G1 Despatches from the Colonial Office, 153–165, 402–437
G2 [Supplementary] Despatches from the Colonial Office, 7–8
G4 Despatches referred to the Executive Council, 14–18
G6 Despatches from the British Minister at Washington, 10–16
G7 Despatches from the Lieutenant-Governors, 11
G8A Records from the Lieutenant-Governor's Office: Nova Scotia, 1, 5
G8B Do., New Brunswick, 41–46, 62–66 (copies are available at the New Brunswick Museum)
G8C Do., British Columbia, 2–5, 9–12, 21–23
G8D Do., Prince Edward Island, 30–34, 58–59, 68
G9 Drafts of Despatches to the Colonial Office, 38–44
G10 Drafts of Secret and Confidential Despatches to the Colonial Office, 1–2
G11 Drafts of Despatches to the British Minister at Washington, 184–221, 229–239, 321–328, 466
G12 Letter Books of Despatches to the Colonial Office, 67–70
G13 Telegrams, 1–2
G14 Miscellaneous Records, 14, 44, 74, 76
G17 [Governor General's Internal] Letter Books, 4–6, 8
G18 [Additional] Miscellaneous Records, 14, 59, 67, 71
G19 Records of the Military Secretary, 4, 13, 16–18, 32–33
G20 Civil Secretary's Correspondence, 81–107, 384, 386
G21 Governor General's Numbered Files, 19, 57, 86, 301, 441
G23 Miscellaneous Records relating to Royal Visits, 24

Most series consist of bound volumes, without an index, arranged chronologically. Almost all of the dispatches in the main series contain endorsements, but these notations often hinder rather than aid research, since they usually mention only the most important subject taken up in the dispatch, omitting any reference to lesser matters. Most —but not all—of G 6 and G 11 are available on photostats at the Library of Congress, but since these duplications sometimes omit the various enclosures, the fuller sets of papers should be consulted in Ottawa. Several of the dispatches from these two series also are present in the Notes from the British Legation at the National Archives, for Lord Lyons kept Seward well informed, frequently sending him copies of material that he sent to Monck.

The various "G" series were reorganized in 1940, and an inventory for the record group was published by the Archives in 1953. An exception is G 21, a portion of which became available in 1956, dealing as the series does largely with fairly recent materials. This series has an index and is arranged in reverse order of time, with the exception of the first portion of number 57, which has been calendared. In G 21 only, the numbers used in the notes refer not to single volumes but to sets of volumes. This document group contains material on the St. Albans raid, United States consular appointments, and enlistments. The G 1, 6, 7, 11, and 12 groups remain the key series, however.

To supplement the "G" series, the writer consulted some seventy-seven volumes, under twenty-four subheadings, of Record Group 8, the "C" series, entitled British Military Records. This series includes material on desertion, two volumes of crimping reports, two additional collections specifically relating to defensive activities brought on by the Civil War, volumes on the Fenians, the Canadian Militia, the *Trent* affair, and the defenses of Quebec, the Chief-of-Staff's letterbook, telegrams, and miscellaneous reports and correspondence. Within this record group the Admiralty Pacific Station Records include reports on Canadian defense, the San Juan Island controversy, and additional militia material. There are one or two index and purport books but there are no finding aids for most of these papers.

Record Group 1, the "E" series, State Records of the Executive Council, includes the minutes of the Council, militia records, state books, and the correspondence of the Clerk of the Council. The "E" series is important, for while the author has on occasion referred to Monck's activities almost as though he operated autonomously, he in fact did not, of course, except where he acted in a personal capacity. His decisions and requests were made as Governor General-in-Council. Customs records and miscellaneous correspondence and letterbooks, designated Record Group 19, Department of Finance, were consulted. Inventories for this group, and for Group 8, were published in 1954. Finally, photostats of dispatches to the Lieutenant Governor of Nova Scotia, the originals of which subsequently were seen at the Public Archives of Nova Scotia, were consulted in Manuscript Group 10.

Also of importance are the Colonial Office Records and the Foreign Office Correspondence, the originals of which are in the Public Record Office in London. Microfilms of both groups of papers are now available at the Public Archives, and photocopies of the latter are on deposit at the Library of Congress. From the Colonial Office Records the writer used the correspondence of the Governor General with the

Colonial Secretary, that of the Governor of British Columbia and the Lieutenant Governor of Newfoundland with the Secretary, the commissions and instructions to the lieutenant governors, various supplementary records in CO 42, and the Cardwell Papers (microfilm of P.R.O. 30/48). Much of this material has been available on this side of the Atlantic only since 1954. From the Foreign Office Correspondence the writer used series 5, Instructions, Despatches, and Notes; series 81, Miscellaneous, and Law Officer Reports; series 115, General, with Despatches and Notes; series 97; and the Puget's Sound Agricultural Company dispute records. Where these series seemed incomplete, additional microfilms were obtained—as in the case of the British consular despatches for Eastport and Portland, Maine, and Boston, Massachusetts—from the Public Record Office.

Private Papers

Collections of private papers, except for figures in public life, are less plentiful for the Civil War years than for the period preceding the war. Perhaps this may be explained in part by the fact that cheap postage was introduced in the eighteen-fifties, and people began to treasure their letters less. The writer found it difficult to locate any substantial collections of material relating to merchants or farmers that would throw light on small town and rural opinion during the Civil War, and he has attempted to offset any tendency toward an urban bias by the use of newspapers from the smaller communities. As a general rule the diaries of the period are of little help, for they probably were either too personal to be passed on to public archives or they generally recorded only trivia. It is unfortunate that more letters were not saved, for in them a person was more inclined to express his views (although not necessarily his true views, of course) on current events, not wishing to have his reader think him uninformed, than in his diary, which told abundantly of the weather and often of little else. It is doubly unfortunate that the private papers of Thomas D'Arcy McGee, while originally preserved, apparently were destroyed by fire early in the present century.

But there is much that remains. One of the two or three most valuable collections of private papers in Canada is that of John A. Macdonald at the Public Archives. Splendidly organized, these volumes include special compilations on the St. Albans raid, the Fenians, defense, the militia, McMicken's police force, confederation, and reciprocity, as well as many volumes organized by correspondent, including Cartier, Head, Monck, Brydges, Vankoughnet, Galt, Sandfield Macdonald, McGee, Tupper, Taché, and others. The volumes used in the present study were numbers 14, 50–51, 56, 86, 99–100, 118, 145, 158, 161, 188–189, 191, 194, 202–203, 209, 216, 221–222, 224, 228, 230–235, 238, 246–247, 252–254, 258, 260, 273, 281–282, 293–299, 337–339, 508–511, and Letter Book 6. Recent additions to the Public Archives include a small group of Alexander T. Galt papers and a substantial body of George Brown manuscripts, first opened for general research in 1960, and made available to the writer with the permission of Professor J. M. S. Careless of the University of Toronto.

The Archives yielded many other peripherally useful collections. Among these were the Edward M. Archibald papers, the Baring Brothers papers, partial transcripts of which originally were supplied to the author by Joe Patterson Smith of Illinois College, the Isaac Buchanan papers, the George Taylor Denison papers, diaries, and scrapbooks, the William Denny Family papers, the Colonel C. de Salaberry papers, the diaries of Sir Sandford Fleming, the Glyn, Mills, Company letterbooks, the papers and typescript journal of Marcus Gunn, the Joseph Howe manuscripts, the H. S. Kane papers (containing material on Coursol and the St. Albans raid), the papers of William King, Guillaume Lamothe, H. G. McGillivray, Hamilton Merritt (indexed by Norah Story), and W. C. Milner, the Strathcona papers, the Charles Tupper papers, several items relating to William McDougall, John Dougall, John Sandfield Macdonald, and Thomas D'Arcy McGee, and Simon Fraser's papers on the Grenville Militia. On microfilm the author used the papers of Edward Ellice, the originals of which are in the National Library of Scotland, the James Wickes Taylor papers, the originals being in the Minnesota Historical Society, the papers of William Morris and one item from the Charles Hibbert Tupper papers, two items from the Sir Edmund Head papers, and the diaries of Alexander McNeilledge. Of these collections the papers of Ellice, Denison, Howe, Lamothe, and Taylor were especially valuable. The Howe volumes include various letters pertaining to defense, reciprocity, railways, and the fisheries, and an interesting if erratic manuscript biography of the Nova Scotian by George S. Johnson appears in the Johnson papers. The Lamothe papers had not been processed at the time, and the writer was given permission to use them before they were sorted. They were found to contain, among other valuable items, a handwritten account, presumably by Lamothe, of his efforts to help some of the St. Albans raiders escape from Canada East to Newfoundland or Nova Scotia.

Several other collections of private papers were used in Canada. These include the papers of A. N. Buell, Sir Alexander Campbell, William Canniff, Sir Richard Cartwright, Charles Clarke, the J. T. Gilkison Family, C. S. Gzowski, William Kirby, the Robinson Family, the Strachan Family, and John Twigg, all at the Ontario Provincial Archives; and the Sir Richard Cartwright, J. H. Delamere, Henry Scadding, and Denison Family papers, and the diaries of John Grant, Edward H. Osler, and L. W. Smith, at the Toronto Public Library. The John Charlton papers were read at the University of Toronto. Extracts from the diary of George W. Brown, in private hands, were used, and extracts from some nine other diaries were obtained but not incorporated into the study. Finally, the Archives of the New Brunswick Museum in Saint John yielded the Moses Perley and valuable Sir William Fenwick Williams papers; the disappointing Arthur H. Gordon papers were consulted in their original form at the Bonar Law-Bennett Library of the University of New Brunswick in Fredericton; and a small collection of additional Joseph Howe material was read at the Public Archives of Nova Scotia. In England, one of Goldwin Smith's letters on enlistments was found in the James Bryce Papers at the Bodleian Library, Oxford.

In the United States two manuscript collections were indispensable. The superbly organized papers of William H. Seward at the University of Rochester, which consist of some eighty-four thousand letters in 170 volumes, were given to the Rush Rhees Library by William H. Seward III in 1949. Supplemented with the letters of Thurlow Weed and Frederick Seward and microcards of the papers of Archbishop John Hughes of New York, this collection is one of the finest in America. While no less than seven large cabinets contain material on the Civil War years, use is rendered feasible and even pleasurable by an extensive index of names of correspondents and by an excellent filing system.

Not so the Charles Sumner papers at the Houghton Library, Harvard University, which are organized in a somewhat cumbersome manner. Valuable nonetheless, this material is of great importance for any student of the Senate's role in Civil War diplomacy. Also basic to the period are the papers of Charles Francis Adams, especially the famous diary, available on microfilm from the Massachusetts Historical Society. The Society also houses the substantial John A. Andrew papers and a box of John Brown material. At the New York Public Library the Horace Greeley and Gideon Welles papers, and at the Maryland Historical Society the Reverdy Johnson and Henry Winter Davis papers, yielded a few items of interest. The papers of Joshua Giddings at the Ohio Historical Society were an important corrective to the official voice of the Ohio abolitionist as recorded in his consular dispatches. Several Giddings items also were found in the Gerrit Smith Miller collection at Syracuse University. The Mallet collection at l'Union Saint-Jean-Baptiste d'Amérique in Woonsocket, Rhode Island, was disappointingly thin. One letter from Giddings to William Lloyd Garrison was found in the Garrison collection at the Boston Public Library. The James Miller McKim and Goldwin Smith papers at Cornell University provided an item or two but the latter are of little use for the Civil War period since Smith destroyed most of his papers when he moved to the United States in 1869. The Austin Blair and N. W. Brooks papers at the Detroit Public Library were mildly rewarding, while the Thomas Hines papers at the Filson Club in Louisville were of less value than one would be led to believe by Hines' biographer, who seriously overinflates his hero's place in Confederate affairs. The papers of John A. Dix at the New York State Library, which were searched at the author's request, produced nothing of value.

Several manuscript groups at the Library of Congress collectively proved important, although none alone was of central value. A few Johnson, Seward, Gerrit Smith, Sumner, and Weed papers added little to collections consulted elsewhere. The papers of John Brown, J. C. Bancroft Davis, Zachariah Chandler, Salmon P. Chase, Matthew F. Maury, Justin S. Morrill, Winfield Scott, Edwin M. Stanton, Robert Walker, and Gideon Welles were of marginal value. Although outside the period of this study, the papers of Hamilton Fish were of some aid, as were those of Henry Wilson. The papers, autobiography, and diary of Charles Wilkes were examined for any light they might throw on the *Trent* affair, and the fragmentary papers of James M. Mason and George Sanders produced several items of real value. The diary of Benjamin Moran—later checked against the published version (see below)—was of occasional use, especially in its bitter comments on public opinion in England and on Charles Francis Adams' reaction to that opinion.

Published and Printed Sources

Because of the pivotal nature of the years 1860–1867 in the history of both Canada and the United States, a large number of official and private compilations of documents have been prepared. While the author consulted all such collections known to him, he preferred to turn directly to the document in its original form whenever possible. In the occasional instance where the original manuscript was not available to him or could not be found the writer has cited the document from its printed source, as will be seen from the notes. In a few cases research preceded from the printed version to the original document, but in most cases the writer used the manuscript first and later checked it against any subsequent printings. In a few instances—as with the published version of Moran's diary, *The Journal of Benjamin Moran, 1857–1865* (2 vols., Chicago, 1948–1949), edited by Sarah A. Wallace and Frances E. Gillespie—the standard of accuracy was extremely high, but too often the incidence of minor errors was sufficiently frequent to lead the writer to discount edited collections whenever possible. In any case, very few of the pertinent letters of Seward, Macdonald, or Monck have appeared in print. For example, while Seward's famous "proposition of April 1, 1861," was first printed in the 1880's and subsequently has been reprinted many times, almost none of Seward's letters to anyone other than Charles Francis Adams have been published. Many of the Sumner letters and speeches and Andrew letters cited in the notes have appeared in the *Proceedings* of the Massachusetts Historical Society, the *American Historical Review,* or in Charles Sumner, *His Complete Works* (20 vols., Boston, 1900). Collections of Abraham Lincoln's writings abound, the most recent and fullest being Roy P. Basler, M. D. Pratt, and L. A. Dunlap, eds., *The Collected Works of Abraham Lincoln* (8 vols., New Brunswick, 1953). A very few of the Giddings letters, on reciprocity, have been printed in the *Canadian Historical Review,* XVI (Sept., 1935), 289–295. Many of the papers relating to the activities of the Confederate commissioners have been printed variously in D. S. Freeman, ed., *A Calender of Confederate Papers* . . . (Richmond, 1908), in volume VII of the *Papers* of the Southern Historical Society (1879), and in Richard Rush, *et. al.,* eds., *Official Records of the Union and Confederate Navies in the War of the Rebellion* (30 vols., Washington, 1894–1922), especially volume three of Series II, edited under the supervision of H. K. White.

Several of the diplomatic exchanges between Washington and London have been printed in the *British and Foreign State Papers* (London), published from four to eight years after the dates with which they deal, and in *Papers relating to the Foreign Relations of the United States* (Washington), often cited as *Papers relating to Foreign Affairs* for the years 1861–1868, and at that time published from one to two years after the events. Both compilations are highly selective, occasionally —although not often—in error, and seldom include the British North American side of the triangle. Contrary to the continuing practice of some, it is quite impossible to write even an adequate history of Anglo-American relations from these official source books.

For the author's purposes the standard collections of the lives and letters of the leading Canadian politicians were so many "baked meats at the funeral parlor." Joseph Pope has edited the *Correspondence of Sir John Macdonald* . . . (Toronto [1921]), and J. A. Chisholm has culled the *Speeches and Public Letters of Joseph Howe* (2 vols., Halifax, 1909), but neither book is very rewarding. Alexander Mackenzie, ed., *The Life and Speeches of the Hon. George Brown* (Toronto, 1882), is quite unsatisfactory, for Mackenzie has resorted to considerable editing and cutting, while Charles Murphy, ed., *1925—D'Arcy McGee: A Collection of Speeches and Addresses* . . . (Toronto, 1937), is scarcely better. Other collections of the letters and speeches of Macdonald and McGee exist and were consulted but for various reasons the above, no matter how inadequate, seemed the best. At the moment there is no satisfactory published collection of the letters of any Canadian statesman—philanthropic, educational, and governmental groups in the Dominion not yet having decided to enshrine the Fathers of Confederation as Washington, Adams, Jefferson, Franklin, Monroe, Clay, Calhoun, Lincoln, and the two Roosevelts have been or are being enshrined in the United States.

Certain information can be obtained only from printed primary sources, of course. Among those that the author used are, for British North America, the *Journals* of the Legislative Assembly and of the Legislative Council of the united province of Canada, the *Parliamentary Debates on the Subject of the Confederation of the British North American Provinces* (Quebec, 1865), usually referred to as *Confederation Debates;* the *Canadian Sessional Papers,* the *Journals* of the Legislative Council and House of Assembly of New Brunswick, *Journals and Proceedings* of the Legislative Council and the House of Assembly of Nova Scotia, the *Journals* and *Appendixes* of the Legislative Council and House of Assembly of Prince Edward Island, the *Journals* of the Legislative Council and the House of Assembly of Newfoundland, the official *Gazettes* of the united Canadas, New Brunswick, and Nova Scotia, the *Minutes* of the Council of Vancouver Island, the *Reports* of the Court of Common Pleas and the Court of Queen's Bench for the Canadas, *The Lower Canada Jurist* (Montreal), the *Census of the Canadas: 1860–61* (Quebec, 1863), the special *Census of Nova Scotia* (Halifax, 1862), *Mandements Lettres Pastorales: Circulaires et Autres Documents Publies dans le Diocèse de Montréal* (Montreal, 1887), *Mandements des Evêques de Québec* (Quebec, 1865), the *Annual Reports* of the Anti-Slavery Society of Canada, the *Transactions* of the Board of Agriculture and of the Agricultural Association of Upper Canada, and various printed reports of the Montreal City Council, the Saint John Chamber of Commerce, and other municipal bodies. Most of these official and semi-official journals were used in the Public Archives of Canada, the Parliamentary Library, and the Yale University Library, but the official *Gazettes*, which are quite rare, generally had to be consulted in the law or legislative library of the province concerned. By far the most valuable of these compilations were the various provincial "Hansard's" under their differing and changing titles, listed above.

Official British publications include *Hansard's Parliamentary Debates*, the *Sessional Papers*, statistical abstracts, and various official collections of documents that were issued from time to time (as, for example, *Papers relating to the Seizure of the United States' Steamer 'Chesapeake'* [London, 1864]) and that are cited in the notes, as are a number of Toronto, Montreal, and Halifax imprints of the same nature. Almost all of these official volumes have indexes of a sort, but they are quite inadequate. The researcher is well advised, especially when using the British North American materials, to use the index only as a preliminary guide.

In addition to those collections already mentioned, United and Confederate States materials which were used included the *Congressional Globe*, the various House and Senate Executive and Miscellaneous Documents, the Department of State's printed Circulars, the *Army and Navy Official Gazette* (Washington, 1863–1865), various printed memoranda from the War Department, certain Department of State compilations (e.g., *The Assassination of Abraham Lincoln* . . . [Washington, 1867]), the indispensable 130 volumes of *The War of the Rebellion: A Compilation of the Official Records of the Union and Con-*

federate Armies (Washington, 1880–1901), the *Journal of the Congress of the Confederate States of America, 1861–1865* (7 vols., Washington, 1904–1905), and James D. Richardson, *A Compilation of the Messages and Papers of the Presidents, 1789–1897* (10 vols., Washington, 1896–1899). Richardson, *A Compilation of the Messages and Papers of the Confederacy, including the Diplomatic Correspondence, 1861–1865* (2 vols., Nashville, 1906), contains most of the Benjamin-Thompson exchanges. Despite its title, W. R. Manning, ed., *Diplomatic Correspondence of the United States: Canadian Relations, 1784–1860* (3 vols., Washington, 1940–1943), falls well short (1848) of the period under consideration and has not been continued.

Locally oriented material included the *Annual Reports* of the Boston Board of Trade, the *Proceedings* of the Detroit Commercial Convention of 1865, the *Journal* of the House (Lewiston) and *Annual Reports* of the Adjutant General (Augusta) for Maine, *Annual Reports* of the Adjutant General of New York, *Proceedings* of the Chamber of Commerce of the State of New York, *Annual Reports* of the Adjutant and Inspector General's Office of Vermont, the *Journal* of the Senate of Virginia, *Annual Reports* of the American Missionary Association, and many special collections (e.g., *A Leaf from History: Report of J. Thompson* . . . [Washington, 1868?], or the New York Legislature's *Report of the Select Committee* . . . *on the Reciprocity Treaty* [New York, 1865]). A considerable number of reminiscences, some of value despite their brevity, have appeared in the various publications of the many local Canadian historical societies. Many books written by travelers in the United States and British North America during the war, as well as a large number of autobiographies, were consulted and will be found listed, and on occasion discussed, in the notes.

Contemporary Materials

Newspapers have been discounted as a source by many recent historians who have discovered something that was obvious to the lay reader all along—that the popular press is inevitably biased, often factually inaccurate as to detail, and usually sensational. But once one has acknowledged that opinion cannot be treated as fact and that partisan prejudice leads to a sometimes bizarre mixture of the two, the newspaper still remains—in the present writer's opinion—an extremely important source of information. In his use of the press the author has attempted to cite several supporting references from manuscript materials for each controversial statement. But he also has used the newspapers, especially in Chapter Eleven, as a source of opinion, and the publication of an error may be fully as significant as the publication of accurate news of a verified incident.

During the Civil War years British North America's most widely read newspaper was George Brown's Toronto *Globe*. The *Globe* was by no means free of factual error, and its editor gave it a strong bias, but its bias was clear, its editorials outspoken, and its news coverage wide-ranging. Used with care and balanced against conservative newspapers the *Globe* is an excellent contemporary source. A complete file for the Civil War years is available by combining sets at the Ontario Legislative Library and the Ontario Public Archives.

Next to the *Globe* the most valuable papers were the Toronto *Leader* (O.P.A., P.A.C., T.P.L.), the former's conservative counterpart; the liberal Montreal *Witness* (P.A.C.), the conservative Montreal *Gazette* (P.A.C.), the Charlottetown *Examiner* (microfilm), Fredericton *Head Quarters* (microfilm), Halifax *Morning Chronicle* (microfilm) and *Novascotian* (Public Archives of Nova Scotia), Saint John *New Brunswick Courier* and *Morning Freeman* (both microfilm), Victoria *British Colonist* and *Chronicle* (both microfilm), and two French-language newspapers, *La Minerve* and *Le Canadien* (both P.A.C.) of Montreal and Quebec respectively. Each of these newspapers, whether issued daily or weekly, proved extremely useful. Many other Canadian newspapers were consulted at the Parliamentary Library (which, having suffered from a severe fire in 1952, only recently has been able to make its newspaper collection fully available again), the Public Archives of Canada, the Douglas Library of Queen's University, or in the various provincial archives. The names of some of these newspapers, together with a description of the method of search, appears. in note 36, Chapter Eleven. *The Times* of London is indispensable for a study of this kind, of course, and is readily available on microfilm, together with an excellent index. The *Canadian News*, a commercial sheet published in London, also was of considerable value, and a set is on file at the Public Archives.

For the war period the leading American newspaper remains the New York *Herald*, and a complete file may be consulted at the Library of Congress. The national library is rich in United States newspapers (although notably weak in terms of the British North American press), and in addition to files of the New York *Times*, *Tribune*, and *Sun*, the Buffalo *Commercial Advertiser*, the Chicago *Tribune*, and Detroit *Advertiser and Tribune* and *Free Press*, the writer was able to consult scattered runs of some seven Maine newspapers (e.g., Augusta *Age*, Portland *Daily Eastern Argus*), four and three additional newspapers from Massachusetts and Michigan respectively, several New York papers, eleven Vermont papers for opinion and fact on the St. Albans raid, and a few files from Ohio, Illinois, and the Confederate States.

An extensive collection of New York state newspapers is housed at the University of Rochester, where the writer found the files of the Albany *Commercial*, the Buffalo *Express*, and three Rochester newspapers—*Daily Democrat and American*, *Daily Union and Advertiser*, and *Evening Express*. William H. Seward's personal gift of the Albany *Evening Journal* for 1861–1862 is here as is Manton Marble's gift of a file of his own newspaper, the New York *World*. The fullest contemporary account of the St. Albans raid appeared in the Burlington *Free Press*, a complete file of which is in the Fletcher Free Public Library of Burlington, Vermont. The Cleveland *Leader* has been skillfully and devotedly abstracted under the editorship of that faceless entity, the Works Progress Administration in Ohio, and presented in a series of multigraph source books as *Annals of Cleveland, 1818–1935* (94 vols., Cleveland, 1936–1938), and it is to this compilation that the author's notes refer. A few other newspapers have been consulted in the public libraries and historical societies noted in the Preface.

Another category of contemporary materials is that of pamphlets and magazines. Especially valuable among the latter were *Blackwood's Magazine*, *The Saturday Review* (London), *The Quarterly Review*, *The Lancet*, *The British American Magazine* (Toronto, 1863–1864), the *Canadian Farmer*, which was first issued in 1864 and which contains numerous articles on the reciprocity treaty, the *Canadian Quarterly Review and Family Magazine*, also launched in 1864, and *Trade Review*, a short-lived Canadian periodical established in 1865. Occasional contemporary articles of interest appear in *Harper's Magazine*, *The Atlantic Monthly*, *Macmillan's Magazine*, *Frank Leslie's Illustrated Newspaper*, *DeBow's Review*, *Littell's Living Age*, *The Merchant's Magazine and Commercial Review* and *Continental Monthly*.

The number of pamphlets, polemical and propagandistic, that appeared during the Civil War and that are pertinent to the present subject, is staggering. A separate study well might be written on the efforts of these pamphleteers to achieve by their pens what professional diplomats could or would not do. Many of these pamphlets are listed in the notes. Most of the pamphlets may be found in Ottawa and are noted in Magdalen Casey, *Catalogue of Pamphlets in the Public Archives of Canada* (2 vols., Ottawa, 1931–1932). Others of British North American origin are to be found in the Keefer Collection on railroad history at the Hamilton Public Library, in the Akins Collection at Acadia University in Wolfville, Nova Scotia, the Webster Collection of the New Brunswick Museum, and the Woods Collection at the University of Alberta, Edmonton. A few were found only at the Widener Library at Harvard University, the Illinois State Historical Society, and in the excellent Seward Pamphlet Collection at the University of Rochester. This material ranges from George T. Denison's *Canada: Is She Prepared for War?* (Toronto, 1861) to Joseph Wright's *Self Reliance, or a Plea for the Protection of Canadian Industry* (Dundas [C.W.], 1864).

Last, the author strongly believes in the perhaps outmoded view that it is best to experience a place physically rather than vicariously before attempting to write of it. Few authors can obtain the necessary nuance knowledge, the tone of place, through a library. Whether the historian must, as R. G. Collingwood implies, relive the past through his own experience, or as G. M. Trevelyan asserts, walk over the ground of history, depends upon the particular historian's view of his craft. If he does feel this need, there is an abundance of places that one may visit to invoke the past, from the docks of Victoria to McNab's Island in the harbor of Halifax, past which the *Tallahassee* slipped one night to elude her Federal pursuer, from the sleepy village of St. Albans to the remains of old Fort Garry on the now-tranquil Red River. It is at such places as these, as well as in the exciting chase within the confines of an archive, that the historian finds his pleasure and his reward.

NOTE TO THE SECOND EDITION

IN ADDITION TO THE MINOR MANUSCRIPT SOURCES MENTIONED IN THE PREFACE
to this, second, edition I have also examined the archives and museum
collections of Bermuda, the Confederate Museum in St. George, added
Brougham Papers in University College, London, and post-1960 additions
to the Brown and Galt papers, none of which throw any substantial new
light on the subjects discussed here. Some of the classifications given on
pages 385-86 have been changed ; otherwise the Note on Sources may still
be used as a guide.

Some significant new publications have appeared during the last decade,
of course. Foremost among these are Glyndon G. Van Deusen's *William
Henry Seward* (New York, 1967), Martin B. Duberman's *Charles Francis
Adams, 1807-1886* (Boston, 1961), David Donald's *Charles Sumner and the
Coming of the Civil War* (New York, 1960), James K. Chapman's *The
Career of Arthur Hamilton Gordon, First Lord Stanmore, 1829-1912* (Toronto,
1964), James Osborne McCabe's *San Juan Boundary Question* (Toronto,
1964), Donald F. Warner's *The Idea of Continental Union : Agitation for
the Annexation of Canada to the United States, 1849-1893* (Lexington, Ky.,
1960), Alvin C. Gluek, Jr.'s *Minnesota and the Manifest Destiny of the
Canadian Northwest : A Study in Canadian-American Relations* (Toronto,
1965) ; S.F. Wise and Robert Craig Brown's *Canada Views the United States :
Nineteenth Century Political Attitudes* (Seattle, 1967) ; Brian Jenkins' *Fenians
and Anglo-American Relations during Reconstruction* (Ithaca, 1969) ; and
W.L. Morton's *The Critical Years : The Union of British North America, 1857-
1873* (Toronto, 1964). Most important of all have been Peter Waite's *Confederation and Its Times* (Toronto, 1962) and J.M.S. Careless' *Brown of
the Globe*, II : *Statesman of Confederation* (Toronto, 1963). A number of
disagreements, largely on matters of detail, arise between my own study and the
award-winning *Britain and the Balance of Power in North America 1815-1908*
(London, 1967) by Kenneth Bourne, and it should be read in conjunction with
chapters 6 and 8.

Several articles should also be cited in their proper place in the footnotes,
were this possible. These include Allan Keller, "Canada and the Civil War,"
Civil War Times Illustrated, III (1964), 49-54, which is a summary of the
present book ; Sir John Wheller-Bennett, "The Trent Affair," *History Today*,
XI (1961), 805-15, which summarizes previous knowledge ; Norman B.
Ferris, "The Prince Consort, 'The Times,' and the 'Trent' Affair," *Civil War
History*, VI (1960), 152-56 ; Conway W. Henderson, "The Anglo-American
Treaty of 1862 in Civil War Diplomacy," *ibid.*, XV (1969), 308-19 ; Charles

M. Wilson, "The Hit-and-Run Raid," *American Heritage,* XII (1961), 28-31, 90-93, a popular account ; and Doris W. Dashew, "The Story of an Illusion : The Plan to Trade the *Alabama* Claims for Canada," *Civil War History,* XV (1969), 332-48. None changes any interpretations stated here. Guy Maclean's article, "The Georgian Affair," *CHR,* XLII (1961), differs on some points of detail, however, and should be read along with pages 308-10.

I have followed some of the lines of inquiry suggested in the pages above in a series of articles : " 'A Sacred Animosity' : Abolitionism in Canada, " in Martin B. Duberman, ed., *The Antislavery Vanguard : New Essays on the Abolitionists* (Princeton, 1965), pp. 301-42 ; "William 'Colorado' Jewett of the Niagara Falls Conference." *The Historian,* XXIII (1960), written with Clark C. Spence ; "Raid at St. Albans," *Vermont Life* (1961) ; "A Century of Misunderstanding : Canadian-American Cultural Relations," *International Educational and Cultural Exchange,* I (1965), 6-18 ; and "Sir William Francis Drummond Jervois," *Australian Dictionary of Biography,* IV (Melbourne, forthcoming). The reprint edition referred to on page 177 has not appeared.

Finally, I should note the journal of the Household Brigade, published as *Montreal during the American Civil War* (Montreal, n.d.) ; a useful new M.A. thesis of Dalhousie University by Harry A. Overholtzer, Jr., "Nova Scotia and the United States' Civil War" (1965) ; E.H. Royce's pamphlet, *The St. Albans Raid* (St. Albans, 1959) ; and the several general works which continue to cite the inflated and erroneous Canadian enlistment figures discussed on pages 179 following. In many dozens of local histories published in Canada in honor of the Centennial of 1867 there are ritual paragraphs concerning the Civil War years, seldom shedding any additional light on those years. Three locally-oriented exceptions are Esther Clark Wright, *Samphire Greens : The Story of the Steeves* (Ottawa, n.d.) ; W.A. Kingston, *The Light of Other Days* (n.p., n.d.) ; and William G. Richardson, *The Story of Whittington : A History of the Whittington Community of Dufferin County* ([Shelburne, Ont.], 1963), which tells of Jack Chapman, the Canadian widely believed to have been the sentry who mortally wounded "Stonewall" Jackson. G.F.G. Stanley's *Canada's Soldiers* has been reissued in a revised edition (Toronto, 1960). Surprisingly, very little that has been written since 1960 on the diplomatic history of the Civil War touches on Canada, the exception being John Williams' essay in Harold M. Hyman, ed., *Heard 'Round the World* (Impact of the Civil War Series, Vol. III) New York, 1969.